CULTURAL ANTHROPOLOGY

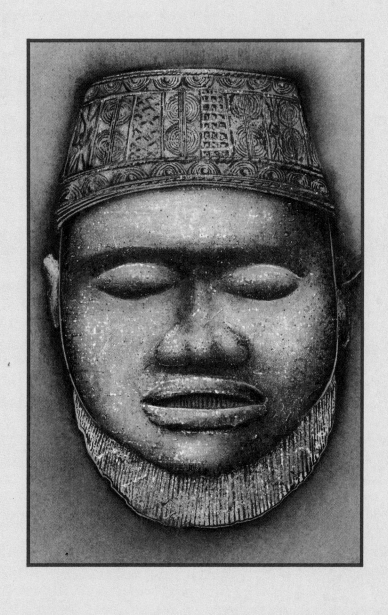

Dr. William A. Haviland is professor of anthropology

at the University of Vermont, where he has taught since

1965. He holds a doctoral degree in anthropology from

the University of Pennsylvania and has published widely

on archaeological, ethnological, and physical anthropo-

logical research carried out in Guatemala, Maine, and

Vermont. Dr. Haviland is a member of many profession-

al societies, including the American Anthropological

ABOUT THE AUTHOR

Association and the American Association for the

Advancement of Science. In 1988, he participated in the

project on "Gender and the Anthropology Curriculum"

sponsored by the American Anthropological Association.

One of Dr. Haviland's greatest loves is teaching,

which originally prompted him to write *Cultural Anthro-*

pology. He says he learns something new every year from

his students about what they need out of their first

college course in anthropology. In addition to writing

Cultural Anthropology, Dr. Haviland has authored several

other popular Harcourt Brace Jovanovich works for

anthropology students.

SEVENTH EDITION

CULTURAL ANTHROPOLOGY

WILLIAM A. HAVILAND

UNIVERSITY OF VERMONT

HARCOURT BRACE JOVANOVICH COLLEGE PUBLISHERS

FORT WORTH PHILADELPHIA SAN DIEGO NEW YORK ORLANDO AUSTIN SAN ANTONIO

TORONTO MONTREAL LONDON SYDNEY TOKYO

Editor-in-Chief	Ted Buchholz
Acquisitions Editor	Chris Klein
Developmental Editor	Karee Galloway
Senior Project Editor	Cliff Crouch
Permissions Editors	Sandra Lord, Barbara McGinnis
Senior Production Manager	Annette Dudley Wiggins
Designers	Linda Miller, Vicki McAlindon Horton

Cover and part opening illustrations by Rebecca Rüegger

Library of Congress Catalog Card Number 92-52939
 International Standard Book Number 0-03-049942-9

Address editorial correspondence to: 301 Commerce Street, Suite 3700
Fort Worth, Texas 76102
Address orders to: 6277 Sea Harbor Drive
Orlando, Florida 32887
1-800-782-4479, or 1-800-433-0001 (in Florida)

Printed in the United States of America
2 3 4 5 6 7 8 9 0 1 2 048 9 8 7 6 5 4 3 2 1

To my wife, Anita

PREFACE

This textbook is designed for introductory anthropology courses at the college level. It deals primarily with cultural anthropology, presenting the key concepts and terminology of that branch of the discipline, but also provides related material on physical anthropology and linguistics.

The aim of the book is to give students a thorough introduction to the principles and processes of cultural anthropology. Because it draws from the research and ideas of a number of schools of anthropological thought, it will expose students to a mix of approaches—evolutionism, historical particularism, diffusionism, functionalism, French structuralism, structural functionalism, and others. This inclusiveness reflects my conviction that each of these approaches has important things to say about human behavior. To restrict oneself to a single approach is to cut oneself off from important insights. Thorough and scholarly in its coverage, the book is nonetheless simply written and attractively designed. Students will find that it pleases as it teaches.

UNIFYING THEME

Although each chapter has been developed as a self-contained unit of study that may be used in any sequence the instructor wishes, a common theme runs through all the chapters. This, along with part introductions that support the theme, serves to convey to students how material in one chapter relates to that in others. The theme is that people maintain cultures to deal with problems, or matters that concern them. Although their cultures must produce behavior that is generally adaptive, or at least not maladaptive, this is not necessarily the same as saying that cultural practices arise because they are adaptive in a particular environment. Thus, the theme cannot be described as a simple kind of environmental adaptation.

FEATURES

READABILITY

The purpose of a textbook is to provide ideas and information, to induce readers to see old things in new ways, and to cause those readers to think about what they see. A book may be elegantly written, handsomely designed, and lavishly illustrated, but if it is not clear, interesting, and comprehensible to the student, it is valueless as a teaching tool. The trick is not just to present facts and concepts but to make them memorable.

The book presents even the most difficult concepts in prose that is clear, straightforward, and easy for today's first- and second-year students to understand, without feeling that they are being "spoken down to." Technical terms, which have been kept to a minimum, appear in boldfaced type, are carefully explained in the text itself, and are defined again in the running glossary in simple, clear language.

EXAMPLES

Because much learning is based on analogy, numerous colorful examples have been used to illustrate, emphasize, and clarify anthropological concepts. A cross-cultural perspective is introduced wherever appropriate, comparing cultural practices in several different societies, often including the student's own. But while the student should be made aware that anthropology has important things to say about the student's own society and culture, the emphasis in introductory cultural anthropology should be on non-Western societies and cultures. North Americans are a distinct minority, accounting for less than a quarter of the world's population. Yet the traditional school curriculum in North America emphasizes its own surroundings and backgrounds, saying little about the rest of the world. In its March 8, 1976 issue (p. 32), the *Chronicle of Higher Education* documented an increasing tendency toward cultural insularity and ethnocentrism in North American higher education. That the problem persists is clear from a report made public in 1989 by the National Governors' Association, which warned that the economic well-being of the United States is in jeopardy because so many of its citizens are ignorant of the languages and cultures of other nations. More than ever, college students need to acquire knowledge about the rest of the world and its peoples. Such a background gives them the global perspective they need to better understand their own culture and society and their place in today's world. Anthropology, with its long-standing commitment to combating ethnocentrism, has a unique obligation to provide this perspective.

ORIGINAL STUDIES

One of the unique features of this textbook is the Original Study that appears in each chapter. These studies consist of selections from case studies and other original works by men and women who have done, or are doing, important anthropological work. Each study, integrally related to the material in the text, sheds additional light on some important anthropological concept or subject area found in the chapter.

The Original Studies give students a feel for how anthropologists actually go about studying humans and their behavior. For example, Chapter 5 includes an Original Study extracted from the *Mbuti Pygmies: Change and Adaptation*, by Colin M. Turnbull, who presents an absorbing picture of a way of growing up that stands in marked contrast to the experience of most students who will use this textbook.

Women have always been an important part of the anthropological enterprise, and students need to realize this. Accordingly, women are well represented as authors of Original Studies in the seventh edition—10 of the 16 are by women alone, and another is jointly authored by a woman and a man.

ANTHROPOLOGY APPLIED

Students are sometimes unaware of the valuable functions anthropological work provides and the many job opportunities that are available outside academia for people with anthropological training. *Anthropology Applied*, a boxed feature appearing in each chapter, focuses on the many practical applications of anthropological knowledge, and the important work being done by anthropologists outside academic settings, and the variety of careers pursued by anthropologists. Each box is designed to expand on subject matter included in the chapter.

EMPHASIS ON GEOGRAPHY

It's necessary in any cultural anthropology textbook to refer frequently to the many different places throughout the world. Today's students are far less knowledgeable about world geography than were students 20 years ago, yet most anthropology textbooks have done little to address this problem. In this edition, a consistent effort has been made to help students identify the regions, countries, and continents as they are discussed. Each Original Study is accompanied by a detailed map that helps the students place the people discussed within a country, continent, and the world itself. In addition, longer discussions of cultures in the body of the text are also accompanied by detailed maps.

Equally important as helping students find specific locations on maps is helping them understand the nature of maps. A new section titled "Putting the World in Perspective" introduces students to some of the main points in the history of cartography, the deceptions necessarily inherent in any two-dimensional map, and the cultural "clues" within each map. This introductory section includes reproductions of several different world maps, each representing a unique view of the world.

PREVIEWS AND SUMMARIES

An old but effective pedagogical technique is repetition: "Tell 'em what you're going to tell 'em, do it, and then tell 'em what you've told 'em." To do just that, each chapter provides preview questions that set up a framework for studying the contents of the chapter. Then each chapter ends with a summary of the most important ideas presented in the chapter. The summaries provide handy reviews without being so long and detailed as to seduce students into thinking they can get by without reading the chapter itself.

SUGGESTED READINGS AND BIBLIOGRAPHY

Each chapter includes a list of suggested readings that will supply inquisitive students with further information about specific anthropological points. In addition, the bibliography at the end of the book lists more than 500 books and articles from scholarly journals and popular magazines on virtually every topic covered in the text.

RUNNING GLOSSARY

A running glossary defines key terms on the same page that they are first introduced, thereby reinforcing the meaning of each new term. It is also useful for chapter review in that students may readily isolate those terms introduced in one chapter from those introduced in others. Because each term is defined in clear, understandable language, less class time is required of the instructor.

ADVANTAGES OF THE SEVENTH EDITION

The planning of the seventh edition of *Cultural Anthropology* was based on extensive review and criticism by users of the sixth edition as well as users of other textbooks. Two major innovations of the sixth edition were kept: inclusion of significant material on gender and on applied anthropology in each and every chapter. The first emphasizes how considerations of gender enter into virtually everything people do. The second, accomplished through the boxed feature *Anthropology Applied*, demonstrates the many practical applications of anthropological knowledge, the important work

being done by anthropologists outside of academic settings, and the variety of careers pursued by anthropologists.

In addition to the new emphasis on geography and the nature of maps discussed above, the major changes in the seventh edition consist of fine tuning and updating. Examples include references to the importance of paralanguage in courtroom proceedings, and a new discussion of language origins, in Chapter 4; thorough revision of the discussion of incest, and a new discussion of polygamy in the United States, in Chapter 8; a discussion of the distinction between *nation* and *state* in Chapter 12; reference to the arts as means of enchantment, and urban legends, in Chapter 14; discussion of the recent plight of the Yanomami in Brazil, in Chapter 15; and reference to recent events in the former Soviet Union, Yugoslavia, Kuwait, and Iraq, as well as to the dumping of toxic substances in the third world by industrial countries, in Chapter 16. Indeed, no chapter has escaped change, which has improved every feature of the book: topic coverage, readability, continuity, photos and other illustrations, Original Studies, *Anthropology Applied* features, summaries, Suggested Readings, running glossary, and bibliography.

In addition to the substantial rewriting and updating of the content, 7 of the 16 Original Studies are new. Included are such topics as "Intellectual Abilities of Chimpanzees" by Jane Goodall (Chapter 3), "Sexism and the English Language" by Deborah Tannen (Chapter 4), "Prestige Economics in Papua New Guinea" by Allen Johnson (Chapter 7), "The Ephemeral Modern Family" by Judith Stacey (Chapter 9), "The Structure of Namibian Society" by Robert Gordon (Chapter 11), "Bye Bye, Ted . . ." by Anthony Parades and Elizabeth D. Purdum (Chapter 13), and "Wauja Organization in Defence of Their Homeland" by Emilienne Ireland (Chapter 15).

SUPPLEMENTS

The ancillaries that accompany *Cultural Anthropology*, Seventh Edition, have been skillfully prepared by James W. Green of the University of Washington and Sue Parman of California State University, Fullerton.

A separate *Study Guide* is provided to aid comprehension of the textbook material. Each chapter begins with a summary and concise learning objectives and then offers chapter exercises, review questions, and a glossary review to help students achieve these objectives. This supplement also includes hints on reading anthropology textbooks, and studying for tests.

An *Instructor's Manual* offers teaching objectives and lecture and class activity suggestions that correspond to each chapter of the textbook. An extensive *Test Bank,* available in both printed and computerized form, offers more than 1200 multiple-choice and true/false questions. Each question is rated according to level of difficulty. A set of 50 color transparencies, developed by Cynthia Mahmood of the University of Maine, Orono, is also available to instructors.

ACKNOWLEDGMENTS

Many people assisted in the preparation of this book, some directly and some indirectly. In the latter category are all of the anthropologists under whom I was privileged to study at the University of Pennsylvania: Robbins Burling, William R. Coe, Carleton S. Coon, Robert Ehrich, Loren Eiseley, J. Louis Giddings, Ward H. Goodenough, A. Irving Hallowell, Alfred V. Kidder II, Wilton M. Krogman, Froelich Rainey, Ruben Reina, and Linton Satterthwaite. They may not always recognize the final product, but they all contributed to it in important ways.

A similar debt is owed to all those anthropologists with whom I have worked or discussed research interests and the field in general. There are too many of them to list here, but they have had an important impact on my thinking and so on this book. Finally, the influence of all those who assisted in the preparation of the first six editions must linger on in this new one.

This revision has also benefited from my continued association with valued colleagues at the University of Vermont: Robert Gordon, William E. Mitchell, Carroll McC. P. Lewin, Stephen L. Pastner, Marjory Power, Peter A. Thomas, and A. Peter Woolfson. All have responded graciously at one time or another to my requests for sources and

for advice about their various fields of expertise. We all share freely our successes and failures in teaching anthropology to introductory students.

In 1984, I was given the opportunity to participate in a free and open discussion between textbook authors and users at the American Anthropological Association's Annual Meeting (a session organized and chaired by Walter Packard and the Council on Anthropology and Education). From this I got a good sense of what instructors at institutions ranging from community colleges to major universities were looking for in anthropology textbooks. Subsequent insights came from a special symposium on the teaching of anthropology at the University of Vermont in 1986 (organized by A. Peter Woolfson), a meeting of textbook authors with members of the "Gender and the Anthropology Curriculum" project at the American Anthropological Association's Annual Meeting in 1988, and a special session on "Central Themes in the Teaching of Anthropology" at the American Anthropological Association's Annual Meeting in 1990 (organized by Richard Furlow). To the organizers and sponsors of all these events, I give my sincere thanks.

Thanks are also due to the anthropologists who made suggestions for this edition. They include: Cliff Boyd, Radford University; Richard Bordner, Chaminade University of Honolulu; Norman E. Whitten, University of Illinois at Urbana-Champaign; Robert Lawless, University of Florida; Donna Birdwell–Pheasant, Lamar University; Roger C. Owen, Queens College; Mirtha Quintanales, Jersey City State College; and Scott Rushforth, New Mexico State University. All of their comments were carefully considered; how I have responded to them has been determined by my own perspective of anthropology, as well as my 27 years of experience with undergraduate students. Therefore, neither they nor any of the other anthropologists mentioned here should be held responsible for any shortcomings in this book.

I also wish to acknowledge my debt to a number of nonanthropologists who helped me with this book. The influence of David Boynton, winner of the 1985 Distinguished Service Award of the American Anthropological Association and my editor at Holt, Rinehart and Winston until his retirement in 1983, I am sure lingers on. Helpful in seeing this edition through to publication have been my new acquisition editor Christopher Klein and developmental editor Karee Galloway; both have been a pleasure to work with. I also thank my skilled editorial, design, and production team: Annette Wiggins, senior production manager; Linda Miller, senior book designer; and Clifford Crouch, senior project editor.

The greatest debt of all is owed my wife, Anita de Laguna Haviland, who has had to put up with my preoccupation with this revision, reminding me when it is time to feed the livestock or play midwife to the sheep in the barn. As if that were not enough, it is she who fed revised text into the word processor, bringing me at last into the world of "high tech" and delivering all my editors from the frustration of dealing with cut-and-paste copy and pencilled-in changes. She has been a source of endless good ideas on things to include and ways to express things. The book has benefited enormously from her involvement.

CONTENTS IN BRIEF

CONTENTS

PART I
ANTHROPOLOGY AND THE STUDY OF CULTURE 1

1
THE NATURE OF ANTHROPOLOGY 4

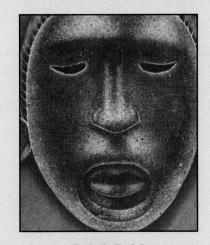

PART II
CULTURE AND SURVIVAL: COMMUNICATING, RAISING, CHILDREN, AND STAYING ALIVE 85

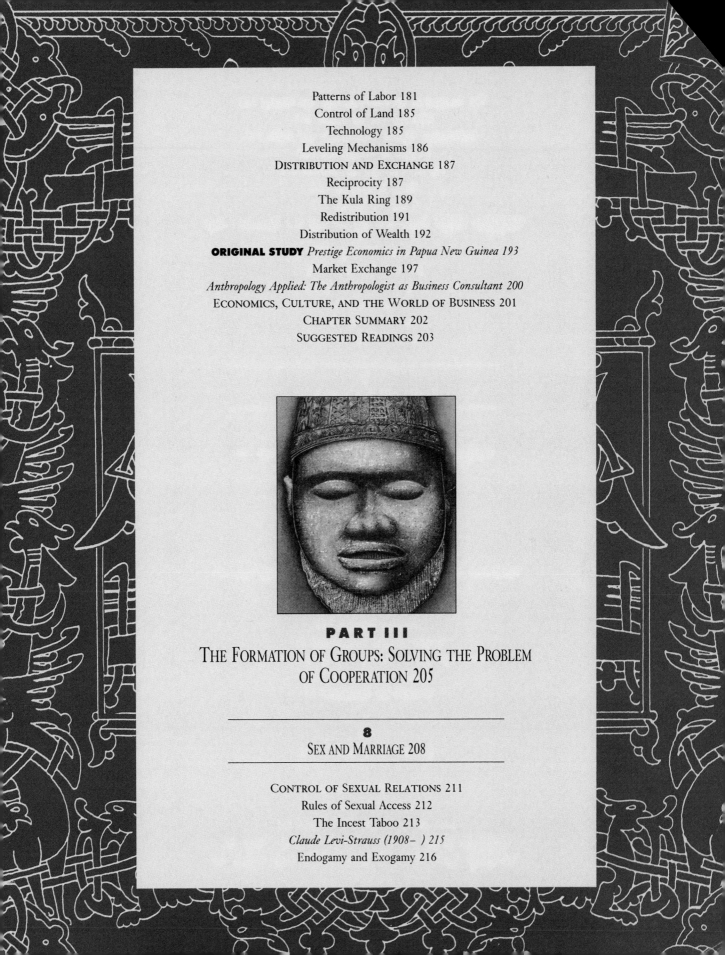

PART III
THE FORMATION OF GROUPS: SOLVING THE PROBLEM OF COOPERATION 205

8
SEX AND MARRIAGE 208

11
GROUPING BY SEX, AGE, COMMON INTEREST, AND CLASS 284

PART IV
THE SEARCH FOR ORDER: SOLVING THE PROBLEM OF DISORDER 307

12
POLITICAL ORGANIZATION AND SOCIAL CONTROL 310

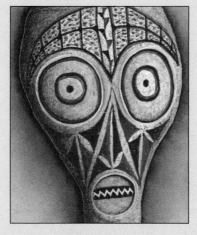

PART V
CHANGE AND THE FUTURE: SOLVING THE PROBLEM
OF ADJUSTING TO CHANGED CONDITIONS 399

Although all humans that we know about are capable of producing accurate sketches of localities and regions with which they are familiar, CARTOGRAPHY (the craft of mapmaking as we know it today) had its beginnings in 13th century Europe, and its subsequent development is related to the expansion of Europeans to all parts of the globe. From the beginning, there have been two problems with maps: the technical one of how to depict on a two-dimensional, flat surface a three-dimensional spherical object, and the cultural one of whose world view they reflect. In fact, the two issues are inseparable, for the particular projection one uses inevitably makes a statement about how one views one's own people and their place in the world. Indeed, maps often shape our perception of reality as much as they reflect it.

PUTTING THE WORLD IN PERSPECTIVE

In cartography, a PROJECTION refers to the system of intersecting lines (of longitude and latitude) by which part or all of the globe is represented on a flat surface. There are more than 100 different projections in use today, ranging from polar perspectives to interrupted "butterflies" to rectangles to heart shapes. Each projection causes distortion in size, shape, or distance in some way or another. A map that shows the shape of land masses correctly will of necessity misrepresent the size. A map that is accurate along the equator will be deceptive at the poles.

Perhaps no projection has had more influence on the way we see the world than that of Gerhardus Mercator, who devised his map in 1569 as a navigational aid for mariners. So well suited was Mercator's map for this purpose that it continues to be used for navigational charts today. At the same time, the Mercator projection became a standard for depicting land masses, something for which it was never intended. Although an accurate navigational tool, the Mercator projection greatly exaggerates the size of land masses in higher latitudes, giving about two-thirds of the map's surface to the northern hemisphere. Thus, the lands occupied by Europeans and European descendents appear far larger than those of other people. For example, North America (19 million square kilometers) appears almost twice the size of Africa (30 million square kilometers), while Europe is shown as equal in size to South America, which actually has nearly twice the land mass of Europe.

A map developed in 1805 by Karl B. Mollweide was one of the earlier equal-area projections of the world. Equal-area projections portray land masses in correct relative size, but, as a result, distort the shape of continents more than other projections. They most often compress and warp lands in the higher latitudes and vertically stretch land masses close to the equator. Other equal-area projections include the Lambert Cylindrical Equal-Area Projection (1772), the Hammer Equal-Area Projection (1892), and the Eckert Equal-Area Projection (1906).

The Van der Grinten Projection (1904) was a compromise aimed at minimizing both the distortions of size in the Mercator and the distortion of shape in equal-area maps such as the Mollweide. Although an improvement, the lands of the northern hemisphere are still emphasized at the expense of the southern. For example, in the Van der Grinten, the Commonwealth of Independent States (the former Soviet Union) and Canada are shown at more than twice their relative size.

The Robinson Projection, which was adopted by the National Geographic Society in 1988 to replace the Van der Grinten, is one of the best compromises to date between the distortion of size and shape. Although an improvement over the Van der Grinten, the Robinson projection still depicts lands in the northern latitudes as proportionally larger at the same time that it depicts lands in the lower latitudes (representing most third-world nations) as proportionally smaller. Like European maps before it, the Robinson projection places Europe at the center of the map with the Atlantic Ocean and the Americas to the left, emphasizing the cultural connection between Europe and North America, while neglecting the geographical closeness of northwestern North America to northeast Asia.

The following pages show four maps that each convey quite different "cultural messages." Included among them is the Peters Projection, an equal-area map that has been adopted as the official map of UNESCO (the United Nations Educational, Scientific, and Cultural Organization), and a map made in Japan, showing us how the world looks from the other side.

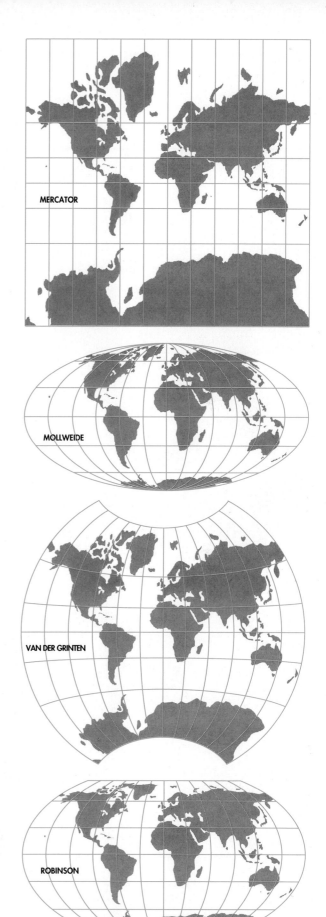

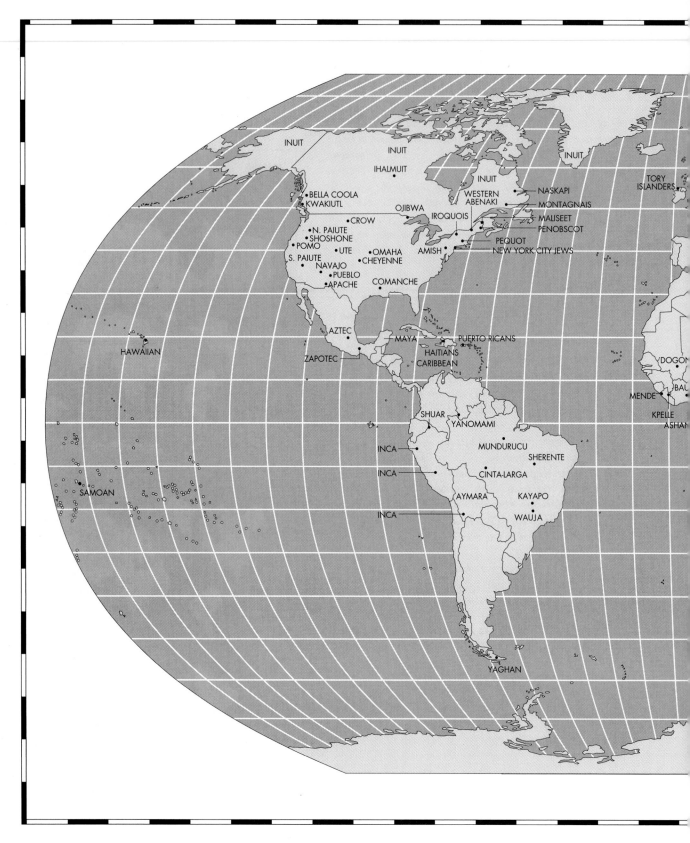

THE ROBINSON PROJECTION *The map above is based on the Robinson Projection, which is used today by the National Geographic Society and Rand McNally. Although the Robinson Projection distorts the relative size of land masses, it does so to a much lesser degree than*

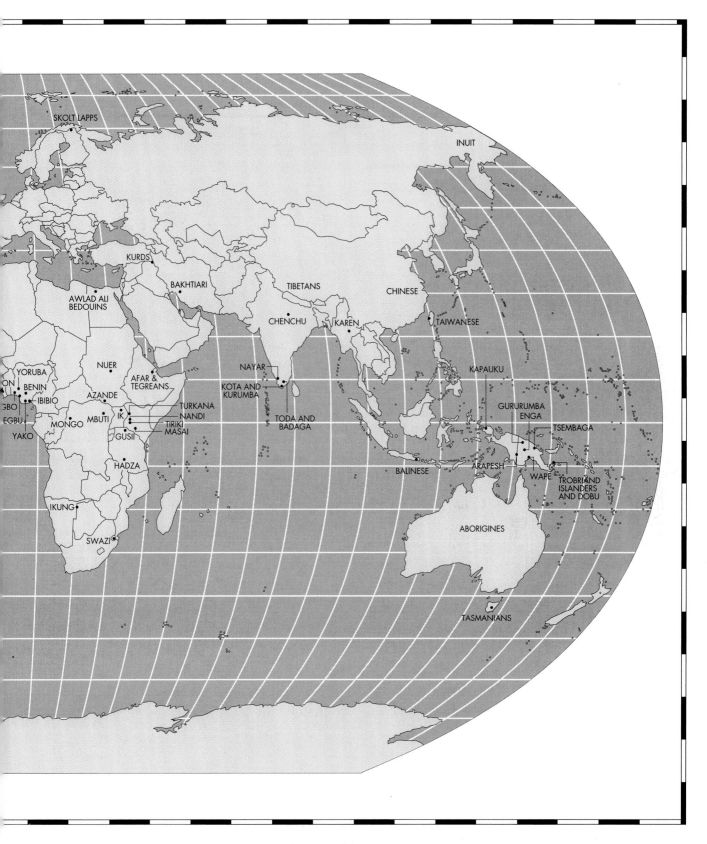

most other projections. Still, it places Europe at the center of the map.
This particular view of the world has been used to identify the location of many of the cultures discussed in this text.

THE PETERS PROJECTION   *The map above is based on the Peters Projection, which has been adopted as the official map of*
UNESCO. While it distorts the shape of continents (countries near the equator are vertically elongated by a ratio of two to one),

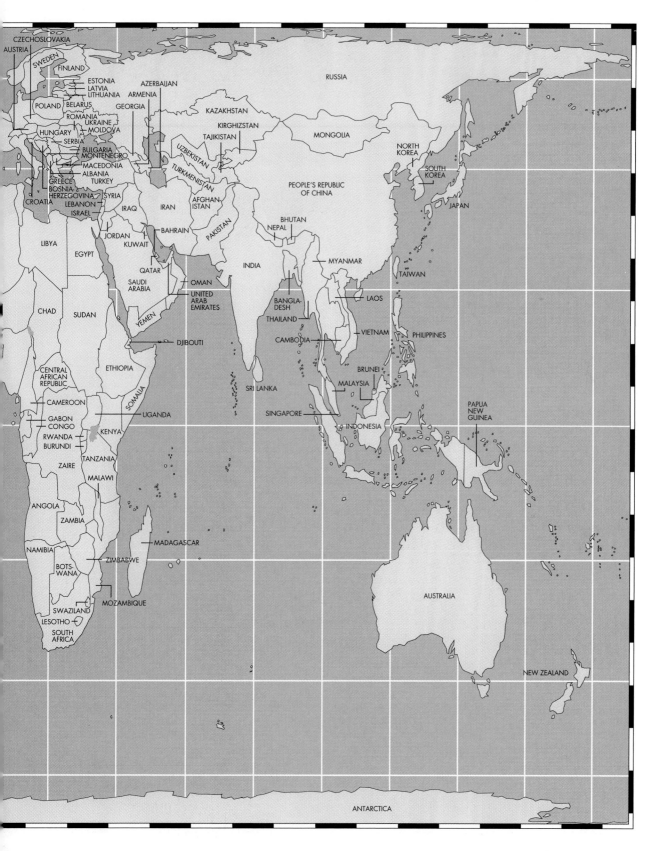

the Peters Projection does show all continents according to their correct relative size. Though Europe is still at the center, it is not shown as larger and more extensive than the third world.

JAPANESE MAP *Not all maps place Europe at the center of the world, as this Japanese map illustrates. Besides reflecting the importance the Japanese attach to themselves in the world, this map has the virtue of showing the*

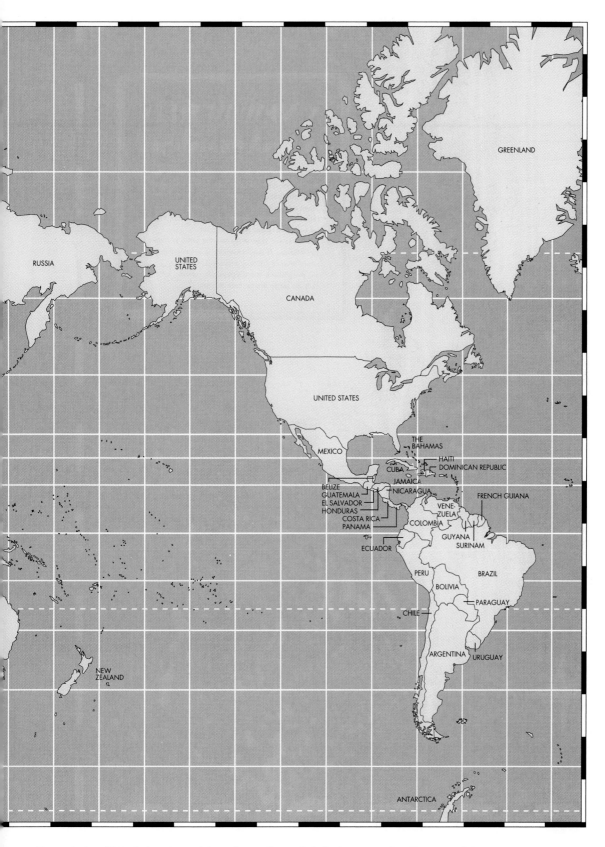

... geographic proximity of North America to Asia, a fact easily overlooked when maps place Europe at their center.

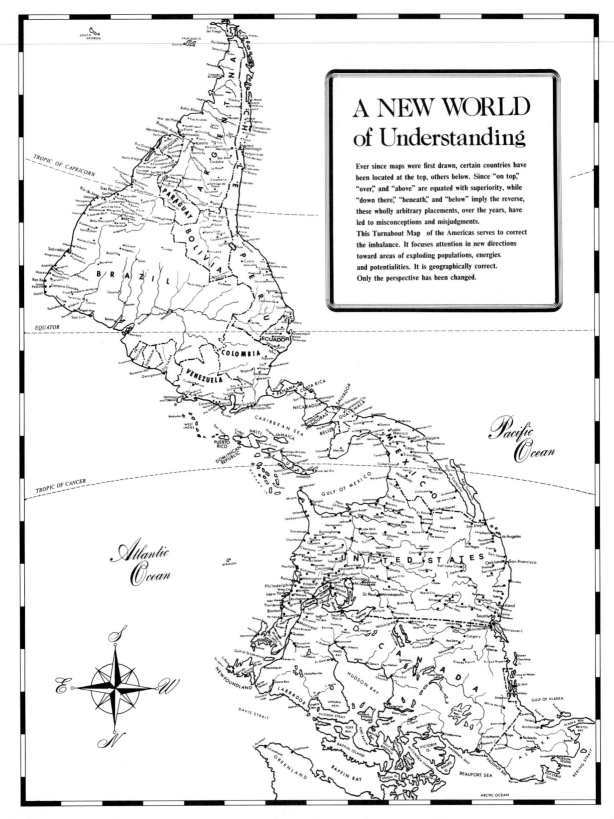

A NEW WORLD of Understanding

Ever since maps were first drawn, certain countries have been located at the top, others below. Since "on top," "over," and "above" are equated with superiority, while "down there," "beneath," and "below" imply the reverse, these wholly arbitrary placements, over the years, have led to misconceptions and misjudgments.

This Turnabout Map of the Americas serves to correct the imbalance. It focuses attention in new directions toward areas of exploding populations, energies and potentialities. It is geographically correct. Only the perspective has been changed.

THE TURNABOUT MAP *The way maps may reflect (and influence) our thinking is exemplified by the "Turnabout Map," which places the South Pole at the top and the North Pole at the bottom. Words and phrases such as "on top," "over," and "above" tend to be equated by some people with superiority. Turning things upside down may cause us to rethink the way North Americans regard themselves in relation to the people of Central and South America.* © 1982 by Jesse Levine Turnabout Map™ —Dist. by Laguna Sales, Inc., 7040 Via Valverde, San Jose, CA 95135

CULTURAL ANTHROPOLOGY

STATUE,

SRI

LANKA

PART I

ANTHROPOLOGY AND THE STUDY OF CULTURE

INTRODUCTION

ANTHROPOLOGY IS THE MOST LIBERATING OF ALL THE SCIENCES. NOT ONLY HAS IT EXPOSED THE FALLACIES OF RACIAL AND CULTURAL SUPERIORITY, BUT ITS DEVOTION TO THE STUDY OF ALL PEOPLES, REGARDLESS OF WHERE AND WHEN THEY LIVED, HAS ►

► cast more light on human nature than all the reflections of sages or the studies of laboratory scientists. If this sounds like the assertion of an overly enthusiastic anthropologist, it is not; it was all said by the philosopher Grace de Laguna in her 1941 presidential address to the Eastern Division of the American Philosophical Association.

The subject matter of anthropology is vast, as we shall see in the first three chapters of this book: It includes everything that has to do with human beings, past and present. Of course, many other disciplines are concerned in one way or another with human beings. Some, such as anatomy and physiology, study humans as biological organisms. The social sciences are concerned with the distinctive forms of human relationships, while the humanities examine the great achievements of human culture. Anthropologists are interested in all of these things too, but they try to deal with them all together, in all places and times. It is this unique, broad perspective that equips anthropologists so well to deal with that elusive thing called human nature.

No single anthropologist is able to investigate personally everything that has to do with people.

For practical purposes, the discipline is divided into various subfields, and individual anthropologists specialize in one or more of these. Whatever their specialization, though, they retain a commitment to a broader, overall perspective of humankind. For example, cultural anthropologists specialize in the study of human behavior, while physical anthropologists specialize in the study of humans as biological organisms. Yet neither can afford to ignore the work of the other, for human behavior and biology are inextricably intertwined, with each affecting the other in important ways. We can see, for example, how biology affects a cultural practice: color-naming behavior. Human populations differ in the density of pigmentation within the eye itself, which in turn affects people's ability to distinguish the color blue from green, black, or both. Consequently, a number of cultures identify blue with green, black, or both. We can see also how a cultural practice may affect human biology, as exemplified by the sickle-cell trait and related conditions. In certain parts of the Old World, when humans took up the practice of farming, they altered the ecology in a way that, by chance, created ideal conditions for the breeding of mosquitoes. As a result, malaria became a serious problem, and a biological response to this was the spread of certain genes that, in substantial numbers of people living in malarial areas, produced a built-in resistance to the disease.

To begin our introduction to the study of cultural anthropology, we will look closely at the nature of the discipline. In Chapter 1 we will see how the field of anthropology is subdivided, how the subdivisions relate to one another, and how they relate to the other sciences and humanities. Following this, we will turn our attention to the core concept of anthropology, the concept of culture. Chapter 2 will discuss the nature of culture and its significance for human individuals and societies. We will conclude this part of the book with a chapter (3) that gives us a look at how human culture began and gained primacy over biological change as the human mechanism for solving the problems of existence. We will see, also, how cultural evolution has its roots in biological evolution, and how it has played a significant role in making human beings what they are today. With these things done, we will have set the stage for a detailed look at the subject matter of cultural anthropology.

1

THE NATURE

OF

ANTHROPOLOGY

In this sixteenth-century depiction of a meeting between Frenchmen and American Indians, the latter look more like costumed Europeans than aboriginal Americans. The tendency to see other people as one has been conditioned to see them, rather than as they are, is still a major problem throughout the world.

WHAT IS ANTHROPOLOGY?

Anthropology, the study of humankind everywhere, throughout time, seeks to produce useful generalizations about people and their behavior and to arrive at the fullest possible understanding of human diversity.

WHAT DO ANTHROPOLOGISTS DO?

Physical anthropologists study humans as biological organisms, tracing the evolutionary development of the human animal and looking at biological variations within the species, past and present. Cultural anthropologists are concerned with human cultures, or the ways of life in societies. Within the field of cultural anthropology are archaeologists, who seek to explain human behavior by studying material objects, usually from past cultures; linguists, who study languages, by which cultures are maintained and passed on to succeeding generations; and ethnologists, who study cultures as they have been observed, experienced, and discussed with persons whose culture they seek to understand.

HOW DO ANTHROPOLOGISTS DO WHAT THEY DO?

Anthropologists, in common with other scientists, are concerned with the formulation and testing of hypotheses, or tentative explanations of observed phenomena. In so doing, they hope to arrive at a system of validated hypotheses or theory, although they recognize that no theory is ever completely beyond challenge. In order to frame hypotheses that are as objective and free of cultural bias as possible, anthropologists typically develop them through a kind of total immersion in the field, becoming so familiar with the minute details of the situation that they can begin to recognize patterns inherent in the data. It is also through fieldwork that anthropologists test existing hypotheses.

For as long as they have been on earth, people have needed answers to questions about who they are, where they came from, and why they act as they do. Throughout most of their history, though, people had no extensive and reliable body of data about their own behavior and background, and so they relied on myth and folklore for their answers to these questions. Anthropology, over the last 200 years, has emerged as a more scientific approach to answering these questions. Simply stated, **anthropology** is the study of humankind everywhere, and throughout time. The anthropologist is concerned primarily with a single species—*Homo sapiens*—the human species, its ancestors, and near relatives. Because anthropologists are members of the species being studied, it is difficult for them to be completely objective. They have found, however, that the use of the scientific approach produces useful generalizations about humans and their behavior. With the scientific approach, anthropologists are able to arrive at a reasonably reliable understanding of human diversity, as well as those things that all humans have in common.

DEVELOPMENT OF ANTHROPOLOGY

Although works of anthropological significance have a considerable antiquity—among others, the accounts of other peoples by Herodotus the Greek, or the Arab Ibn Khaldun, written in the fifth century B.C. and fourteenth century A.D.—anthropology as a distinct field of inquiry is a relatively recent product of Western civilization. In the United States, for example, the first course in general anthropology to carry credit in a college or university was offered at the University of Rochester, but not until 1879. If people have always been concerned about themselves and their origins, why then did it take such a long time for a systematic discipline of anthropology to appear?

The answer to this is as complex as human history. In part, the question of anthropology's late growth may be answered by reference to the limits of human technology. Throughout most of history, people have been restricted in their geographical horizons. Without the means of traveling to distant parts of the world, observation of cultures and peoples far from one's own was a difficult—if not impossible—venture. Extensive travel was usually the exclusive prerogative of a few; the study of foreign peoples and cultures was not likely to flourish until adequate modes of transportation and communication could be developed.

This is not to say that people have always been unaware of the existence of others in the world who look and act differently from themselves. The Old and New Testaments of the Bible, for example, are full of references to diverse peoples, among them Jews, Egyptians, Hittites, Babylonians, Ethiopians, Romans, and so forth. Different though they may have been, however, these peoples were at least familiar to one another, and familiar differences are one thing, while unfamiliar differences are another. It was the massive encounter with hitherto unknown peoples, which came as Europeans sought to extend their trade and political influence to all parts of the world, that focused attention on human differences in all their glory.

Another significant element that contributed to the slow growth of anthropology was the reluctance of Europeans to recognize the common humanity that they share with all people everywhere. Societies that did not subscribe to the fundamental cultural values of Europeans were often regarded as merely savage or barbarian. It was not until the late eighteenth century that a significant number of Europeans considered the behavior of foreigners to be at all relevant to an understanding of themselves. This awareness of human diversity, coming at a time when there were increasing efforts to explain things in terms of natural laws, cast doubts on the traditional biblical mythology, which no longer adequately "explained" human diversity. From the reexamination that followed came the awareness that the study of "savages" is a study of all mankind.

ANTHROPOLOGY AND THE OTHER SCIENCES

It would be incorrect to infer from the foregoing that serious attempts were never made to analyze human diversity before the eighteenth century. Anthropology is not the only discipline that studies people. In this respect it shares its objectives with the other social and natural sciences. Anthropo-

In the United States, anthropology began in the nineteenth century, when a number of dedicated amateurs went into the field to determine whether prevailing ideas about so-called savage peoples were valid. Shown here are Alice Fletcher, who spent the better part of 30 years documenting the ways of the Omaha Indians, and Frank Hamilton Cushing, who lived four and a half years with the Zuni in New Mexico.

gists do not think of their findings as something quite apart from those of psychologists, economists, sociologists, or biologists; rather, they welcome the contributions these other disciplines have to make to the common goal of understanding humanity, and they gladly offer their own findings for the benefit of these other disciplines. Anthropologists do not expect, for example, to know as much about the structure of the human eye as anatomists, or as much about the perception of color as psychologists. As synthesizers, however, they are better prepared to understand these things, in analyzing color-naming behavior in different human societies, than any of their fellow scientists. Because they look for the broad basis of human behavior without limiting themselves to any single social or biological aspect of that behavior, anthropologists can acquire an especially extensive overview of the complex biological and cultural organism that is the human being.

THE DISCIPLINE OF ANTHROPOLOGY

Anthropology is traditionally divided into four fields: physical anthropology and the three branches of cultural anthropology, which are archaeology, linguistic anthropology, and ethnology. **Physical anthropology** is concerned primarily with humans as biological organisms, whereas **cultural anthropology** deals with humans as cultural animals. Both, of course, are closely related; we cannot understand what people do unless we know what

Anthropology: The study of humankind, in all times and places.

people are. And we want to know how biology does and does not influence culture, as well as how culture affects biology.

PHYSICAL ANTHROPOLOGY

Physical anthropology (or, alternatively, biological anthropology) is the branch of anthropology that focuses on humans as biological organisms, and one of its many interests is human evolution. Whatever distinctions people may claim for themselves, they are mammals—specifically, primates—and, as such, they share a common ancestry with other primates, most specifically apes and monkeys. Through the analysis of fossils and the observation of living primates, the physical anthropologist tries to trace the ancestry of the human species in order to understand how, when, and why we became the kind of animal we are today.

Physical anthropology: The systematic study of humans as biological organisms.

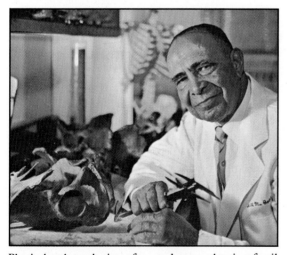

Physical anthropologists often study more than just fossil skulls. W. Montague Cobb, for many years head of the anatomy department in Howard University's medical school, specialized in research on aging in the adult human skeleton. This expertise made him a valued expert consultant to the FBI and similar agencies on forensic matters.

Another major concern of physical anthropology is the study of present-day human variation. Although we are all members of a single species, we differ from one another in many obvious and not so obvious ways. We differ not only in such visible traits as the color of our skins or the shape of our noses, but also in such biochemical factors as our blood types and our susceptibility to certain diseases. The modern physical anthropologist applies genetics and biochemistry to achieve fuller understanding of human variation and the ways in which it relates to the different environments in which people have lived.

CULTURAL ANTHROPOLOGY

Because the capacity for culture is rooted in our biological natures, the work of the physical anthropologist provides a necessary background for the cultural anthropologist. In order to understand the work of the cultural anthropologist, we must clarify what we mean when we refer to culture. The subject will be taken up in more detail in Chapter 2, but for our purposes here, we may think of culture as the often unconscious standards by which societies—groups of people—operate. These standards are learned rather than acquired through biological inheritance. Since they determine, or at least guide, the day-to-day behavior of the members of a society, human behavior is above all cultural behavior. The manifestations of culture may vary considerably from place to place, but no person is "more cultured" in the anthropological sense than any other.

Just as physical anthropology is closely related to the other biological sciences, cultural anthropology is closely related to the other social sciences. The one to which it has most often been compared is sociology, since the business of both is the description and explanation of behavior of people within a social context. Sociologists, however, have concen-

---

Cultural anthropology: The branch of anthropology that focuses on human behavior.

ANTHROPOLOGY APPLIED

FORENSIC ANTHROPOLOGY

In the public mind, anthropology is often identified with the recovery of the bones of remote human ancestors, the uncovering of ancient campsites and "lost cities," or the study of present-day tribal peoples whose way of life is erroneously seen as being something "out of the past." What people are often unaware of are the many practical applications of anthropological knowledge. One field of applied anthropology—known as **forensic anthropology**—specializes in the identification of human skeletal remains for legal purposes. Forensic anthropologists are routinely called upon by police and other authorities to identify the remains of murder victims, missing persons, or people who have died in disasters such as plane crashes. From skeletal remains, the forensic anthropologist can establish the age, sex, race, and stature of the deceased, and often whether they were right- or left-handed, exhibited any physical abnormalities, or evidence of trauma (broken bones and the like). In addition, some details of an individual's health and nutritional history can be read from the bones.

One well-known forensic anthropologist is Clyde C. Snow, who has been practicing in this field for 35 years, first for the Federal Aviation Administration and more recently as a freelance consultant.* In addition to the usual police work, Snow has studied the remains of Custer and his men from the battlefield at Little Big Horn, and in 1985, he went to Brazil, where he identified the remains of the notorious Nazi war criminal Josef Mengele. He

also has been instrumental in establishing the first forensic team devoted to documenting cases of human rights abuses around the world. This began in 1984, when he went to Argentina at the request of a newly elected civilian government as part of a team to help with the identification of remains of the *desaparecidos*, or "disappeared ones," the 9,000 or more people who were eliminated by government death squads during seven years of military rule. A year later, he returned to give expert testimony at the trial of nine junta members, and to teach Argentineans how to recover, clean, repair, preserve, photograph, x-ray, and analyze bones.

Besides providing factual accounts of the fate of victims to their surviving kin, and refuting the assertions of revisionists that the massacres never happened, the work of Snow and his Argentinean associates was crucial in convicting several military officers of kidnapping, torture, and murder. Subsequently, Snow and two of his Argentine associates were invited to the Philippines to look into the disappearance of 600 or more suspected victims of the Marcos regime. Similar requests from other South American countries, from Guatemala to Chile, in addition to work for regular clients in the U.S. such as the medical examiners' offices of Oklahoma, Cook County, Illinois, and the FBI, keep Snow busy. Although not all cases he investigates involve abuse of police powers, when this is an issue, it is often the investigators who bring the culprits to justice. To quote Snow: "Of all the forms of murder, none is more monstrous than that committed by a state against its own citizens. And of all murder victims, those of the state are the most helpless and vulnerable since the very entity to which they have entrusted their lives and safety becomes their killer." Thus, it is especially important that states be called to account for their deeds.

Forensic anthropology: Field of applied physical anthropology that specializes in the identification of human skeletal remains for legal purposes.

*SOURCE: Christopher Joyce, *Witnesses from the Grave: The Stories Bones Tell*. Boston: Little, Brown, 1991.

trated heavily on studies of people living in modern —or at least recent—North American and European societies, thereby increasing the probability that their theories of human behavior will be **culture-bound:** that is, based on assumptions about the world and reality that are part of the sociologists'

own culture. Cultural anthropologists, while not immune to culture-bound theorizing, constantly seek to minimize the problem by studying the whole of humanity in all times and places, and do not limit themselves to the study of recent Western peoples; anthropologists have found that to fully

Sociologists interview, and administer questionnaires to, *respondents*, while psychologists experiment with *subjects*. Anthropologists, by contrast, learn from *informants*.

Culture-bound: Theories about the world and reality based on the assumptions and values of one's own culture.

understand human behavior, all humans must be studied. More than any other feature, this unique cross-cultural and evolutionary perspective distinguishes cultural anthropology from the other social sciences. It provides anthropology with a far richer body of data than that of any other social science, and it can also be applied to any current issue. As a case in point, two different anthropologists have tested independently the validity of the argument that a high degree of military sophistication acts as a deterrent to war. By comparing the frequency of war in a number of different types of cultures, both found that the more sophisticated a community is militarily, the more frequently it engages in aggressive war and is attacked in turn. This at least suggests that as we ourselves expand our arsenal and develop new weapons systems, we will increase, rather than decrease, the likelihood of war.[1]

The emphasis cultural anthropology places on studies of prehistoric or more recent non-Western cultures has often led to findings that dispute existing beliefs arrived at on the basis of Western studies. Thus, cultural anthropologists were the first to point out

> that the world does not divide into the pious and the superstitious; that there are sculptures in jungles and paintings in deserts; that political order is possible without centralized power and principled justice without codified rules; that the norms of reason were not fixed in Greece, the evolution of morality not consummated in England. . . . We have, with no little success, sought to keep the world off balance; pulling out rugs, upsetting tea tables, setting off firecrackers. It has been the office of others to reassure; ours to unsettle.[2]

Although the findings of cultural anthropologists have often challenged the conclusions of sociologists, psychologists, and economists, anthropology is absolutely indispensable to them as the testing ground for their theories. It is to these disciplines what the laboratory is to physics and chemistry.

Cultural anthropology may be divided into the areas of archaeology, linguistic anthropology, and ethnology (often called sociocultural anthropology; Fig. 1.1). Although each has its own special interests and methods, all deal with cultural data. The archaeologist, the linguist, and the ethnologist take different approaches to the subject, but each gathers and analyzes data that are useful in explaining

[1]John H. Bodley, *Anthropology and Contemporary Human Problems* (Palo Alto, Calif.: Mayfield, 1985), p. 207.

[2]Clifford Geertz, "Distinguished Lecture: Anti Anti-Relativism," *American Anthropologist* 86 (June 1984):275.

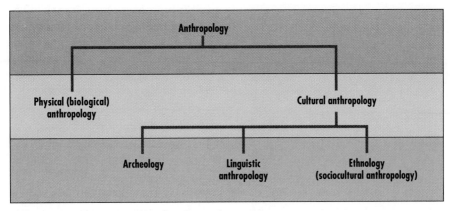

Figure 1.1   The subfields of anthropology.

similarities and differences between human cultures, as well as the ways that cultures everywhere develop, adapt, and continue to change.

ARCHAEOLOGY

Archaeology is the branch of cultural anthropology that studies material remains in order to describe and explain human behavior. Traditionally, it has focused on the human past, for material products of behavior, rather than behavior itself, are all that survive of that past. The archaeologist studies the tools, pottery, and other enduring relics that remain as the legacy of extinct cultures, some of them as much as 2.5 million years old. Such objects, and the way they were left in the ground, reflect certain aspects of human behavior. For example, shallow, restricted concentrations of charcoal, that include oxidized earth, bone fragments, and charred plant remains as well, and near which are pieces of fire-cracked rock, pottery, and tools suitable for food preparation, indicate cooking and associated food processing. From such remains much can be learned about a people's diet and subsistence activi-

ties. Thus the archaeologist is able to find out about human behavior in the past, far beyond the mere 5,000 years to which historians are limited by their dependence upon written records. By contrast, archaeologists are not limited to the study of prehistoric societies, but may also study those for which historic documents are available to supplement the material remains that people left behind them. In most literate societies, written records are associated with governing elites, rather than with people at the "grass roots." Thus, while documents can tell archaeologists much that they might not know from archaeological evidence alone, it is equally true that archaeological remains can tell historians much about a society that is not apparent from its written documents.

Although archaeologists have concentrated on the human past, increasing numbers of them are concerned with the study of material objects in contemporary settings. One example is the University of Arizona's "Garbage Project," which, by a carefully controlled study of household waste, continues to produce information about contemporary social issues. One aim of this project has been to test the validity of interview-survey techniques, upon which sociologists, economists, other social scientists, and policymakers rely heavily for their data. The tests clearly show a significant difference between what people say they do and what garbage analysis shows they actually do. For example, in 1973, conventional techniques were used to construct and administer a questionnaire to find out about the rate of alcohol consumption in Tucson. In

---

Archaeology: The study of material remains, usually from the past, to describe and explain human behavior.

Archaeologists study material remains to learn about human behavior. Shown here is an exposed burial at the ancient Maya site of Cuello, in Belize.

one part of town, 15 percent of respondent households admitted consuming beer, and no household reported consumption of more than eight cans a week. Analysis of garbage from the same area, however, demonstrated that some beer was consumed in over 80 percent of households, and 50 percent discarded more than eight empty cans a week. Another interesting finding of the Garbage Project is that when beef prices reached an all-time high in 1973, so did the amount of beef wasted by households (not just in Tucson, but other parts of the country as well). Although common sense would lead us to suppose just the opposite, high prices and scarcity correlate with more, rather than less, waste. Obviously, such findings are important, for they suggest that ideas about human behavior based on conventional interview-survey techniques alone may be seriously in error.

In 1987, the Garbage Project began a program of test excavations in landfills in various parts of the country. From this work has come the first reliable data on what materials actually go into landfills and what happens to them once there. And once again, we are finding that our existing beliefs are at odds with the actual situation. For example, biodegradable materials, like newspapers, take a much longer time to decay when buried in deep compact landfills than anyone previously expected. This kind of information is vital if the U.S. is ever to solve its waste disposal problems.

LINGUISTIC ANTHROPOLOGY

Perhaps the most distinctive human feature is the ability to speak. Humans are not alone in the use of symbolic communication. Studies have shown that the sounds and gestures made by some other animals—especially by apes—may serve functions comparable to those of human speech; yet no other animal has developed so complex a system of symbolic communication as have humans. Ultimately, language is what allows people to preserve and transmit their culture from generation to generation.

The branch of cultural anthropology that studies human languages is called **linguistic anthropology**. Linguistics may deal with the description of a language (the way a sentence is formed or a verb conjugated) or with the history of languages (the way languages develop and influence each other with the passage of time). Both approaches yield valuable information, not only about the ways in which people communicate but about the ways in which they understand the world around them as well. The "everyday" language of North Americans, for example, includes a number of slang words, such as *dough, greenback, dust, loot, cash, bucks, change,* and *bread,* to identify what a Papuan would recognize only as *money.* Such phenomena help identify things that are considered of special importance to a culture. Through the study of linguistics, the anthropologist is better able to understand how people perceive themselves and the world around them.

Linguistic anthropology: The branch of cultural anthropology that studies human language.

Anthropological linguists may also make a significant contribution to our understanding of the human past. By working out the genealogical relationships among languages and examining the distributions of those languages, they may estimate how long the speakers of those languages have lived where they do. By identifying those words in related languages that have survived from an ancient ancestral tongue, they can also suggest where the speakers of the ancestral language lived, as well as how they lived.

ETHNOLOGY

As the archaeologist has traditionally concentrated on cultures of the past, so the **ethnologist,** or sociocultural anthropologist, concentrates on cultures of the present. While the archaeologist focuses on the study of material objects to learn about human behavior, the ethnologist concentrates on the study of human behavior as it can be seen,

Ethnologist: An anthropologist who studies cultures from a comparative or historical point of view.

Ethnographers (such as Marjory Shostak, shown here with the !Kung of Africa's Kalahari Desert) learn about the cultures of other people by actually living among them.

Ethnography: The systematic description of a culture based on firsthand observation.

experienced, and discussed with those whose culture is to be understood.

Fundamental to the ethnologist's approach is descriptive **ethnography.** Whenever possible, the ethnologist becomes ethnographer by going to live among the people under study. Through **participant observation**—eating a people's food, speaking their language, and personally experiencing their habits and customs—the ethnographer is able to understand their way of life to a far greater extent than any non-participant anthropologist ever could; one learns a culture best by learning how to behave acceptably in the society in which one is doing fieldwork. To become a participant observer in the culture under study does not mean that the ethnographer must join in a people's battles in order to study a culture in which warfare is prominent; but by living among a warlike people, the ethnographer should be able to understand the role of warfare in the overall cultural scheme. He or she must be a meticulous observer in order to be able to get a broad overview of a culture without emphasizing one of its parts to the detriment of another. Only by discovering how all cultural institutions—social, political, economic, religious—relate to one another can the ethnographer begin to understand the cultural system. Anthropologists refer to this as the **holistic perspective,** and it is one of the fundamental principles of anthropology. Robert Gordon, an anthropologist from Namibia, speaks of it in this way: "Whereas the sociologist or the political scientist might examine the beauty of a flower petal by petal, the anthropologist is the

Participant observation: In ethnography, the technique of learning a people's culture through direct participation in their everyday life over an extended period of time.

Holistic perspective: A fundamental principle of anthropology, that things must be viewed in the broadest possible context, in order to understand their interconnections and interdependence.

person that stands on the top of the mountain and looks at the beauty of the field. In other words, we try and go for the wider perspective."[3]

So basic is ethnographic fieldwork to ethnology that the British anthropologist C.G. Seligman once asserted, "Field research in anthropology is what the blood of the martyrs is to the church."[4] Something of its flavor is conveyed by the experience of one young anthropologist working in Thailand.

[3]Robert Gordon, Interview for Coast Telecourses, Inc., Los Angeles, December 4, 1981.

[4]I.M. Lewis, *Social Anthropology in Perspective* (Harmondsworth, England: Penguin, 1976), p. 27.

ORIGINAL STUDY

PARTICIPANT OBSERVATION ON A MOTORCYCLE[5]

A short while after arriving in the field in southern Thailand, I managed to acquire a motorcycle. While I did not actually possess a licence to ride it, some kind words to those in high places by patrons who had taken me under their wing had cleared the way for me to be turned loose on the roads of Thailand without hindrance unless, it was sharply stressed, I was foolish enough to get involved in an accident. At an early stage I had wondered whether I should mention that my licence at home had been repossessed by a couple of incredulous policemen who took a very dim view of creative driving, but I felt that to try and explain this in Thai would probably lead to misunderstandings, and might well have caused my hosts unnecessary anxiety.

Come St. David's Day, the inevitable accident occurred. I had been on an afternoon jaunt on my freshly cleaned motorcycle, merrily weaving through the traffic, and thinking how interesting it was that Thai motorists actually lived out the theory of loose structure in their driving. During this course of musing I decided to make a right-hand turn, and still being rather set in my Western ways, slowed down to do so. This was an ethnocentric mistake. As I began to turn, another motorcyclist, complete with an ice chest full of fish and a large basket of oranges on the pillion seat, decided that this was the ideal moment to overtake. I was much too slow, he was far too fast, and our subjective constructions of existence spectacularly collided with the limits of the material world.

What followed was actually quite pleasurable for the brief but slow-motion moments it lasted. A massive surge of metal, flesh, fish, and disintegrating oranges swept me from behind, then passed overhead in a surrealistic collage as my body easily performed a series of gymnastic stunts that I had been totally unable to master at school. As always in life, the brief pleasure had to be repaid with an extended flood of unwelcome pain, relieved only by the happy realization that I, and the other motorist who had flown so gracefully above me, had narrowly but successfully avoided truncating our skulls on a Burmese ebony tree.

Anxious to reassure myself that nothing was broken, I got quickly to my feet, dusted myself off, and walked over to switch off my motorcycle engine, which by now was making a maniacal noise without its exhaust pipe. Then I walked back to the other rider, who was still lying rigidly on his back and wondering whether he should believe what was happening. I politely asked him if he was all right, but the hypothesis that in a crisis everyone reverts to speaking English clearly required some revision. Months of Thai lessons began to trickle back, but far too slowly, and in the meantime he had also stood up. It was only then that I realized the pair of us had been surrounded by a rather large crowd of onlookers.

Television in Thailand does not commence broadcasting until 4:30 p.m. so our little accident had a good audience, with local residents coming out of their houses and shops, and cars, motorcycles, and trucks stopping to take in the scene. The other rider began talking to some people near him, and a shopkeeper who knew me came and asked if I was all right. From that moment, I never had a chance to speak to the other rider again. We were slowly but surely separated, each of us in the centre of a group, the two groups gathering slightly apart from one another. I had a sudden and horrible realization that I was in the middle of one of those dispute settlement cases that I had intermittently dozed through as an undergraduate. With an abrupt and sickening shock, participant observation had become rather too much participation and too little cosy observation.

Some of the other rider's newly acquired entourage came over to ask the fringes of my group what exactly had happened. I pleaded my version to those standing close to me, and it was then relayed—and, I should add, suitably amended—back through the throng to be taken away and compared with the other rider's tale of woe. While this little contest was going on, a number of people from both groups were inspecting the rather forlorn wreckages of our motorcycles and debating over which one appeared to be more badly damaged. "Look at this!" someone cried, lifting a torn section of the seat and helpfully making the tear more ostentatious in the process. "But look at this!" came the reply, as someone else wrenched a limply hanging indicator light completely off its mounting. After a series of such exchanges, the two groups finally agreed that both motorcycles were in an equally derelict state, though I could not help feeling, peering from the little prison within my group of supporters, that those judging the damage to the machines had played a more than passive role in ensuring a parity of demolition.

Physical injuries were the next to be subjected to this adjudication process. I found my shirt being lifted up, and a chorus of oohs and aahs issuing from the crowd, as someone with jolly animation prodded and pinched the large areas of my back which were now bravely attempting to stay in place without the aid of skin. My startled eyes began looking in opposite directions at the same time, while somewhat less than human groans gargled out of my mouth. From similar sounds in the distance I deduced that the other poor rider was being subjected to similar treatment. He frankly looked rather the worse for wear than I did, but whenever his group claimed this, my supporters would proceed to show just what excruciating pain I was suffering by prodding me in the back and indicating my randomly circumambulating eyes as if to say "see, we told you so."

On issues of damage, both mechanical and physical, we were adjudged by the two groups to be fairly evenly scored. Fault in relation to road rules had never been an issue. Then came a bit of a lull, as if something serious was about to happen. A senior person from the other group came over and spoke to me directly, asking if I wanted to call the police. A hush fell over everyone. I, of course, was totally terrified at the prospect—no licence, visions of deportation, and so far only one meagre book of field notes to my name. I put on my best weak pathetic smile and mumbled that I thought it was not really necessary unless the other chap insisted. A culturally appropriate move: everyone looked happily relieved, and the other rider's spokesman said generously that it would only be a waste of time and cause unnecessary bother to bring the police out on an errand like this. It was to be a few months before I realized that, like many other motorcyclists, the other rider was also probably roaming the roads without a licence, and that in this part of the country calling the police was generally regarded as a last, and unsporting, resort.

The final agreement was that we should settle our own repairs—to both body and vehicle—and let the matter rest. A visible sigh of relief passed through the two groups that had gathered, and they slowly began to disperse. For the first time since the collision, I saw the other rider face to face, so I walked towards him to offer my apologies. I never managed to reach him. The dispersing groups froze in horror, then quickly regathered around me. "What is wrong now?" I was interrogated on all sides. Was I not happy with the result? I had clearly made a serious blunder, and it took a while to settle things down once more. A perceptive shopkeeper from nearby grabbed my arm and dragged me off to his shop for coffee, explaining to me that the matter had been settled and that further contact for any reason with the other rider or his group would only prolong an unpleasant situation that could now be forgotten by all involved.

So it was that later that evening I was able to start my second book of field notes with an entry on dispute settlement, though painful twinges up my back and throbbing between the ears made me wish I had relied on some other informant to provide the ethnographic details. I made a silent vow to myself to discontinue this idiosyncratic method of participant observation, and managed to some extent to keep the vow for the rest of my stay. Thereafter I successfully steered clear of motorcycle accidents, and instead got shot at, electrocuted, and innocently involved in scandal and otherwise abused. But all that, as they say, is another story.

[5]Andrew Cornish, "Participant Observation on a Motorcycle," *Anthropology Today*, 3(6) (December 1987): 15–16. By permission of the Royal Anthropological Institute of Great Britain and Ireland.

The popular image of ethnographic fieldwork is that it takes place among far-off, exotic peoples. To be sure, a lot of ethnographic work has been done in places like Africa, the islands of the Pacific Ocean, the deserts of Australia, and so on. One very good reason for this is that non-Western peoples have been too often ignored by other social scientists. Still, anthropologists have recognized from the start that an understanding of human behavior depends upon knowledge of all cultures and peoples, including their own. During the years of the Great Depression and World War II, for example, many anthropologists in the United States worked in settings ranging from factories to whole communities. One of the landmark studies of this period was W. Lloyd Warner's study of "Yankee City" (Newburyport, Massachusetts). Less well known is that it was an anthropologist, Philleo Nash, working at the time in the White House under presidents Franklin Roosevelt and Harry Truman, who was instrumental in desegregating the U.S. armed forces and moving the national government into the field of civil rights.

In the 1950s, the availability of large amounts of money for research in foreign lands diverted attention from work at home. More recently, as political unrest made fieldwork increasingly difficult to carry out, there was renewed awareness of important anthropological problems that need to be dealt with in North American society. Many of these problems involve people that anthropologists have studied in other settings. Thus, as Hispanic Americans have moved into the cities of the United States, or as refugees have arrived from southeast Asia, anthropologists have been there not just to study them, but to help them adjust to their new circumstances. Simultaneously, anthropologists are applying the same research techniques that served them so well in the study of non-Western peoples to the study of such diverse things as street gangs, corporate bureaucracies, religious cults, health care delivery systems, schools, and how people deal with consumer complaints.

An important discovery from such research is that it produces knowledge that usually does not emerge from the kinds of research done by other social scientists. For example, the theory of cultural deprivation arose during the 1960s as a way of explaining the educational failure of many children of minorities. In order to account for their lack of

Anthropologists carry out fieldwork at home as well as abroad. Known on the road as "Dr. Truck," Michael Agar spends much of his time in the cabs of eighteen-wheelers studying the culture of independent truckers.

achievement, some social scientists proposed that such children were culturally deprived. They then proceeded to "confirm" this idea by studying children, mostly from American Indian, black, and Hispanic populations, interpreting the results through the protective screen of their theory. By contrast, ethnographic research on the cultures of "culturally deprived" children reveals a different story. Far from being culturally deprived, they have elaborate, sophisticated, and adaptive cultures that are simply different from the ones espoused by the educational system. Although some still cling to it, the cultural-deprivation theory is culture-bound, and is merely a way of saying that people are deprived of the speaker's culture. One cannot argue that such children do not speak adequate Spanish, black English, or whatever, or that they do not do well the things that are considered rewarding in *their* cultures.

Much though it has to offer, the anthropological study of one's own culture is not without its own special problems. Sir Edmund Leach, a noted British anthropologist, puts it in the following way:

> Surprising though it may seem, fieldwork in a cultural context of which you already have intimate

first-hand experience seems to be much more difficult than fieldwork which is approached from the naive viewpoint of a total stranger. When anthropologists study facets of their own society their vision seems to become distorted by prejudices which derive from private rather than public experience.[6]

Probably the most successful anthropological studies of their own culture by North Americans have been done by those who first worked in some other culture. Lloyd Warner, for example, had studied the Murngin of Australia before he tackled Newburyport. In addition to studying a culture outside of their own before North Americans try to study the familiar, much is to be gained by encouraging anthropologists from Africa, Asia, and South America to do fieldwork in North America. From their outsiders' perspective come insights all too easily overlooked by an insider. Nonetheless, the special difficulties of studying one's own culture can be overcome; what it requires is an acute awareness of those difficulties.

Although ethnographic fieldwork is basic to ethnology, it is not the sole occupation of the ethnologist. What it provides is the basic data the ethnologist may then use to study one particular aspect of a culture by comparing it with that same aspect in others. Anthropologists constantly make such cross-cultural comparisons, and this is another hallmark of the discipline. Interesting insights into our own practices may come from cross-cultural comparisons, as when one compares the time that people devote to what we consider to be "housework." In North American society, people generally believe that the ever-increasing output of household appliance consumer goods has resulted in a steady reduction in housework, with a consequent increase in leisure time. Thus, consumer appliances have become principal indicators of a high standard of living. Anthropological research among food foragers (people who rely on wild plant and animal resources for subsistence), however, has shown that they work far less at household tasks, and indeed less at all subsistence pursuits, than do people in industrialized societies. Aboriginal Australian women, for example, devote an average of approximately 20 hours per week to collecting and preparing food, as well as other domestic chores, whereas

women in the rural United States in the 1920s, without the benefit of laborsaving appliances, devoted approximately 52 hours a week to their housework. Some 50 years later, contrary to all expectations, urban U.S. women who were not working for wages outside their homes were putting 55 hours a week into their housework, in spite of all their "laborsaving" dishwashers, washing machines, clothes dryers, vacuum cleaners, food processors, and microwave ovens.[7]

Cross-cultural comparisons highlight alternative ways of doing things, and so have much to offer North Americans, significant numbers of whom, opinion polls show, continue to doubt the effectiveness of their own ways of doing things. In this sense, one may think of ethnology as the study of alternative ways of doing things. At the same time, by making systematic cross-cultural comparisons, ethnologists seek to arrive at valid conclusions concerning the nature of culture in all times and places.

ANTHROPOLOGY AND SCIENCE

The chief concern of all anthropologists is the careful and systematic study of humankind. Anthropology has been called a social or a behavioral science by some, a natural science by others, and one of the humanities by still others. Can the work of the anthropologist properly be labeled scientific? What exactly do we mean by the term *science*?

Science is a powerful and elegant way people have hit upon to understand the workings of the visible world and universe. Science seeks testable explanations for observed phenomena in terms of the workings of hidden but universal and immutable principles, or laws. Two basic ingredients are essential for this: imagination and skepticism. Imagination, though capable of leading us astray, is required in order that we may imagine the ways in which phenomena might be ordered, and think of old things in new ways. Without it, there can be no science. Skepticism is what allows us to distinguish fact from fancy, to test our speculations, and to prevent our capricious imaginations from running away with us.

[6]Edmund Leach, *Social Anthropology* (Glasgow: Fontana Paperbacks, 1982), p. 124.

[7]Bodley, *Anthropology*, p. 69.

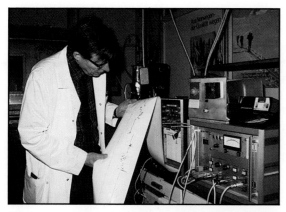

To many people, a scientist is someone who works in a laboratory, carrying out experiments with the aid of specialized equipment. Contrary to such a stereotypical image, not all scientists are white men in lab coats, not all work in laboratories, and experimentation is not the only technique they use.

In their search for explanations, scientists do not assume that things are always as they appear on the surface. After all, what could be more obvious than that the earth is a stable entity, around which the sun travels every day? And yet, it isn't so. Supernatural explanations are rejected, as are all explanations and appeals to authority that are not supported by strong observational evidence. Because explanations are constantly challenged by new observations and novel ideas, science is self-correcting; that is, inadequate explanations are sooner or later shown up as such, and are replaced by more reliable explanations.

The scientist begins with an **hypothesis,** or tentative explanation of the relationship between certain phenomena. By gathering various kinds of data that seem to support such generalizations, and, equally important, by showing that alternative hypotheses are false, and should be eliminated from consideration, the scientist arrives at a system of validated hypotheses, or **theory.** Although a theory

Hypothesis: A tentative explanation of the relation between certain phenomena.

Theory: A system of validated hypotheses that explains phenomena systematically.

is actually a well-supported body of knowledge, no theory is acknowledged to be beyond challenge. Truth, in science, is not considered to be absolute, but rather a matter of varying degrees of probability; what is considered to be true is what is most probable. This is true of anthropology, just as it is true of biology or physics. As our knowledge expands, the odds in favor of some theories over others are generally increased, but sometimes old "truths" must be discarded as alternative theories are shown to be more probable.

DIFFICULTIES OF THE SCIENTIFIC APPROACH

Straightforward though the scientific approach may appear to be, there are serious difficulties in its application in anthropology. One of them is that once one has stated a hypothesis, one is strongly motivated to verify it, and this can cause one unwittingly to overlook negative evidence, not to mention all sorts of other unexpected things. This is a familiar problem in science; as paleontologist Stephen Jay Gould put it, "The greatest impediment to scientific innovation is usually a conceptual lock, not a factual lock."[8] In the fields of cultural anthropology there is a further difficulty: In order to arrive at useful theories concerning human behavior, one must begin with hypotheses that are as objective and as little culture-bound as possible. And here lies a major—some people would say insurmountable—problem: It is difficult for someone who has grown up in one culture to frame objective hypotheses about another that are not culture-bound.

As one example of this sort of problem, we may look at attempts by archaeologists to understand the nature of settlement in the Classic period of Maya civilization. This civilization flourished between

[8]Stephen Jay Gould, *Wonderful Life* (New York: Norton, 1989), p. 226.

Nagasaki one month after the atomic bomb blast of August 9, 1945. Japan surrendered less than a week after the blast. Late in World War II, however, anthropologists and other social scientists working for the U.S. government had predicted a Japanese surrender without the need to drop nuclear bombs.

A.D. 250 and 900 in what is now northern Guatemala, Belize, and adjacent portions of Mexico and Honduras. Today much of this region is covered by a dense tropical forest of the sort that people of European background find difficult to deal with. In recent times this forest has been inhabited by few people, who sustain themselves through slash-and-burn farming. (After cutting and burning the natural vegetation, crops are grown for only two years or so before fertility is exhausted and a new field must be cleared.) Yet numerous archaeological sites, featuring temples sometimes as tall as a modern 20-story building, other sorts of monumental architecture, and carved monuments are to be found there. Because of their cultural bias against tropical forests as places to live, and against slash-and-burn farming as a means of raising food, North American and European archaeologists asked the question: How could the Maya have maintained large, permanent settlements on the basis of slash-and-burn farming? The answer seemed self-evident—they couldn't; therefore, the great archaeological sites must have been ceremonial centers inhabited by

few, if any, people. Periodically a rural peasantry, living scattered in small hamlets over the countryside, must have gathered in these centers for rituals, or to provide labor for their construction and maintenance.

This view was the dominant one for several decades, and it was not until 1960 that archaeologists working at Tikal, one of the largest of all Maya sites, decided to ask the simplest and least biased questions they could think of: Did anyone live at this particular site on a permanent basis; if so, how many, and how were they supported? Working intensively over the next decade, with as few preconceived notions as possible, the archaeologists were able to establish that Tikal was a huge settlement inhabited by tens of thousands of people, who were supported by intensive forms of agriculture. It was this work at Tikal that paved the way for a new understanding of Classic Maya civilization totally at odds with the older, culture-bound ideas.

Recognizing the problem of framing hypotheses that are not culture-bound, anthropologists have relied heavily on a technique that has proved

The unique character of anthropology among the social sciences in North America owes a great deal to these three men, all educated in the natural sciences: Franz Boas (1858–1942), in physics; Frederic Ward Putnam (1839–1915), in zoology; and John Wesley Powell (1834–1902), in geology. Although not the first to teach anthropology, Boas (and his students) made such courses a common part of college and university curricula. Similarly, Putnam established anthropology in the museum world, as did Powell in government.

successful in other fields of the natural sciences. As did the archaeologists working at Tikal, they immerse themselves in the data to the fullest extent possible. By doing so, they become so thoroughly familiar with the minute details that they can begin to see patterns inherent in the data, many of which might otherwise have been overlooked. These patterns are what allow the anthropologist to frame hypotheses, which then may be subjected to further testing.

This approach is most easily seen in ethnographic fieldwork, but it is just as important in archaeology. Unlike many social scientists, the ethnographer usually does not go into the field armed with prefigured questionnaires; rather, the ethnographer recognizes that there are probably all sorts of unguessed things, to be found out only by maintaining as open a mind as one can. This is not to say that anthropologists never use questionnaires, for sometimes they do. Generally, though, they use them as a means of supplementing or clarifying information gained through some other means. As the fieldwork proceeds, ethnographers sort their complex observations into a meaningful whole, sometimes by formulating and testing limited or low-level hypotheses, but as often as not by making use of intuition and playing hunches. What is important is that the results are constantly scrutinized for consistency, for if the parts fail to fit together in a manner that is internally consistent, then the eth-

nographer knows that a mistake has been made and that further work is necessary.

The contrast between the anthropological and other social-science approaches is dramatically illustrated by the following example—one of several —presented by Robert Chambers in his book *Rural Development*. Since Chambers is a highly respected professional in the field of international development, and not an anthropologist, he can scarcely be accused of trying to promote his own discipline at the expense of others.

> Sean Conlin lived as a social anthropologist in a village in Peru. While he was there a sociologist came and carried out a survey. According to the sociologist's results, people in the village invariably worked together on each other's individually owned plots of land. That was what they told him. But in the period of over a year during which Conlin lived in the village, he observed the practice only once. The belief in exchange relations was, he concludes, important for the people's understanding of themselves, but it was not an economic fact.[9]

This does not mean that all sociological research is bad and all anthropological research is good; merely that reliance on questionnaire surveys is a risky business, no matter who does it. Robert Chambers sums up the difficulties:

[9]Robert Chambers, *Rural Development: Putting the Last First* (New York: Longman, 1983), p. 51.

Unless careful appraisal precedes drawing up a questionnaire, the survey will embody the concepts and categories of outsiders rather than those of rural people, and thus impose meanings on the social reality. The misfit between the concepts of urban professionals and those of poor rural people is likely to be substantial, and the questions asked may construct artificial chunks of 'knowledge' which distort or mutilate the reality which poor people experience. Nor are questionnaire surveys on their own good ways of identifying causal relationships—a correlation alone tells us nothing definite about cause—or of exploring social relationships such as reciprocity, dependence, exploitation and so on. Their penetration is usually shallow, concentrating on what is measurable, answerable, and acceptable as a question, rather than probing less tangible and more qualitative aspects of society. For many reasons—fear, prudence, ignorance, exhaustion, hostility, hope of benefit—poor people give information which is slanted or false.

For these and many other reasons, conventional questionnaire surveys have many drawbacks if the aim is to gain insight into the lives and conditions of the poorer rural people. Other methods are required, either alone, or together with surveys. But extensive questionnaire surveys pre-empt resources, capturing staff and finance, and preventing other approaches.[10]

The end result of archaeological or ethnographic fieldwork, if properly carried out, is a coherent

[10]Ibid., p. 51.

account of a culture, which provides an explanatory framework for understanding the behavior of the people who have been studied. And this, in turn, is what permits the anthropologist to frame broader hypotheses about human behavior. Plausible though such hypotheses may be, however, the consideration of a single society is generally insufficient for their testing. Without some basis for comparison, the hypothesis grounded in a single case may be no more than an historical coincidence. A single case may be adequate, however, to cast doubt on, if not refute, a theory that had previously been held to be valid. The discovery in 1948 that aborigines living in Australia's Arnhem Land put in an average work day of less than 6 hours, while living well above a level of bare sufficiency, was enough to call into question the widely accepted notion that food-foraging peoples are so preoccupied with finding food that they lack time for any of life's more pleasurable activities. Even today, economists are prone to label such peoples as backward (some examples will be given in Chapter 6 and the Introduction to Part V), even though the observations made in the Arnhem Land study have since been confirmed many times over in various parts of the world.

Hypothetical explanations of cultural phenomena may be tested by the comparison of archaeological and/or ethnographic data for several societies

Ju/wasi family members relax in their Kalahari Desert home. Like most food foragers, these people spend only a small percentage of their time working—in this case, no more than about 20 hours a week.

found in a particular region. Nonhistorical, controlled comparison provides a broader context for understanding cultural phenomena than does the study of a single culture. The anthropologist who undertakes such a comparison may be more confident that the conditions believed to be related really are related, at least within the region that is under investigation; however, an explanation that is valid in one region is not necessarily so in another.

Ideally, theories in cultural anthropology are generated from worldwide comparisons. The cross-cultural researcher examines a worldwide sample of societies in order to discover whether or not hypotheses proposed to explain cultural phenomena seem to be universally applicable. Because the sample is selected at random, it is probable that the conclusions of the cross-cultural researcher will be valid; however, the greater the number of societies being examined, the less likely it is that the investigator will have a detailed understanding of all the societies encompassed by the study. The cross-cultural researcher depends upon other ethnographers for data. It is impossible for any single individual personally to perform in-depth analyses of a broad sample of human cultures throughout the world.

In anthropology, cultural comparisons need not be restricted to ethnographic data. Anthropologists can, for example, turn to archaeological data to test hypotheses about culture change. Cultural characteristics thought to be caused by certain specified conditions can be tested archaeologically by investigating situations where such conditions actually occurred. Also useful are data provided by the ethnohistorian. **Ethnohistory** is a kind of historic ethnography that studies cultures of the recent past through the accounts of explorers, missionaries, and traders and through the analysis of such records as land titles, birth and death

records, and other archival materials. The ethnohistorical analysis of cultures, like archaeology, is a valuable approach to understanding change. By examining the conditions believed to have caused certain phenomena, we can discover whether or not those conditions truly precede those phenomena.

Ethnohistorical research, like the field studies of archaeologists, is valuable for testing and confirming hypotheses about culture. And like much of anthropology, it has practical utility as well. In the United States, ethnohistorical research has flourished, for it often provides the key evidence necessary for deciding legal cases involving Native American land claims.

ANTHROPOLOGY AND THE HUMANITIES

Although the sciences and humanities are often thought of as mutually exclusive approaches to learning, they come together in anthropology. That is why, for example, anthropological research is funded not only by such "hard science" agencies as the National Science Foundation, but also by such organizations as the National Endowment for the Humanities. The humanistic side of anthropology is perhaps most immediately evident in its concern with other cultures' languages, values, and achievements in the arts and literature (oral literature, among peoples who lack writing). Beyond this, anthropologists remain committed to the proposition that one cannot fully understand another culture by observing it; one must *experience* it as well. Thus, ethnographers spend prolonged periods of time living with the people whom they study, sharing their joys and suffering their deprivations, including sickness and, sometimes, premature death. They are not so naive as to believe that they can be, or even should be, dispassionate about the people whose trials and tribulations they share. As Robin Fox puts it, "our hearts, as well as our brains, should be with our men and women."[11] Nor are anthropologists so self-deceived as to believe that they can avoid dealing with the moral and political consequences of their findings.

Ethnohistory: The study of cultures of the recent past through oral histories, accounts left by explorers, missionaries, and traders, and through the analysis of such records as land titles, birth and death records, and other archival materials.

[11]Robin Fox, *Encounter with Anthropology* (New York: Dell, 1968), p. 290.

Given their intense encounters with other peoples, it should come as no surprise that anthropologists have amassed as much information about human frailty and nobility—the stuff of the humanities—as any other discipline. Small wonder, too, that above all they intend to avoid allowing a "coldly" scientific approach to blind them to the fact that human societies are made up of individuals with rich assortments of emotions and aspirations that demand respect. Anthropology has sometimes been called the most human of the sciences, a designation in which anthropologists take considerable pride.

QUESTIONS OF ETHICS

The kinds of research carried out by anthropologists, and the settings within which they work, raise a number of important questions concerning ethics. Who will make use of the findings of anthropologists, and for what purposes? In the case of a militant minority, for example, will others use anthropological data to suppress that minority? And what of traditional communities around the world? Who is to decide what changes should, or should not, be introduced for community "betterment"? By whose definition is it betterment—the community's or that of a remote national government? Then there is the problem of privacy. Anthropologists deal with people's private and sensitive matters, including things that people would not care to have generally known about them. How does one write about such matters and at the same time protect the privacy of informants? Not surprisingly, because of these and other questions, there has been much discussion among anthropologists over the past two decades on the subject of ethics.

The present consensus among anthropologists about the ethics of their profession was summed up by Laura Nader in an interview:

> Anthropologists have obligations to three different sets of people. First, to the people that we study; secondly, to the profession which expects us to report back our findings; and thirdly, to the organizations that fund the research. Some people would order them differently—one, two, three, three, two, one, or whatever—but those three are in the minds of most anthropologists. Now, sometimes the obligations con-

flict. If I do fieldwork among a group of people and I learn certain things that, if revealed, might come back to hurt them, then reporting my findings back to the profession is going to be secondary because first and foremost I have to protect my informants because they trusted me. In the case of the Zapotec, I was dealing with very sensitive materials about law and disputes and conflicts and so forth. And I was very sensitive about how much of that to report while people were still alive and while things might still be warm, so I waited on that. I'm just finishing my Zapotec monograph now. I've written certain things, but I waited for the most part, and I feel comfortable now releasing that information. With regard to a funder in that case, it was the Mexican government, and I feel that I have written enough to have paid off the $1200 which they gave me to support that work for a year. So, I've not felt particularly strained for my Zapotec work in those three areas. On energy research that I've done, it's been another story. Much of what people wanted me to do energy research for was . . . to tell people in decision-making positions about American consumers in such a way that they could be manipulated better, and I didn't want to do that. So what I said was I would be willing to study a vertical slice. That is, I would never study the consumer without studying the producer. And once you take a vertical slice like that, then it's fair because you're telling the consumer about the producer and the producer about the consumer. But just to do a study of consumers for producers, I think I would feel uncomfortable.[12]

ANTHROPOLOGY AND CONTEMPORARY LIFE

Anthropology, with its long-standing commitment to understanding people in all parts of the world, coupled with its holistic perspective, is better equipped than any other discipline to grapple with a problem of overriding importance for all of humanity in this last quarter of the twentieth century. An inescapable fact of life is that North Americans live in a global community in which all the world's people are interdependent. Although there is widespread awareness of this in the business communi-

[12]Laura Nader, Interview for Coast Telecourses, Inc., Los Angeles, December 3, 1981.

Like the ethnologist, the religious missionary lives among an unfamiliar "people under study." But where the missionary seeks to transform people (through spiritual conversion), the ethnologist seeks instead to investigate and comprehend them just as they are, through *participant observation.*

ty, which relies on foreign sources for raw materials, sees the non-Western world as its major area for market expansion, and is more and more making its products abroad, citizens of the United States are on the whole as ignorant about the cultures of the rest of the world as they have ever been. As a result, they are poorly equipped to handle the demands of living in the modern world.

Anthropologist Dennis Shaw sums up the implications of this state of affairs:

Such provinciality raises questions about the welfare of our nation and the global context in which it is a major force. We have, as a nation, continued to interpret the political actions of other nations in terms of the cultural and political norms of our own culture and have thus made major misinterpretations of global political affairs. Our economic interests have been pursued from the perspective of our own cultural norms, and thus, we have failed to keep up with other nations that have shown a sensitivity to cultural differences. Domestically, a serious question can be raised about the viability of a democracy in which a major portion of the electorate is basically ignorant of the issues which our political leaders must confront. Internationally, one can speculate about the well-being of a world in which the citizens of one of the most powerful nations are seriously deficient in their ability to evaluate global issues.[13]

Former ambassador Edwin Reischauer put it more tersely: "Education is not moving rapidly enough in the right directions to produce the knowledge about the outside world and attitudes toward other peoples that may be essential for human survival."[14] What anthropology has to contribute to contemporary life, then, is an understanding of, and way of looking at, the world's peoples, faculties which are nothing less than basic skills for survival in the modern world.

Chapter Summary

Throughout human history, people have needed to know who they are, where they came from, and why they behave as they do. Traditionally, myths and legends provided the answers to these questions. Anthropology, as it has emerged over the last 200 years, offers another approach to answering the questions people ask about themselves.

Anthropology is the study of humankind. In employing a scientific approach, anthropologists seek to produce useful generalizations about humans and their behavior and to arrive at a reasonably objective understanding of human diversity. The two major fields of anthropology are physical and cultural anthropology. Physical anthropology focuses on humans as biological organisms. Particular emphasis is given by physical anthropologists to tracing the evolutionary development of the human animal and studying biological variation within the species today. Cultural anthropologists study humans in terms of their cultures, the often unconscious standards by which societies operate.

Three areas of cultural anthropology are archaeology, anthropological linguistics, and ethnology. Archaeologists study material objects usually from past cultures in order to explain human behavior.

Linguists, who study human languages, may deal with the description of a language or with the history of languages. Ethnologists concentrate on cultures of the present or recent past; in doing comparative studies of culture, they may also focus on a particular aspect of culture, such as religious or economic practices, or as ethnographers, they may go into the field to observe and describe human behavior as it can be seen, experienced, and discussed with persons whose culture is to be understood.

Anthropology is unique among the social and natural sciences in that it is concerned with formulating explanations of human diversity based on a study of all aspects of human biology and behavior in all known societies, rather than in European and North American societies alone. Thus anthropologists have devoted much attention to the study of non-Western peoples.

Anthropologists are concerned with the objective and systematic study of humankind. The anthropologist employs the methods of other scientists by developing a hypothesis, or assumed explanation, using other data to test the hypothesis, and ultimately arriving at a theory—a system of

[13]Dennis G. Shaw, "A Light at the End of the Tunnel: Anthropological Contributions Towards Global Competence," *Anthropology Newsletter,* 25 (November 1984):16.

[14]Quoted in Susan L. Allen, "Media Anthropology: Building a Public Perspective," *Anthropology Newsletter,* 25 (November 1984):6.

validated hypotheses. The data used by the cultural anthropologist may be field data of one society or comparative studies of numerous societies.

In anthropology, the humanities and sciences come together into a genuinely human science. Anthropology's link with the humanities can be seen in its concern with people's values, languages, arts, and literature—oral as well as written—but above all in its attempt to convey the experience of living as other people do. As both science and humanity, anthropology has essential skills to offer the modern world, where understanding the other people with whom we share the globe has become a matter of survival.

Suggested Readings

Lett, James. *The Human Enterprise: A Critical Introduction to Anthropological Theory.* Boulder, Colo.: Westview, 1987.
Part 1 examines the philosophical foundations of anthropological theory, paying special attention to the nature of scientific inquiry and the mechanisms of scientific progress. Part 2 deals with the nature of social science as well as the particular features of anthropology.

Peacock, James L. *The Anthropological Lens: Harsh Light, Soft Focus.* New York: Cambridge University Press, 1986.
This lively and innovative book manages to give the reader a good understanding of the diversity of activities undertaken by anthropologists, while at the same time identifying the unifying themes that hold the discipline together.

Spradley, James P. *The Ethnographic Interview.* New York: Holt, Rinehart and Winston, 1979.
This contains one of the best discussions of the nature and value of ethnographic research to be found. The bulk of the book is devoted to a step-by-step, easy-to-understand account of how one carries out ethnographic research with the assistance of "informants." Numerous examples drawn from the author's own research in such diverse settings as Skid Row, courtrooms, and bars make for interesting reading. A companion volume, *Participant Observation,* is also highly recommended.

Vogt, Fred W. *A History of Ethnology.* New York: Holt, Rinehart and Winston, 1975.
This history of cultural anthropology attempts to describe and interpret the major intellectual strands, in their cultural and historical contexts, that influenced the development of the field. The author tries for a balanced view of this subject rather than one that would support a particular theoretical position.

CHAPTER

2

THE NATURE

OF

CULTURE

A cow-powered irrigation system in Egypt. All over the world, people have worked out their own solutions to particular problems of existence. Though sometimes construed as old-fashioned, traditional ways often offer more workable solutions than so-called modern ways.

WHAT IS CULTURE?

Culture consists of the abstract values, beliefs, and perceptions of the world that lie behind people's behavior, and which are reflected in their behavior. These are shared by members of a society, and when acted upon, they produce behavior considered acceptable within that society. Cultures are learned, largely through the medium of language, rather than inherited biologically, and the parts of a culture function as an integrated whole.

HOW IS CULTURE STUDIED?

Anthropologists, like children, learn about a culture by experiencing it and talking about it with those who live by its rules. Of course, anthropologists have less time to learn, but are more systematic in the way they learn. Through careful observation and discussion with informants who are particularly knowledgeable in the ways of their culture, the anthropologist abstracts a set of rules in order to explain how people behave in a particular society.

WHY DO CULTURES EXIST?

People maintain cultures to deal with problems or matters that concern them. To survive, a culture must satisfy the basic needs of those who live by its rules, provide for its own continuity, and provide an orderly existence for the members of a society. In doing so, a culture must strike a balance between the self-interests of individuals and the needs of society as a whole. And finally, a culture must have the capacity to change in order to adapt to new circumstances or to altered perceptions of existing circumstances.

Students of anthropology are bound to find themselves studying a seemingly endless variety of human societies, each with its own distinctive system of politics, economics, and religion. Yet for all this variation, these societies have one thing in common. Each is a collection of people cooperating to ensure their collective survival and well-being. In order for this to work, some degree of predictable behavior is required of each individual within the society, for group living and cooperation are impossible unless individuals know how others are likely to behave in any given situation. In humans, it is culture that sets the limits of behavior and guides it along predictable paths.

THE CONCEPT OF CULTURE

The **culture** concept was first developed by anthropologists toward the end of the nineteenth century. The first really clear and comprehensive definition was that of the British anthropologist Sir Edward Burnett Tylor. Writing in 1871, Tylor defined culture as "that complex whole which includes knowledge, belief, art, law, morals, custom and any other capabilities and habits acquired by man as a member of society." Since Tylor's time, definitions of culture have proliferated. In the 1950s, the late A.L. Kroeber and Clyde Kluckhohn combed the literature and collected over a hundred definitions of culture. Recent definitions tend to distinguish more clearly between actual behavior on the one hand and the abstract values, beliefs, and perceptions of the world that lie behind that behavior on the other. To put it another way, culture is not observable behavior, but rather the values and beliefs that people use to interpret experience and generate behavior, and which are reflected in their behavior. An acceptable modern definition of culture, then, runs as follows: Culture is a set of rules

---

Culture: A set of rules or standards shared by members of a society, which, when acted upon by the members, produce behavior that falls within a range of variation the members consider proper and acceptable.

---

or standards that, when acted upon by the members of a society, produce behavior that falls within a range of variance the members consider proper and acceptable.

CHARACTERISTICS OF CULTURE

Through the comparative study of many different cultures, anthropologists have arrived at an understanding of the basic characteristics that all cultures share. A careful study of these helps us to see the importance and the function of culture itself.

CULTURE IS SHARED

Culture is a set of shared ideals, values, and standards of behavior; it is the common denominator that makes the actions of individuals intelligible to the group. Because they share a common culture, people can predict how others are most likely to behave in a given circumstance and react accordingly. A group of people from different cultures, stranded over a period of time on a desert island, might appear to become a society of sorts. They would have a common interest—survival—and would develop techniques for living and working together. Each of the members of this group, however, would retain his or her own identity and cultural background, and the group would disintegrate without further ado as soon as its members were rescued from the island. The group would have been merely an aggregate in time and not a cultural entity. **Society** may be defined as a group of people occupying a specific locality, who are dependent on each other for survival and who share a common culture. The way in which these people depend upon each other can be seen in such things as their economic systems and their family relationships; moreover, members of a society are held together by a sense of group identity. The relation-

---

Society: A group of people who occupy a specific locality and who share common cultural traditions.

Social structure: The relationships of groups within a society that hold it together.

---

ships that hold a society together are known as its **social structure.**

Culture and society are two closely related concepts, and anthropologists study both. Obviously, there can be no culture without a society, just as there can be no society without individuals. Conversely, there are no known human societies that do not exhibit culture. Some other species of animals, however, do lead a social existence. Ants and bees, for example, instinctively cooperate in a manner that clearly indicates a degree of social organization, yet this instinctual behavior is not a culture. One can, therefore, have a society (but not a *human* society) without a culture, even though one cannot have a culture without a society. Whether or not there exist animals other than humans that are capable of culture is a question that will be dealt with shortly.

While a culture is shared by members of a society, it is important to realize that all is not uniformity. In any human society, there is at the very least some difference between the roles of men and women. This stems from the fact that women give birth but men do not, and that there are obvious differences between male and female anatomy. What every culture does is to give meaning to these differences by explaining them and specifying what is to be done about them. Every culture as well specifies how the two kinds of people resulting from the differences should relate to each other and to the world at large. Since each culture does this in its own way, there is tremendous variation from one society to another. Anthropologists use the term **gender** to refer to the cultural elaborations and meanings assigned to the biological differentiation between the sexes.

The distinction between sex, which is biological, and gender, which is cultural, is an important one. Presumably, gender differences are as old as human culture—about 2.5 million years—and arose from the biological differences between early human males and females. Back then, males were about twice the size of females, as they are today among such species as gorillas, orangutans, and baboons. As humans evolved, however, the biological differences between the two sexes were radically reduced. Thus, whatever biological basis there once was for gender role differences has largely disappeared. Nevertheless, cultures have maintained some differentiation of gender roles ever since, although these differences are far greater in some societies than others. Paradoxically, gender differences were far more extreme in late nineteenth and early twentieth century Western

---

Gender: The elaborations and meanings assigned by cultures to the biological differentiation of the sexes.

In all societies, children's play is used both consciously and unconsciously to teach gender roles.

(European and European-derived) societies than they are among most historically known food-foraging peoples whose ways of life, though not unchanged, are more like those of the late Stone Age ancestors of Western peoples. In other words, differences between the behavior of men and women in North American and Western societies today, which are thought by many to be rooted in human biology, are not so rooted at all. Rather, they appear to have been recently elaborated in the course of history.

In addition to cultural differences along lines of sex, there will also be some age variation. In any society, children are not expected to behave as adults, and the reverse is equally true. Besides age and sex variation, there may be variation among subgroups in societies. These may be occupational groups, where there is a complex division of labor, or social classes in a stratified society, or ethnic groups in some other societies. When such groups exist within a society, each functioning by its own distinctive standards of behavior while at the same time sharing some standards in common, we speak

Subcultural variation: A distinctive set of standards and behavior patterns by which a group within a larger society operates.

of **subcultural variation.** The word *subcultural*, it should be noted, carries no connotation of lesser status relative to the word *cultural*. The degree to which subcultures are tolerated varies greatly from one society to another. Consider, for example, the following case from the *Wall Street Journal* of May 13, 1983:

SALT LAKE CITY—Police called it a cross-cultural misunderstanding. When the man showed up to buy the Shetland pony advertised for sale, the owner asked what he intended to do with the animal.

"For my son's birthday," he replied, and the deal was closed.

The buyer thereupon clubbed the pony to death with a two-by-four, dumped the carcass in his pickup truck and drove away. The horrified seller called the

Funerals have become commonplace in Guatemala, a prime example of a pluralistic society in which cultural differences have escalated into bloodshed and violence. Thousands of Indian men, women, and children have been killed by the forces of a government controlled by a non-Indian minority. Those not killed are systematically deprived of the means of providing for their own well-being.

Pluralistic societies: Societies in which there exists a diversity of cultural patterns.

police, who tracked down the buyer. At his house they found a birthday party in progress. The pony was trussed and roasting in a luau pit.

We don't ride horses, we eat them, explained the buyer, a recent immigrant from Tonga.

Raised here is the issue of so-called **pluralistic societies,** in which subcultural variation is especially marked and few standards, if any, are held in common. Pluralistic societies are, in effect, multicultural, and could not have existed before the first politically centralized states arose a mere 5,000 years ago. With the rise of the state, it became possible to bring about the political unification of two or more formerly independent societies, each with its own culture, thereby creating what amounts to a higher-order social entity that transcends the theoretical one culture–one society linkage. Plural societies are characterized by a particular problem: The groups within them, by virtue of their marked degree of subcultural variation, are all essentially operating by different sets of rules. This can create problems, given the fact that social living demands predictable behavior. In a culturally plural society, it may become difficult for the members of any one subgroup to comprehend the different standards by which the others operate. At the least, this can lead to major misunderstandings, as in the case of the Utah Tongans cited above.

It can, however, go far beyond mere misunderstanding, in which case violence and bloodshed may result. Many cases might be cited, but one that we shall look at in some detail in a later chapter (16) is Guatemala, where a government distrustful of its Indian population unleashed a reign of terror against it.

One example of a subculture in the United States can be seen in the Amish.[1] The old-order Amish originated in Austria and Moravia during the Reformation; today members of this order number

[1]John Hostetler and Gertrude Huntington, *Children in Amish Society* (New York: Holt, Rinehart and Winston, 1971).

The Amish people have maintained a distinctive agrarian way of life in the midst of industrialized North American society. By administering their own schools to instill Amish values in their children, prohibiting mechanized vehicles and equipment, and dressing in their characteristic plain clothing, they perpetuate their own special identity.

about 60,000 and live mainly in Pennsylvania, Ohio, and Indiana. They are pacifistic, agrarian people whose lives focus on their religious beliefs. They value simplicity, hard work, and a high degree of neighborly cooperation. They dress in a distinctive, plain garb, and even today rely on the horse for transportation as well as agricultural work. They rarely mingle with non-Amish.

The goal of Amish education is to teach reading, writing, and arithmetic and to instill Amish values in their children. They reject "worldly" knowledge and the idea of schools producing good citizens for the state. The Amish insist that their children attend school near home and that teachers be committed to Amish values. Their nonconformity to the standards of the larger culture has caused frequent conflict with state authorities, as well as legal and personal harassment. The Amish have resisted all attempts to force their children to attend regular public schools. Some compromise has been necessary, and "vocational training" has been introduced beyond the elementary school level to fulfill state requirements. The Amish have succeeded in gaining control of their schools and maintaining their way of life, but they are a beleaguered, defensive culture, more distrustful than ever of the larger culture around them.

The experience of the Amish is one example of the way a subculture may be dealt with by the larger culture within which it functions. Different as they are, the Amish actually practice many values that our country respects in the abstract: thrift, hard work, independence, a close family life. The degree of tolerance accorded to them may also be due in part to the fact that the Amish are white Europeans. American Indian subcultures have been treated differently by whites, who came as conquerors and often defined Indian values as "savage." For over 400 years, Europeans and their descendants in what is now the United States have generally accepted the notion that the American Indian cultures were doomed to disappear; yet they are still very much with us, even if in altered form.

In every culture, there are persons whose idiosyncratic behavior has earned them the terms of "eccentric," "crazy," or "queer." Such persons are looked upon suspiciously by society, and if their behavior becomes too idiosyncratic, are sooner or later excluded from participating in the activities of the group. Such exclusion acts to keep what is defined as deviant behavior outside the group. On the other hand, what is regarded as deviant in one society may not be in another. In many American Indian societies, for example, individuals were permitted to assume for life the role normally associated with people of the opposite sex. Thus, a man could dress as a woman and engage in what were conventionally defined as "female" activities; conversely, women could achieve renown in activities normally in the masculine domain. In effect, four different gender identities were available: masculine men, feminine men, feminine women, and masculine women. Furthermore, masculine women and feminine men were not merely accepted, but were highly respected.

Because individuals who share a culture tend to marry within their society and thus to share certain physical characteristics, some people mistakenly believe that there is a direct relationship between culture and race. Research has shown that racial characteristics represent biological adaptations to climate and have nothing to do with differences in intelligence or cultural superiority. Some North American blacks have concluded that they have more in common with black Africans than they do with those North Americans who are light-skinned and straight-haired. Yet if they suddenly had to live in a traditional Bantu society, they would find themselves lacking the cultural knowledge to be successful members of this group. The culture they share with white North Americans is more significant than the physical traits they share with the Bantu.

CULTURE IS LEARNED

All culture is learned rather than biologically inherited, prompting the anthropologist Ralph Linton to refer to it as humanity's "social heredity." One learns one's culture by growing up with it and the process whereby culture is transmitted from one generation to the next is called **enculturation.**

Most animals eat and drink whenever the urge arises. Humans, however, do most of their eating and drinking at certain culturally prescribed times and feel hungry as those times approach. These eating times vary from culture to culture. Similarly, a North American's idea of a comfortable way to sleep will vary greatly from that of a Japanese. The need to sleep is determined by biology; the way it is satisfied is cultural.

Through enculturation one learns the socially appropriate way of satisfying one's biologically determined needs. It is important to distinguish between the needs themselves, which are not learned, and the learned ways in which they are satisfied. The biological needs of humans are the same as those of other animals: food, shelter, companionship, self-defense, and sexual gratification. Each culture determines in its own way how these needs will be met.

Not all learned behavior is cultural. A dog may learn tricks, but this behavior is reflexive, the result of conditioning by repeated training, not the product of enculturation. On the other hand, nonhuman primates are capable of forms of cultural behavior. A chimpanzee, for example, will take a twig and strip it of all leaves in order to make a tool with which termites may be extracted from a hole. Such toolmaking, learned by imitating other chimpanzees, is unquestionably a form of cultural behavior

Enculturation: The process by which a society's culture is transmitted from one generation to the next.

ANTHROPOLOGY APPLIED

NEW HOUSES FOR APACHE INDIANS

The United States, in common with the other industrialized countries of the world, has within it a number of more or less separate subcultures. Those who live by the standards of one particular subculture have their closest relationships with one another, receiving constant reassurance that their perceptions of the world are the only correct ones, and coming to take it for granted that the whole culture is as they see it. As a consequence, members of one subcultural group frequently have trouble understanding the needs and aspirations of other such groups. For this reason anthropologists, with their special understanding of cultural differences, are frequently employed as go-betweens in situations requiring interaction between peoples of differing cultural traditions.

As an example, George S. Esber, Jr., while still a graduate student in anthropology, was hired to work with architects and a band of Apache Indians in designing a new community for the Apaches.* Although architects began with an awareness that cross-cultural differences in the use of space exist, they had no idea of how to get relevant information from the Indians. For their part, the Apaches had no explicit awareness of their needs, for these were based on unconscious patterns of behavior. Moreover, the idea that patterns of behavior could be acted out unconsciously was an alien idea to them.

Esber's task was to persuade the architects to hold back on their planning long enough for him to gather, through fieldwork and review of written records, the kind of data from which Apache housing needs could be abstracted. At the same time, he had to overcome Apache

anxieties over an outsider coming into their midst to learn about matters as personal as their daily lives. With these things accomplished, Esber was able to identify and successfully communicate to the architects features of Apache life with important implications for community design. At the same time, discussions of findings with the Apaches themselves enhanced awareness of their own unique needs.

As a result of Esber's work, in 1981, the Apaches were able to move into houses that had been designed with *their* participation, for *their* specific needs. Among other things, account was taken of the Indians' need to ease into a social situation, rather than to jump right in. Apache etiquette requires that all people be in full view of each other, so each can assess from a distance the behavior of others, in order to act appropriately with them. This requires a large, open living space. At the same time, hosts must be able to offer food to guests as a prelude to further social interaction. Thus, cooking and dining areas cannot be separated from living space. Nor can standard middle-class Anglo kitchen equipment be installed; the need for handling large quantities of food requires large pots and pans, for which extra large sinks and cupboards are necessary. In such ways were the new houses made to accommodate long-standing native traditions.

*See George Esber, "Designing Apache Houses with Apaches." In: *Anthropological Praxis: Translating Knowledge into Action*, edited by Robert M. Wulff and Shirley J. Fiske. Boulder, Colo.: Westview, 1987.

once thought to be exclusively human. Even more impressive indications of ape capabilities are afforded by long-term studies of young captive apes who have been taught how to "talk" with humans through American Sign Language or some other system (see Chapter 3). These, as well as observations of apes in the wild, reveal a degree of intelligence and capacity for conceptual thought hitherto unsuspected for nonhuman animals.

There has been a good deal of debate among scientists about the validity of studies of the linguistic and conceptual abilities of captive apes. (The issues will be more fully discussed in Chapter

4.) Those who are skeptical of the studies feel that the researchers are projecting too much of themselves into their interpretations, ascribing human attributes to nonhuman animals. To be sure, it is easy to see animals as pseudo-human (Garfield the cat, Kermit the frog, and Miss Piggy illustrate the point); on the other hand, the idea that there is a deep and unbridgeable gap between humans and animals is deeply embedded in Western culture, as exemplified by Judaic and Christian beliefs. Scientists are, after all, products of their own culture, and it seems likely that much of the resistance to what studies of captive apes seem to be telling us—that

LESLIE A. WHITE

(1900–1975)

Leslie White was a major theoretician in North American anthropology who saw culture as consisting of three essential components, which he referred to as the techno-economic, the social, and the ideological. White defined the techno-economic aspect of a culture as the way in which members of the culture deal with their environment, and it is this aspect that then determines the social and ideological aspects of the culture.

Although he acknowledged the importance of symbols, White considered the manner in which culture adapts to its environment to be the most significant factor in its development. Hence his strategy has been labeled the **cultural materialist approach.** In *The Evolution of Culture* (1959), White stated his basic law of evolution, that culture evolves in proportion to the increased output of energy on the part of each individual, or to the increased efficiency with which that energy is put to work. In other words, culture develops in direct response to technological "progress." A problem with White's position is his failure to account for the fact that "technological progress" may occur in response to purely cultural stimuli. In this respect, his theories were heavily influenced by nineteenth-century notions of human progress.

the differences between us and them are more of degree than kind—stems from this cultural bias.

Koko the gorilla "talks" with researcher Penny Patterson. Language experiments with captive apes reveal a degree of intelligence and capacity for conceptual thought long believed impossible for nonhuman animals.

Cultural materialist approach: The approach to anthropology that regards the manner in which a culture adapts to its environment as the most significant factor in its development.

What seems to be true, then, is that the cultural capacity of apes is more impressive than was once thought. This should not be surprising, though, given the degree of biological similarity between apes and humans (discussed in Chapter 3). One should not conclude from this, however, that humans are no more than some kind of "naked ape." Let us not forget that the languages used by captive apes were not thought up by, nor learned from, some other ape. The differences between apes and humans *are* of degree, rather than kind, but the degree does make a difference.

A.R. RADCLIFFE-BROWN

(1881–1955)

The British anthropologist A.R. Radcliffe-Brown was an originator of the structural-functionalist school of thought. He and his followers maintained that each custom and belief of a society has a specific function that serves to perpetuate the structure of that society—its ordered arrangement of parts—so that the society's continued existence is possible. The work of the anthropologist, then, was to study the ways in which customs and beliefs function to solve the problem of maintaining the system. From such studies should emerge universal laws of human behavior.

The value of the structural-functionalist approach is that it caused anthropologists to analyze cultures as systems, and to examine the interconnections between their various parts. It also gave a new dimension to comparative studies, as present-day societies were compared in terms of structural-functional similarities and differences rather than their presumed historical connections. Contrary to Radcliffe-Brown's original theory, universal laws of human behavior have not emerged, however, and the questions remain: Why do particular customs arise in the first place, and how do cultures change?

CULTURE IS BASED ON SYMBOLS

When anthropologist Leslie White observed that all human behavior originates in the use of symbols, he expressed an opinion shared by all anthropologists. Art, religion, and money involve the use of symbols. We are all familiar with the fervor and devotion that religion can elicit from a believer. A Christian cross, an Islamic crescent, a Jewish Star of David, or any object of worship may bring to mind centuries of struggle and persecution or may stand for a whole philosophy or creed. The most important symbolic aspect of culture is language—the substitution of words for objects.

Through language, humans are able to transmit culture from one generation to another. In particular, language makes it possible to learn from cumulative, shared experience.[2] Without it, one could not inform others about events to which they were not a party. We shall consider the important relationship between language and culture in greater detail in Chapter 4.

CULTURE IS INTEGRATED

For purposes of comparison and analysis, anthropologists customarily break a culture down into many seemingly discrete parts, even though such distinctions are arbitrary. The anthropologist who examines one aspect of a culture invariably finds it necessary to examine others as well. This tendency for all aspects of a culture to function as an interrelated whole is called **integration**.

Integration: The tendency for all aspects of a culture to function as an interrelated whole.

[2]Ward H. Goodenough, "Evolution of the Human Capacity for Beliefs," *American Anthropologist*, 92(1990), p. 605.

The integration of the economic, political, and social aspects of a culture can be illustrated by the Kapauku Papuans, a mountain people of western New Guinea (now Irian Jaya), studied in 1955 by the North

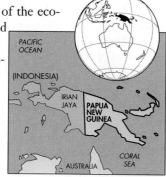

PACIFIC OCEAN

(INDONESIA)

IRIAN JAYA

PAPUA NEW GUINEA

AUSTRALIA

CORAL SEA

American anthropologist Leopold Pospisil.[3] The Kapauku economy relies on plant cultivation, along with pig breeding, hunting, and fishing. Although plant cultivation provides most of the people's food, it is through pig breeding that men achieve political power and positions of legal authority.

Among the Kapauku, pig breeding is a complex business. Raising lots of pigs, obviously, requires lots of food to feed them. This consists primarily of sweet potatoes, grown in garden plots. Some essential gardening activities, however, can be performed only by women. Furthermore, pigs must be cared for by women. So, to raise lots of pigs, a man has to have lots of women in the household. The way he gets them is by marrying them. In Kapauku society, multiple wives (polygyny) are not only permitted,

[3]Leopold Pospisil, *The Kapauku Papuans of West New Guinea* (New York: Holt, Rinehart and Winston, 1963).

they are highly desired. For each wife, however, a man must pay a bride price, which can be expensive. Furthermore, wives have to be compensated for their care of pigs. Put simply, it takes pigs, by which wealth is measured, to get wives, which are necessary to raise pigs in the first place. Needless to say, this requires considerable entrepreneurship. It is this ability that produces leaders in Kapauku society.

The interrelatedness of the various parts of Kapauku culture is even more complex than this. For example, one condition conducive to polygyny is a surplus of adult women. In the Kapauku case, warfare is endemic, regarded as a necessary evil. By the rules of Kapauku warfare, men get killed but women do not. This system works to promote the kind of imbalance of sexes that facilitates polygyny. Polygyny also tends to work best if wives come to live in their husband's village, rather than the other way around, which is the case among the Kapauku. Thus, the men of a village are "blood" relatives of one another. Given this, a patrilineal (descent reckoned through men) emphasis in Kapauku culture is not unexpected.

These examples by no means exhaust the interrelationships to be found in Kapauku culture. For example, both patrilineality and endemic warfare tend to promote male dominance, and so it is not surprising to find that positions of leadership in Kapauku society are held exclusively by men, who

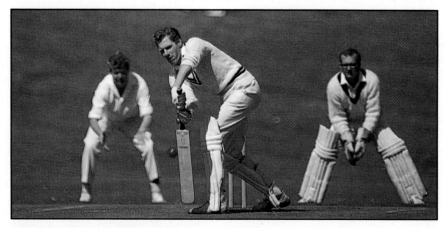

Describing another culture is like trying to describe an unfamiliar game. These men are playing cricket, a game especially popular in Great Britain. Though cricket is in some ways similar to baseball, to describe it in the language of baseball would provide at best a caricature of the game as the British know it. The problem in anthropology is how to describe another culture for an audience unfamiliar with it so that the description is not a caricature.

appropriate the products of women's labor in order to effect their political "games." Assertions to the contrary not withstanding, male dominance is by no means characteristic of all human societies. Rather, as in the Kapauku case, it arises only under particular sets of circumstances which, if changed, will alter the way in which men and women relate to one another.

From what has been said so far, one might suppose that the various parts of a culture must operate in perfect harmony at all times. The analogy would be that of a machine; all parts must be compatible and complementary or it won't run. Try putting diesel fuel in the tank of a car that runs on gasoline and you've got a problem; one part of the system is no longer compatible with the rest. To a degree, this is true of all cultures. A change in one part of a culture usually will affect other parts, sometimes in rather dramatic ways. This point, to which we will return later in this chapter, is of particular importance today as diverse agents seek to introduce changes of all sorts into societies all around the world.

At the same time that we must recognize that a degree of harmony is necessary in any properly functioning culture, we should not assume that complete harmony is required. Because no two individuals experience the enculturation process in precisely the same way, no two individuals perceive their culture in exactly the same way, and so there is always some potential for change in any culture. So we should speak, instead, of a strain to consistency in culture. So long as the parts are reasonably consistent, a culture will operate reasonably well. If, however, that strain to consistency breaks down, a situation of cultural crisis ensues.

STUDYING CULTURE IN THE FIELD

Armed, now, with some understanding of what culture is, the question arises: How does an anthropologist study culture in the field? Culture, being a set of rules or standards, cannot itself be directly observed; only actual behavior is observable. What the anthropologist must do is to abstract a set of rules from what is observed and heard in order to explain social behavior, much as a linguist, from the way people speak a language, tries to develop a set of rules to account for the ways those speakers combine sounds into meaningful phrases.

To pursue this further, consider the following discussion of exogamy—marriage outside one's own group—among the Trobriand Islanders, as described by Bronislaw Malinowski.

> If you were to inquire into the matter among the Trobrianders, you would find that. . . . the natives show horror at the idea of violating the rules of exogamy and that they believe that sores, diseases, even death might follow clan incest. [But] from the viewpoint of the native libertine, *suvasova* (the breach of exogamy) is indeed a specially interesting and spicy form of erotic experience. Most of my informants would not only admit but did actually boast about having committed this offense.[4]

Malinowski himself determined that although such breaches did occasionally occur, they were much less frequent than gossip would have it. Had Malinowski relied solely on what the Trobrianders told him, his description of their culture would have been inaccurate. The same sort of discrepancy between cultural ideals and the way people really do behave can be found in any culture. In Chapter 1 we saw another example from contemporary North America in our discussion of the Garbage Project.

From these examples, it is obvious that an anthropologist must be cautious, if a realistic description of a culture is to be given. To play it safe, data drawn in three different ways ought to be considered. First, the people's own understanding of the rules they share—that is, their notion of the way their society *ought* to be—must be examined. Second, the extent to which people believe they are observing those rules—that is, how they think they actually do behave—needs to be looked at. Third, the behavior that can be directly observed should be considered—in the example of the Trobrianders, whether or not the rule of *suvasova* is actually violated. As we see here, and as we saw in our discussion of the Garbage Project, the way people think they should behave, the way in which they think they do behave, and the way in which they actually behave may be three distinctly different things. By carefully evaluating these elements, the anthropologist can draw up a set of rules that

---

[4]Bronislaw Malinowski, *Argonauts of the Western Pacific* (New York: Dutton, 1922).

BRONISLAW MALINOWSKI

(1884–1942)

The Polish-born Bronislaw Malinowski argued that people everywhere share certain biological and psychological needs and that the ultimate function of all cultural institutions is to fulfill those needs. Everyone, for example, needs to feel secure in relation to the physical universe. Therefore, when science and technology are inadequate to explain certain natural phenomena—such as eclipses or earthquakes—people develop religion and magic to account for those phenomena and to restore a feeling of security. The nature of the institution, according to Malinowski, is determined by its function.

Malinowski outlined three fundamental levels of needs which he claimed had to be resolved by all cultures:

1. A culture must provide for biological needs, such as the need for food and procreation.
2. A culture must provide for instrumental needs, such as the need for law and education.
3. A culture must provide for integrative needs, such as religion and art.

If anthropologists could analyze the ways in which a culture fills these

needs for its members, Malinowski believed that they could also deduce the origin of cultural traits. Although this belief was never justified, the quality of data called for by Malinowski's approach set new standards for ethnographic fieldwork. He himself showed the way with his work in the Trobriand Islands between 1915 and 1918. Never before had such in-depth work been done, nor had such insights been gained into the workings of another culture. Such was the quality of Malinowski's Trobriand research that, with it, ethnography can be said to have come of age as a scientific enterprise.

actually may explain the acceptable behavior within a culture.

Of course, the anthropologist is only human. It is difficult to completely cast aside one's own personal feelings and biases, which have been shaped by one's own culture. Yet it is important to make every effort to do just this, for otherwise one may seriously misinterpret what one sees. As a case in point, we may see how the male bias of Western culture caused Malinowski to miss important things in his pioneering study of the Trobriand Islanders.

CULTURE AND PROCESS

In the course of their evolution humans, like all animals, have been continually faced with the prob-

---

Adaptation: A process by which organisms achieve beneficial adjustment to an available environment and the results of that process—the characteristics of organisms that fit them to the particular set of conditions of the environment in which they are generally found.

---

lem of adapting to their environment. The term **adaptation** refers to a natural (rather than willful) process by which organisms achieve a beneficial adjustment to an available environment, and the results of that process—the possession of characteristics that permit organisms to overcome the hazards, and secure the resources that they need, in the particular environments in which they live. With the exception of humans, organisms have generally adapted as natural selection has provided

ORIGINAL STUDY

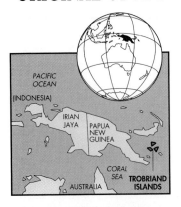

THE IMPORTANCE OF TROBRIAND WOMEN[5]

Walking into a village at the beginning of fieldwork is entering a world without cultural guideposts. The task of learning values that others live by is never easy. The rigors of fieldwork involve listening and watching, learning a new language of speech and actions, and most of all, letting go of one's own cultural assumptions in order to understand the meanings others give to work, power, death, family, and friends. As my fieldwork in the Trobriand Islands of Papua New Guinea was no exception, I wrestled doggedly with each of these problems. Doing research in the Trobriand Islands created one additional obstacle. I was working in the footsteps of a celebrated anthropological ancestor, Bronislaw Kasper Malinowski. . . .

In 1971, before my first trip to the Trobriands, I thought I understood many things about Trobriand customs and beliefs from having read Malinowski's exhaustive writings. Once there, however, I found that I had much more to discover about what I thought I already knew. For many months I worked with these discordant realities, always conscious of Malinowski's shadow, his words, his explanations. Although I found significant differences in areas of importance, I gradually came to understand how he reached certain conclusions. The answers we both received from informants were not so dissimilar, and I could actually trace how Malinowski had analyzed what his informants told him in a way that made sense and was scientifically significant—given what anthropologists generally then recognized about such societies. Sixty years separate our fieldwork, and any comparison of our studies illustrates not so much Malinowski's mistaken interpretations but the developments in anthropological knowledge and inquiry from his time to mine.

This important point has been forgotten by those anthropologists who today argue that ethnographic writing can never be more than a kind of fictional account of an author's experiences. Although Malinowski and I were in the Trobriands at vastly different historical moments and there also are many areas in which our analyses differ, a large part of what we learned in the field was similar. From the vantage point that time gives to me, I can illustrate how our differences, even those that are major, came to be. Taken together, our two studies profoundly exemplify the scientific basis that underlies the collection of ethnographic data. Like all such data, however, whether researched in a laboratory or a village, the more we learn about a subject, the more we can refine and revise earlier assumptions. This is the way all sciences create their own historical developments. Therefore, the lack of agreement between Malinowski's enthnography and mine must not be taken as an adversarial attack against an opponent. Nor should it be read as an example of the writing of enthnography as "fiction" or "partial truths." Each of our differences can be traced historically within the discipline of anthropology.

My most significant point of departure from Malinowski's analyses was the attention I gave to women's productive work. In my original

In the Trobriand Islands, women's wealth consists of skirts and banana leaves, large quantities of which must be given away upon the death of a relative.

research plans, women were not the central focus of study, but on the first day I took up residence in a village I was taken by them to watch a distribution of their own wealth—bundles of banana leaves and banana fiber skirts—which they exchanged with other women in commemoration of someone who had recently died. Watching that event forced me to take women's economic roles more seriously than I would have from reading Malinowski's studies. Although Malinowski noted the high status of Trobriand women, he attributed their importance to the fact that Trobrianders reckon descent through women, thereby giving them genealogical significance in a matrilineal society. Yet he never considered that this significance was underwritten by women's own wealth because he did not systematically investigate the women's productive activities. Although in his field notes he mentions Trobriand women making these seemingly useless banana bundles to be exchanged at a death, his published work only deals with men's wealth.

My taking seriously the importance of women's wealth not only brought women as the neglected half of society clearly into the ethnographic picture but also forced me to revise many of Malinowski's assumptions about Trobriand men. For example, Trobriand kinship as described by Malinowski has always been a subject of debate among anthropologists. For Malinowski, the basic relationships within a Trobriand family were guided by the matrilineal principle of "mother-right" and "father-love." A father was called "stranger" and had little authority over his own children. A woman's brother was the commanding figure and exercised control over his sister's sons because they were members of his matrilineage rather than their father's matrilineage.

According to Malinowski, this matrilineal drama was played out biologically by the Trobrianders' belief that a man has no role as genitor. A man's wife is thought to become pregnant when an ancestral spirit enters her body and causes conception. Even after a child is born, Malinowski reported, it is the woman's brother who presents a harvest of yams to his sister so that her child will be fed with food from its own matrilineage, rather than its father's matrilineage. In this way, Malinowski conceptualized matrilineality as an institution in which the father of a child, as a member of a *different* matrilineage, was excluded not only from participating in procreation but also from giving any objects of lasting value to his children, thus provisioning them only with love.

In my study of Trobriand women and men, a different configuration of matrilineal descent emerged. A Trobriand father is not a "stranger" in Malinowski's definition, nor is he a powerless figure as the third party to the relationship between a woman and her brother. The father is one of the most important persons in his child's life, and remains so even after his child grows up and marries. Even a father's procreative importance is incorporated into his child's growth and development. A Trobriand man gives his child many opportunities to gain things from his matrilineage, thereby adding to the available resources that he or she can draw upon. At the same time, this giving creates obligations on the part of a man's children toward him that last even beyond his death. Therefore, the roles that men and their children play in each other's lives are worked out through extensive cycles of exchanges, which define the strength of their relationships to each other and eventually benefit the other members of both their matrilineages. Central to these exchanges are women and their wealth.

That Malinowski never gave equal time to the women's side of things, given the deep significance of their role in societal and political life, is not surprising. Only recently have anthropologists begun to understand the importance of taking women's work seriously. In some cultures, such as the Middle East or among Australian aborigines, it is extremely difficult for ethnographers to cross the culturally bounded ritual worlds that separate women from men. In the past, however, both women and men ethnographers generally analyzed the societies they studied from a male perspective. The "women's point of view" was largely ignored in the study of gender roles, since anthropologists generally perceived women as living in the shadows of men—occupying the private rather than the public sectors of society, rearing children rather than engaging in economic or political pursuits.

[5]Annette B. Weiner, *The Trobrianders of Papua New Guinea.* Copyright © 1987 by Holt, Rinehart and Winston, Inc. Reprinted by permission of Harcourt Brace Jovanovich, Inc. Pp. 4–7.

What is adaptive at one time may not be at another. In the United States, one major source of fruits and vegetables is California's Central Valley, where vast irrigation works have made the desert bloom. As happened in ancient Mesopotamia, evaporation concentrates salts in the water, but here pollution is made worse by chemical fertilizers. These are now accumulating in the soil and threaten to make the valley a desert again.

them with advantageous anatomical and physiological characteristics. For example, a body covering of hair, coupled with certain other physiological mechanisms, protects mammals from extremes of temperature; specialized teeth help them to procure the kinds of food they need; and so on. Humans, however, have come to depend more and more on cultural adaptation. For example, biology has not provided them with built-in fur coats to protect them in cold climates, but it has provided them with the ability to make their own coats, build fires, and erect shelters to protect themselves against the cold. More than this, culture enables people to utilize a wide diversity of environments. By manipulating environments through cultural means, people have been able to move into the Arctic, the Sahara, and have even gotten to the moon. Through culture the human species has secured not just its survival but its expansion as well.

This is not to say that everything that humans do they do *because* it is adaptive to a particular environment. For one thing, people don't just react to an environment as given; rather, they react to it as they perceive it, and different groups of people may perceive the same environment in radically differ-

ent ways. They also react to things other than the environment: their own biological natures, for one, and their beliefs, attitudes, and the consequences of their own behavior, for others. All of these things present them with problems, and people maintain cultures to deal with problems, or matters that concern them. To be sure, their cultures must produce behavior that is generally adaptive, or at least not maladaptive, but this is not the same as saying that cultural practices necessarily arise because they are adaptive in a given environment. The fact is, current utility of a custom is an unreliable guide to its origin.

A further complication is the relativity of any given adaptation: What is adaptive in one context may be seriously maladaptive in another. For example, the sanitation practices of food-foraging peoples—their toilet habits and methods of garbage disposal—are appropriate to contexts of low population levels and some degree of residential mobility. These same practices, however, become serious health hazards in the context of large, fully sedentary populations. Similarly, behavior that is adaptive in the short run may be maladaptive over the long run. Thus, the development of irrigation in ancient

Mesopotamia (modern-day Iraq) made it possible over the short run to increase food production, but over the long run it favored the gradual accumulation of salts in the soils. This, in turn, contributed to the collapse of civilization there after 2000 B.C. Similarly, the development of prime farmland today in places like the eastern United States for purposes other than food production makes us increasingly dependent on food raised in marginal environments. High yields are presently possible through the application of expensive technology, but continuing loss of topsoil, increasing salinity of soils through evaporation of irrigation waters, and silting of irrigation works, not to mention impending shortages of water and fossil fuels, make continuing high yields over the long term unlikely.

CULTURAL ADAPTATION

A good example of the way cultural factors are involved in a people's adaptation is afforded by the Yanomami, a people who inhabit the tropical forests of Venezuela and Brazil.[6] Their adaptation to their sociopolitical environment is as important as their adaptation to nature, and their adjustment to it affects the way they are distributed over the land, their patterns of migration, and the kinds of relationships they maintain with their neighbors.

The Yanomami are a fiercely combative people who inhabit villages of 40 to 250 persons. Village life revolves around the cultivation of a plantain garden and warring against other villages. Because peace is so uncertain, a village must be prepared to evacuate, either to a new location or to the parent village, on very short notice. Since the garden is of such economic importance, however, abandoning it to start a new one elsewhere is seen as a formidable task, and is resisted except in the most extreme situations. Alliances are therefore made with neighboring villages, so that one village joins another's war parties, or takes in the inhabitants of another village during times of need.

The Yanomami are so combative that in a village of 100 people there is bound to be feuding and bloodshed, necessitating a split, with the dissident

[6]Napoleon A. Chagnon, *Yanomamö: The Fierce People*, 3rd ed. (New York: Holt, Rinehart and Winston, 1988).

faction going off to establish a new garden. Although Yanomami try to avoid the establishment of a new garden because of the labor and uncertainty of the first harvest, their conflicts force them to this decision frequently. While they are a gardening people, their choice of a garden site is based on political considerations.

FUNCTIONS OF CULTURE

A culture cannot survive if it does not successfully deal with basic problems. A culture must provide for the production and distribution of goods and services considered necessary for life. It must provide for biological continuity through the reproduction of its members. It must enculturate new members so that they can become functioning adults. It must maintain order among its members, as well as between them and outsiders. Finally, it must motivate its members to survive and engage in those activities necessary for survival.

CULTURE AND CHANGE

All cultures change over time, although not always as rapidly or as massively as many are doing today. Changes take place in response to such events as environmental crises, intrusion of outsiders, or modification of behavior and values within the culture. In North American culture, clothing fashions change frequently. In the past few decades it has become culturally permissible for men and women alike to bare more of their bodies not just in swimming but in dress as well. Along with this has come greater permissiveness about the body in photographs and movies. Finally, the sexual attitudes and practices of North Americans have become less restrictive. Obviously these changes are interrelated, reflecting an underlying change in attitudes toward cultural rules regarding sex.

Culture change can bring unexpected and often disastrous results. A case in point are the droughts that have periodically afflicted so many peoples living in Africa just south of the Sahara Desert, particularly in the mid-1980s. Native to this region are a number of pastoral nomadic peoples, whose

Clothing fashions change frequently in the United States, as illustrated by these photos from different eras of men in their swimsuits.

lives are centered on cattle and other livestock, which they herd from place to place as required for pasturage and water. For thousands of years these people have been able to go about their business, efficiently utilizing vast areas of arid lands in ways that allowed them to survive severe droughts many times in the past. Unfortunately for them, their nomadic life-style, which makes it difficult to impose controls upon them and takes them across international boundaries at will, makes them a source of annoyance to the governments of the post-colonial states of the region. Seeing nomads as a challenge to their authority, these governments have gone all out to convert them into sedentary villagers. Overgrazing has resulted from this loss of mobility, and the problem has been compounded by government efforts to involve the pastoralists in a market economy by encouraging them to raise many more animals than required for their own needs, in order to have a surplus to sell. The resultant devastation, where there had previously been no significant overgrazing or erosion, now makes droughts far more disastrous than they would otherwise be, and places the former nomads' very existence in jeopardy.

CULTURE, SOCIETY, AND THE INDIVIDUAL

Ultimately, a society is no more than a union of individuals, all of whom have their own special needs and interests. If a society is to survive, it must succeed in balancing the self-interest of its members against the demands of the society as a whole. To accomplish this, a society offers rewards for adherence to its cultural standards. In most cases, these rewards assume the form of social acceptance. In contemporary North American society, a man who holds a good job, is faithful to his wife, and goes to church services, for example, may be elected "model citizen" by his neighbors. In order to ensure the survival of the group, each person must learn to postpone certain immediate satisfactions. Yet the needs of the individual cannot be suppressed too far, lest levels of stress become too much to bear. Hence, a delicate balance always exists between an individual's personal interests and the demands made upon each person by the group. Take, for example, the matter of sex which,

like anything that people do, is shaped by culture. Sex is important in any society, for it helps to strengthen cooperative bonds between men and women, as well as to ensure the perpetuation of the society itself. Yet sex can be disruptive to social living; if who has sexual access to whom is not clearly spelled out, competition for sexual privileges can destroy the cooperative bonds on which human survival depends. Uncontrolled sexual activity, too, can result in reproductive rates that cause a society's population to outstrip its resources. Hence, as it shapes sexual behavior, every culture must balance the needs of society against the need for sufficient individual gratification, lest frustration build up to the point of being disruptive in itself.

Not just in sex, but in all things, cultures must strike a balance between the needs of individuals and those of society. When those of society take precedence, then people experience excessive stress. Symptomatic of this are increased levels of mental illness and behavior regarded as antisocial: violence, crime, abuse of alcohol and other drugs, suicide, or simply alienation. If not corrected, the situation can result in cultural breakdown.

Just as problems develop if the needs of society take precedence over those of the individual, so also do they develop if the balance is upset in the other direction. This is precisely what has happened among the Ik, a Ugandan people who at one time were forcibly uprooted from their homeland in order to create a national park.[7] This caused severe disruption of their traditional ways, and placed them in a situation where resources are no longer adequate to meet their needs. Among the Ik today, every individual past the age of three is responsible for his or her own well-being; no one is expected to do anything for anyone else. Once they are weaned, children are "turned loose" to find their own food, and no child expects to be fed by a parent, any more than the aged or infirm expect to be fed by their children. Any who are unable to find their own food die. In this society people have died while their husbands or wives were plump and healthy; those who go out and get food, returning well fed at the end of the day, wouldn't dream of bringing any

---

[7]Colin M. Turnbull, *The Mountain People* (New York: Simon & Schuster, 1972).

A drug bust in Miami. Increasing substance abuse may be considered one symptom of a culture's inability to satisfy the needs or wants of individuals who live by its rules.

back to share with a sick wife, husband, or child. The Ik show us what can happen to a people whose individuals are required to fend for themselves. They are dying out morally as well as physically, and there is now no one alive among them who can remember a single act of kindness.

EVALUATION OF CULTURE

We have knowledge of diverse cultural solutions to the problems of human existence. The question often arises, Which is best? In the nineteenth century Western peoples had no doubts about the answer—Western civilization was obviously the peak of human development. At the same time, though, anthropologists were intrigued to find that *all* cultures with which they had any familiarity saw themselves as the best of all possible worlds. Commonly, this was reflected in a name for the society which, roughly translated, meant "we human beings" as opposed to "you subhumans." We now

know that any culture that is functioning adequately regards itself as the best, a view reflecting the phenomenon known as **ethnocentrism.** Hence, the nineteenth-century Westerners were also displaying their ethnocentrism.

Anthropologists have been actively engaged in the fight against ethnocentrism ever since they started to live among so-called savage peoples and discovered that they were just as human as anyone else. As a consequence, anthropologists began to examine each culture on its own terms, asking whether or not the culture satisfied the needs and expectations of the people themselves. If a people practiced human sacrifice, for example, they asked whether or not the taking of human life was

Ethnocentrism: The belief that one's own culture is superior in every way to all others.

Cultural relativism: The thesis that because cultures are unique, they can be evaluated only according to their own standards and values.

acceptable according to native values. The idea that a culture must be evaluated according to its own standards, and those alone, is called **cultural relativism.** One could say, for instance, that the ritual killing of other human beings may be acceptable in some societies, yet it is a custom that North Americans, among other peoples, would not wish to emulate, no matter how functional it may be to some other group of people.

While cultural relativism may be preferable to the ethnocentric approach, both positions represent extreme viewpoints. These may be characterized as, on the one hand, "We are right and everyone else is wrong," and on the other as "Anything goes,

An Ik child in the unused kitchen of her family compound. Her parents were unable to feed her, and when she persisted in her demands, they shut her in. Too weak to break out, she died there; a few days later her body was unceremoniously thrown out. Such acts have become standard among the Ik.

no matter how reprehensible." As practiced today, cultural relativism requires suspension of judgement, not forever, but only until practices are understood in their own terms. Only then may another culture be evaluated. A still useful formula for this was proposed more than 30 years ago by the anthropologist Walter Goldschmidt. In his approach the important question to ask is, How well does a given culture satisfy the physical and psychological needs of those whose behavior it guides? Specific indicators are to be found in the nutritional status and general physical and mental health of its population, the incidence of crime and delinquency, the demographic structure, stability and tranquility of domestic life, and the group's relationship to its resource base. The culture of a people who experience high rates of malnutrition, crime, delinquency, suicide, emotional disorders and despair, and environmental degradation may be said to be operating less well than that of another people who exhibit few such problems. In a well-working culture, people "can be proud, jealous, and pugnacious, and live a very satisfactory life without feeling '*angst*,' 'alienation,' 'anomie,' 'depression,' or any of the other pervasive ills of our own inhuman and civilized way of living."[8] It is when people feel helpless to effect their own lives in their own societies, when traditional ways of coping no longer seem to work, that the symptoms of cultural breakdown become prominent.

A culture is essentially a system to ensure the continued well-being of a group of people; therefore, it may be termed successful so long as it secures the survival of a society in a way that its members recognize as reasonably fulfilling. What complicates matters is that any society is made up of groups with different interests, raising the possibility that some peoples' may be served better than others. Therefore, a culture which is quite fulfilling for one group within a society may be less so for another. For this reason, the anthropologist must always ask: Whose needs, and whose survival, is best served by the culture in question? Only by looking at the overall situation can a reasonably objective judgement be made as to how well a culture is working.

[8]Robin Fox, *Encounter with Anthropology* (New York: Dell, 1968), p. 290.

Chapter Summary

Culture, to the anthropologist, is a set of rules or standards that, when acted upon by the members of a society, produce behavior that falls within a range of variance the members consider proper and acceptable.

All cultures share certain basic characteristics; study of these sheds light on the nature and function of culture itself. Culture is a set of shared ideals, values, and standards of behavior. It cannot exist without society: a group of people occupying a specific locality who are dependent on each other for survival. Society is held together by relationships determined by social structure or social organization. Culture cannot exist without society, although one can have society, as do creatures like ants and bees, without culture. All is not uniformity within a culture, one reason being that there is some difference between male and female roles in any human society. Anthropologists use the term *gender* to refer to the elaborations or meanings cultures assign to the biological differences between men and women. Age variation is also universal, and in some cultures there is subcultural variation as well. A subculture shares certain overarching assumptions of the larger culture, while observing a set of rules that is distinctively different. Pluralistic societies are those in which subcultural variation is particularly marked. They are characterized by a number of groups operating under different sets of rules. One example of a subculture in the United States is that of the Amish.

In addition to being shared, all cultures are learned. Individual members of a society learn the accepted norms of social behavior through the process of enculturation. Another characteristic is that culture is based on symbols. It is transmitted through the communication of ideas, emotions, and desires expressed in language. Finally, culture is integrated, so that all aspects of a culture function as an integrated whole. In a properly functioning culture, though, total harmony of all elements is approximated, rather than completely achieved.

The job of the anthropologist is to abstract a set of rules from what he or she observes in order to explain the social behavior of people. To arrive at a realistic description of a culture, free from personal and cultural assumptions, the anthropologist must (1) examine a people's notion of the way their society ought to function; (2) determine how a people think they behave; and (3) compare these with how a people actually do behave. The anthropologist must also be as free as possible of the biases of his or her own culture.

Cultural adaptation has enabled humans, in the course of evolution, to survive and expand in a variety of environments. Sometimes, though, what is adaptive in one set of circumstances, or over the short run, is maladaptive in another set of circumstances, or over the long run.

To survive, a culture must satisfy the basic biological needs of its members, provide for their continuity, and maintain order among its members and between its members and outsiders.

All cultures change over time, sometimes because the environment they must cope with has changed, sometimes as the result of the intrusion of outsiders, or because values within the culture have undergone modification. Sometimes the unforeseen consequences of change are disastrous for a society.

A society must strike a balance between the self-interest of individuals and the needs of the group. If one or the other becomes paramount, the result may be cultural breakdown.

Ethnocentrism is the worldwide tendency to regard one's own culture as better than all others. One concept anthropologists use to counter ethnocentrism is cultural relativism, which involves examining each culture on its own terms, according to its own standards. The least biased measure of a culture's success, however, employs criteria indicative of its effectiveness at securing the survival of a society in a way that its members see as being reasonably fulfilling.

Suggested Readings

Brown, Donald E. *Human Universals*. New York: McGraw-Hill, 1991.
The message of this book is that we should not let our fascination with the diversity of cultural practices interfere with the study of human universals: those things that all cultures share in spite of their differences. Important though the differences are, the universals have special relevance for our understanding of the nature of all humanity, and raise issues that transcend the boundaries of biological and social science, as well as the humanities.

Gamst, Frederick C., and Edward Norbeck. *Ideas of Culture: Sources and Uses*. New York: Holt, Rinehart and Winston, 1976.
This is a book of selected writings, with editorial comments, about the culture concept. From these selections one can see how the concept has grown, as well as how it has given rise to narrow specializations within the field of anthropology.

Goodenough, Ward H. *Description and Comparison in Cultural Anthropology*. Chicago: Aldine, 1970.
The major question to which Goodenough addresses himself is how the anthropologist is to avoid ethnocentric bias when studying culture. His approach relies on models of descriptive linguistics. A large part of the book is concerned with kinship and terminology, with a discussion of the problems of a universal definition of marriage and the family. This is a particularly lucid discussion of culture, its relation to society, and the problem of individual variance.

Keesing, Roger M. *Cultural Anthropology: A Contemporary Perspective*. New York: Holt, Rinehart and Winston, 1976.
This book approaches anthropology by tackling the important problems of cultural anthropology, discussing them through ethnographic examples and theoretical considerations. In the process the author takes a critical stance toward conventional anthropological thinking and practice.

Linton, Ralph. *The Study of Man: An Introduction*. New York: Appleton, 1963.
Linton wrote this book in 1936 with the intention of providing a general survey of the field of anthropology. His study of social structure is still illuminating today. This book is regarded as a classic and is an important source historically.

CHAPTER

3

THE BEGINNINGS

OF

HUMAN CULTURE

By studying primates that are closely related to us, like these lowland gorillas, we can discover which characteristics we do and do not share with them. The former characteristics we presumably owe to a common ancestry; the latter are what make us distinctly human.

TO WHAT GROUP OF ANIMALS DO HUMANS BELONG? Humans are classified by biologists as belonging to the Primate Order, a group that also includes lemurs, indriids, lorises, tarsiers, monkeys, and apes. By studying the anatomy and behavior of monkeys and apes, the primates most closely related to us, we draw closer to understanding how and why humans developed as they did.

WHEN AND HOW DID HUMANS EVOLVE? Present evidence suggests that humans evolved from the small, apelike ramapithecines, which lived between 15 and 8 million years ago. By 4 million years ago *Australopithecus,* apparently a descendant of ramapithecines, had become fully adapted for moving about on the open savanna on its hind legs in the distinctive human manner. Otherwise, the behavior of this human ancestor probably was comparable to that of modern-day chimpanzees.

WHEN AND HOW DID HUMAN CULTURE EVOLVE? Human culture appears to have developed as some populations of *Australopithecus* began making stone tools with which they could butcher animals for their meat. Actually, the earliest stone tools and evidence of significant meat eating date to between 2.5 and 2 million years ago, along with the appearance of the genus *Homo,* whose brain was significantly enlarged over that of *Australopithecus.* From then on the increasing importance of culture in human survival favored the evolution of a better brain, which in turn made possible improvement in culture as the vehicle through which humans secured their survival. By about 100,000 years ago the human brain had reached its modern size, but culture has continued to evolve and change down to the present time.

Early forerunners of humanity, like all other creatures, depended a great deal on physical attributes for survival. Although learned behavior was certainly important to them, much of what they did was still dictated by their biological natures. In the course of evolution, however, humans came to rely increasingly on learned behavior as an extremely effective way of adapting to the environment. They learned to manufacture and utilize tools; they organized into social units more proficient at foraging for food than their ancestors had been; and eventually they learned to preserve their traditions and knowledge, to bridge past and present, through the use of symbols. In other words, humans acquired the ability to produce culture.

This ability has made humans the most influential creatures on this planet. Humans do not merely adapt to the environment; they attempt to mold and manipulate it to suit needs and desires that they themselves define. If they manage to avoid self-destruction through misuse of their technology,

their medical technology may eventually enable them to control genetic inheritance and thus the future course of their biological evolution. Space technology may enable them to propagate their species in extraterrestrial environments. And computer technology enables them to correlate and organize an ever-increasing amount of knowledge as they attempt to keep pace with the changes they themselves have brought about.

Humans have gotten where they are today in an extraordinarily short period of time; culture, as we know it, came into existence a mere 2.5 million years ago. By looking backwards in order to see where we came from, and how we got to be the way we are today, we may gain insights into how culture came into being, and how it increasingly took on the job of solving the problems of human existence. In the process, we may gain a fuller understanding of the nature of culture itself.

HUMANS AND THE OTHER PRIMATES

Humans are classified by biologists as belonging to the **Primate Order,** a group of mammals that also includes lemurs, indriids, lorises, tarsiers, monkeys, and apes. One might properly question the value of studying primates other than humans, when it is humans and their distinctive cultural capacities that concern us. Humans, however, did not start out as cultural beings—they did not even start out as humans. Their roots, like those of the other living primates, lie in ancient times and in less specialized biological creatures; their development was influenced by the same evolutionary processes. By studying the environment of those times, the anatomical features that evolved in the context of that environment, and the rudimentary cultural adaptations of those primates to which we are related, we may draw closer to an understanding of how and why humans developed as they did.

Modern lemurs represent highly evolved variants of an early primate model. In them, primate characteristics are not as prominent as they are in monkeys, apes, and humans.

Primate Order: That group of mammals including lemurs, indriids, lorises, tarsiers, monkeys, apes, and humans.

The first primates came into being at a time when a new, mild climate favored the spread of dense tropical and subtropical forests over much of the earth, including North and South America, southeast Asia, the Middle East, and most of Africa. Forestation set the stage for the evolutionary development from a relatively inconspicuous ground existence to tree living.

EVOLUTION THROUGH ADAPTATION

The term *adaptation* refers to both a process by which organisms achieve a beneficial adjustment to an available environment and the results of that process—the characteristics of organisms that fit them to the particular set of conditions of the environment in which they are generally found. The process of **natural selection** favors not just the survival of well-adapted individuals, but the propagation of their genetic traits. Although some individuals less suited to the environment may in fact survive, they often do not reproduce; they may be incapable of attracting mates, or they may be sterile, or they may produce offspring that do not survive after birth.

By chance, the ancestral primates possessed certain characteristics that allowed them to adapt to life in the forests. Their relatively small size allowed them to utilize the smaller branches of trees; larger and heavier competitors and predators could not follow. The move to the smaller branches also opened up an abundant new food supply. The primates were able to gather leaves, flowers, fruits, insects, birds' eggs, and even nesting birds, rather than having to wait for them to fall to the ground.

The move to an arboreal existence brought a combination of the problems of earthbound existence and those of flight. In their move into space, birds developed a highly stereotyped behavior pattern, keyed to the problems of flight. Animals living

---

Natural selection: The evolutionary mechanism by which individuals with characters best suited to a particular environment survive and reproduce with greater frequency than do those without them.

---

on the ground developed a slower-paced, more flexible relationship to the environment.

The tree-dwelling primates, however, were obliged to develop both flexible behavior and virtually automatic mechanisms for moving through the trees; for if they were no longer limited to roaming around on the ground, they also no longer had the certainty of a substantial surface directly beneath their feet. Initial forays into the trees must have included many errors in judgement and coordination, leading to falls that injured or killed those who were poorly adapted to arboreal life. Natural selection favored those who judged depth correctly and gripped the branches tightly. Although it is likely that the early primates who took to the trees were in some measure preadapted—that is, they already possessed features potentially useful to tree dwellers even though they had lived on the ground —the transition to life in the trees required important physical adjustments. The way in which early primates adapted has considerable relevance for their human descendants.

ANATOMICAL ADAPTATION

From the study of both ancient and modern primates, anthropologists have worked out a list of characteristics common to them all.

PRIMATE DENTITION

The diet available to arboreal primates—shoots, leaves, insects, and soft fruits—required relatively unspecialized teeth, compared to those found in other mammals. On the evidence of comparative anatomy and the fossil record, the mammals ancestral to the primates possessed three incisors, one canine, four premolars, and three molars on each side of the jaw, top and bottom, for a total of 44 teeth. The incisors (in the front of the mouth) were used for gripping, and cutting, canines (behind the incisors) for tearing and shredding, and molars and premolars (the "cheek teeth") for grinding and chewing food.

The evolutionary trend for primate dentition has generally been toward economy, with fewer smaller teeth doing more work. In the early stages, one incisor on each side of the upper and lower jaws

was lost, further differentiating primates from other mammals. The canines of most of the primates grew longer, forming daggerlike teeth that enabled them to rip open tough husks of fruit and other foods. Over the millennia, the first and second premolars became smaller and eventually disappeared altogether; the third and fourth premolars grew larger and added a second pointed projection, or cusp, thus becoming "bicuspid." The molars also evolved from a three-cusp to a four- and even five-cusp pattern. Thus the functions of grasping, cutting, and grinding were served by different kinds of teeth.

SENSE ORGANS

The primates' adaptation to life in the trees involved changes in the form and function of their sensory apparatus. To mammals living on the ground, the sense of smell is of great importance, for it enables them to operate at night, as well as to sense what is out of sight—to "see around corners," as it were. Not only can they sniff out their food, but they can be warned of the presence of hidden predators. Up in the trees, though, primates are out of the way of most predators, and good vision is a better guide than smell in judging correctly where the next branch is. Accordingly, the sense of smell declined in primates, while that of sight became highly developed.

Traveling through trees demands judgements concerning depth, direction, distance, and the relationships of objects hanging in space, such as vines or branches. In tarsiers, monkeys, apes, and humans, this is achieved through stereoscopic color vision. The ability to see the world in the three dimensions of height, width, and depth requires two eyes set next to each other on the same plane so that the visual fields of the two eyes overlap. Stereoscopic color vision appears to have led to increased brain size in the visual area in primates and a greater complexity at nerve connections.

A more acute sense of touch also characterized the arboreal primates. An effective feeling and grasping mechanism helped prevent them from falling and tumbling while speeding through the trees. The early mammals from which primates

The abilities to judge depth correctly and to grasp branches firmly are of obvious use to animals as active in the trees as this South American squirrel monkey.

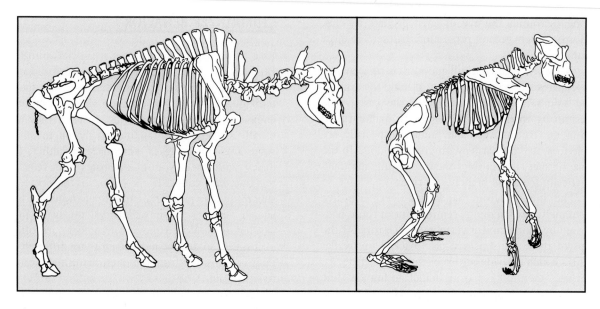

Figure 3.1 Skeletons of a bison (*left*) and gorilla (*right*). Note where the skulls and vertebral columns are joined; in the bison (as in most mammals), the skull projects forward from the vertebral column, but in the semierect gorilla, the vertebral column is well down beneath the skull.

evolved possessed tiny hairs that gave them extremely sensitive tactile capacities. In primates these hairs were replaced by sensitive pads on the tips of the animals' fingers and toes.

THE PRIMATE BRAIN

The most outstanding characteristic of primate evolution has been the great increase in size of the brain. The cerebral hemispheres—the areas of conscious thought—have grown dramatically, and in monkeys, apes, and humans they completely cover the cerebellum, the part of the brain that coordinates the muscles and maintains body equilibrium.

One of the main reasons for this change is probably the primates' arboreal existence. An animal living in the trees is constantly acting and reacting to the environment. Messages from the hands and feet, eyes and ears, as well as from the sensors of balance, movement, heat, touch, and pain, are simultaneously relayed to the cortex. Obviously the cortex had to develop considerably in order to receive, analyze, and coordinate these impressions and transmit the appropriate response back down the motor nerves to the proper receptor. The enlarged cortex not only made the primates

more efficient in the daily struggle for survival, but also prepared the way for cerebration, or thought—an ability that played a decisive role in the emergence of humanity.

THE PRIMATE SKELETON

The skeleton gives a vertebrate animal its basic shape or silhouette, supports the soft tissues, and helps protect vital internal organs. The opening of the skull through which the spinal cord passes and connects to the brain is an important clue to evolutionary relationships. In primates, the trend is for this opening to shift forward, toward the center of the skull's base, so that it faces downward, rather than directly backward, as in dogs and other mammals (Fig. 3.1). This shift enables the backbone to join the skull at the center of its base, a more advantageous arrangement for an animal that assumes an upright posture at least occasionally. The head is thus balanced on the vertebral column, instead of projecting forward from it.

In most primates, the snout or muzzle portion of the skull was reduced as the sense of smell declined. The smaller snout offers less interference with stereoscopic vision and enables the eyes to be placed in a more frontal position. A solid wall of

bone surrounds the eye in most primate species, affording them greater protection than seen in most mammals.

Below the primate skull and neck is the clavicle, or collarbone. It acts as a strut, placing the arms at the side rather than in front of the body, thus permitting them to swing sideways and outward from the trunk. Apes and humans especially are able to move their arms with great freedom. In the case of apes, this enables them to swing and hang vertically from the branches of trees.

The limbs end in hands and feet with five extremely flexible digits, reminiscent of those possessed by more ancient vertebrate ancestors. At the tips of these are sensitive pads backed up by flat nails, which provide an excellent grasping device for use when moving from branch to branch. The thumb and great toe are opposable to varying degrees, so food can easily be handled and branches grasped.

Hindsight allows us to see that the primitive primate hand was to prove a valuable asset to late primates. It was, in part, unspecialized hands capable of grasping that enabled hominids to manufacture and utilize tools and thus alter the course of their evolution.

ADAPTATION THROUGH BEHAVIOR

Important though anatomical adaptation has been to the primates, it has not been the only way of coping with the environment. Studies of monkeys and apes living today indicate that learned social behavior plays an important role in adaptation. The range of behavior shown by living primates is great, but by looking at the behavior of the species most closely related to humans—chimpanzees in particular, and the other great apes as well—or ones like baboons that have adapted to environments somewhat similar to those faced by our own ancestors millions of years ago, we may discover clues to those patterns that contributed to the emergence of human cultural behavior. Unfortunately, space does not permit us to survey the behavior of all these species here. Instead, we shall look at the behavior of our closest genetic relative—the chimpanzee—even though we must realize that no living primate represents a precise analogue for the behavior of our own ancient ancestors.

CHIMPANZEE BEHAVIOR

Like all primates, chimpanzees are social animals.[1] In their native haunts, the largest organizational unit is the community, composed of 50 or more individuals. Rarely, however, do all these animals come together at a single time. Instead, they are usually to be found ranging singly or in small subgroups consisting of adult males together, females with their young, or males and females together with young. In the course of their travels, subgroups may join forces and forage together, but sooner or later these will break up again into smaller units. When they do, members are often exchanged, so that the new subunits are different in their composition from the ones that initially came together.

Although relationships between individuals within the community are relatively harmonious, dominance hierarchies, in which some animals outrank and can dominate others, do exist. Generally, males outrank females, although high-ranking females may dominate low-ranking males. While physical strength and size play a role in determining an animal's rank, what really counts is the rank of its mother, how effective it is at enlisting the aid of other individuals and, in the case of males, how motivated they are to achieve high status. Highly motivated males may bring considerable intelligence and ingenuity to bear in their quest for high rank. For example, one chimp in the community studied by Jane Goodall, a pioneer in the study of primate behavior, was able to figure out how to incorporate noisy kerosene cans into his charging displays, thereby intimidating all the other males. As a result, he rose from relatively low status to the number one (alpha) position.

Grooming, the ritual cleaning of another chimp's coat to remove parasites and other matter, is a common chimpanzee pastime. Besides being hygienic, it is as well a gesture of friendliness, submission, appeasement, or closeness. Group sociability, an important behavioral trait probably found among human precursors, is also expressed in embracing, touching, and the joyous welcoming of other chimps. Group protection and coordination of group efforts is facilitated by visual and

[1]The following summary of chimpanzee behavior is based upon Jane Goodall, *The Chimpanzees of Gombe: Patterns of Behavior* (Cambridge, Mass.: Belknap Press, 1986).

Among chimpanzees, as among most primates, the mother-infant bond is strong. This mother is playfully tickling her offspring.

vocal communication, including warning calls, threat calls, and gathering calls.

The sexes intermingle continually and, as with humans, there is no fixed breeding season. Sexual activity, however—initiated by either the male or the female—occurs only during the period each month when the female is receptive to impregnation. Once impregnated, females are not sexually receptive until their offspring are weaned, at about four years of age. To a degree, chimps are promiscuous in their sexual behavior, and 12 to 14 males have been observed to have as many as 50 copulations in one day with a single female. Nevertheless, dominant males try to monopolize females when the latter are most receptive sexually, although cooperation from the female is usually required for this to succeed. An alpha male, however, is able to monopolize females to some extent, and some alphas have been seen to monopolize several females at the same time.

In most primate species, females and their offspring constitute the core of the social system, and chimps are no exception. The mother-infant bond is especially strong for the first five years, but a close association commonly continues after this.

Although females sometimes leave the group into which they were born, when they do so, their young sons and daughters accompany them. Commonly sons, and often daughters, remain with their mothers for life. Unlike humans, the young chimp must be ready at birth to go everywhere with its mother, for its very survival depends on its ability to remain close to her. Males are generally attentive to juveniles and may share in parental responsibilities. At the least, they provide both mother and infant with protection from other animals, even though they may wander off to forage by themselves. This grouping of adult male (or males), often several adult females, and juveniles suggests what the forerunner of human family groupings may have been like.

Chimpanzees show a remarkable dependence upon learned behavior. Born without built-in responses that will dictate its behavior in complex situations, the young chimp learns how to interact with others, and even manipulate them for his or her own benefit, by trial and error, social facilitation, observation and imitation, and practice. Mistakes made along the way often result in reprimands administered by other members of the group.

This chimpanzee is using a tool to fish for termites.

Among the many things that young chimpanzees learn from adults is how to make and use tools. Not only do they modify objects to make them suitable for particular purposes, but chimps can to some extent modify them to regular and set patterns. They can also pick up and even prepare objects for use at some other location, and they can use objects as tools to solve new and novel problems. For example, chimps have been observed using grass stalks, twigs that they have stripped of leaves, and sticks up to three feet long to fish for termites. They insert the stick into a termite nest, wait a few minutes, pull the stick out, and eat the insects clinging to it.

Other examples of chimpanzee use of objects as tools involve leaves, used as wipes, or as sponges to get water out of a hollow to drink. Large sticks may serve as clubs or as missiles (as may stones) in aggressive or defensive displays. Stones and rocks are also used as hammers and anvils to open palm nuts and hard fruits. Interestingly, tool use to fish for termites is most often exhibited by females, whereas aimed throwing of rocks and sticks is most often exhibited by males. Such tool-using behavior, which young animals learn from their mothers and other adults in their group, may reflect one of the preliminary adaptations that, in the past, led to human cultural behavior.

Fruits, other plant foods, and invertebrate animals constitute the usual chimpanzee diet. Occasionally, however, they will kill and eat other small to medium-sized animals, something that is unusual among primates. Although chimpanzee females sometimes hunt, males do so far more frequently. When on the hunt, they may spend up to two hours watching, following, and chasing intended prey. Moreover, in contrast to the usual practice of each animal finding its own food, hunting among chimpanzees frequently involves teamwork to trap and kill prey. The most sophisticated examples of this occur when hunting baboons; once a potential victim has been partially isolated from its troop, three or more adults will carefully position themselves so as to block off escape routes while another climbs towards the prey for the kill. Once a kill has been made, it is common for most of those present to get a share of the meat, either by grabbing a piece as chance affords, or by sitting and begging for a piece. Modern-day chimps may be recent meat eaters; living at the edge of the savanna, they may be just starting to utilize a food source that human ancestors tapped in similar circumstances millions of years earlier.

The more we learn about chimpanzees in particular, and apes in general, the more we become aware of a degree of intelligence and capacity for conceptual thought hitherto unsuspected for any nonhuman primate.

ORIGINAL STUDY

THE INTELLECTUAL ABILITIES OF CHIMPANZEES[2]

The mid-sixties saw the start of a project that, along with other similar research, was to teach us a great deal about the chimpanzee mind. This was Project Washoe, conceived by Trixie and Allen Gardner. They purchased an infant chimpanzee and began to teach her the signs of ASL, the American Sign Language used by the deaf. Twenty years earlier another husband and wife team, Richard and

Cathy Hayes, had tried, with an almost total lack of success, to teach a young chimp, Vikki, to talk. The Hayes's undertaking taught us a lot about the chimpanzee mind, but Vikki, although she did well in IQ tests, and was clearly an intelligent youngster, could not learn human speech. The Gardners, however, achieved spectacular success with their pupil, Washoe. Not only did she learn signs easily, but she quickly began to string them together in meaningful ways. It was clear that each sign evoked, in her mind, a mental image of the object it represented. If, for example, she was asked, in sign language, to fetch an apple, she would go and locate an apple that was out of sight in another room.

Other chimps entered the project, some starting their lives in deaf signing families before joining Washoe. And finally Washoe adopted an infant, Loulis. He came from a lab where no thought of teaching signs had ever penetrated. When he was with Washoe he was given no lessons in language acquisition—not by humans, anyway. Yet by the time he was eight years old he had made fifty-eight signs in their correct contexts. How did he learn them? Mostly, it seems, by imitating the behaviour of Washoe and the other three signing chimps, Dar, Moja and Tatu. Sometimes, though, he received tuition from Washoe herself. One day, for example, she began to swagger about bipedally, hair bristling, signing *food! food! food!* in great excitement. She had seen a human approaching with a bar of chocolate. Loulis, only eighteen months old, watched passively. Suddenly Washoe stopped her swaggering, went over to him, took his hand, and moulded the sign for food (fingers pointing towards mouth). Another time, in a similar context, she made the sign for *chewing gum*—but with *her* hand on *his* body. On a third occasion Washoe, apropos of nothing, picked up a small chair, took it over to Loulis, set it down in front of him, and very distinctly made the *chair* sign three times, watching him closely as she did so. The two food signs became incorporated into Loulis's vocabulary but the sign for chair did not. Obviously the priorities of a young chimp are similar to those of a human child!

When news of Washoe's accomplishments first hit the scientific community it immediately provoked a storm of bitter protest. It implied that chimpanzees were capable of mastering a human language, and this, in turn, indicated mental powers of generalization, abstraction and concept-formation as well as an ability to understand and use abstract symbols. And these intellectual skills were surely the prerogatives of *Homo sapiens*. Although there were many who were fascinated and excited by the Gardners' findings, there were many more who denounced the whole project, holding that the data was suspect, the methodology sloppy, and the conclusions not only misleading, but quite preposterous. The controversy inspired all sorts of other language projects. And, whether the investigators were sceptical to start with and hoped to disprove the Gardners' work, or whether they were attempting to demonstrate the same thing in a new way, their research provided additional information about the chimpanzee's mind.

And so, with new incentive, psychologists began to test the mental abilities of chimpanzees in a variety of different ways; again and again the results confirmed that their minds are uncannily like our own. It had long been held that only humans were capable of what is called 'cross-modal transfer of information'—in other words, if you shut your eyes and someone allows you to feel a strangely shaped potato, you will subsequently be able to pick it out from other differently shaped potatoes simply by looking at them. And vice versa. It turned out that chimpanzees can 'know' with their eyes what they 'feel' with their fingers in just the same way. In fact, we now know that some other non-human primates can do the same thing. I expect all kinds of creatures have the same ability.

Then it was proved, experimentally and beyond doubt, that chimpanzees could recognize themselves in mirrors—that they had, therefore, some kind of self-concept. In fact, Washoe, some years previously, had already demonstrated the ability when she spontaneously identified herself in the mirror, staring at her image and making her name sign. But that observation was merely anecdotal. The proof came when chimpanzees who had been allowed to play with mirrors were, while anaesthetized, dabbed with spots of odourless paint in places, such as the ears or the top of the head, that they could see only in the mirror. When they woke they were not only fascinated by their images, but immediately investigated, with their fingers, the dabs of paint.

The fact that chimpanzees have excellent memories surprised no one. Everyone, after all, has been brought up to believe that an elephant never forgets, so why should a chimpanzee be any different? The fact that Washoe spontaneously gave the name-sign of Beatrice Gardner, her surrogate mother, when she saw her after a separation of eleven years was no greater an accomplishment than the amazing memory shown by dogs who recognize their owners after separations of almost as long—and the chimpanzee has a much longer life span than a dog. Chimpanzees can plan ahead, too, at least as regards the immediate future. This, in fact, is well illustrated at Gombe, during the termiting season: often an individual prepares a tool for use on a termite mound that is several hundred yards away and absolutely out of sight.

This is not the place to describe in detail the other cognitive abilities that have been studied in laboratory chimpanzees. Among other accomplishments chimpanzees possess premathematical skills: they can, for example, readily differentiate between *more* and *less*. They can classify things into specific categories according to a given criterion— thus they have no difficulty in separating a pile of food into *fruits* and *vegetables* on one occasion, and, on another, dividing the same pile of food into *large* versus *small* items, even though this requires putting some vegetables with some fruits. Chimpanzees who have been taught a language can combine signs creatively in order to describe objects for which they have no symbol. Washoe, for example, puzzled her caretakers by asking, repeatedly, for a *rock berry*. Eventually it transpired that she was referring to Brazil nuts which she had encountered for the first time a while before. Another language-trained chimp described a cucumber as a *green banana,* and another referred to an Alka-Seltzer as a *listen drink.* They can even invent signs. Lucy, as she got older, had to be put on a leash for her outings. One day, eager to set off but having no sign for *leash,* she signalled her wishes by holding a crooked index finger to the ring on her collar. This sign became part of her vocabulary. Some chimpanzees love to draw, and especially to paint. Those who have learned sign language sometimes spontaneously label their works, 'This [is] apple'—or bird, or sweetcorn, or whatever. The fact that the paintings often look, to our eyes, remarkably unlike the objects depicted by the artists either means that the chimpanzees are poor draughtsmen or that we have much to learn regarding ape-style representational art!

People sometimes ask why chimpanzees have evolved such complex intellectual powers when their lives in the wild are so simple. The answer is, of course, that their lives in the wild are not so simple! They use and need—all their mental skills during normal day-to-day life in their complex society. They are always having to make choices—where to go, or with whom to travel. They need highly developed social skills—particularly those males who are ambitious to attain high positions in the dominance hierarchy. Low-ranking chimpanzees must learn deception—to conceal their intentions or to do things in secret—if they are to get their way in the presence of their superiors. Indeed, the study of chimpanzees in the wild suggests that their intellectual abilities evolved, over the millennia, to help them cope with daily life. And now, the solid core of data concerning chimpanzee intellect collected so carefully in the lab setting provides a background against which to evaluate the many examples of intelligent, rational behaviour that we see in the wild.

[2]From *Through a Window: My Thirty Years with the Chimpanzees of Gombe,* by Jane Goodall. Copyright © 1990 by Soko Publications Ltd. Reprinted by permission of Houghton Mifflin Co. All rights reserved.

HUMAN ANCESTORS

Studies in genetics, biochemistry, and anatomy confirm that the chimpanzee is our closest living relative (Fig. 3.2). At the genetic level, we are at least 98 percent identical, from which it is estimated that our evolutionary lines must have separated from a common ancestral stock somewhere between 5.5 and 8 million years ago. Fossils, on the other hand, tell us that humans were going their separate evolutionary way by at least 4 million years ago. The best evidence is that our ancestry lies among a group of apelike animals known as *ramapithecines* that lived in parts of Asia, Africa, and Europe between 15 and 8 million years ago. In many respects, the skull and limb bone fragments that we have of this primate are remarkably orangutanlike. Ramapithecine teeth, while not quite like

Ramapithecines: Apelike primates living between 15 and 8 million years ago, some of which were probably ancestral to the hominids.

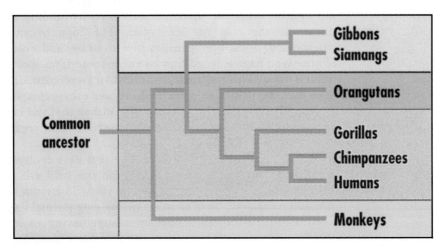

Figure 3.2 The relationships among the various catarrhine primates, as revealed by molecular similarities and differences. It is difficult to take seriously any date in excess of eight million years for the origin of the separate lineages for chimpanzees and humans.

The skull of an Asian ramapithecine is remarkably similar to that of the modern orangutan—so much so that an ancestor-descendant relationship is probable. The last common ancestor of chimpanzees, gorillas, and humans may lie among African ramapithecines.

those of any living ape, are also more like those of orangutans than they are like those of African apes. Still, the incisors are a bit more vertically placed in the mouth, the canines are smaller relative to the molars and premolars, the molar enamel is noticeably thicker, and the tooth row tends to be slightly more V-shaped than is usual in apes. According to David Pilbeam, who has made a study of these and contemporary primate fossils his life work: "Any of [the ramapithecines] would make excellent ancestors for the living hominoids: human bipeds, chimpanzee and gorilla knucklewalkers, orangutan contortionists."[3]

Molar teeth like those of the ramapithecines, having low crown relief, thick enamel, and surfaces poorly developed for cutting, are found in a number of modern primates. Some of these species are terrestrial and some are arboreal, but all have one thing in common: they eat very hard nuts, fruits with very tough rinds, and some seeds. This provides them with a rich source of easily digested nutrients that are not accessible to species with thin molar enamel that is incapable of standing up to the

[3]David Pilbeam, *Human Origins.* David Skamp Distinguished Lecture in Anthropology, Indiana University, 1986:6.

stresses of tough rind removal or nut cracking. Thus, the ramapithecines probably ate food similar to that eaten by these latter-day nut crackers.

Analysis of materials from deposits in which ramapithecine fossils have been found suggests utilization of a broad range of habitats, including tropical rain forests as well as drier bush country. Of particular interest to us, from the standpoint of human origins, are those populations that lived on the edge of open country, where food could be obtained through foraging on the ground out in the open, as well as in the trees of the forests. As it happened, there was a climatic shift under way, causing a gradual but persistent breaking up of forested areas, with a consequent expansion of open savanna country. Under such circumstances, it seems likely that those populations of ramapithecines living at the edge of the forests were obliged to supplement food from the forest more and more with other foods readily available on the open savannas. Consistent with this theory, late ramapithecine fossils are typically found in association with greater numbers of the remains of animals adapted to grasslands than are earlier ones.

Because ramapithecines already had large, thickly enameled molars, those that had to were capable of dealing with the tough and abrasive foods available on the savanna. What they lacked, however, were canine teeth of sufficient size to have served as effective "weapons" of defense. By contrast, most modern monkeys and apes that spend much time down on the ground rely heavily for defense on the massive, fang-like canines possessed by the males. Since catlike predators were even more numerous on the savanna then than now, ramapithecines, especially the smaller ones (which probably weighed no more than about 40 pounds), would seem to have been very vulnerable primates indeed. Probably the forest fringe was more than just a source of foods different from those of the savanna; its trees would have provided refuge when danger threatened. Yet, with continued expansion of savanna country, trees for refuge would have become fewer and farther between.

Slowly, however, physical and behavioral changes must have improved these primates' chances for survival on the savanna. For one thing, those that were able to gather food on the ground and then

The modern ape most like (although not identical to) the ramapithecine is the orangutan. Chimpanzees and gorillas, like humans, have come to differ more from the ancestral condition than have these Asian apes.

A gorilla mother and her offspring. The ability of these apes to carry their infants is limited by the need to use their arms in locomotion.

carry it to the safety of a tree probably had a better rate of survival than those that did not. Although many species of monkeys have cheek pouches in which to carry food, apes do not. Occasionally, modern apes will assume a bipedal stance in order to transport food in their arms, but they are quite awkward about it. The center of gravity, however, is higher in the body of modern apes than it seems to have been in their earlier ancestors, so that bipedal food transport may not have been quite so awkward for the ramapithecines, especially the smaller ones.

Food may not have been the only thing transported. Among modern primates, infants must be able to cling to their mothers in order to be transported, but since the mother is using her forelimbs in locomotion, either to walk, climb, or swing by, she can't very well carry her infant. Chimpanzee infants, for example, must cling for themselves to their mothers, and even at the age of four, they make long journeys on her back. Injuries caused by falling from the mother are a significant cause of infant mortality. Thus, females able to carry their infants would have made a significant contribution to the survival of their offspring.

Other advantages of at least the occasional assumption of a bipedal stance would have been the ability to scan the savanna, so that predators could be spotted before they got too close. Such scanning can be seen from time to time among baboons and chimps today when out on the savanna, even though their anatomy is less suited for this than the ramapithecines' was. In addition, bipedalism would

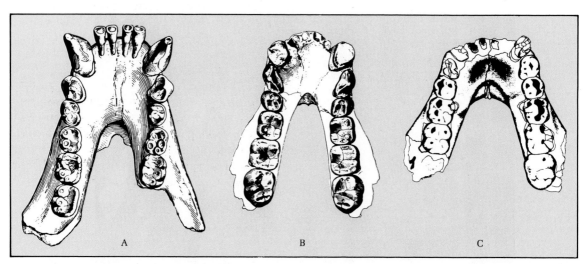

Figure 3.3   The lower jaws of *Dryopithecus* (A), an early ape; a ramapithecine (B); and *Australopithecus* (C) from Laetoli, East Africa. The latter is a hominid who lived nearly four million years ago. All have comparably small teeth at the very front of the jaw, relative to the cheek teeth. There is a general similarity between (A) and (B), as well as between (B) and (C). The major difference between the ramapithecine and *Australopithecus* is that the rows of cheek teeth are farther apart in the hominid.

Hominid: A member of the human family.

Australopithecus: The first undoubted hominid; lived between 1 and 4 or 6 million years ago, and included one (or two) robust species and one (or two) smaller, lightly built species.

---

have facilitated the use of hands to wield and throw things at predators. Among primates, "threat gestures" typically involve shaking branches and large sticks; while on the ground, chimpanzees have been observed throwing rocks at leopards. Lacking the large body size and formidable canines of chimps, there is every reason to suppose that the ramapithecines, when away from the trees and faced by a predator, indulged in the same kind of behavior.

One final incentive to stand bipedally would be to make use of one of the more abundant food sources on the savanna—the thorn bushes that provide edible seeds, leaves, and pods that would have been too high to pick while standing on four (or three) feet. At the same time, the bushes are too spiny and flimsy to be climbed.

Although the ramapithecines display a number of features from which our own may be derived (Fig. 3.3), and some may occasionally have walked bipedally, they were much too apelike to be considered **hominids**—members of the human family. The first undoubted hominid and one who walked about in a fully human manner, is *Australopithecus*, who had appeared on the scene by 4 million years ago.

THE FIRST HOMINID

Most anthropologists recognize at least two distinct species of *Australopithecus: A. africanus* and *A. robustus.* Some refer to the latter as *A. boisei*, while others would reserve this name for a third, super-robust species. Finally, a fourth species, *A. afarensis*, has been applied to the earliest *Australopithecus* fossils.

In spite of differences of opinion over the exact number of species, it is generally agreed that there

were basically two kinds of *Australopithecus*. One, represented by *A. robustus* and *A. boisei*, was heavy with a robust frame and jaws that are massive relative to the size of the brain case. The other, represented by *A. africanus* and *A. afarensis*, was smaller and more lightly built, or **gracile**. Although they argue over details, anthropologists agree that the robust forms lie outside of our own ancestry, and ultimately became extinct. Most anthropologists also agree that gracile *Australopithecus* was anatomically suitable to have given rise both to the robust forms as well as to the genus *Homo*, to which we belong. Present evidence suggests that, by 2.5 million years ago, this differentiation from the gracile ancestral stock into robust *Australopithecus* and early *Homo* was well under way (Fig. 3.4).[4]

None of these early hominids were as large as most modern people, although even the gracile forms were more muscular for their size. The structure and size of the teeth are more like those of modern people than they are like those of apes, and the condition of the molars indicates that food was chewed in hominid fashion: that is, with a grinding motion, rather than simple up and down movement of the jaws. Unlike the apes, no gap exists between the canines and the teeth next to them on the lower jaw, except occasionally in the case of the earliest ones, *A. afarensis*. The large jaw is very similar to that of early *Homo*, although some apelike features are still apparent in the jaw of *A. afarensis*. The brain–body ratio, which permits a rough estimate of *Australopithecus'* intelligence, suggests that this was comparable to that of modern chimpanzees or gorillas.

Australopithecus fossils have also provided anthropology with two striking facts. First, by at least 4 million years ago, this hominid was fully bipedal, walking erect. Second, hominids acquired their erect bipedal posture long before they acquired their highly developed and enlarged brain. Bipedalism was an important adaptive feature in the

---

[4]Donald Johanson and James Shreeve, *Lucy's Child* (New York: Avon, 1989), p. 132.

Gracile: Small and lightly built.

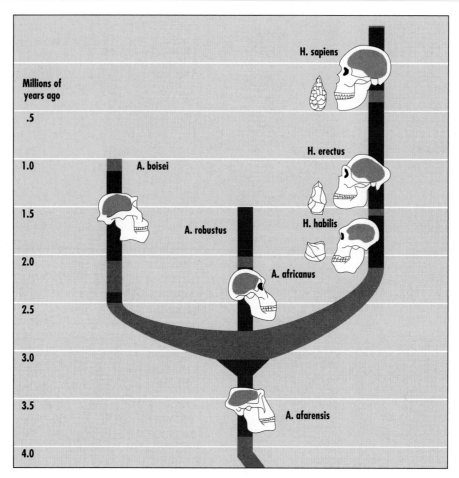

Figure 3.4   A plausible view of early human evolution.

savanna environment. A biped could not run as fast as a quadruped, but could travel long distances in search of food without tiring. It could carry food to places where it could be eaten in relative safety, and it could carry infants, rather than relying on the latter to hang on for themselves. And, standing erect on the open savanna, it could see farther and spot both food and predators.

Although an accomplished biped, evidence from the arm, hand, and foot skeletons of *Australopithecus* indicates that these hominids had not given up tree climbing altogether. One reason may be that trees, sparsely distributed though they were on the savanna, continued to be important places of refuge in a land teeming with dangerous predatory animals. Another is that food was still to be found in trees. Dental and skeletal evidence suggests that the males, who were about twice the size of the females, fed more often on the ground and lower levels of trees than females, who had a higher proportion of fruit in the diet.[5] Something like this pattern is seen today among orangutans, where it is a response to highly dispersed resources. As a consequence, food to which males have access is of lower quality than that eaten by females, and they must consume more of it. A major difference, of course, is that orangutan males still forage in the forest, whereas *Australopithecus* did not. In such a situation, these latter may have been tempted to try out supplementary sources of food on the ground, especially as existing sources became scarcer, as they likely did; a cold, dry episode has been identified in the crucial period between 2.6 and 2.3

[5]William R. Leonard and Michelle Hegman, "Evolution of P_3 Morphology in *Australopithecus afarensis*," *American Journal of Physical Anthropology*, 73(1987):61.

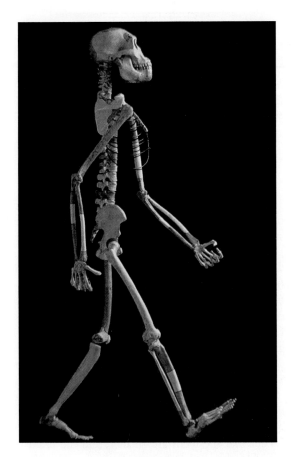

Sufficient parts of the skeleton of "Lucy," a hominid that lived between 2.6 and 3.3 million years ago, survived to permit this reconstruction. Her hip and leg bones reveal that she moved around in a fully human manner.

Footprints of *Australopithecus* from Laetoli, Tanzania.

million years ago. The major new source was animal flesh, but as we shall see, the activities of females were as important as those of males in upping the amount of meat in the hominid diet.

EARLY HOMO

Increased consumption of meat on the part of evolving hominids is a point of major importance. Out on the savanna, it is hard for a primate with a digestive system like that of humans to satisfy its amino-acid requirements from available plant resources. Moreover, failure to do so has serious consequences: growth depression, malnutrition, and ultimately death. The most readily accessible plant sources would have been the proteins available in leaves and legumes (nitrogen-fixing plants, familiar modern examples being beans and peas). The problem is, these are hard for primates like us to digest, unless they are cooked. The leaves and legumes available contain substances that cause the proteins to pass right through the gut without being absorbed.

Chimpanzees have a similar problem when out on the savanna. In such a setting, they spend about 37 percent of their time going after insects such as ants and termites on a year-round basis, while at the same time increasing their predation on eggs and vertebrate animals. Such animal foods not only are easily digestible, but they provide high-quality proteins that contain all the essential amino acids, in just the right percentages. No one plant food does

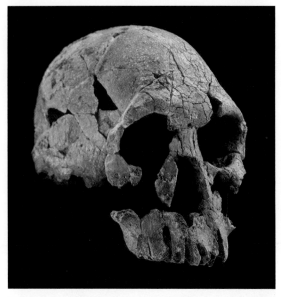

This skull of the genus *Homo,* found in the early 1970s near Lake Turkana, Kenya, is nearly two million years old.

this by itself. Only the right combination of plants can provide what meat does by itself in the way of amino acids. Moreover, there is abundant meat to be had on the savanna. We should not be surprised, then, if our own ancestors solved their "protein problem" in much the same way that chimps on the savanna do today.

Much of a popular nature has been written about the addition of meat to the hominid diet, often with numerous colorful references to "killer apes." Such references are quite misleading, not only because hominids are not apes but also because they obtained their meat, not by killing live animals, but by scavenging, or even by stealing it from other predators. What is significant is that teeth like those possessed by *Australopithecus* are poorly suited for meat eating. Even chimpanzees, whose canine teeth are far larger and sharper, frequently have trouble tearing through the skin of other animals. What hominids need for efficient utilization of meat, in the absence of teeth like those possessed by carnivorous animals, are sharp tools for butchering. The earliest tools of this sort, which were found in Ethiopia, are about 2.5 million years old. The only tools used before this time were probably heavy sticks to dig up roots or ward off animals, unshaped stones to use as missiles for defense or to crack open nuts, and perhaps simple carrying devices made of knotted plant fibers.

Oldowan tools: The earliest identifiable stone tools; first appeared 2.5 million years ago.

Paleolithic: The Old Stone Age, characterized by chipped stone tools.

The earliest *identifiable* tools consist of a number of implements made by striking flakes from the surface of a stone core, leaving either a one- or two-faced tool. The resultant choppers, scrapers, flakes, gouging tools, and hammerstones were used for cutting meat, scraping hides, and cracking bones to extract marrow. These, together with the cores from which they were struck, are known as **Oldowan tools.** Their appearance marks the beginning of the **Paleolithic,** or Old Stone Age.

Since the late 1960s, a number of the deposits in South and East Africa that have produced Oldowan tools have also produced the fossil remains of a lightly built hominid with a body all but indistinguishable from that of gracile *Australopithecus,*[6] except that the teeth are smaller, and the brain is significantly larger, relative to body size. This latter means that there was a marked advance in information-processing capacity over that of *Australopithecus.* Since major brain-size increase and tooth-size reduction are important trends in the evolution of the genus *Homo,* but not of *Australopithecus,* it looks as if these hominids were evolving in a more human direction. It is significant that the earliest fossils to exhibit this trend appeared 2.4 million years ago, soon after the earliest evidence of stone toolmaking and increased consumption of meat.

ENLARGEMENT OF THE HOMINID BRAIN

The significance of meat eating and stone toolmaking for future human evolution was enormous. Not only did it provide a secure source of high quality

[6]Roger Lewin, "The Earliest 'Humans' Were More Like Apes," *Science,* 236(1987):1062.

protein, but as an accidental by-product, it made possible the development of larger brains. The nutritive demands of nerve tissue, of which the brain is made, are high—higher, in fact, than the demands of the other types of tissue in the human body. One can meet these demands on a vegetarian diet, but the overall nutritive value of a given amount of such food is less than that of the same amount of meat. Thus, the use of meat in addition to vegetable foods ensured that a reliable source of high-quality nutrition would be available to support a more highly developed brain, once it evolved. But more than this, animals that live on plant foods must eat large quantities of vegetation, and this consumes much of their time. Meat eaters, by contrast, have no need to eat so much, or so often. Consequently, meat-eating hominids may have had more leisure time available to explore and manipulate their environment; like lions and leopards, they would have time to spend lying around and playing.

As already noted, early *Homo* got meat by scavenging from carcasses of dead animals, rather than hunting live ones. We know this because the marks of stone tools on the bones of animals that were butchered commonly overlie marks made by the teeth of carnivores. Clearly, early *Homo* did not get to them first. Because carcasses are usually widely scattered, the only way these early hominids could have gotten a reasonably steady supply of meat would have been to do on the ground what vultures do in the air: range over vast areas in search of dead animals.[7] Bipedal locomotion allowed them to do just that, without tiring, in an energetically efficient way. Thus bipedalism, which arose for reasons having nothing to do with scavenging, made it possible for our ancestors to take up a new mode of life on the savanna.

While finding carcasses is one thing, it is quite another to get a portion of the meat. Since early hominids lacked size and strength to drive off predators, or to compete directly with other scavengers attracted to kills, they must have had to rely on their wit and cunning for success. One may imagine them lurking in the vicinity of a kill, sizing up the situation as the predator ate its fill while hyenas and other scavengers gathered, and devising strategies to outwit them all so as to grab a piece of the carcass. A hominid depending on stereotyped instinctual behavior in such a situation would have been at a competitive disadvantage. One that could anticipate problems, devise distractions, bluff competitors into temporary retreat, and recognize, the instant it came, its opportunity to rush in and grab what it could of the carcass, stood a much better chance of surviving, reproducing, and proliferating.

Several lines of evidence suggest it was probably early *Homo* males, rather than the females, who scavenged for food. As already noted, somewhat different foraging patterns on the part of gracile *Australopithecus* appear to have predisposed the males more than the females in this direction. Furthermore, without contraceptive devices and formulas that could be bottle fed to infants, females in their prime, when not pregnant, must have had infants to nurse. While this would not have restricted their local mobility, any more than it does a female ape or monkey, it would have been less easy for them than for males to range over the vast distances (on the order of 20 square miles) necessary to search out carcasses. Another necessity for the successful scavenger would have been the ability to mobilize rapidly high bursts of energy, in order to elude successfully carnivorous competitors at the scavenging site. Although anatomical and physiological differences between the sexes in humans today are relatively insignificant compared to early *Homo* (whose males were about twice the size of females[8]), as a general rule, men can still run faster than women (even though some women can certainly run faster than some men). Finally, even for the smartest and swiftest individuals, scavenging would have been a risky business. To place early *Homo* females at risk would have been to place their offspring, actual and potential, at risk as well. Males, on the other hand, would have been relatively expendable, for, to put the matter bluntly, a very few males are capable of impregnating a large number of females. In evolutionary terms, the population that places its males at risk is less likely to jeopardize its chances for reproductive success than is the one that places its females at risk.

Although we should not assume that early *Homo* had meat on a daily basis, a reasonably steady supply would have required that substantial amounts of time and energy be devoted to the search for

[7]Roger Lewin, "Four Legs Bad, Two Legs Good," *Science*, 235(1987):969.

[8]Lewin, "The Earliest 'Humans' Were More Like Apes," 1062.

carcasses, and food gathered by females and shared with males could have supplied the latter with both. Among modern apes and monkeys, food is rarely shared between adults, the one notable exception being the chimpanzee. Although they rarely share other foods, adult males almost always share meat, frequently with females. Thus, increased consumption of meat on the part of early *Homo* may have promoted the sharing of food between the sexes, although not necessarily between mated males and females; it could just as well have been between brothers and sisters or mothers and sons. On the other hand, the potential to be constantly receptive sexually on the part of females may have promoted sharing between a male and one or more sex partners, for among most monkeys and apes, males attempt to monopolize females when the latter are at the height of sexual receptivity. As discussed in Chapter 8, the ability to respond sexually at any time that is characteristic of the human female alone among the primates probably was an incidental by-product of bipedal locomotion; hence, it should have been characteristic of the earliest hominids.

For this new pattern of sharing to work, females, no less than the males, had to "sharpen their wits." Although they continued to gather the same kinds of foods that their ancestors had been eating all along, instead of consuming all this food themselves as they gathered it (as other primates do), they had to gather enough to share with the males, from whom they got a portion of the meat. To do this, they had to plan ahead so as to know where food would be found in sufficient quantities; they had to figure out ways to transport it to some previously agreed-upon location for division, while at the same time taking precautions to prevent either spoilage or loss to such animals as rats and mice. These altered female activities, therefore, played a key role in the development of better brains.

Finally, toolmaking itself played a role in the evolution of the human brain, first by putting a premium on manual dexterity and fine manipulation, as opposed to hand use emphasizing power rather than precision. This in turn put a premium on improved organization of the nervous system. Second, the transformation of a lump of stone into a "chopper," "knife," or "scraper" is a far cry from what a chimpanzee does when it uses stones to crack open nuts, or transforms a stick into a termite probe. While the probe is not unlike the stick, the stone tool *is* unlike the lump of stone. Thus, the

This late *H. erectus* skull from Petralona, Greece, like its contemporaries from Africa and Asia, retains much of the shape of earlier *erectus* skulls, but its brain is a bit larger.

toolmaker must have in mind an abstract idea of the tool to be made, as well as a specific set of steps that will accomplish the transformation. Furthermore, only certain kinds of stone have the flaking properties that will allow the transformation to take place, and the toolmaker must know about these.

In sum, a combination of factors, all associated in one way or another with the addition of more meat into the human diet, imposed strong selective pressures for better brains in early *Homo*, for both males and females. From this point on, the record is one of increasing brain size relative to body size, and increasing cultural development, each presumably acting to promote the other.

Although early *Homo* is best known from fossils found in South Africa, Tanzania, and Kenya, similar fossils have been found in Java, suggesting that these early ancestors of ours were widespread in the Old World tropics (Fig. 3.5). Even more widespread, however, was the next figure in human evolution, ***Homo erectus,*** whose remains have been found not only in Africa and Southeast Asia but up into Europe and China as well.

Homo erectus: Species of *Homo* preceding and ancestral to *Homo sapiens.*

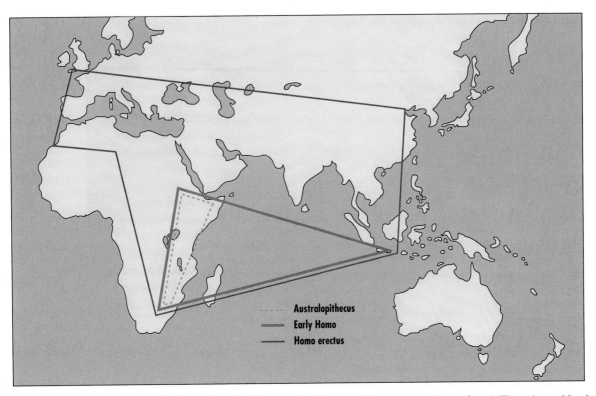

Figure 3.5 Areas in which fossils of *Australopithecus*, early *Homo* and *H. erectus* have been found. There has evidently been a steady expansion of hominid populations into new areas as the efficiency of cultural adaptation has increased.

HOMO ERECTUS

In spite of their broad distribution, fossils of *H. erectus* reveal no more significant physical variations than are to be seen in modern human populations. These fossils indicate that *H. erectus* had a body much like our own, though with heavier musculature and a smaller birth canal. Differences in body size between the sexes were considerably reduced compared to early *Homo*. Brain size was significantly larger than in early *Homo*, and well within the lower range of modern brain size. The dentition was fully human, though relatively large by modern standards. As one might expect, given its larger brain, *H. erectus* outstripped its predecessors in cultural development. In Africa, the Oldowan chopper was transformed into the more sophisticated hand ax (the Stone Age equivalent of "building a better mousetrap"). In parts of Europe chopper tools continued to be made, but later, in both Africa and Europe, the hand ax appears further refined and developed.

During this time, tool kits also began to diversify, indicating the increased efficiency of *H. erectus* in adapting to diverse environments. At first the hand axes—shaped by regular blows that gave them a larger and finer cutting edge than chopper tools—were probably all-purpose implements, useful in food processing, hide scraping, and defense. But *H. erectus* then developed cleavers (like hand axes, but without points), which could be used for killing as well as butchering; several different types of scrapers, which would be used for processing hides for bedding and clothing; and flake tools to cut meat and process vegetables. Adaptation to specific regions is also indicated by different assortments of tools in the various regions inhabited by *H. erectus*.

The improved technological efficiency of *H. erectus* is also evident in the selection of raw materials. Instead of making a few large tools out of large pieces of stone, a new emphasis was placed on smaller tools that were more economical of raw materials. Moreover, new techniques were developed to produce thinner, straighter, and sharper

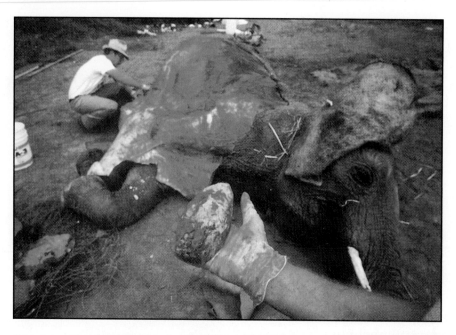

Experimentation on an elephant that died of natural causes demonstrates the effectiveness of Acheulean tools. Simple flakes of flint slice through the thick hide easily, while hand axes sever large muscles. With such tools, two men can each butcher 100 pounds of meat in an hour.

tools. The use of a hard wooden baton for flaking produced shallow flake scars, rather than the crushed edge found on the older tools. By first preparing a flat platform on a core, from which flakes could be struck off, even sharper and thinner implements could be made. The toolmaker could also shape the core so that flake points 3 to 6 inches long could be struck off all ready to use.

By 700,000 years ago—as attested by an identifiable hearth in a rock shelter in Thailand—*H. erectus* learned how to use fire.[9] Studies of modern humans indicate that they can remain reasonably comfortable down to 50° F with a minimum of clothing so long as they are active; below that temperature, the extremities cool to the point of pain. Thus, dispersal of early humans into regions where winter temperatures regularly went below 50°, as they must have in China and Europe, was probably not possible without fires to keep warm. As one would expect, evidence does not suggest the presence of *H. erectus* in China and Europe until ca. 700,000 years ago.

[9]Geoffrey Pope, "Bamboo and Human Evolution," *Natural History* (Oct. 1988):56.

In addition to keeping them warm, use of fire enabled *H. erectus* to cook food, a significant step in human cultural adaptation. This altered the forces of natural selection, which previously favored individuals with heavy jaws and large, sharp teeth (food is tougher and needs more chewing when it is uncooked), thus paving the way for reduction in tooth size as well as supportive facial architecture. Cooking did more than this, though; because it detoxifies a number of otherwise poisonous plants, alters digestion-inhibiting substances so that important vitamins, minerals, and proteins can be absorbed while in the gut, rather than just passing through unused, and makes complex carbohydrates like starch—high-energy foods—digestible, the basic resources available to humans were substantially increased and made more secure.

Like tools, then, fire gave people more control over their environment. It may have been used, if not by *H. erectus,* then by subsequent hominids, to frighten away cave-dwelling predators so that they might live in the caves themselves; and it could then be used to provide warmth and light in these cold and dark habitations. Even more, it modified the natural succession of day and night, perhaps en-

Archaeologists working at the hearth in Kao Poh Nam rockshelter in Thailand. This hearth testifies to human use of fire 700,000 years ago.

couraging *H. erectus* to stay up after dark to review the day's events, and plan the next day's activities. That *H. erectus* was capable of at least some planning is implied by the existence of populations in temperate climates, where the ability to anticipate the needs of the winter season by preparing in advance to protect against the cold would have been crucial for survival.[10]

As *H. erectus* became technologically more proficient, hunting began to replace scavenging as the means by which meat, animal hides, and sinew were procured. The sophistication of hunting techniques in use by 400,000 years ago suggests, however, more than just greater technological capability; it also reflects an increased organizational ability. For example, excavations in Kenya at Olorgesailie indi-

cate that group hunting techniques were used 400,000 years ago to ambush and kill a group of at least 63 baboons of a species larger than today's savanna baboon.

With *H. erectus*, then, we find a clearer manifestation of the interplay among cultural, physical, and environmental factors than ever before. Social organization and technology developed along with an increase in brain size and complexity. Cultural adaptations such as cooking and more complex tool kits facilitated dental reduction; and dental reduction in turn encouraged an even heavier reliance upon tool development and facilitated the development of language. Improvements in communication and social organization brought about by language undoubtedly contributed to the use of improved methods of food gathering, as well as hunting, a population increase, and territorial expansion. Evidence from tools and fossils indicates that just as

[10]Ward H. Goodenough, "Evolution of the Human Capacity for Beliefs," *American Anthropologist*, 92(1990):601.

H. erectus was able to move into areas previously uninhabited by hominids (Europe and northern China), *Homo sapiens*—the subject of our next discussion—was able to live in areas previously uninhabited by *H. erectus*.

HOMO SAPIENS

At various sites in Europe and Africa, a number of hominid fossils have been found that date between roughly 300,000 and 200,000 years ago. Some of these—most commonly the African fossils, but also a skull from southern France—have been called *Homo erectus;* others—most commonly skulls from Steinheim, Germany, and Swanscombe, England—have been called **Homo sapiens**. In fact, all show a mixture of characteristics of both forms, which is what one would expect of remains transitional between the two. For example, skulls from Ethiopia, Steinheim, and Swanscombe had rather large brains for *Homo erectus*. Their overall appearance, however, is different from skulls like ours. They are large and robust, with their maximum breadth lower on the skull, and they had more prominent brow ridges, larger faces, and bigger teeth. Even a skull from Morocco, which had a rather small brain for *Homo sapiens*, looks surprisingly modern from the back. Finally, the various jaws from Morocco and France seem to combine features of *Homo erectus* with those of the European Neandertals.

Whether one chooses to call these early humans primitive *H. sapiens* or advanced, *H. erectus* seems to be a matter of taste; both names are in keeping with their apparently transitional status.

ARCHAIC *HOMO SAPIENS*

The abundance of human fossils postdating 200,000 years ago is in marked contrast to the paucity of earlier fossils. All are assignable to *Homo sapiens*, though a distinction is made between archa-

Homo sapiens: The modern human species.

Neandertal skull from La Ferrassie, France.

ic *H. sapiens* which, by about 30,000 years ago, had been supplanted everywhere by anatomically modern *H. sapiens*.

No representatives of archaic *H. sapiens* are better known than the **Neandertals**, which are represented by numerous fossils from Europe, the Middle East, and south central Asia. These extremely muscular people, while having brains of modern size, possessed faces distinctively different from those of modern humans. Midfacial projection of their noses and teeth formed a kind of prow, at least in part to sustain the large size of their front teeth. Over the eyes were prominent brow ridges, and on the back of the skull, a bony mass provided for attachment of powerful neck muscles.

Living in other parts of the world were variants of archaic *H. sapiens* that lacked the extreme midfacial projection and massive muscle attachments on the back of the skull characteristic of the Neandertals. In 1931, for example, a number of interesting skulls were found in Java, near the Solo River, which suggest a being with features common to *H.*

Neandertal: Representative of "archaic" *Homo sapiens* in Europe and the Middle East, living from about 100,000 years ago to about 35,000 years ago.

Mousterian: Toolmaking tradition of the Neandertals of Europe, southwest Asia, and North Africa.

erectus, Neandertal, and more modern *H. sapiens*. These Solo fossils look like robust versions of some more recent Southeast Asian populations or, if one looks backwards, somewhat less primitive versions of the *H. erectus* populations that preceded them in this region. Fossils from various parts of Africa, the most famous being a skull from Broken Hill in Zambia, show a similar combination of ancient and modern traits. Finally, equivalent remains have been found at several localities in China.

Adaptations to the environment on the part of archaic *Homo sapiens* were, of course, both physical and cultural, but the capacity for cultural adaptation was predictably superior to what it had been. Neandertal's extensive use of fire, for example, was essential to survival in an arctic climate like that of Europe at the time. They lived in small bands or single-family units, both in the open and in caves, and undoubtedly communicated by speech (see Chapter 4). Evidence of deliberate burials seems to reflect complex ritual behavior. Moreover, the remains of an amputee discovered in Iraq and an arthritic man unearthed in France imply that Neandertals cared for the disabled, an unprecedented example of social concern.

Hunting techniques improved along with social organization and a more developed technology in weapon- and toolmaking. The toolmaking tradition of all but the latest Neandertals (whose technology was comparable to that of anatomically modern *H. sapiens*),[11] is called **Mousterian** after a site (Le Mousier) in France. Mousterian tools date from 100,000 to 40,000 years ago, and characterized this period in Europe, North Africa, and western Asia.

Mousterian tools are generally lighter and smaller than those of earlier traditions. Whereas previously only two or three flakes could be obtained from the entire core, Neandertal toolmakers obtained many more smaller flakes, which they skillfully retouched and sharpened. Their tool kits also contained a greater variety of types than the earlier ones: hand axes, flakes, scrapers, borers, notched flakes for shaving wood, and many types of points that could be attached to wooden shafts to make spears. This variety of tools facilitated more effective utilization of food resources and enhanced the quality of clothing and shelter.

Improved ability in cultural adaptation no doubt is related to the fact that, with archaic *H. sapiens*, the human brain had achieved modern size. Such a brain made possible not only sophisticated technology but also conceptual thought of considerable sophistication. Evidence for this is provided by the ceremonial burial of the dead, as well as by objects of apparently symbolic significance. These latter consist of nonutilitarian items, such as pendants, and carved and engraved markings on objects that would have required some form of linguistic explanation.

One of the great debates in anthropology today is whether one, some, or all populations of the archaic species played a role in the evolution of modern *H. sapiens*. With the evident exception of those Neandertals who coexisted between 90,000 and 30,000 years ago with anatomically modern humans in Europe and the Middle East, the fossil evidence suggests that local populations in eastern and southern Asia, as well as Africa, made the transition from *Homo erectus* to modern *sapiens*. On the other hand, a comparison of molecular data from modern human populations living in diverse geographical regions suggests that all modern people are derived from one single population of archaic *H. sapiens* that lived in Africa (although some argue in favor of Asia). Although modern features do seem to appear earlier in African fossils than in those from other regions, this "Eve hypothesis" has been criticized on several grounds. For one thing, it conflicts with the fossil evidence for continuity between older and more recent populations not just in Africa but in China, southeast Asia, and parts of the Middle East, even if not in Europe and other parts of western Asia. Furthermore, even well established molecular techniques sometimes yield conflicting results and may be upset by extraneous factors.[12] In this case, the techniques used are

[11]Paul Mellars, "Major Issues in the Emergence of Modern Humans," *Current Anthropology*, 30(1989):356–357.

[12]Roger Lewin, "Molecular Clocks Turn a Quarter Century," *Science*, 239(1988):562; Timothy Rowe, "New Issues for Phylogenetics," *Science*, 239(1988):1184.

new, and so may not yield results that are as reliable as we would like.

Taking a cautious approach, all that can be said at the moment is that *at least* one population of archaic *H. sapiens* evolved into modern humans. The basic difference between the two is that the modern face is less massive, as is the bony architecture at the rear of the skull that provided attachment needed for the neck musculature to compensate for the weight of a massive face.

UPPER PALEOLITHIC PEOPLES

Between about 200,000 and 90,000 years ago, the only hominid present in the world was archaic *H. sapiens*. By 30,000 years ago, only anatomically modern peoples who possessed a physical appearance similar to our own were present. These more modern representatives of *Homo sapiens* are often referred to as **Cro-Magnons,** after the French rock

Cro-Magnons: The Upper Paleolithic peoples of Europe.

Upper Paleolithic: The late Old Stone Age; began about 35,000 years ago.

Upper Paleolithic peoples: The first people of modern appearance, who lived in the last part of the Old Stone Age.

shelter in which their bones were first found. Since the name really refers to **Upper Paleolithic** remains from Europe, it is best to refer to human remains from other parts of the world not as Cro-Magnons, but as those of **Upper Paleolithic peoples.**

Cro-Magnon and other Upper Paleolithic remains reveal considerable physical variability, as is usual in human populations. Generally speaking, however, these people had characteristically modern-looking faces. As suggested in our discussion of *H. erectus,* specialized tools and cooking helped achieve this modernization by gradually assuming the chewing and softening functions once served by large teeth and heavy jaws. Selection seems to have favored diminished muscles for chewing, and

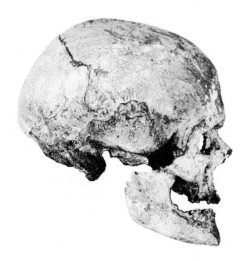 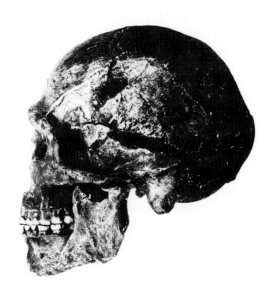

Left, the original Cro-Magnon skull, which differs very little from modern European skulls. *Right,* a much earlier, anatomically modern skull from the 90,000-year-old site of Qafzeh, Israel.

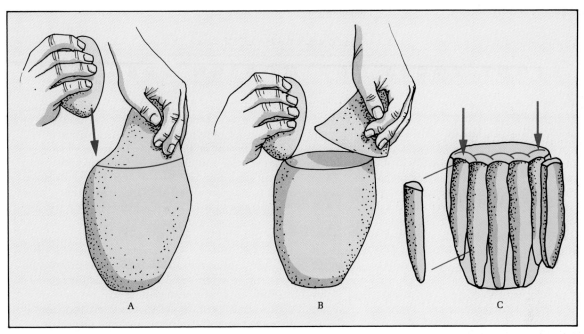

Figure 3.6   During the Upper Paleolithic, a new technique was devised to manufacture blades. The stone is broken to create a striking platform, then vertical blades are flaked off the sides to form sharp-edged tools.

consequently the bones to which these muscles were attached became less massive.

At this point in human evolution, culture had become a more potent force than biology. As the smaller features of Upper Paleolithic peoples suggest, physical bulk was no longer required for survival. New technological developments had contributed to the increasing complexity of the brain by the time of archaic *H. sapiens*, and this complexity now enabled people to create a still more sophisticated technology. Similarly, conceptual thought and symbolic behavior seem to have developed beyond what we saw in the case of archaic *H. sapiens*. More than ever, intelligence henceforth provides the key to humanity's increased reliance on cultural rather than physical adaptation.

In Upper Paleolithic times, human intelligence enabled people to manufacture tools that surpassed the physical equipment of predators and to develop more efficient means of social organization and cooperation—all of which made them far more proficient at hunting and fishing as well as at gathering. Cultural adaptation also became highly specific and regional, thus increasing human chances for survival under a variety of environmental conditions. Instead of manufacturing crude all-purpose tools, Upper Paleolithic populations of the savanna, forest, and shore all developed specialized devices suited to the resources of their particular environment and the different seasons in which they were being used. It also permitted human habitation of new areas, such as Australia and the Americas.

This degree of specialization naturally required improved manufacturing techniques. The blade method of manufacture (Fig. 3.6), used widely in Europe and western Asia, required less raw material than before, and resulted in smaller and lighter tools with a better ratio between weight of flint and length of cutting edge. The pressure-flaking technique—in which a bone, antler, or a wooden tool was used to press off small flakes from a flint core—gave the toolmaker greater control over the shape of the tool than was possible with percussion flaking.

Although invented by Mousterian toolmakers, the burin—a stone tool with chisel-like edges—came into common use in the Upper Paleolithic. The burin provided an excellent means of carving bone and antler, used for such tools as fishhooks

ANTHROPOLOGY APPLIED

STONE TOOLS FOR MODERN SURGEONS

In 1975, Don Crabtree, then at the Idaho State University Museum, underwent heart surgery; in 1980, an anonymous patient in Boulder, Colorado, underwent eye surgery; and in 1986, David Pokotylo of the Museum of Anthropology at the University of British Columbia underwent reconstructive surgery on his hand. What these operations had in common was that the scalpels used were not of surgical steel. Instead, they were made of obsidian (a naturally occurring volcanic "glass") by the Upper Paleolithic blade technique. In all three cases, the scalpels were handmade by archaeologists who specialized in the study of ancient stone tool technology: Crabtree himself, Payson Sheets at the University of Colorado, and Pokotylo with his colleague Len McFarlane (who hafted the blades) of the Museum of Anthropology.

The reason for the use of scalpels modeled on ancient stone tools, rather than modern steel, or even diamond scalpels, is because the obsidian is superior in almost every way: 210 to 1050 times sharper than surgical steel, 100 to 500 times sharper than a razor blade, and three times sharper than a diamond blade (which costs many times more and cannot be made with more than 3mm of cutting edge), obsidian blades are easier to cut with, and do less damage in the process (under a microscope, incisions made with the sharpest steel blades show torn ragged edges and are littered with bits of displaced flesh).* As a consequence, the surgeon has better control over what she or he is doing, the incisions heal faster with less scarring, and with less pain.

In order to develop and market obsidian scalpels, Sheets has formed a corporation in partnership with Boulder Colorado eye surgeon Dr. Firmon Hardenbergh. So far, they have developed a means of producing cores of uniform size from molten glass, as well as a machine to detach blades from the cores. Once this equipment is tested and refined, they hope to go into production for the surgical supply trade.

*Payson D. Sheets, "Dawn of a New Stone Age in Eye Surgery" in *Archaeology: Discovering Our Past,* by Robert J. Sharer and Wendy Ashmore (Palo Alto, Calif.: Mayfield, 1987), p.231.

and harpoons. The atlatl, which consisted of a piece of wood with a groove in it for holding and throwing a spear, also appeared at this time. By using the atlatl, a hunter increased the force behind the spear throw. The bow and arrow went even beyond this. The bowstring increased the force on the arrow, enabling it to travel farther and with greater effectiveness than if it had been thrown by hand.

One important aspect of Upper Paleolithic culture is the art of this period. As far as we know, humans had not produced art work of this caliber before; therefore, the level of artistic proficiency is certainly amazing. Tools and weapons were decorated with engravings of animal figures; pendants were made of bone and ivory as were female figurines; and there was sculpting in clay. More spectacular, and quite unlike anything undertaken by the earlier Neandertals, are the cave paintings in Spain and France. Made with mineral oxide pig-

ments, these skillfully executed paintings almost exclusively depict animals that were hunted by Upper Paleolithic peoples. It is not known for certain why other subject matter was not chosen, nor compositional background provided for the animals portrayed. It is also curious that later paintings are found in the darkest recesses of the caves, suggesting that they served other than a decorative function. Some anthropologists suggest that these paintings served a magical or religious function having to do with control over the animals represented, or a symbolic function having to do with male initiation ceremonies. In any case, they reflect a remarkably developed aesthetic sensibility.

With the end of the Upper Paleolithic, with anatomically modern varieties of humans on the scene, as well as cultures comparable to those known for recent food-foraging peoples, we have reached a logical place to end our examination of the beginnings of human culture. Ending our examination of human cultural development here should not be taken to mean that human evolution stopped at the end of the Paleolithic. Since then, the human species has continued to change biologically, even though it remains the same species now as then. Culture, too, has continued to change, and revolutionary developments in cultural evolution, such as the development of food production and, later, civilization, came after the Paleolithic. These developments will be touched upon in subsequent chapters, especially Chapters 6 and 15.

This Upper Paleolithic cave painting of a bull indicates an artist who was not only skilled but also thoroughly familiar with the anatomy of the animal depicted.

Chapter Summary

Anthropology includes the study of primates other than humans in order to explain why and how humans developed as they did. As the early primates became tree dwellers, various modifications took place—in dental characteristics, sense organs, the brain, and skeletal structure—that helped them to adapt to their environment. At the same time, learned social behavior became increasingly important to them. Through the study of the behavior of present-day primates, anthropologists seek clues with which to reconstruct behavior patterns that may have characterized those apelike primates ancestral to both humans and present-day apes.

Like all monkeys and apes, chimpanzees live in structured social groups and express their sociability through communication by visual and vocal signals. They also exhibit learning, but unlike most other primates, they can make and use tools.

The earliest undoubted member of the human family was *Australopithecus,* who was living in Africa by 4 million years ago. Anthropologists recognize two kinds of *Australopithecus,* a gracile (small, lightly built) and a robust form. This hominid, fully bipedal (able to walk and run erect) was well equipped for generalized food gathering in the savanna environment. Although still strikingly apelike from the waist up, *Australopithecus* had a fully human dentition, many features of which are easily derivable from the earlier ramapithecines. Some of these ramapithecines lived under conditions that forced them to spend considerable time on the ground, and they appear to have had the capacity for at least occasional bipedal locomotion.

It appears that an early form of gracile *Australopithecus* gave rise to an early form of the genus *Homo.* It is of major significance that members of this new genus were both meat eaters and makers of stone tools. Toolmaking enabled early *Homo* to process meat so that it could be eaten; because making tools from stone depended on fine manipulation of the hands, it put a premium on more developed brains. So, too, did the analytic and planning abilities required to scavenge meat from

the carcasses of dead animals, and to gather the surplus of other wild foods for sharing.

Homo erectus exhibited a nearly modern body, a brain close in size to the modern human brain, and fully human dental characteristics. The ability to use fire provided a further means of controlling the environment. The technological efficiency of *H. erectus* is evidenced in a refined toolmaking, with the development of the hand axe and, later, specialized tools for hunting, butchering, food processing, hide scraping, and defense. In addition, hunting techniques ultimately developed by *H. erectus* reflected a considerable advance in organizational ability.

By 100,000 years ago, hominids possessed the brain capacity of true *Homo sapiens.* Apparently several local variations of archaic *H. sapiens,* including the Neandertals, existed. Their capacity for cultural adaptation was considerable, doubtless because their fully modern brains made possible not only sophisticated technology but sophisticated conceptual thought as well. Those who lived in Europe used fire extensively in their arctic climate, lived in small bands, and communicated by speech. Remains indicate the existence of ritual behavior, and the aged and infirm were cared for.

Evidence indicates that at least one population of archaic *H. sapiens* evolved into modern humans. Cro-Magnons and other Upper Paleolithic peoples possessed physical features similar to those of modern human populations as sheer physical bulk gave way to smaller features. The art work of Cro-Magnon cultures surpasses any undertaken by previous humans. Cave paintings found in Spain and France, which most anthropologists believe served a religious purpose, attest to a highly sophisticated aesthetic sensibility.

What we have seen is a close interrelation between developing culture and developing humanity. The critical importance of culture as the human adaptive mechanism seems to have imposed selective pressures favoring a better brain, and a better brain, in turn, made possible improved cultural adaptation. Indeed, it seems fair to say that modern humans look the way they do today because cultural adaptation came to play such an important role in the survival of our ancient ancestors. Because cultural adaptation worked so well, human populations were able to grow, probably very slowly, causing a gradual expansion into previously uninhabited parts of the world. And this, too, affected cultural adaptation, as adjustments were made to meet new conditions.

Suggested Readings

Campbell, Bernard G. *Humankind Emerging,* 5th ed. Boston: Little, Brown, 1988.
An up-to-date introduction to human evolution that is not only highly informative and readable, but lavishly illustrated with photographs, drawings, and charts drawn from Time-Life's *Emergence of Man* and *Life Nature Library* series.

Johanson, Donald, and James Shreeve. *Lucy's Child: The Discovery of a Human Ancestor.* New York: Avon, 1989.
This book tells the story of the discovery of the fossils of *Australopithecus* and early *Homo* and what they have to tell us about the early stages of human evolution. It reads like a first-rate detective story, at the same time giving good descriptions of the various forms of *Australopithecus*, and early *Homo*, one of the best discussions of the issues involved in the arguments over when (and why) *Homo* appeared, and one of the best accounts of how paleoanthropologists analyze their fossils.

Goodall, Jane. *Through a Window.* Boston: Houghton Mifflin, 1990.
This fascinating book is a personal account of Goodall's experience over 30 years of studying wild chimpanzees in Tanzania. A pleasure to read and a fount of information on the behavior of these apes, the book is profusely illustrated as well.

Jolly, Allison. *The Evolution of Primate Behavior,* 2nd ed. New York: Macmillan, 1985.
The first edition of this book was the standard text on primate behavior for 13 years. In this as in the original edition, the author surveys current knowledge about primate behavior and its relevance for human behavior. Comprehensive and still reasonably up-to-date, the book is also exciting, amusing, and well illustrated.

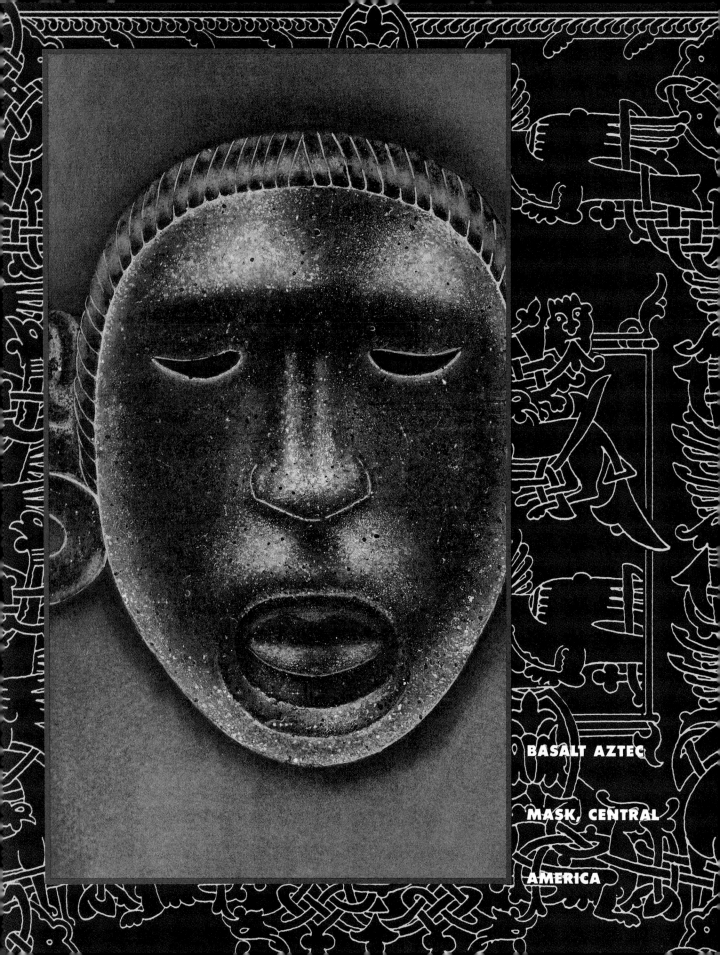

BASALT AZTEC

MASK, CENTRAL

AMERICA

PART II

CULTURE
AND
SURVIVAL:
COMMUNICATING,
RAISING
CHILDREN,
AND
STAYING
ALIVE

INTRODUCTION

ALL LIVING CREATURES FACE

A FUNDAMENTAL PROBLEM

IN COMMON—THAT OF

SURVIVAL. SIMPLY PUT,

UNLESS THEY ADAPT

THEMSELVES TO SOME

AVAILABLE ENVIRONMENT,

THEY CANNOT SURVIVE.

ADAPTATION REQUIRES THE

DEVELOPMENT OF ▶

▶ behaviors that will help an organism use the environment to its advantage—to find food and sustenance, avoid hazards, and (if the species is to survive) reproduce its own kind. In turn, organisms need to have the biological equipment that allows development of appropriate patterns of behavior. For the hundreds of millions of years of life on earth, biological adaptation has been the primary means by which the problem of survival has been solved. This is accomplished as organisms of a particular kind, whose biological equipment is best suited to a particular way of life, produce more offspring than those whose equipment is not. In this way, advantageous characteristics become more common in succeeding generations, while less advantageous ones become less common.

By two million years ago, some time after the line of human evolution had branched off from apes, a new means of dealing with the problems of existence had come into being. Early hominids began to rely more on what their minds could invent, rather than on what their bodies were capable of. Although the human species has not freed itself entirely, even today, from the forces of biological adaptation, it has come to rely primarily on culture—a body of learned traditions that, in essence, tells people how to live—as the medium through which the problems of human existence are solved. The consequences of this are profound. As evolving hominids unconsciously came to rely more on cultural as opposed to biological solutions to their problems, their chances of survival improved. For example, when hominids added scavenging to their subsistence practices some 2.5 million years ago, the resources available to them increased substantially. Moreover, the tools and techniques that made this new way of life possible made our ancient ancestors less vulnerable to predators than

they had been before. Thus life became a bit easier, and with humans, as with other animals, this generally makes for easier reproduction. A slow but steady growth of human populations followed the development of scavenging and gathering.

Among most mammals, population growth frequently leads to the dispersal of fringe populations into regions previously uninhabited by the species. There they find new environments, to which they must adapt or face extinction. This pattern of dispersal seems to have been followed by the evolving human species, for not long after the invention of scavenging and gathering, humans began to spread geographically, inhabiting new and even harsh environments. As they did so, they devised cultural rather than biological solutions to their new problems of existence. This is illustrated by human habitation of cold regions of the world, which was not dependent on the evolution of humans capable of growing heavy coats of fur, as do other mammals that live in such regions. Instead, humans had the ability to devise forms of clothing and shelter that, coupled with the use of fire, enabled them to overcome the cold. Moreover, this "cold adaptation" could be rapidly changed in the face of different circumstances. The fact is that cultural equipment and techniques can be changed drastically in less than a single generation, whereas biological change takes many generations to accomplish.

As the medium through which humans handle the problems of existence, culture is basic to human survival. It cannot do its job, though, unless it deals successfully with certain basic problems. Because culture is learned and not inherited biologically, its transmission from one person to another, and from one generation to the next, depends on an effective system of communication that must be far more complex than that of any other animal. Thus, a first requirement for any culture is providing a means of communication among individuals. All cultures do this through some form of language, the subject of Chapter 4.

In human societies each generation learns its culture anew. The learning process itself is thus crucial to a culture's survival. A second requirement of culture, then, is the development of reliable means by which individuals learn the behavior expected of them as members of their community, and how children learn appears to be as important as what they learn. Since to a large extent adult personality is the product of life experiences, the ways children are raised and educated play a major part in the shaping of their later selves: the ability of individuals to function properly as adults depends, to a degree, upon how effectively their personalities have been shaped to fit their culture. As we see in Chapter 5, findings have emerged from anthropological investigations in these areas which have implications for human behavior that go beyond anthropology.

Important as effective communication and education are for the survival of a culture, they are of no avail unless the culture is able to satisfy the basic needs of the individuals who live by its rules. A third requirement of culture, therefore, is the ability to provide its members with food, water, and protection from the elements. Chapter 6 discusses the ways in which cultures handle people's basic needs and the ways societies adapt through culture to the environment. Since this leads to the production, distribution, and consumption of goods—the subject matter of economic anthropology—we conclude this section with a chapter (Chapter 7) on economic systems.

CHAPTER

4

LANGUAGE

AND

COMMUNICATION

Although humans rely primarily on language for communication, it is by no means the only system used. These children are communicating with one another by means of facial gestures.

WHAT IS LANGUAGE?

Language is a system of sounds that, when put together according to certain rules, results in meanings that are intelligible to all speakers. Although humans rely primarily on language to communicate with one another, it is not their sole means of communication. Other means of communication are paralanguage, a system of extralinguistic noises that accompany language, and kinesics, a system of body motions used to convey messages.

HOW IS LANGUAGE RELATED TO CULTURE?

Languages are spoken by people, who are members of societies which have their own distinctive cultures. Social variables, such as class, gender, and status of the speaker, will influence people's use of language. Moreover, people communicate what is meaningful to them, and what is or is not meaningful is defined by their particular culture. In fact, our use of language affects, and is affected by, our culture.

HOW DID LANGUAGE BEGIN?

Many theories have been proposed to account for the origin of language, several of them quite farfetched. One theory held by anthropologists today is that human language began as a tool to communicate and implement intentions within a social setting. As such, it represents an outgrowth of abilities possessed as well by the great apes. A key factor in its elaboration seems to have been the importance of planning ahead for future contingencies on the part of our ancient ancestors.

All normal humans have the ability to talk, and in many societies they may spend a considerable part of each day doing so. Indeed, **language** is so much a part of our lives that it permeates everything we do, and everything we do permeates language. There is no doubt that our ability to speak rests squarely upon our biological organization. We are "programmed" to speak, although only in a general sort of way. Beyond the cries of babies, which are not learned but which do communicate, humans must learn how to speak. We must be taught to speak a particular language, and any normal child from anywhere in the world readily learns whatever language is spoken where she or he happens to be reared.

Language is a system for the communication, in **symbols,** of any kind of information. In the sense that nonhuman animals also communicate certain kinds of information systematically, we may speak of animal language. "Symbol" in our definition, however, means any kind of sound or gesture to which cultural tradition has given meaning as standing for something, and not one that has a natural or self-evident meaning, which we call a **signal.** A tear is a signal of crying, and crying is a signal of some kind of emotional or physical state; the word *crying,* however, is a symbol, a group of sounds to which we have learned to assign the meaning of a particular action, and which we can use to communicate that meaning whether or not anyone around us is actually crying.

At the moment, language experts are not certain whether to give credit to animals, such as bees,

dolphins, or chimpanzees, for the ability to use symbols as well as signals, even though these animals and many others have been found to communicate in remarkable ways. Some apes have been taught the American Sign Language for the Deaf, with results such as those noted in the Original Study for Chapter 3. Even among vervet monkeys, calls are not mere indexes of degree of arousal or fear. As primatologist Allison Jolly notes:

> They mean something in the outside world; they include which direction to look in or where to run. There is an audience effect: calls are given when there is someone appropriate to listen . . . monkey calls are far more than involuntary expressions of emotion.[1]

What are the implications of this for our understanding of the nature and evolution of language? No final answer will be evident until we have a better understanding of animal communication than we now have. What we can be sure of is that animal communication cannot be dismissed as a set of simple reflexes or fixed action patterns, even though we cannot yet claim that animal communication presents a complete model for the evolution of human language.[2] The fact is that human culture, as we know it, is ultimately dependent on a system of communication far more complex than that of any other animal. The reason for this is the sheer amount of what must be learned by each individual from other individuals in order to control the knowledge and rules for behavior necessary for full participation in his or her society. Of course, learning can and does take place in the absence of language by observation and imitation, guided by a limited number of signs or symbols. All known cultures, however, are so rich in content that they require systems of communication that not only can give precise labels to various classes of phenomena, but also permit people to think and talk about their own and others' experiences in the past and future as well as the present. The central and most highly developed human system of communication is language. Knowledge of the workings of language, then, is essential to a full understanding of culture.

Language: A system of communication using sounds that are put together in meaningful ways according to a set of rules.

Symbols: Sounds or gestures that stand for meanings among a group of people.

Signal: A sound or gesture that has a natural or self-evident meaning.

---

[1] Allison Jolly, "Thinking Like a Vervet," *Science,* 251(1991):574.

[2] Charles T. Snowden, "Language Capabilities of Nonhuman Animals," *Yearbook of Physical Anthropology,* 33(1990):233.

Animals use signals to indicate their feelings and intentions. Here, one hyena uses a snarl to challenge another.

THE NATURE OF LANGUAGE

Any human language—English, Mandarin Chinese, Swahili, or whatever—is obviously a means of transmitting information and sharing with others both cultural and individual experiences. Because we tend to take language for granted, it is perhaps not so obvious that language is also a system that enables us to translate our concerns, beliefs, and perceptions into symbols that can be understood and interpreted by others. This is done by taking a few sounds—no language uses more than about fifty—and developing rules for putting them together in meaningful ways. The many such languages presently in existence all over the world—an estimated 3,000 different ones—may well astound and mystify us by their great variety and complexity; but this should not blind us to the fact that all languages, as far back as we can trace them, are organized in the same basic way.

The roots of **linguistics**—the modern scientific study of language—go back a long way, to the works of ancient grammarians in India more than 2,000 years ago. With the age of exploration and discovery, the scientific study of language was given impetus by the accumulation of facts: the collection of sounds, words, and sentences from all sorts of different languages, chiefly those encountered in exotic lands by European explorers, invaders, and missionaries. The great contribution of the nineteenth century was the discovery of system, regularity, and relationships in the data and the tentative formulation of some laws and regular principles. In the twentieth century, while we are still collecting data, we have made considerable progress in the reasoning process, testing and working from new and improved theories. Insofar as theories and facts of language are verifiable by independent researchers looking at the same materials, there may now be said to be a science of linguistics.

Linguistics: The modern scientific study of all aspects of language.

THE SOUND AND SHAPE OF LANGUAGE

How can an anthropologist, a missionary, a social worker, or a medical worker approach and make sense of a language that has not already been analyzed and described, or for which there are no immediately available materials? There are hundreds of such languages in the world; fortunately, some fairly efficient methods have been developed to help with the task. It is a painstaking process to unravel a language, but it is ultimately rewarding and often even fascinating for its own sake.

The process requires first a trained ear and a thorough understanding of the way speech sounds are produced. Otherwise, it will be extremely difficult to write out or make intelligent use of any data. To satisfy this preliminary requirement, most people need special training in **phonetics,** or the systematic study of the production, transmission, and reception of speech sounds.

PHONOLOGY

To analyze and describe any new language, an inventory of all of its sounds and an accurate way of writing them down are needed. Some sounds of other languages may be very much like the sounds

---

Phonetics: The study of the production, transmission, and reception of speech sounds.

A portable tape recorder is an important tool for the modern linguist. Here, a group of !Kung listen to playback of stories recorded in the field.

Table 4.1   Phonetic vowel symbols (Sapir System)*

i (Fr. *fini*)	*ü* (Fr. *lune*)	*i*	*u̇* (Swed. *hus*)	*ï*	*u* (Ger. *gut*)
ι (Eng. *bit*)	*ü̈* (Ger. *Mütze*)	*ι*	*v̇*	*ï*	*v* (Eng. *put*)
e (Fr. *été*)	*ö* (Fr. *peu*)	—	*ȯ*	*α* (Eng. *but*)	*o* (Ger. *so*)
ε (Eng. *men*)	*ɔ̈* (Ger. *Götter*)	—	*ɔ̇*	*a* (Ger. *Mann*)	*ɔ* (Ger. *Volk*)
—	*ω̈* (Fr. *peur*)	—	*ω̇*	—	*ω* (Eng. *law*)
ä (Eng. *man*)	—	*à* (Fr. *patte*)	—	—	—

*The symbol *ə* is used for an "indeterminate" vowel.
SOURCE: George L. Trager, *Language and Languages* (San Fransisco: Chandler Publishing Company, 1972), p. 304.

of English, others may be sounds that we have never consciously produced; but since we all have the same vocal equipment, we are all able, with practice, to reproduce all the sounds that anyone else makes. Once we have knowledge of all of the possible sounds in a language, we can study the patterns these sounds take as they are used to form words. This study, by which we discover the underlying rules that tell us which combinations of sounds are permissible in the language and which are not, is known as **phonology.**

The first step in studying any particular language, once a number of utterances have been collected, is to isolate the **phonemes,** or the smallest classes of sound that make a difference in

Phonology: The study of the sound patterns of language.

Phonemes: In linguistics, the smallest classes of sound that make a difference in meaning.

meaning. We can then analyze the **allophones,** the actual sounds that belong to each of these classes. This isolation and analysis may be done by a process called the minimal-pair test: The linguist tries to find two short words that appear to be exactly alike except for one sound, such as *bit* and *pit* in English. If the substitution of [b] for [p] in this minimal pair makes a difference in meaning, which it does in English, then those two sounds have been identified as members of distinct phonemes of the language and will require two different symbols to record. If, however, the linguist finds two different pronunciations, as when "butter" is pronounced "budder," and then finds that there is no difference in their meaning for a native speaker, the sounds represented will be considered allophones of the same phoneme. In such cases, for economy of representation only, one of the two symbols will be used to

Allophones: In linguistics, different sounds belonging to the same sound class, or phoneme.

record that sound wherever it is found. For greater accuracy and to avoid confusion with the various sounds of one's language, the symbols of a phonetic alphabet, such as was developed by Edward Sapir for the American Anthropological Association (Table 4.1, previous page), can be used to distinguish between the sounds of most languages in a way comprehensible to anyone who knows the system.

MORPHOLOGY

The process of making and studying an inventory of sounds may, of course, be a long task; concurrently, the linguist may begin to work out all groups or combinations of sounds that seem to have meaning. These are called **morphemes** and they are the smallest units that have meaning in the language (unlike phonemes which, while making a difference in meaning, have no meaning by themselves). They may consist of words or parts of words. A field linguist can abstract morphemes and their meanings from speakers of a language by means of pointing or gesturing to elicit words and their meanings, but the ideal situation is to have an informant, a person who knows enough of a common second language, so that approximate translations can be made more efficiently and confidently. It is pointless to write down data without any suggestion of meaning for them. *Cat* and *dog* would, of course, turn out to be morphemes, or meaningful combinations of sounds, in English. By pointing to two of either of them, the linguist could elicit *cats* and *dogs*. This indicates that there is another unit that carries meaning, an -*s*, that may be added to the original morpheme to mean "plural." When the linguist finds that this -*s* cannot occur in the language unattached, it will be identified as a **bound morpheme;** because *dog* and *cat* can occur unat-

---

Morphemes: In linguistics, the smallest units of sound that carry a meaning.

Bound morpheme: A sound that can occur in a language only in combination with other sounds, as *s* in English to signify the plural.

Free morphemes: Morphemes that can occur unattached in a language; for example, *dog* and *cat* are free morphemes in English.

Allomorphs: Variants of a single morpheme.

---

tached to anything, they are called **free morphemes.** Because the sound represented as *s* is actually different in the two words (*s* in *cats* and *z* in *dogs*), the linguist will conclude that the sounds *s* and *z* are **allomorphs** of the plural morpheme; that is, they are two varieties of the same morpheme (even though they may be two different phonemes), occurring in different contexts but with no difference in meaning.

GRAMMAR AND SYNTAX

The next step is to put morphemes together to form phrases or sentences. This process is known as identifying the syntactic units of the language, or the meaningful combination of morphemes in larger chains or strings. One way to do this is to use a method called **frame substitution.** By proceeding slowly at first, and relying on pointing or gestures, the field linguist can elicit such strings as *my cat, your cat,* or *her cat,* and *I see your cat; she sees my cat.* This begins to establish the rules or principles of phrase and sentence making, the **syntax** of the language.

Further success of this sort of linguistic study depends greatly on individual ingenuity, tact, logic, and experience with language. A language may make extensive use of kinds of utterances that are

---

Frame substitution: A method used to identify the syntactic units of language. For example, a category called "nouns" may be established as anything that will fit the substitution frame "I see a [   ]."

Syntax: In linguistics, the rules or principles of phrase and sentence making.

not found at all in English, and which an English-speaking linguist may not, therefore, even think of asking for. Furthermore, certain speakers may pretend not to be able to say (or may truly not be able to say) certain things considered by their culture to be impolite, taboo, or inappropriate for mention to outsiders. It may even be unacceptable to point, in which case the linguist will have to devise roundabout ways of eliciting words for objects.

The **grammar** of the language will ultimately consist of all observations about its morphemes and syntax. Further work may include the establishment, by means of substitution frames, of all the **form classes** of the language: that is, the parts of speech or categories of words that work the same way in any sentence. For example, we may establish a category we call "nouns," defined as anything that will fit the substitution frame "I see a [   ]." We simply make the frame, try out a number of words in it, and have a native speaker indicate "yes" or "no" for whether the words work. In English, the words *house* and *cat* will fit this frame and will be said to belong to the same form class, but the word *think* will not. Another possible substitution frame for nouns might be "The [   ] died," in which the word *cat* will fit, but not the word *house*. Thus we can identify subclasses of our nouns: in this case, what we can call "animate" or "inanimate" subclasses. The same procedure may be followed for all the words of the language, using as many

Grammar: The entire formal structure of a language consisting of all observations about the morphemes and syntax.

Form classes: The parts of speech or categories of words that work the same way in any sentence.

Descriptive linguistics: The study of language concerned with registering and explaining all the features of a language at one point in history.

different frames as necessary, until we have a lexicon, or dictionary, that accurately describes the possible uses of all the words in the language.

One of the strengths of modern **descriptive linguistics** is the objectivity of its methods. A descriptive linguist will not approach a language with the idea that it must have nouns, verbs, prepositions, or any other of the form classes identifiable in English. The linguist instead sees what turns up in the language and makes an attempt to describe it in terms of its own inner workings. For convenience, morphemes that behave approximately like English nouns and verbs may be labeled as such, but if it is thought that the terms are misleading, the linguist may instead call them "x-words" and "y-words," or "form class A" and "form class B."

PARALANGUAGE

Although humans rely primarily on language for their communication, it is by no means the only system used. How often has it been remarked, "It's not what he said so much as how he said it"? What the speaker is concerned with in this phrase is **paralanguage,** a less developed system of communication than language, which always accompanies it. Paralanguage may be defined as a system of extralinguistic noises that generally accompany language. Though not our primary means of communication, its importance should not be underestimated. Recent studies have shown, for example, that subliminal messages communicated by seemingly minor differences in phraseology, tempo,

Paralanguage: The extralinguistic noises that accompany language, for example, those of crying or laughing.

Shown here are different gender signals sent by men and women in North America. While women tend to hold their arms and legs together, men hold theirs apart.

length of answers, and the like are far more important in courtroom proceedings than even the most perceptive trial lawyer may have realized. Among other things, how a witness gives testimony alters the reception it gets from jurors, and bears on the witness' credibility where inconsistencies exist in testimony.

VOICE QUALITIES

While it is not always easy for the linguist to distinguish between the sounds of language and paralinguistic noises, two different kinds of the latter have been identified. The first has to do with **voice qualities,** which operate as the background characteristics of a speaker's voice. These involve pitch range (from low- to high-pitched); lip control (from closed to open); glottis control (sharp to smooth transitions in pitch); articulation control (forceful or relaxed speech); rhythm control (smooth or jerky setting off of portions of vocal activity); resonance (from vibrant to thin); and tempo (an increase or decrease from the norm).

Voice qualities are capable of communicating much about the state of being of the person who is speaking, quite apart from what is being said. An obvious example of this is slurred speech, which may indicate that the speaker is intoxicated. Or, if someone says rather languidly, coupled with a restricted pitch range, that she or he is delighted with something, it probably indicates that the person isn't delighted at all. The same thing said more rapidly, with increasing pitch, might indicate that the speaker really is genuinely excited about the matter. While the speaker's state of being is affected by his or her anatomical and physiological status, it is also markedly affected by the individual's overall self-image in the given situation. If an individual is made to feel anxious by being crowded in some way, or by some aspects of the social situation, for example, this anxiety will probably be conveyed by certain voice qualities.

Voice qualities: In paralanguage, the background characteristics of a speaker's voice.

VOCALIZATIONS

The second kind of paralinguistic noises consists of **vocalizations.** Instead of being background characteristics, these are actual identifiable noises

Vocalizations: Identifiable paralinguistic noises that are turned on and off at perceivable and relatively short intervals.

Vocal characterizers: In paralanguage, sound productions such as laughing or crying that humans "speak through."

that, unlike voice qualities, are turned on and off at perceivable and relatively short intervals. They are, nonetheless, separate from language sounds. One category of vocalizations are **vocal characterizers:** the sounds of laughing or crying, yelling or whispering, yawning or belching, and the like. One "talks through" vocal characterizers, and they are generally indicative of the speaker's attitude. If one yawns while speaking to someone, for example, this may indicate an attitude of boredom on the part of the speaker. Breaking, an intermittent tensing and relaxing of the vocal musculature producing a tremulousness while speaking, may indicate great emotion on the part of the speaker.

Another category of vocalizations consists of **vocal qualifiers.** These are of briefer duration than vocal characterizers, being limited generally to the space of a single intonation, rather than over whole phrases. They modify utterances in terms of intensity—loud versus soft; pitch—high versus low; and extent—drawl versus clipping. These indicate the speaker's attitude to specific phrases such as "get out." The third category consists of **vocal segregates.** These are somewhat like the actual sounds of language, but they don't appear in the kinds of sequences that can be called words. Examples of vocal segregates familiar to English-speaking peoples are such substitutes for language as *shh, uh-uh,* or *uh-huh.*

Vocal qualifiers: In paralanguage, sound productions of brief duration that modify utterances in terms of intensity.

KINESICS

Kinesics may be thought of as a system for communication through motion. Familiar to many through the phrase "body language," kinesics is a system of postures, facial expressions, and bodily motions that convey messages. These messages may be communicated directly, as in the case of gestures. For example, in North America scratching one's scalp, biting one's lip, or knitting one's brows are ways of conveying doubt. A more complex example is afforded by the gender signals sent by North American men and women. Although there is some regional and class variation, women when standing generally bring their legs together, at times to the point that the upper legs cross, either in a full leg cross with feet still together, the outer sides of the feet parallel to each other, or in standing knee over knee. The pelvis is carried rolled slightly forward. The upper arms are held close to the body, and in movement, the entire body from neck to ankle is presented as a moving whole. Men, by contrast, hold their legs apart, with the upper legs at a 10- or 15-degree angle. Their pelvis is carried in a slightly rolled-back position. The arms are held out at 10 to 15 degrees from the body, and they are moved independently of the body. Finally, a man may subtly wag his hips with a slight right and left presentation, with a movement involving a twist at the base of the rib cage and at the ankles.

Such gender markers are not the same as invitations to sexual activity. Rather, they are conventions inscribed on the body through imitation and subtle training. In any culture, as little girls grow up, they imitate their mothers or other older women; little boys do the same with their fathers or other older men. In our own culture, by the time

Vocal segregates: In paralanguage, sound productions that are similar to the sounds of language, but do not appear in sequences that can properly be called words.

Kinesics: A system of postures, facial expressions, and body motions that convey messages.

Some kinesic gestures that humans use are also used by other primates.

we become adults, we have acquired a host of gender markers that intrude into every moment of our lives, so much so that we are literally at a loss if we do not know the sex of someone with whom we must interact. This is easily verified, as the philosopher Marilyn Frye suggests:

> . . . To discover the differences in how you greet a woman and how you greet a man, for instance, just observe yourself, paying attention to the following sorts of things: frequency and duration of eye contact, frequency and type of touch, . . . physical distance maintained between bodies, how and whether you smile . . . , whether your body dips into a shadow curtsey or bow. That I have two repertories for handling introductions to people was vividly confirmed for me when a student introduced me to his friend, Pat, and I really could not tell what sex Pat was. For a moment I was stopped cold, completely incapable of action. I felt myself helplessly caught between two paths—the one I would take if Pat were female and the one I would take if Pat were male. Of course the paralysis does not last. One is rescued by one's ingenuity and good will: one can invent a way to behave as one says "How do you do?" to a human being. But the habitual ways are not for humans: they are one way for women and another for men.[3]

[3]Marilyn Frye, "Sexism," in *The Politics of Reality* (New York: The Crossing Press, 1983), p. 20.

Often, kinesic messages complement spoken messages, as by nodding the head while affirming something verbally. Other examples are punching the palm of the hand for emphasis, raising the head and brows when asking a question, or using the hands to illustrate what is being talked about. Such gestures are rather like bound morphemes—they have meaning but don't stand alone, except in particular situations, such as a nodded response to a question.

Although little scientific notice was taken of kinesics prior to the 1950s, there has since been a great deal of research, particularly among North Americans. Cross-cultural research has shown, however, that there is a good deal of similarity around the world in such basic facial expressions as smiling, laughing, crying, and the facial expressions of anger. More specifically, there is great similarity in the routine for greeting over a distance around the world. Europeans, Balinese, Papuans, Samoans, !Kung, and at least some South American Indians all smile and nod, and if the individuals are especially friendly, they will raise their eyebrows with a rapid movement, keeping them raised for a fraction of a second. All of this signals a readiness for contact. The Japanese, however, suppress the eyebrow flash, regarding it as indecent, which goes to show that there are important differences, as well as similarities, cross-culturally. This can be seen in kinesic expressions for "yes" and "no." In our culture, one

There is a great deal of similarity around the world in such basic facial expressions as smiling, laughing, crying, and anger. Shown here are smiling children from Asia, Africa, and South America.

nods the head for "yes" or shakes it for "no." The people of Sri Lanka, like us, will nod to answer "yes" to a factual question, but if asked to do something, a slow sideways movement of the head means "yes." In Greece, the nodded head means "yes," but "no" is indicated by jerking the head back so as to lift the face; at the same time, the eyes are often closed and the eyebrows lifted.

LINGUISTIC CHANGE

In our discussion of the sound and shape of language, we looked briefly at the internal organization of language—its phonology, morphology, syntax, and grammar. It is the descriptive approach to language that is concerned with registering and explaining all the features of any one particular language at any one time in its history. Descriptive linguistics concentrates, for example, on the way modern French or Spanish function now, as if they were separate systems, consistent within themselves, without any reference to historical reasons for their development. Yet languages, like cultures, have histories. The Latin *ille* ("that") is identifiable as the origin of both French *le* ("the") and Spanish *el* ("the"), even though the descriptive linguist treats *le* and *el* only as they function in the modern language, where the meaning "that" is no longer

relevant and very few native speakers are aware that they are speaking modern derivatives of Latin.

Historical linguistics, by contrast, investigates relationships between earlier and later forms of the same language, antecedents in older languages for developments in modern ones, and questions of relationships between older languages. Historical linguists, for example, attempt to identify and explain the development of early medieval spoken Latin into later medieval French and Spanish by investigating both natural change in the original language and the influence of contacts with the "barbarian" invaders from the north. There is no conflict between historical and descriptive linguists, the two approaches being recognized as interdependent. Even a modern language is constantly changing, and it changes according to principles that can be established only historically.

Historical linguists have achieved considerable success in working out the genealogical relation-

Historical linguistics: The study of relationships between earlier and later forms of a language, antecedents in older languages of developments in modern languages, and relationships among older languages.

Language family: A group of languages that are ultimately descended from a single ancestral language.

Language subgroups: Languages of a family that are more closely related to one another than they are to other languages of the same family.

Linguistic divergence: The development of different languages from a single ancestral language.

ships between different languages, and these are reflected in schemes of classification. For example, English is one of a number of languages classified in the Indo-European **language family.** (Fig. 4.1) This family is subdivided into some 11 **language subgroups,** which reflect the fact that there has been a long period of **linguistic divergence** from an ancient unified language (referred to as Proto-Indo-European) into separate "daughter" languages. English is one of a number of languages in the Germanic subgroup (Fig. 4.2). These languages are the result of further linguistic divergence; all are more closely related to one another than they are to the languages of other subgroups of the Indo-European family.

Historical linguists have been successful in describing the changes that have taken place as lan-

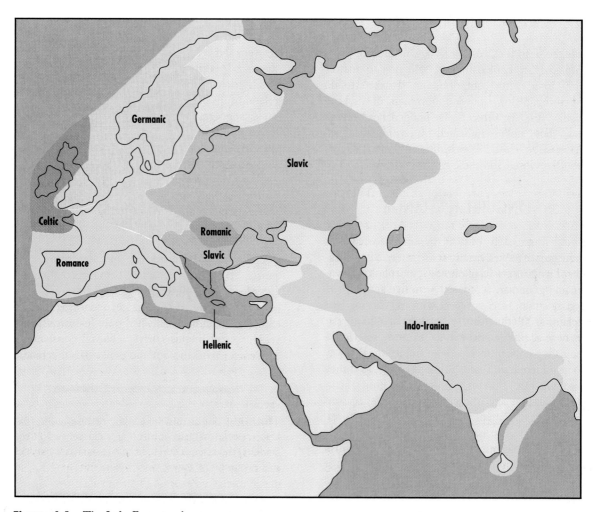

Figure 4.1   The Indo-European languages.

guages have diverged from more ancient parent languages. They have also developed means of estimating when certain migrations, invasions, and contacts of peoples have taken place, on the basis of linguistic similarities and differences. The concept of linguistic divergence, for example, is used to suggest the time at which one group of speakers of a language separated from another group. A more complicated technique, known as **glottochronology,** was developed by Swadesh and Lees in the early 1950s to try to date the divergence of related languages, such as Latin and Greek, from an earlier common language. The technique is based on the assumption that changes in a language's **core vocabulary**—pronouns, lower numerals, and names for parts of the body and natural objects— change at a more or less constant rate. By applying a logarithmic formula to two related core vocabularies, one should be able to determine how many years the languages have been separated. Although not as precise as this might suggest, glottochronology provides a useful way of estimating when languages may have separated.

While many of the changes that have taken place in the course of linguistic divergence are well known, their causes are not. One force for linguistic change is borrowing by one language from another, and languages do readily borrow from one another; but if borrowing were the sole force for change, linguistic differences would be expected to become less pronounced through time. Through the study of modern languages in their cultural settings, one can begin to understand the forces for change. One such force is novelty, pure and simple. There seems to be a human tendency to admire the person who comes up with a new and clever idiom, a new and useful word, or a particularly stylish pronunciation, so long as these do not seriously interfere with communication. Indeed, in linguistic matters, complexity tends to be admired, while

---

Glottochronology: In linguistics, a method of dating divergence in branches of language families.

Core vocabulary: In language, pronouns, lower numerals, and names for body parts and natural objects.

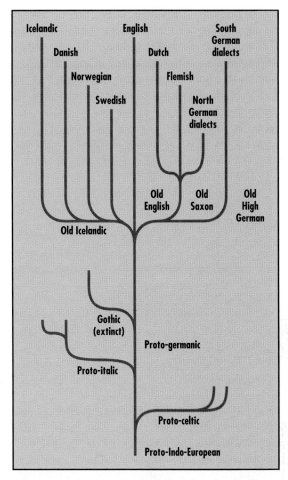

Figure 4-2 English is one of a group of languages in the Germanic subgroup of the Indo-European family. This diagram shows its relationship to other languages in the same subgroup. Its root is proto-Indo-European, a language spoken by a people who spread westward over Europe, bringing with them their own customs and language.

simplicity seems dull. Hence, about as fast as a language may be simplified, purged of needlessly complex constructions or phrases, new ones will arise.

Group membership also plays a role in linguistic change. Part of this is functional: professions, sects, or other groups in a society often have need of special vocabularies to be able to communicate effectively about their special interests. Beyond this, special vocabularies may serve as labeling devices; those who use such vocabularies are set off as a group from those who do not, and this helps to create a strong sense of group identity.

When a military officer speaks of "incontinent ordinance" and "collateral damage," a physician of "exsanguination," a dentist of the "oral cavity," or an anthropologist of "the structural implications of matrilateral cross-cousin marriage," they express, in part at least, their membership in a profession and their command of its language. For insiders, professional terminology reinforces their sense of belonging to a select "in-group"; to outsiders it often seems an unneeded and pretentious use of "bafflegab" where perfectly adequate and simple words would do as well. Whether needed or not, professional terminology does serve to differentiate language and to set the speech of one group apart from that of others. Therefore, it is a force for stylistic divergence.

Phonological differences between groups may be regarded in the same light as vocabulary differences. In a class-structured society, for example, members of the upper class may try to keep their pronunciation distinct from that of lower classes. An example of a different sort is afforded by coastal communities in the state of Maine, in particular, though it may be seen to varying degrees elsewhere along the New England coast. In the past, people in these communities developed a style of pronunciation quite distinct from the styles of "inlanders." More recently, as outsiders have moved into these coastal communities, either as summer people or as permanent residents, the traditional coastal style has come to identify those who adhere to traditional coastal values, as opposed to those who do not.

One other far-reaching force for linguistic change is **linguistic nationalism,** an attempt by whole nations to proclaim their independence by purging their vocabularies of "foreign" terms. This phenomenon is particularly characteristic of the formerly colonized countries of Africa and Asia today. It is by no means limited to those countries, however, as one can see by periodic French attempts to purge their language of such Americanisms as *le hamburger*. Also in the category of linguistic nationalism are revivals of languages long out of common use, such as Gaelic and Yiddish.

Linguistic nationalism: The attempt by nations to proclaim independence by purging their languages of foreign terms.

LANGUAGE IN ITS CULTURAL SETTING

Rewarding though it is to analyze language as a system in which linguistic variables dependent upon other linguistic phenomena operate, it is important to remember that languages are spoken by people, who are members of societies, each of which has its own distinctive culture. Individuals tend to vary in the ways they use language, and as the preceding discussion suggests, social variables such as class and status of the speaker will also influence their use of language. Moreover, people choose words and sentences so as to communicate meaning, and what is meaningful in one culture may not be in another. The fact is that our use of language affects, and is affected by, our culture.

The whole question of the relationships between language and culture is the province of **ethnolinguistics,** an outgrowth of both ethnology and descriptive linguistics, which has become almost a separate field of inquiry. Ethnolinguistics is concerned with every aspect of the structure and use of language that has anything to do with society, culture, and human behavior.

LANGUAGE AND THOUGHT

An important ethnolinguistic concern of the 1930s and 1940s was the question of whether language might indeed determine culture. Do we see and react differently to the colors blue and green, with different cultural symbolism for the two different colors, only because our language has different names for these two neighboring parts of the unbroken color spectrum? When anthropologists noticed that some cultures lump together blue and green with one name, they began to wonder about this question. The American linguist Edward Sapir first formulated the problem, and his student, Benjamin Lee Whorf, drawing on his experience with the language of the Hopi Indians, developed a

---

Ethnolinguistics: The study of the relation between language and culture.

ANTHROPOLOGY APPLIED

LANGUAGE RENEWAL AMONG THE NORTHERN UTE

On April 10, 1984, the Northern Ute Tribe became the first community of American Indians in the United States to affirm the prerogative of its members to regain and maintain fluency in their ancestral language, as well as their option to use it as a means of communication throughout their lives. Like many other American Indian tribes, these people had experienced a decline in fluency in their native tongue as they had interacted more and more intensively with non-Indians who spoke English. Once the on-reservation boarding school closed in 1953, Ute children had to attend schools where teachers and most other students were ignorant of the Ute language. Outside the classroom as well, children and adults alike were increasingly surrounded by English as they sought employment off the reservation, traded in non-Indian communities, or were exposed to television and other popular media. By the late 1960s, although Ute language fluency was still highly valued, many members of the community could no longer speak it.

Alarmed by this situation, the group of Ute parents and educators that supervises federally funded tutorial services to Indian students decided that action needed to be taken, lest their native language be lost altogether. With the assistance of other community leaders, they launched discussions into what might be done about the situation, and invited anthropologist William L. Leap to join in these discussions. Previously, Leap had worked on language education with other tribes, and he was subsequently hired by the Utes to assist them in their efforts at linguistic renewal.

Leap began work for the Northern Utes in 1978, and his first task was to carry out a first-ever reservation-wide language survey.* This found, among other things, that inability to speak Ute did not automatically imply loss of skill; evidently, many nonspeakers retained a "passive fluency" in the language and could understand it, even though they couldn't speak it. Furthermore (and quite contrary to expectations), children who were still able to speak Ute had fewer problems with English in school than did nonspeakers.

Over the next few years, Leap helped set up a Ute language renewal program within the tribe's Division of Education, wrote several grant requests to obtain funding, led staff training workshops in linguistic transcription and grammatical analysis, provided technical assistance in designing a practical writing system for the language, and supervised data gathering sessions with already fluent speakers of the language. With the establishment in 1980 of an in-school program to provide developmental Ute and English instruction to Indian and other interested children, he became staff linguist. In this capacity he helped train the language teachers (all of whom were Ute, and none of whom had degrees in education); carried out research that resulted in numerous technical reports, publications, and in-service workshops; helped prepare a practical Ute language handbook for home use; prepared the preliminary text for the tribe's statement of policy on language, and then helped persuade the governing body to accept it. By 1984, not only did this policy become official, but several language development projects were in place on the reservation, all monitored and coordinated by a tribally sanctioned language and culture committee. Supported by both tribal and federal funds, these involved the participation of persons with varying degrees of familiarity with the language. Although literacy was not a goal, down-to-earth needs resulted in development of practical writing systems, and a number of people in fact became literate in Ute. One important reason for all this success was the involvement of the Ute people in all stages of development; not only did these projects originate in response to their own expressed desires, they were active participants in all discussions and made decisions at each stage of activities, participating not just as individuals, but as members of family, kin, community, and band.

* See William L. Leap, "Tribally Controlled Culture Change: The Northern Ute Language Renewal Project." In: *Anthropological Praxis: Translating Knowledge into Action*, edited by Robert M. Wulff and Shirley J. Fiske (Boulder, Colo.: Westview, 1987).

full-fledged theory, sometimes called the **Whorfian hypothesis.** Whorf proposed that a language is not simply an encoding process for voicing our ideas and needs but is rather a shaping force, which, by providing habitual grooves of expression that predispose people to see the world in a certain way, guides their thinking and behavior. The problem is a little like the old question of the chicken or the egg, and some later formulations of Whorf's theory about which came first, thinking and behavior

Whorfian hypothesis: The hypothesis, proposed by the linguist B. L. Whorf, which states that language, by providing habitual grooves of expression, predisposes people to see the world in a certain way and so guides their thinking and behavior.

or language, have since been criticized as both logically unsound and not amenable to any experimentation or proof. Its primary value is that it focused attention on the relationships between language and culture.

The opposite point of view is that language reflects reality. In this view, language mirrors cultural reality, and as the latter changes, so too will language. Some support for this is provided by studies of blue-green color terms. It has been shown that eye pigmentation acts to filter out the shorter wavelengths of solar radiation. Color vision is thus limited through a reduced sensitivity to blue and confusion between the short visible wavelengths. The effect shows up in color-naming behavior, where green may be identified with blue,

blue with black, or both green and blue with black. The severity of visual limitation, as well as the extent of lumping of color terms, depends on the density of eye pigmentation characteristic of the people in a given society.

These findings do not mean that language merely reflects reality, any more than thinking and behavior are determined by language. The truth of the matter is more as anthropologist Peter Woolfson has put it:

> Reality should be the same for us all. Our nervous systems, however, are being bombarded by a continual flow of sensations of different kinds, intensities, and durations. It is obvious that all of these sensations do not reach our consciousness; some kind of filtering system reduces them to manageable propositions. The Whorfian hypothesis suggests that the filtering system is one's language. Our language, in effect, provides us with a special pair of glasses that heightens certain perceptions and dims others. Thus, while all sensations are received by the nervous system, only some are brought to the level of consciousness.[4]

[4]Peter Woolfson, "Language, Thought, and Culture," in *Language*, ed. Virginia P. Clark, Paul A. Escholz, and Alfred F. Rosa (New York: St. Martin's, 1972), p. 4.

The nature of language allows bland euphemisms to obscure brutal realities, such as this, the gruesome aftermath of a 1991 mass execution committed inside Iraq. George Orwell wrote that through linguistic manipulation such an event "is called *elimination of unreliable elements.* . . . A mass of Latin words falls upon the facts like soft snow, blurring the outlines and covering up all the details."

So important are cattle to the Nuer of southern Sudan that they have more than 400 names to describe them.

Linguists are finding that although language is generally flexible and adaptable, once a terminology is established, it tends to perpetuate itself and to reflect and reveal the social structure and the common perceptions and concerns of a group. For example, English is richly endowed with words having to do with war, the tactics of war, and the hierarchy of officers and fighting men. It is rich, too, in militaristic metaphors, as when we speak of conquering space, fighting the battle of the budget, carrying out a war on poverty, making a killing on the stock market, shooting down an argument, or bombing out on an exam. An observer from an entirely different and perhaps warless culture could understand a great deal about the importance of warfare in our lives, as well as how we go about conducting it, simply from what we have found necessary to name and how we talk. Similarly, anthropologists have noted that the language of the Nuer, a nomadic people of Africa, is rich in words and expressions having to do with cattle; not only are more than 400 words used to describe cattle, but Nuer boys actually take their names from them. Thus, by studying the language we can determine the importance of cattle to Nuer culture, attitudes toward cattle, and the whole etiquette of human and

cattle relationships. A people's language does not, however, prevent them from thinking in new and novel ways. If this leads to important changes in common perceptions and concerns, then language can be expected to change accordingly.

KINSHIP TERMS

In the same connection, anthropologists have paid considerable attention to the way people name their relatives in various societies. Further observations on the question of kinship terms will be found in Chapter 10. In English we have terms to identify brother, sister, mother, father, grandmother, grandfather, granddaughter, grandson, niece, nephew, mother-in-law, father-in-law, sister-in-law, and brother-in-law. Some people also distinguish first and second cousin and great-aunt and great-uncle. Is this the only possible system for naming relatives and identifying relationships? Obviously not. We could have separate terms, as some cultures do, for younger brother and older brother, for mother's sister and father's sister, and so on. What we can describe in English with a phrase, if pressed to do so, other languages make explicit from the outset, and vice versa: A number of languages use the same word to denote both a brother and a cousin, and a mother's sister may also be called by the same term as one's mother.

What do kinship terms reveal? From them, we can certainly gain a good idea of how the family is structured, what relationships are considered especially important, and sometimes what attitudes toward relationships may prevail. Caution is required, however, in drawing conclusions from kinship terms. Just because we do not distinguish linguistically in English between our mother's parents and our father's parents (both are simply grandmother and grandfather), does that mean that we do not know which is which? Certainly not. Nevertheless, non-anthropologists, when confront-

ed with a kinship system in which the same term is applied to father's brother as to father, frequently make the mistake of assuming that "these people don't know who their own father is."

LANGUAGE AND GENDER

Throughout history, human beings have handled the relationship between men and women in many different ways, and here again language can be revealing. In English-speaking societies, for example, men and women use the language in different ways, revealing a deep-seated bias against women, the following Original Study argues.

ORIGINAL STUDY

SEXISM AND THE ENGLISH LANGUAGE[5]

There are many ways that women talk that make sense and are effective in conversations with women but appear powerless and self-deprecating in conversations with men. One such pattern is that many women seem to apologize all the time. An apology is a move that frames the apologizer as one-down. This might seem obvious. But the following example shows that an apparent apology may not be intended in that spirit at all.

A teacher was having trouble with a student widely known to be incorrigible. Finally, she sent the boy to the principal's office. Later the principal approached her in the teachers' lounge and told her the student had been suspended. The teacher replied "I'm sorry," and the principal reassured her, "It's not your fault." The teacher was taken aback by the principal's reassurance, because it had not occurred to her that the student's suspension might be her fault until he said it. To her, "I'm sorry" did not mean "I apologize"; it meant "I'm sorry to hear that." "I'm sorry" was intended to establish a connection to the principal by implying, "I know you must feel bad about this; I do too." She was framing herself as connected to him by similar feelings. By interpreting her words of shared feeling as an apology, the principal introduced the notion that she might be at fault, and framed himself as one-up, in a position to absolve her of guilt.

The continuation of this story indicates that these different points of view may be associated with gender. When this teacher told her grown daughter about the incident, the daughter agreed that the principal's reaction had been strange. But when she told her son and husband, they upbraided her for apologizing when she had not been at fault. They too interpreted "I'm sorry" as apology.

There are several dynamics that make women appear to apologize too much. For one thing, women may be more likely to apologize because they do not instinctively balk at risking a one-down position. This is not to say that they relish it, just that it is less likely to set off automatic alarms in their heads. But another factor is that women are heard as apologizing when they do not intend to do so. Women frequently say "I'm sorry" to express sympathy and concern, not apology.

This confusion is rooted in the double meaning of the word *sorry*. This double meaning is highlighted in the following anecdote. A twelve-year-old Japanese girl living in the United States was writing a letter of condolence to her grandmother in Japan because her grandfather had died. The girl was writing in Japanese, but she was more accustomed to English. She began in the appropriate way: "I'm so sorry that Grandfather died." But then she stopped and looked at what she had written. "That doesn't sound right," she said to her mother. "I didn't kill him." Because she was writing in a language that was not second nature to her, this girl realized that an expression most people use automatically had a different meaning when interpreted literally. "I'm sorry," used figuratively to express regret, could be interpreted literally to mean "I apologize."

The difference between ritual and literal uses of language is also at play in the following example. A businesswoman named Beverly returned from an out-of-town trip to find a phone message on her answering machine from her division head. The message explained that he had found an enormous number of errors in a report written by her assistant. He told her that he had indicated the errors, returned the report to the assistant, and arranged for the deadline to be extended while she typed in the corrections. Beverly was surprised, since she had read and approved the report before leaving on vacation, but she said, "I'm sorry"—and was offended when he said, "I'm not blaming anyone." This seemed to imply that he *was* blaming her, since he introduced the idea.

Beverly asked her assistant to show her the lengthy corrected report and became angry when she saw that half the pages had "errors" marked, but few were actually errors. Nearly all involved punctuation, and most were matters of stylistic preference, such as adding commas after brief introductory phrases or before the conjunction *and*. In a large number of cases, she felt that her division head had introduced punctuation errors into sentences that were grammatically correct as they stood.

Later that day she encountered the division head at an office party and announced as soon as she saw him that she was angry at him and told him why. She realized by his reaction that she had offended his sensibilities by raising the matter in front of someone else. She immediately apologized for having blurted out her anger rather than expressing it more diplomatically, and she later visited him in his office to apologize again. She was sure that if she apologized for having confronted him in the wrong way at the wrong time, he would counterapologize for having overcorrected the report and for going

directly to the assistant instead of through her. Instead, he generously said, "I accept your apology," and affably changed the subject to office politics.

Now accepting an apology is arguably quite rude. From the point of view of connection, an apology should be matched. And from the perspective of status, an apology should be deflected. In this view, a person who apologizes takes a one-down position, and accepting the apology preserves that asymmetry, whereas deflecting the apology restores balance. Although she felt immediately uncomfortable, Beverly did not realize until after she had left the office, all smiles and goodwill, that not only had her division head rudely accepted her apology, but he had not offered a balancing one.

Women's and men's differential awareness of status may have been the cause of Beverly's problem in a more fundamental way too. She felt quite friendly with her division head; she liked him; she had come to think of him as a friend. For her, as for many women, being friends means downplaying if not obliterating status differences. When she blurted out her anger, she was not thinking of herself as upbraiding a superior in front of others. To the extent that he remained aware of the difference in their status despite their friendly relationship, to accept her criticism would have amounted to public humiliation. Had she focused on their status differences rather than their friendship, she would not have approached him as she did. She would not, for example, have taken that tack with the company president.

Nowhere is the conflict between femininity and authority more crucial than with women in politics. The characteristics of a good man and a good candidate are the same, but a woman has to choose between coming across as a strong leader or a good woman. If a man appears forceful, logical, direct, masterful, and powerful, he enhances his value as a man. If a woman appears forceful, logical, direct, masterful, or powerful, she risks undercutting her value as a woman.

As Robin Lakoff shows in *Language and Woman's Place*, language comes at women from two angles: the words they speak, and the words spoken about them. If I wrote, "After delivering the acceptance speech, the candidate fainted," you would know I was talking about a woman. Men do not faint; they pass out. And these terms have vastly different connotations that both reflect and affect our images of women and men. *Fainting* conjures up a frail figure crumpling into a man's rescuing arms, the back of her hand pressed to her forehead—probably for little reason, maybe just for dramatic effect. *Passing out* suggests a straightforward fall to the floor.

An article in *Newsweek* during the 1984 presidential campaign quoted a Reagan aide who called Ferraro "a nasty woman" who would "claw Ronald Reagan's eyes out." Never mind the nastiness of the remark and of the newsmagazine's using it to open its article. Applied to a man, *nasty* would be so tame as to seem harmless. Furthermore, men don't claw; they punch and sock, with correspondingly more forceful results. The verb *claw* both reflects and reinforces the stereotypical metaphor of women as cats. Each time someone uses an expression associated with this metaphor, it reinforces it, suggesting a general "cattiness" in women's character.

Even when seeming to praise Ferraro, the article used terms drenched in gender. She was credited with "a striking gift for tart political rhetoric, needling Ronald Reagan on the fairness issue and twitting the Reagan-Bush campaign for its reluctance to let Bush debate her." If we reversed subject and object, *needling* and *twitting* would not sound like praise for Reagan's verbal ability—or any man's. (I will refrain from commenting on the connotations of *tart,* assuming the word's double meaning was at least consciously unintended.)

In his book *The Language of Politics,* Michael Geis gives several examples of words used to describe Ferraro that undercut her. One headline called her "spunky," another "feisty." As Gels observes, *spunky* and *feisty* are used only for creatures that are small and lacking in real power; they could be said of a Pekingese but not a Great Dane, perhaps of Mickey Rooney but not of John Wayne—in other words, of any average-size woman, but not of an average-size man.

I am sure that the journalists who wrote these descriptions of Ferraro came to praise her, not to bury her. Perhaps they felt they were choosing snappy, eye-catching phrases. But their words bent back and trivialized the vice presidential candidate, highlighting, even if unintentionally, the incongruity between her images as a woman and as a political leader. When we think we are using language, our language is using us.

It's not that journalists, other writers, or everyday speakers are deliberately, or even unintentionally, "sexists" in their use of language. The important point is that gender distinctions are built into language. The words available to us to describe women and men are not the same words. And, most damaging of all, through language, our images and attitudes are buttressed and shaped. Simply by understanding and using the words of our language, we all absorb and pass on different, asymmetrical assumptions about men and women.

Body language is eloquent too. Political candidates necessarily circulate photographs of their families. In the typical family photograph, the candidate looks straight out at the camera, while his wife gazes up at him. This leads the viewer's eye to the candidate as the center of interest. In a well-publicized family photograph, Ferraro was looking up at her husband and he was looking straight out. It is an appealing photo, which shows her as a good woman, but makes him the inappropriate center of interest, just as his finances became the center of interest in candidate Ferraro's financial disclosure. Had the family photograph shown Ferraro looking straight out, with her husband gazing adoringly at her, it would not have been an effective campaign photo, because she would have looked like a domineering wife with a namby-pamby for a husband.

Ironically, it is probably more difficult for a woman to hold a position of authority in a relatively [fluid] society like that of the United States than in more [rigidly] hierarchical ones. An American woman who owned and edited an English-language magazine in Athens told me that when Greeks came to the magazine to do business, as soon as they realized that she was the boss, they focused their attention on her. But if her male assistant editor was in the room, Americans were irresistibly drawn to address themselves to him. It

seems that Greeks' sensitivity to the publisher's status overrode their awareness of her gender, but Americans, who are less intimidated by status than Greeks, could not rise above their awareness of gender.

⁵Deborah Tannen, *You Just Don't Understand: Women and Men in Conversation* (New York: William Morrow, 1990), pp. 231–234 and 241–244.

SOCIAL DIALECTS

In our previous discussion of linguistic change, phonological and vocabulary differences between groups were noted as important forces for linguistic change. Varying forms of a language that are similar enough to be mutually intelligible are known as **dialects,** and the study of dialects is a concern of **sociolinguistics.** Technically, all dialects are languages—there is nothing partial or sublinguistic about them—and the point at which two different dialects become distinctly different languages is roughly the point at which speakers of one are almost totally unable to communicate with speakers of the other. Boundaries may be psychological, geographical, social, or economic, and they are not always very clear. Frequently, there is a transitional territory, or perhaps a buffer zone, where features of both are found and understood, as between central and southern China. If you learn the Chinese of Beijing, you cannot communicate with the waiter in your local Chinese restaurant who comes from Canton or Hong Kong, although both languages—or dialects—are conventionally called Chinese.

A classic example of the kind of dialect that may set one group apart from others within a single

Dialects: Varying forms of a language that reflect particular regions or social classes and that are similar enough to be mutually intelligible.

Sociolinguistics: The study of the structure and use of language as it relates to its social setting.

society is one spoken by many American inner-city blacks. Educator Dorothy Seymour provides the following example:

"C'mon, man, le's git goin'!" called the boy to his companion. "Dat bell ringin'. It say, 'Git in rat now!'" He dashed into the school yard.

"Aw, f'get you," replied the other. "Whe' Richuh? Whe' da' muvvah? He be goin' to schoo'."

"He in de' now, man!" was the answer as they went through the door.

In the classroom they made for their desks and opened their books. The name of the story they tried to read was "Come." It went:

> Come, Bill, come
> Come with me.
> Come and see this.
> See what is here.

The first boy poked the second. "Wha' da' wor'?"

"Da' wor' *is*, you dope."

"*Is*? Ain't no wor' *is*. You jivin' me? Wha' da' wor' mean?"

"Ah dunno. Jus' *is*."⁶

Unfortunately, there is a widespread perception among middle-class whites and blacks alike that this dialect is somehow substandard or defective. Rather, it is a highly structured mode of speech, capable of expressing anything its speakers care to express, often in creative ways (as in "rapping"). Many of its distinctive features stem from retention of sound patterns, grammatical devices, and even words of the West African languages spoken by the ancestors of today's American blacks. Compared to black English, the standard English dialect lacks certain sounds, contains some sounds that are unnecessary for which others may serve just as well, doubles and drawls some of its vowel sounds in sequences that

⁶ Dorothy Z. Seymour, "Black Children, Black Speech," in *Language Awareness,* 4th ed., ed. Paul Escholz, Alfred Rosa, and Virginia Clark (New York: St. Martin's Press, 1986), p. 74.

Because they are culture-bound, standardized tests devised by people from one subcultural background usually fail to measure what they are supposed to when administered to those from another background.

are unusual and difficult to imitate, lacks a method of forming an important tense (the habitual), requires too many ways of indicating tense, plurality, and gender, and doesn't mark negatives in such a way as to make a strong negative statement.

Because their dialect differs so much from standard English, and has been stigmatized so often, speakers of black English frequently find themselves at a disadvantage outside of their own communities. In schools, for example, African-American children may be seen by teachers as deficient in verbal skills and may even be wrongly diagnosed as learning-impaired. The great challenge for the schools is to find ways of teaching these children how to use standard English in those situations where it is to their advantage to do so, without denigrating their ability to use the dialect of their own community. The Reverend Martin Luther King, Jr., was particularly skilled at switching back and forth, depending on the situation in which he was speaking. Less consciously, we all do the same sort of thing when we switch from formality to informality in our speech, depending upon where we are and to whom we are talking. The process of changing from one level of language to another as the situation demands, whether from one language to another or from one dialect of a language to another, is known as **code switching,** and it has been the subject of a number of sociolinguistic studies.

Code switching: The process of changing from one level of language to another.

OTHER SOCIOLINGUISTIC CONCERNS

Of the many other concerns of sociolinguistics today we can only mention that we also find investigations of children's languages and word games, the structure of folktales and folk songs, bilingualism and multilingualism, pidgin languages and creoles ("trade languages" with simple grammars and mixed vocabularies, developed to enable peoples of widely different languages to communicate), linguistic borrowing and innovation, formulas of address and politeness, secret languages, magic languages, and myth. The list increases and has begun to duplicate many of the concerns of other fields or disciplines. Almost every aspect of anthropology and sociology has a linguistic side or a relevance to linguistics. This new field of sociolinguistics proves to be not one field but many, and it is providing an opportunity for some productive cooperation and sharing between disciplines.

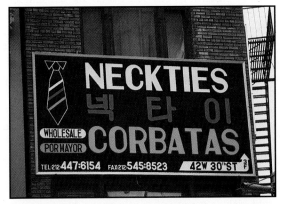

Multilingualism is likely to be important in pluralistic societies. Because a people's language is attuned to their traditional ways of thinking about themselves and the world around them, retention of their language helps preserve cultural traditions. It also proclaims their distinctive identity within the wider society. Unfortunately, the more divergent cultural traditions are within a society, the more difficult it appears to be to make a pluralistic society work, because of the attendant problems and frictions.

THE ORIGINS OF LANGUAGE

A realization of the central importance of language for human culture leads inevitably to speculation about how language might have started in the first place. The question of the origin of language has long been a popular subject, and some reasonable and many not so reasonable theories have been proposed: Exclamations became words, sounds in nature were imitated, or people simply got together and assigned sounds to objects and actions. The main trouble with past theories is that there was so little in the way of evidence that theorizing often reached the point of wild speculation. The result was a reaction against such theorizing, exemplified by the ban imposed in 1866 by the Société de Linguistique de Paris against papers on linguistic origins. Now there is more evidence to work with—better knowledge of primate brains, new studies of primate communication, more information on the development of linguistic competence in children, more human fossils that can be used to tentatively reconstruct what ancient brains and vocal tracts were like, and a better understanding of early hominid ways of life. We still can't prove how and when human language developed, but we can speculate much less wildly than was once the case.

Attempts to teach other primates to talk like humans have not been successful. In one famous experiment in communication that went on for seven years, for example, the chimpanzee Vikki learned to voice only a few words, such as "up," "mama," and "papa." This inability to speak is not the result of any obvious sensory or perceptual deficit, and apes can in fact produce many of the sounds used in speech. Evidently, their failure to speak has to do with either a lack of motor control mechanisms to produce articulation of speech, or simply a lack of motivation to communicate vocally.

Better results have been achieved through non-vocal methods. Chimpanzees and gorillas in the wild make a variety of vocalizations, but these are often emotional, rather than propositional. In this sense, they are equivalent to human paralanguage. Much of their communication takes place by kinesic means—the use of specific gestures and postures. Indeed, some of these, such as kissing and embracing, are in virtually universal use today among humans, as well as apes. Recognizing the importance of gestural communication to apes,

Allen and Beatrice Gardner began teaching the American Sign Language, used by the deaf, to their young chimpanzee Washoe, the first of several who have since learned to sign. (See the Original Study in Chapter 3.) With vocabularies of over 400 signs, chimps have shown themselves to be able to transfer each sign from its original referent to other appropriate objects and even pictures of objects. Their vocabularies include verbs, adjectives, and words like "sorry" and "please"; furthermore, they can string signs together properly to produce original sentences. Even more impressive, Washoe has been observed spontaneously teaching her own adopted offspring how to sign.

Other chimpanzees have been taught to communicate by other means. One named Sarah learned to converse by means of pictographs—designs such as squares and triangles—on brightly colored plastic chips. Each pictograph stands for a noun or a verb. Sarah can also produce new sentences of her own. Another chimpanzee, Lana, learned to converse by means of a computer with a keyboard somewhat like that of a typewriter, but with symbols rather than letters. One of the most adept with this system is a pygmy chimpanzee named Kanzi who, rather than being taught by a human, learned it as an infant from its mother and soon went on to surpass her abilities.

Chimps have not been the only subjects of ape language experiments. In one project, the American Sign Language was taught to a young gorilla, Koko, whose accomplishments are familiar to millions of readers of the *National Geographic* magazine. Koko's working vocabulary—those signs used regularly and appropriately—consists of over 500 signs. She knows about 500 more, however, and uses as many as 251 of them in a single hour. She not only responds to and asks questions, but she refers to events removed in time and space. This last characteristic, **displacement,** is one of the distinctive characteristics of human speech. Koko has now been joined by a young gorilla named Michael, and the two regularly use sign language to converse with each other.

Displacement: The ability to refer to things and events removed in time and space.

Humans talk, while other primates communicate largely through gestures. Still, humans have not abandoned gestural language altogether, as we see here.

A basic issue raised by these language studies is the question: Do the animals really *know* that a sign can stand for an object in time and space, and that a name can be used to convey information to other beings? After all, say the skeptics, even pigeons can be taught to peck selectively at red keys to obtain food and green keys to obtain water. Might not the apes be doing a very clever version of this? The answer that has emerged is that apes (and even monkeys) do indeed possess competence that goes far beyond the automatic responses that pigeons and other animals learn to give in response to their trainers' cues. What has become clear is that a number of capabilities necessary for language are possessed by both monkeys and apes. These include categorization of experience; perception and categorization of things in structural arrangements; abstraction of higher-order from lower-order categories on the basis of common features in spite of obvious differences; potential for making analogies; intuitive grasping or perceiving of relationships that would, if expressed in language, constitute propositions; and the ability to act on these perceptions in the definition and pursuit of goals.[7] Given these capabilities in both apes and monkeys, it is likely that they arose even before the first hominids appeared on the scene.

In a recent discussion of language origins, anthropologist Ward Goodenough argues that our earliest ancestors were able at the onset to make the kinds of discriminations involved in human languages in order to respond selectively to a wide range of sounds; they were able as well to produce vocal sounds that were distinct in intonation; and they already used vocalizations to some degree (as do apes today) in order to communicate and implement intentions in social interaction. Subsequent elaboration of these abilities allowed the development of phonologically segmented verbal signs that served mainly to enable individuals to identify things of social importance to one another more precisely and to allow them to make the kinds of two-word utterances that human children today make in their early stages of language learning. As Goodenough notes:

> A limited vocabulary of arbitrary signs that can be freely combined in two-word utterances allows for a great deal of communication. It enables individuals to make wants clear to others and to communicate intentions and internal feeling states. Some intentions and feeling states are communicable without such rudimentary language, as is clearly shown in the behavior of chimpanzees. Nevertheless the possibilities for such communication are expanded considerably by a very limited set of verbal symbols.[8]

[7] Ward H. Goodenough,"Evolution of the Human Capacity for Beliefs," *American Anthropologist*, 92(1990):599.

[8] Goodenough: pp. 604-605.

Thus a rudimentary language, lacking both grammar and syntax, is seen as arising early in hominid evolution as a tool to communicate and implement intentions within a social setting, especially the group that lives together.

Useful though simple two-word utterances may be, if one wishes to communicate information beyond rudimentary statements like "baby hurt," especially with respect to events removed in time and space, something more is needed; specifically, organizational conventions of the kind that constitute grammar and syntax. With the development of these, the accumulation of knowledge from shared knowledge became possible. Just when this took place has been a matter of considerable debate, though all would agree that spoken languages with grammar and syntax are at least as old as anatomically modern *Homo sapiens*. There is, however, no anatomical evidence to support arguments that Neandertals and other representatives of archaic *H. sapiens* were incapable of grammatically structured spoken language. In fact, the ability to plan ahead for changes in seasonal conditions crucial to survival in the temperate and subarctic climates in which many populations of archaic *H. sapiens* lived would not have been possible without use of such a language. Since the first hominid to live under cold climate conditions was *H. erectus*, whose vocal tract and brain were intermediate between that of *H. sapiens* and earlier *Australopithecus*, we may suppose that the development of grammar and syntax began as much as 700,000 years ago. Indeed, the appearance of a few evidently symbolic objects in deposits left by *Homo erectus* strongly implies more than a rudimentary linguistic ability, for such objects can have no shared meaning in the absence of explanation.

The search for a truly primitive language spoken by a living people that might show the processes of language just beginning or developing has been abandoned, no doubt permanently. Is there such a thing as a primitive language? So far, all human languages that have been described and studied, even among people with something approximating a Stone Age culture, are highly developed, complex, and capable of expressing infinite meanings. The truth is that people have been talking in this world for an extremely long time, and every known language, wherever it is, now has a long history and has developed subtleties and complexities that strongly resist any label of "primitivism." What a language may or may not express is not a measure of its age, but of its speakers' way of life, reflecting what they want or need to share and communicate with others.

Chapter Summary

Anthropologists need to understand the workings of language, because it is through language that people in every culture are able to share their experiences, concerns, and beliefs, over the past and in the present, and to communicate these to the next generation. Language makes communication of infinite meanings possible by employing a few sounds that, when put together according to certain rules, result in meanings that are intelligible to all speakers.

Linguistics is the modern scientific study of all aspects of language. Phonetics focuses on the production, transmission, and reception of speech sounds. Phonology studies the sound patterns of language in order to extract the rules that govern the way sounds are combined. Morphology is concerned with the smallest units of meaningful combinations of sounds—morphemes—in a language. Syntax refers to the principles according to which phrases and sentences are built. The entire formal structure of a language, consisting of all observations about its morphemes and syntax, constitutes the grammar of a language.

Paralanguage, which always accompanies language, is a less developed means of communication than language and involves such noises as voice qualities and vocalizations. Another means of communication is kinesics, a system of body motions used to convey messages.

Descriptive linguistics registers and explains the features of a language at a particular time in its history. Historical linguistics investigates relationships between earlier and later forms of the same language. A primary concern of historical linguists is to identify the forces behind the changes that have taken place in languages in the course of linguistic divergence. Historical linguistics also provides a means of roughly dating certain migrations, invasions, and contacts of people.

Ethnolinguistics deals with language as it relates to society, culture, and human behavior. Some linguists, following Benjamin Lee Whorf, have proposed that language shapes the way people think and behave. Others argue that language reflects reality. Although linguists find language flexible and adaptable, they have found that once a terminology is established, it tends to perpetuate itself and to reflect much about the speakers' beliefs and social relationships. Kinship terms, for example, help reveal how a family is structured, what relationships are considered close or distant, and what attitudes toward relationships are held. Similarly, gender language reveals how the men and women in a society relate to one another.

A social dialect is the language of a group of people within a larger one, all of whom may speak more or less the same language. Sociolinguists are concerned with whether dialect differences reflect cultural differences. They also study code switching—the process of changing from one level of language to another as the situation demands—for much the same reason.

One theory of language origins is that early hominids, by developing potentials exhibited also by apes and monkeys, began using simple vocal utterances as a tool to communicate and implement intentions within a social setting. With the movement of *Homo erectus* out of the tropics, the need to plan for future needs in order to survive seasons of cold temperatures favored the development of the grammar and syntax necessary to communicate information about events removed in time and space.

For some time linguists searched for a truly primitive language spoken by some living group that would reveal language in its very early state. This search has been abandoned. All languages that have been studied, including those of people with "primitive" cultures, are complex, sophisticated, and able to express a wide range of experiences. What a language is capable of expressing has nothing to do with its age, but with the kind of culture its speakers share and wish to communicate.

Suggested Readings

Birdwhistell, Ray L. *Kinesics and Context*. Philadelphia: University of Pennsylvania Press, 1970.
Kinesics was first delineated as an area for anthropological research by Birdwhistell, so this book is particularly appropriate for those who wish to know more about the phenomenon.

Crane, L. Ben, Edward Yeager, and Randal L. Whitman. *An Introduction to Linguistics*. Boston: Little, Brown, 1981.
A book that gives balanced coverage to all subfields of linguistics, including topics traditionally ignored in textbooks.

Eastman, Carol M. *Aspects of Language and Culture*, 2nd ed. Novato, Calif.: Chandler and Sharp, 1990.
The bulk of this book is devoted to the subjects of worldview, ethnography of communication, nonverbal behavior, animal communication, discourse pragmatics, conversational analysis, semiotics, and ethnicity. A single chapter deals with linguistics as a field tool.

Hickerson, Nancy Parrot. *Linguistic Anthropology*. New York: Holt, Rinehart and Winston, 1980.
A description and explanation of what anthropological linguistics is all about, written so as to be understood by beginning students.

Lehmann, Winifred P. *Historical Linguistics, An Introduction*, 2nd ed. New York: Holt, Rinehart and Winston, 1973.
In recent years, historical linguistics has tended to be overshadowed by descriptive linguistics. Historical linguistics, however, remains an active and changing field, and this book is a good introduction to it.

Patterson, Francine, and Eugene Linden. *The Education of Koko*. New York: Holt, Rinehart and Winston, 1981.
A fascinating and readable account of the longest continuing study of an ape's linguistic abilities ever undertaken. In it, Patterson deals with the various criticisms that have been leveled at ape-language studies.

Trager, George L. "Paralanguage: A First Approximation," in *Language in Culture and Society*, ed. Dell Hymes, New York: Harper & Row, 1964, pp. 274–279.
The author is the pioneer in paralinguistic research, and in this article he discusses what paralanguage is, why it should be studied, and how.

5

GROWING

UP

HUMAN

A Gilbert Island man and his son. In some societies men play an active role in rearing their children, while in others they largely ignore children below the age of puberty. These and other cultural differences in child-rearing practices, and their possible effects on adult personalities, have long been of interest to anthropologists.

WHAT IS ENCULTURATION?

Enculturation is the process by which culture is passed from one generation to the next. It begins soon after birth, as self-awareness—the ability to perceive oneself as an object in time and space and to judge one's own actions—starts to develop. For self-awareness to function, the individual must be provided with a behavioral environment. First, one learns about a world of objects other than self, and these are always perceived in terms that are specified by the culture in which one grows up. Along with this, one is provided with spatial, temporal, and normative orientations.

WHAT IS THE EFFECT OF ENCULTURATION ON ADULT PERSONALITY?

Studies have shown that there is some kind of nonrandom relationship between enculturation and personality development, although it is also clear that each individual begins with certain broad potentials and limitations that are genetically inherited. In some cultures certain child-rearing practices seem to promote the development of compliant personalities, while in others different practices seem to promote more independent, self-reliant personalities.

ARE DIFFERENT PERSONALITIES CHARACTERISTIC OF DIFFERENT CULTURES?

Although cultures vary a great deal in terms of the personality traits that are looked upon with admiration or disapproval, it is difficult to characterize cultures in terms of particular personalities. Of the several attempts that have been made, the concept of modal personality is the most satisfactory. This recognizes that in any human society there will be a range of individual personalities, but that some will be more "typical" than others.

DO CULTURES DIFFER IN WHAT THEY REGARD AS ABNORMAL PERSONALITIES?

A normal personality may be thought of as one that approximates the modal personality of a particular culture. Since modal personalities may differ from one culture to another, and since cultures may differ in the range of variation they will accept, it is clear that abnormal personality is a relative concept. A particular personality regarded as abnormal in one culture may not be so regarded in another.

In 1690, John Locke presented his *tabula rasa* theory in his *Essay Concerning Human Understanding*. This theory held that the newborn human was like a blank slate, and what the individual became in life was written on the slate by his or her life experiences. The implication is that all individuals are biologically identical at birth in their potential for personality development and that their adult personalities are exclusively the products of their postnatal experiences, which will differ from culture to culture. Stated in these terms, the theory is not acceptable, for we know that each person is born with unique inherited tendencies that will influence his or her adult personality. It is also known, however, that genetic inheritance sets certain broad potentials and limitations and that life experiences, particularly in the early years, are critically important in the shaping of individual personalities. Since different cultures handle the raising and education of children in different ways, these practices and their effects on personalities are important subjects of anthropological inquiry. Such studies gave rise to the subfield of psychological anthropology and are the subjects of the present chapter.

THE SELF AND ITS BEHAVIORAL ENVIRONMENT

Because culture is created and learned rather than biologically inherited, all societies must somehow ensure that culture is adequately transmitted from one generation to the next. This process of transmission is known as **enculturation,** and it begins soon after birth. The first agents of enculturation in all societies are the members of the household into which a person is born. At first, the most important member of this household is the newborn's mother, but other members of the household soon come to play roles in the process. Just who these others are depends on how households are structured in the particular society (Chapter 9). In our own, they usually include the father or stepfather and the

Enculturation: The process by which a society's culture is transmitted from one generation to the next.

A chimpanzee mother with her offspring. The basic primate child-rearing unit consists of a mother and her offspring; to this humans have added an adult male. In some societies, this male is the mother's husband; in others, her brother.

child's siblings. In other societies the father may have little contact with his children in their early years; indeed, there are societies where men do not even live with the mothers of their children. In such instances, brothers of the child's mother usually have important responsibilities toward their nieces and nephews. In many societies, grandparents, other wives of the father, brothers of the father or sisters of the mother, not to mention their children, are also likely to be key players in the enculturation process.

As the young person matures, individuals outside the household are brought into the process. These usually include other kin, and certainly the individual's peers. The latter may be included informally in the form of play groups or formally in age associations, where children actually teach other children. In some societies, and our own is a good example, professionals are brought into the process of enculturation to provide formal instruction, although in many societies, children are pretty much allowed to learn through observation and participation, at their own speed.

THE SELF

Enculturation begins with the development of **self-awareness**—the ability to identify oneself as an object, to react to oneself, and to appraise or evaluate oneself. People do not have this ability at birth, even though it is essential for existence in human societies. It is self-awareness that permits one to assume responsibility for one's conduct, to learn how to react to others, and to assume a variety of roles. An important aspect of self-awareness is the attachment of positive value to the self. This is necessary in order to motivate individuals to act to their advantage rather than disadvantage. Self-identification by itself is not sufficient for this.

Self-awareness does not come all at once. In modern North American society, for example, self and nonself are not clearly distinguished until about

---

Self-awareness: The ability to identify oneself as an object, to react to oneself, and to appraise oneself.

---

two years of age. This development of self-awareness in children from North America, however, may lag somewhat behind other cultures, since self-awareness develops in concert with neuromotor development, and this occurs at a slower rate in infants from North America than in infants in many, perhaps even most, non-Western societies. The reasons for this are not yet clear, although the amount of human contact and stimulation that infants receive probably plays an important role. For example, at 15 weeks of age, the home-reared infant in North America is in contact with its mother for about 20 percent of the time, on the average. At the same age, infants in the traditional !Kung society of South Africa's Kalahari Desert are in close contact with their mothers about 70 percent of the time. Moreover, their contacts are not usually limited to their mothers; they include numerous other adults and children of virtually all ages. In the United States and Canada, something approximating these same conditions is now being provided by day-care centers. So long as their personnel remains stable and (ideally) is recruited from the same neighborhood as the child, these centers should have a positive effect on the cognitive and social development of the very young children enrolled in them.

In the development of self-awareness, *perception*— a kind of vague awareness of one's existence —precedes *conception*, or more specific knowledge of the interrelated needs, attitudes, concerns, and interests that define what one is. This involves a cultural definition of self, and in this definition language plays a crucial role. So it is that in all cultures individuals master personal and possessive pronouns at an early age. Personal names, too, are important devices for self-identification in all cultures. Then, as infancy gives way to early childhood, the "I" or "me" is increasingly separated from the environment.

THE BEHAVIORAL ENVIRONMENT

For self-awareness to emerge and function, basic orientations are necessary to structure the psychological field in which the self is prepared to act. Thus, each individual must learn about a world of objects other than self. The basis of this world of other-than-self is what we would think of as the

The Ituri Forest, in the geographical heart of Africa, is viewed in very different ways by the people who live there. Mbuti foragers view it with affection; like a benevolent parent, it provides them with sustenance, protection, and security. Village-dwelling farmers, by contrast, view the forest with misgiving and hostility, as something they must constantly struggle to control.

objective environment of things. The objective environment, though, is organized culturally and mediated symbolically through language. Putting this another way, we might say that the objective world is perceived through cultural glasses. Those attributes of the environment that are culturally significant are singled out for attention and labeled; those that are not may be ignored or lumped together in broad categories. Culture, however, also *explains* the perceived environment. This is important, for it provides the individual with an orderly, rather than chaotic, universe within which to act. Behind this lies a powerful psychological drive to reduce uncertainty, the product of a universal human need for a balanced and integrated perspective on the relevant universe. When confronted with ambiguity and uncertainty, people invariably strive to clarify and give structure to the situation; they do this, of course, in ways that their particular culture tells them are appropriate. Indeed, the greater the lack of structure and certainty, the greater individual suggestibility and persuadability tend to be. Thus, we should not be surprised to find that explanations of the universe are never entirely objective in nature.

The behavioral environment in which the self acts involves more than object orientation alone. Action requires spatial orientation, or the ability to get from one object, or place, to another. In all societies, names and significant features of places are important means of discriminating and representing points of reference for spatial orientation. Individuals must know where they have been, and will be, to get from one place to another. They also need to maintain a sense of self-continuity, so that past actions are connected with those in the present and future. Hence, temporal orientation is also part of the behavioral environment. Just as the perceived environment is organized in cultural terms, so too are time and space.

A final aspect of the behavioral environment is the normative orientation. Values, ideals, and standards, which are purely cultural in origin, are as much a part of the individual's behavioral environment as are trees, rivers, and mountains. Without them one would have nothing by which to judge either one's own actions or those of others. In short, the self-appraisal aspect of self-awareness could not be made functional.

Like any aspect of culture, conceptions of the self vary considerably from one society to another. The Penobscot Indians, a people who at one time relied on fishing, hunting, and the gathering of wild plants (food foraging) for subsistence, and whose descendants still live today in the woodlands of northeastern North America, serve as an example.[1]

THE PENOBSCOT

When first encountered by Europeans, the Penobscot conceived of each individual as being made up of two parts—the body and a "vital self." The latter was dependent on the body, yet was able to disengage itself from the body and travel about for short periods of time, to perform overt acts and to interact with other "selves." It was activity on the part of the vital self that was thought to occur in dreams. So long as the vital self returned to the body before the passage of too much time, the individual remained in good health; if, however, the vital self was prevented from returning to the body, then the individual sickened and died. Along with this dual nature of the self went a potential for every individual to work magic. Theoretically, it was possible to send one's own vital self out to work mischief on others, just as it was possible for others to lure one's vital self away from the body, resulting in sickness and eventual death.

To many people today, the traditional Penobscot concept of self may seem strange. The British colonists of New England regarded such ideas as false and shot through with superstition, even though their own concept of self at the time was every bit as supernaturalistic. To the Indians their concept made sense, for it adequately accounted for

their experience, regardless of its rightness or wrongness in any objective sense. Furthermore, the Penobscot view of self is relevant for anyone who wishes to understand Penobscot behavior in the days when the British and French first tried to settle in North America. For one thing, it was responsible for an undercurrent of suspicion and distrust of strangers, as well as the individual secretiveness that characterized Penobscot society at the time. This propensity for individual secretiveness made it difficult for a potentially malevolent stranger to gain control of an individual's vital self. Also, the belief that dreams are real experiences, rather than expressions of unconscious desires, could impose burdens of guilt and anxiety on individuals who dreamed of doing things not accepted as proper. Finally, individuals indulged in acts that would strike many people today as quite mad. A case in point is a Penobscot Indian who spent the night fighting for his life with a fallen tree. To the Indian, this was a metamorphosed magician who was out to get him, and it would have been madness *not* to try to overcome his adversary.

The behavioral environment in which the Penobscot self operated consisted of a flat world, which these people conceived as being surrounded on all sides by salt water. They could actually see the latter downstream, where the Penobscot River reached the sea. The river itself was the spatial reference point and was as well the main artery for canoe travel in the region. The largest of a number of waterways, it flowed through forests abounding with game. Like humans, each animal was also composed of a body and a vital self. Along with the animals were various quasi-human supernatural beings that inhabited bodies of water and mountains or roamed freely through the forest. One of these, *Gluskabe*, created the all-important Penobscot River by killing a greedy giant frog that had monopolized the world's water supply. Gluskabe was also responsible for a number of other natural features of the world, often as a by-product of punishment (such as that of the giant frog) for transgressions of the moral code. Indeed, individuals had to be concerned about their behavior vis-à-vis both animals and these quasi-human beings or they, too, would come to various kinds of grief. Hence, these supernaturals not only "explained" many otherwise unexplainable natural phenomena to the Penobscot but were also important in structuring the Penob-

[1]Frank G. Speck, "Penobscot Shamanism," *Memoirs of the American Anthropological Association*, 6 (1920):239–288.

Patterns of affect: How people feel about themselves and others.

scot moral order. To the Penobscot, all of this was quite believable; the lone hunter, for example, off for extended periods in the forest, knew he would hear in the night the cry of *Pskedemus,* the swamp woman. And a Penobscot accepted the fact that his or her vital self routinely traveled about while the body slept, interacting with various of these supernatural beings.

Penobscot concepts of the self and behavioral environment have changed considerably since the seventeenth century, though no less so than those of the descendants of the early Europeans who first came to New England. Both groups may now be said to hold modern beliefs about the nature of their selves and the world they live in. The old beliefs were associated with **patterns of affect**—how people *feel* about themselves and others—which differed considerably in American Indian and European cultures. This is significant, for as the Chinese-born anthropologist Francis Hsu has pointed out, patterns of affect are likely to persist over thousands of years, even in the face of far-reaching changes in all other aspects of culture.[2] A failure to understand this point seems to be partially responsible for the generally negative attitude, on the part of many non-Indians, to claims for a variety of rights on the part of American Indians like the Penobscot. Although vast changes have taken place in the external trappings (clothing, housing, transport, etc.) of American Indian cultures, many less visible, but basic, elements of American Indian cultures have persisted even into the 1990s.

PERSONALITY

In the process of enculturation we have seen that each individual is introduced to the concepts of self and the behavioral environment characteristic of his

or her culture. The result is that a kind of cognitive or mental map of the operating world is built up, in terms of which the individual will think and act. It is each individual's map of how to run the maze of life. This cognitive map is an integrated, dynamic system of perceptual assemblages, including the self and its behavioral environment. When we speak of an individual's **personality**, we are generalizing about that individual's cognitive map over time. Hence, personalities are products of enculturation, as experienced by individuals, each with a particular genetic makeup. "Personality" does not lend itself to a formal definition, but for our purposes we may take it as the distinctive way a person thinks, feels, and behaves.

THE DEVELOPMENT OF PERSONALITY

Although *what* one learns is important to personality development, most anthropologists assume that *how* one learns is no less important. With the psychoanalytic theorists, anthropologists view adult personality as having been strongly influenced by early childhood experiences. Indeed, many anthropologists have been strongly attracted by Freudian psychoanalytic theory, but with a critical eye. Psychoanalytic literature tends to be long on concepts, speculation, and clinical data, but short on less culture-bound studies. Anthropologists, for their part, are most interested in studies that seek to prove, modify, or at least shed light on the role of early childhood experiences on personality. For example, in Western societies, men have traditionally been expected to be tough, aggressive, assertive, dominant, self-reliant and achievement oriented, whereas women have been expected to be passive, obedient, compliant, loyal, and caring. To many, these personality differences between the sexes seem so "natural" that they seem biologically grounded and therefore inescapable, unchangeable, and universal. But are they? Have anthropologists

Personality: The distinctive way a person thinks, feels, and behaves.

[2]Francis L.K. Hsu, "Role, Affect, and Anthropology," *American Anthropologist,* 79 (1977):807.

MARGARET MEAD

1901–1978

Although all of the natural and social sciences are able to look back and pay homage to certain "founding fathers," anthropologists take pride in the fact they have a number of "founding mothers" to whom they also pay homage. One is Margaret Mead, who was encouraged by her teacher, Franz Boas, to pursue a career in anthropology at a time when most other academic disciplines rarely accepted women into their ranks. In 1925, she set out for Samoa in order to test the theory (widely accepted at the time) that the biological changes of adolescence could not be accomplished without a great deal of stress, both social and psychological. In her book

Coming of Age in Samoa: A Psychological Study of Primitive Youth for Western Civilization, she concluded that adolescence does not have to be a time of stress and strain, but that cultural conditions may make it so. Published in 1928, this book is generally credited as marking the beginning of the field of culture and personality.

Pioneering works are never without their faults, and *Coming of Age* is no exception, as Mead herself recognized. It would be strange indeed had we not learned more about becoming adults, both in Samoa and elsewhere, since 1928. Highly publicized criticism of Mead's Samoa study that began after her death, however, was more a "media

event" than a scientific discourse; among other things, it misrepresented both her work and anthropology itself.

While not the last word on Samoan youth, Mead's book stands as a landmark for several reasons: Not only was it a deliberate test of a Western psychological hypothesis; it also showed psychologists the value of modifying intelligence tests so as to be appropriate for the population under study. Furthermore, by emphasizing the lesson to be drawn for Mead's own society, it laid the groundwork for the popularization of anthropology and advanced the cause of applied anthropology.

identified any psychological or personality characteristics which universally differentiate men and women?

As Margaret Mead's pioneering studies suggested, and subsequent cross-cultural studies have confirmed, there are no absolute personality differences between men and women. Among the Arapesh of New Guinea it is not just the women, but the men, too, who are gentle and nonaggressive, while among the Mundugamor (also of New Guinea), both sexes are angry and aggressive. In yet another New Guinea society, the Tchambuli, it is the men who decorate themselves, are vain, and interested in art, theatre, and petty gossip, whereas the women are unadorned, brisk and efficient in such practical tasks as raising children, fishing, and marketing.

Clearly, although each culture has different expectations for male-female behavior, the criteria of differentiation in one may bear no relation to those in another, and may in fact be poles apart. From this we may conclude that there is no inevitability to the physical, political, and economic dominance that men have traditionally exerted over women in Western societies, and that other arrangements are possible.

To understand the importance of child-rearing practices for the development of gender-related personality characteristics, we may look briefly at how children grow up among !Kung food foragers of Africa's Kalahari Desert, as compared with how they grow up in sedentary villages in the same region, where people tend small herds of goats and plant gardens for their livelihood.[3] In the former instance, dominance and aggressiveness are not tolerated in either sex; men are as mild-mannered as the women, while women are as energetic and self-reliant as the men.

In the villages, by contrast, men and women exhibit personality characteristics approximating those that have traditionally been thought of as typically masculine and feminine in Western societies. Among the food foragers, children of both sexes receive lengthy, intensive care from their mothers, whose attention is not diverted by the birth of new offspring until after the passage of many years. This is not to say that they are constantly with their children, for they are not; when they go gathering in the bush, they do not always take their offspring with them. At such times, the children will be supervised by their fathers or other adults of the community, one-third to one-half of whom are always to be found in camp on any given day. Because these include men as well as women, children are as much habituated to the male as to the female presence.

Fathers, too, spend much time interacting with their offspring. Although they may correct their children's behavior, so may women. Thus, among !Kung foragers, no one grows up to respect or fear male authority any more than that of women. In fact, instead of being punished, a child who misbehaves will simply be carried away and interested in some other more inoffensive activity. Nor are boys or girls assigned tasks to do; both sexes do equally little work, instead spending much of their time in play groups that include members of both sexes of widely different age. Thus, !Kung children have few experiences that set one sex apart from another. While older ones do amuse and monitor younger ones, this is done spontaneously rather than as an assigned chore, and the burden does not fall any more heavily on girls than boys.

[3]Patricia Draper, "!Kung Women: Contrasts in Sexual Egalitarianism in Foraging and Sedentary Contexts," in *Toward an Anthropology of Women*, ed. Rayna Reiter (New York: Monthly Review Press, 1975), pp. 77–109.

Among the sedentary villagers, women spend much of their time in and around the home preparing food and attending to other domestic chores, as well as tending the children. The work of men, by contrast, requires them to spend many hours outside the household. As a result, children are less habituated to their presence. This remoteness, coupled with their more extensive knowledge of the outside world, tends to enhance their influence within the household.

Within village households, sex-role typing begins early as girls, as soon as they are old enough, are expected to attend to many of the needs of their younger siblings, thereby allowing the mother more time to attend to her other domestic tasks. This not only shapes, but limits the behavior of girls, who cannot range as widely or explore as freely and independently as they could without little brothers and sisters in tow. Indeed, they must stay close to home, be more careful, more obedient, and more sensitive to the wishes of others than they otherwise might be. Boys, by contrast, have little to do with the handling of infants, and when they are assigned work, it generally takes them away from the household. Thus, the space that girls occupy becomes restricted and they are trained in behaviors that promote passivity and nurturance, whereas boys begin to become the distant, controlling figures they will be as adults.

From this comparison, we may begin to understand how a society's economy helps structure the way a child is brought up, and how this, in turn, influences the adult personality. It also shows that there are alternatives to the way that children are raised in Western societies and that by changing the conditions in which our children grow up, we might make it significantly easier for men and women to interact on an equal basis than has been the case so far. Thus, child rearing emerges as not only an anthropological problem, but a practical one as well.

DEPENDENCE TRAINING

Although Margaret Mead compared sex and temperament in three different societies in the early 1930s, most cross-cultural studies of the effects of child rearing on personality have been carried out more recently by John and Beatrice Whiting and Irving L. Child, or their associates. Their work has

Among traditional !Kung, fathers spend much time with their children, interacting with them in nonauthoritarian ways, and children grow up to view male authority and female authority as being equivalent.

Dependence training: Child-rearing practices that foster compliance in the performance of assigned tasks and dependence on the domestic group, rather than reliance on oneself.

demonstrated a number of apparent regularities. For example, it is possible to distinguish at a broad level of generalization between two different patterns of child rearing, which we may label for convenience "dependence training" and "independence training."[4]

Dependence training tends to ensure compliance in the performance of assigned tasks and to keep individuals within the group. This pattern is typically associated with extended families, which consist of several husband-wife-children groups within the same household, and which are most apt to be found in societies in which the economy is based on subsistence farming. Such families are important, for they provide the large labor force

[4] Eric Wolf, *Peasants* (Englewood Cliffs, N.J.: Prentice-Hall, 1966), pp. 69–70.

necessary to till the soil, tend whatever flocks are kept, and carry out other part-time economic pursuits considered necessary for existence. Such large families, however, have built into them certain tensions that are potentially disruptive. For example, one of the adults typically makes the important family decisions, which must be followed by all other family members. In addition, the in-marrying spouses—husbands and/or wives—must subordinate themselves to the will of the group, which may be quite difficult for them. Dependence training helps to keep these potential problems under control, and involves both supportive and punitive aspects. On the supportive side, indulgence is shown to young children, particularly in the form of prolonged oral gratification. Nursing continues for several years and is virtually on demand. This may be interpreted as rewarding the child for seeking support within the family, the main agent in meeting the child's needs. Also on the supportive side, children at a relatively early age are assigned a number of childcare and domestic tasks, all of which make significant and obvious contributions to the family's welfare. Thus, family members all actively work to help and support one another. On the punitive side, behavior that is interpreted by the

The White Man's Bad Medicine, by American Indian artist Jerome Tiger (1941–1967). In the 1950s, in an effort to end its special relationship with American Indians, the federal government terminated its establishment of, and aid to, some Indian reservations. This termination policy led many Indians to relocate to urban areas. As a people whose definition of self springs from the group into which they were born, separation from family and kin led many to severe depression and related problems.

adults as aggressive or sexual is apt to be actively discouraged. Moreover, the adults tend to be quite insistent on overall obedience, which is seen as rendering the individual subordinate to the group. This combination of encouragement and discouragement ideally produces individuals who are obedient, supportive, noncompetitive, generally responsible, and who will stay within the fold and not do anything potentially disruptive. Indeed, their very definition of self comes from their affiliation with a group, rather than from the mere fact of their individual existence.

INDEPENDENCE TRAINING

By contrast, **independence training** emphasizes individual independence, self-reliance, and personal achievement. It is typically associated with societies in which nuclear families, consisting of a husband, wife, and their offspring, are independent rather than a part of some larger household group. Independence training is particularly characteristic of industrial societies such as that of the United

Independence training: Child-rearing practices that promote independence, self-reliance, and personal achievement on the part of the child.

States, where self-reliance and personal achievement, especially on the part of men, are important traits for survival. Again, this pattern of training involves both encouragement and discouragement. On the negative side, little emphasis is placed on prolonged oral gratification, and feeding is prompted more by schedule than demand. In the U.S., for example, people like to establish a schedule as soon as possible, and it is not long before they start feeding infants baby food, and even try to get them to feed themselves. Many parents are delighted if they can prop their infants up in the crib or playpen so that they can hold their own bottles. In fact, infants do not receive the amount of attention they so often do in nonindustrialized societies. In the United States a mother may be very affectionate

In North American society, independence training pits individuals against one another through games and other forms of competition.

with her 15-week-old infant during the 20 percent of the time she is in contact with it, but for the other 80 percent of the time the infant is more or less on its own. Collective responsibility is not encouraged in children; they are not given responsible tasks to perform until later in childhood, and these are generally few in number. Furthermore, their contribution to the welfare of the family is often not immediately apparent to the child, to whom the tasks appear arbitrary as a result.

Displays of aggression and sexuality are encouraged, or at least tolerated to a greater degree than where dependence training is the rule. In schools, and even in the family, competition is emphasized. In the United States, we have gone to the extreme of turning the biological functions of infancy—eating, sleeping, crying, and elimination—into contests between parents and offspring. In our schools, considerable resources are devoted to competitive sports, but competition is fostered within the classroom as well: overtly, through such devices as spelling bees and competition for prizes, and covertly through such devices as grading on a curve. The latter practice, widely utilized for certain heavily enrolled courses on some college campuses, condemns some students to failure, irrespective of how well they actually do, so long as most of the class does better. This puts students in competition with each other, for one soon learns that one's own chances for a decent grade depend, as much as anything, on other members of the class not doing well themselves. If the stakes are high, students may devote considerable effort to placing obstacles in the way of classmates, so that they are prevented from doing too well. Thus, by the time one has grown up in U.S. society, regardless of what one may think about it, one has received a clear message: success is something that comes at someone else's expense. "Even the team spirit, so loudly touted" in school athletics (or out of school in Little League baseball and the like), "is merely a more efficient way, through limited cooperation, to 'beat' a greater number of people more efficiently."[5]

In sum, independence training generally encourages individuals to seek help and attention, rather than to give it, and to try to exert individual dominance. Such qualities are useful in societies with social structures that emphasize personal achievement and where individuals are expected to look out for their own interests.

COMBINED DEPENDENCE/INDEPENDENCE TRAINING

In food-foraging societies, child-rearing practices combine elements of independence and dependence training. "Share and share alike" is the order of the day, and so competitive behavior, which can interfere with the cooperation on which all else depends, is discouraged. Thus, infants receive much in the way of positive, affectionate attention from adults, along with prolonged oral gratification. This, as well as low pressure for compliance and a lack of emphasis on competition, encourages individuals to be more supportive of one another than is often the case in modern industrial societies. At the same time, personal achievement and independence are encouraged, for those individuals most capable of self-reliance are apt to be the most successful in the food quest.

In the United States, the argument has sometimes been made (though not by anthropologists) that "permissive" child rearing produces irresponsible adults. Since the practices of food foragers seem to be about as permissive as they can get, and yet socially responsible adults are produced, it is worth taking a closer look at how this is achieved. In the following Original Study, we see how children grow up among the Mbuti, hunters and gatherers who live in Zaire's Ituri forest.

[5]Colin M. Turnbull, *The Human Cycle* (New York: Simon & Schuster, 1983), p. 74.

ORIGINAL STUDY

GROWING UP AMONG THE MBUTI[6]

In the first three years of life every Mbuti alive experiences almost total security. The infant is breast-fed for those three years, and is allowed almost every freedom. Regardless of gender, the infant learns to have absolute trust in both male and female parents. If anything, the father is just another kind of mother, for in the second year the father formally introduces the child to its first solid food. There used to be a beautiful ritual in which the mother presented the child to the father in the middle of the camp, where all important statements are made (anyone speaking from the middle of the camp must be listened to). The father took the child and held it to his breast, and the child would try to suckle, crying *"ema, ema,"* or "mother." The father would shake his head, and say "no, father . . . *eba,*" but like a mother (the Mbuti said), then give the child its first solid food.

At three the child ventures out into the world on its own and enters the *bopi,* what we might call a playground, a tiny camp perhaps a hundred yards from the main camp, often on the edge of a stream. The *bopi* were indeed playgrounds, and often very noisy ones, full of fun and high spirits. But they were also rigorous training grounds for eventual economic responsibility. On entry to the *bopi,* for one thing, the child discovers the importance of age as a structural principle, and the relative unimportance of gender and biological kinship. The *bopi* is the private world of the children. Younger youths may occasionally venture in, but if adults or elders try, as they sometimes do when angry at having their afternoon snooze interrupted, they invariably get driven out, taunted, and ridiculed. Children, among the Mbuti, have rights, but they also learn that they have responsibilities. Before the hunt sets out each day it is the children, sometimes the younger youths, who light the hunting fire.

Ritual among the Mbuti is often so informal and apparently casual that it may pass unnoticed at first. Yet insofar as ritual involves symbolic acts that represent unspoken, perhaps even unthought, concepts or ideals, or invoke other states of being, alternative frames of mind and reference, then Mbuti life is full of ritual. The hunting fire is one of the more obvious of such rituals. Early in the morning children would take firebrands from the *bopi,* where they always lit their own fire with embers from their family hearths, and set off on the trail by which the hunt was to leave that day (the direction of each day's hunt was always settled by discussion the night before). Just a short distance from the camp they lit a fire at the base of a large tree, and covered it with special leaves that made it give off a column of dense smoke. Hunters leaving the camp, both men and women, and such youths and children as were going with them, had to pass by this fire. Some did so casually, without stopping or looking, but passing through the smoke. Others reached into the smoke with their hands as they passed, rubbing the smoke into their bodies. A few always stopped, for a moment, and let the smoke envelop them, only then almost dreamily moving off.

For the Mbuti, education into social consciousness begins literally at the mother's breast. Nursed virtually on demand for the first three years of life, an infant learns to have absolute trust in his or her parents.

And indeed it *was* a form of intoxication, for the smoke invoked the spirit of the forest, and by passing through it the hunters sought to fill themselves with that spirit, not so much to make the hunt successful as to minimize the sacrilege of killing. Yet they, the hunters, could not light the fire themselves. After all, they were already contaminated by death. Even youths, who daily joined the hunt at the edges, catching any game that escaped the nets, by hand, if they could, were not pure enough to invoke the spirit of forestness. But young children were uncontaminated, as yet untainted by contact with the original sin of the Mbuti. It was their responsibility to light the fire, and if it was not lit then the hunt would not take place, or as the Mbuti put it, the hunt *could* not take place.

In this way even the children in Mbuti society, at the first of the four age levels that dominate Mbuti social structure, are given very real social responsibility and see themselves as a part of that structure, by virtue of their purity. After all, they have just been born from the source of all purity, the forest itself. By the same reasoning, the elders, who are about to return to that ultimate source of all being, through death, are at least closer to purity than the adults, who are daily contaminated by killing. Elders no longer go on the hunt. So, like the children, the elders have important sacred ritual responsibilities in the Mbuti division of labor by age. In the *bopi* the children play, but they have no "games" in the strict sense of the word. Levi-Strauss has perceptively compared games with rituals, suggesting that whereas in a game the players start theoretically equal but end up unequal, in a ritual just the reverse takes place. All are equalized. Mbuti children could be seen every day playing in the *bopi*, but not once did I see a game, not one activity that smacked of any kind of competition, except perhaps that competition that it is necessary for us all to feel from time to time, competition with our own private and personal inadequacies. One such pastime (rather than game) was tree climbing. A dozen or so children would climb up a young sapling. Reaching the top, their weight brought the sapling bending down until it almost touched the ground. Then all the children leapt off together, shrieking as the young tree sprang upright again with a rush. Sometimes one child, male or female, might stay on a little too long, either out of fear, or out of bravado, or from sheer carelessness or bad timing. Whatever the reason, it was a lesson most children only needed to be taught once, for the result was that you got flung upward with the tree, and were lucky to escape with no more than a few bruises and a very bad fright.

Other pastimes taught the children the rules of hunting and gathering. Frequently elders, who stayed in camp when the hunt went off, called the children into the main camp and enacted a mock hunt with them there. Stretching a discarded piece of net across the camp, they pretended to be animals, showing the children how to drive them into the nets. And, of course, the children played house, learning the patterns of cooperation that would be necessary for them later in life. They also learned the prime lesson of egality, other than for purposes of division of labor, making no distinction between male and female, this nuclear family or that. All in the *bopi* were *apua'i* to each other, and so they would remain throughout their lives. At every age level—childhood, youth, adulthood, or old age—everyone of that level is *apua'i* to all the others. Only adults sometimes (but so rarely that I think it was only done as a kind of joke, or possibly insult) made the distinction that the Bira do, using *apua'i* for male and *amua'i* for female. Male or female, for the Mbuti, if you are the same age you are *apua'i*, and that means that you share everything equally, regardless of kinship or gender.

Sometime before the age of puberty boys or girls, whenever they feel ready, move back into the main camp from the *bopi* and join the youths. This is when they must assume new responsibilities, which for the youths are primarily political. Already, in the *bopi*, the children become involved in disputes, and are sometimes instrumental in settling them by ridicule, for nothing hurts an adult more than being ridiculed publicly by children. The art of reason, however, is something they learn from the youths, and it is the youths who apply the art of reason to the settlement of disputes.

When puberty comes it separates them, for the first time in their experience, from each other as *apua'i*. Very plainly girls are different from boys. When a girl has her first menstrual period the whole camp celebrates with the wild *elima* festival, in which the girl, and some of her chosen girl friends, are the center of all attention, living together in a special *elima* house. Male youths sit outside the *elima* house and wait for the girls to come out, usually in the afternoon, for the *elima* singing. They sing in antiphony, the girls leading, the boys responding. Boys come from neighboring territories all around, for this is a time of courtship. But there are always eligible youths within the camp as well, and the *elima* girl may well choose girls from other territories to come and join her, so there is more than enough excuse for every youth to carry on several flirtations, legitimate or illegitimate. I have known even first cousins to flirt with each other, but learned to be prudent enough not to pull out my kinship charts and point this out—well, not in public anyway.

The *elima* is more than a premarital festival, more than a joint initiation of youth into adulthood, and more than a rite of passage through puberty, though it is all those things. It is a public recognition of the opposition of male and female, and every *elima* is used to highlight the *potential* for conflict that lies in that opposition. As at other times of crisis, at puberty, a time of change and uncertainty, the Mbuti bring all the major forms of conflict out into the open. And the one that evidently most concerns them is the male/female opposition.

The adults begin to play a special form of "tug of war" that is clearly a ritual rather than a game. All the men are on one side, the women on the other. At first it looks like a game, but quickly it becomes clear that the objective is for *neither* side to win. As soon as the women begin to win, one of them will leave the end of the line and run around to join the men, assuming a deep male voice and in other ways ridiculing manhood. Then, as the men begin to win, a male will similarly join the women, making fun of womanhood as he does so. Each adult on changing sides attempts to outdo all the others in ridiculing the opposite sex. Finally, when nearly all have switched sides, and sexes, the ritual battle between the genders simply collapses into hysterical laughter, the contestants letting go of the rope, falling onto the ground, and rolling over with mirth. Neither side wins, both are equalized very nicely, and each learns the essential lesson, that there should be *no* contest.

[6]From *Mbuti Pygmies: Change and Adaptation*, by Colin M. Turnbull, pp. 39–47. Copyright © 1983 by Holt, Rinehart and Winston. Reprinted by permission of Harcourt Brace Jovanovich, Inc.

It must be stressed that no particular system of child rearing is inherently better or worse than any other; what matters is whether the system is functional or dysfunctional in the context of a particular society. If compliant adults, who are accepting of authority, are required, then independence training will not work well in that society. Nor will dependence training serve very well a society in which adults are expected to be independent, self-reliant, and questioning of authority. Sometimes, however, inconsistencies develop, and here we may look again at North American society. As we have seen, independence training generally tends to be stressed in the United States, where we often speak in glowing terms of the worth of personal independence, the dignity of the individual, and so on. Our pronouncements, however, do not always suit our actions. In spite of the professed desire for personal independence, there seems to be a strong underlying desire for compliance. This may be seen in the criticism of "whistle blowers" in government bureaus, who, if they don't lose their jobs, are often shunted to one side and passed by when the rewards are handed out. In business as well as in government, there is a tendency for the rewards to be given to those who go along with the system, while criticism, no matter how constructive, is a risky business. In corporate, as well as government bureaucracies, the ability to please, not shake up the system, is what is required for success. Yet, in spite of pressures for compliance, which would be most effectively served by dependence training, we continue to raise our children to be independent, and then wonder why they so often refuse to behave in ways adults would have them behave.

GROUP PERSONALITY

From studies such as those reviewed here, it is clear that personality, child-rearing practices, and other aspects of culture are interrelated in some kind of nonrandom way. Whiting and Child have argued that the child-rearing practices of a society originate in basic customs surrounding nourishment, shelter, and protection, and that these child-rearing practices in turn produce particular kinds of adult personalities.[7] The trouble is that correlations do not prove cause and effect. We are still left with the fact that, however logical it may seem, such a causal chain remains an unproved hypothesis.

The existence of a close, if not causal, interrelationship between child-rearing practices and personality, coupled with variation in child-rearing practices from one society to another, have led to a number of attempts to characterize groups in terms of particular kinds of personalities. Indeed, common sense suggests that personalities appropriate for one culture may be less appropriate for some others. For example, an egocentric, aggressive personality would be out of place where cooperation and sharing are the keys to success. Or, in the context of traditional Penobscot Indian culture, which we examined briefly earlier in this chapter, an open and extroverted personality would seem inappropriate, for it would be inconsistent with the prevailing conception of the self. Unfortunately,

[7]John W.M. Whiting and Irvin L. Child, *Child Training and Personality: A Cross-cultural Study* (New Haven, Conn.: Yale University Press, 1953).

Yanomami men display their fierceness. While flamboyant, belligerent personalities are especially compatible with the Yanomami ideal that men should be fierce, some are quiet and retiring.

common sense, like conventional wisdom in general, isn't always true. The question is worth asking: Can we describe a group personality without falling into stereotyping? The answer appears to be a qualified yes; in an abstract way, we may speak of a generalized "cultural personality" for a society, so long as we do not expect to find a uniformity of personalities within that society. Put another way, each individual develops certain personality characteristics that, from common experience, resemble those of other people. Yet, because each individual is exposed to unique experiences as well, may react to common experiences in novel ways, and brings to these experiences a unique (except for the case of identical twins) genetic potential, each also acquires distinct personality traits. Because individual personalities differ, the organization of diversity is important to all cultures.

As an example of the fact that individual personalities in traditional societies are far from uniform,

consider the case of the Yanomami, whom we discussed in Chapter 2. Among them, individual men strive to achieve a reputation for fierceness and aggressiveness that they are willing to defend at the risk of serious personal injury and death. And yet there are men among the Yanomami who are quiet and somewhat retiring. In any gathering of these people, the quiet ones are all too easily overlooked by outsiders, when so many others are in the front row pushing and demanding attention. Not only do traditional societies include a range of personalities, but some of those personalities may resemble in many ways those of some individuals in U.S. society. Ruth Landes once observed an Ojibwa Indian shaman at Emo, Ontario, who displayed what she judged to be the same sort of "cold, moralistic, driven personality" as ex-President Richard Nixon.[8]

[8] Ruth Landes, "Comment," *Current Anthropology,* 23 (1982):401.

RUTH FULTON BENEDICT

1887–1947

Ruth Benedict came late to anthropology; upon her graduation from Vassar College, she taught high school English, published poetry, and tried her hand at social work. In anthropology, she developed the idea that culture was a projection of the personality of those who created it. In her most famous book *Patterns of Culture* (1934), she compared the cultures of three peoples—the Kwakiutl of western Canada, the Zuni of the southwestern United States, and the Dobuans of New Guinea. She held that each was comparable to a great work of art, with an internal coherence and consistency of its own. Seeing the Kwakiutl as egocentric, individualistic, and ecstatic in their rituals, she labeled their cultural configuration "Dionysian"; the Zuni, whom she saw as living by the golden mean, wanting no part of excess of disruptive psychological states, and distrusting of individualism, she characterized as "Apollonian." The Dobuans, whose culture seemed magic-ridden, with everyone fearing and hating everyone else, she characterized as "paranoid."

Although *Patterns of Culture* still enjoys popularity in some nonanthropological circles, anthropologists have long since abandoned its approach as impressionistic and not susceptible to replication. To compound the problem, Benedict's characterizatons of cultures are misleading (the supposedly "Apollonian" Zunis, for example, indulge in such seemingly "Dionysian" practices as sword swallowing and walking over hot coals), and the use of such value-laden terms as "paranoid" prejudices others toward a culture. Nonetheless, the book did have an enormous and valuable influence in focusing attention on the problem of the interrelation between culture and personality, and in popularizing the reality of cultural variation.

MODAL PERSONALITY

Obviously, any fruitful approach to the problem of group personality must recognize that each individual is unique to a degree in both inheritance and life experiences, and that we should expect a range of personality types in any society. In addition, personality traits that may be regarded as appropriate in men may not be so regarded in women, and vice versa. Given all this, we may focus our attention on the **modal personality** of a group, defined as the

Modal personality: The personality typical of a society as indicated by the central tendency of a defined frequency distribution.

personality typical of a culturally bounded population, as indicated by the central tendency of a defined frequency distribution. Modal personality is a statistical concept, and, as such, it opens up for investigation the questions of how societies organize diversity and how diversity relates to culture change. Such questions are easily overlooked if one associates one particular type of personality with one particular culture, as older approaches (like that of Ruth Benedict, described in the box above) tended to do. At the same time, modal personalities of different groups can be compared.

Data on modal personality are best gathered by means of psychological tests administered to a sample of the population in question. Those most often used include the Rorschach, or "ink-blot" test, and the Thematic Apperception Test (TAT). The latter consists of pictures, which the individual tested is asked to explain, or to tell what is going on. There are, as well, other sorts of projective tests that have been used at one time or another; all have in common a purposeful ambiguity, so that the individual tested has to structure the situation before responding. The idea is that one's personality is projected into the ambiguous situation. Along with the use of such tests, observations recording the frequency of certain behaviors, the collection and analysis of life histories and dreams, and the analysis of oral literature are also helpful in eliciting data on modal personality.

While having much to recommend it, the concept of modal personality as a means of dealing with group personality nevertheless presents certain difficulties. One of these is the complexity of the measurement techniques themselves, which may be difficult to carry out in the field. For one thing, an adequate representative sample of subjects is necessary. The problem here is twofold: making sure that the sample is genuinely representative and having the time and personnel necessary to administer the tests, conduct interviews, and so on, all of which can be lengthy proceedings. Also, the tests themselves constitute a problem, for those devised in one cultural setting may not be appropriate in another. This is more of a problem with the TAT than with some other tests, although different pictures have been devised for other cultures. Still, to minimize any hidden cultural bias, it is best not to rely on projective tests alone. In addition to all this, there are often language problems, which may lead to misinterpretation. Furthermore, the field investigator may be in conflict with cultural values. A people like the Penobscot, whose concept of self we surveyed earlier, would not take kindly to revealing their dreams to strangers. Finally, there is the question of what is being measured. Just what, for example, is aggression? Does everyone define it the same way? Is it a legitimate entity, or does it involve other variables?

NATIONAL CHARACTER

No discussion of group personality would be complete without a consideration of national character, which popular thought all too often ascribes to the citizens of many different countries. The novelist Henry Miller epitomizes this view when he says, "Madmen are logical—as are the French," suggest-

ing that Frenchmen, in general, are overly rational. A Parisian, on the other hand, might view North Americans as maudlin and unsophisticated. Similarly, we all have in mind some image, perhaps not well defined, of the "typical" Russian or Japanese or Englishman. Essentially, these are simply stereotypes. We might well ask, however, if these stereotypes have any basis in fact. Is there, in reality, such a thing as national character?

Some anthropologists have thought that maybe the answer is yes. Accordingly, national character studies were begun that sought to discover basic personality traits shared by the majority of the peoples of modern countries. Along with this went an emphasis on child-rearing practices and education as the factors theoretically responsible for such characteristics. Margaret Mead, Ruth Benedict, Weston LaBarre, and Geoffrey Gorer conducted pioneering studies of national character, using relatively small samples of informants. During World War II, techniques were developed for studying "culture at a distance" through the analysis of newspapers, books, and photographs. By investigating memories of childhood and cultural attitudes, and by examining graphic material for the appearance of recurrent themes and values, researchers attempted to portray national character.

THE JAPANESE

At the height of World War II, Geoffrey Gorer attempted to determine the underlying reasons for the "contrast between the all-pervasive gentleness of family life in Japan, which has charmed nearly every visitor, and the overwhelming brutality and sadism of the Japanese at War." Strongly under the influence of Freud, Gorer sought his causes in the toilet-training practices of the Japanese, which he believed were severe and threatening. He suggested that because Japanese infants were forced to control their sphincters before they had acquired the necessary muscular or neurological development, they grew up filled with repressed rage. As adults, the Japanese were able to express this rage in their ruthlessness in war.[9]

In the midst of war, Gorer was unable to do fieldwork in Japan. After the war was over, though,

[9]Geoffrey Gorer, "Themes in Japanese Culture," *Transactions of the New York Academy of Sciences,* Series II, 5 (1943).

the toilet-training hypothesis was tested, at which time it was found that the severity of Japanese toilet training was a myth. Children were not subject to severe threats of punishment. Nor were all Japanese soldiers brutal and sadistic in war; some were, but then so were some North Americans. Also, the participation of many Japanese in postwar peace movements in the Far East hardly conformed to the wartime image of brutality.

Gorer's study, along with others by Benedict and LaBarre, was most important, not in revealing the importance of Japanese sphincters on the national character, but in pointing out the dangers of generalizing from insufficient evidence and employing simplistic individual psychology to explain complex social phenomena.

OBJECTIONS TO NATIONAL CHARACTER STUDIES

Critics of national character theories have emphasized the tendency for such work to be based on unscientific and overgeneralized data. The concept of modal personality has a certain statistical validity, they argue, but to generalize the qualities of a complex nation on the basis of such limited data is to lend insufficient recognition to the countless

Core values: Those values especially promoted by a particular culture.

individuals who vary from the generalization. Further, such studies tend to be highly subjective; for example, the tendency during the late 1930s and 1940s for anthropologists to characterize the German people as aggressive paranoids was obviously a reflection of wartime hostilities rather than scientific objectivity.

It has also been pointed out that occupational and social status tends to cut across national boundaries. A French farmer may have less in common with a French factory worker than he does with a German farmer. Yet in spite of all the difficulties, not to mention the valid criticisms of past studies, Francis Hsu, in his presidential address to the American Anthropological Association in 1978, asserted that there is a new urgency to studies of national character, and that without them, we will probably never really understand what motivates the leaders and civil servants of modern nations.[10] Hsu's approach has been to study the **core values**

[10]Francis L.K. Hsu, "The Cultural Problem of the Cultural Anthropologist," *American Anthropologist*, 81 (1979):528.

The core values of Chinese culture promote the assimilation of the individual into a larger group. By contrast, the core values of American culture promote the autonomy of the individual.

of a nation's culture and related personality traits. The Chinese, he suggests, value kin ties and cooperation above all else. To them, mutual dependence is the very essence of personal relationships, and has been for thousands of years. Compliance and subordination of one's will to that of family and kin transcends all else, while self-reliance is neither promoted nor a source of pride. Following the 1949 revolution, Mao Zedong sought to expand the sphere of affect to the nation as a whole, presenting himself as the "father" of all citizens.

Perhaps the core value held in highest esteem by North Americans of European descent is that of "rugged individualism," at least for men (only recently has this become recognized as a valid ideal for women). Nowadays, each individual alone is supposed to be able to achieve anything he or she likes, given a willingness to work hard enough. From their earliest years, individuals are subjected to relentless pressures to excel and, as we have already noted, competition and winning are seen as crucial to this. Undoubtedly, this contributes to the "restlessness" and "drivenness" of North American society, and to the degree that it motivates individuals to work hard and to go where the economy needs them, it fits well with the needs of an industrial society. Thus, while the Chinese are firmly bound into a larger group to which they have lifelong obligations, North Americans are isolated from all other kin save husband or wife (and something like 50 percent of marriages end in divorce). Even parents and children have no legal obligations to one another, once the latter have reached the age of majority. This isolation of the individual has been suggested as one reason for the North American obsession with pets. A dog or a cat may partially compensate for limited opportunities to maintain close affective ties with other human beings.

ABNORMAL PERSONALITY

The concept of modal personality holds that a range of personalities will exist in any society. The modal personality itself may be thought of as normal for that society, but may in fact be shared by less than half the population. What of those personalities that differ from the norm? The Dobuans of New

Guinea and certain Plains Indians furnish examples of normal and abnormal behavior strikingly different from our own.

NORMAL AND ABNORMAL BEHAVIOR

The individual man in Dobu whom the other villagers considered neurotic and thoroughly disoriented was a man who was naturally friendly and found activity an end in itself. He was a pleasant fellow who did not seek to overthrow his fellows or to punish them. He worked for anyone who asked him, and he was tireless in carrying out their commands. In any other Dobuan, this would have been scandalous behavior, but in him it was regarded as merely silly. The village treated him in a kindly fashion, not taking advantage of him, nor making sport of or ridiculing him, but he was definitely regarded as one who stood outside the normal conventions of behavior.

Among certain Plains Indians, a man, compelled by supernatural spirits, could assume women's attire and perform woman's work; he could even marry another man, although not all men who assumed a woman's identity were homosexuals, nor did all homosexuals behave in this way. Under this institution of the "berdache," an individual would find himself living in a dramatically different manner from most men; yet, although the berdache was rare among Indians, it was *not* looked upon as the behavior of an abnormal individual. Quite the contrary, for the berdache was often sought out as a curer, artist, matchmaker, and companion of warriors, because of the great spiritual power he was thought to possess.

In Western societies like the United States, behavior like that of the Plains Indian berdaches has traditionally been regarded as abnormal. If a man dresses as a woman, it is generally regarded as a cause for concern and is likely to lead to psychiatric intervention. Nor have jobs traditionally filled by women been seen as desirable for men. By contrast, women are much more free to wear masculine-style clothing and to assume jobs more usually held by men, even though to do so may cause them to be branded as somehow "unfeminine." What lies behind this are traditional values (jobs traditionally associated with men have been more highly valued than those associated with women) and a pattern of

Among North American Indians of the Great Plains, some men dressed and acted like women without being regarded as abnormal. By contrast, such behavior in Western society has traditionally been regarded as abnormal.

child rearing that creates problems of gender identity for both sexes, although of a different sort for each sex.

As Nancy Chodorow has argued, in our society, girls have traditionally been raised by women, usually their mothers, and most still are. Thus, feminine role models are constantly available and easily understandable. Very early, girls begin to do the things that women do, and gradually and continuously acquire the identity deemed appropriate for their sex. Once they enter school, however, they learn that women are not all-powerful and prestigious, that it is men who generally run things, and who are portrayed as the ones who have most advanced human progress. As a consequence, a girl finds that the feminine identity, which has become so easy for her, leaves much to be desired. Under

the circumstances, she is bound to feel a certain resentment towards it.

Boys have a different problem; like girls, they, too, begin their lives in a feminine world. With adult men out of the house working, not only is a male model rarely present, but it is the mother who seems to be all-powerful. Under these conditions, boys begin to develop a feminine identity with its expected compliant personality. In keeping with all this, it used to be that boys were even dressed as girls (dresses for little boys were not dropped from the Sears catalogue until 1940) until the age thought proper to "graduate" into less feminine attire arrived. Once out of the house and in school, boys learn that they must switch from a female to male identity; in a sense, they must renounce femininity and prove their maleness, in a way that girls do not have to prove their femaleness. Generally speaking, the more distant a boy's father (or other male companion of his mother), the greater the boy's insecurity in his male identity and the greater his compulsion to be seen as really masculine. To do this, he must strive all the harder to be aggressive and assert his dominance, particularly over women.

Nancy Chodorow sums up the situation as follows:

Sex-role ideology and socialization for these roles seem to ensure that neither boys nor girls can attain both stable identity and meaningful roles. The tragedy of woman's socialization is not that she is left unclear, as is the man, about her basic sexual identity. This identity is ascribed to her, and she does not need to prove to herself or to society that she has earned it or continues to have it. Her problem is that this identity is clearly devalued in the society in which she lives. This does not mean that women too should be required to compete for identity, to be assertive and to need to achieve—to "do" like men. Nor does it suggest that it is not crucial for everyone, men and women alike, to have a stable sexual identity. But until male "identity" does not depend upon men's proving themselves, their "doing" will be a reaction to insecurity, not a creative exercise of their humanity, and woman's "being," far from being an easy and positive acceptance of self, will be a resignation to inferiority. And as long as women must live through their children, and men do not genuinely contribute to socialization and provide easily accessible role models, women will continue to bring up sons whose sexual identity depends upon devaluing femininity inside

and outside themselves, and daughters who must accept this devalued position and resign themselves to producing more men who will perpetuate the system that devalues them.[11]

This example shows us how a culture may itself actually induce certain kinds of psychological conflicts, with important consequences for the entire society. Although the conditions under which children are raised in our society are now changing, we have a long way to go before the conflicts just described become things of the past. But what has seemed normal in the past may become "abnormal" in the future.

The standards that define normal behavior for any culture are determined by that culture itself. Obviously, no society could survive if suicide were looked upon as normal behavior; yet each culture determines for itself the circumstances under which suicide may be acceptable. The Aymara of the Bolivian Andes, for example, disapprove of suicide, but a man possessed by spirits of the dead, which cannot be exorcised, may take his own life and yet be remembered with respect. Given his affliction, suicide is considered to be perfectly reasonable. Moral acts are those that conform to cultural standards of good and evil, and each society determines those standards for itself. Morality is thus based on culturally determined ideals.

Is all this to suggest that "normalcy" is a meaningless concept as it is applied to personality? Within the context of a given culture, the concept of normal personality is quite meaningful. A.I. Hallowell somewhat ironically observed that it is normal to share the delusions traditionally accepted by one's society. Abnormality involves the development of a delusional system not sanctioned by the culture. The individual who is disturbed because he or she cannot adequately measure up to the norms of society, and yet be happy, may be termed neurotic. When one's delusional system is so different from that of one's society that it in no way reflects its norms, the individual may be termed psychotic.

Culturally induced conflicts, if severe enough, may not only produce psychosis but determine the form of the psychosis as well. In a culture that

encourages aggressiveness and suspicion, the madman is that individual who is passive and trusting. In a culture that encourages passivity and trust, the madman is that individual who is aggressive and suspicious. Just as each society establishes its own norms, each individual is unique in his or her perceptions. Many anthropologists see the only meaningful criterion for personality evaluation as the correlation between personality and social conformity.

While it is true that culture defines what is and is not normal behavior, the situation is complicated by findings suggesting that major categories of mental disorders may be universal types of human affliction. Take, for example, the case of schizophrenia, probably the most common of all psychoses, and one which may be found in any culture, no matter how it may manifest itself. Individuals afflicted by schizophrenia experience distortions of reality that impair their ability to function adequately, and so they withdraw from the social world into their own psychological shell, from which they do not emerge. Although environmental factors play a role, there is evidence that schizophrenia is caused by a biochemical disorder for which there is an inherited tendency. One of its more severe forms is paranoid schizophrenia. Those suffering from it fear and mistrust almost everyone; they hear voices that whisper dreadful things to them and they are convinced that someone is "out to get them." Acting on this conviction, they engage in bizarre types of behavior, which leads to their removal from society, usually to a mental institution.

A precise image of paranoid schizophrenia is one of the so-called **ethnic psychoses** known as *Windigo*. Such psychoses involve symptoms of mental disorder specific to particular ethnic groups (Table 5.1, p. 140). Windigo psychosis is limited to northern Algonkian Indian groups such as the Chippewa, Cree, and Ojibwa. In their traditional belief systems, these northern Indians recognized the existence of cannibalistic monsters called

[11]Nancy Chodorow, "Being and Doing: A Cross-cultural Examination of the Socialization of Males and Females," in *Woman in Sexist Society*, ed. Vivian Gornick and Barbara K. Moran (New York: Basic Books, 1971), p. 193.

Ethnic psychoses: Mental disorders specific to particular ethnic groups.

ANTHROPOLOGY APPLIED

ANTHROPOLOGISTS AND MENTAL HEALTH

One consequence of development in the newly emerged states of Africa, Asia, and Central and South America, is a rising incidence of related mental disturbances among their people. Similarly, mental health problems abound among ethnic minorities living within industrialized countries. Unfortunately, orthodox approaches to mental health have not been successful at dealing with these problems, for a number of reasons. For one, different ethnic groups have different attitudes towards mental disorders than do medical practitioners. For another, the diverse conditions under which different ethnic groups live produce culturally patterned health conditions, including culture-bound syndromes not recognized by the orthodox medical profession. Among Puerto Ricans, for example, a widely held belief is that spirits are active in the world, and that they influence human behavior. Thus, for someone with a psychiatric problem, it makes sense to them to go to a native spiritist for help. In a Puerto Rican community, going to a spiritist is normal. Not only does the client not understand the symbols of psychiatry, but to go to a psychiatrist seems to imply that he or she is "crazy" and requires restraint, or removal from the community.

Although practitioners of Western medicine have often regarded spiritists and other folk healers as ignorant, if not outright fraudulent, efforts were begun in the 1950s to experiment with community-based treatment in which psychiatrists cooperated with traditional healers. Since then, this approach has gained widespread accept-

ance in many parts of the world, as when (in 1977) the World Health Organization advocated cooperation between health professionals and native specialists (including herbalists and midwives). As a consequence, many anthropologists have found work as cultural brokers, studying the cultural system of the client population and explaining this to the health professionals, while at the same time explaining the world of the psychiatrists to the folk healers and the client population.

As an example, as a part of the Miami Community Mental Health Program, a field team led by an anthropologist was set up to work with the Puerto Rican community of Dade County.* Like other ethnic communities in the area, this one was characterized by low incomes, high rents, and a plethora of health (including mental health) problems, yet health facilities and social service agencies were underutilized. Working in the community, the team successfully built up support networks among the Puerto Ricans, involving extended families, churches, clubs, and spiritists. At the same time, they gathered information about the community, which was provided to appropriate social service agencies. At the Dade County Hospital, team members acted as brokers between the psychiatric personnel and their Puerto Rican clients, and a training program was implemented for the mental health staff.

* See John Van Willigan, *Applied Anthropology* (South Hadley, Mass.: Bergin and Garvey, 1986), pp. 128–129 and 133–139.

Windigos. Individuals afflicted by the psychosis developed the delusion that falling under control of these monsters, they themselves were being transformed into Windigos, with a craving for human flesh. At the same time, they saw people around them turning into various edible animals—fat, juicy beavers, for instance. Although the victim of Windigo psychosis developed the exaggerated fear of actually eating another human being, there are no known instances where this was actually done, at least as the result of the psychosis alone. For this reason, some anthropologists have doubted the

existence of the psychosis; nevertheless, fear of cannibalism was real enough to the Indians.

At first, Windigo psychosis seems quite different from Western clinical cases of paranoid schizophrenia, but a closer look suggests otherwise; the disorder was merely being expressed in ways compatible with traditional northern Algonkian culture. Ideas of persecution, instead of being directed toward other humans, are directed toward supernatural beings (the Windigo monsters); cannibalistic panic replaces homosexual panic, and the like. The northern Algonkian Indian, like the Westerner,

Table 5.1   Patterns of Behavior Considered to Be Culture-Bound Disorders

Name of disorder	Culture	Description
Amok	Malaya (also observed in Java, Philippines, Africa, and Tierra del Fuego)	A disorder characterized by sudden, wild outbursts of homicidal aggression in which the afflicted person may kill or injure others. The rage disorder is usually found in males who are rather withdrawn, quiet, and inoffensive prior to the onset of the disorder. Stress, sleep deprivation, extreme heat, and alcohol are among the conditions thought to precipitate the disorder. Several stages have been observed: Typically in the first stage the person becomes more withdrawn; then a period of brooding follows in which a loss of reality contact is evident. Ideas of persecution and anger predominate. Finally, a phase of automatism, or *amok*, occurs, in which the person jumps up, yells, grabs a knife, and stabs people or objects within reach. Exhaustion and depression usually follow, with amnesia for the rage.
Anorexia nervosa	Western countries	A disorder occurring most frequently among young women in which a preoccupation with thinness produces a refusal to eat. This condition can result in death.
Latah	Malay	A fear reaction often occurring in middle-aged women of low intelligence who are subservient and self-effacing. The disorder is precipitated by the word *snake* or by tickling. It is characterized by *echolalia* (repetition of the words and sentences of others). The disturbed individual may also react with negativism and the compulsive use of obscene language.
Koro	Southeast Asia (particularly Malay Archipelago)	A fear reaction or anxiety state in which the person fears that his penis will withdraw into his abdomen and he will die. This reaction may appear after sexual overindulgence or excessive masturbation. The anxiety is typically very intense and of sudden onset. The condition is "treated" by having the penis held firmly by the patient or by family members or friends. Often the penis is clamped to a wooden box.
Windigo	Algonquian Indians of Canada and northern U.S.	A fear reaction in which a hunter becomes anxious and agitated, convinced that he is bewitched. Fears center around his being turned into a cannibal by the power of a monster with an insatiable craving for human flesh.
Kitsunetsuki	Japan	A disorder in which victims believe that they are possessed by foxes and are said to change their facial expressions to resemble foxes. Entire families are often possessed and banned by the community. This reaction occurs in rural areas of Japan where people are relatively uneducated.
Pibloktoq and other arctic hysterias	Circum-polar peoples from Lapland eastward across Siberia, northern Alaska and Canada to Greenland	A disorder brought on by fright, which is followed by a short period of bizarre behavior; victim may tear clothes off, jump in water or fire, roll in snow, try to walk on the ceiling, throw things and thrash about and "speak in tongues." Outburst followed by return to normal behavior.

Based on Robert C. Carson, James N. Butcher, and James C. Coleman, *Abnormal Psychology*, 8th ed. (Glenview, Illinois: Scott, Foresman, 1990, p. 85.

expresses his or her problem in terms compatible with the appropriate view of the self and its behavioral environment. The northern Algonkian, though, was removed from society, not by being committed to a mental institution, but by being killed.

Windigo behavior has seemed exotic and dramatic to the Westerner. When all is said and done, however, the imagery and symbolism that a psychotic person has to draw upon is that which his or her culture has to offer, and in northern Algonkian culture, these involve myths in which cannibal giants figure prominently. By contrast, the delusions of Irish schizophrenics draw upon the images and symbols of Irish Catholicism, and feature Virgin and Savior motifs. Anglo-Americans, on the other hand, tend toward secular or electromagnetic persecution delusions. The underlying structure of the mental disorder is the same in all cases, but its expression is culturally specific.

Of interest to anthropologists are the effects of child-care centers on maternal development. Among monkeys and apes, infants deprived of maternal attention and affection do not develop normally—if they survive at all. Among humans, persons who are not strangers to the child may substitute for the mother with no ill effects on the child's development. However, if child-care personnel are not recruited from the same neighborhood, and there is high turnover, children who spend eight to ten hours a day in such a center may become unable to form social bonds.

CURRENT TRENDS IN PSYCHOLOGICAL ANTHROPOLOGY

Although they may now be criticized for being impressionistic and not susceptible to replication, rather than scientific, the classic studies of Benedict, Mead, and other pioneers in the investigation of culture and personality remain important for their contribution to the realization that human behavior is relative. The concept of cultural relativity resulting from the study of many societies undermined the ethnocentrism common to all human groups. Anthropologists have established that cultures are indeed different and that these differences are associated with personality differences.

By 1960, however, there was a sense that a point of diminishing returns had been reached in the study of personality differences between cultures. Instead of looking at individual differences within cultures as annoying distortions of norms, many culture and personality specialists began to look more closely at these differences in order to understand better such behavior as the altered states of consciousness employed by religious practitioners in many of the world's societies. Others began to devote more attention to the study of cognitive processes—how people think and perceive the world in which they live. By observing how individual members of particular societies segment, interpret, and express reality through language, anthropologists should be able to draw general conclusions about the implicit mental representations of reality in the minds of these individuals— their cognitive "models" of the world around them. This, of course, continues an interest in the self and its behavioral environment, as discussed earlier in this chapter.

An interest in psychoanalytical theory has always characterized culture and personality studies, but current investigators are combining psychoanalytically based theories with biological and social variables to discover, analyze, and explain the laws of cultural dynamics. Thus, current studies are examining human genetic and ecological processes that are entirely independent of culture, but that cause change in the human biological system upon which culture depends.

Studies of child-rearing practices, a central concern of culture and personality studies from their earliest days, have burgeoned into a specialized field in their own right. Today cross-cultural studies of physiological maturation, interpersonal contacts, group composition, and the like are emphasized, often to test the theories developed in the other social and behavioral sciences. They have been broadened, however, to embrace the new subfield of educational anthropology. Similarly, the old interest in abnormal personality has given birth to numerous cross-cultural studies of mental health and illness, which are now part of the new specialty called medical anthropology.

In sum, the field of culture and personality has expanded and become a highly varied field. As a reflection of this, specialists began in the 1960s to refer to their field as psychological anthropology. This anthropological specialty is flourishing today, and we shall deal with some of its findings in later chapters of this book, as in our discussion of revitalization movements in Chapters 12 and 15.

Chapter Summary

Enculturation, the process by which culture is passed from one generation to the next, begins soon after birth. Its first agents are the members of an individual's household, but later, in some societies, this role is assumed by professionals. For enculturation to proceed, individuals must possess self-awareness, or the ability to perceive themselves as objects in time and space and to judge their own actions. A major facet of self-awareness is a positive view of the self, for it is this that motivates persons to act to their advantage rather than disadvantage.

Several requirements involving one's behavioral environment need to be met in order for emerging self-awareness to function. The individual first needs to learn about a world of objects other than self; this environment is perceived in terms compatible with the values of the culture into which one is born. Also required is a sense of both spatial and temporal orientation. Finally, the growing individual needs a normative orientation, or an understanding of the values, ideals, and standards that constitute the behavioral environment.

Personality is a product of enculturation and refers to the distinctive ways a person thinks, feels, and behaves. With the psychoanalysts, most anthropologists believe that adult personality is shaped by early childhood experiences. A prime goal of anthropologists has been to produce objective studies that test this theory. Cross-cultural studies of gender-related personality characteristics, for example, show that there are no absolute personality differences between men and women. Instead, a society's economy helps structure the way children

are brought up, which in turn influences their adult personalities.

Anthropologists John and Beatrice Whiting, and Irvin Child, on the basis of cross-cultural studies, have established the interrelation of personality, child-rearing practices, and other aspects of culture. One may speak, for example, of dependence training. Usually associated with traditional farming societies, it tries to ensure that members of society will willingly and routinely work for the benefit of the group, performing the jobs assigned to them. At the opposite extreme, independence training, typical of societies characterized by independent nuclear families, puts a premium on self-reliance and independent behavior. Although a society may emphasize one sort of behavior over the other, it may not emphasize it to the same degree in both sexes. Whiting and Child believe that child-rearing practices have their roots in a society's customs surrounding the meeting of the basic physical needs of its members; these practices, in turn, develop particular kinds of adult personalities.

Anthropologists have long worked on the problem of whether it is possible to delineate a group personality without falling into stereotyping. Each culture chooses, from the vast array of possibilities, those traits that it sees as normative or ideal. Individuals who conform to these traits are rewarded; the rest are not. The modal personality of a group is the personality typical of a culturally bounded population, as indicated by the central tendency of a defined frequency distribution. As a statistical concept, it opens up for investigation how societies organize the diverse personalities of their members, some of which conform more than others to the modal "type."

National character studies have focused on the modal characteristics of modern countries. They have then attempted to determine the child-rearing practices and education that shape such a personality. Investigators during World War II interviewed foreign-born nationals and analyzed other sources in an effort to depict national character. Many anthropologists believe that national character theories are based on unscientific and overgeneralized data. Others believe that new studies of national character, without the flaws of past studies, are needed, if we are really to understand what motivates the leaders and civil servants of modern states.

What defines normal behavior in any culture is determined by the culture itself, and morality is defined by culturally determined ideals. Abnormality involves developing a delusional system not accepted by the culture. Culturally induced conflicts not only can produce psychosis but can determine the form of the psychosis as well.

Current studies in psychological anthropology are combining traditional psychoanalytically based theories with biological and social factors to explain culture and cultural dynamics. Attention is also being given to cognitive processes of the mind, which are the basic mechanisms responsible for such cultural expression as language, myth, and art. At the same time, cross-cultural studies of child-rearing and mental health have become established as anthropological subfields in their own right.

Suggested Readings

Barnouw, Victor. *Culture and Personality*, 4th ed. Homewood, Ill.: Dorsey Press, 1985.
A recent revision of a well-respected text designed to introduce students to psychological anthropology.

Hunt, Robert C., ed. *Personalities and Cultures: Readings in Psychological Anthropology*. Garden City, N.Y.: Natural History Press, 1967.
The 18 articles included in this book focus on various aspects of culture and personality. Attention is given to psychological and sociocultural variables and the relationships between them.

Norbeck, Edward, Douglas Price Williams, and William McCord, eds. *The Study of Personality: An Interdisciplinary Appraisal*. New York: Holt, Rinehart and Winston, 1968.
The volume contains addresses given at Rice University in 1966. Its objective is to review and appraise knowledge and theories concerning personality in several scholarly fields (psychology, anthropology, sociology, philosophy of science, and so forth). It also discusses factors that influence the formation of personality, and the personalities of social and psychiatric deviates.

Wallace, Anthony F.C. *Culture and Personality*, 2nd ed. New York: Random House, 1970.
The logical and methodological foundations of culture and personality as a science form the basis of this book. The study is guided by the assumptions that anthropology should develop a scientific theory about culture, and that a theory pretending to explain or predict cultural phenomena must reckon with noncultural phenomena (such as personality) as well.

Whiting, John W.M., and I. Child. *Child Training and Personality: A Cross-cultural Study*. New Haven, Conn.: Yale University Press, 1953.
How culture is integrated though the medium of personality processes is the main concern of this study. It covers both the influence of culture on personality and personality on culture. It is oriented toward testing general hypotheses about human behavior in any and all societies, rather than toward a detailed analysis of a particular society.

CHAPTER

6

PATTERNS

OF

SUBSISTENCE

CHAPTER PREVIEW

A Chinese man tends to ducks raised for market. The basic business of culture is securing the survival of those who live by its rules, and so the study of subsistence activities is an important aspect of anthropological study.

WHAT IS ADAPTATION?

Adaptation refers to the process of interaction between changes an organism makes on its environment and changes the environment makes in the organism. This kind of two-way adjustment is necessary for the survival of all life forms, including human beings.

HOW DO HUMANS ADAPT?

Humans adapt through the medium of culture, as they develop ways of doing things that are compatible with the resources they have available to them and are within the limitations of the environment in which they live. In a particular region, people living in similar environments tend to borrow from one another customs that seem to work well in those environments. Once achieved, adaptations may be remarkably stable for long periods of time, even thousands of years.

WHAT SORTS OF ADAPTATIONS HAVE HUMANS ACHIEVED THROUGH THE AGES?

Food foraging is the oldest and most universal type of human adaptation. To it we owe such important elements of social organization as the sexual division of labor, food sharing, and a home base as the center of daily activity and where food sharing is accomplished. Quite different adaptations, involving farming and animal husbandry, began to develop in some parts of the world between 9,000 and 11,000 years ago. Horticulture—the cultivation of domestic plants by means of simple hand tools—made possible more permanent settlements and a reorganization of the division of labor. Under pastoralism—reliance on raising herds of domestic animals—nomadism continued, but new modes of interaction with other peoples were developed. Urbanism began to develop as early as 5,000 years ago in some places, as intensive agriculture produced sufficient food to support full-time specialists of various sorts. With this went a further transformation of the social fabric.

Several times today you will interrupt your activities to eat or drink. You may take this very much for granted, but if you went totally without food for as long as a day, you would begin to feel the symptoms of hunger: weakness, fatigue, headache. After a month of starvation, your body would probably never repair the damage. A mere week to ten days without water would be enough to kill you.

All living beings, and people are no exception, must satisfy certain basic needs in order to stay alive. Among these needs are food, water, and shelter. Humans may not live by bread alone, but nobody can live long without any bread at all; and no creature could long survive if its relations with its environment were random and chaotic. Living beings must have regular access to a supply of food and water and a reliable means of obtaining and using it. A lion might die if all its prey disappeared, if its teeth and claws grew soft, or if its digestive

A Tsembaga man tends an oven in which a pig, dedicated to the red spirits, is cooked. Such pig feasts help control the size of the pig population and ensure that people have access to high-quality protein in times of crisis.

Horticulture: Cultivation of crops using hand tools such as digging sticks or hoes.

---

system failed. Although people face these same sorts of problems, they have an overwhelming advantage over other creatures; people have culture. If our meat supply dwindles, we can turn to some vegetable, like the soybean, and process it to taste like meat. When our tools fail, we replace them or invent better ones. Even when our stomachs are incapable of digesting food, we can predigest food by boiling or pureeing. We are, however, subject to the same needs and pressures as all living creatures, and it is important to understand human behavior from this point of view. The crucial concept that underlies such a perspective is **adaptation**, that is, how humans manage to deal with the contingencies of daily life. Dealing with these contingencies is the basic business of all cultures.

ADAPTATION

The process of adaptation establishes a moving balance between the needs of a population and the potential of its environment. One illustration of this process can be seen in the case of the Tsembaga, Papua New Guinea highlanders who support themselves chiefly through **horticulture**—the cultivation of crops carried out with simple hand tools.[1] Although they also raise pigs, they eat them only under conditions of illness, injury, warfare, or celebration. At such times the pigs are sacrificed to ancestor spirits, and their flesh is ritually consumed by those people involved in the crisis. (This guarantees a supply of high-quality protein when it is most needed.)

In precolonial times the Tsembaga and their neighbors were bound together in a unique cycle of pig sacrifices that served to mark the end of

---

[1]Roy A. Rappaport, "Ritual Regulation of Environmental Relations among a New Guinea People," in *Environment and Cultural Behavior*, ed. Andrew P. Vayda (Garden City, N.Y.: Natural History Press, 1969), pp. 181–201.

hostilities between groups. Frequent hostilities were set off by a number of ecological pressures, in which pigs were a significant factor. Since very few pigs were normally slaughtered and their food requirements were great, they could very quickly literally eat a local group out of house and home. The need to expand food production in order to support the prestigious but hungry pigs put a strain on the land best suited for farming. Therefore, when one group had driven another off its land, hostilities ended, and the new residents celebrated their victory with a pig festival. Many pigs were slaughtered, and the pork was widely shared among allied groups. Even without hostilities, festivals were held whenever the pig population became unmanageable, every five to ten years, depending on the groups' success at farming. Thus the cycle of fighting and feasting kept the balance among humans, land, and animals.

The term *adaptation* also refers to the process of interaction between changes an organism makes in its environment and changes the environment makes in the organism. The spread of the gene for sickle-cell anemia is a case in point. Long ago, in the Old World tropics west of India, a genetic mutation appeared in human populations, causing the manufacture of red blood cells that take on a sickle shape under conditions of low oxygen pressure. Since persons who receive a gene for this trait from each parent usually develop severe anemia and die in childhood, selective pressure was exerted against the spread of this gene in the local gene pool.

Then slash-and-burn horticulture was introduced into this tropical region, creating a change in the natural environment by removal—through cutting (slashing) and burning—of the natural vegetative cover. This was conducive to the breeding of mosquitos that carry the parasite causing falciparum malaria. When transmitted to humans, the parasites live in the red blood cells and cause a disease that is always debilitating and very often fatal. Individuals who received the gene for the sickle-cell trait from only one parent, however, while receiving one "normal" gene from the other, turned out to have a specific natural defense against the parasite. The gene's presence caused only some of the cells to take on a sickle shape; when those cells circulated through the spleen, which routinely screens out all damaged or worn red blood cells, the infected cells and the parasites along with them were destroyed. Since these individuals were therefore resistant to malaria, they were favored by selection, and the sickling trait became more and more frequent in the population. Thus, while people changed their environment, their environment also changed them.

The case of sickle-cell anemia is a neat illustration of the relativity of any adaptation. In malarial areas, the gene responsible for this condition is adaptive for human populations, even though some individuals suffer as a result of its presence. In nonmalarial regions, however, it is positively maladaptive, for it confers no advantage at all on human populations living under such conditions, at the same time that some individuals die as a result of its presence.

THE UNIT OF ADAPTATION

The unit of adaptation includes both organisms and environment. Organisms exist as members of populations; populations, in turn, must have the flexibility to cope with variability and change within the environment. In biological terms, this means that different organisms within the population have somewhat differing genetic endowments. In cultural terms, it means that there is variation among individual skills, knowledge, and personalities. Organisms and environments form interacting systems. People might as easily be farmers as fisherfolk, but we do not expect to find farmers north of the Arctic Circle or people who fish for a living in the Sahara Desert.

We might consider the example of a group of lakeside fisherfolk. The people live off fish, which, in turn, live off smaller organisms. Those animals, in turn, consume green plants; plants liberate minerals from water and mud, and, with energy from sunlight, transform them into proteins and carbohydrates. Dead plant and animal matter is decomposed by bacteria, and chemicals are returned to the

▬▬▬▬ ▭▭▭ ▬▬▬▬

Ecosystem: A system, or a functioning whole, composed of both the physical environment and the organisms living within it.

▬▬▬▬ ▭▭▭ ▬▬▬▬

soil and water. Some energy escapes from this system in the form of heat. Evaporation and rainfall constantly recirculate the water. People add chemicals to the system in the form of their wastes, and, if they are judicious, they may help to regulate the balance of animals and plants.

Some anthropologists have borrowed the ecologists' concept of **ecosystem.** An ecosystem is composed of both the physical environment and the organisms living within it. The system is bound by the activities of the organisms, as well as by such physical processes as erosion and evaporation.

Human ecologists are generally concerned with detailed microstudies of particular human ecosystems; they emphasize that all aspects of human culture must be considered, not just the most obvious technological ones. The Tsembaga's attitude toward pigs and the cycle of sacrifices have important economic functions; we see them in this way, but the Tsembaga do not. They are motivated by their belief in the power and needs of their ancestral spirits. Although the pigs are consumed *by* the living, they are sacrificed *for* ancestors. Human ecosystems must often be interpreted in cultural terms.

EVOLUTIONARY ADAPTATION

Adaptation must also be understood from an historical point of view. In order for an organism to fit into an ecosystem, it must have the potential to adjust to or become a part of it. The Comanche, whose history began in the harsh, arid country of southern Idaho, provide a good example.[2] In their original home they subsisted on wild plants, small animals, and occasionally larger game. Their material equipment was simple and limited to what could be transported by their women. The size of

[2]Ernest Wallace and E. Adamson Hoebel, *The Comanches* (Norman: University of Oklahoma Press, 1952).

The Indian tribes of the North American plains, such as the Sioux, Crow, and Comanche, show a great deal of cultural similarity because they had to adapt to similar environmental conditions. *(For a map of American Indian culture areas, see Figure 6.1.)*

their groups was restricted, and what little social power could develop was in the hands of the shaman, who was a combination of medicine man and spiritual guide.

At some point in their nomadic history, the Comanche moved onto the Great Plains, where buffalo were abundant and the Indians' potential as hunters could be fully developed. As larger groups could be supported by the new food supply, the need arose for a more complex political organization. Hunting ability thus became a means to acquire political power.

Eventually the Comanche acquired horses and guns from whites, which greatly enhanced their hunting prowess, and the great hunting chiefs became powerful indeed. The Comanche became raiders to get horses, since they did not breed them for themselves, and their hunting chiefs evolved

Preadaptations: In culture, existing customs which, by chance, have potential for a new cultural adaptation.

into war chiefs. The once "poor" and peaceful hunter-gatherers of the Great Basin became wealthy and warlike, dominating the Southwest from the borders of New Spain (Mexico) in the south to those of New France (Louisiana) and the fledgling United States in the east and north. In moving from one environment to another, and in evolving from one way of life to a second, the Comanche made the most of their developing potentials, or cultural **preadaptations.**

Sometimes societies that have developed independently find similar solutions to similar problems. For example, another group that moved out onto the Great Plains and took up a form of Plains Indian culture, similar in many ways to that of the Comanche, were the Cheyenne. Yet their cultural background was quite different; formerly, they were settled farmers with social, political, and religious institutions quite unlike those of the Comanche back in their ancestral homeland. The development of similar cultural adaptations to similar environmental conditions by peoples whose ancestral cultures were quite different is called **convergent evolution.**

Somewhat similar to the phenomenon of convergent evolution is **parallel evolution,** the difference being that similar adaptations are achieved by peoples whose ancestral cultures were already somewhat similar. For example, the development of farming in southwest Asia and Mesoamerica took

Convergent evolution: In cultural evolution, the development of similar adaptations to similar environmental conditions by peoples whose ancestral cultures were quite different.

Parallel evolution: In cultural evolution, the development of similar adaptations to similar environmental conditions by peoples whose ancestral cultures were similar.

To say that a society is stable is not to say that it is unchanging. Shown here is a descendant of the western Abenaki, a people who maintained a stable way of life (in what is now Vermont, New Hampshire, and southern Quebec) for 5,000 years, even as they frequently incorporated new elements into their culture. Even today, 400 years after the Abenaki's first contact with Europeans, many of their traditions continue to be important to them.

place independently, as people in both places, whose ways of life were already similar, went on to become dependent on a narrow range of plant foods which themselves depended upon human intervention for their protection and reproductive success.

It is important to recognize that stability as well as change is involved in evolutionary adaptation, and that once a satisfactory adaptation is achieved, too much in the way of change may cause it to break down.

Thus, episodes of major change may be followed by long periods of relative stability. For example, by 3500 B.C., a way of life had evolved in northwestern New England and southern Quebec that was well attuned to the environmental conditions of the times.[3] Since those conditions remained more or less the same over the next 5,000 years or so, it is understandable that people's life ways remained so as well. This is not to say that change was entirely

[3]William A. Haviland and Marjory Power, *The Original Vermonters,* 2nd ed. (Hanover, N.H.: University Press of New England, in press).

absent, for it was not. ("Stable" does not mean static.) From time to time, people refined and enhanced their way of life, as when hunting methods were improved first by adoption of the spear thrower and later the bow and arrow; when cooking was improved by the substitution of pottery vessels for containers made from animal hide, wood, or bark; when transport was improved by the replacement of heavy and cumbersome dugouts by sturdy, yet lightweight birchbark canoes; or when people began to supplement the products of hunting, gathering, and fishing with limited cultivation of corn, beans, and squash. In spite of these changes, however, the native peoples of the region still basically retained the unique structure of their culture, and tended toward a balance with their resource base, well into the seventeenth century, when the culture began to adjust to pressures associated with the European settling of North America. Such long-term stability by no means implies stagnation, backwardness, or failure to progress; rather, it is indicative of success. Had this culture not effectively satisfied people's physical and psychological needs, it never would have endured as it did for thousands of years.

CULTURE AREAS

The aboriginal **culture area** of the Great Plains (Fig. 6.1) was a geographic region in which there existed a number of societies with similar ways of life. Thirty-one politically independent peoples (of which the aforementioned Cheyenne and Comanche were but two) faced a common environment, in which the buffalo was the most obvious and practical source of food as well as materials for clothing and shelter. Living close by each other, they were able to share new inventions and discoveries. They reached a common and shared adaptation to a particular ecological zone.

The Indians of the Great Plains were, at the time of contact with Europeans, invariably buffalo hunt-

Culture area: A geographic region in which a number of different societies follow similar patterns of life.

ers, dependent upon this animal for food, clothing, shelter, and bone tools. Each nation was organized into a number of warrior societies, and prestige came from hunting and fighting skills. Their camps were typically arranged in a distinctive circular pattern. Many religious rituals, such as the Sun Dance, were practiced throughout the plains region.

Sometimes geographic regions are not uniform in climate and topography, and so new discoveries do not always spread from one group to another. Moreover, within a culture area, there are variations between local environments, and these favor variations in adaptation. The Great Basin of the western United States—an area embracing the states of Nevada and Utah, with adjacent portions of California, Oregon, Wyoming, and Idaho—is a case in point.[4] The Great Basin Shoshone Indians were divided into a northern and a western group, both primarily nomadic hunters and gatherers. In the north, a relative abundance of game animals provided for the maintenance of larger populations, requiring a great deal of cooperation among local groups. The western Shoshone, on the other hand, were almost entirely dependent upon the gathering of wild plants for their subsistence, and as these varied considerably in their seasonal and local availability, the western Shoshone were forced to cover vast distances in search of food. Under such conditions, it was most efficient to travel in groups of but a few families, only occasionally coming together with other groups, and not always with the same ones.

The Shoshone were not the only inhabitants of the Great Basin. To the south lived the closely related Paiutes. They, too, were hunter-gatherers living under the same environmental conditions as the Shoshone, but the Paiute managed their food resources more actively by diverting small streams to irrigate wild crops. They did not plant and cultivate these, but they were able to secure higher yields than their northern neighbors. Hence, their populations were larger than those of the Shoshone, and they led a more settled existence.

To deal with variations within a given region, Julian Steward proposed the concept of **culture**

[4]Julian H. Steward, *Theory of Culture Change: The Methodology of Multilinear Evolution* (Urbana: University of Illinois Press, 1972).

Culture type: The view of a culture in terms of the relation of its particular technology to the environment exploited by that technology.

type, a culture considered in terms of a particular technology and its relationship with those environmental features that technology is equipped to deal with. The example of the Great Plains shows how technology helps decide just which environmental features will be useful. Those same prairies that once supported buffalo hunters now support grain

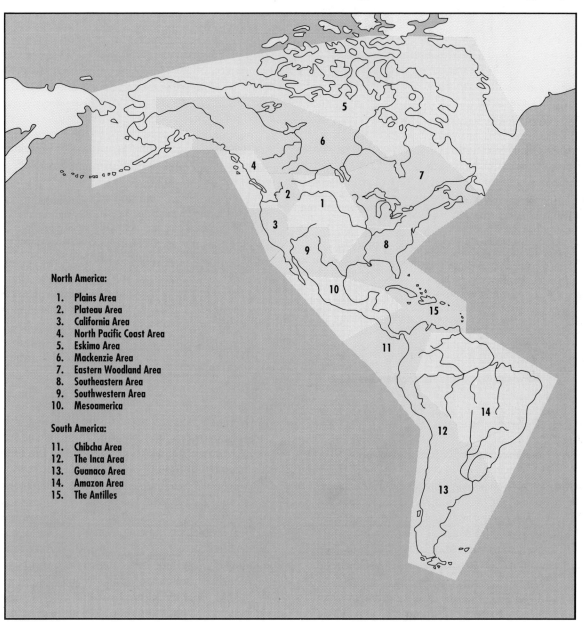

North America:

1. Plains Area
2. Plateau Area
3. California Area
4. North Pacific Coast Area
5. Eskimo Area
6. Mackenzie Area
7. Eastern Woodland Area
8. Southeastern Area
9. Southwestern Area
10. Mesoamerica

South America:

11. Chibcha Area
12. The Inca Area
13. Guanaco Area
14. Amazon Area
15. The Antilles

Figure 6.1 The culture-area concept was developed by North American anthropologists in the early part of the twentieth century. This map shows culture areas that have been defined for the Americas. Within each numbered area there is an overall similarity of native cultures, which is not as apparent when the native cultures of one area are compared with those of another.

JULIAN H. STEWARD

(1902–1972)

This North American developed an approach that he called **cultural ecology**—that is, the interaction of specific cultures with their environments. Initially, Steward was struck by a number of similarities in the development of urban civilizations in both Peru and Mesoamerica and noted that certain developments were paralleled in the urban civilizations of the Old World. He identified the constants and abstracted from them his laws of cultural development. Steward proposed three fundamental procedures for cultural ecology:

1. The interrelationship of a culture's technology and its environment must be analyzed. How effectively does the culture take advantage of available resources to provide food and housing for its members?
2. The pattern of behavior associated with a culture's technology must be analyzed.

How do members of the culture go about performing the work that is necessary for their survival?
3. The relationship between those behavior patterns and the rest of the cultural system must be determined. How does the work they do to survive affect the people's attitudes and outlooks? How is their survival behavior linked to their social activities and their personal relationships?

Cultural ecology: The study of the interaction of specific human cultures with their environment.

---

farmers. The Indians were prevented from farming the plains not for environmental reasons, nor for lack of knowledge about farming, since some of them, like the Cheyenne, had been farmers before they moved onto the plains. They did not farm because the buffalo herds provided abundant food without farming, and because farming would have been difficult without the steel-tipped plow that was needed to break up the compacted prairie sod. The farming potential of the Great Plains was simply not a relevant feature of the environment, given the available resources and technology before the coming of the Europeans.

CULTURE CORE

Environment and technology are not the only factors that determine a society's way of subsistence; social and political organization also affect the application of technology to the problem of staying alive. In order to understand the rise of irrigation agriculture in the great centers of ancient civilization, such as China, Mesopotamia, and Mesoamerica, it is important to note not only the technological and environmental factors that made possible the building of large-scale irrigation works but also the social and political organization needed to mobilize the many workers necessary to build and maintain the systems. One must examine the monarchies and priesthoods that organized the work and decided where the water would be used and how the agricultural products of this joint venture would be distributed.

━━━━━━━━━━━━━━━━━━

Culture core: The features of a culture that play a part in matters relating to the society's way of making a living.

Ethnoscientists: Anthropologists who seek to understand the principles behind folk ideologies and the way these ideologies help a people survive.

━━━━━━━━━━━━━━━━━━

Those features of a culture that play a part in the society's way of making its living are called its **culture core.** This includes the society's productive techniques and its knowledge of the resources available to it. It encompasses the patterns of labor involved in applying those techniques to the local environment. For example, do people work every day for a fixed number of hours, or is most work concentrated during certain times of the year? The culture core also includes other aspects of culture that bear on the production and distribution of food. An example of the way ideology can indirectly affect subsistence can be seen in a number of cultures where religion may lead to failure to utilize foods that are both locally available and nutritionally valuable. One reported example of this is the taboo that some Inuit of the Canadian Arctic follow, which forbids the hunting of seals in the summer. It has been said that if land game fails, a whole group will starve, even though seals are available to them.[5]

A number of anthropologists, known as **ethnoscientists,** are attempting to understand the principles behind folk ideologies and the way those principles usually help keep a people alive. The Tsembaga, for example, avoid certain low-lying, marshy areas, because they believe those areas are inhabited by red spirits who punish trespassers. Western science, by contrast, interprets those areas as the home of mosquitos, and the "punishment" as malaria. Whatever Westerners may think of the Tsembaga's belief in red spirits, it is a useful one; it keeps them away from marshy areas just as surely as does the recognition of malaria. If we want to understand why people in other cultures behave the way they do, we must understand their system of

thought from their point of view as well as our own. Not all such beliefs are as easy to translate into our terms as are those of the Tsembaga red spirits.

━━━━━━━━━━━━━━━━━━

THE FOOD-FORAGING WAY OF LIFE

At present, perhaps a quarter of a million people—less than 0.00005 percent of a world population of over five billion—support themselves chiefly through hunting, fishing, and the gathering of wild plant foods. Yet, before the domestication of plants and animals, which began a mere 10,000 years ago, all people supported themselves through some combination of plant gathering, hunting, and fishing. Of all the people who have *ever* lived, 90 percent have been food foragers, and it was as food foragers that we became truly human, acquiring the basic habits of dealing with one another and with the world around us that still guide the behavior of individuals, communities, and nations. Thus, if we would know who we are and how we came to be, if we would understand the relationship between environment and culture, and if we would comprehend the institutions of the food-producing societies that have arisen since the development of farming and animal husbandry, we should turn first to the oldest and most universal of fully human life-styles, the food-foraging adaptation. The beginnings of this we examined in Chapter 3.

When food foragers had the world to themselves some 10,000 years ago, they had their pick of the best environments. These have long since been appropriated by farming and, more recently, by industrial societies. Today, most food foragers are to be found only in the world's marginal areas—frozen Arctic tundra, deserts, and inaccessible forests. These habitats, although they may not support large or dense agricultural societies, provide a good living for food-foraging peoples.

Until recently it was assumed that a food-foraging life in these areas was difficult, and that one had to work hard just to stay alive. Behind this view lies the Western notion of progress, which is actually a culturally conditioned bias. This predisposes us to see what is new as generally preferable to what is old, and to read human history as a more or less steady climb up an evolutionary ladder of progress. Thus, if food foraging as a way of life is

[5]Annemarie deWaal Malefijt, *Religion and Culture: An Introduction to Anthropology of Religion* (London: Macmillan, 1969), pp. 326–327.

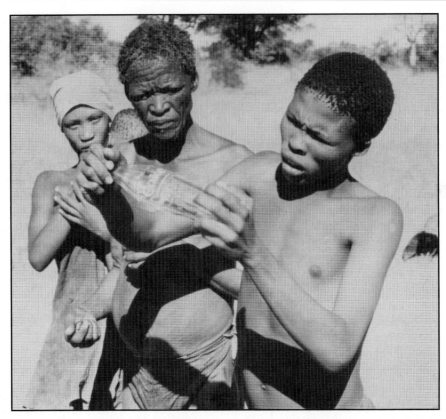

Scene from the comedic film *The Gods Must Be Crazy*. Such entertainments play off of the inaccurate stereotype of food-foraging peoples as "living fossils" out of a timeless, unchanging past.

much older than industrial civilization (which it is), the latter must be intrinsically better than the former. Hence, food-foraging societies are referred to as primitive, backward, or undeveloped, terms by which economists, politicians, and other members of industrial or would-be industrial societies express their disapproval. In reality, food-foraging societies are very highly developed, but in a way quite different from industrial societies.

Detailed studies have revealed that life in food-foraging societies is far from being "solitary, poor, nasty, brutish, and short," as the philosopher Thomas Hobbes asserted over 300 years ago. Rather, their diets are well-balanced and ample, and they are less likely to experience severe famine than are farmers. While their material comforts are limited, so are their desires. On the other hand, they have plenty of time in which to concentrate on family ties, social life, and spiritual development. The !Kung (the ! refers to a click—the tongue tip is pressed against the roof of the mouth and drawn

sharply away) of South Africa's Kalahari Desert—scarcely what one would call a lush environment—obtain a better than adequate diet in an average workweek of about 20 hours. If one adds in time spent making and repairing equipment, the total rises to just over 23 hours, while the equivalent of our "housework" adds another 19 hours. The total, just over 42 hours (44.5 for men, 40.1 for women), is still less than the time spent on the job, and on maintenance tasks and housework in North America today.[6] Their lives are rich in human warmth and aesthetic experience, displaying a balance of work and love, ritual, and play that many of us might envy. Small wonder that some anthropologists have gone so far as to label this "the original affluent society." The !Kung are not exceptional among food foragers today; one can only wonder about the level of affluence achieved by their ancient counter-

[6]Elizabeth Cashdan, "Hunters and Gatherers: Economic Behavior in Bands," in *Economic Anthropology*, ed. Stuart Plattner (Stanford, Calif.: Stanford University Press, 1989), pp. 23–24.

parts who lived in lusher environments with more secure and plentiful supplies of food.

All modern food foragers have had some degree of interaction with neighbors whose ways of life often differ radically from their own. The Mbuti of Zaire's Ituri rain forest (see the Original Study in Chapter 5), for example, live in a complex patron-client relationship with their neighbors, Bantu- and Sudanic-speaking peoples who are farmers. They exchange meat and other products of the forest for farm produce and manufactured goods. During part of the year, they live in their patron's village and are incorporated into his kin group, even to the point of allowing him to initiate their sons.

While some modern food foragers, like the Mbuti, have continued to maintain traditional ways, while adapting to neighbors and traders, various others have reverted to this way of life after giving up other modes of subsistence. Some, like the Cheyenne of the Great Plains, were once farmers, while others, like many of the !Kung of Southern Africa, were once pastoral nomads. Nor are such reversions things of the past. In the 1980s, when a world economic recession led to the abandonment of many sheep stations in the Australian outback, a number of aboriginal peoples returned to a food-foraging way of life, thereby emancipating them-

Members of industrialized societies are not immune to the lure of food foraging. Many find pleasure in occasionally foraging for wild foods, as the author is shown doing here—digging for clams. Some, such as commercial fishers, forage full time.

selves from a dependency on the government into which they had been forced.

An important point that emerges from the preceding discussion is this: People in the world today who subsist by hunting, fishing, and gathering wild plants are not necessarily following an ancient way of life because they don't know any better; they may be doing it through deliberate choice. In many cases, they find such satisfaction in living the way they do that they go to great lengths to avoid adopting other ways of life.

CHARACTERISTICS OF THE FOOD-FORAGING LIFE

Food foragers are, by definition, people who do not farm or practice animal husbandry. Hence, they must accommodate their places of residence to naturally available food sources. This being the case, it is no wonder that they move about a great deal. Such movement is not aimless wandering, but is done within a fixed territory or home range. Some, like the !Kung, who depend on the reliable and highly drought-resistant Mongongo nut, may keep to fairly fixed annual routes and cover only a restricted territory. Others, such as the Great Basin Shoshone, must cover a wider territory; their course is determined by the local availability of the erratically productive pine nut. A crucial factor in

Human groups (including food foragers) do not exist in isolation except occasionally, and even then not for long. The snowmobile this Alaskan native is using is indicative of his links with the wider world. In the past, Alaskan natives were regular participants in a trade network of such vast extent that Alaskan furs, walrus ivory, and hides were reaching Europe before people there had any inkling that the lands of the western hemisphere even existed.

Carrying capacity: The number of people who can be supported by the available resources at a given level of technology.

Density of social relations: Roughly, the number and intensity of interactions among the members of a camp or other residential unit.

---

this mobility is the availability of water. The distance between the food supply and water must not be so great that more energy is required to fetch water than can be obtained from the food.

Another characteristic of the food-foraging adaptation is the small size of local groups, which usually include fewer than 100 people. Although no completely satisfactory explanation of group size has yet been offered, it seems certain that both ecological and social factors are involved. Among those suggested are the **carrying capacity** of the land, the number of people who can be supported by the available resources at a given level of food-getting techniques, and the **density of social relations,** roughly the number and intensity of interactions between camp members. More people means a higher social density, which, in turn, means more opportunities for conflict.

Both carrying capacity and social density are complex variables. Carrying capacity involves not only the immediate presence of food and water but the tools and work necessary to secure them, as well as short- and long-term fluctuations in their availability. Social density involves not only the number of people and their interactions but also the circumstances and quality of those interactions and the mechanisms for regulating them. A mob of a hundred angry strangers has a different social density than the same number of neighbors enjoying themselves at a block party.

Among food-foraging populations, social density seems always to be in a state of flux, as people spend more or less time away from camp and as they move to other camps, either on visits or more permanently. Among the !Kung, for example, exhaustion of local food resources, conflict within the group, or the desire to visit friends or relatives living elsewhere, cause people to leave one group for another. As Richard Lee notes:

The !Kung love to go visiting, and the practice acts as a safety valve when tempers get frayed. In fact, the !Kung usually move, not when their food is exhausted, but rather when only their patience is exhausted.[7]

If a camp has so many children as to create a burden for the working adults, some young families may be encouraged to join others where there are fewer children. Conversely, groups with few children may actively recruit families with young children in order to ensure the group's survival. Redistribution of people, then, is an important mechanism for regulating social density, as well as for assuring that the size and composition of local groups is suited to local variations in resources. Thus, cultural adaptations serve to help transcend the limitations of the physical environment.

In addition to seasonal or local adjustments, long-term adjustments to resources must be made. Most food-foraging populations seem to stabilize in numbers well below the carrying capacity of their land. In fact, the home ranges of most food foragers can support from three to five times as many people as they typically do. In the long run, it may be more adaptive for a group to keep its numbers low, rather than to expand indefinitely and risk being cut down by a sudden and unexpected natural reduction in food resources. The population density of food-foraging groups rarely exceeds one person per square mile, a very low density; yet their resources could support greater numbers.

Just how food-foraging peoples regulate population size has come to be understood only recently. Typically, such peoples nurse their infants several times each hour over a period of as many as four or five years. The constant stimulation of the mother's nipple is known to suppress the level of hormones that promote ovulation, making conception unlikely, especially if their work happens to keep the mothers physically active, and they do not have large stores of body fat to draw on for energy.[8] By prolonging nursing over several years, women avoid giving birth except at widely spaced intervals, and the total number of offspring remains low.

[7]Richard Lee, *The Dobe !Kung: Foragers in a Changing World* (New York: Holt, Rinehart and Winston, 1984). p. 60.

[8]Peter T. Ellison, "Human Ovarian Function and Reproductive Ecology: New Hypotheses," *American Anthropologist* 92(1990), pp. 933–952.

THE IMPACT OF FOOD FORAGING ON HUMAN SOCIETY

Although much has been written on the theoretical importance of hunting in shaping the supposedly competitive and aggressive nature of the human species, most anthropologists are unconvinced by these arguments. The fact is that most known food-foraging peoples are remarkably unaggressive and place more emphasis on cooperation than they do on competition. It does seem likely, however, that three crucial elements of human social organization did develop along with food foraging. The first of these is the sexual division of labor. Some form of division of labor by sex, however modified, has been observed in all human societies, and is probably as old as human culture (see Chapter 3). There is some tendency in contemporary Western society to do away with such division, as we shall see in the next chapter. One may ask what the implications are for future cooperative relationships between men and women, a problem we will discuss further in Chapters 8 and 9.

SUBSISTENCE AND SEX ROLES

The hunting and butchering of large game as well as the processing of hard or tough raw materials are almost universally masculine occupations. Women's work, by contrast, usually consists of gathering and processing a variety of vegetal foods, as well as various other domestic chores. Historically, this pattern appears to have its origin in an earlier era, in which males, who were twice the size of females, got meat by scavenging from the carcasses of dead animals, butchered it with stone tools, and shared it with females (see Chapter 3). The latter, for their part, gathered wild plant foods, probably utilizing digging sticks and carrying devices made of soft, perishable materials. As the hunting of live animals replaced scavenging as a source of meat, and the biological differences between the sexes were reduced to minor proportions, the essence of the original division of labor was maintained nonetheless.

Among food foragers today, the work of women is no less arduous than that of men. !Kung women, for example, may walk as much as 12 miles a day two or three times a week to gather food, carrying not only their children, but on the return home, anywhere from 15 to 33 pounds of food. Still, they don't have to travel quite so far afield as do men on the hunt, nor is their work usually quite so dangerous. Finally, their tasks require less rapid mobility, do not require complete and undivided attention, and are readily resumed after interruption. All of this is compatible with those biological differences which do remain between the sexes. Certainly women who are pregnant, or have infants to nurse, cannot as easily travel long distances in pursuit of game as can men. In addition to wide-ranging mobility, the successful hunter must also be able to mobilize rapidly high bursts of energy. Although some women can certainly run faster than some men, it is a fact that in general men can run faster than women, even when the latter are not pregnant or encumbered with infants. Because human females must be able to give birth to infants with relatively large heads, their pelvic structure differs from that of human males to a greater degree than among most other species of mammals. As a consequence, the human female is not as well equipped as is the human male where rapid and prolonged mobility are required.

To say that differing sex roles among food foragers is compatible with the biological differences between men and women is *not* to say that it is biologically determined. Among the Indians of the Great Plains of North America, for example, there are numerous reported cases of women who gained fame as hunters and warriors, both regarded as men's activities. There is even one case of a Gros Ventre girl captured by the Crow who became one of their chiefs, so accomplished was she at what were considered to be masculine pursuits. Conversely, any young man for whom masculine pursuits seemed uncongenial, could assume the dress and demeanor of women, providing he had the necessary skills to achieve success in feminine activities. Although sexual preferences might enter into the decision to assume a feminine identity, not all such individuals were homosexuals, nor did all homosexuals assume a woman's role. Clearly, sexual preference was of lesser importance than occupation and appearance. In fact, the sexual division of labor is nowhere near as rigid among food foragers as it is in most other types of society. Thus, !Kung

Food foragers always have a division of labor in which women prepare food and men hunt, as shown here among the !Kung.

men willingly and without embarrassment, as the occasion demands, will gather wild plant foods, build huts and collect water, all clearly regarded as women's work.

The nature of women's work in food-foraging societies is such that it can be done while taking care of children. It can also be done in company with other women, which helps alleviate somewhat the monotony of the work. In the past, there was a tendency to underestimate the contribution made by the food-gathering activities of women to the survival of their group. Most modern food foragers obtain 60 to 70 percent of their diets from plant foods, with perhaps some fish and shellfish provided by women.

Although women in food-foraging societies may spend some time each day gathering plant food, men do not spend all or even the greatest part of their time in hunting. The amount of energy expended in hunting, especially in hot climates, is often greater than the energy return from the kill. Too much time spent at hunting might actually be counterproductive. Energy itself is derived primarily from plant carbohydrates, and it is the woman gatherer who brings in the bulk of the calories. A certain amount of meat in the diet, though, guarantees high-quality protein that is less easily obtained from plant sources, for meat contains exactly the right balance of all of the amino acids (the building blocks of protein), that are required by the human body. This is important, for the entire spectrum must be provided in the proper balance at the same meal, if their full value is to be realized, and the lack of just one prevents full utilization of the others. No one plant food does this by itself, and in order to get by without meat, one must hit on exactly the right combination of plants together to provide the essential amino acids in the right proportions.

FOOD SHARING

A second key feature of human social organization associated with food foraging is the sharing of food between adults, something that is very rare among nonhuman primates. It is easy enough to see why sharing takes place, with women supplying one kind of food and men another. Among the !Kung, women have control over the food that they collect, and can share it with whomever they choose. Men, by contrast, are constrained by rules which specify how much meat is to be distributed, and to whom. Thus, a hunter has little effective control over the meat he brings into camp. For the individual hunter, meat sharing is really a way of storing it for the future; his generosity, obligatory though it might be, gives him a claim on the future kills of other hunters. As a cultural trait, food sharing has the obvious survival value of distributing resources needed for subsistence.

Although carnivorous animals often share food, the few examples of food sharing among nonhuman primate adults all involve groups of male chimpanzees cooperating in a hunt and later sharing the spoils, frequently with adult females as well as juveniles. What this suggests is that the origins of food sharing and the division of labor are related to a shift in food habits from infrequent to more frequent meat eating. This seems to have occurred with the appearance of the earliest members of the genus *Homo* some 2.5 million years ago.

A final distinctive feature of the food-foraging economy is the importance of the camp as the center of daily activity and the place where food sharing actually occurs. Among nonhuman primates, activities tend to be divided between feeding areas and sleeping areas, and the latter tend to be shifted each evening. Food-foraging people, however, live in camps of some permanence, ranging from the dry-season camps of the !Kung that serve for the entire winter to the dry-season camps of the Hadza of Tanzania, oriented to the hunt and serving for several days or at most a week or two. Moreover, human camps are more than sleeping areas; people are in and out all day, eating, working, and socializing in camps to a greater extent than any other primates.

CULTURAL ADAPTATIONS AND MATERIAL TECHNOLOGY

The mobility of food-foraging groups may depend on the availability of water, as in the case of the !Kung; of pine nuts, as in the Shoshone example; or of game animals, as among the Hadza. Hunting styles and equipment may also play a role in determining population size and movement. Some Mbuti hunt with nets. This requires the cooperation of 7 to 30 families; consequently, their camps are relatively large. The camps of those Mbuti who hunt with bow and arrow number from three to six families. Too many archers in the same locale means that each must travel a great distance daily to keep out of another's way. Only during midsummer do the archers collect into larger camps for religious ceremonies, matrimonial arrangements, and social exchange. At this time the bowmen turn to communal hunts. Without nets they are less effective than their neighbors, and it is only when the net-hunters are widely dispersed in the pursuit of honey that the archers can come together.

EGALITARIAN SOCIETY

An important characteristic of the food-foraging society is its egalitarianism. Food foragers are usually highly mobile and, lacking animal or mechanical means of transportation, they must be able to travel without many encumbrances, especially on food-getting expeditions. Their material goods must be limited to the barest essentials, which include implements that serve for hunting, gathering, fishing, building, and making tools, cooking utensils, traps, and nets. There is little chance for the accumulation of luxuries or surplus goods, and the fact that no one owns significantly more than another helps to limit status differences. Age and sex are usually the only sources of important status differences in food-foraging societies.

It is important to realize that status differences by themselves do not imply any necessary inequality, a point that has all too often been misunderstood, especially where relations between men and women are concerned. In the following Original Study, anthropologist Eleanor Leacock argues that, in egalitarian societies, egalitarianism applies as much to women as to men.

Food foragers make no attempt to accumulate surplus foodstuffs, often an important source of status in agrarian societies. To say that they do not accumulate food surpluses, however, is not to say that they live constantly on the verge of starvation. Their environment is their storehouse, and, except in the coldest climates (where a surplus must be put by to see people through the lean season), or in

ORIGINAL STUDY

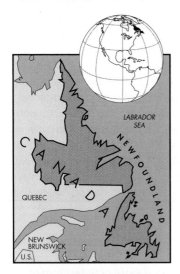

MEN AND WOMEN IN EGALITARIAN SOCIETIES[9]

With regard to the autonomy of women, nothing in the structure of egalitarian band societies necessitated special deference to men. There were no economic and social liabilities that bound women to be more sensitive to men's needs and feelings than vice versa. This was true even in hunting societies, where women did not furnish a major share of the food. The record of seventeenth century Montagnais-Naskapi life in *The Jesuit Relations* makes this clear. [The Montagnais and Naskapi live on the Labrador peninsula of Newfoundland and Quebec, Canada.] Disputes and quarrels among spouses were virtually nonexistent, Le Jeune reported, since each sex carried out its own activities without "meddling" in those of the other. Le Jeune deplored the fact that the Montagnais "imagine that they ought by right of birth, to enjoy the liberty of wild ass colts, rendering no homage to any one whomsoever." Noting that women had "great power," he expressed his disapproval of the fact that men had no apparent inclination to make their wives "obey" them or to enjoin sexual fidelity upon them. He lectured the Indians of this failing, reporting in one instance, "I told him then that he was the master, and that in France women do not rule their husbands." Le Jeune was also distressed by the sharp and ribald joking and teasing into which women entered along with the men. "Their language has the foul odor of the sewers," he wrote. The *Relations* reflect the program of the Jesuits to "civilize" the Indians, and during the course of the seventeenth century they attempted to introduce principles of formal authority, lectured the people about obeying newly elected tribal chiefs, and introduced disciplinary measures in the effort to enforce male authority upon women. No data are more illustrative of the distance between hierarchical and egalitarian forms of organization than the Jesuit account of these efforts.

Nonetheless, runs the argument for universal female subservience to men, the hunt and war, male domains, are associated with power and prestige to the disadvantage of women. What about this assumption?

Answers are at several levels. First, it is necessary to modify the exaggerations of male as hunter and warrior. Women did some individual hunting . . . and they participated in hunting drives that were often of great importance. Men did a lot of nonhunting. Warfare was minimal or nonexistent. The association of hunting, war, and masculine assertiveness is not found among hunter-gatherers except, in a limited way, in Australia. Instead, it characterizes horticultural societies in certain areas, notably Melanesia and the Amazon lowlands.

It is also necessary to reexamine the idea that these male activities were in the past more prestigious than the creation of new human beings. I am sympathetic to the skepticism with which women may view the argument that their gift of fertility was as highly valued as or more highly valued than anything men did. Women are too commonly told today to be content with the wondrous ability to give birth and with the presumed propensity for "motherhood" as defined in saccharine terms. They correctly read such exhortations as saying, "Do not fight for a change in status." However, the fact that childbearing is associated with women's present oppression does not mean this was the case in earlier social forms. To the extent that hunting and warring (or, more accurately, sporadic raiding, where it existed) were areas of male ritualization, they were just that: areas of male ritualization. To a greater or lesser extent women participated in the rituals, while to a greater or lesser extent they were also involved in ritual elaborations of generative power, either along with men or separately. To presume the greater importance of male than female participants, or to casually accept the statements to this effect of later-day male informants, is to miss the basic function of dichotomized sex-symbolism in egalitarian society. Dichotomization made it possible to ritualize the reciprocal roles of females and males that sustained the group. As ranking began to develop, it became a means of asserting male dominance, and with the full-scale development of classes, sex ideologies reinforced inequalities that were basic to exploitative structures.

Much is made of Australian aboriginal society in arguments for universal deference of women toward men. The data need ethnohistorical review, since the vast changes that have taken place in Australia over the last two centuries cannot be ignored in the consideration of ritual life and of male brutality toward women. Disease, outright genocidal practices, and expulsion from their lands reduced the population of native Australians to its lowest point in the 1930s, after which the cessation of direct genocide, the mission distribution of foods, and the control of infant mortality began to permit a population increase. The concomitant intensification of ceremonial life is described as follows by Godelier:

> This . . . phenomenon, of a politico-religious order, of course expresses the desire of these groups to reaffirm their cultural identity and to resist the destructive pressures of the process of domination and acculturation they are undergoing, which has robbed them of their land and subjected their ancient religious and political practices to erosion and systematic extirpation.

Thus ceremonial elaboration was oriented toward renewed ethnic identification, in the context of oppression. Furthermore, on the reserves, the economic autonomy of women vis-à-vis men was undercut by handouts to men defined as heads of families and by sporadic opportunities for wage labor open to men. To assume that recent ritual data reflect aboriginal Australian symbolic structures as if unchanged is to be guilty of freezing these people in some timeless "traditional culture" that does not change or develop, but only becomes lost; it is to rob them of their history. Even in their day [the nineteenth century], Spencer and Gillen noted the probable decline in women's ceremonial participation among the Arunta.

Allusions to male brutality toward women are common for Australia. Not all violence can be blamed on European colonialism, to be sure, yet it is crass ethnocentrism, if not outright racism, to assume that the grim brutality of Europeans toward the Australians they were literally seeking to exterminate was without profound effect. A common response to defeat is to turn hostility inward. The process is reversed when people acquire the political understanding and organizational strength to confront the source of their problems, as has recently been happening among Australian Aborigines.

References to women of recent times fighting back publicly in a spirited style, occasionally going after their husbands with both tongue and fighting club, and publicly haranguing both men and women bespeak a persisting tradition of autonomy. In relation to "those reciprocal rights and duties that are recognized to be inherent in marriage," Kaberry writes:

> I, personally, have seen too many women attack their husbands with a tomahawk or even their own boomerangs, to feel that they are invariably the victims of ill treatment. A man may perhaps try to beat his wife if she has not brought in sufficient food, but I never saw a wife stand by in submission to receive punishment for her culpable conduct. In the quarrel she might even strike the first blow, and if she were clearly in danger of being seriously hurt, then one of the bystanders might intervene, in fact always did within my experience.

Nor did the man's greater strength tell in such a struggle, for the wife "will pack up all her goods and chattels and move to the camp of a relative . . . till the loss of an economic partner . . . brings the man to his senses and he attempts a reconciliation." Kaberry concludes that the point to stress about this indispensability of a woman's economic contribution is "not only her great importance in economics, but also her power to utilize this to her own advantage in other spheres of marital life."

A further point also needs stressing: such quarrels are not, as they may first appear, structurally at the same level as similar quarrels in our own society. In our case, reciprocity in marital rights and duties is defined in terms of a social order in which subsistence is gained through paid wage labor, while women supply socially essential but unpaid services within a household. A dichotomy between "public" labor and "private" household service marks the household "slavery" of women. In all societies, women use the resources available to them to manipulate their situation to their advantage as best they can, but they are in a qualitatively different position, structurally, in our society from that in societies where what has been called the "household economy" is the *entire* economy. References to the autonomy of women when it comes to making decisions about their own lives are common for such societies. Concomitant autonomy of attitude is pointed out by Kaberry, again, for the Kimberly peoples: "The women, as far as I could judge from their attitudes," she writes, "remained regrettably profane in their attitude towards the men." To be sure, they much admired the younger men as they paraded in their ceremonial finery, but "the praise uttered was in terms that suggested that the spectators regarded the men as potential lovers, and not as individuals near unto gods." In summary, Kaberry argues that "there can be no question of identifying the sacred inheritance of the tribe only with the men's ceremonies. Those of the women belong to it also." As for concepts of "pollution," she says, "the women with regard to the men's rituals are profane and uninitiated; the men with regard to the women's ritual are profane and uninitiated."

The record on women's autonomy and lack of special deference among the seventeenth-century Montagnais-Naskapi is unambiguous. Yet this was a society in which the hunt was overwhelmingly important. Women manufactured clothing and other necessities, but furnished much less food than was the usual case with hunter-gatherers. In the seventeenth century, women as well as men were shamans, although this is apparently no longer remembered. As powerful shamans, they might exhort men to battle. Men held certain feasts to do with hunting from which women were excluded. Similarly, men were excluded from women's feasts about which we know nothing but that they were held. When man needed more than public teasing to ensure his good conduct, or in times of crisis, women held their own councils. In relation to warfare, anything but dominance-deference behavior is indicated. In historic times, raids were carried on against the Iroquois, who were expanding their territories in search of furs. The fury with which women would enjoin men to do battle and the hideous and protracted intricacies of the torture of captives in which they took the initiative boggle the mind. Getting back at the Iroquois for killing their menfolk was central, however, not "hailing the conquering hero."

[9]Eleanor Burke Leacock, "Women's Status in Egalitarian Society: Implications for Social Evolution," in *Myths of Male Dominance: Collected Articles on Women Cross Culturally* (New York: Monthly Review Press, 1981) pp. 140–145. Copyright © 1981 by Eleanor Leacock.

---

times of acute ecological disaster, there is always some food to be found in a group's territory. Because food resources are typically distributed equally throughout the group (share and share alike is the order of the day), no one achieves the wealth or status that hoarding might bring. In such a society, wealth is a sign of deviance rather than a desirable characteristic.

The food forager's concept of territory contributes as much to social equality as it does to the equal distribution of resources. Most groups have home ranges, which they utilize and within which access to resources is open to all members: What is available to one is available to all. If a Mbuti hunter discovers a honey tree, he has first rights; but when he has taken his share, others have a turn. In the

unlikely possibility that he does not take advantage of his discovery, others will. No one owns the tree; the system is first come, first served. Therefore, knowledge of the existence of food resources circulates quickly throughout the entire group.

Families move easily from one group to another, settling in any group where they have a previous kinship tie. The composition of groups is always shifting. This loose attitude toward group membership promotes the widest access to resources and, at the same time, is a device that maintains a balance between populations and resources.

The food forager pattern of generalized exchange, or sharing without any expectation of a direct return, also serves the ends of resource distribution and social equality. A !Kung man or woman spends as much as two-thirds of his or her day visiting others or receiving guests; during this time, many exchanges of gifts take place. To refuse to share—to hoard—would be morally wrong. By sharing whatever is at hand, the !Kung achieve social leveling and assure their right to share in the windfalls of others.

FOOD-PRODUCING SOCIETY

As we saw in Chapter 3, it was toolmaking that allowed humans to become meat eaters as well as consumers of plant foods. The next truly momentous event in human history was the domestication of plants and animals (Fig. 6.2). The transition from food forager to food producer (the available evidence suggests this change began 9,000 to 11,000 years ago) has been termed revolutionary. By changing the way they provided for their subsistence, people changed the very nature of human society itself.

Just why this change came about is one of the important questions in anthropology; since food production by and large requires more work than food foraging, is more monotonous, is often a less secure means of subsistence, and requires people to eat more of the foods that food foragers eat only when they have no other choice, it can be assumed that people probably did not become food producers through choice. Initially, it appears that food production came about as a largely unintended by-product of existing food-management practices which, by chance, promoted the development of new varieties of particular plants and animals. Subsequently, many populations adopted farming out of necessity in situations where population growth outstripped peoples' ability to sustain themselves through food foraging. For them, food production became a subsistence option of last resort.

THE SETTLED LIFE OF FARMERS

Whatever the causes, one of the most significant correlates of this new way of life was the development of permanent settlements, in which families of farmers lived together. The task of food production lent itself to a different kind of social organization; the hard work of some members of the group

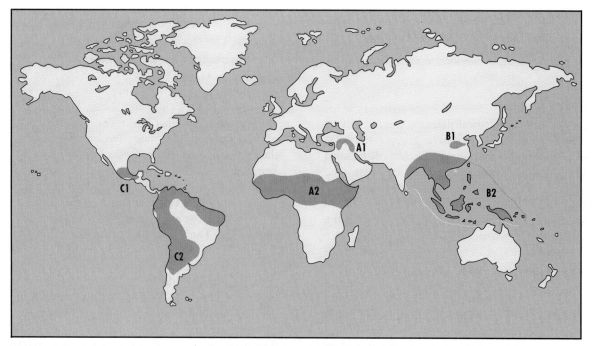

Figure 6.2   Areas of early plant and animal domestication: A1, Southwest Asia; A2, Central Africa; B1, China; B2, Southeast Asia; C1, Mesoamerica; C2, South America; C3, eastern North America.

While it supports larger and more sedentary populations than food foraging, farming generally requires longer and more monotonous work.

could provide food for all, thus freeing certain people to devote their time to inventing and manufacturing the equipment needed for a new way of life. Harvesting and digging tools, pottery for storage and cooking, clothing made of woven textiles, and housing made of stone, wood, or sun-dried bricks were some of the results of this combination of new living conditions and altered division of labor.

The transition also brought important changes in social structure. At first, social relations were egalitarian and hardly different from those that prevailed among food foragers. As settlements grew, however, and large numbers of people began to share the same important resources, such as land and water, society became more elaborately structured. Multi-family kinship groups such as lineages, which do not commonly play a large part in the social order of food foragers, were probably the organizing units; as will be discussed in Chapter 10, they provide a convenient way to handle the problems of land use and ownership that arise in food-producing societies.

Humans adapted to this new settled life in a number of ways. For example, some societies became horticultural—small communities of gardeners working with simple hand tools and using neither irrigation nor the plow. Horticulturists typically cultivate several varieties of crops together in small gardens they have cleared by hand. Production is for subsistence, rather than to produce a surplus for sale; however, the politics of horticultural communities commonly involve periodic feasts, in the course of which substantial amounts of produce and other gifts are given away in order to gain prestige. Such prestige is the basis for the political power of leaders, who play important roles in production, exchange, and resource allocation.

Technologically more complex than the horticulturists are intensive agriculturalists, whose practices usually result in far more modification of the landscape and ecology than do those of horticulturalists. Employed are such techniques as irrigation, fertilizers, and the wooden or metal plow pulled by harnessed draft animals, or in the developed countries of the world, tractors, to produce food on larger plots of land. Such farmers are able to grow sufficient food to provide not just for their own needs, but for those of full-time specialists of various sorts as well. This surplus may be sold for cash, or it may be coerced out of the farmers through taxes, or rent paid to owners of the land. These landowners and other specialists typically reside in substantial towns or cities, where political power is centralized, in the hands of a socially elite class of people. The distinction between horticulturalist and agriculturalist is not always an easy one to make. For example, the Hopi Indians of the North American Southwest traditionally employed irrigation in their farming, while at the same time using simple hand tools. Moreover, they produced for their own immediate needs, and lived in towns without centralized political government.

As food producers, people have developed several major crop complexes: two adapted to seasonal uplands and two to tropical wetlands. In the dry uplands of southwest Asia, for example, they time their agricultural activities with the rhythm of the changing seasons, cultivating wheat, barley, flax, rye, and millet. In the tropical wetlands of southeast Asia, rice and tubers such as yams and taro are cultivated. In the Americas, people have adapted to environments similar to those of the Old World, but have cultivated different plants. Maize, beans, squash, and the potato are typically grown in drier areas, whereas manioc is extensively grown in the tropical wetlands.

HORTICULTURE: THE GURURUMBA

A good example of a horticultural society that has adapted to its environment successfully are the Gururumba, a people numbering about 1,121 who live in six villages spread over 30 square miles in the Upper Asaro valley of New Guinea. Because of the elevation, the climate is cool and damp, and the area receives about 100 inches of rain a year.[10]

Each Gururumba village has a number of gardens separated by fences; several small families may have plots inside each fenced area. Every adult is involved in food production, with a strict division of labor according to sex. Men plant and tend sugarcane, bananas, taro, and yams, while women cultivate sweet potatoes and a variety of green vegetables. A family's social prestige is partially based on the neatness and productivity of its garden. Crops are rotated, but fertilizers are not used. Each gardener maintains more than one plot and uses different soils and different ecological zones for different crops; thus, the gardens are

ready for harvesting at different times of the year, assuring a constant food supply. (Another technologically simple cultivating technique commonly used by horticultural societies, but not the Gururumba, is the slash-and-burn method, in which trees are cut, allowed to dry for several months, then set afire. The ashes provide nutrients for the soil, which is then seeded and cultivated.) Since rainfall is plentiful, the Gururumba do not irrigate their gardens, and although some plots are planted on slopes with angles of 45 degrees, terracing is not practiced. Simple hand tools, such as digging sticks made of wood or ground stone, are used by the men to break the soil.

Like many such societies in New Guinea and Melanesia (the islands nearby), Gururumba society is knit together through a complex system of gift exchange, in which men lavish gifts on one another and so accumulate a host of debtors. The more a man gives away, the more is owed him, and hence the more prestige he has. For this reason every man keeps two gardens, one with crops to fulfill his everyday needs and one with "prestige" crops for his exchange needs. Although the crops planted in the latter gardens are not special, particular care is given to this garden to assure crops of the finest quality. A man anticipates a major occasion when he will have to give a feast, such as a daughter's wedding or a son's initiation, by planting his prestige garden a year in advance.

The second major feature of the Gururumba subsistence pattern, also common throughout this culture area, is the keeping of pigs. Pigs are raised not primarily for food but as gift-exchange items to raise social prestige. Every five to seven years, a huge pig feast, called an *idzi namo* ("pig flute") is held. Hundreds of pigs are killed, cooked, and distributed, simultaneously abolishing old obligations and creating new ones for the clan that gives the feast. As was the case among the Tsembaga whom we met earlier in this chapter, the pig feast helps the Gururumba get rid of a pig population that has grown too large to continue feeding; it also provides occasional animal protein in their diet.

---

[10]Most of the following information is taken from Philip L. Newman, *Knowing the Gururumba* (New York: Holt, Rinehart and Winston, 1965).

PASTORALISM: THE BAKHTIARI

One of the more striking examples of human adaptation to the environment is the **pastoralist,** who lives in societies in which animal husbandry is viewed as the ideal way of making a living and in which movement of all or part of the society is considered a normal and natural part of life. This cultural aspect is vitally important, for while economic analysis of some groups may show that they earn more from nonpastoral sources, the concept of nomadic pastoralism remains central to their own identities. These societies are built around a pastoral economic specialization, but imbued with values far beyond just doing a job. This distinguishes them from American ranchers, who likewise have a pas-

---

Pastoralist: Member of a society in which animal husbandry is regarded as the ideal way of making a living, and in which movement of all or part of the society is considered a normal and natural way of life.

This garden in Papua New Guinea is being worked by a woman with her child.

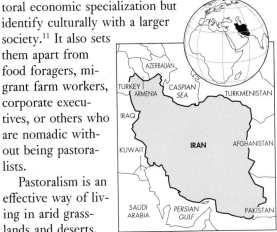

toral economic specialization but identify culturally with a larger society.[11] It also sets them apart from food foragers, migrant farm workers, corporate executives, or others who are nomadic without being pastoralists.

Pastoralism is an effective way of living in arid grasslands and deserts, such as those that stretch eastward from the dry country of North Africa through the Arabian Desert, across the plateau of Iran and into Turkestan and Mongolia. One group of people living in this belt of arid lands is the Bakhtiari, a fiercely independent people who live in the south Zagros mountains of western Iran, where they tend herds of goats and fat-tailed sheep.[12] Although some of the Bakhtiari own horses and most own donkeys, these are used only for transport; the animals around which these people's life revolves are the sheep and goat.

The harsh, bleak environment dominates the lives of these people: It determines when and where they move their flocks, the clothes they wear, the food they eat, and even their dispositions—they have been called "mountain bears" by Iranian townspeople. In the Zagros are ridges that reach altitudes of 12,000 to 14,000 feet. Their steep, rocky trails and escarpments challenge the hardiest and ablest climbers; jagged peaks, deep chasms, and watercourses with thunderous torrents also make living and traveling hazardous.

The pastoral life of the Bakhtiari revolves around two seasonal migrations to find better grazing lands for the flocks. Twice yearly the people move: in the fall, from their *sardsir,* or

[11]Thomas J. Barfield, "Introduction," *Cultural Survival Quarterly,* 8(Spring 1984):2.

[12]Material on the Bakhtiari is drawn mainly from Frederik Barth, "Nomadism in the Mountain and Plateau Areas of South West Asia," *The Problems of the Arid Zone* (UNESCO, 1960), pp. 341–355; from Carleton S. Coon, *Caravan: The Story of the Middle East,* 2nd ed. (New York: Holt, Rinehart and Winston, 1958), Chap. 13; and from Philip C. Salzman, "Political Organization among Nomadic Peoples," *Proceedings of the American Philosophical Society,* 111 (1967):115–131.

Pastoral nomads with their camels on the move in one of their seasonal migrations.

summer quarters in the mountains, and in the spring, from their *garmsir*, or winter quarters in the lowlands. In the fall, before the harsh winter comes to the mountains, the nomads load their tents and other belongings on donkeys and drive their flocks down to the warm plains that border Iraq in the west; grazing land here is excellent and well watered in the winter. In the spring, when the low-lying pastures dry up, the Bakhtiari return to the mountain valleys, where a new crop of grass is sprouting. For this trek, they split into five groups, each containing about 5,000 individuals and 50,000 animals.

The return trip north is the more dangerous because the mountain snows are melting and the gorges are full of turbulent, ice-cold water rushing down from the mountain peaks. This long trek is further impeded by the kids that are born in the spring, just before migration. Where the water courses are not very deep, the nomads ford them. Deeper channels, including one river that is a half-mile wide, are crossed with the help of inflatable goatskin rafts, on which are placed infants, the elderly and infirm, and lambs and kids; the rafts are then pushed by the men swimming alongside in the icy water. If they work from dawn to dusk, the nomads can get all of the people and animals across the river in five days. Not surprisingly, dozens of sheep are drowned each day at the river crossing.

In the mountain passes, where a biting wind numbs the skin and brings tears to the eyes, the Bakhtiari must make their way through slippery unmelted snow. Climbing the steep escarpments is dangerous, and the stronger men must often carry their own children and the newborn kids on their shoulders as they make their way over the ice and snow to the lush mountain valley that is their goal. During each migration the people may cover as many as 200 miles, and the trek can take weeks, because the flocks travel slowly and require constant attention. The nomads have fixed routes and a somewhat definite itinerary; generally, they know where they should be and when they should be there. On the drive the men and boys herd the sheep and goats, while the women and children ride the donkeys along with the tents and other equipment.

When they reach their destination, the Bakhtiari live in black tents of goat's-hair cloth woven by the women. The tents have sloping tops and vertical sides, held up by wooden poles. Inside, the furnishings are sparse. Rugs woven by the women or heavy felt pads cover the floor. Against one side of the tent are blankets; containers made of goatskin, copper utensils, clay jugs, and bags of grain line the opposite side. Bakhtiari tents provide an excellent example of adaptation to a changing environment. The goat's-hair cloth retains heat and repels water during the winter and keeps out heat during the summer. These portable homes are very easy to erect, take down, and transport.

Sheep and goats are central to Bakhtiari subsistence. The animals provide milk, cheese, butter, meat, hides, and wool, which is woven into clothes, tents, storage bags, and other essentials by the women or sold in towns. The people also engage in very limited horticulture; they own lands that contain orchards, and the fruit is consumed by the nomads or sold to townspeople. The division of labor is according to sex. The men, who take great pride in their marksmanship and horsemanship, engage in a limited amount of hunting on horseback, but their chief task is the tending of the flocks. The women cook, sew, weave, care for the children, and carry fuel and water.

The Bakhtiari have their own system of justice, including laws and a penal code. They are governed by tribal leaders, or *khans*, who are elected or inherit their office. Most of the *khans* grew wealthy when oil was discovered in their homeland around the start of the twentieth century, and many of them are well educated, having attended Iranian or foreign universities. Despite this, and although some of them own houses in cities, the *khans* spend much of their lives among their people.

INTENSIVE AGRICULTURE AND NONINDUSTRIAL CITIES

With the intensification of agriculture, some farming communities grew into cities (Fig. 6.3), in which individuals who had previously been engaged in agriculture were freed to specialize in other activities. Thus, such craftspeople as carpenters, blacksmiths, sculptors, basketmakers, and stonecutters contribute to the vibrant, diversified life of the city.

Unlike horticulturalists and pastoralists, city dwellers are only indirectly concerned with adapting to their natural environment. Far more important is the need to adapt to living and getting along with their fellow urbanites. To an important degree, this is true as well for the farmers who provide the city dwellers with their food. Under the political control of an urban elite, much of what

they do is governed by economic forces over which they have little, if any, control. Urbanization brings with it a new social order; marked inequality develops as society becomes stratified and people are ranked according to the kind of work they do, or the family they are born into. As social institutions cease to operate in simple, face-to-face groups of relatives, friends, and acquaintances, they become more formal and bureaucratic, with specialized political institutions.

With urbanization came a sharp increase in the tempo of human cultural evolution. Writing was invented, trade intensified and expanded, the wheel and the sail were invented, and metallurgy and other crafts were developed. In many early cities, monumental buildings, such as royal palaces and temples, were built by thousands of men, often slaves taken in war; these feats of engineering still amaze modern architects and engineers. The inhabitants of these buildings—the ruling class composed of nobles and priests—formed a central government that dictated social and religious rules; in turn, the rules were carried out by the merchants, soldiers, artisans, farmers, and other citizens.

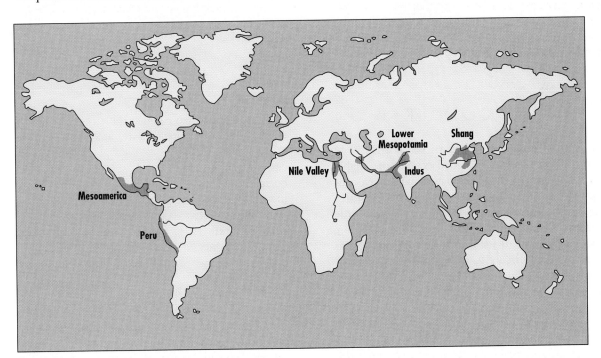

Figure 6.3 Locations of major early civilizations. Those of North and South America developed wholly independently of those in Africa and Asia. Chinese civilization may well have developed independently of southwest Asian (including the Nile and Indus) civilization.

One form of intensive agriculture, the *chinampa*, was perfected in ancient Mexico. This is a modern *chinampa* garden on the Gulf Coast of Mexico.

AZTEC CITY LIFE

The Aztec empire, which flourished in Mexico in the sixteenth century, is a good example of a highly developed urban society among non-Western peoples.[13] The capital city of the empire, Tenochtitlán (modern-day Mexico City), was located in a fertile valley 7,000 feet above sea level. Its population, along with that of its sister city, Tlatelolco, was about 200,000 in 1519, when Cortes first saw it. This makes it five times more populous than the city of London at the same time. The Aztec metropolis sat on an island in the middle of a salt lake, which has since dried up, and two aqueducts brought in fresh water from springs on the mainland. A 10-mile dike rimmed the eastern end of the city to ward off floodwaters originating in the neighboring lakes during the rainy season.

As in the early cities of southwest Asia, the foundation of Aztec society was agriculture. Corn was the chief crop. Each family, allotted a plot of land by its lineage, cultivated any of a number of crops, including beans, squash, gourds, peppers, tomatoes, cotton, and tobacco. Unlike Old World societies, however, only a few animals were domesticated; these included dogs

[13]Most of the following information is taken from Frances F. Berdan, *The Aztecs of Central Mexico* (New York: Holt, Rinehart and Winston, 1982).

ANTHROPOLOGY APPLIED

ECONOMIC DEVELOPMENT IN TROPICAL FORESTS

Prime targets for development in the world today, in the eyes of governments and private corporations alike, are vast tracts of tropical forests. On a global basis, forests are being rapidly cleared for lumber and fuel, as well as to make way for farms, ranches, mines, and other forms of economic development. The world's largest uninterrupted tracts are the forests of the Amazon and Orinoco of South America, which are being destroyed at the rate of about four percent a year. Just what the rate is for the world no one is quite sure, but it is clearly accelerating. And already there are signs of trouble, as extensive tracts of once-lush growth have been converted to semi-desert. What happens is that essential nutrients are lost, either through erosion (which increases by several orders of magnitude under deforestation), or by leaching (percolating) too deeply, as soils are exposed to the direct force of the heavy tropical rains.

The problem is that developers, until recently, have lacked reliable models by which the long-term impact of their actions might be assessed. Such a model now exists, thanks to the efforts of archaeologists unraveling the mystery of how the ancient Maya of Central America, in a tropical rain-forest setting, carried out large-scale urban construction and sustained huge numbers of people successfully for two millennia. The key to the Maya success was their implementation of sophisticated prac-

tices to reduce regionwide processes of nutrient loss, deterioration of soil structure, destabilization of water flows, soil erosion, and loss of productive components of their environment.* These included construction of terraces, canals, and raised fields, the fertility of which was maintained through mulching with water plants and the addition of organic wastes. Coupled with this, crops were planted in such a way as to produce complex patterns of foliage distribution, canopy heights, and nutrient demands. Far different from "modern" monocrop agriculture, this reduced the impact on the soils of intensive farming, while making maximum use of nutrients and enhancing their cycling in the system.

In Mexico, where population growth has threatened the country's ability to provide sufficient food for its people, archaeologists and agriculturists are already cooperating to apply our knowledge of ancient Maya techniques to the problems of modern food production in the tropics. Application of these techniques in other tropical forested countries, such as Brazil, could do much to alleviate food shortages, without the environmental degradation caused by more conventional methods of development.

*Don S. Rice and Prudence M. Rice, "Lessons from the Maya" *Latin American Research Review*, 1984, 19(3):24–28.

and turkeys (both for eating). Many of the plots in which crops were grown around Tenochtitlán were actually constructed artificially in the shallow waters of the surrounding lake. Canals between these *chinampas* not only facilitated transport, but were also a source of water plants used for heavy mulching. In addition, muck rich in fish feces was periodically dredged from the canals and spread over the gardens to maintain their fertility. Even today, *chinampas* can be found at Xochimilco, a few miles outside Mexico City.

Aztec agricultural success provided for an increasingly large population and the diversification of labor. Skilled artisans, such as sculptors, silversmiths, stoneworkers, potters, weavers, feather workers, and painters were able to make good

livings by pursuing these crafts exclusively. Since religion was central to the operation of the Aztec social order, these craftspeople were continuously engaged in the manufacture of religious artifacts, clothing, and decorations for buildings and temples. Other nonagricultural specialists included some of the warriors, the traveling merchants, or *pochteca*, the priests, and the government bureaucracy of nobles.

As specialization increased, both among individuals and cities of the Aztec empire, the market became an extremely important economic and social institution. In addition to the daily markets in each city, there were larger markets in the various cities held at different times of year. Buyers and sellers traveled to these from the far reaches of the

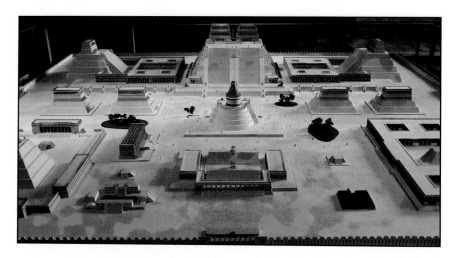

Model of the center of Tenochtitlán, the Aztec capital city.

empire. The market at Tlatelolco, Tenochtitlán's sister city, was so huge that the Spanish compared it to those of Rome and Constantinople. At the Aztec markets, barter was the primary means of exchange. At times, however, cacao beans, gold dust, crescent-shaped knives, and copper were used as a kind of currency. In addition to its obvious economic use, the market served social functions: people went there not only to buy or to sell but to meet other people and to hear the latest news. A law actually required that each person go to market at least once within a specified number of days; this ensured that the citizenry was kept informed of all important news. The other major economic institution, trade networks between the Aztec capital and other cities, brought goods such as chocolate, vanilla beans, and pineapples into Tenochtitlán.

The Aztec social order was stratified into three main classes: nobles, commoners, and serfs. The nobles operated outside the lineage system on the basis of land and serfs allotted them by the ruler, from conquered peoples. The commoners were divided into lineages, on which they were dependent for land. Within each of these, individual status depended on the degree of descent from the founder: those more closely related to the lineage founder had higher status than those whose kinship was more distant. The third class in Aztec society consisted of serfs bound to the land and porters employed as carriers by merchants. Lowest of this class were the slaves. Some had voluntarily sold themselves into bondage; others were captives taken in war.

The Aztecs were governed by a semidivine king, who was chosen by a council of nobles, priests, and leaders from among candidates of royal lineage. Although the king was an absolute monarch, the councilors advised him on affairs of state. A vast number of government officials oversaw various functions, such as the maintenance of the tax system, the courts of justice, management of government storehouses, and control of military training.

The typical Aztec city was rectangular and reflected the way the land was divided among the lineages. In the center was a large plaza containing the temple and the house of the city's ruler. At Tenochtitlán, with a total area of about 20 square miles, a huge temple and two lavish palaces stood in the central plaza, also called the Sacred Precinct. Surrounding this area were other ceremonial buildings belonging to each lineage.

As in a modern city, housing in Tenochtitlán ranged from squalid to magnificent. On the outskirts of the city, on *chinampas*, were the farmers' hovels, huts of thatched straw and wattle smeared with mud. In the city proper were the houses of the middle class—graceful, multi-roomed, single- and two-story stone and mortar buildings, each of which surrounded a flower-filled patio and rested on a stone platform for protection against floods. It is estimated that there were about 60,000 houses in

Tenochtitlán. The focal points of the city were the *teocallis,* or pyramidal temples, at which religious ceremonies, including human sacrifice, were held. The 100-foot-high double temple dedicated to the war god and the rain god was made of stone and featured a steep staircase that led to a platform with an altar, a chamber containing shrines, and an antechamber for the priests.

The palace of the emperor Moctezuma boasted numerous rooms for attendants and concubines, a menagerie, hanging gardens, and a swimming pool. Since Tenochtitlán sat in the middle of a lake, it was unfortified and connected to the mainland by three causeways. Communication among different parts of the city was easy, and one could travel either by land or by water. A series of canals, with footpaths running beside them, ran throughout the city. The Spaniards who came to this city reported that thousands of canoes plied the canals, carrying passengers and cargo around the city; these Euro-peans were so impressed by the communication network that they called Tenochtitlán the Venice of the New World.

NONINDUSTRIAL CITIES IN THE MODERN WORLD

Tenochtitlán is a good example of the kind of urban settlement that was characteristic of most ancient, nonindustrial civilizations. Commonly termed **preindustrial cities,** they are apt to be thought of as

Preindustrial cities: The kinds of urban settlements that are characteristic of nonindustrial civilizations.

The modern industrial city is a very recent human development, although its roots lie in the so-called preindustrial city. The widespread belief that preindustrial cities are things of the past and that industrial cities are things of the future is based upon culture-bound assumptions rather than established facts.

things of the past, or as little more than stages in some sort of inevitable progression toward the kinds of industrial cities one finds today in places like Europe and North America. This view obscures the fact that preindustrial cities are far from uncommon in the world today—especially in third-world countries. Furthermore, industrial cities have not yet come close to demonstrating that they have the long-term viability shown by nonindustrial cities, which in some parts of the world have been around for not just hundreds but thousands of years.

Chapter Summary

To meet their requirements for food, water, and shelter, people must adjust their behavior to suit their environment. This adjustment, which involves both change and stability, is a part of adaptation. Adaptation means that there is a moving balance between a society's needs and its environmental potential. Adaptation also refers to the interaction between an organism and its environment, with each causing changes in the other. Adaptation is a continuing process, and it is essential for survival. An ecosystem is bound by the activities of organisms and by physical forces such as erosion. Human ecosystems must be considered in terms of all aspects of culture.

To fit into an ecosystem an organism must be able to adapt or become a part of it. Once such a fit is achieved, stability may serve the organism's interest more than change.

A culture area is a geographical region in which various societies follow similar patterns of life. Since geographical regions are not always uniform in climate and topography, new discoveries do not always spread to every group. Environmental variation also favors variation in technology, since needs may be quite different from area to area.

Julian Steward used the concept of culture type to explain variations within geographical regions. In this view a culture is considered in terms of a particular technology and of the particular environmental features that technology is best suited to deal with.

The social and political organization of a society are other factors that influence how technology is to be used to ensure survival. Those features of a culture that play a part in the way the society makes

a living are its culture core. Anthropologists can trace direct relationships between types of culture cores and types of environments.

The food-foraging way of life, the oldest and most universal type of human adaptation, requires that people move their residence according to changing food sources. For as yet unknown ecological and social factors, local group size is kept small. One explanation contends that small sizes fit land capacity to sustain the groups. Another states that the fewer the people, the less the chance of social conflict. The primary mechanism for regulation of population size among food foragers is frequent stimulation of the female nipple, which prevents ovulation, as infants nurse several times an hour over several years.

Three important elements of human social organization probably developed along with scavenging and hunting for meat. These are a sexual division of labor, food sharing, and the camp as the center of daily activity and the place where food sharing takes place.

A characteristic of food-foraging societies is their egalitarianism. Since this way of life requires mobility, people accumulate only the material goods necessary for survival, so that status differences are limited to those based on age and sex. Status differences associated with sex, however, do not imply subordination of women to men. Food resources are distributed equally throughout the groups; thus no individual can achieve the wealth or status that hoarding might bring.

The reason for the transition from food foraging to food production, which began about 11,000 to 9,000 years ago, was likely the unforeseen result of

increased management of wild food resources. One correlate of the food-producing revolution was the development of permanent settlements, as people practiced simple horticulture, using neither the plow nor irrigation nor intensive agriculture—a more complex activity that requires irrigation, fertilizers, and draft animals. Pastoralism is a means of subsistence that relies on raising herds of domesticated animals, such as cattle, sheep, and goats. Pastoralists are usually nomads, moving to different pastures as required for grass and water.

Cities developed as intensified agriculture techniques created a surplus, freeing individuals to specialize full time in other activities. Social structure becomes increasingly stratified with the development of cities, and people are ranked according to the work they do and the family they are born into. Social relationships grow more formal, and centralized political institutions are formed.

One should not conclude that there is inevitability to the sequence from food foraging, through horticultural/pastoral, to intensive agricultural, nonindustrial urban, and then industrial societies, even though these did appear in that order. Where older adaptations continue to prevail, it is because conditions are such that they continue to work so well, and provide such satisfaction, that the people who maintain them prefer them to the alternatives of which they are aware. It is not because of any "backwardness" or ignorance. Modern food-forager, horticultural, pastoral, nonindustrial, and industrial urban societies are all highly evolved adaptations, each in its own particular way.

Suggested Readings

Bates, Daniel G., and Fred Plog. *Human Adaptive Strategies*. New York: McGraw-Hill, 1991.
This book takes an ecological approach to understanding human cultural diversity. A chapter each is devoted to hunting and gathering, horticultural, pastoral, intensive agricultural, and industrial societies, with a final chapter devoted to change and development. Theoretical issues are made easy to grasp through use of readable ethnographic cases.

Lustig-Arecco, Vera. *Technology: Strategies for Survival*. New York: Holt, Rinehart and Winston, 1975.
Although the early anthropologists devoted a good deal of attention to technology, the subject fell into neglect early in the twentieth century. This is one of the few recent studies of the subject. The author's particular interest is the technoeconomic adaptation of hunters, pastoralists, and farmers.

Oswalt, Wendell H. *Habitat and Technology*. New York: Holt, Rinehart and Winston, 1972.
The author develops a taxonomy that permits precise cross-cultural comparisons of the complexity of manufactures. The research is based on a systematic analysis of the known manufactures of non-Western peoples. Shelters, tools, clothing, implements, and cultivated foodstuffs are considered.

Schrire, Carmel, ed. *Past and Present in Hunter Gatherer Studies*. Orlando, Fla.: Academic Press, 1984.
This collection of papers demolishes many a myth (including several held by anthropologists) about food-foraging societies. Especially recommended is the editor's introduction, titled "Wild Surmises on Savage Thoughts."

Vayda, Andrew, ed. *Environment and Cultural Behavior: Ecological Studies in Cultural Anthropology*. Garden City, N.Y.: Natural History Press, 1969.
The focus of the studies collected here is the interrelationship between cultural behavior and environmental phenomena. The writers attempt to make cultural behavior intelligible by relating it to the material world in which it develops. This volume includes articles concerning population, divination, ritual, warfare, food production, climate, and diseases.

ECONOMIC

SYSTEMS

The fundamental characteristic of the market in non-Western societies is that it always means a literal market place, *where actual goods are exchanged. At this market in Marrakesh, Morocco, people exchange items they have produced for things they need but can get only from others.*

HOW DO ANTHROPOLOGISTS STUDY ECONOMIC SYSTEMS?

Anthropologists study the means by which goods are produced, distributed, and consumed in the context of the total culture of particular societies. Although they have borrowed theories and concepts from economists, most anthropologists feel that principles derived from the study of Western market economies have limited applicability to economic systems where people do not produce and exchange goods for profit.

HOW DO THE ECONOMIES OF NONINDUSTRIAL PEOPLES WORK?

In non-Western, nonindustrial societies there is always a division of labor by age and sex, with some additional craft specialization. Land and other valuable resources are usually controlled by groups of relatives, such as bands or lineages, and individual ownership is rare. Production takes place in the quantity and at the time required, and most goods are consumed by the group that produces them. Leveling mechanisms ensure that no one accumulates significantly more goods than anyone else.

HOW AND WHY ARE GOODS EXCHANGED IN NONINDUSTRIAL SOCIETIES?

Nonindustrial peoples exchange goods through the processes of reciprocity, redistribution, and market exchange. Reciprocity involves the exchange of goods and services of roughly equivalent value, and it is often undertaken for ritual purposes or in order to gain prestige. Redistribution requires some sort of government and/or religious elite to collect and then reallocate resources, in the form of either goods or services. Market exchange, which in nonindustrial societies means going to a specific place for direct exchange of goods, also serves as entertainment and as a means of exchanging important information. The latter are frequently primary motivating forces bringing people into the marketplace.

An economic system may be defined as one by which goods are produced, distributed, and consumed. Because a people, in pursuing a particular means of subsistence, necessarily produces, distributes, and consumes things, our earlier discussion of patterns of subsistence (Chapter 6) involved us with economic matters. Yet there is much more to economic systems than we have so far covered. This chapter looks at aspects of economic systems —specifically, systems of production, exchange, and redistribution—that require more discussion than we were able to give them in the last chapter.

ECONOMIC ANTHROPOLOGY

It is perhaps in the study of the economies of nonliterate peoples that we are most apt to fall prey to interpreting anthropological data in terms of our own technologies, our own values of work and property, and our own determination of what is rational. Take, for example, the following statement from just one respected textbook in economics: "In all societies, the prevailing reality of life has been the inadequacy of output to fill the wants and needs of the people."[1] What this assertion fails to realize is that in many societies people's wants are maintained at levels that can be fully and continuously satisfied, and without jeopardizing the environment. In such societies, things are produced in the quantity and at the time required, and to do more than this makes no sense at all. Thus, no matter how hard people may work when hard work is called for, at other times they will have available hours, days, or even weeks on end to devote to "unproductive" (in the economic sense) activities. To Western observers, such people are apt to appear lazy (Fig. 7.1); "instead of disciplined workers, they are reluctant and untrained laborers."[2] If the people happen to be hunters and gatherers, even the hard work is likely to be misinterpreted. In Western culture, hunting is often defined as a sport; hence, the men in food-foraging societies are often misperceived as spending virtually all of their time in

[1]Robert L. Heilbroner and Lester C. Thurow, *The Economic Problem*, 6th ed. (Englewood Cliffs, N.J.: Prentice-Hall, 1981), p. 327.

[2]Ibid., p. 609.

recreational pursuits, while the women are seen as working themselves to the bone.

To understand how the schedule of wants or demands of a given society is balanced against the supply of goods and services available, it is necessary to introduce a noneconomic variable—the anthropological variable of culture. In any given economic system, economic processes cannot be interpreted without culturally defining the demands and understanding the conventions that dictate how and when they are satisfied. The fact is, the economic sphere of behavior is *not* separate from the social, religious, and political spheres, free to follow its own purely economic logic. To be sure, economic behavior and institutions can be analyzed in purely economic terms, but to do so is to ignore crucial noneconomic considerations.

As a case in point, we may look briefly at yam production among the Trobriand Islanders, who

Trobriand Island men devote a great deal of time and energy to raising yams not for themselves, but to give to others. These yams, which have been raised by men related through marriage to a chief, are about to be loaded into the chief's yam house.

```
┌────────────────────────────────────────────────────────────────┐
│  The Chief Registrar of Natives,            N.A.D. Form No 54/____│
│        NAIROBI.                                                   │
│                                                                   │
│        COMPLAINT OF DESERTION OF REGISTERED NATIVE.               │
│                                                                   │
│  Native's Certificate No. _____ Name _____    │
│  The above native deserted from my employ _____    │
│                                            (date)                 │
│                                                                   │
│  He was engaged on _____ on _____ days verbal contract  │
│                     (date)                                        │
│                                   _____ months written contract│
│                                                                   │
│  at _____ │
│                         (place)           (Contract No.)          │
│                                                                   │
│      I wish to prosecute him for this offence and hereby agree to │
│  appear as a witness or to produce evidence if and when called    │
│  upon.                                                            │
│                                                                   │
│                            _____   │
│                                     Signature of Employer         │
│                                                                   │
│  Address _____                                │
│                                                                   │
│  Date    _____                                │
└────────────────────────────────────────────────────────────────┘
```

Figure 7.1 People with industrial economies frequently misunderstand the work ethic in so-called tribal societies. Thus the British in colonial Kenya thought it necessary to teach natives "the dignity of labor," and made it a crime for a tribal person to quit work without authorization.

inhabit a group of coral atolls that lie north of New Guinea's eastern end.[3] Trobriand men spend a great deal of their time and energy raising yams, not for themselves or their own households, but to give others, normally their sisters and married daughters. The purpose of this yam production is not to provision the households of those to whom they are given, as most of what people eat they grow for themselves in gardens in which they plant taro, sweet potatoes, tapioca, greens, beans, and squash, as well as breadfruit and banana trees. The reason for a man to give yams to a woman is to show his support for her husband, and to enhance his own influence. Once received by the woman, they are loaded into her husband's yam house, symbolizing his worth as a man of power and influence in his community. Some of these yams he may use to purchase a variety of things, including armshells, shell necklaces and earrings, betel nuts, pigs, chickens, locally produced goods such as wooden bowls, combs, floor mats, lime pots, or even magic spells. Some he must use to discharge obligations, as in the

presentation of yams to the relatives of his daughter's husband when she marries, or the payments that must be made following the death of a member of his lineage (a group of relatives descended, in this case through women, from a common ancestor).

Finally, any man who aspires to high status and power is expected to show his worth by organizing a yam competition, in the course of which huge quantities of yams are given away to invited guests. As anthropologist Annette Weiner explains: "A yam house, then, is like a bank account; when full, a man is wealthy and powerful. Until yams are cooked or they rot, they may circulate as limited currency. That is why, once harvested, the usage of yams for daily food is avoided as much as possible."[4]

By giving yams to his sister or daughter, a man not only expresses his confidence in the woman's husband, he also makes the latter indebted to him. Although the recipient rewards the gardener and his helpers by throwing a feast, at which they are fed cooked yams, taro and—what everyone especially looks forward to—ample pieces of pork, this

---

[3]Annette B. Weiner, *The Trobrianders of Papua New Guinea*, (New York: Holt, Rinehart and Winston, 1988).

[4]Ibid., p. 86.

in no way pays off the debt. Nor does the gift of a stone axe blade (another valuable in the Trobriand system), which may reward an especially good harvest. The debt can only be repaid in women's wealth, which consists of bundles of banana leaves, and skirts made of the same material which have been dyed red. Although the bundles are of no utilitarian value, extensive labor is invested in their production, and large quantities of them, along with skirts, are regarded as essential in paying off all the members of other lineages that were close to a recently deceased relative in life, and who assisted with the funeral. At the same time, the wealth and vitality of the dead person's lineage is measured by the quality and quantity of the bundles and skirts so distributed. Because a man has received yams from his wife's brother, he is obligated to provide her with yams with which she can purchase the necessary bundles and skirts, over and above those she herself has produced, in order to help with payments following the death of a member of her lineage. Because deaths are unpredictable, and can occur at any time, a man must have yams available for his wife when she needs them. This, and the fact that she may require all of his yams, acts as an effective check on a man's wealth.

Like people the world over, the Trobriand Islanders assign meanings to objects that make them worth far more than their cost in labor or the materials of which they are made. Yams, for example, establish long-term relationships that lead to other advantages, such as access to land, protection, assistance, and other kinds of wealth. Thus, yam exchanges are as much social and political, as they are economic transactions. Banana leaf bundles and skirts, for their part, are symbolic of the political state of lineages, and of their immortality. In their distribution, which is related to rituals associated with death, we see how men in Trobriand society are ultimately dependent on women and their valuables. So important are these matters to the Trobrianders that even in the face of Western money, education, religion, and law, these people remain as committed today as in the past to yam cultivation and the production of women's wealth. Looked at in terms of Western economics, this appears to make little sense, but looked at in terms of Trobriand values and concerns, it makes a great deal of sense.

RESOURCES

In every society there are customs and rules governing the kinds of work that are done, who does the work, who controls the resources and tools, and how the work is accomplished. Raw materials, labor, and technology are the productive resources that a social group may use to produce desired

Often, work considered inappropriate for men (or for women) in one society is performed by them in another. Shown here are a Chinese man sewing and Guajiro women carrying heavy loads.

goods and services. The rules surrounding the use of these are embedded in the culture and determine the way the economy operates.

PATTERNS OF LABOR

In every human society, there has always been a division of labor by both sex and age; such division is an elaboration of patterns found among all higher primates. The former increases the chances that the learning of necessary skills will be more efficient, since only half the adult repertoire needs to be learned by any one individual. The latter provides sufficient time for those skills to be developed.

SEXUAL DIVISION OF LABOR

The sexual division of labor in human societies of all sorts has been studied extensively by anthropologists, and we discussed some aspects of it in the preceding chapter, as well as in Chapter 3. Whether men or women do a particular job varies from group to group, but much work has been set apart as the work of either one sex or the other. For example, we have seen that the tasks most often regarded as women's work tend to be those that can be carried out near home and that are easily resumed after interruption. The tasks most often regarded as men's work tend to be those that require physical strength, rapid mobilization of high bursts of energy, frequent travel at some distance from home, and assumption of high levels of risk and danger. There are, however, plenty of exceptions, as in those societies where women regularly carry burdensome loads, or put in long hours of hard work cultivating crops in the fields. In some societies, women perform almost three-quarters of all work, and there are even societies where women serve as warriors. In the nineteenth-century kingdom of Dahomey, in West Africa, thousands served in the armed forces of the Dahomean King, and in the eyes of some observers, were better fighters than their male counterparts. There are also references to women warriors in ancient Ireland, archaeological evidence exists of their presence among the Vikings, and among the Abkhasians of Georgia, women were trained in weaponry until quite recently. Clearly, the sexual division of labor cannot be explained simply as a consequence of male strength, expendability, or female reproductive biology.

Instead of looking for biological imperatives to explain the sexual division of labor, a more productive strategy is to examine the kinds of work done by men and women in the context of specific societies, to see how it relates to other cultural and historical factors. What we find are three different configurations, one featuring flexibility and sexual integration, another rigid segregation by sex, and a third featuring elements of the other two.[5] The flexible/integrated pattern is exemplified by people like the !Kung (whose practices we examined in Chapter 6), and is seen most often among food foragers and subsistence farmers. In such societies, up to 35 percent of activities are performed by both sexes with approximately equal participation, while those tasks deemed appropriate for one sex may be performed by the other, without loss of face, as the situation warrants. Where these practices prevail, boys and girls grow up in much the same way, learn to value cooperation over competition, and become equally habituated to adult men and women, who interact with one another on a relatively equal basis.

Sexually segregated societies are those in which almost all work is rigidly defined as either masculine or feminine, so that men and women rarely engage in joint efforts of any kind. In such societies, it is inconceivable that someone would even think of doing something considered to be the work of the opposite sex! This pattern is frequently seen in pastoral nomadic, intensive agricultural, and industrial societies, in which men's work keeps them outside the home for much of the time. Thus, boys and girls alike are raised primarily by women, who encourage compliance in their charges. At some point, however, boys must undergo a role reversal to become like men who are supposed to be tough, aggressive, and competitive, and to do this, they must prove their masculinity in ways that women do not have to prove their feminine identity. Commonly, this involves assertions of male superiority, and hence authority, over women. Historically, sexually segregated societies have often imposed their control on those featuring sexual integration, upsetting the egalitarian nature of the latter.

[5]Peggy Reeves Sanday, *Female Power and Male Dominance: On the Origins of Sexual Inequality* (Cambridge, England: Cambridge University Press, 1981), pp. 79–80.

In the third, or dual sex configuration, men and women carry out their work separately, as in sexually segregated societies, but the relationship between them is one of balanced complimentarity, rather than inequality. Although competition is a prevailing ethic, each sex manages its own affairs, and the interests of both men and women are represented at all levels. Thus, as in sexually integrated societies, neither sex exerts dominance over the other. The dual sex orientation may be seen among certain Native American peoples whose economies were based upon subsistence farming, as well as among several West African kingdoms, including that of the aforementioned Dahomeans.

AGE DIVISION OF LABOR

A division of labor according to age is also typical of human societies. Among the !Kung, for example, children are not expected to contribute significantly to subsistence until they reach their late teens. Their equivalent of retirement comes somewhere around the age of 60. Elderly people, while they will usually do some foraging for themselves, are not expected to contribute much food. On the other hand, older men and women alike play an essential role in spiritual matters; being freed from food taboos and other restrictions that apply to younger adults, they may handle ritual substances considered dangerous to those still involved with hunting or having children. By virtue of their old age, they also remember things that happened far in the past. Thus, they are repositories of accumulated wisdom —the living libraries of a nonliterate people—and are able to suggest solutions to problems that younger adults have never before had to face. Thus, they are far from being unproductive members of society.

In many nonindustrial societies, not just older people but children as well may make a greater contribution to the economy in terms of work and responsibility than is common in our own. For instance, in Maya communities in southern Mexico and Guatemala, young children not only look after their younger brothers and sisters but help with housework as well. Girls begin to make a substantial contribution to the work of the household by the age of 7 or 8, and by the time they are 11, are constantly busy grinding corn, making tortillas,

Among the Maya, young boys make a substantial contribution to work in the fields. Among food foragers, large numbers of children are a burden to women; in agrarian societies, the work they contribute to the family makes them an economic asset.

fetching wood and water, sweeping the house, and so forth. Boys have less to do, but are given small tasks, such as bringing in the chickens or playing with a baby; by the time they are 12, however, they are carrying toasted tortillas to the men out working in the fields, and returning with loads of corn.[6]

COOPERATION

Cooperative work groups can be found everywhere in nonliterate as well as literate and in nonindustrial as well as industrial societies. Often, if the effort involves the whole community, there is a festive spirit to the work. Jomo Kenyatta, the anthropologist who went on to become a respected statesman

[6]Evon Z. Vogt, *The Zinacantecos of Mexico, a Modern Maya Way of Life* (New York: Holt, Rinehart and Winston, 1970), pp. 62–67.

as well as "father" of an independent Kenya, described the time of enjoyment after a day's labor in his country:

> If a stranger happens to pass by, he will have no idea that these people who are singing and dancing have completed their day's work. This is why most Europeans have erred by not realizing that the African in his own environment does not count hours or work by the movement of the clock, but works with good spirit and enthusiasm to complete the tasks before him.[7]

Among the !Kung, women go out to gather wild plant foods about three times a week. Although they may go out alone, they more often go out in groups, talking loudly as they go. This not only turns what might otherwise seem a monotonous task into a social occasion, it also causes large animals—potential sources of danger—to move elsewhere.

In most human societies, the basic unit within which cooperation takes place is the household. It is a unit of production and consumption at one and the same time; only in industrial societies have these two things been separated. The Maya farmer, for

[7]Melville Herskovits, *Economic Anthropology: A Study in Comparative Economics*, 2nd ed. (New York: Knopf, 1952), p. 103.

example, unlike his North American counterpart, is not so much running a commercial enterprise as he is a household. He is motivated by a desire to provide for the welfare of his own family; each family, as an economic unit, works as a group for its own good. Cooperative work may be undertaken outside of the household, however, for other reasons, though not always voluntarily. It may be part of fulfilling duties to in-laws; it may be performed for political officials or priests, by command. Thus, institutions of family, kinship, religion, and the state all may act as organizing elements that define the nature and condition of each worker's cooperative obligations.

CRAFT SPECIALIZATION

In nonindustrial societies, where division of labor occurs along lines of age and sex, each person in the society has knowledge and competence in all aspects of work appropriate to his or her age and sex. In modern industrial societies, by contrast, there exists a greater diversity of more specialized tasks to be performed, and no individual can even begin to have knowledge of all those appropriate for his or her age and sex. Yet even in nonindustrial

In nonindustrial societies, households produce much of what they consume. Among the Maya, men work in the fields to produce food for the household; women prepare the food and perform other chores that can be done in or near the house.

In industrial societies, people do not have unrestricted access to the means of production, nor do they generally produce directly for their own consumption. Instead, they often work for strangers, at monotonous tasks, and in depersonalized settings. Such conditions contribute to alienation, a major problem in industrial societies.

societies, there is some specialization of craft. This is often minimal in food-foraging societies, but even here the arrow points of one man may be in some demand because of his particular skill at making them. Among people who produce their own food, there is apt to be more in the way of specialization. In the Trobriand Islands, for example, if one wanted stone to make axe blades, one had to travel some distance to a particular island where the appropriate kind of stone was quarried; clay pots, on the other hand, were made by people living on yet another island.

An example of specialization can be seen among Afar tribesmen of Ethiopia's Danakil depression. They are miners of salt, which since ancient times has been widely traded in East Africa. The salt is mined from the crust of an extensive salt plain in the north part of the depression, and to get it is a risky and difficult business. L.M. Nesbitt, the first European to successfully traverse the depression, labeled it "the hell-hole of creation."[8] The heat is extreme during the day, with shade temperatures between 140° and 156° F not unusual. Shade is not

to be found on the salt plain, however, unless a shelter of salt blocks is built. Nor is there food or water for man or beast. To add to the difficulty, until recently the Muslim Afars and the Christian Tegreans, highlanders who also mine salt, were mortal enemies.

Successful mining, then, requires skill at planning and organization, as well as physical strength and the will to work under the most trying conditions.[9] Pack animals to carry the salt have to be fed in advance, for to carry sufficient fodder for them interferes with their ability to carry out salt. Food and water must be carried for the miners, who usually number 30 to 40 per group. Travel is planned to take place at night to avoid the intense heat of day. In the past, measures to protect against attack had to be taken. Finally, timing is critical; a party has to get back to sources of food and water before their own supplies are too long exhausted, and before their animals are unable to continue farther.

[8]L.M. Nesbitt, *Hell-Hole of Creation* (New York: Knopf, 1935).

[9]Haile Michael Mesghinua, "Salt Mining in Enderta," *Journal of Ethiopian Studies*, 4, No.2(1966): Kevin O'Mahoney, "The Salt Trade," *Journal of Ethiopian Studies*, 8, No.2(1970).

CONTROL OF LAND

All societies have regulations that determine the way valuable land resources will be allocated. Food foragers must determine who can hunt game and gather plants and where these activities take place. Horticulturists must decide how their farmland is to be acquired, worked, and passed on. Pastoralists require a system that determines rights to watering places and grazing land, as well as the right of access to land over which they move their herds. Full-time or intensive agriculturalists must have some means of determining title to land and access to water supplies for irrigation purposes. In our own industrialized Western society, a system of private ownership of land and rights to natural resources generally prevails. Although elaborate laws have been established to regulate the buying, owning, and selling of land and water resources, if individuals wish to reallocate valuable farmland, for instance, for another purpose, they are generally able to do so.

In nonindustrial societies, land is often controlled by kinship groups such as the lineage (discussed in Chapter 10) or band, rather than by individuals. For example, among the !Kung, each band of anywhere from 10 to 30 people lives on roughly 250 square miles of land, which they consider to be their territory—their own country. These territories are defined not in terms of boundaries, but rather in terms of waterholes that are located within them. The land is said to be "owned" by those who have lived the longest in the band, usually a group of brothers and sisters or cousins. Their ownership, however, is more symbolic than real. They cannot sell (or buy) land, but their permission must be asked by outsiders to enter the territory. To refuse such permission, though, would be unthinkable.

The practice of defining territories on the basis of core features, be they waterholes (as among the !Kung), distinctive features of the landscape where ancestral spirits are thought to dwell (as among Australian aborigines), watercourses (as among Indians of the northeastern United States), or whatever, is typical of food foragers. Territorial boundaries are left vaguely defined, at best. The adaptive value of this is clear; the size of band territories, as well as the size of the bands themselves, can adjust to keep pace with availability of resources in any given place. Such adjustment would be more diffi-

---

Technology: Tools and other material equipment, together with the knowledge of how to make and use them.

---

cult under a system of individual ownership of clearly bounded land.

Among some West African farmers, a feudal system of land ownership prevails, by which all land belongs to the head chief. He allocates it to various subchiefs, who in turn distribute it to lineages; lineage leaders then assign individual plots to each farmer. Just as in medieval Europe, these African people owe allegiance to the subchiefs (or nobles) and the principal chief (or king). The people who work the land must pay taxes and fight for the king when necessary. The people, in a sense, "own" the land and transmit their ownership to their heirs. No one, however, can give away, sell, or otherwise dispose of a plot of land without approval from the elder of the lineage. When an individual no longer needs the land that has been allocated, the lineage head rescinds title to it and reallocates it to someone else in the lineage. The important operative principle here is that the system extends the right of the individual to use land for a certain period of time, but the land is not "owned" outright. This serves to maintain the integrity of valuable farmland as such, preventing its loss through subdivision and conversion to other uses.

TECHNOLOGY

All societies have some means of creating and allocating the tools and other artifacts used in the production of goods and passed on to succeeding generations. The number and kinds of tools a society uses—which, together with the knowledge of how to make and use them, constitute its **technology**—are related to the life-styles of its members. Food foragers and pastoral nomads, who are frequently on the move, are apt to have fewer and simpler tools than the more sedentary farmer, in part because a great number of complex tools would decrease their mobility.

Nonetheless, food foragers make and use a variety of tools, many of which are ingenious in their effectiveness. Some of these they make for

their own individual use, but codes of generosity are such that a person may not refuse giving or loaning what is requested. Thus, tools may be given or loaned to others in exchange for the products resulting from their use. For example, a !Kung who gives his arrow to another hunter has a right to a share in any animals that the hunter may kill. Game is thought to "belong" to the man whose arrow killed it.

Among horticulturists, the axe, machete, and digging stick or hoe are the primary tools. Since these are relatively easy to produce, every person can make them. Although the maker has first rights to their use, when that person is not using them, any member of the family may ask to use them and usually is granted permission to do so. To refuse would cause the tool owner to be treated with scorn for this singular lack of concern for others. If another relative helps raise the crop that is traded for a particular tool, that relative becomes part-owner of the implement, and it may not be traded or given away without his or her permission.

In sedentary communities, which farming makes possible, tools and other productive goods become more complex and more difficult and costlier to make. Where this happens, individual ownership in them usually becomes more absolute, as do the conditions under which persons may borrow and use such equipment. It is easy to replace a knife lost by a relative during palm cultivation, but much more difficult to replace an iron plow or a power-driven threshing machine. Rights to the ownership of complex tools are more rigidly applied; generally the person who has supplied the funds for the purchase of a complex piece of machinery is considered the sole owner and may decide how and by whom it will be used.

LEVELING MECHANISMS

In spite of the increased opportunities for people in sedentary farming communities to accumulate belongings, limits on property acquisition may be as prominent in them as among nomadic peoples. In such communities, social obligations compel people to divest themselves of wealth, and no one is permitted to accumulate too much more than others. Greater wealth simply brings greater obligation to give. Anthropologists refer to such obligations as **leveling mechanisms**.

Leveling mechanism: A societal obligation compelling a family to distribute goods so that no one accumulates more wealth than anyone else.

Leveling mechanisms are found in communities where property must not be allowed to threaten a more or less egalitarian social order, as in many Maya villages and towns in the highlands of Mexico and Guatemala. In these communities, cargo systems function to siphon off any excess wealth that people may accumulate. A cargo system is a civil-religious hierarchy, which, on a revolving basis, combines most of the civic and ceremonial offices of a community. All offices are open to all men, and eventually virtually every man has at least one term in office, each term lasting for one year. The scale is pyramidal, which is to say that more offices exist at the lower levels, with progressively fewer at the top. For example, in a community of about 8,000 people, there may be four levels of offices with 32 on the lowest level, 12 on the next one up, 6 on the next, and 2 at the top. Offices at the lower level include those for the performance of various menial chores, such as sweeping and carrying messages. The higher offices are those of councilmen, judges, mayors, and ceremonial positions. These positions are regarded as burdens, for which one receives no pay. Instead, the officeholder is expected to pay for the food, liquor, music, fireworks, or whatever is required for community festivals or for banquets associated with the transmission of office. After holding a cargo position, a man usually has a period of rest, during which he may accumulate sufficient resources to campaign for a higher office. Each male citizen of the community is socially obligated to serve in the system at least once, and social pressure to do so is such that it drives individuals who have once again accumulated excess wealth to apply for higher offices in order to raise their social status. Thus, while some individuals have appreciably more prestige than others in their community, no one has appreciably more material wealth than anyone else.

In addition to equalizing wealth, the cargo system accomplishes other things as well. Through its system of offices, it ensures that necessary services within the community are performed. Members are

also pressured into investing their resources in their own community, rather than elsewhere. Finally, it keeps goods in circulation, rather than sitting around "gathering dust" somewhere.

DISTRIBUTION AND EXCHANGE

In our own money economy, there is a two-step process between labor and consumption. The money received for labor must be translated into something else before it is directly consumable. In societies with no such medium of exchange, the rewards for labor are usually direct. The workers in a family group consume what they harvest; they eat what the hunter or gatherer brings home; they use the tools that they themselves make. But even where there is no formal medium of exchange, some distribution of goods takes place. Karl Polanyi, an economist, classified the cultural systems of distributing material goods into three modes: reciprocity, redistribution, and market exchange.[10]

[10]Karl Polanyi, "The Economy as Instituted Process," in *Economic Anthropology: Readings in Theory and Analysis,* ed. Edward E. LeClair, Jr., and Harold K. Schneider (New York: Holt, Rinehart and Winston, 1968), pp. 122–143.

Reciprocity: The exchange of goods and services, of approximately equal value, between two parties.

RECIPROCITY

Reciprocity refers to a transaction between two parties, whereby goods and services of roughly equivalent value are exchanged. This may involve gift giving, but in non-Western societies, pure altruism in gift giving is as rare as it is in the U.S. or any other Western society. The overriding motive is to fulfill social obligations and perhaps to gain a bit of prestige in the process. It might be best compared in North American society to someone who gives a party. He or she may go to great lengths to impress others by the excellence of the food and drink served, not to mention the quality of wit and conversation of those in attendance. The expectation is that, sooner or later, he or she will be invited to similar parties by some, although perhaps not all, of the guests.

Social customs dictate the nature and occasion of exchange. When an animal is killed by a group of

!Kung cutting up meat, which will then be shared by others in the camp. The food distribution practices of such food foragers constitute an example of generalized reciprocity.

Generalized reciprocity: A mode of exchange in which neither is the value of the gift calculated nor the time of repayment specified.

hunters in Australia, the meat is divided among the families of the hunters and other relatives. Each person in the camp gets a share, the size depending on the nature of the person's kinship tie to the hunters. The least desirable parts may be kept by the hunters themselves. When a kangaroo is killed, for example, the left hind leg goes to the brother of the hunter, the tail to his father's brother's son, the loins and the fat to his father-in-law, the ribs to his mother-in-law, the forelegs to his father's younger sister, the head to his wife, and the entrails and the blood to the hunter. If there were arguments over the apportionment, it would be because the principles of distribution were not being followed properly. The hunter and his family would seem to fare badly according to this arrangement, but they have their turn when another man makes a kill. The giving and receiving is obligatory, as is the particularity of the distribution. Such sharing of food reinforces community bonds and ensures that everyone eats. It might also be viewed as a way of saving perishable goods. By giving away part of his kill, the hunter gets a social IOU for a similar amount of food in the future. It is a little bit like putting money in a time-deposit savings account.

The food-distribution practices just described for Australian hunters constitute an example of **generalized reciprocity.** This may be defined as exchange in which neither is the value of what is given calculated nor the time of repayment specified. Gift giving, in the altruistic sense, also falls in this category. Most commonly, generalized reciprocity occurs among close kin or people who otherwise have very close ties with one another.

Balanced reciprocity: A mode of exchange in which the giving and the receiving are specific as to the value of the goods and the time of their delivery.

Negative reciprocity: A form of exchange in which the giver tries to get the better of the exchange.

Balanced reciprocity differs, in that it is not part of a long-term process. The giving and receiving, as well as the time involved, are more specific. Examples of balanced reciprocity among the Crow Indians are related by Robert Lowie.[11] A woman skilled in the tanning of buffalo hides might offer her services to a neighbor who needed a new cover for her tepee. It took an expert to design a tepee cover, which required from 14 to 20 skins. The designer might need as many as 20 collaborators, whom she instructed in the sewing together of the skins and whom the tepee owner might remunerate with a feast. The designer herself would be given some kind of property by the tepee owner. In another example from the Crow, Lowie relates that if a married woman brought her brother a present of food, he might reciprocate with a present of 10 arrows for her husband, which rated as the equivalent of a horse.

Giving, receiving, and sharing as so far described constitute a form of social security or insurance. A family contributes to others when they have the means and can count on receiving from others in time of need. A leveling mechanism is at work in the process of generalized or balanced reciprocity, promoting an egalitarian distribution of wealth over the long run.

Negative reciprocity is a third form of exchange, in which the giver tries to get the better of the deal. The parties involved have opposed interests, usually are members of different communities, and are not closely related. The ultimate form of negative reciprocity is to take something by force. Less extreme forms involve the use of guile and deception, or at the least hard bargaining. Among the Navajo, according to the anthropologist Clyde Kluckhohn, "to deceive when trading with foreign peoples is morally accepted."[12]

[11]Robert Lowie, *Crow Indians* (New York: Holt, Rinehart and Winston, 1956), p. 75. Original edition, 1935.

[12]Clyde Kluckhohn, quoted in Marshall Sahlins, *Stone Age Economics* (Chicago: Aldine, 1972), p. 200.

BARTER AND TRADE

Exchange that takes place within a group of people generally takes the form of generalized or balanced reciprocity. When it takes place between two groups, there is apt to be at least a potential for hostility and competition. Therefore, such exchange may well be in the form of negative reciprocity, unless some sort of arrangement has been made to ensure at least an approach to balance. Barter is one form of negative reciprocity by which scarce items from one group are exchanged for desirable goods from another group. Relative value is calculated, and despite an outward show of indifference, sharp trading is more the rule, when compared to the reciprocal nature of the exchanges within a group.

An arrangement that partook partly of balanced reciprocity and partly of barter existed between the Kota, in India, and three neighboring peoples who traded their surplus goods and certain services with the Kota. The Kota were the musicians and artisans for the area. They exchanged iron tools with the other three groups and provided the music essential for ceremonial occasions. The Toda furnished the Kota with ghee (a kind of butter) for certain ceremonies and buffalo for funerals; relations between the Kota and the Toda were friendly. The Badaga were agricultural and traded their grain for music and tools. Between the Kota and Badaga there was a feeling of great competition, which sometimes led to one-sided trading practices; it was usually the Kota who procured the advantage. The forest-dwelling Kurumba, who were dreaded sorcerers, had honey, canes, and occasionally fruits to offer, but their main contribution was protection against the supernatural. The Kota feared the Kurumba, and the Kurumba took advantage of this in their trade dealings, so that they always got more than they gave. Thus there was great latent hostility between these two tribes.

Silent trade is a specialized form of barter in which no verbal communication takes place. In fact,

it may involve no actual face-to-face contact at all. Such is the case with many forest-dwelling people in the world. Carleton Coon has described how this system works:

> The forest people creep through the lianas to the trading place, and leave a neat pile of jungle products, such as wax, camphor, monkeys' gall bladders, birds' nests for Chinese soup. They creep back a certain distance, and wait in a safe place. The partners to the exchange, who are usually agriculturalists with a more elaborate and extensive set of material possessions but who cannot be bothered stumbling through the jungle after wax when they have someone else to do it for them, discover the little pile, and lay down beside it what they consider its equivalent in metal cutting tools, cheap cloth, bananas, and the like. They too discreetly retire. The shy folk then reappear, inspect the two piles, and if they are satisfied, take the second one away. Then the opposite group comes back and takes pile number one, and the exchange is completed. If the forest people are dissatisfied, they can retire once more, and if the other people want to increase their offering they may, time and again, until everyone is happy.[13]

The reasons for silent trade can only be postulated, but in some situations trade may be silent for lack of a common language. More often it may serve to control hostility so as to keep relations peaceful. In a very real sense, good relations are maintained by preventing relations. Another possibility, which does not exclude the others, is that it makes exchange possible where problems of status might make verbal communication unthinkable. In any event, it provides for the exchange of goods between groups in spite of potential barriers.

THE KULA RING

Although we tend to think of trade as something undertaken for purely practical purposes, in order to gain access to necessary goods and services, not all trade is motivated by economic considerations. A classic example of this is the Kula ring (also referred to as the Kula), a Trobriand Island inter-island trading system in which prestige items are ceremoniously exchanged. Malinowski first described the Kula in 1920, but it is still going strong

Silent trade: A form of barter in which no verbal communication takes place.

[13]Carleton S. Coon, *A Reader in General Anthropology* (New York: Holt, Rinehart and Winston, 1948), p. 594.

today.[14] From their coral atolls, men periodically set sail in their canoes in order to exchange shell valuables with their Kula partners, who live on far distant islands. These voyages take men away from their homes for weeks, even months, at a time, and may expose them to various hardships along the way. The valuables consist of red shell necklaces, which always circulate in a clockwise direction, and ornate white armshells, which move in the opposite direction (Fig. 7.2). These objects are ranked according to their size, color, how finely polished they are, and their particular histories. Such is the fame of some that, when they appear in a village, they create a sensation. No one man holds these valuables for very long; at most, perhaps ten years. To hold on to an armshell or necklace too long risks disrupting the "path" that it must follow, as it is passed from one partner to another.

Although men on Kula voyages may use the opportunity to trade for other things, this is not the reason for such voyages, nor is the Kula necessary for trade to take place. In fact, overseas trade is regularly undertaken without the exchange of shell valuables. Instead, Trobriand men seek to create history through their Kula exchanges. By circulating armbands and necklaces that accumulate the histories of their travels and names of those who have possessed them, men proclaim their individual fame and talent, gaining considerable influence for themselves in the process. Although the idea is to match the size and value of one shell for another, men draw on all their negotiating skills, material resources, and magical expertise to gain access to the strongest partners and most valuable shells; thus, an element of negative reciprocity enters in as a man may divert shells from their proper "paths," or entice others to compete for whatever necklaces and armbands he may have to offer. But when all is said and done, success is limited, for while a man may keep a shell for five or ten years, sooner or later it must be passed on to others.

The Kula is a most elaborate complex of ceremony, political relationships, economic exchange, travel, magic, and social integration. To see it only in its economic aspects is to misunderstand it completely. The Kula demonstrates once more how inseparable economic matters are from the rest of culture, and shows that economics is not a realm

unto itself. This is just as true in societies of modern industrial countries as it is in Trobriand society; when the U.S. stopped trading with South Africa, for instance, it was for political rather than economic reasons. Similarly, retail activity in the U.S. peaks in December for religious, rather than purely economic reasons.

These photos show Kula valuables, and a canoe used for Kula voyages.

---

[14]Annette B. Weiner, *The Trobrianders of Papua New Guinea*, pp. 139–157.

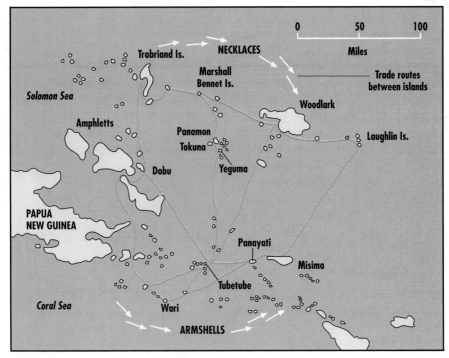

Figure 7.2 The ceremonial trading of necklaces and armbands in the Kula ring encourages trade throughout Melanesia.

REDISTRIBUTION

In nonindustrial societies, where there is a sufficient surplus to support a government, income is siphoned into the public coffers in the form of gifts, taxes, and the spoils of war, then distributed again. The chief or king has three motives in disposing of this income: The first is to maintain his position of superiority by a display of wealth; the second is to assure those who support him an adequate standard of living; and the third is to establish alliances outside of his territory.

The administration of the Inca empire in Peru was one of the most efficient the world has ever known, both in the collection of taxes and methods of control.[15] A census was kept of the population and resources. Tributes in goods and, more important, in services were levied. Each craftsman had to produce a specific quota of goods from materials supplied by overseers. Forced labor might be used for agricultural work or work in the mines. Forced labor was also employed in a program of public works, which included a remarkable system of roads and bridges throughout the mountainous terrain, aqueducts that guaranteed a supply of water, and storehouses that held surplus food for use in times of famine. Careful accounts were kept of income and expenditures. A governmental bureaucracy had the responsibility for seeing that production was maintained and that commodities were distributed according to the regulations set forth by the ruling powers.

Through the activities of the government, **redistribution** took place. The ruling class lived in great luxury, but goods were redistributed to the common people when necessary. Redistribution is a pattern of distribution by which the exchange is not between individuals or between groups, but, rather,

[15]J. Alden Mason, *The Ancient Civilizations of Peru* (Baltimore, Md.: Penguin, 1957).

Redistribution: A form of exchange in which goods flow into a central place, such as a market, and are distributed again.

by which a proportion of the products of labor is funneled into one source and is parceled out again as directed by a central administration. Taxes are a form of redistribution in the United States; people pay taxes to the government, some of which support the government itself, while the rest is redistributed in the form of either cash (as in the case of welfare payments, government loans, or subsidies to business) or services (as in the case of food and drug inspection, construction of freeways, support of the military, and the like). For redistribution to be possible, a society must have a centralized system of political organization, as well as an economic surplus over and above people's immediate needs.

DISTRIBUTION OF WEALTH

In societies in which people devote most of their time to subsistence activities, gradations of wealth are small, kept that way through leveling mechanisms and systems of reciprocity, which serve to distribute in a fairly equitable fashion what little wealth exists.

Display for social prestige, which economist Thorstein Veblen called **conspicuous consumption,** is a strong motivating force for the distribution of wealth in societies where some substantial surplus is produced. It has, of course, long been recognized that conspicuous consumption plays a prominent role in Western societies, as individuals compete with one another for prestige. Indeed, some North Americans spend much of their lives trying to impress others, and this requires the display of items symbolic of prestigious positions in life. The ultimate prestigious status is that of someone who doesn't have to work for a living, and here lies the irony: People may work long and hard in order to acquire the things that will make it appear as if they belong to a nonworking class of society. This all fits very nicely into an economy based on consumer wants:

Conspicuous consumption: A term coined by Thorstein Veblen to describe the display of wealth for social prestige.

Conspicuous consumption: Fur coats do not keep their wearers any warmer than other kinds of coats that are far less expensive and easier to care for. Furthermore, such coats would be more comfortable to wear with the fur inside rather than outside.

> In an expanding economy based on consumer wants, every effort must be made to place the standard of living in the center of public and private consideration, and every effort must therefore be lent to remove material and psychological impediments to consumption. Hence, rather than feelings of restraint, feelings of letting-go must be in the ascendant, and the institutions supporting restraint must recede into the background and give way to their opposite.[16]

A form of conspicuous consumption may occur in nonindustrial societies, as illustrated by the lavish feasts given by Big Men in many societies of Papua New Guinea. In the course of these feasts, food and various other items of wealth, laboriously accumulated over several preceding months, are all given away to others. To Western observers, such grandiose displays are apt to be seen as wasteful in the extreme, but to the people involved, these giveaways accomplish important social and political goals, as the analysis on the page opposite shows.

In the case of these Big Man feasts, a surplus is created for the express purpose of gaining prestige through a display of wealth and generous giving of gifts. But, unlike conspicuous consumption in

[16]Jules Henry, "A Theory for an Anthropological Analysis of American Culture," in *Anthropology and American Life,* ed. Joseph G. Jorgensen and Marcello Truzzi (Englewood Cliffs, N.J.: Prentice-Hall, 1974), p. 14.

ORIGINAL STUDY

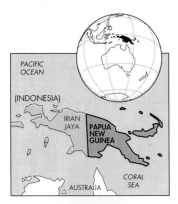

PRESTIGE ECONOMICS IN PAPUA NEW GUINEA[17]

The average Enga patrilineage group [people who trace their descent back through men to a particular male ancestor] numbers about 33 and . . . [constitutes a] . . . close knit extended family. . . . At the next level, however, is the Enga subclan, a group numbering about 90 members that owns a sacred dance ground and a sacred grove of trees. Members of a subclan are required to pool wealth for bride payments whenever any of their members marries and in support of one of their members who is striving to become a Big Man. A subclan is in competition with other subclans for prestige, which affects its members' ability to obtain wives and their desirability as partners in regional alliances. An individual householder is motivated to contribute to his subclan's political and economic activities, therefore, because his immediate family's self-interest is intimately bound with that of the subclan.

The Enga subclan is a unit approximately the size of the largest corporate kin groups in societies occupying the less densely populated highland fringe of New Guinea, such as the Tsembaga [see Chapter 6]. But the Enga are organized into a still higher level grouping, the clan, which averages about 350 members and is the ultimate owner and defender of the territory of the clan, from which all clan members ultimately derive their subsistence. Clans own carefully defined territories and defend them both in battle and on ceremonial occasions. They are led by Big Men who speak for their clans in interclan relations and who work within their clans to mobilize the separate households for military, political, and ceremonial action.

Like the subclan, the clan is an arena for dramatic public activities. The clan owns a main dance ground and an ancestral cult house. At these ceremonial centers, public gatherings take place that emphasize the unity of the group as against other clans. Sackschewsky . . . sees this as an essential tactic to overcome the fierce independence of Enga households, where "each man makes his own decisions." Such familistic independence creates problems for Big Men, who encourage interfamily unity in the effort to enhance the strength of their own clans in a fiercely competitive and dangerous social environment.

Let us imagine the problems faced by the members of an Enga clan. They are trying to make an adequate subsistence from small amounts of intensely utilized land. Surrounding them is a world of enemies ready to drive them from their land and seize it at the first sign of weakness. They must attempt to neutralize this external threat by several means: (1) by maintaining a large, unified group, they show strength in numbers, making others afraid to attack them; (2) by collaborating in the accumulation of food and wealth to be generously given away at ceremonies, they make themselves attractive as feasting partners; and (3) by being strong and wealthy, they become attractive as allies for defensive purposes, turning their neighbors either into friends or into outnumbered enemies. These three goals can be

In Papua New Guinea, Big Men must host impressive competitive feasts to advertise the size and wealth of their clans. Although done for political purposes, they require months of hard work to amass the necessary food—like the cooked pigs shown here—and wealth, which are then given away to others.

achieved only if each member of a clan is willing to fight on behalf of other members, to avoid fighting within the clan (even though it is with his clan members that a man is most directly in competition for land, since they are his most immediate neighbors), and to give up a share of his precious household accumulation of food and wealth objects in order that his Big Man may host an impressive feast.

This dependence of the household on the economic and political success of the clan is the basis of the Big Man's power. A Big Man is a local leader who motivates his followers to act in concert. He does not hold office and has no ultimate institutional power, so he must lead by pleading and bullyragging. His personal characteristics make him a leader . . . : He is usually a good speaker, convincing to his listeners; he has an excellent memory for kinship relations and for past transactions in societies where there is no writing; he is a peacemaker whenever possible, arranging compensatory payments and fines in order to avoid direct violent retribution from groups who feel they have been injured; and, when all else fails, he leads his followers into battle.

Of great importance in this system is the exchange of brides between patrilineal groups, for which payments of food, especially pigs, and wealth objects are required. An individual's political position —which affects his access to land, pigs, and other necessities— depends on alliances formed via his own marriage and those of his close kin. A Big Man, skilled as a negotiator and extremely knowledgeable about the delicate web of alliances created across the generations by a myriad of previous marriages and wealth payments, can help a group to marry well and maintain its competitive edge. By arranging his own marriages, of course, the Big Man can not only increase the number of alliances in which he is personally involved, but he can also bring more women, which is to say, more production of sweet potatoes and pigs, under his control. Hence, as he strengthens his group, he does not neglect his own personal power, as measured by his control of women, pigs, and wealth objects. His efforts both public and personal come together most visibly when he succeeds in hosting a feast.

Among the most dramatic economic institutions on earth, the Melanesian feasts have fascinated economic anthropologists. The Big Man works for months, painfully acquiring food and wealth from his reluctant followers, only to present them in spectacular accumulations —as *gifts* to his allies. But the generosity has an edge, as the Kawelka Big Man Ongka put it: "I have won. I have knocked you down by giving so much . . . " And the Big Man expects that his turn will come to be hosted by his allies, when they will be morally bound to return his gift with an equivalent or larger one. The "conspicuous consumption" and underlying competitiveness of these displays of generosity have been regarded as so similar to philanthropy in our own economy as to seem to close the gap between "primitive" and "modern" economies.

But the Big Man feast must be understood in context. Similar to the famous potlatch of the northwest coast of North America, these feasts do not exist merely as arenas for grandiose men to flaunt their ambition. As analyzed for the northwest coast, the competitive feast is the most dramatic event in a complex of interactions that maintain what Newman . . . calls "the intergroup collectivity." We must remember that, beyond the Enga clan, there is no group that can guarantee the rights of the individual, in the sense that the modern state does for us. Beyond the clan are only allies, strangers, and enemies. Many of them covet the desirable lands of other clans, and, if they sense weakness, they will strike. Small groups—weak in numbers and vulnerable to attack—must seek to swell their numbers and to attract allies in other clans. Thus an individual family's access to the means of subsistence depends on the success of its clan in the political arena, ultimately in the size of fighting force that can be mounted from within the clan and recruited from allied clans.

In the absence of courts and constitutions regulating intergroup relations, the Big Men assume central importance. It is they who maintain and advertise their group's attractiveness as allies (hence the bragging and showmanship that accompany Big Man feasts), who mediate disputes to avoid the dangerous extremity of homicidal violence, who remember old alliances and initiate new ones. Despite the public competitiveness between Big Men as they attempt to humiliate one another with generosity, over time they develop relationships of a predictable, even trustworthy, nature with other Big Men, lending intergroup stability in an unstable world.

A good example of this stabilizing effect is seen in the *Te* cycle, a series of competitive exchanges that link many Central Enga clans. Starting at one end of the chain, initiatory gifts of pigs, salt, and other valuables are given as individual exchanges from one partner to the next down the chain of clans. Big Men do not have to be directly involved, since such individual exchanges follow personal lines of alliance. But because the gifts are flowing in one direction down the chain of clans, after a time the giving clans begin to demand repayment. As this signal passes through the system, individuals amass pigs for larger feasts at the opposite, or receiving end, of the chain. These larger interclan ceremonies are full of oratory and display that serve to advertise the size and wealth of individual clans. Over a period of months a series of large gifting ceremonies move back up the chain of clans toward the beginning. The emphasis on prestige in these ceremonies is certainly gratifying to the participants, but it serves larger purposes: to maintain peace by substituting competitive feasting for open warfare, to establish and reinforce alliances, and to advertise a clan's attractiveness as an ally and fearsomeness as an enemy.

The central points to note from this example are the following:

1. The high population density of the Enga . . . implies two related developments: First, there is little wild forest left and virtually no supply of wild foods for the diet; and, second, the best horticultural land is fully occupied and in permanent use. These two primary consequences of population growth have further implications.

2. One is an intensive mode of food production that does not rely so much on regeneration of natural soil fertility through fallowing as upon mounding and the addition of green manure to soils. Because of the Enga's reliance on pigs, these fields must support not only the human population but also that of the pigs, who consume as much garden produce as humans do. The labor costs of pigs therefore include both producing their food and building fences to control their predation of gardens. Although the Enga populations are able to provide their basic nutritional needs in this manner, other highland groups with similar economies do show some signs of malnutrition, suggesting that overall production is not much more than adequate.

3. Furthermore, with land scarce, warfare shows a clear emphasis on territorial expansion and displacement. In response to this basic threat to their livelihood, families participate, albeit somewhat reluctantly, in the political activities of the lineage and clan. Although these activities often appear belligerent and can lead to warfare by deflecting hostilities outside the clan or local alliance of clans, it remains true that they have the primary function of preventing violence and stabilizing access to land.

The three major paths for creating alliances are marriage exchanges, sharing of food at feasts (commensality), and an intricate web of debt and credit established through exchanges of food and wealth objects. All of these together constitute the prestige economies for which such groups are famous. Crucial junctures in the prestige economy are occupied by Big Men, who earn their status by personally managing the complex alliances that provide a degree of security to otherwise vulnerable groups of closely related kin.

[17]From *Economic Anthropology*, edited, with an Introduction, by Stuart Plattner, with the permission of the publisher, Stanford University Press. Copyright ©1989 by the Board of Trustees of the Leland Stanford Junior University.

The Chicago Commodities Exchange, where people are buying and selling, even though no goods are physically present.

Western societies, the emphasis is not on the hoarding of goods which would make them unavailable to others. Instead, the emphasis is on giving away, or at least getting rid of, one's wealth goods. Thus, these feasts serve as a leveling mechanism, preventing some individuals from accumulating too much wealth at the expense of other members of society.

MARKET EXCHANGE

To an economist, market exchange has to do with the buying and selling of goods and services, with prices set by powers of supply and demand. Just where the buying and selling takes place is largely irrelevant. Although some market transactions do take place in a specific identifiable location—much of the trade in cotton, for example, takes place in the New Orleans Cotton Exchange—it is also quite

possible for two North Americans to buy and sell goods without ever being on the same side of the continent as each other. When people talk about a market in today's world, the particular place where something is sold is often not important at all. For example, think of the way people speak of a market for certain types of automobiles, or for mouthwash.

Market exchange may also take place in the non-Western world, usually in societies with a state type of political organization. In such cases, an actual market*place* plays far more prominent a role than in our system. The chief goods exchanged in non-Western markets are material items produced by people, who bring to the market the produce and animals they have grown and raised and the handicrafts they have made. These they sell or exchange for items they want and cannot produce themselves. Land, labor, and occupations are not bought and sold as they are through the Western market economy. In other words, what happens in the market-

In non-Western societies, the market is an important focus of social as well as economic activity. Here, men in a Peruvian market socialize while women sell goods.

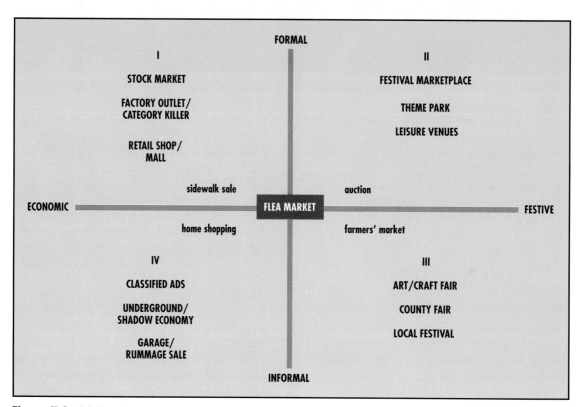

Figure 7.3   Marketplace structure and function may range from formal to informal and from economic to festive, as this diagram suggests.

place has nothing to do with the price of land, the amount paid for labor, or the cost of services. The market is local, specific, and contained. Prices are apt to be set on the basis of face-to-face bargaining, rather than by market forces wholly removed from the transaction itself. Nor need some form of money be involved; instead, goods may be directly exchanged between the specific individuals involved.

Some noneconomic aspects of marketplaces in nonindustrial societies overshadow the strictly economic aspects. Social relationships are as important in the marketplace as they are in other aspects of the economy. For example, dancers and other enter-

tainers perform in the marketplace. It is customary for people to gather there to hear news. In ancient Mexico, under the Aztecs, people were required by law to go to market at specific intervals, to be informed as to what was going on. Government officials held court and settled judicial disputes at the market. Above all, the market is a gathering place where people renew friendships, see relatives, gossip, and keep up with the world.

In the United States, as part of a reaction to the increasingly intangible nature of our economic system, there has been something of a revival and proliferation of flea markets (Fig. 7.3), where, for a small fee, anyone may display and sell handicrafts,

A New Jersey flea market. Such markets are common weekend events in many parts of the United States.

ANTHROPOLOGY APPLIED

THE ANTHROPOLOGIST AS BUSINESS CONSULTANT

When people learn that the head of the Cultural Analysis group at Planmetrics, a Chicago-based consulting firm, Steve Barnett, holds a Ph.D. in anthropology from the University of Chicago, their reaction is usually one of surprise. In the public mind, people with advanced degrees in anthropology are supposed to work in exotic, faraway places like remote islands, deep forests, hostile deserts, or arctic wastes—not in the world of business. After all, when anthropology makes the pages of the *New York Times*, is it not to report the "discovery" of a "last surviving Stone-Age tribe," the uncovering of some ancient "lost city," or the recovery of bones of some remote human ancestor, usually in some out-of-the-way part of the world?

As we saw in the first chapter of this book, anthropologists have had a long-standing interest in their own culture, and increasing numbers of them, as applied anthropologists, are putting their expertise to work in attempts to find solutions to problems of various sorts. Since 1972, the number of anthropologists going into business has grown fivefold. Some, like Steve Barnett, solve problems having to do with consumer behavior, and his clients are some of the country's largest corporations. Others like Peter Reynolds and Sunny Baker, co-founders of the Seattle consulting firm, Corporate Anthropology Group, may be called upon when companies feel a need to change their corporate culture. Their clients include such firms as Microsoft, CAE Systems and Rohm; demand for anthropologists is particularly strong in Silicon Valley, where job-hopping and rapid changes can be a source of corporate instability.

What anthropologists have to offer the corporate world are skills in analyzing everyday life that other social and behavioral scientists do not have. For example, instead of using the polling techniques market researchers prefer, Barnett relies on participant observation. Thus when Kimberly Clark hired him to help with the redesign of disposable diapers, he recorded on videotape 200 hours of diaper changing at a daycare center, which he then analyzed as if it were a ritual in another culture in order to develop meaningful categories by which to understand the diaper-changing process. Similar techniques were used in studies of dishwashing and dusting for Procter and Gamble. Unlike interviews and questionnaires, the techniques traditionally used in ethnographic fieldwork are less likely to be tinged by politics, personal biases, and *post hoc* rationalization. As John Seely Brown, director of Xerox Corporation's Palo Alto Research Center points out, anthropologists can deliver "dramatic improvements in productivity. To get these, companies have to go beyond industrial psychology and reengineer the business process. They have to work from the bottom up. And anthropology is the field most attuned to that."

Stimulating though it may be, the life of an anthropologist working for business may not always be easy. Managers may be inclined to tune out when anthropologists start talking about values. For another, the anthropologist must always keep in mind the welfare of those being studied, be they corporate employees or potential consumers so that their best interests are not ignored or violated by those paying for the services of the anthropologist. This, though, is no different from the problems faced by ethnographers in more traditional settings, who must always be on guard that their findings not be used by governments or other powerful organizations in ways that are harmful to those they study.

* Christina Elnora Garza, "Studying the Natives on the Shop Floor," *Business Week*, Sept. 30, 1991, p. 74. See also Tamar Lewin, "Casting an Anthropological Eye on American Consumers," *New York Times*, May 11, 1986, p. 6F; and Sana Siwolop, "What's an Anthropologist Doing in My Office?," in *Applying Anthropology*, ed. by Aaron Podolefsky and Peter J. Brown (Mountain View, Calif.: Mayfield, 1991), pp. 34–35.

---

secondhand items, farm produce, and paintings in a face-to-face setting. There is excitement in the search for bargains and an opportunity for haggling. A carnival atmosphere prevails, with eating, laughing, and conversation, and items may even be bartered without any cash passing hands. These flea markets, or farmers' markets, are similar to the markets of non-Western societies.

ECONOMICS, CULTURE, AND THE WORLD OF BUSINESS

At the start of this chapter, we noted that it is perhaps in the study of the economies of nonliterate peoples that we are most apt to fall prey to our own ethnocentric biases. The misunderstandings that result are of major importance to us in the modern world in at least two ways. For one, they encourage development schemes in third-world countries that all too often result in poverty, poor health, discontent, and a host of other ills. In northeastern Brazil, for example, development of large-scale plantations to grow sisal for export took over numerous small farms on which peasants grew food to feed themselves. With this development, many peasants joined the ranks of the unemployed. Being unable to earn enough money to satisfy their minimal nutritional needs, the incidence of malnutrition rose dramatically. Similarly, development projects in Africa, designed to bring about changes in local hydrology, vegetation, and settlement patterns—and even programs aimed at reducing certain diseases—have frequently led directly to *increased* disease rates.[18] Fortunately, there is now a growing awareness on the part of development officials that future projects are unlikely to succeed without the expertise that anthropologically trained people can bring to bear.

Achieving an understanding of the economic systems of other peoples that is not bound by the hopes and expectations of our own culture has also become a matter of import for corporate executives in today's world. At least, recognition of how embedded such systems are within the cultures of which they are parts could avoid problems of the sort experienced by a large Manhattan-based cosmetics manufacturer. About to come out with an ad in Italy featuring a model holding some flowers, it was discovered that the flowers were the kind traditionally given at Italian funerals. Along the same lines, the Chevrolet Nova did not sell well in Spanish-speaking countries because in Spanish *no va* means "no go." Anthropologists Edward and Mildred Hall describe another case of the same sort:

Remains of a "model village" built especially for the Mbuti to bring them out of the forest and integrate them into Zaire's national life. The rectangular shapes and inflexible architecture of these villages are so foreign to the Mbuti that even those who stay build traditional huts behind the abandoned model homes. Mostly, though, these villages quickly become death traps, breeding malaria, dysentery, yaws, and sexually transmitted diseases, spread by truckers up and down the road. The third world is strewn with failed development projects conceived by well-meaning but uninformed planners.

> José Ybarra and Sir Edmund Jones are at the same party and it is important for them to establish a cordial relationship for business reasons. Each is trying to be warm and friendly, yet they will part with mutual distrust and their business transaction will probably fall through. José, in Latin fashion, moved closer and closer to Sir Edmund as they spoke, and this movement was miscommunicated as pushiness to Sir Edmund, who kept backing away from this intimacy, and this was miscommunicated to José as coldness.[19]

Where third-world countries are involved, the chances for cross-cultural misunderstandings increase dramatically. The executives of major corporations realize their dependency on these countries for raw materials, they are increasingly inclined to manufacture their products in them, and they see their best potential for market expansion as lying in the third world. That is why business recruiters on college campuses in the United States are on the lookout for job candidates with the kind of understanding of the world that anthropology provides.

---

[18]John H. Bodley, *Victims of Progress*, 2nd ed. (Palo Alto, Calif.: Mayfield, 1982), p. 153.

[19]Edward T. Hall and Mildred Reed Hall, "The Sounds of Silence," in *Anthropology 86/87*, ed. Elvio Angeloni (Guilford, Conn.: Dushkin, 1986), p. 65.

Chapter Summary

An economic system is the means by which goods are produced, distributed, and consumed. The study of the economics of nonliterate, nonindustrial societies can be undertaken only in the context of the total culture of each society. Each society solves the problem of getting its living by allocating raw materials, land, labor, and technology, and distributing goods according to its own priorities.

The work people do is a major productive resource, and the allotment of work is always governed by rules according to sex and age. Only a few broad generalizations can be made covering the kinds of work performed by men and women. Instead of looking for biological imperatives to explain the sexual division of labor, a more productive strategy is to examine the kinds of work done by men and women in the context of specific societies to see how it relates to other cultural and historical factors. The cooperation of many people working together is a typical feature of both nonliterate and literate societies. Specialization of craft is important even in societies with a very simple technology.

All societies regulate the way that the valuable resources of land will be allocated. In nonindustrial societies, individual ownership of land is rare; generally land is controlled by kinship groups, such as the lineage or band. This system provides for greater flexibility of land use, since the size of the band territories, or of the bands themselves, can be adjusted according to availability of resources in any particular place. The technology of a people, in the form of the tools they use, is related to their mode of subsistence. In food-foraging societies, codes of generosity promote free access to tools, even though these may have been made by individuals for their own use. In sedentary, farming communities, there is greater opportunity to accumulate material belongings, and inequalities of wealth may develop. In many such communities, though, a relatively egalitarian social order is maintained through the operation of leveling mechanisms.

Nonliterate people consume most of what they produce themselves, but they do exchange goods. The processes of distribution that may be distinguished are reciprocity, redistribution, and market exchange. Reciprocity is a transaction between individuals or groups, involving the exchange of goods and services of roughly equivalent value. Usually it is prescribed by ritual and ceremony.

Barter and trade take place between groups. There are elements of reciprocity in trading exchanges, but there is a greater calculation of the relative value of goods exchanged. Barter is one form of negative reciprocity, by which scarce goods from one group are exchanged for desirable goods from another group. Silent trade, which need not involve face-to-face contact, is a specialized form of barter in which no verbal communication takes place. It is one means by which the potential dangers of negative reciprocity may be controlled. A classic example of exchange between groups that partook of both reciprocity and sharp trading was the Kula ring of the Trobriand Islanders.

Strong centralized political organization is necessary for redistribution to take place. The government assesses each citizen a tax or tribute, uses the proceeds to support the governmental and religious elite, and redistributes the rest. The collection of taxes and delivery of government services and subsidies in the United States is a form of redistribution.

Display for social prestige is a motivating force in societies, including our own, where there is some surplus of goods produced. In our society, goods that are accumulated for display generally remain in the hands of those who accumulated them, whereas in other societies they are generally given away; the prestige comes from publicly divesting oneself of valuables.

Exchange in the marketplace serves to distribute goods in a district. In nonindustrial societies, the marketplace is usually a specific site where material items produced by the people are exchanged. It also functions as a social gathering place and a news medium.

The anthropological approach to economics has taken on new importance in today's world of international development and commerce. Without it, development schemes in the third world are prone to failure, and international trade is handicapped as a result of cross-cultural misunderstandings.

Suggested Readings

Dalton, George. *Traditional Tribal and Peasant Economies: An Introductory Survey of Economic Anthropology.* Reading, Mass.: Addison-Wesley, 1971.
This is just what the title says it is, by a major specialist in economic anthropology.

Leclair, Edward E., Jr., and Harold K. Schneider, eds. *Economic Anthropology: Readings in Theory and Analysis.* New York: Holt, Rinehart and Winston, 1968.
A selection of significant writings in economic anthropology from the preceding 50 years. In the first section are theoretical papers covering major points of view, and in the second are case materials selected to show the practical application of the various theoretical positions.

Nash, Manning. *Primitive and Peasant Economic Systems.* San Francisco: Chandler, 1966.
This book studies the problems of economic anthropology, especially the dynamics of social and economic change, in terms of primitive and peasant economic systems. The book is heavily theoretical, but draws on the author's fieldwork in Guatemala, Mexico, and Burma.

Plattner, Stuart, ed. *Economic Anthropology.* Stanford, Calif.: Stanford University Press, 1989.
This is the first comprehensive text in economic anthropology to appear since the 1970s. Twelve scholars in the field contributed chapters on a variety of issues ranging from economic behavior in foraging, horticultural, "preindustrial" state, peasant, and industrial societies to sex roles, common-property resources, informal economics in industrial societies, and mass-marketing in urban areas.

Rathje, William, and Cullen Murphy, *Rubbish!: The Archaeology of Garbage.* New York: HarperCollins, 1992.
While much has been said in this chapter about the production and consumption of goods, often we don't think much about what happens *after* consumption. This book, a study of the University of Arizona Garbage Project written by its director, dispels some myths about patterns of consumption, biodegradability, and the so-called garbage crisis.

BRASS MASK, WEST AFRICA

PART III

THE FORMATION OF GROUPS: SOLVING THE PROBLEM OF COOPERATION

INTRODUCTION

ONE OF THE MOST

IMPORTANT THINGS TO

EMERGE FROM

ANTHROPOLOGICAL STUDY IS

THE REALIZATION OF JUST

HOW FUNDAMENTAL

COOPERATION IS TO HUMAN

SURVIVAL. THROUGH

COOPERATION, ALL KNOWN

HUMANS HANDLE EVEN ▶

▶ the most basic problems of existence, the need for food and protection—not only from the elements but from predatory animals and even each other. To some extent, this is true not only for humans, but for monkeys and apes as well. Baboons, for example, protect themselves against predators by traveling about in large troops which include males as well as females with their young. Owing to their much larger size and far more formidable canine teeth, the males are a more credible threat to predators than are the females. Within the troop, females provide themselves and their infants with protection against harassment from other baboons by forming friendships with particular males. Among humans, males still usually bear primary responsibility for their group's defense, even though the anatomical and physiological differences between the sexes have been reduced to relatively minor proportions compared to what we see in most monkeys and apes. Moreover, women are potentially as capable of fighting as are men, and in some societies women do bear arms. But what sets humans apart from other primates even more, is some form of cooperation in subsistence activities on a regular basis. At the least, this takes the form of the sexual division of labor as seen among food-foraging peoples. Such cooperation is not customary among nonhuman primates; adult chimpanzees, for example, may cooperate to get meat, and share it when they get it, but they don't get meat very often, and they don't normally share other kinds of food the way humans regularly do.

Just as cooperation seems to be basic to human nature, so the organization of groups is basic to effective cooperation. Humans form many kinds of groups, and each is geared to solving different kinds of problems with which people must cope. Social groups are important to humans also because they give identity and support to their members. The basic building block of human

societies is the household, within which economic production, consumption, inheritance, child rearing, and shelter are organized and carried out. Usually, the core of the household consists of some form of family, a group of relatives that stems from the parent-child bond and the interdependence of men and women. Although it may be structured in many different ways, however structured, the family provides for economic cooperation between men and women, while furnishing at the same time the kind of setting within which child rearing may take place. Another problem faced by all human societies is the need to control sexual activity, and this is the job of marriage. Given the close connection between sexual activity and the production of children, who must then be nurtured, a close interconnection between marriage and family is to be expected.

Many different marriage and family patterns exist the world over, but all societies have some form of marriage and most (but not all) have some form of family organization. As we shall see in Chapters 8 and 9, the forms of family and marriage organization are to a large extent shaped by the specific kinds of problems people must solve in particular situations.

The solutions to some organizational challenges are beyond the scope of family and household. These include such matters as defense, allocation of resources, and provision of work forces for tasks too large to be undertaken by a family. Some societies develop formal political systems to perform these functions. Nonindustrial societies frequently meet these challenges through kinship groups, which we discuss in Chapter 10. These large, cohesive groups of individuals base their loyalty to one another on descent from a common ancestor or their relationship to a living individual. In societies where a great number of people are linked by kinship, these groups serve the

important function of precisely defining the social roles of their members. In this way they reduce the potential for tension that might arise from the sudden and unexpected behavior of an individual. They also provide their members with material security and moral support through religious and ceremonial activities.

Other important forms of human social groups are the subjects of Chapter 11. Where kinship ties do not provide for all of the organizational needs of a society, grouping by age or sex, or both, is one force that may be used to create social groups. In North America, as well as in many non-Western countries, today and in the past, the organization of persons by age is common. In many areas of the world, too, social groups based on the common interests of their members serve a vital function. In industrializing countries, they may help to ease the transition of rural individuals into the urban setting. Finally, groups based on social rank are characteristic of the world's civilizations, past and present. Such groups are referred to as social classes, and they are always ranked high versus low relative to one another. Class structure involves inequalities between classes and frequently is the means by which one group may dominate large numbers of other people. To the extent that social class membership cuts across lines of kinship, residence, age, or other group membership, it may work to counteract tendencies for a society to fragment into discrete special-interest groups. Paradoxically, it does so in a way which is itself divisive, in that class distinctions systematically deprive people of equal access to important resources. Thus, class conflict has been a recurrent phenomenon in class-structured societies, in spite of the existence of political and religious institutions that function to preserve the status quo.

8

SEX

AND

MARRIAGE

A Masai wedding ceremony. In all societies, marriage establishes a continuing sexual relationship between a man and a woman, backed by legal, economic, and social forces. Thus, unlike mating (which is biological), marriage is distinctively cultural.

WHAT IS MARRIAGE?

Marriage is a transaction and resulting contract in which a woman and a man are recognized by society as having a continuing claim to the right of sexual access to each other, and in which the woman involved is eligible to bear children. Although in many societies, husbands and wives live together as members of the same household, this is not true in all societies. And though most marriages around the world tend to be to a single spouse, most societies permit, and regard as most desirable, marriage of a single individual to multiple spouses.

WHAT IS THE DIFFERENCE BETWEEN MARRIAGE AND MATING?

All animals, including humans, mate—that is, they form a sexual bond with individuals of the opposite sex. In some species, the bond lasts for life, but in some others, it lasts no longer than a single sex act. Thus, some animals mate with a single individual of the opposite sex, while others mate with several. Only marriage, however, is backed by social, legal, and economic forces. Consequently, while mating is biological, marriage is cultural.

WHY IS MARRIAGE UNIVERSAL?

A problem universal to all human societies is the need to control sexual relations, in order that they not introduce a disruptive, combative influence into society. Because the problem it deals with is universal, it follows that marriage should be universal. The specific form marriage takes is related to who has rights to offspring that normally result from sexual intercourse, as well as how property is distributed.

Among the Trobriand Islanders, whose yam exchanges and Kula voyages we examined in Chapter 7, children who have reached the age of seven or eight years begin playing erotic games with each other and imitating adult seductive attitudes. Within another four or five years they begin to pursue sexual partners in earnest, changing partners often, experimenting sexually first with one, and then another. By the time they are in their mid-teens, meetings between lovers take up most of the night, and affairs between them are apt to last for several months. Ultimately, lovers begin to meet the same partner again and again, rejecting the advances of others. When the couple is ready, they appear together one morning outside the young man's house, as a way of announcing their intention to be married.

For young Trobrianders, attracting sexual partners is an important business, and they spend a great deal of time making themselves look as attractive and seductive as possible. Youthful conversations during the day are loaded with sexual innuendos, and magical spells as well as small gifts are employed to entice a prospective sex partner to the beach at night, or to the house in which boys sleep apart from their parents. Because girls, too, sleep apart from their parents, youths and adolescents have considerable freedom in arranging their love affairs. Boys and girls play this game as equals, with neither sex being more dominant than the other.

As anthropologist Annette Weiner points out, all of this sexual activity is not a frivolous, adolescent pastime. Attracting lovers

To attract lovers, young Trobriand Islanders must look as attractive and seductive as possible. The young men shown here have decorated themselves with Johnson's Baby Powder, while the young girl's beauty has been enhanced by decorations given by her father.

is the first step toward entering the adult world of strategies, where the line between influencing others while not allowing others to gain control of oneself must be carefully learned. . . . Sexual liaisons give adolescents the time and occasion to experiment with all the possibilities and problems that adults face in creating relationships with those who are not relatives. Individual wills may clash, and the achievement of one's desire takes patience, hard work, and determination. The adolescent world of lovemaking has its own dangers and disillusionments. Young people, to the degree they are capable, must learn to be both careful and fearless.[1]

The Trobriand attitude towards adolescent sexuality stands in marked contrast to that of North American society. Theoretically, North Americans are not supposed to have sexual relations outside of wedlock, although there is a considerable discrepancy between theory and practice. Nonetheless, premarital sexual activity in our society cannot be conducted with the openness and approval that characterizes the Trobriand situation. As a consequence, it is not subject to the kind of social pressures from the community at large that prepare traditional Trobriand youths for the adult world after marriage.

CONTROL OF SEXUAL RELATIONS

One distinctively human characteristic is the ability of the human female, like the human male, to engage in sexual relations at any time she wants, or whenever her culture deems it appropriate. While this ability to perform at any time when provided with the appropriate cue is not unusual on the part of male mammals in general, it is unusual on the part of females. Although female primates, whose offspring are weaned but who have not yet become pregnant again, are likely to engage in sexual activity around the time of ovulation (approximately once a month), they are otherwise little interested in such activity. Only the human female may be willing to engage in sex at any point in her cycle, or even when she is pregnant. In some societies, intercourse during pregnancy is thought to promote the growth of the fetus. Among Trobriand

[1]Annette B. Weiner, *The Trobrianders of Papua New Guinea* (New York: Holt, Rinehart and Winston, 1988), p. 71.

Attempts by males to dominate females may introduce a competitive, combative element into social relations. Among gorillas, male silverbacks maintain absolute breeding rights over females in their group. All other adult males must acknowledge this dominance or leave the group and attempt to lure females from other groups.

Islanders, for example, a child's identity is thought to come from its mother, but it is the father's job to build up and nurture the child, which he begins to do before birth through frequent intercourse with its mother.

On the basis of clues from the behavior of other primates, anthropologists have speculated about the evolutionary significance of this human female sexuality. The best current explanation is that it arose as a side effect of persistent bipedal locomotion in early hominids.[2] The energetic requirements of this form of locomotion are such that endurance is impossible without a hormone output that is significantly greater than that of other primates. These hormones catalyze the steady release of muscular energy that is required for endurance; at the same time, they make us the "sexiest" of all primates. This is not to say that either men or women are simply at the mercy of their hormones where sex is concerned, for in the human species, both males and females have voluntary control over sex. People engage in it when it suits them to do so, and when it is deemed appropriate.

[2]James N. Spuhler, "Continuities and Discontinuities in Anthropoid-Hominid Behavioral Evolution: Bipedal Locomotion and Sexual Reception," in *Evolutionary Biology and Human Social Behavior*, ed. N.A. Chagnon and William Irons (North Scituate, Mass.: Duxbury Press, 1979), pp. 454–461.

Although developed as an accidental by-product of something else, a common phenomenon in evolution, the ability of females as well as males to engage in sex at any time would have been advantageous to early hominids to the extent that it acted, not alone but with other factors, to tie members of both sexes more firmly to the social groups so crucial to their survival. At the same time, however, that sexual activity can reinforce group ties, it can also be disruptive. This stems from the common primate characteristic of male dominance.

On the average, males are bigger and more muscular than females, although this differentiation has become drastically reduced in modern *Homo sapiens* compared to the earliest hominids. Among other primates, the males' larger size allows them to try to dominate females when the latter are at the height of their sexuality; this trait can be seen among baboons, gorillas, and, though less obviously, chimpanzees (significantly, the size difference between male and female chimpanzees is not as great as among baboons or gorillas, but it is still substantially greater than among modern humans). With early hominid females potentially ready for sexual intercourse at any time, dominant males may have attempted to monopolize females; an added inducement could have been the prowess of the female at food gathering. (In food-foraging societies, the bulk of the food is usually provided by the gathering activities of women.) In any event, a tendency to monopolize females would introduce the kind of competitive, combative element into hominid groupings that one sees among many other primate species—one that cannot be allowed to disrupt harmonious social relationships. The solution to this problem is to bring sexual activity under cultural control. Thus, just as a culture tells people what, when, and how they should eat, so does it tell them when, where, how, and with whom they should have sex.

RULES OF SEXUAL ACCESS

We find that everywhere societies have cultural rules that seek to control sexual relations. In the United States and Canada, the official ideology has been that all sexual activity outside of wedlock is taboo. One is supposed to establish a family, which is done through marriage. With this, a person establishes a continuing claim to the right of sexual access to another person. Actually very few known societies—only about 5 percent—prohibit all sexual involvement outside of marriage, and even North American society has become less restrictive. Among other peoples, as we have already seen, things are often done quite differently. As a further example, we may look at the Nayar peoples of India *(see map opposite).*[3]

The Nayar constitute a landowning, warrior caste (rather than an independent society) from southwest India. Among them, estates are held by corporations of sorts, which are made up of kinsmen related in the female line. These kinsmen all live together in a large household, with the eldest male serving as manager.

Three transactions that take place among the Nayar are of concern to us here. The first occurs shortly before a girl undergoes her first menstruation. It involves a ceremony that joins together in a temporary union the girl with a young man. This union, which may or may not involve sexual relations, lasts for a few days and then breaks up. There is no further obligation on the part of either individual, although the woman and her future children will probably mourn for the man when he dies. What this transaction does is to establish the girl's eligibility for sexual activity with men who are approved by her household. With this, she is officially an adult.

The second transaction takes place when a girl enters into a continuing sexual liaison with an approved man. This is a formal relationship, which requires the man to present her with gifts three times each year until such time as the relationship may be terminated. In return, the man may spend the nights with her. In spite of continuing sexual privileges, however, the man has no obligation to support his sex partner economically, nor is her home regarded as his home. In fact, she may have such an arrangement with more than one man at a time. Regardless of how many men are involved with a single woman, this second Nayar transaction, which is their version of marriage, clearly specifies who has sexual access to whom, so as to avoid

[3]My interpretation of the Nayar follows Ward H. Goodenough, *Description and Comparison in Cultural Anthropology* (Chicago: Aldine, 1970), pp. 6–11.

conflict. We may define **marriage** as a transaction and resulting contract in which a woman and man are recognized by society as having a continuing claim to the right of sexual access to each other, and in which the woman involved is eligible to bear children. Thus defined, marriage is universal, presumably because the problems with which it deals are universal. As the Nayar case demonstrates, however, marriage need not have anything to do with beginning a new family, or even establishing a cooperative economic relationship between people of opposite sexes.

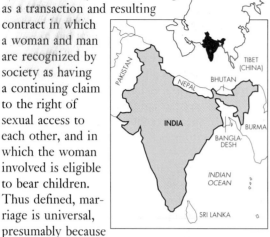

In the absence of effective birth-control devices, the usual result of sexual activity is that, sooner or later, the woman becomes pregnant. When this happens among the Nayar, some man must formally acknowledge paternity. This is done by his making gifts to the woman and the midwife. Though he may continue to take much interest in the child, he has no further obligations, for the education and support of the child are the responsibility of the child's mother's brothers, with whom the child and its mother live. What we have in this third transaction is one that establishes the legitimacy of the child. In this sense, it is the counterpart of the registration of birth in North American culture, in which motherhood and fatherhood are spelled out. In Western societies generally, the father is supposed to be the mother's husband, but in numerous other societies, there is no such necessity.

Marriage: A transaction and resulting contract in which a woman and a man are recognized by society as having a continuing claim to the right of sexual access to each other, and in which the woman involved is eligible to bear children.

Affinal kin: Relatives by marriage.

Conjugal bond: The bond between a man and a woman who are married.

Consanguineal kin: Relatives by birth; that is, "blood" relatives.

Before leaving the Nayar, it is important to note that there is nothing here comparable to the family as we know it in North America. The group that forms the household does not include **affinal kin,** or those individuals joined by a **conjugal bond** established by marriage. As will be seen in Chapter 9, a household doesn't have to be a family as we know it. Among the Nayar the household is composed wholly of what we often call "blood" relatives, which are technically known as **consanguineal kin.** Sexual relations are with those who are not consanguineal kin, and so live in other households. This brings us to another human universal, the incest taboo.

THE INCEST TABOO

No human society has ever been found to be without a rule, called the **incest taboo,** that prohibits sexual relations at least between parents and children of opposite sex, and usually siblings as well. The universality of this rule, save for a few exceptions involving siblings, has fascinated anthropologists and other students of human behavior. It has become something of a challenge for anthropologists to explain why incest should commonly be regarded as such a loathsome thing.

Many explanations have been given. Of those that have gained some popularity at one time or

---

Incest taboo: The prohibition of sexual relations between specified individuals, usually parent-child and sibling relations at a minimum.

---

another, the simplest and least satisfactory is based on human nature—that is, some instinctive horror of incest. It has been documented that human beings raised together have less sexual attraction for one another, but by itself this argument may simply substitute the result for the cause. The incest taboo ensures that children and their parents, who are constantly in intimate contact, avoid regarding one another as sexual objects. Besides this, if there were an instinctive horror of incest, we would be hard pressed to account for the far from rare violations of the incest taboo, such as occur in North American society (an estimated 10–14 percent of our children under 18 years of age in the United States have been involved in incestuous relations[4]), or for cases of institutionalized incest, such as that which required the head of the Inca empire in Peru to marry his own sister.

Various psychological explanations of the incest taboo have been advanced at one time or another. Sigmund Freud tried to account for it in his psychoanalytic theory of the unconscious. According to him, the son desires the mother, creating a rivalry with the father. (Freud called this the Oedipus complex.) He must suppress these feelings or earn the wrath of the father, who is far more powerful than he. Similarly, the attraction of the daughter to the father, or the Electra complex, places her in rivalry with her mother. Freud's theory can be viewed as an elaboration of the reasons for a deep-seated aversion to sexual relations within the family. Some other psychologists have endorsed the belief that young children can be emotionally scarred by sexual experiences, which they may have interpreted as violent and frightening acts of aggression. The incest taboo thus protects children against sexual advances by older members of the family. A closely related theory is that the incest taboo helps prevent girls who are socially and emotionally too young for motherhood from becoming pregnant.

Early students of genetics thought that the incest taboo precluded the harmful effects of inbreeding. While this is so, it is also true that as with domestic animals, inbreeding can increase desired characteristics as well as detrimental ones. Further-

more, undesirable effects will show up sooner than would otherwise be the case, so that whatever genes are responsible for them are quickly eliminated from the population. On the other hand, preference for a genetically different mate does tend to maintain a higher level of genetic diversity within a population, and in evolution this generally works to a species' advantage. Without genetic diversity, a species cannot adapt biologically to a changed environment when and if this becomes necessary.

A truly convincing explanation of the incest taboo has still to be advanced. Certainly, there are persistent hints that it may be a cultural elaboration of an underlying biological tendency toward avoidance of inbreeding. Studies of animal behavior have

In ancient Egypt, where both men and women inherited family wealth, brother-sister marriages served to keep property intact among nobles and farmers alike.

[4]Patricia Whelehan, "Review of *Incest, a Biosocial View,*" *American Anthropologist* 87 (1985):678.

CLAUDE LÉVI-STRAUSS

(1908–   )

Claude Lévi-Strauss is the leading exponent of French structuralism, which sees culture as a surface representation of underlying mental structures that have been affected by a group's physical and social environment as well as its history. Thus, cultures may vary considerably, even though the structure of the human thought processes responsible for them is the same everywhere.

Human thought processes are structured, according to Lévi-Strauss, into contrastive pairs of polar opposites, such as light versus dark, good versus evil, nature versus culture, raw versus cooked. The ultimate contrastive pair is that of "self" versus "others," which is necessary for true symbolic communication to take place, and upon which culture depends. Communication is a reciprocal exchange, which is extended to include goods and marital partners. Hence, the incest taboo stems from this fundamental contrastive pair of "self" versus "others." From this universal taboo stem the many and varied marriage rules that have been described by ethnographers.

shown such a tendency to be common among those species that are relatively large, long-lived, slow to mature, and intelligent. Humans qualify for membership in this group on all counts. So do a number of other primates, including those most closely related to humans—chimpanzees. Although they exhibit few sexual inhibitions, chimpanzees do tend to avoid inbreeding between siblings and between females and their male offspring. So perhaps the tendency for human children to look for sex partners outside the group in which they have been raised is not just the result of the incest taboo after all. Support for this appears to come from studies that show that children raised together on an Israeli kibbutz, although not required or even encouraged to do so, almost invariably marry outside their group. In this case however, appearances seem to be deceiving. For one thing, there is hardly a kibbutz without a report of heterosexual relationships be-

tween adolescents who have grown up together since infancy.[5] As for actual marriage, most Israeli youths leave the kibbutz in their late teens for service in the armed forces. Thus, they are away from the kibbutz precisely when they are most ready to consider marriage. Consequently, those most available as potential spouses are from other parts of Israel. An even greater challenge to the "biological avoidance" theory, however, is raised by detailed census records made in Roman Egypt that conclusively demonstrate that brother-sister marriages were not only common, but preferred by ordinary members of the farming class.[6]

If indeed there is a biological basic for inbreeding avoidance among humans, it clearly is far from being completely effective in its operation. Nor is its mechanism understood; to say that certain genes program specifically for inbreeding avoidance, as some have argued, is not warranted on the basis of existing evidence.

[5]Gregory C. Leavitt, "Sociobiological Explanations of Incest Avoidance: A Critical Review of Evidential Claims," *American Anthropologist* 92(1990):973.

[6]Ibid., p. 982.

ENDOGAMY AND EXOGAMY

Whatever its cause, the utility of the incest taboo can be seen by examining its effects on social structure. Closely related to prohibitions against incest are rules against **endogamy,** or marriage within a particular group of individuals. If the group is defined as one's immediate family alone, then almost all societies prohibit endogamy and practice **exogamy,** or marriage outside the group. On the other hand, a society that practices exogamy at one level may practice endogamy at another. Among the Trobriand Islanders, for example, each individual has to marry outside of his or her own clan and lineage (exogamy). However, since eligible sex partners are to be found within one's own community, village endogamy, though not obligatory, is commonly practiced.

Sir Edward Tylor long ago advanced the proposition that alternatives to inbreeding were either "marrying out or being killed out."[7] Our ancestors, he suggested, discovered the advantage of intermarriage to create bonds of friendship. Claude Lévi-Strauss elaborated on this premise. He saw exogamy as the basis of a distinction between early hominid life in isolated endogamous groups and the life of *Homo sapiens* in a supportive society with an accumulating culture. Alliances with other groups, established and strengthened by marriage ties, make possible a sharing of culture. Building on Levi-Strauss' work, anthropologist Yehudi Cohen suggests that exogamy was an important means of promoting trade between groups, thereby ensuring access to needed goods and resources not otherwise available. Noting that incest taboos necessitating exogamy are generally most widely extended in the least complex of human societies, but do not extend beyond parents and siblings in industrialized societies, he argues that as formal governments and other

---

Endogamy: Marriage within a particular group or category of individuals.

Exogamy: Marriage outside the group.

---

[7]Quoted in Roger M. Keesing, *Cultural Anthropology: A Contemporary Perspective* (New York: Holt, Rinehart and Winston, 1976), p. 286.

Monogamy: Marriage in which an individual has a single spouse.

---

institutions have come to control trade, the need for extended taboos has been removed. Indeed, he suggests that this may have reached the point where the incest taboo is becoming obsolete altogether.

In a roundabout way, exogamy also helps to explain some exceptions to the incest taboo, such as that of obligatory brother and sister marriage within the royal families of ancient Egypt, the Inca empire, and Hawaii. Members of these royal families were considered semidivine, and their very sacredness kept them from marrying mere mortals. The brother and sister married so as *not* to share their godliness, thereby maintaining the "purity" of the royal line, not to mention control of royal property. By the same token, in Roman Egypt, where property was inherited by women as well as men, and where there was a particularly tight relationship between land and people, brother-sister marriages among the farming class acted to prevent fragmentation of a family's holdings.

THE DISTINCTION BETWEEN MARRIAGE AND MATING

Having defined marriage in terms of sexual access, it is important at this point to make clear the distinction between systems of marriage and mating. All animals, including humans, mate; some for life and some not, some with a single individual of the opposite sex, and some with several. Only marriage, however, is backed by legal, economic, and social forces. Even among the Nayar, where marriage seems to involve little else than a sexual relationship, a woman's husband is legally obligated to provide her with gifts at specified intervals. Nor may a woman legally have sex with a man to whom she is not married. Thus, while mating is biological, marriage is cultural.

The distinction between marriage and mating may be seen by looking, briefly, at practices in North American society, in which **monogamy**— the taking of a single spouse—is the only legally

In the United States, as in most Western countries, monogamy is the only legally recognized form of marriage. Nevertheless, about half of all marriages end in divorce, and most divorced people remarry at least once. Thus, serial monogamy is far from uncommon.

recognized form of marriage. Not only are other forms not legally sanctioned, but systems of inheritance, by which property and wealth are transferred from one generation to the next, are predicated upon the institution of monogamous marriage. Mating patterns, by contrast, are frequently *not* monogamous. Not only is adultery far from rare in the United States and Canada, but it has become increasingly acceptable for individuals of the opposite sex—particularly young people who have not yet married—to live together outside of wedlock. None of these arrangements, however, are legally sanctioned. Even married couples who do not engage in sexual activity outside of wedlock frequently mate with one or more individuals of the opposite sex; after all, over 50 percent of first marriages in the U.S. end in divorce, and most divorced people ultimately remarry.

Among primates in general, monogamous mating patterns are not common. Although some smaller species of South American monkeys, a few island-dwelling populations of leaf-eating Old World monkeys, and all of the smaller apes (gibbons and siamangs) do mate for life with a single individual of the opposite sex, none of these are closely related to human beings, nor do "monogamous"

primates ever display the degree of anatomical differences between males and females that is characteristic of our closest primate relatives, or that were characteristic of our own ancient ancestors. Thus it is not likely that the human species began its career as one with monogamous mating patterns. Certainly, one cannot say (as some have tried to assert) that the human species is, by nature, monogamous in its mating behavior.

MARRIAGE AND THE FAMILY

Although, as we saw in our discussion of the Nayar, marriage does not have to result in the formation of a new family, it can easily serve this purpose, in addition to its main function of indicating who has continuing sexual access to whom. This is precisely what is done in most human societies. Consequently, some mention of family organization—otherwise discussed in Chapter 9—is necessary before we can proceed further with our discussion of marriage. If we were to define the family in terms with which we are familiar, as requiring fathers, mothers, and children, then we would have to say that people like the Nayar (who, as we shall see in

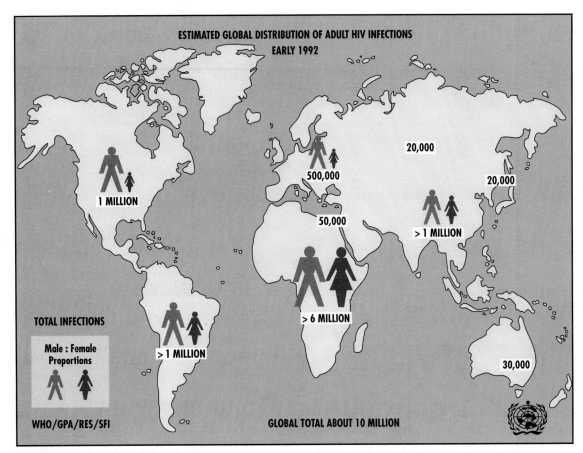

Figure 8.1   Estimated global distribution of adult HIV infections, early 1992. Courtesy of the World Health Organization.

Family: A residential kin group composed of a woman, her dependent children, and at least one adult male joined through marriage or blood relationship.

Consanguine family: A family consisting of related women, their brothers, and the offspring of the women.

Nuclear family: A family unit consisting of husband, wife, and dependent children.

Chapter 9, do not constitute a unique case) do not have families. We can, however, define the **family** in a less ethnocentric way as a group composed of a woman and her dependent children and at least one adult male joined through marriage or blood relationship.[8] The Nayar family is a **consanguine** one, consisting as it does of women with their brothers and the dependent offspring of the women. In such

societies, men and women get married, but do not live together as members of a single household. Rather, they spend their lives in the households in which they grew up, with the men "commuting" for sexual activity with their wives. Economic cooperation between men and women takes place between sisters and brothers, rather than husbands and wives.

Conjugal, as opposed to consanguine, families, are formed on the basis of marital ties between husband and wife. Minimally, a conjugal family consists of a married couple with their dependent children, otherwise known as the **nuclear family;**

[8]Goodenough, *Description*, p. 19.

ANTHROPOLOGY APPLIED

ANTHROPOLOGY AND AIDS

In North America, the 1960s and the 1970s were a time of social turmoil involving, among other things, significant changes for some in sexual values and practices. With this rebellion developed new life-styles—including sexual experimentation with many different partners and techniques. Inevitably, these changes were reflected in the health problems of such sexually active individuals. In particular, the incidence of sexually transmitted diseases (STDs) of all kinds has skyrocketed. Among these diseases is Acquired Immune-Deficiency Syndrome, or AIDS, which can be transmitted through intravenous drug use and blood transfusions as well as sexual intercourse. In the United States, AIDS was unknown before the mid-1970s; since then, it has possibly become the most serious menace to public health in the twentieth century. By the beginning of 1992, more than one million people in the United States were infected with the AIDS virus.

Worldwide, AIDS now spreads primarily through heterosexual transmission; and in the U.S. today, the rate of AIDS transmission among heterosexuals (especially among intravenous drug users and their sexual partners) may possibly be rising even as it appears to be levelling off among homosexual and bisexual men.

During its first decade in the U.S., however, AIDS affected primarily the homosexual male population. In San Francisco's homosexual community, the first cases appeared in 1979, and by 1980 it had become evident that a major epidemic was under way. As part of a concerted effort to deal with this situation, a group at the University of California, San Francisco began a team effort to learn more about the disease, and to begin efforts at prevention and health education based on current knowledge of AIDS. Included on the team was E. Michael Gorman, a medical anthropologist with training in epidemiology and infectious disease who had extensive experience working with the city's homosexual population on health-related issues. Data gathered by the team included information on demography, medical history, sexual history, social factors, alcohol and drug usage, and sexual contacts. Gaining information on history posed a particular challenge, requiring knowledge and understanding of various aspects of homosexual male sexual behavior and the distinctive cultural themes of the homosexual subcultures.

As Gorman points out, the participation of a medical anthropologist, and use of anthropological methodologies were of great relevance in many respects:

> Epidemiological inquiry focuses primarily on the determinants of disease in human population. In this context, anthropological knowledge assisted in the more precise definition of the epidemiological variables of interest: person, time, and place. Specific knowledge of the population at risk and familiarity with the cultural context also aided in the process of investigating the epidemic. Experience with the community and understanding of its mores and history likewise facilitated the research process and brought community needs such as health education, risk reduction information, and prevention generally to the attention of the investigators.*

No less important than the research is prevention, for in the absence of either a cure or a vaccine (neither of which is on the horizon), the only effective way to deal with AIDS is through education and the development of risk-reduction strategies. Here, the input of anthropologists is especially valuable in designing and implementing prevention programs tailored (as they must be) to the concerns of particular high-risk populations, each of which has its distinctive subculture. Finally, anthropologists are highly qualified to act as culture brokers, clarifying issues and positions to both public health officials and the communities they seek to serve.

*SOURCE: E. Michael Gorman, "The AIDS Epidemic in San Francisco: Epidemiological and Anthropological Perspectives," in *Applying Anthropology, An Introductory Reader*, ed. Aaron Podolefsky and Peter J. Brown. (Mountain View, Calif.: Mayfield, 1989): 197–198.

other forms of conjugal families are polygynous and polyandrous families, which may be thought of as aggregates of nuclear families with one spouse in common. A polygynous family includes the multi-

ple wives of a single husband, while a polyandrous family includes the multiple husbands of a single wife. Both are often lumped together under the heading of polygamous families.

FORMS OF MARRIAGE

Monogamy is the form of marriage with which we are most familiar. It is also the most common, but for economic rather than moral reasons. In many polygynous societies, a man must be fairly wealthy to be able to afford **polygyny,** or marriage to more than one wife. Among the Kapauku of western New Guinea,[9] the ideal is to have as many wives as possible, and a woman actually urges her husband to spend money on acquiring additional wives. She even has the legal right to divorce him if she can prove that he has money for bride price and refuses to remarry. As we saw in Chapter 2, wives are desirable because they work in the fields and care for pigs, by which wealth is measured, but not all men are wealthy enough to afford bride price for multiple wives.

Among the Turkana, a pastoral nomadic people of northern Kenya, the number of animals at a family's disposal is directly related to the number of adult women available to care for them. The more wives a man has, the more women there are to look after the livestock, and so the more substantial the family's holdings can be. Thus, it is not uncommon for a man's existing wife to actively search for another woman to marry her husband. Again, however, a substantial bride price is involved in marriage, and only men of wealth and prominence can afford large numbers of wives.

Although most marriages around the world tend to be monogamous, polygyny is the preferred form in by far a majority of the world's societies. Even in the United States, an estimated 50,000 people in the Rocky Mountain states live in households made up of a man with two or more wives. In spite of its illegality, law enforcement officials have adopted a "live and let live" attitude toward polygyny. Nor are those involved in such marriages uneducated.

Polygyny: The marriage custom of a man having several wives at the same time; a form of polygamy.

[9]Leopold Pospisil, *The Kapauku Papuans of West New Guinea,* (New York: Holt, Rinehart and Winston, 1963).

One woman—a lawyer and one of nine co-wives—expresses her attitude as follows:

> I see it as the ideal way for a woman to have a career and children. In our family, the women can help each other care for the children. Women in monogamous relationships don't have that luxury. As I see it, if this life style didn't already exist, it would have to be invented to accommodate career women.[10]

Polygyny is particularly common in societies that support themselves by growing crops, and the bulk of the farm work is done by women. Under these conditions, women are valued as workers as well as child bearers. Because the labor of wives in polygynous households generates wealth and little support is required from husbands, the wives' bargaining position within the household is a strong one. Often, they have considerable freedom of movement and some economic independence from sale of crops. Commonly, each wife within the household lives with her children in her own dwelling, apart from her co-wives and husband, who occupy other houses within some sort of larger household compound (note that the terms *house* and *household* need not be synonymous; a household may consist of several houses together, as here). Because of this residential autonomy, fathers are usually remote from their sons, who grow up among women. As noted in Chapter 5, this is the sort of setting conducive to the development of aggressiveness in adult males, who must prove their masculinity. As a consequence, a high value is often placed on military glory, and one reason for going to war is to capture women, who may then become a warrior's co-wives. This wealth-increasing pattern is found in its fullest elaboration in sub-Saharan Africa, though it is known elsewhere as well (the Kapauku are a case in point). Moreover, it is still intact in the world today, as its wealth-generating properties at the household level have made it an economically productive system.[11]

In societies practicing wealth-generating polygyny, most men and women do enter into polygy-

[10]Dirk Johnson, "Polygamists Emerge From Secrecy, Seeking Not Just Peace But Respect," *New York Times,* April 9, 1991, p. A22.

[11]Douglas R. White, "Rethinking Polygyny: Co-Wives, Codes and Cultural Systems," *Current Anthropology* 29(1988):529–572.

Where polygynous marriages occur, a man's wives may occupy separate dwellings in a larger household, like the one shown here. Thus, children usually have a close relationship with their mother, but a distant one with their father.

nous marriages, although some are able to do this earlier in life than others. In societies in which men are more heavily involved in productive work, generally only a small minority of marriages are polygynous. Under these circumstances, women are more dependant on men for support so that they are valued as child bearers more than for the work they do. This makes them especially vulnerable if they prove incapable of bearing children, which is one reason a man may seek another wife. Another reason for a man to take on secondary wives is to demonstrate his high position in society. But in societies in which men do most productive work, the men must work exceptionally hard to support more than one wife, and few actually do so. Usually, it is the exceptional hunter, or a shaman ("medicine man") in a food-foraging society, or a particularly wealthy man in an agricultural or pastoral society who is most apt to practice polygyny. When he does, it is usually of the sororal type, in which the women he marries are sisters. Having already lived together before marriage, they continue to do so with their husband, instead of occupying separate dwellings of their own.

Polyandry: The marriage custom of a woman having several husbands at one time; a form of polygamy.

Although monogamy and polygyny are the most common forms of marriage in the world today, other forms do occur, however rarely. **Polyandry,** the marriage of one woman to several men at the same time, is known in only a few societies, perhaps in part because a man's life expectancy is shorter than a woman's, and male infant mortality is high, so a surplus of men in a society is unlikely. Another reason is that it limits a man's descendants more than any other pattern. Fewer than a dozen societies are known to have favored polyandry, but they involve people as widely separated from one another as the eastern Inuit (Eskimos), Marquesan Islanders of Polynesia, and Tibetans. In Tibet, where inheritance is in the male line and arable land is limited, the marriage of brothers to a single woman averted the danger of constantly subdividing farm lands among all the sons of any one landholder.

Group marriage: Marriage in which several men and women have sexual access to one another.

Levirate: A marriage custom according to which a widow marries a brother of her dead husband.

Sororate: A marriage custom according to which a widower marries his dead wife's sister.

Serial monogamy: A marriage form in which a man or a woman marries or lives with a series of partners in succession.

Group marriage, in which several men and women have sexual access to one another, also occurs only rarely. Even in communal groups today, among young people seeking alternatives to modern marriage forms, group marriage seems to be a transitory phenomenon, despite the publicity it may sometimes receive.

THE LEVIRATE AND THE SORORATE

If a husband dies, leaving a wife and children, it is often the custom that the wife marry one of the brothers of the dead man. This custom, called the **levirate,** not only provides social security for the widow and her children but also is a way for the husband's family to maintain their rights over the wife's sexuality and her future children: It acts to preserve relationships previously established. When a man marries the sister of his dead wife, it is called the **sororate;** in essence, a family of "wife givers" supplies one of "wife takers" with another

spouse to take the place of the one who died. In societies that have the levirate and sororate, the relationship between the two families is maintained even after the death of a spouse; and in such societies, an adequate supply of brothers and sisters is generally ensured by the structure of the kinship system (discussed in Chapter 10), in which individuals whom we would call "cousins" are classified as brothers and sisters.

SERIAL MONOGAMY

A form of marriage becoming increasingly common in North American society today is **serial monogamy,** in which the man or the woman marries a series of partners in succession. Currently, more than 50% of first marriages end in divorce.[12] Upon

[12] Judith Stacey, *Brave New Families* (New York: Basic Books, 1990), pp. 15 and 286 (n46).

Although standards of feminine beauty change, the great emphasis Western cultures place on it is illustrated by Vanna White's role as a model to turn letters on the television show *Wheel of Fortune*. Lillie Langtry (1852–1929), a celebrated British actress, represented an earlier standard of beauty.

dissolution, the children of each marriage more often than not remain with the mother. This pattern is an outgrowth of one first described by sociologists and anthropologists among West Indians and lower-class urban blacks in the United States. Early in life, women begin to bear children by men who are not married to them. To support themselves and their children, the women must look for work outside of the household, but to do so they must seek help from other kin, most commonly the children's mother's mother. As a consequence, households are frequently headed by women (on the average, about 32% are so headed in the West Indies). After a number of years, however, an unmarried woman usually does marry a man, who may or may not be the father of some or all of her children. Under conditions of poverty, where this pattern has been most common, women are driven to seek this male support, owing to the difficulties of supporting themselves and their children, while at the same time fulfilling their domestic obligations.

In the United States, with the rise of live-in premarital arrangements between couples, the increasing necessity for women to seek work outside the home, and rising divorce rates, a similar pattern is becoming more common among middle-class whites. In 90% of divorce cases, it is the woman who assumes responsibility for any children; furthermore, of all children born in the U.S. today, 25% are born out of wedlock. Frequently isolated from kin or other assistance, women in single-parent households commonly find it difficult to cope. To be sure, fathers of children are usually expected to provide child support, but in 50% of the cases of children born out of wedlock, paternity cannot be established. Furthermore, failure of fathers to live up to their obligations is far from rare. One solution for unmarried women is to marry (often, to remarry), to get the assistance of another adult.

CHOICE OF SPOUSE

The Western ideal that an individual should be free to marry whomever he or she chooses is an unusual arrangement, certainly not one universally embraced. However desirable such an ideal may be in the abstract, it is fraught with difficulties, and

certainly contributes to the apparent instability of marital relationships in modern North American society. Part of the problem is the great emphasis that our culture places on the importance of youth and glamour—especially on the part of women—for romantic love. Female youth and beauty are perhaps most glaringly exploited by the women's wear, cosmetics, and beauty parlor industries, but the film, television, and music industries have

Marriage is a means of creating alliances between two groups of people—the relatives of the bride and those of the groom. Since such alliances have important economic and political implications, the decision has traditionally not been left in the hands of two young and inexperienced people. At the top is a Moroccan bride, whose marriage has been arranged by her parents and those of the groom. Immediately above is a scene from the wedding of Prince Charles and Lady Diana in England.

generally not lagged far behind; nor do advertisements for cigarettes, liquor, soft drinks, beer, automobiles, and a host of other products that make liberal use of young, glamorous women. As anthropologist Jules Henry once observed, "Even men's wear and toiletries could not be marketed as efficiently without an adoring, pretty woman (well under thirty-five years of age) looking at a man wearing a stylish shirt or sniffing at a man wearing a deodorant."[13] By no means are all North Americans taken in by this, but it does tend to nudge people in such a way that marriages may all too easily be based on trivial and transient characteristics. In no other part of the world are such chances taken with something as momentous as marriage.

In many societies, marriage and the establishment of a family are considered far too important to be left to the whims of young people. The marriage

of two individuals who are expected to spend their whole lives together and raise their children together is incidental to the more serious matter of making allies of two families by means of the marriage bond. Marriage involves a transfer of rights between families, including rights to property and rights over the children, as well as sexual rights. Thus, marriages tend to be arranged for the economic and political advantage of the family unit.

Arranged marriages are not commonplace in North American society, but they do occur. Among ethnic minorities, they may serve to preserve traditional values that people fear might otherwise be lost. Among families of wealth and power, marriages may be arranged by segregating their children in private schools and carefully steering them toward "proper" marriages. A careful reading of announced engagements in the society pages of the *New York Times* provides clear evidence of such family alliances. The following Original Study illustrates how marriages may be arranged in societies where such practices are commonplace.

[13]Jules Henry, "The Metaphysic of Youth, Beauty, and Romantic Love," in *The Challenge to Women*, ed. Seymour Farber and Roger Wilson (New York: Basic Books, 1966).

ORIGINAL STUDY

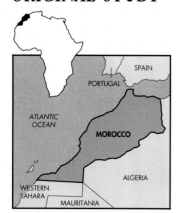

ENGAGEMENT AND MARRIAGE IN A MOROCCAN VILLAGE[14]

Marriages in Sidi Embarek are all arranged by the parents of the couple involved, although the parties on occasion may make suggestions, or veto those of their parents. The author heard an older woman describe, with obvious glee, how she had foiled her parents' plans for her. The prospective groom's family sent a donkey bearing baskets full of ripe grapes and a large sack of *henna* (a cosmetic made of powdered leaves, used to color hair red in the U.S.) as a gift. To show her disapproval, Fatna dumped all the grapes on the ground, sprinkled the *henna* over them, and set the chickens loose in the mess—and ran away to hide. When her parents found her, they chained her ankles together so she could not run far, and went ahead with the wedding plans. But Fatna was not about to be subdued, and a girl friend helped her remove the chain from one ankle. She put this over her shoulder and ran off to a nearby French farm where she knew some Moroccan workers, and they interceded with the owner. He let her stay, and when her parents came for her persuaded them to delay the marriage. According to Fatna, she was fourteen at the time, and she did not marry (and then it was someone else) for another several years.

Legally, a girl now has the right to refuse the match and is asked if she agrees to it during the engagement ceremony, but the legal prerogative does not always match the reality of the situation. If a girl fears a beating, or lack of further support from her family, she will agree publicly to the marriage, whatever her personal preferences (which are just beginning to be important in village marriages). Traditionally, marriage is an alliance between two families. It was said to often be of the patrilateral parallel cousin type, in which a boy married his father's brother's daughter, which had the effect of keeping jointly owned property in the same patrilineal family. Since the families involved were related and may even have lived together as an extended family, it also meant that it was easier to assess both the types of relationships being entered into and the characters of the actors. Data collected in Sidi Embarek, however, show that in only three of twenty-four cases did persons related by blood (not only parallel cousins) marry, while in the other twenty-one marriages the partners were unrelated. While this was not a random or representatively selected sample, it does indicate that marriage often occurs between unrelated couples.

Since marriage is mainly an alliance between two families, the partners do not have expectations of Western-style "love" (although movies and magazines are beginning to arouse such expectations), but rather work as a partnership with the object of raising a family. In this context, arranged marriages are not resented, as many Western observers suspect, but rather accepted as the most sensible way to go about the matter. Even if a girl and boy in the village decide they want to marry, the decision is probably based on only a few meetings, since the sexes do not usually mix and in rural Morocco there is nothing like the custom of dating. Parents have more experience in life and more knowledge of the families which may be involved, so they are the logical agents.

The age at marriage of village girls is considerably higher than was that of their mothers. Many women recall that they had barely reached puberty when they were married ("I hardly had any breasts yet"), were afraid of their husbands, and ran away several times before finally settling down. There is now a Moroccan law setting the minimum age at marriage for girls as sixteen years and boys as eighteen, but this can easily be circumvented (an agreement with the proper official, or a change in the birth certificate) and is thus unlikely to be the cause of the higher age at marriage, now usually seventeen or eighteen for girls and the early or mid-twenties for boys. Unmarried teenage girls are still seen as a threat to the family honor, and in other rural regions of Morocco (e.g., the Southeast, near the Sahara) may still be married when they are eleven or twelve years old. The higher age at marriage in Sidi Embarek is probably due to the general lack of agriculturally based extended families living as a single household unit that could absorb and support the new couple. Marriages now usually do not occur until the male has a job with which he can support his new family, and when the job is not involved with family agriculture (and given the general shortage of jobs available), he is usually in his twenties before he can afford to be married. Thus age at marriage is higher, and most girls approve of this (although some of the boys get impatient). However, girls are still regarded as likely to be old maids if they are not married by the time they are twenty.

It is the male's family which selects the wife for its son and makes the first overtures to her family. The first sign the girl has of her impending marriage (it is improper for a father and daughter to discuss such things) is a visit paid to her home by a few female members of the groom's family, including his mother. While the males of the groom's family are important in selecting with which family they desire further ties, since they are men they can play little part in personally assessing the worthiness of the proposed bride. The women of the family are given this task, both because they can interact with her face-to-face, and because they will be more accurate judges of her housekeeping skills. In fact, household skills and honor are highly correlated; one would not expect to find an honorable girl a sloppy housekeeper, and a messy house suggests also a looseness in a woman's moral character. In this way, even if the women have been overruled initially by the men in the choice of the bride, they still have the opportunity to influence the decision in their favor.

If the groom's family is pleased with the reputation, demeanor (very shy and retiring), and household skills of the potential bride, males of the two families discuss the bride price (*sdaq* in Morocco, *mahr* in classical Arabic and in the Middle East). This sum is included in the marriage contract, and may either be given as a large lump sum to the family of the bride, or given only in part at the marriage with the other portion to be paid only in case of divorce or death of the husband. In either case, the bride price contributes to the stability of the marriage. A man considers seriously before divorcing a woman when it means he will have to pay her family additional money. Even if he has paid the total amount initially, he must still raise the bride price for another wife, for men seldom live as bachelors. Usually his family contributes to the bride price, and their hesitance to invest any further money leads them to put pressure on him to sustain his current marriage.

The inflation of bride prices in recent years is a problem for many bachelors and has also contributed to the rising age at marriage. The family of a country girl in 1972 demanded $100.00 or $200.00, while that of a city girl asked between $700.00 and $1,000.00 (village girls fell in between), in a country where the per capita income was then $80.00 a year. Divorcees and widows are much more easily attainable; their price fell within the $20.00 to $40.00 range (and did not require a large wedding celebration either), but usually only a man who has in some way lost his first wife will marry a woman who is not a virgin.

The Moroccan case also refutes (once again) those who suggest that a bride price involves the "selling" of a daughter. The money is paid to the bride's father, but it is used to buy jewelry for the bride or household furnishings for the new couple, and to finance the elaborate and costly wedding celebration. Guests do bring gifts, but these are usually something personal for the bride (such as a slip or nightgown) or cash, and are not large enough to furnish a house. The bride's father may manage to retain some of the money (for this reason some prospective grooms attempt to provide the furnishings themselves rather than giving cash to the bride's family to do so, confident that in this way they can be more economical), but not a great deal in any case.

Rather, he is expected to contribute a similar sum as a dowry, to be used for the celebration, the bride's garments, and household furnishings.

If a bride price is agreed upon by the two families, there are exchanges of gifts and meals between them and a contract is prepared. The legal part of the ceremony of signing the marriage contract in rural Morocco (literally, "they do the paper") is considered as part of the engagement, but is actually also the only legal part of the marriage. If one decides afterwards to break the "engagement," one must obtain a divorce. The marriage is usually not consummated until months or even years later at a marriage ceremony (which is purely secular and consists of several days of celebration and feasting), but it is legally binding from the signing of the contract at the engagement.

The signature of the contract is done at home in the presence of a judge or his assistant and attended by members of each family. The bride is present but is spoken for by her father (or other male relative) except when asked if she agrees to the marriage. Otherwise she maintains a demure silence, her eyes cast down.

[14]Susan S. Davis, *Patience and Power, Women's Lives in a Moroccan Village* (Rochester, Vt.: Shenkman Books, Inc., 1987), pp. 26–30. Reprinted by permission of Shenkman Books, Inc.

COUSIN MARRIAGE

In the Original Study, mention was made of **patrilateral parallel-cousin marriage**, in which a man marries his father's brother's daughter. Although not obligatory, such marriages have been favored historically among Arabs, the ancient Israelites, and also in ancient Greece and traditional China. All of these societies are hierarchial in nature—that is, some people have more property than others—and although male dominance and descent are emphasized, property of interest to men is inherited by daughters as well as sons. Thus, when a man marries his father's brother's daughter (or, from the woman's point of view, her father's brother's son), property is retained within the single male line of descent. In these societies, generally speaking, the greater the property, the more this form of parallel cousin marriage is apt to occur.

Matrilateral cross-cousin marriage—that is, of a man to his mother's brother's daughter, or a woman to her father's sister's son—is a preferred form of marriage in a variety of societies ranging from food foragers (Australian aborigines, for example) to intensive agriculturists (as among various peoples of South India). Among food-foraging peoples, who inherit relatively little in the way of property from adults, such marriages help establish and maintain ties of solidarity between social groups. In agricultural societies, on the other hand, the transmission of property is once again an important determinant. In societies in which descent is traced exclusively in the female line, for instance, property and important rights usually pass

Patrilateral parallel-cousin marriage: Marriage of a man to his father's brother's daughter, or a woman to her father's brother's son.

Matrilateral cross-cousin marriage: Marriage of a woman to her father's sister's son, or a man to his mother's brother's daughter.

from a man to his sister's son; under cross-cousin marriage, sister's son is at the same time the man's daughter's husband.

MARRIAGE EXCHANGES

In the Trobriand Islands, when a young couple decides to get married, they sit in public on the veranda of the young man's adolescent retreat, where all may see them. Here they remain until the bride's mother brings the couple cooked yams, which they then eat together, making their marriage official. This is followed a day later by the presentation of three long skirts to the bride by the husband's sister, a symbol of the fact that the sexual freedom of adolescence is now over for the newly wed woman. This is followed up by a large presen-

Bride price: Compensation paid by the groom or his family to the bride's family upon marriage.

Bride service: A designated period of time after marriage during which the groom works for the bride's family.

tation of uncooked yams by the bride's father and her mother's brother, who represent both her lineage and that of her father. Meanwhile, the groom's father and mother's brother—representing his father's and his own lineages—collect such valuables as stone axe blades, clay pots, money, and the occasional Kula shell to present to the young wife's maternal kin and father. After the first year of the marriage, during which the bride's mother continues to provide the couple's meals of cooked yams, each of the young husband's relatives who provided valuables for his father and mother's brother to present to the bride's relatives will receive yams from her maternal relatives and father. All of this gift giving back and forth between the lineages to which the husband and wife belong, as well as those of their fathers, serve to bind the four parties together in a way that people respect, honor the marriage, and create obligations on the part of the woman's kin to take care of her husband in the future.

As among the Trobriand Islanders, marriages in many human societies are formalized by some sort of economic exchange. Among the Trobrianders, this takes the form of a gift exchange, as described above. Far more common is **bride price**, sometimes called bride wealth. This involves payments of money or other valuables to a bride's parents or other close kin. This usually happens in societies where the bride will become a member of the household in which her husband grew up; it is they who will benefit from her labor, as well as the offspring she produces. Thus, her family must be compensated for their loss. Other forms of compensation are an exchange of women between families—my son will marry your daughter if your son will marry my daughter—or **bride service,** a period of time during which the groom works for the bride's family. In a number of societies more or less restricted to the western, southern, and eastern

On the day that her marriage is announced, the Trobriand Islander bride must give up the provocative miniskirts she has worn until then for longer skirts, the first of which are provided by the groom's sister. This change announces that her days of sexual freedom are past.

Dowry: Payment of a woman's inheritance at the time of her marriage, either to her or to her husband.

margins of Eurasia, in which the economy is based on intensive agriculture, women often bring a **dowry** with them at marriage. In effect, a dowry is a woman's share of parental property which, instead of passing to her upon her parents' death, is distributed to her at the time of her marriage. This is not to say that she retains control of this property after marriage; in a number of European countries, for example, a woman's property falls exclusively under the control of her husband. Having benefitted by what she has brought to the marriage, however, he is obligated to look out for her future well-being, even after his death. Thus, one of the functions of dowry is to ensure a woman's support in widowhood (or after divorce), an important consideration in a society where men carry out the bulk of productive work, and women are valued for their reproductive potential, but not the work they do. In such societies, women incapable of bearing children are especially vulnerable, but the dowry they bring with them at marriage helps protect them against desertion. Another function of dowry is to reflect the economic status of the woman in societies where differences in wealth are important. Thus, the property that a woman brings with her at marriage demonstrates that the man is marrying a woman whose standing is on a par with his own. It also permits women, with the aid of their parents and kin, to compete through dowry for desirable (that is, wealthy) husbands.

RELATIONSHIPS MODELED ON MARRIAGE

As we have seen, marriage, although defined in terms of a continuing sexual relationship between individuals of opposite sex always involves various other nonsexual rights and obligations as well. In some societies, however, marriage-like arrangements may occur between individuals of the same sex. Although not marriage in the technical sense of our definition, they are clearly modeled on marriage, and represent legal fictions designed to deal with problems for which ordinary marriage offers no satisfactory solution. Such is the case with woman/woman marriage, a practice sanctioned in

In some societies, when a woman marries, she receives her share of the family inheritance (her dowry), which she brings to her new family (unlike the bride price, which passes from the groom's to the bride's family). Shown here is a traditional dowry presentation in Czechoslovakia.

many societies of sub-Saharan Africa, although in none does it involve more than a small minority of all women.

Although details differ from one society to another, woman/woman marriages among the Nandi of western Kenya may be taken as reasonably representative of such practices in Africa.[15] The Nandi are a pastoral people who also do considerable farming. Control of most significant property and the primary means of production—livestock and land—is exclusively in the hands of men, and may only be transmitted to their male heirs, usually their sons. Since polygyny is the preferred form of marriage, a man's property is normally divided equally among his wives for their sons to inherit. Within the household, each wife has her own house in which she lives with her children, but all are under the authority of the woman's husband, who is a remote and aloof figure within the household. In such situations, the position of a woman who bears no sons is difficult; not only does she not help perpetuate her husband's male line—a major concern among the Nandi—but she has no one to inherit the proper share of her husband's property.

To get around these problems, a woman of advanced age to whom no sons have been born may become a female husband by marrying a young woman. The purpose of this arrangement is for the wife to provide the male heirs that her female husband could not. To accomplish this, the woman's wife enters into a sexual relationship with a man other than her female husband's; usually it is one of his male relatives. No other obligations exist between this woman and her male sex partner, and it is her female husband who is recognized as the social and legal father of any children born under these conditions.

In keeping with her role as female husband, this

woman is expected to abandon her female gender identity and, ideally, dress and behave as a man. In practice, the ideal is not completely achieved, for the habits of a lifetime are difficult to reverse. Generally it is in the context of domestic activities, which are most highly symbolic of female identity, that female husbands most completely assume a male identity.

For the individuals who are parties to woman/woman marriages, there are several advantages. By assuming male identity, a barren or son-less woman raises her status considerably, and even achieves near equality with men, who otherwise occupy a far more favored position in Nandi society than do women. A woman who marries a female husband is usually one who is unable to make a good marriage, often because she has lost face as a consequence of premarital pregnancy. By marrying a female husband, she too raises her status, and secures legitimacy for her children. Moreover, a female husband is usually less harsh and demanding, spends more time with her, and allows her a greater say in decision making than does a male husband. The one thing she may not do is engage in sexual activity with her marriage partner; in fact, female husbands are expected to abandon sexual activity altogether, even with their male husbands, to whom they remain married even though the woman now has her own wife.

DIVORCE

Like marriage, divorce in non-Western societies is a matter of great concern to the families of the couple. Since marriage is less often a religious than an economic matter, divorce arrangements can be made for a variety of reasons and with varying degrees of difficulty.

Among the Gusii of Kenya, sterility or impotence were grounds for a divorce. Among the Chenchu of Hyderabad and the Caribou Indians of Canada, divorce was discouraged after children were born, and a couple were usually urged by their families to adjust their differences. By contrast, in the southwestern United States, a Hopi woman might divorce her husband at any time merely by placing his belongings outside the door to indicate he was no longer welcome. Divorce was fairly common among the Yahgan, who lived at the

---

[15]The following is based on Regina Smith Obler, "Is the Female Husband a Man? Woman/Woman Marriage Among the Nandi of Kenya," *Ethnology* 19(1980):69–88.

southernmost tip of South America, and was seen as justified if the husband was considered cruel or failed as a provider.

Divorce in these societies seems familiar and even sensible, considered in the light of our own entangled arrangements. In one way or another, the children are taken care of. An adult unmarried woman is almost unheard of in most non-Western societies; a divorced woman will soon remarry. In many societies, economic considerations are often the strongest motivation to marry. A man of New Guinea does not marry because of sexual needs, which he can readily satisfy out of wedlock, but because he needs a woman to make pots and cook his meals, to fabricate nets and weed his plantings. A man without a wife among the Australian aborigines is in an unsatisfactory position, since he has no one to supply him regularly with food or firewood.

It is of interest to note that divorce rates in Western societies are low when compared to those in some societies, notably matrilineal societies such as that of the Hopi. Yet they are high enough to cause many North Americans to worry about the future of marriage and the family in the contemporary world. Undoubtedly, the causes of divorce in our society are many and varied. Among them are the trivial and transient characteristics that we have already mentioned, on which marriages may all too easily be based. Beyond this, marriage is supposed to involve an enduring supportive, intimate bond between a man and woman, full of affection and love. In this relationship, we are supposed to find escape from the pressures of the competitive workaday world, as well as from the legal and social constraints that so affect our behavior outside the family. Yet, in a society in which people are brought up to seek individual gratification, where this often is seen to come through competition at someone else's expense (see Chapter 5), and in which women have traditionally been expected to be submissive to men, it should not come as a surprise to find that the reality of marriage does not always live up to the ideal. Harsh treatment and neglect of spouses—usually wives by husbands—in our society is neither new nor rare; furthermore, we are more tolerant of violence directed against spouses and children than we are against outsiders. As anthropologists Collier, Rosaldo, and Yanagisako have observed, "a smaller percentage of homicides involving family members are prosecuted than those

In Europe, where both men and women inherit family wealth, the "marriage" of women to the Church as nuns passed wealth that might otherwise have gone to husbands and offspring to the Church instead.

involving strangers. We are faced with the irony that in our society the place where nurturance and noncontingent [unconditional] affection are supposed to be located is simultaneously the place where violence is most tolerated."[16] What has happened in recent years is that we have become less inclined to moral censure of those—women especially—who seek escape from unsatisfactory marriages. No longer are people as willing to stick it out at all costs, no matter how intolerable the situation. Thus, divorce is increasingly seen and exercised as a sensible reaction to marriages that don't work.

[16]Jane Collier, Michelle Z. Rosaldo and Sylvia Yanagisako, "Is There a Family? New Anthropological Views," in *Rethinking the Family: Some Feminist Problems*, ed. Barrie Thorne and Marilyn Yalom (New York: Longman, 1982), p. 36.

Chapter Summary

Among primates, the human female is unique in her ability to engage in sexual behavior whenever she wants or whenever her culture tells her it is appropriate, irrespective of whether or not she is fertile. While such activity may reinforce social bonds between men and women, it can also be disruptive, so that in every society there are rules that govern sexual access.

The near universality of the incest taboo, which forbids sexual relations between parents and their children, and usually between siblings, has long interested anthropologists, but a truly convincing explanation of the taboo has yet to be advanced.

Endogamy is marriage within a group of individuals; exogamy is marriage outside the group. If the group is limited to the immediate family, all societies can be said to prohibit endogamy and practice exogamy. At the same time, societies that practice exogamy at one level may practice endogamy at another. Community endogamy, for example is a relatively common practice. In a few societies, royal families are known to have practiced endogamy rather than exogamy among siblings, in order to preserve intact the purity of the royal line.

Although defined in terms of a continuing sexual relationship between a man and woman, marriage should not be confused with mating. Although mating takes place within marriage, it often takes place outside of it as well. Unlike mating, marriage is backed by social, legal, and economic forces. In some societies, new families are formed through marriage, but this is not true for all societies.

Monogamy, or the taking of a single spouse, is the most common form of marriage, primarily for economic reasons. A man must have a certain amount of wealth to be able to afford polygyny, or marriage to more than one wife at the same time. On the other hand, in societies where most of the productive work is done by women, polygyny may serve as a means of generating wealth for a household. Although few marriages in a given society

may be polygynous, it is regarded as an appropriate, and even preferred, form of marriage in the majority of the world's societies. Since few communities have a surplus of men, polyandry, or the custom of a woman having several husbands, is uncommon. Also rare is group marriage, in which several men and several women have sexual access to one another. The levirate ensures the security of a woman by providing that a widow marry her husband's brother; the sororate provides that a widower marry his wife's sister.

Serial monogamy is a form in which a man or woman marries a series of partners. In recent decades, this pattern has become increasingly common among middle-class Americans as individuals divorce and remarry.

In many industrialized countries of the West, marriages run the risk of being based solely on an ideal of romantic love in which youthful beauty is emphasized. In no other parts of the world would marriages based on such "trivial"and transitory characteristics be expected to work. In non-Western societies, economic considerations are of major concern in arranging marriages. Love follows rather than precedes marriage. The family arranges marriages in societies in which it is the most powerful social institution. Marriage serves to bind two families as allies.

Preferred marriage partners in many societies are cross-cousins (mother's brother's daughter if a man; father's sister's son if a woman), or less commonly, parallel cousins on the paternal side (father's brother's son or daughter). Cross-cousin marriage is a means of establishing and maintaining solidarity between groups. Marriage to a paternal parallel cousin serves to retain property within a single male line of descent.

In many societies, marriages are formalized by some sort of economic exchange. Sometimes, this takes the form of reciprocal gift exchange between the bride's and groom's relatives. More common is bride price, the payment of money or other valuables from the groom's to the bride's kin; this is characteristic of societies in which the women will work and bear children for the husband's family. An alternative arrangement is for families to exchange daughters. Bride service occurs when the groom is expected to work for a period of time for the bride's family. Dowry is the payment of a woman's inheritance at the time of marriage to her or her husband; its purpose is to ensure support for women in societies where most productive work is done by men, and women are valued for their reproductive potential alone.

In some societies, arrangements exist between individuals that are modelled on marriage. One example is woman/woman marriage, as practiced by a small minority of women in many African societies. Such arrangements provide a socially approved way to deal with problems for which conventional marriage offers no satisfactory solution.

Divorce is possible in all societies, though reasons for divorce as well as its frequency vary widely from one society to another. In the United States, factors contributing to the breakup of marriages may include the transitory characteristics on which many marriages are based, and the difficulty of establishing a supportive, intimate bond in a society in which people are brought up to seek individual gratification, often through competition at someone else's expense.

Suggested Readings

duToit, Brian M. *Human Sexuality: Cross Cultural Readings*. New York: McGraw-Hill, 1991.
Of the numerous texts that deal with most aspects of human sexuality, this is the only one which adequately recognizes that most peoples in the world do things differently than North Americans. This reader deals cross-culturally with such topics as the menstrual cycle, pair-bonding, sexuality, pregnancy and childbirth, childhood, puberty, birth control, sexually transmitted diseases, sex roles, and the climacteric.

Goodenough, Ward H. *Description and Comparison in Cultural Anthropology*. Chicago: Aldine, 1970.
The book illustrates the difficulties anthropologists confront in describing and comparing social organization cross-culturally. The author begins with an examination of marriage and family, clarifying these and related concepts in important ways.

Goody, Jack. *Production and Reproduction: A Comparative Study of the Domestic Domain*. Cambridge, England: Cambridge University Press, 1976.
This book is especially good in its discussion of the interrelationship between marriage, property, and inheritance. Although the book is cross-cultural in approach, readers will be fascinated by its many insights into the history of marriage in the Western world.

Mair, Lucy. *Marriage*. Baltimore, Md.: Penguin, 1971.
Dr. Mair traces the evolution of marriage and such alternative relationships as surrogates and protectors. Commenting upon marriage as an institution and drawing her examples from tribal cultures, Dr. Mair deals with the function, rules, symbolic rituals, and economic factors of marriage. She also discusses the self-determining behavior of "serious free women" as an important factor in social change.

FAMILY

AND

HOUSEHOLD

CHAPTER PREVIEW

A Laotian father bathes his son. Caring for children is one of the basic functions of the family.

WHAT IS THE FAMILY?

The human family is a group composed of a woman, her dependent children, and at least one adult male joined through marriage or blood relationship. The family may take many forms, ranging all the way from a single married couple with their children, as in North American society, to a large group composed of several brothers and sisters with the sisters' children, as in southwest India among the Nayar. The particular form taken by the family is related to particular social, historical, and ecological circumstances.

WHAT IS THE DIFFERENCE BETWEEN FAMILY AND HOUSEHOLD?

Households are task-oriented residential units within which economic production, consumption, inheritance, child rearing, and shelter is organized and carried out. In the vast majority of human societies, households either consist of families, or else their core members constitute families, even though some members of the household may not be relatives of the family around which it is built. In some societies, although households are present, families are not. Furthermore, in some societies where families are present, they may be less important in peoples' thinking than the households of which they are parts.

WHAT ARE SOME OF THE PROBLEMS OF FAMILY AND HOUSEHOLD ORGANIZATION?

Although families and households exist to solve in various ways problems with which all peoples must deal, the different forms that they may take are all accompanied by their own characteristic problems. Where families and households are small and relatively independent, as they are in North American society, individuals are isolated from the aid and support of kin and must fend for themselves in many situations. By contrast, families that include several adults within the same large household must find ways of controlling various kinds of tensions that invariably exist between their members.

235

The family, long regarded by North Americans as a critically necessary, core social institution, today has become a matter for controversy and discussion. Women going outside the home to take jobs rather than staying home with children, young couples living together without the formality of marriage, and soaring divorce rates have raised questions about the functions of the family in North American society and its ability to survive in a period of rapid social change. Evidence of the widespread interest in these questions can be seen in the convening, in 1980, of a White House Conference on Families.

Does the family, as presently constituted in North America, offer the best environment for bringing up children? Does it impose an inferior status on the woman, confined and isolated in the home, performing household and child-raising chores? Does the man, locked into an authoritarian role, suffer unduly in his personal development from bearing the primary responsibility for support of the family? Are there adequate substitutes for people who have no family to care for them, such as old people and orphans? If the family as people in the United States know it today is found wanting, what are the alternatives?

Historical and cross-cultural studies of the family offer as many different family patterns as the fertile human imagination can invent. The one

This grouping of a pregnant woman, her husband, and her son typifies the North American ideal of the nuclear family. (The pony is optional.)

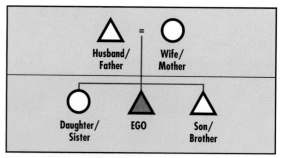

Figure 9.1   Anthropologists use diagrams of this sort to illustrate the relationships formed through marriage. The diagram always begins with a hypothetical individual called Ego, and then demonstrates the kinship and marital ties in Ego's immediate family. This diagram shows the relationships in nuclear families, such as those found in North American society. Only two generations are represented, but all possible relationships between the individuals can be determined from the diagram.

considered normal or natural by most North Americans—a discrete and independent living unit consisting of the nuclear family (Fig. 9.1)—is in fact no more normal or natural than any other, and cannot be used as the standard against which other forms should be measured. Neither universal, nor even common among human societies, the independent nuclear family emerged only recently in human history. Its roots go back to a series of regulations promoted by the Roman Catholic Church in the fourth century A.D. which prohibited close marriages, discouraged adoption, and condemned polygyny, concubinage, divorce, and remarriage (all of which had previously been perfectly respectable, as the Old Testament of the Bible, among other sources, makes clear). Not only did this strengthen the conjugal tie between a single man and woman, at the expense of consanguineal or "blood" ties, it also ensured that large numbers of people would be left with no male heirs. It is a biological fact that 20 percent of all couples will have only daughters, and another 20 percent will have no children at all. By eliminating polygyny, concubinage, divorce, remarriage, and discouraging adoption, the Church removed the means by which people overcame these odds and made sure that they would have male heirs. The result of all this was to facilitate the transfer of property from families to the Roman Catholic Church, which rapidly became the largest landowner in most European countries, a position it has retained to this day. By weaving itself into the fabric of domestic life, of heirship, and marriage, the Roman Catholic Church gained tremendous control over the grass roots of society.[1]

With the industrialization of Europe and North America, the nuclear family became further isolated from other kin. One reason for this is that industrial economies require a mobile labor force; people must be prepared to move to where the jobs are, something that is most easily done without excess

kin in tow. Another reason is that the family came to be seen as a kind of refuge from a public world that people saw as threatening to their sense of privacy and self-determination.[2] Within the family, relationships were supposed to be enduring and noncontingent, entailing love and affection, based upon cooperation, and governed by feeling and morality. Outside the family, where people sold their work and negotiated contracts, relationships

[1]Jack Goody, *The Development of the Family and Marriage in Europe* (Cambridge: Cambridge University Press, 1983), pp. 44–46.

[2]Jane Collier, Michelle Z. Rosaldo, and Sylvia Yanagisako, "Is There a Family? New Anthropological Views," in *Rethinking the Family: Some Feminist Problems*, ed. Barrie Thorne and Marilyn Yalom (New York: Longman, 1982), pp. 34–35.

The Holy Family of Christianity. Mary's husband, Joseph, was her cousin (her father's brother's son), and was himself the product of a leviratic marriage. Even though both of these kinds of marriage were considered proper in the early days of Christianity, they were not allowed by the Church after the fourth century.

increasingly were seen as competitive, temporary, and contingent upon performance, requiring buttressing by law and legal sanction. Such views were most widely held in the late nineteenth and early twentieth centuries, and in the United States, nuclear family households reached their highest frequency around 1950, when three-fifths of all households conformed to this model. Since then, things have changed, and twice as many U.S. households are now headed by divorced, separated, and never-married individuals as are headed by a member of a traditional nuclear family.[3] This situation has come about as increasingly large numbers of people have found more intimacy and emotional support in relationships outside the family and have become less inclined to tolerate the harsh treatment and neglect of children and spouses, especially wives, that have been all too common within families.

[3]Judith Stacey, *Brave New Families* (New York: Basic Books, 1990), pp. 5 and 10.

The family as it has emerged in Europe and North America, then, is the product of particular historical and social circumstances; where these have differed, so have family forms. Thus, how men and women in other societies live together must be studied, not as bizarre and exotic forms of human behavior, but as logical outcomes of peoples' experience living in particular times, places, and social situations.

FAMILY AND SOCIETY

Although many North Americans continue to think of families as standing in opposition to the rest of society, the truth is that they are affected by, and in turn affect, the values and structure of the society in which they are embedded. For a closer look at this, we may take a more detailed look at the rise and fall of nuclear families in the United States.

ORIGINAL STUDY

THE EPHEMERAL MODERN FAMILY[4]

Now that the "modern" [i.e. independent nuclear] family system has almost exited from its historical stage, we can perceive how peculiar, ephemeral, and internally contradictory was this once-revolutionary gender and kinship order. Historians place the emergence of the modern American family among white middle-class people in the late eighteenth century; they depict its flowering in the nineteenth century and chart its decline in the second half of the twentieth. Thus, for white Americans, the history of modern families traverses the same historical trajectory as that of modern industrial society. What was modern about upper-middle-class family life in the half century after the American Revolution was the appearance of social arrangements governing gender and kinship relationships that contrasted sharply with those of "traditional," or premodern, patriarchal corporate units.

The premodern family among white Colonial Americans, an institution some scholars characterize as "the Godly family," was the constitutive element of Colonial society. This integrated economic, social, and political unit explicitly subordinated individual to corporate family interests and women and children to the authority of the household's patriarchal head. Decisions regarding the timing and crafting of premodern marriages served not the emotional needs of individuals but the economic, religious, and social purposes of larger kin groups, as these were interpreted by patriarchs who controlled access to land, property, and craft skills. Nostalgic images of "traditional" families rarely recall their instability or diversity. Death visited Colonial homes so frequently that second marriages and blended households composed of stepkin were commonplace. With female submission thought to be divinely prescribed, conjugal love was a fortuitous bonus, not a prerequisite of such marriages. Similarly the doctrine of innate depravity demanded authoritarian parenting to break the will and save the souls of obstinate children, a project that required extensive paternal involvement in child rearing. Few boundaries between family and work impeded such patriarchal supervision, or segregated the sexes who labored at their arduous and interdependent tasks in close proximity. Boundaries between public and private life were equally permeable. Communities regulated proper family conduct, intervening actively to enforce disciplinary codes, and parents exchanged their children as apprentices and servants.

Four radical innovations differentiate modern from premodern family life among white Americans: (1) Family work and productive work became separated, rendering women's work invisible as they and their children became economically dependent on the earnings of men. (2) Love and companionship became the ideal purposes of marriages that were to be freely contracted by individuals. (3) A doctrine of privacy emerged that attempted to withdraw middle-class family relationships from public scrutiny. (4) Women devoted increased attention to nurturing fewer and fewer children as mothering came to be exalted as both a natural and demanding vocation.

The rise of the modern American family accompanied the rise of industrial capitalist society, with its revolutionary social, spatial, and temporal reorganization of work and domestic life. The core premises and practices of the new family regime were far more contradictory than those of the premodern family order. Coding work as masculine and home as feminine modern economic arrangements deepened the segregation of the sexes by extracting men from, and consigning white married women to, an increasingly privatized domestic domain. The institutionalized subordination of these wives to their husbands persisted; indeed, as factory production supplanted domestic industry, wives became increasingly dependent on their spouse's earnings. The doctrine of separate gender spheres governing the modern family order in the nineteenth century was so potent that few married women among even the poorest of native white families dared to venture outside their homes in search of income.

The proper sphere of working-class married white women also was confined to the home. Yet few working-class families approximated the modern family ideal before well into the twentieth century. Enduring conditions of poverty, squalor, disease, and duress rivaling those in industrializing England, most immigrant and native white working-class families in nineteenth-century America depended on supplementary income. Income from women's out work, child labor, lodgers, and the earnings of employed unmarried sons and daughters supplemented the meager and unreliable wages paid to working men. Not until the post-World War II era did substantial numbers of working-class households achieve the "modern family" pattern.

If the doctrine of separate, and unequal, gender spheres limited women's domain and rendered their work invisible, it also enhanced their capacity to formulate potent moral and political challenges to patriarchy. Men ceded the domains of child rearing and virtue to "moral" mothers who made these responsibilities the basis for expanding their social influence and political rights. This and the radical ideologies of individualism, democracy, and conjugal love, which infused modern family culture, would lead ultimately to its undoing. It is no accident, historians suggest, that the first wave of American feminism accompanied the rise of the modern family.

With rearview vision one glimpses the structural fragility of the modern family system, particularly its premise of enduring voluntary commitment. For modern marriages, unlike their predecessors, were properly affairs not of the purse but of the heart. A romantic "until death do us part" commitment volunteered by two young adults acting largely independent of the needs, interests, or wishes of their kin was the vulnerable linchpin of the modern family order. It seems rather remarkable, looking back, that during the first century of the modern family's cultural ascendancy, death did part the vast majority of married couples. But an ideology of conjugal love and companionship implies access to divorce as a safety valve for failures of youthful judgment or the vagaries of adult affective development. Thus, a statistical omen of the internal instability of this form of marriage lies in the unprecedented rise of divorce rates that accompanied the spread of the modern family. Despite severe legal and social restrictions, divorce rates began to climb at least as early as the 1840s. They have continued their ascent ever since, until by the middle of the 1970s divorce outstripped death as a source of marital dissolution. A crucial component of the modern family system, divorce would ultimately prove to be its Achilles' heel.

For a century, as the cultural significance of the modern family grew, the productive and even the reproductive work performed within its domain contracted. By the end of the "modern" industrial era in the 1950s, virtually all productive work had left the home. While advances in longevity stretched enduring marriages to unprecedented lengths, the full-time homemaker's province had been pared to the chores of housework, consumption, and the cultivation of a declining number of progeny during a shortened span of years.

Those Americans, like myself, who came of age at that historic moment were encouraged to absorb a particularly distorted impression of the normalcy and timelessness of the modern family system. The decade between the late 1940s and the late 1950s represents an aberrant period in the history of this aberrant form of family life. Fueled in part, as historian Elaine May has suggested, by the apocalyptic Cold War sensibilities of the post-World War II nuclear age, the nation indulged in what would prove to be a last-gasp orgy of modern nuclear family domesticity. Three-fifths of American households conformed to the celebrated breadwinner-fulltime homemaker modern form in 1950, as substantial sectors of working-class men began at long last to secure access to a family wage. A few years later Walt

Disney opened the nation's first family theme park in southern California, designed to please and profit from the socially conservative fantasies of such increasingly prosperous families.

The aberrant fifties temporarily reversed the century's steady decline in birth rates. The average age of first-time visitors to the conjugal altar also dropped to record lows. Higher percentages of Americans were marrying than ever before or since, and even the majority of white working-class families achieved coveted homeownership status. It was during this time that Talcott Parsons provided family sociology with its most influential theoretical elaboration of the modern American family, of how its nuclear household structure and complementary division of roles into female "expressive" and male "instrumental" domains was sociologically adaptive to the functional demands of an industrial society. Rare are the generations, or even the sociologists, who perceive the historical idiosyncrasies of the normal cultural arrangements of their time.

The postwar baby boom was to make the behaviors and beliefs of that decade's offspring disproportionately significant for the rest of their lives. The media, the market, and all social and political institutions would follow their development with heightened interest. Thus, a peculiar period in U.S. family history came to set the terms for the waves of rebellion against, and nostalgia for, the passing modern family and gender order that have become such prominent and disruptive features of the American political landscape. The world's first generation of childhood television viewers grew up, as I did, inundated by such weekly paeans to the male breadwinner nuclear household and modern family ideology as *Father Knows Best, Leave It to Beaver,* and *Ozzie and Harriet.* Because unusual numbers of us later pushed women's biological "clock" to its reproductive limits, many now find ourselves parenting (or choosing not to) in the less innocent age of *Thirtysomething, Kate and Allie,* and *Who's the Boss.* For beneath the sentimental gloss that the fifties enameled onto its domestic customs, forces undermining the modern family of the 1950s accelerated while those sustaining it eroded. In the midst of profamily pageantry, nonfamily households proliferated. As the decade drew to a close, the nation entered what C. Wright Mills, with characteristic prescience, termed its "postmodern period." The emergent postindustrial economy shifted employment from heavy industries to nonunionized clerical, service, and new industrial sectors. Employers found themselves irresistibly attracted to the nonunionized, cheaper labor of women and, thus, increasingly to that of married women and mothers.

One glimpses the ironies of class and gender history here. For decades industrial unions struggled heroically for a socially recognized male breadwinner wage that would allow the working class to participate in the modern gender order. These struggles, however, contributed to the cheapening of female labor that helped gradually to undermine the modern family regime. Escalating consumption standards, the expansion of mass collegiate coeducation, and the persistence of high divorce rates then gave more and more women ample cause to invest a portion of their identities in the "instrumental" sphere of paid labor. Thus, middle-class women began to abandon their confinement in the modern family just as working-class women were approaching its access ramps. The former did so, however, only after the wives of working-class men had pioneered the twentieth-century revolution in women's paid work. Entering employment during the catastrophic 1930s, participating in defense industries in the 1940s, and raising their family incomes to middle-class standards by returning to the labor force rapidly after child rearing in the 1950s, working-class women quietly modeled and normalized the postmodern family standard of employment for married mothers. Whereas in 1950 the less a man earned, the more likely his wife was to be employed, by 1968 wives of middle-income men were the most likely to be in the labor force.

[4]Judith Stacey, *Brave New Families* (New York: Basic Books, 1990), pp. 6–11.

FUNCTIONS OF THE FAMILY

Among humans, reliance on group living for survival is a basic characteristic. We have inherited this from our primate ancestors, though we have developed it in our own distinctively human ways. Even among monkeys and apes, group living requires the participation of adults of both sexes. Among those species which, like us, have taken up life on the ground, as well as among those species most closely related to us, adult males are normally much larger and stronger than females, and their teeth are usually more efficient for fighting. Thus, they are essential for the group's defense. Moreover, the close and prolonged relationship between infants and their mothers, without which the infants cannot survive, renders the adult primate female less well suited than the males to handle defense.

NURTURANCE OF CHILDREN

Taking care of the young is primarily the job of the adult primate female. Primate babies are born relatively helpless and remain dependent upon their mothers for a longer time than any other animals (a chimpanzee, for example, cannot survive without its mother until it reaches the age of four or even five). This dependence is not only for food and physical care, but, as a number of studies have shown, primate infants deprived of normal maternal attention will not grow and develop normally, if they survive at all. The protective presence of adult males shields the mothers from both danger and harassment from other troop members, allowing them to give their infants the attention they require.

Among humans, the sexual division of labor has been developed beyond that of other primates. Until the recent advent of synthetic infant formulas, human females have more often than not been occupied much of their adult lives with child rearing. And human infants need no less active mothering than do the young of other primates. For one thing, they are even more helpless at birth, and for another, the period of infant dependency is longer in humans. Besides all this, studies have shown that human infants, no less than other primates, need more than just food and physical care if they are to develop normally. But among humans, unlike other primates, all this mothering does not have to be provided by the infant's biological mother. Not only may other women provide the child with much of the attention it needs, but so may men. In many societies children may be handled and fondled as much by men as by women, and in some societies men are more nuturant to children than are women.

In all human societies, even though women may be the primary providers of childcare, they have other responsibilities as well. While many of the economic activities that they have traditionally

A female baboon with her infant and male friend. Baboon males are protective of their female friends, even though they are not always the fathers of their friends' infants. Thus shielded from danger and harassment from other troop members, females are able to give their infants the attention they require to survive.

engaged in have been compatible with their child-rearing role, and have not placed their offspring at risk, this cannot be said of all of them. As a case in point, the common combination of childcare with food preparation, especially if cooking is done over an open fire, creates a potentially hazardous situation for children. With the mother (or other caregiver) distracted by some other task, the child may all too easily receive a severe burn, or bad cut, with serious consequences. What can be said is that the economic activities of women have generally complemented those of men, even though in some societies, individuals may perform tasks normally assigned to the opposite sex, as the occasion dictates. Thus, men and women could share the results of their labors on a regular basis, as was discussed in Chapters 6 and 7.

An effective way both to facilitate economic cooperation between the sexes while at the same time providing for a close bond between mother and child is through the establishment of residential groups that include adults of both sexes. The differing nature of male and female roles, as these are defined by different cultures, requires a child to have an adult of the same sex available to serve as a proper model for the appropriate adult role. The presence of adult men and women in the same residential group provides for this. As defined in Chapter 8, a family is a residential group composed of a woman, her dependent children, and at least one male joined through marriage or consanguinal ("blood") relationship.

Well-suited though it may be for the task, we should not suppose that the family is the only unit capable of providing these conditions. In fact, other arrangements are possible, as on the Israeli kibbutz where groups of children are raised by paired teams of male and female specialists. In many food-foraging societies (the !Kung and Mbuti, discussed in Chapters 5 and 6 are good examples), all adult members of a community share in the responsibilities of child care. Thus, when parents go off to hunt or to collect plants and herbs, they may leave their children behind, secure in the knowledge that they will be looked after by whatever adults remain in the camp. Yet another arrangement may be seen among the Mundurucu of the Amazon, a horticultural people of South America's Amazon forest. Their children live in houses with their mothers, apart from all men until the age of thirteen, whereupon the boys leave their mothers' houses to go live with the men of the village. Because Mundurucu men and women do not live together as members of discrete residential units, it cannot be said that families are present in their society.

FAMILY AND HOUSEHOLD

Although it is often stated that some form of family is present in all human societies, the Mundurucu case just cited demonstrates that this is not so. In Mundurucu villages, the men all live together in a single house with all boys over the age of thirteen; women live with others of their sex as well as younger boys in two or three houses grouped around that of the men. As among the Nayar (discussed in Chapter 8), married men and women are members of separate households, meeting periodically for sexual activity.

Although the family is not universally present in human societies, the **household**, defined as the

---

Household: The basic residential unit in which economic production, consumption, inheritance, child rearing, and shelter are organized and carried out; may or may not be synonymous with family.

---

basic residential unit within which economic production, consumption, inheritance, child rearing, and shelter are organized and carried out, is universally present. Among the Mundurucu of the Amazon, the men's house constitutes one household, and the women's houses constitute others. Although in this case, as in many,  each house is in effect a household; there are a number of societies in which households are made up of two or more houses together, as we shall see later in this chapter.

In many human societies, most households in fact constitute families, although other sorts of households may be present as well (single parent households, for example, in the United States and many Caribbean countries). Often, a household may consist of a family along with some more distant relatives of family members. Or, coresidents may be unrelated, as in the case of service personnel in an elaborate royal household, apprentices in the household of craft specialists, or low status clients of rich and powerful patrons. In such societies, even though people may think in terms of house-

One alternative to the family as a child-rearing unit is the Israeli kibbutz. Here, children of a kibbutz are shown on their playground.

A celebration at the palace in the Yoruba city of Oyo, Nigeria. As is usual in societies in which royal households are found, that of the Yoruba includes many individuals not related to the ruler, as well as the royal family itself.

holds, rather than families, it is the latter around which the households are built. Thus, even though the family is not universal, in the vast majority of human societies, the basic core of the household is the family.

FORM OF THE FAMILY

As suggested earlier in this chapter, the family may take any one of a number of forms in response to particular social, historical, and ecological circumstances. At the outset, a distinction must be made between **conjugal families**, which are formed on the basis of marital ties, and consanguine families, which are not. As defined in Chapter 8, consanguine families consist of related women, their brothers, and the women's offspring. Such families are not common; the classic case is the Nayar household group. The Nayar are not unique, how-

Conjugal Family: A family consisting of one or more men married to one or more women, and their offspring.

ever, and consanguine families are found elsewhere, for example, among the Tory Islanders, a Roman Catholic, Gaelic-speaking fisher folk living off the coast of Ireland. These people do not marry until they are in their late twenties or early thirties, by which time there is tremendous resistance to breaking up existing household arrangements. The Tory Islanders look at it this way: "Oh, well, you get married at that age, it's too late to break up arrangements that you have already known for a long time. . . . You know, I have my sisters and brothers to look after, why should I leave home to go live with a husband? After all, he's got his sisters and his brothers looking after him."[5] Because the community numbers only a few hundred people, husbands and wives are within easy commuting distance of each other.

THE NUCLEAR FAMILY

The form of conjugal family most familiar to most North Americans is the nuclear family, which in spite of its decline is still widely regarded as the

[5]Robin Fox, Interview for Coast Telecourses, Inc., in Los Angeles, December 3, 1981.

standard in the United States and Canada. In these countries it is not considered desirable for young people to live with their parents beyond a certain age, nor is it considered a moral responsibility for a couple to take their aged parents into their home when the old people are no longer able to care for themselves. For this there are retirement communities and nursing homes, and to take aged parents into one's own home is commonly regarded as not only an economic burden, but as a threat to the privacy and independence of the household.

The nuclear family is also apt to be prominent in societies, such as the Inuit (of northern Canada, Alaska, Siberia, and Greenland), that live in harsh environments. In the winter the Inuit husband and wife, with their children, roam the vast arctic wilderness in search of food. The husband hunts and makes shelters. The wife cooks, is responsible for the children, and makes and keeps the clothing in good repair. One chore is to chew her husband's boots to soften the leather for the next day, so that he can resume his search for game. The wife and her children could not survive without the husband, and life for a man is unimaginable without a wife.

Certain parallels can be drawn between the nuclear family in industrial societies and families living under especially harsh environmental condi-

tions. In both cases, the family is an independent unit that must be prepared to fend for itself; this creates a strong dependence of individual members on one another. There is minimal help from outside in the event of emergencies or catastrophes. When their usefulness is at an end, the elderly are cared for only if it is feasible. In the event of death of the mother or father, life becomes precarious for the child. Yet this form of family is well adapted to a life that requires a high degree of geographical mobility. For the Inuit, this mobility permits the hunt for food; for North Americans, it is the hunt for jobs and improved social status that requires a mobile form of family unit.

Not even among the Inuit, however, is the nuclear family as isolated from other kin as it has become among most North Americans. When Inuit

Among the Inuit, nuclear families (such as the one shown here) are the norm, although they are not as isolated from other kin as nuclear families in the United States may be.

Extended family: A collection of nuclear families, related by ties of blood, that live together in one household.

families are off by themselves, it is regarded as a matter of temporary expediency; most of the time, they are found in groups of at least a few families together, with members of one having relatives in all of the others.[6] Thus families cooperate with one another on a daily basis, sharing food and other resources, looking out for each other's children, and sometimes even eating together. The sense of shared responsibility for each other's children, and general welfare, in Inuit multi-family groups contrasts with families in the United States, which are basically "on their own." Here the state has assigned sole responsibility to the family for childcare and the welfare of its members, with relatively little assistance from outside.[7] To be sure, families can and often do help one another out, but they are under no obligation to do so. In fact, once children reach the age of majority, parents have no further legal obligation to them, nor do the children to their parents. When families do have difficulty fulfilling their assigned functions—as is increasingly the case—even though it be through no fault of their own, less support is available to them from the community at large than in most of the world's "stateless" societies, including that of the Inuit.

THE EXTENDED FAMILY

In North America, nuclear families have not always had the degree of independence that they came to have with the rise of industrialism. In an earlier, more agrarian era, the small nuclear family commonly was part of a larger **extended family**. This kind of family, in part conjugal and in part consanguine, might include grandparents, mother and father, brothers and sisters, perhaps an uncle and

Extended families, like this one in Yuba City, California, are still found in some parts of North America.

aunt, and a stray cousin or two. All these people, some related by blood and some by marriage, lived and worked together. Because members of the younger generation brought their spouses (husbands or wives) to live in the family, extended families, like consanguine families, had continuity through time. As older members died off, new members were born into the family.

Such families have survived until recently, in some communities, as along the Maine coast.[8] There they developed in response to a unique economy featuring a mix of farming and seafaring, coupled with an ideal of self-sufficiency. Because family farms were incapable of providing self-sufficiency, seafaring was taken up as an economic alternative. Seagoing commerce, however, was periodically afflicted by depression, and so family farming remained important as a cushion against economic hard times. The need for sufficient manpower to tend the farm, while at the same time furnishing officers, crew, or (frequently) both for locally owned vessels, was satisfied by the practice of a couple, when they married, settling on the farm of either the bride's or the groom's parents. Thus, most people spent their lives cooperating on a day-to-day basis in economic activities with close relatives, all of whom lived together (even if in separate houses) on the same farm.

[6]Nelson H.H. Graburn, *Eskimos Without Igloos: Social and Economic Development in Sugluk* (Boston: Little, Brown, 1969) pp. 56–58.

[7]Collier, Rosaldo, and Yanagisako, pp. 28–29.

[8]William A. Haviland, "Farming, Seafaring, and Bilocal Residence on the Coast of Maine," *Man in the Northeast*, 6 (Fall 1973):31–44.

Members of modern Maya extended families carry out various activities on the household plaza; here, women weave and family members interact with outsiders.

The Maya of Guatemala and southern Mexico also live in extended family households.[9] In many of their communities, sons bring their wives to live in houses built on the edges of a small open plaza, on one edge of which their father's house already stands. Numerous household activities take place out on this plaza; here women may weave, men may receive guests, and children play together. The head of the family is the sons' father, who makes most of the important decisions. All members of the family work together for the common good and deal with outsiders as a single unit.

Extended families living together in single households were important social units among the Hopi Indians of Arizona.[10] Ideally, the head of the household was an old woman; her married daughters, their husbands, and their children lived with her. The women of the household owned land, but it was tilled by the men (usually their husbands). When extra help was needed during the harvest, for example, other male relatives, or friends, or persons designated by local religious organizations, formed work groups and turned the hard work into a festive occasion. The women performed household tasks, such as the making of pottery, together.

The 1960s saw a number of attempts on the part of some young people in the United States to reinvent a form of extended family living. Their

families were groups of unrelated nuclear families that held property in common and lived together. It is further noteworthy that the life-style of these modern families often emphasized the kinds of cooperative ties to be found in the rural North American extended family of old, which provided a labor pool for the many tasks required for economic survival. In some of them the members even reverted to old traditional gender roles; the women took care of the child-rearing and household chores, while the men took care of those tasks that took people outside of the household itself.

RESIDENCE PATTERNS

Where some form of conjugal or extended family is the norm, family exogamy requires that either the husband or wife, if not both, must move to a new household upon marriage. There are five common patterns of residence that a newly married couple may adopt:

1. As just described for the Maya, a woman may go to live with her husband in the household in which he grew up; this is known as **patrilocal residence.**

Patrilocal residence: A residence pattern in which a married couple lives in the locality associated with the husband's father's relatives.

[9]Evon Z. Vogt, *The Zinacantecos of Mexico, A Modern Maya Way of Life* (New York: Holt, Rinehart and Winston, 1970), pp. 30–34.

[10]C. Daryll Forde, *Habitat, Economy and Society* (New York: E.P. Dutton, 1950), pp. 225–245.

2. As among the Hopi, the man may leave the family in which he grew up to go live with his wife in her parents' household; this is called **matrilocal residence.**

3. As in the case of extended families on the coast of Maine, a married couple may have the option of choosing whether to live matrilocally or patrilocally, an arrangement that is labelled **ambilocal residence.**

4. As in most of modern North America, a married couple may form a household in an independent location, an arrangement referred to as **neolocal residence.**

5. The final pattern, to which we will return below for an example, is far less common than any of the others; this is **avunculocal residence,** in which a married couple goes to live with the groom's mother's brother.

There are variations of these patterns, but they need not concern us here.

Why do postmarital patterns of residence differ so from one society to another? Briefly, the prime determinants of residence are ecological circumstances, although other factors enter in as well. If these make the role of the man predominant in subsistence, patrilocal residence is a likely result. This is even more likely if in addition men own property that can be accumulated, if polygyny is customary, if warfare is prominent enough to make cooperation among men especially important, and if there is elaborate political organization, in which men wield authority. These conditions are most often found together in societies that rely on animal husbandry or intensive agriculture, or both, for

Matrilocal residence: A residence pattern in which a married couple lives in the locality associated with the wife's relatives.

Ambilocal residence: A pattern in which a married couple may choose either matrilocal or patrilocal residence.

Neolocal residence: A pattern in which a married couple may establish their household in a location apart from either the husband's or the wife's relatives.

Avunculocal residence: Residence of a married couple with the husband's mother's brother.

This photo, taken in 1911, shows a Hopi woman making piki bread. Traditional Hopi households are made up of women who are "blood" relatives of one another, with their unmarried sons and husbands. The latter are given roofs over their heads in return for their labor on the women's fields.

their subsistence. Where patrilocal residence is customary, it is often the case that the bride must move to a different band or community. In such cases, her parents' family is not only losing the services of a useful family member, they are losing her potential offspring as well. Hence, some kind of compensation to her family, most commonly bride price, is usual.

Matrilocal residence is a likely result if ecological circumstances make the role of the woman predominant in subsistence. It is found most often in horticultural societies, where political complexity is relatively uncentralized, and where cooperation among women is important. Under matrilocal residence, men usually do not move very far from the family in which they were raised, and so they are available to help out there from time to time. Therefore, marriage usually does not involve compensation to the groom's family.

Ambilocal residence is particularly well suited to situations where economic cooperation of more people than are available in the nuclear family is needed, but where resources are limited in some way. Because one can join either the bride's or the groom's family, family membership is flexible, and one can go where the resources look best, or where one's labor is most needed. This was once the situation on the peninsulas and islands along the coast of Maine, where extended family households were based upon ambilocal residence. The same pattern of residence is particularly common among food-foraging peoples, as among the Mbuti of Africa's Ituri forest. Typically, a Mbuti marries someone from another band, so that each individual has in-laws who live elsewhere. Thus, if foraging is bad in their part of the forest, there is somewhere else to go where food may be more readily available. Ambilocality greatly enhances the Mbutis' opportunity to find food. It also provides a place to go if a dispute breaks out with someone in the band in which one is currently living. Consequently, Mbuti camps are constantly changing their composition as people split off to go live with their in-laws, while others are joining from other groups. For a people like food foragers, who find their food in nature, and who maintain an egalitarian social order, ambilocal residence can be a crucial factor in both survival and conflict resolution.

Neolocal residence occurs where the independence of the nuclear family is emphasized. In industrial societies like the United States, where most economic activity occurs outside rather than inside the family, and where it is important for individuals to be able to move where jobs are to be found, neolocal residence is better suited than any of the other patterns.

Avunculocal residence is favored by the same factors that promote patrilocal residence, but only in societies in which descent through women is deemed crucial for the transmission of important rights and property. Such is the case among the people of the Trobriand Islands, where each individual is a member from birth of a group of relatives, all of whom trace their descent back through their mother, their mother's mother and so on to the one woman from whom all others are descended. Each of these descent groups holds property, consisting of hamlet sites, bush and garden lands and, in some cases, beach fronts, to which members have rights of access. These properties are controlled each generation by a chief or other

This Trobriand Islander chief, shown in front of his house, will be succeeded by his sister's son. Hence, men who will become chiefs live avunculocally.

leader who inherits these rights and obligations, but because descent is traced exclusively through women, these cannot be inherited by a man from his father. Thus, succession to positions of leadership passes from a man to his sister's son. For this reason, a man who is in line to take over control of his descent group's assets will take his wife to live with the one he will succeed—his mother's brother. This enables him to observe how the older man takes care of his hamlet's affairs, as well as to learn the oral traditions and magic that he will need to be an effective leader.

Although Trobriand leaders and chiefs live avunculocally, most married couples in this society live patrilocally. This allows sons to fulfill their obligations to their fathers, who helped build up and nurture them when they were small; in return, the sons will inherit personal property such as clay pots and valuable stone axe-blades from their fathers. This also gives men access to land controlled by their fathers' descent groups in addition to their own, enabling them to improve their own economic and political position in Trobriand society. In short, here, as in any human society, practical considerations play a central role in determining where people will live following marriage.

Shown here is a North African Bedouin man with his two wives. In polygynous families, ways must be found to prevent tensions between co-wives from erupting into conflict.

PROBLEMS OF FAMILY AND HOUSEHOLD ORGANIZATION

Effective though the family may be at organizing economic production, consumption, inheritance and child rearing, at the household level, relationships within the family inevitably involve a certain amount of conflict and tension. This is not to say that they may not also involve a great deal of warmth and affection, for indeed they may. Nevertheless, at least the potential for conflict is always there, and must be dealt with lest families become dysfunctional. Different forms of families are associated with different sorts of tensions, and the means employed to manage these tensions differ accordingly.

POLYGAMOUS FAMILIES

A major source of tension within polygamous families is the potential for conflict that exists between the multiple spouses of the one individual to whom they are married. For example, under polygyny (the most common form of polygamy), the several wives of a man must be able to get along with a minimum of bickering and jealousy. One way to handle this is through sororal polygyny, or marriage to women who are sisters. Presumably, women who have grown up together can get along as co-wives of a man more easily than women who grew up in different households and have never had to live together before. Another mechanism is to provide each wife with a separate apartment or house within a household compound, and perhaps require the husband to adhere to a system of rotation for sleeping purposes. The latter at least prevents the husband from playing obvious favorites among his wives. Although polygyny can be difficult for the women involved, this is not always the case. In some polygynous societies, women enjoy considerable economic autonomy, and in societies where women's work is hard and boring, polygyny can provide a means of sharing the work load and alleviating boredom through sociability.

EXTENDED FAMILIES

Extended families too, no matter how well they may work, have their own potential areas of stress. Decision making in such families usually rests with an older individual, and other family members must defer to the elder's decisions. Among a group of siblings, an older one usually has the authority. Then there is the problem of in-marrying spouses, who must adjust their ways to conform to the expectations of the family into which they have come to live. To combat these problems, cultures rely on various techniques to enforce harmony, including such things as dependence training and the concept of "face," or honor. Dependence training, discussed in Chapter 5, is typically associated with extended family organization, and raises people who are more inclined to accept their lot in life than are individuals who have been raised to be independent. One of the many problems faced by young people in North American society who have experimented with extended family living is that they have generally been raised to be independent, making it hard to defer to the wishes of others, when they are in disagreement.

The concept of "face" may constitute a particularly potent check on the power of senior members of extended families. Among pastoral nomads of North Africa, for example, young men can escape from the ill-treatment of a father or older brother by leaving the patrilocal extended family to join the family of his maternal relatives, in-laws, or even an unrelated family willing to take him in.[11] Because men lose face if their sons or brothers flee in this way, they are generally at pains to control their behavior in order to prevent this from happening. Women, who are the in-marrying spouses, may also return to their natal families if they are mistreated in their husbands' families. A woman who does this exposes her husband and his family to scolding by her kin, again causing loss of face.

Effective though such techniques may be in societies which stress the importance of the group over the individual, and where loss of face is to be avoided at almost any cost, not all conflict may be avoided. When all else fails to restore harmony, siblings may be forced to demand their share of family assets in order to set up separate households, and in this way, new families may come into being. Divorce, too, may be possible, although the ease with which this may be accomplished varies considerably from one society to another. In societies that practice matrilocal residence, divorce rates tend to be high, reflecting the ease with which unsatisfactory marriages may be terminated. In some (not all) societies with patrilocal residence, by contrast, divorce may be all but impossible, at least for women (the in-marrying spouses). This was the case in traditional China, for example, where women were raised to be cast out of their families.[12] When they married, they exchanged their dependence on fathers and brothers for absolute dependence on husbands, and later in life, sons. Without divorce as an option, to protect themselves against ill-treatment, women went to great lengths to develop the strongest bond possible between themselves and their sons, in order that the latter would rise to their mothers' defense when necessary. So single-minded were many women in developing such relationships with their sons that they often made life miserable for their daughters-in-law, who were seen as competitors for their sons' affections.

[11]Lila Abu-Lughod, *Veiled Sentiments: Honor and Poetry in a Bedouin Society* (Berkeley, Calif.: University of California Press, 1988), pp. 99–103.

[12]Margery Wolf, *Women and the Family in Rural Taiwan* (Stanford, Calif.: Stanford University Press, 1972), pp. 32–35.

Some young North Americans have attempted to re-create the extended family through the formation of communes. These attempts sometimes run into trouble as young people face unexpected stress resulting from extended family organization.

NUCLEAR FAMILIES

Just as extended families have built into them particular sources of stress and tensions, so too do nuclear families, especially in modern industrial societies where the family has lost one of its chief reasons for being: its economic function as a basic unit of production. Instead of staying within the fold, working with and for each other, one or both adults must seek work outside of the family. Furthermore, their work may keep them away for prolonged periods of time. If both spouses are employed, (as is increasingly the case, since couples find it ever more difficult to maintain their desired standard of living on a single income), the requirement for workers to go where their jobs take them may pull the husband and wife in different directions. On top of all this, neolocal residence tends to isolate husbands and wives from both sets of kin. Because clearly established patterns of responsibility no longer exist between husbands and wives, couples must work these out for themselves. Two things make this difficult, one being the traditional dependence of women on men that has for so long been a feature of Western society. In spite of changes in the direction of greater equality between men and women, often the partners to a marriage do not come to it as equals. The other problem is the great emphasis North American society places on the pursuit of individual gratification through competition, often at someone else's expense. The problem is especially acute if the husband and wife grew up in households with widely divergent outlooks on life and ways of doing things. Furthermore, being isolated from their kin, there is no one on hand to help stabilize the new marriage; for that matter, intervention of kin would likely be regarded as interference.

Isolation from kin also means that a young mother-to-be must face pregnancy and childbirth without the aid and support of female kin with whom she already has a relationship, and who have been through pregnancy and childbirth themselves. Instead, she must turn for advice and guidance to physicians (who are more often men than women), books, and friends and neighbors who are themselves likely to be inexperienced. The problem continues through motherhood, in the absence of experienced women within the family, as well as a clear model for child rearing. So reliance on physicians, books, and mostly inexperienced friends for advice and support continues. The problems are exacerbated, for families differ widely in the ways in which they deal with their children. In the competitive society of the United States, the children themselves recognize this and often use such differences against their parents to their own ends.

A further problem connected with the raising of children confronts the woman who has devoted herself entirely to this task: What will she do when the children are gone? One possible answer to this, of course, is to pursue some sort of career, but this, too, may present problems. She may have a husband with traditional values who believes that a woman's place is in the home. Or it may be difficult to begin a career in middle age. To begin a career earlier, though, may involve difficult choices: Should she have her career at the expense of having children, or should she have both simultaneously? If the

latter, there are not likely to be kin available to look after the children, as there would be in an extended family, and so arrangements must be made with people who are non-kin. And, of course, all of these thorny decisions must be made without the aid and support of kin.

The impermanence of the nuclear family itself may constitute a problem, in the form of anxieties over old age. Once the children are gone, who will care for the parents in their old age? In North American society, there is no *requirement* for their children to do so. The problem does not arise in an extended family, where one is cared for from womb to tomb.

FEMALE-HEADED HOUSEHOLDS

In North America, as increasing numbers of adults have sought escape from dysfunctional nuclear families through divorces, and as young adults have become more sexually active outside of wedlock, there has been a dramatic rise in the incidence of single-parent households headed by women. Currently there are twice as many households in the U.S. headed by divorced, separated and never-married individuals as there are occupied by traditional nuclear families.[13] In the vast majority of cases, as we saw in Chapter 8, any children remain with their mother, who then faces the problem of having to provide for them as well as for herself. In the case of divorces, fathers are usually required to pay child support, but they are not always able or willing to do this, and when they are, the amount is often not sufficient to pay for all the food, clothes, and medical care that are needed, let alone the cost of childcare so that the woman can seek income-producing work outside the house in order to support herself. As in the case of working women who remain with their husbands, kin may not be available to look after the children, and so outside help must be sought and (usually) paid for, thereupon making it even more difficult for the woman to support herself adequately. To compound the problem, women frequently lack the skills necessary to secure other than menial and low-paying jobs, not having acquired such skills earlier, raising children instead. Even when they do have skills, women are generally not paid as much as are men who hold the

---

[13]Judith Stacey, *Brave New Families*, pp. 5 and 15.

ANTHROPOLOGY APPLIED

DEALING WITH INFANT MORTALITY

In 1979 Dr. Margaret Boone, an anthropologist who now works as a social science analyst with the Program Evaluation and Methodology Division of the United States government's General Accounting Office, began a residency on the staff of Washington, D.C.'s only public hospital. Her task was to gain an understanding of the sociocultural basis of poor maternal and infant health among inner-city blacks—something about which little was known at the time—and to communicate that understanding to the relevant public and private agencies, as well as to a wider public. As Dr. Boone put it:

> The problem was death—the highest infant death rate in the United States. In Washington, D.C., babies were dying in their first years of life at the highest rate for any large American city, and nobody could figure out why.*

In Washington, as in the rest of the United States, infant mortality is mainly a black health problem because of the large and increasing number of disadvantaged black women; black infants die at almost twice the rate of white infants. In the hospital in which Boone worked, the population served was overwhelmingly poor and black.

For the next year and a half, Boone worked intensively, reviewing medical, birth, and death records; carrying out statistical analyses; and interviewing women whose infants had died, as well as nurses, physicians, social workers, and administrators. As she herself points out, no matter how important the records review and statistical analyses were (and they were important), her basic understanding of reproduction in the inner-city black community came from the daily experience working in the "community center" for birth and death, which was the hospital—classic anthropological participant observation.

What Boone found out was that infant death and miscarriage are associated with the absence of prenatal care, smoking, the consumption of alcohol, psychological distress during pregnancy and hospitalization, evidence of violence, ineffective contraception, rapid childbearing in the teens (average age at first pregnancy was 18), and the use of several harmful drugs together (contrary to everyone's expectations, heroin abuse was less important a factor than alcohol abuse, and drug abuse in general was no higher among women whose infants died than among those whose infants did not). Cultural factors found to be important include a belief in a birth for every death, a high value placed on children, a value on gestation without necessarily any causal or sequential understanding of the children it will produce, a lack of planning ability, distrust of both men and women, and a separation of men's roles from the process of family formation (indeed, three-quarters of the women in Boone's study were unmarried at the time of delivery). Of course, some of these factors were already known to be related to infant mortality, but many were not.

As a consequence of Boone's work, there have been important changes in policies and programs relating to infant mortality. It is now widely recognized that the problem goes beyond mere medicine, and that medical solutions have gone about as far as they can go. Only by dealing with the social and cultural factors connected to poor black health in the inner city will further progress be made, and new service delivery systems are slowly emerging to reflect this fact.

*Elizabeth S. Boone, "Practicing Sociomedicine: Redefining the Problem of Infant Mortality in Washington, D.C.," in *Anthropological Praxis: Translating Knowledge into Action*, ed. Robert M. Wulff and Shirley J. Fiske (Boulder, Colo.: Westview Press, 1987), p. 56.

same jobs. Not surprisingly, as the number of female-headed households has increased, so has the number of women (and, of course, their children) who live below the governmentally established poverty line. Over one-third of all female-headed households in the U.S. now fall into this category, and one quarter of all children are considered poor (Fig. 9.2).

Single parent households headed by women are neither new, nor are they restricted to industrial-

ized societies like the United States. They have been known and studied for a long time in the countries of the Caribbean basin, where men have historically been exploited as a cheap source of labor on plantations. Under such conditions, men have no power and few economic rewards; hence they are tenuously attached at best to any particular household. These are held together by women, who as producers of subsistence foods, provide the means of economic survival for households. Similar

---

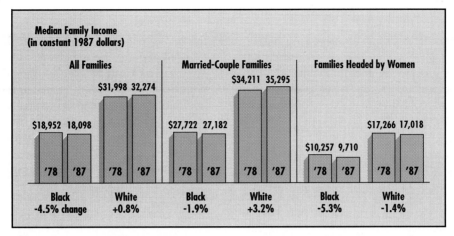

Figure 9.2 Median family income: Married-couple families and female-headed families compared. Source: Center on Budget and Policy Priorities, based on Bureau of the Census data.

female-headed households are becoming increasingly common in other third-world countries, too, as development projects increasingly restrict the ability of women to earn a living wage (reasons for this are discussed in Chapters 15 and 16). Thus, women constitute the majority of the poor, the underprivileged, and the economically and socially disadvantaged in most of the world's societies, just as is coming to be the case in the United States. In third-world countries, the situation has been made worse by reforms required by the International Monetary Fund (IMF) in order to renegotiate payment of foreign debts. Cutbacks in government education, health, and social programs for debt service have their most direct (and negative) impact on women and children, at the same time that further development designed to increase foreign exchange (for debt repayment and the financing of further industrialization) also comes at the expense of women and children. Meanwhile, the prices people must pay for basic necessities of life increase (to cut down on unfavorable balances of trade). If a women is *lucky*, the wage she earns to buy bread for herself and her children remains constant, even if low, while the price she must pay for that bread continues to rise.

At the start of this chapter we posed a number of questions relating in one way or another to the effectiveness of the family, as we know it today in North America, in meeting human needs. From what we have just discussed, it is obvious that neolocal nuclear families impose considerable anxiety and stress upon the individuals in such families. Deprived of the security and multiplicity of emo-

tional ties to be found in polygamous, extended, or consanguine families, if something goes wrong, it is potentially more devastating to the individuals involved. On the other hand, it is also obvious that

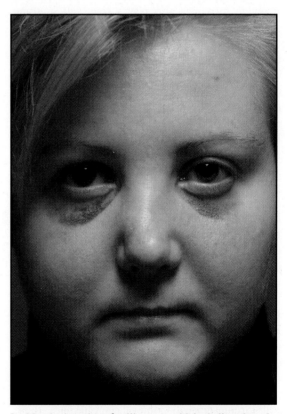

In North America, families are widely believed to be places of refuge from the rough-and-tumble outside world. Yet domestic violence is far from rare, and women and children are the usual victims.

alternative forms of family and household organization come complete with their own distinctive stresses and strains. To the question, which of the alternatives is preferable?, one must answer: It depends on what problems one wishes to overcome, and what price one is willing to pay.

In the United States, problems inherent in the traditional nuclear family have led to a marked decline in the percentage of households occupied by such families. At the same time, the conditions that gave rise to these families in the first place have changed. So far, no single family structure or ideology has arisen to supplant the nuclear family, nor can we predict which (if any) of the alternatives will gain preeminence in the future. The only thing of which we can be certain is that family and household arrangements, not just in the U.S. but throughout the world, will continue to evolve, as they always have, as the conditions to which they are sensitive change.

Chapter Summary

Dependence on group living for survival is a basic human characteristic. Nurturance of children has traditionally been the job of the adult female, although men may also play a role, and in some societies are even more involved with their children than are women. In addition to at least some childcare, women also carry out other economic tasks that complement those of men. The presence of adults of both sexes in a residential group is advantageous, in that it provides the child with an adult model of the same sex, from whom can be learned the gender-appropriate role as defined in that society.

One definition of the family that attempts to avoid ethnocentrism defines it as a group composed of a woman and her dependent children, with at least one adult male joined through marriage or blood relationship. In most human societies, families either constitute households, or else households are built around them. Although families are not universally present in human societies, households are. Households are defined as the basic residential units in which economic production, consumption, inheritance, child rearing, and shelter are organized and carried out.

Far from being a stable, unchanging entity, the family may take any one of a number of forms in response to particular social, historical, and ecological circumstances. Conjugal families are those formed on the basis of marital ties. The smallest conjugal unit of mother, father, and their dependent children is called the nuclear family. Contrasting with the conjugal is the consanguine family, consisting of women, their brothers, and the dependent children of the women. The nuclear family, the ideal in North American society, is also found in societies that live in harsh environments, such as the Inuit. In industrial societies as well as societies that exist in particularly harsh environments, the nuclear family has to be able to look after itself. The result is that individual members are strongly dependent on very few people. This form of family is well suited to the mobility required in food-foraging groups and in industrial societies as well, where frequent job changes necessitate family mobility. Among food foragers, however, the nuclear family is not as isolated from other kin as in modern industrial society.

Characteristic of many nonindustrial societies is the large extended, or conjugal-consanguineal family. Ideally, some of an extended family's members are related by blood, others are related by marriage, and all live and work together as members of a single household. Conjugal, or extended, families are based upon five basic residence patterns: patrilocal, matrilocal, ambilocal, neolocal, and avunculocal.

Different forms of family organization are accompanied by their own distinctive problems. In polygamous families there is the potential for conflict among the several spouses of the one individual to whom they are married. One way to ameliorate this problem is through sororal polygyny. In extended families, the matter of decision making may be the source of stress, resting as it does with an older individual whose views may not coincide with those of the younger family members. In-marrying spouses in particular may have trouble complying with the demands of the family in which they must now live.

In neolocal, nuclear families, individuals are isolated from the aid and support of kin, and so husbands and wives must work out their own solutions to the problems of living together and having children. The problems are especially difficult in North American society, owing to the inequality that still persists between men and wom-en, the great emphasis placed on individualism and competition, and an absence of clearly understood patterns of responsibility between husbands and wives, as well as a clear model for child rearing.

In North America, one alternative to the independent nuclear family, and one which is now twice as common, is the single parent household, usually headed by a woman. Female-headed households are also common in third-world countries. Because the women in such households are hard pressed to provide adequately for themselves as well as for their children, more and more women in the United States and abroad find themselves sinking ever more deeply into poverty.

Suggested Readings

Fox, Robin. *Kinship and Marriage in an Anthropological Perspective*. Baltimore, Md.: Penguin, 1968.
Fox's book is a good introduction to older, orthodox theories about the family.

Goody, Jack. *The Development of the Family and Marriage in Europe*. Cambridge: Cambridge University Press, 1983.
An historical study which shows how the nature of the family changed in Europe, in response to regulations introduced by the Catholic Church in order to weaken the power of kin groups and gain access to property. Explains how European patterns of kinship and marriage came to differ from those of the ancient circum-Mediterranean world, and those that succeeded them in the Middle East and North Africa.

Netting, R.M., R.R. Wilk, and E.J. Arnould, eds. *Households: Comparative and Historical Studies of the Domestic Group*. Berkeley, Calif.: University of California Press, 1984.
This collection of essays by 20 anthropologists and historians focuses on how and why households vary within and between societies, and over time within single societies.

Stacey, Judith. *Brave New Families*. New York: Basic Books, 1990.
Written by a sociologist, this book (subtitled *Stories of Domestic Conflict in Late Twentieth Century America*) takes an anthropological approach to understanding the changes affecting family structure in the United States. Her conclusion is that "the family" is *not* here to stay, nor in her view should we wish otherwise. For all the difficulties attendant on "the family's demise," alternative arrangements do open up hopeful possibilities for the future.

Thorne, Barrie, and Marilyn Yalom, eds. *Rethinking the Family: Some Feminist Questions*. New York: Longman, 1982.
As anthropologists have paid more attention to how institutions and practices work from a woman's perspective, they have reexamined existing assumptions about families in human societies. The twelve original essays in this volume, by scholars in the fields of economics, history, law, literature, philosophy, psychology, and sociology as well as anthropology, examine such topics as the idea of the monolithic family, the sexual division of labor and inequality, motherhood, parenting, and mental illness and relations between family, class, and state. Especially recommended is the essay: "Is There a Family? New Anthropological Views."

10

KINSHIP

AND

DESCENT

On this altar, King Yax-Pac of the ancient Maya city of Copan portrays himself and his predecessors, thereby tracing his descent back to the founder of the dynasty. In many human societies, such genealogical connections are used to define each individual's rights, privileges, and obligations.

WHAT ARE DESCENT GROUPS?
A descent group is a kind of kinship group in which being a lineal descendant of a particular real or mythical ancestor is a criterion of membership. Descent may be reckoned exclusively through men, exclusively through women, or through either at the discretion of the individual. In some cases, two different means of reckoning descent are used at the same time, to assign individuals to different groups for different purposes.

WHAT FUNCTIONS DO DESCENT GROUPS SERVE? Descent groups of various kinds—lineages, clans, phratries, and moieties—are convenient devices for solving a number of problems that commonly confront human societies: how to maintain the integrity of resources that cannot be divided without being destroyed; provide work forces for tasks that require a labor pool larger than households can provide; and allow members of one sovereign local group to claim support and protection from members of another. Not all societies have descent groups; in many food-foraging and industrial societies, some of these problems are often handled by the kindred, a group of people with a living relative in common. The kindred, however, does not exist in perpetuity, as does the descent group, nor is its membership as clearly and explicitly defined. Hence, it is generally a weaker unit than the descent group.

HOW DO DESCENT GROUPS EVOLVE? Descent groups arise from extended family organization, so long as there are problems of organization that such groups help to solve. This is most apt to happen in food-producing as opposed to food-foraging societies. First to develop are localized lineages, followed by larger, dispersed groups such as clans and phratries. With the passage of time, kinship terminology itself is affected by and adjusts to the kinds of descent or other kinship groups that are important in a society.

All societies have found some form of family and/or household organization a convenient way to deal with problems faced by all human groups: how to facilitate economic cooperation between the sexes, how to provide a proper setting within which child rearing may take place, and how to regulate sexual activity. Efficient and flexible though family and household organization may be in rising to challenges connected with such problems, the fact is that many societies confront problems that are beyond the ability of family and household organization to deal with. For one, there is often a need for some means by which members of one sovereign local group can claim support and protection from individuals in another. This can be important for defense against natural or human-made disasters; if people have the right of entry into local groups other than their own, they are able to secure protection or critical resources when their own group cannot provide them. For another, there frequently is a need for a way to share rights in some means of production that cannot be divided without its destruction. This is often the case in horticultural societies, where division of land is impractical beyond a certain point. It can be avoided if ownership of land is vested in a corporate group that exists in perpetuity. Finally, there is often a need for some means of providing cooperative work forces for tasks that require more participants than can be provided by households alone.

There are many ways to deal with these sorts of problems. One is through the development of a formal political system, with personnel to make and enforce laws, keep the peace, allocate resources, and perform other regulatory and societal functions. A more common way in nonindustrial societies—especially horticultural and pastoral societies —is through the development of kinship groups.

DESCENT GROUPS

A common way of organizing a society along kinship lines is by creating what anthropologists call descent groups. A **descent group** is any publicly recognized social entity in which being a lineal descendant of a particular real or mythical ancestor is a criterion of membership. Members of a descent group trace their connections back to a common

---

Descent group: Any publicly recognized social entity such that being a lineal descendant of a particular real or mythical ancestor is a criterion of membership.

---

ancestor through a chain of parent-child links. In this feature, we may have an answer to why descent groups are found in so many human societies. They appear to stem from the parent-child bond, which is built upon as the basis for a structured social group. This is a convenient thing to seize upon, and the addition of a few nonburdensome obligations and avoidances acts as a kind of glue to help hold the group together.

To operate most efficiently, membership in a descent group ought to be clearly defined. Otherwise, membership overlaps and it is not always clear where one's primary loyalty belongs. There are a number of means by which membership can be restricted. It can be done on the basis of where you live; for example, if your parents live patrilocally, you might automatically be assigned to your father's descent group. Another way is through choice; each individual might be presented with a number of options, among which he or she may choose. This, though, introduces a possibility of competition and conflict as groups vie for members, and may not be desirable. The most common way to restrict membership is by making sex jurally relevant. Instead of tracing membership back to the common ancestor, sometimes through men and sometimes through women, one does it exclusively through one sex. In this way, each individual is automatically assigned to his or her mother's or father's group, and that group only.

UNILINEAL DESCENT

Unilineal descent (sometimes called unilateral descent) establishes descent-group membership exclusively through the male or the female line. In non-Western societies, unilineal descent groups are quite common. The individual is assigned at birth to membership in a specific descent group, which may be traced either by **matrilineal descent,** through the female line, or by **patrilineal descent,**

LEWIS HENRY MORGAN

(1818-1881)

This major theoretician of nineteenth-century North American anthropology has been regarded as the founder of kinship studies. In *Systems of Consanguinity and Affinity of the Human Family* (1871), he classified and compared the kinship systems of peoples around the world in an attempt to prove the Asiatic origin of American Indians. In doing so, he developed the idea that the human family had evolved through a series of evolutionary stages, from primitive promiscuity on the one hand to the monogamous, patriarchal family on the other. Although subsequent work showed Morgan to be wrong about this and a number of other things, his work showed the potential value of studying the distribution of different kinship systems in order to frame hypotheses of a developmental or historical nature and, by noting the connection between terminology and behavior, showed the value of kinship for sociological study. Besides his contributions to kinship and evolutionary studies, he produced an ethnography of the Iroquois, which still stands as a major source of information.

Unilineal descent: Descent that establishes group membership exclusively through either the mother's or the father's line.

Matrilineal descent: Descent traced exclusively through the female line for purposes of group membership.

Patrilineal descent: Descent traced exclusively through the male line for purposes of group membership.

---

through the male line, depending on the society. In patrilineal societies the males are far more important than the females, for it is they who are considered to be responsible for the perpetuation of the group. In matrilineal societies, this responsibility falls on the female members of the group.

There seems to be a close relation between the descent system and the economy of a society. Generally, patrilineal descent predominates where the man is the breadwinner, as among pastoralists and intensive agriculturalists, where male labor is a prime factor. Matrilineal descent is important mainly among horticulturists with societies in which women are the breadwinners. Numerous matrilineal societies are found in Southern Asia, one of the cradles of food production in the Old World. Matrilineal systems exist as well in India, Sri Lanka, Indonesia, Sumatra, Tibet, South China, and many Indonesian islands. They were also prominent in parts of pre-Columbian North America, and still are in parts of Africa.

It is now recognized that in all societies, the kin of both mother and father are important components of the social structure. Just because descent may be reckoned patrilineally, for example, does not mean that maternal relatives are necessarily unimportant. It simply means that, for purposes of *group membership*, the mother's relatives are being excluded. Similarly, under matrilineal descent, the father's relatives are being excluded for purposes of group membership. By way of example, we have already seen in the two preceding chapters how important paternal relatives are among the matrilin-

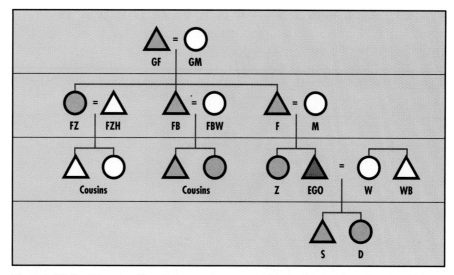

Figure 10.1 How patrilineal descent is traced. Only the individuals symbolized by a colored circle or triangle are in the same descent group as Ego. The abbreviation F stands for *father*, B for *brother*, H for *husband*, S for *son*, M for *mother*, Z for *sister*, D for *daughter*, and W for *wife*.

eal Trobriand Islanders. Although children belong to their mother's descent groups, fathers play an important role in nurturing and building them up. Upon marriage, the bride's and groom's paternal relatives contribute to the exchange of gifts that takes place, and throughout life, a man may expect his paternal kin to assist him in improving his economic and political position in society. Eventually, sons may expect to inherit personal property from their fathers.

PATRILINEAL DESCENT AND ORGANIZATION

Patrilineal descent (sometimes called agnatic or male descent) is the more widespread of the two systems of unilineal descent. The male members of a patrilineal descent group trace through other males their descent from a common ancestor (Fig. 10.1). Brothers and sisters belong to the descent group of their father's father, their father, their father's siblings, and their father's brother's children. A man's son and daughter also trace their descent back through the male line to their common ancestor. In the typical patrilineal group, the responsibility for training the children rests with the father or his elder brother. A woman belongs to the same descent group as her father and his

brothers, but her children cannot trace their descent through them. A person's paternal aunt's children, for example, trace their descent through the patrilineal group of her husband.

Traditional China: A Patrilineal Society

Up until World War II, rural Chinese society was strongly patrilineal. Since then, there have been considerable changes, although vestiges of the old system persist, to varying degrees in different regions. Traditionally, the basic unit for economic cooperation was the large extended family, typically including aged parents, their sons, their sons' wives and sons' children.[1] Residence, therefore, was patrilocal, as defined in Chapter 9. As in most patrilocal societies, then, children grew up in a household dominated by their father and his male relatives. The father himself was a source of discipline, from whom a child would maintain a respectful social distance. Often, the father's brother and his sons were members of the same household. Thus, one's paternal uncle was rather like a second father, and was treated with obedience and respect, while his sons were like one's own brothers. Accordingly, kinship terms applied to one's own

[1]Most of the following is from Fei Hsiaotung, *Peasant Life in China* (London: Kegan, Paul, Trench and Truber, 1939).

father and brothers were extended to the father's brother and his sons as well. When families became too large and unwieldy, as frequently happened, one or more sons would move elsewhere to establish their own separate households; when one did so, however, the tie to his natal household remained strong.

Important though family membership was for each individual, it was the *tsu* that was regarded as the primary social unit. Each *tsu* consisted of men who traced their ancestry back through the male line to a common ancestor, usually within about five generations. Although a woman belonged to the *tsu* of her father, for all practical purposes she was absorbed by that of her husband, with whom she went to live upon marriage. Nonetheless, members of her natal *tsu* retained some interest in her after her departure. Her mother, for example, would come to assist her in the birth of her children, and her brother or some other male relative would look after her interests, perhaps even intervening if the woman was badly treated by her husband or other members of his family.

The function of the *tsu* was to assist its members economically, and to come together on ceremonial occasions such as weddings, funerals, or to make offerings to the ancestors. Recently deceased ancestors, up to about three generations back, were given offerings of food and paper money on the anniversaries of their births and deaths, while more distant ancestors were collectively worshipped five times a year. Each *tsu* maintained its own place for storage of ancestral tablets, on which the names of all members were recorded. In addition to its economic and ritual functions, the *tsu* also functioned as a legal body, passing judgement on errant members.

Just as families periodically split up into new ones, so would the larger descent groups periodically splinter along the lines of its main family branches. Causes included disputes among brothers over management of land holdings, or suspicion of unfair division of profits. When such separation occurred, a representative of the new *tsu* would return periodically to the ancestral temple in order to pay respect to the ancestors and record recent births and deaths in the official genealogy. Ultimately, though the tie to the old *tsu* would still be recognized, a copy of the old genealogy would be made and brought home to the younger *tsu*, following which only its births and deaths would be recorded. In this way, over many centuries, a whole

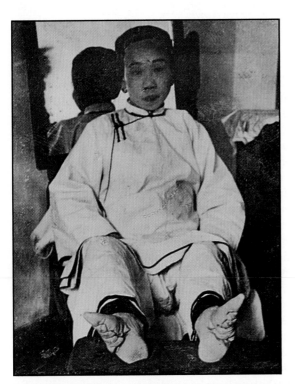

In patrilineal societies, the dominance of men over women sometimes goes to the extreme of inflicting physical as well as social disabilities. In the nineteenth century, Chinese women had their feet tightly bound, while in North America, women often tightly corseted themselves.

hierarchy of descent groups developed, with all persons having the same surname considering themselves to be members of a great patrilineal clan. With this went surname exogamy, which is still widely practiced today even though clan members no longer carry on ceremonial activities together.

The patrilineal system reached throughout rural Chinese social relations. Children owed obedience and respect to their fathers and older patrilineal relatives in life, and had to marry whomever their parents chose for them. It was the duty of sons to care for their parents when they became old and helpless, and even after death, sons had ceremonial obligations to them. Inheritance passed from fathers to sons, with an extra share going to the eldest, since he ordinarily made the greater contribution to the household, and had the greater responsibility to his parents after their deaths. Women, by contrast, had no claims on their families' heritable property. Once married, a woman was in effect cast off by her own patrilineal kin (even though they might continue to take an interest in her) in order to produce children for her husband's family and *tsu*.

As the preceding suggests, a patrilineal society is very much a man's world; no matter how valued they may be, women inevitably find themselves in a difficult position. How they cope with this can be seen by looking more closely at the way women relate to one another in traditional Chinese society.

ORIGINAL STUDY

COPING AS A WOMAN IN A MAN'S WORLD[2]

Women in rural Taiwan do not live their lives in the walled courtyards of their husbands' households. If they did, they might be as powerless as their stereotype. It is in their relations in the outside world (and for women in rural Taiwan that world consists almost entirely of the village) that women develop sufficient backing to maintain some independence under their powerful mothers-in-law. A successful venture into the men's world is no small feat when one recalls that the men of a village were born there and are often related to one another, whereas the women are unlikely to have either the ties of childhood or the ties of kinship to unite them. All the same, shared interests, and common problems of women are reflected in every village in a loosely knit society that can when needed be called on to exercise considerable influence.

Women carry on as many of their activities as possible outside the house. They wash clothes on the riverbank, clean and pare vegetables at a communal pump, mend under a tree that is a known meetingplace, and stop to rest on a bench or group of stones with other women. There is a continual moving back and forth between kitchens, and conversations are carried on from open doorways through the long, hot afternoons of summer. The shy young girl who enters the village as a bride is examined as frankly and suspiciously by the women as an animal that is up for sale. If she is deferential to her elders, does not criticize or compare her new world unfavorably with the one she has left, the older residents will gradually accept her presence on the edge of their conversations and stop changing the topic to general subjects when she brings the family laundry to scrub on the rocks near them. As the young bride meets other girls in her position, she makes allies for the future, but she must also develop relationships with the older women. She learns to use considerable discretion in making and receiving confidences, for a girl who gossips freely about the affairs of her husband's household may find herself always on the outside of the group, or worse yet, accused of snobbery. I described in The House of Lim the plight of Lim Chui-ieng, who had little village backing in her troubles with her husband and his family as a result of her arrogance toward the women's community. In Peihotien the young wife of the storekeeper's son suffered a similar lack of support. Warned by her husband's parents not to be too "easy" with the other villagers lest they try to buy things on credit, she obeyed to the point of being considered unfriendly by the women of the village. When she began to have serious troubles with her husband and eventually his family, there was no one in the village she could turn to for solace, advice, and most important, peacemaking.

Once a young bride has established herself as a member of the women's community, she has also established for herself a certain amount of protection. If the members of her husband's family step beyond the limits of propriety in their treatment of her—such as refusing to allow her to return to her natal home for her brother's wedding or beating her without serious justification—she can complain to a woman friend, preferably older, while they are washing vegetables at the communal pump. The story will quickly spread to the other women, and one of them will take it upon herself to check the facts with another member of the girl's household. For a few days the matter will be thoroughly discussed whenever a few women gather. In a young wife's first few years in the community, she can expect to have her mother-in-law's side of any disagreement given fuller weight than her own—her mother-in-law has, after all, been a part of the community a lot longer. However, the discussion itself will serve to curb many offenses. Even if the older woman knows that public opinion is falling to her side, she will be somewhat more judicious about refusing her daughter-in-law's next request. Still, the daughter-in-law who hopes to make use of the village forum to depose her mother-in-law or at least gain herself special privilege will discover just how important the prerogatives of age and length of residence are. Although the women can serve as a powerful protective force for their defenseless younger members, they are also a very conservative force in the village.

Taiwanese women can and do make use of their collective power to lose face for their menfolk in order to influence decisions that are ostensibly not theirs to make. Although young women may have little or no influence over their husbands and would not dare express an unsolicited opinion (and perhaps not even a solicited one) to their fathers-in-law, older women who have raised their sons properly retain considerable influence over their sons' actions, even in activities exclusive to men. Further, older women who have displayed years of good judgement are regularly consulted by their husbands about major as well as minor economic and social projects. But even men who think themselves free to ignore the opinions of their women are never free of their own concept, face. It is much easier to lose face than to have face. We once asked a male friend in Peihotien just what "having face" amounted to. He replied, "When no one is talking about a family, you can say it has face." This is precisely where women wield their power. When a man behaves in a way that they consider wrong, they talk about him—not only among themselves, but to their sons and husbands. No one "tells him how to mind his own business," but it becomes abundantly clear that he is losing face and by continuing in this manner may bring shame to the family of his ancestors and descendants. Few men will risk that.

The rules that a Taiwanese man must learn and obey to be a successful member of his society are well developed, clear, and relatively easy to stay within. A Taiwanese woman must also learn the rules, but if she is to be a successful woman, she must learn not to stay within them, but to appear to stay within them; to manipulate them, but not to appear to be manipulating them; to teach them to her children, but not to depend on her children for her protection. A truly successful Taiwanese woman is a rugged individualist who has learned to depend largely on herself while appearing to lean on her father, her husband, and her son. The contrast between the terrified young bride and the loud, confident, often lewd old woman who has outlived her mother-in-law and her husband reflects the tests met and passed by not strictly following the rules and by making purposeful use of those who must. The Chinese male's conception of women as "narrow-hearted" and socially inept may well be his vague recognition of this facet of women's power and technique.

[2]Margery Wolf, *Women and the Family in Rural Taiwan* (Stanford, Calif.: Stanford University Press, 1972), pp. 37-41.

MATRILINEAL DESCENT AND ORGANIZATION

In one respect, matrilineal descent is the opposite of patrilineal: It is reckoned through the female line (Fig. 10.2). The matrilineal pattern differs from the patrilineal, however, in that descent does not automatically confer authority. Thus, while patrilineal societies are patriarchal, matrilineal societies are not matriarchal. Although descent passes through the female line, and women may have considerable power, they do not hold exclusive authority in the descent group: They share it with men. These are the brothers, rather than the husbands, of the women through whom descent is reckoned. Apparently, the adaptive purpose of the matrilineal system is to provide continuous female solidarity within the female work group. Matrilineal systems are usually found in farming societies in

which women perform much of the productive work. Because women's work is regarded as so important to the society, matrilineal descent prevails.

In the matrilineal system, brothers and sisters belong to the descent group of the mother's mother, the mother, the mother's siblings, and the mother's sister's children. Males belong to the same descent group as their mother and sister, but their children cannot trace their descent through them. For example, the children of a man's maternal uncle are considered members of the uncle's wife's matrilineal descent group. Similarly, a man's own children belong to his wife's, but not his, descent group.

Although not true of all matrilineal systems, a common feature is the weakness of the tie between husband and wife. The wife's brother, and not the husband-father, distributes goods, organizes work,

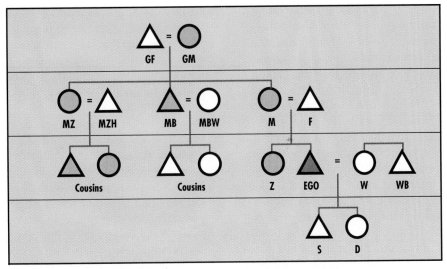

Figure 10.2   This diagram, which traces descent matrilineally, can be compared with that in Figure 10.1, showing patrilineal descent. The two patterns are virtually mirror images. Note that a male Ego cannot transmit descent to his own children.

settles disputes, administers inheritance and succession rules, and supervises rituals. The husband has legal authority not in his own household but in that of his sister. Furthermore, his property and status are inherited by his sister's son, rather than his own. Thus, brothers and sisters maintain life-long ties with one another, whereas marital ties are easily severed. In matrilineal societies, unsatisfactory marriages are more easily ended than in patrilineal societies.

The Hopi: A Matrilineal Society

In northeastern Arizona are the villages, or pueblos, of the Hopi Indians, a farming people whose ancestors have lived in the region for at least 2,000 years. Their society is divided into a number of named clans, based strictly on matrilineal descent.[3] Each individual is assigned from birth to the clan of his or her mother, and so important is this affiliation that, in a very real sense, a person has no identity apart from it. Two or more clans together constitute larger, supraclan units, or phratries, of which there are nine in Hopi society. Within each of these, member clans are expected to support one

another and to observe strict exogamy. Because members of all nine phratries can be found living in any given pueblo, marriage partners can always be found in one's home community. This same dispersal of membership provides individuals with rights of entry into villages other than their own.

Although clans are the major units in Hopi thinking, the functional units consist of subclans, or lineages, of which there are several per village. Each is headed by a senior woman—usually the eldest, although it is her brother or maternal uncle who keeps the sacred "medicine bundle" and plays an active role in running lineage affairs. The woman, however, is not a mere figurehead; she may act as mediator to help resolve disputes between members of the group; nor does she yield any authority to her brother or uncle. Although these men have the right to offer her advice and criticism, they are equally obligated to listen to what she has to say. Most female authority, however, is exerted within the household, and here men clearly take second place. These households consist of the women of the lineage with their husbands and unmarried sons, all of whom used to live in sets of adjacent rooms in single large tenements. Nowadays, nuclear families often live (frequently with a maternal relative or two) in separate houses, but pickup trucks enable related households to maintain close contacts and to cooperate as before.

[3]Most of the following is from John C. Connelly, "Hopi Social Organization" in the *Handbook of North American Indians, Vol. 9, Southwest,* ed. Alfonso Ortiz (Washington, D.C.: Smithsonian Institution, 1979), pp. 539–553.

Lineages function as landholding corporations, allocating land for the support of member households. These lands are farmed by "outsiders," the husbands of the women whose lineage owns the land, and it is to these women that the harvest belongs. Thus, Hopi men spend their lives laboring for alien lineages (their wives'), in return for which they are given food and shelter (by their wives). Although sons learn from their fathers how to farm, a man has no real authority over his son (the two belong to different lineages). Thus, when parents have difficulty with an unruly child, it is the mother's brother who is called upon to mete out punishment. Male loyalties are therefore divided, between their wives' households on the one hand, and their sisters' on the other. If at any time, a man is perceived as being an unsatisfactory husband, his wife has merely to place his belongings outside the door, and the marriage is over.

In addition to their economic and legal functions, lineages play a role in Hopi ceremonial activities. Although membership in the associations that actually perform ceremonies is open to all who have the proper qualifications for membership, they are all owned and managed by clans, and in each

village, a leading lineage acts as its clan's representative. Owned by this lineage is a special house in which the clan's religious paraphernalia is stored and cared for by the "clan mother." Together with her brother, the clan's "Big Uncle," she helps manage ceremonial activity. While most of the associations that do the actual performing are controlled by men, women still have vital roles to play. For example, they provide the cornmeal, symbolic of natural and spiritual life, that is a necessary ingredient in virtually all ceremonies.

Prior to the imposition by the U.S. government in 1936 of a different system, each Hopi pueblo was politically autonomous, with its own chief and village council. Here again, however, descent group organization made itself felt, for the council was made up of men who inherited their positions through their clans. Moreover, the powers of the chief and his council were limited; the chief's major job was to maintain harmony between his village and the spiritual world, and whatever authority he and his council wielded was directed at coordination of community effort, not enforcement of unilateral decrees. Decisions were made on the basis of consensus, and women's views had to

The buildings shown in this 1914 photograph of a traditional Hopi village housed women who were matrilineal relatives of one another—together with their husbands and children.

ANTHROPOLOGY APPLIED

FEDERAL RECOGNITION FOR AMERICAN INDIANS

In 1981, the Washington (D.C.) Association of Professional Anthropologists bestowed its first annual Praxis Award on James Wherry,* for his use of anthropological knowledge to win federal recognition for the Houlton Band of Maliseet Indians in Maine. The Praxis Award is an international competition open to all projects, programs, or activities that illustrate the translation of anthropological knowledge into action. As a consequence of their recognition, the Houlton Band became eligible to receive services and contracts from the Bureau of Indian Affairs and Indian Health Services, and to share in the settlement of the Maine Indian Land Claim, with which they could purchase land to be held in trust for them. With these arrangements, they were transformed from a poor and powerless minority into a semisovereign people with the means to establish their own land base, and a broad range of programs controlled by themselves.

The Houlton Band is one of more than 100 American Indian communities that were forgotten or overlooked by the federal government over the past 200 years, owing to drastic depopulation, forced removals, and other dislocations in the regions in which they lived. Under the U.S. Constitution, Indians are a federal responsibility, but without official recognition, Indian communities are unable to gain access to government health, education, and other services that derive from treaty obligations of the United States towards Indian tribes. As a result,

unrecognized Indians are poorer, less well educated, and subject to more serious health problems than are those in recognized tribes. Most unrecognized groups are landless, and some have disintegrated through lack of protection by the federal government.

In 1978, federal regulations were adopted by which unrecognized American Indian communities could petition for acknowledgment, and several such petitions are now pending. To secure recognition, communities must provide extensive ethnohistorical, genealogical, and ethnographic information on their origins, development, and present social and political organization. Genealogical data are especially important, for genealogies of all present tribal members are required. Moreover, traditional communities often were structured on the basis of kinship and descent, and recurring marriages between families have been an important means by which community organization has been perpetuated and identity maintained. Since the gathering of such data has long been an anthropological specialty, American Indian communities commonly turn to anthropologists like James Wherry to assist in meeting the criteria required for recognition.

* James Wherry now serves as socio-economic development specialist of the Mashantucket Pequot Tribe, an American Indian community in Connecticut that won federal recognition in 1983.

be considered, as well as those of men. Once again, although positions of authority were held by men, women had considerable control over their decisions in a behind-the-scene way. These men, after all, lived in households that were controlled by women, and their position within them depended largely on how well they got along with the senior women. Outside the household, refusal to play their part in the performance of ceremonies gave women the power of the veto. Small wonder, then, that Hopi men readily admit that "women usually get their way."[4]

[4]Alice Schlegel, "Male and Female in Hopi Thought and Action," in *Sexual Stratification*, ed. Alice Schlegel (New York: Columbia University Press, 1977), p. 254.

DOUBLE DESCENT

Double descent, or double unilineal descent, whereby descent is reckoned both patrilineally and matrilineally at the same time, is very rare. In this system descent is matrilineal for some purposes and patrilineal for others. Generally, where double

Double descent: A system according to which descent is reckoned matrilineally for some purposes and patrilineally for others.

Ambilineal descent: Descent in which the individual may affiliate with either the mother's or the father's descent group.

descent is reckoned, the matrilineal and patrilineal groups take action in different spheres of society.

For example, among the Yakö of eastern Nigeria, property is divided into patrilineal line possessions and matrilineal line possessions.[5] The patrilineage owns perpetual productive resources, such as land, whereas the matrilineage owns consumable property, such as livestock. The legally weaker matrilineal line is somewhat more important in religious matters than the patrilineal line. Through double descent, a Yakö individual might inherit grazing lands from the father's patrilineal group and certain ritual privileges from the mother's matrilineal line.

AMBILINEAL DESCENT

Unilineal descent provides an easy way of restricting descent group membership so as to avoid problems of divided loyalty and the like. A number of societies, many of them in the Pacific and in Southeast Asia, accomplish the same thing in other ways, though perhaps not quite so neatly. The resultant descent groups are known as ambilineal, nonunilineal, or cognatic. **Ambilineal descent** provides a measure of flexibility not normally found under unilineal descent; each individual has the option of affiliating with either the mother's or the father's descent group. In many of these societies an individual is allowed to belong to only one group at any one time, regardless of how many groups he or she may be eligible to join. Thus, the society may be divided into the same sorts of discrete and separate groups of kin as in a patrilineal or matrilineal society. There are other cognatic societies, however, such as the Samoans of the South Pacific or the Bella Coola and the southern branch of the Kwakiutl of the Pacific Northwest

This photo shows three generations of a Jewish family. Close family ties have always been important in eastern European Jewish culture. To maintain such ties in the United States, the descendants of eastern European Jews developed ambilineal descent groups.

coast, which allow overlapping membership in a number of descent groups. As anthropologist George Murdock observed, too great a range of individual choice interferes with the orderly functioning of any kin-oriented society.

An individual's plural membership almost inevitably becomes segregated into one primary membership, which is strongly activated by residence, and one or more secondary memberships in which participation is only partial or occasional.[6]

Ambilineal Descent among New York City Jews

For an example of ambilineal organization we might easily turn to a traditional, non-Western society, as we have for patrilineal and matrilineal organization. Instead, we shall turn to contemporary North American society, in order to dispel the common notion that descent groups are necessarily incompatible in structure and function with the demands of modern, industrial society. In fact, large corporate descent groups that hold assets in common and exist in perpetuity are to be found in the city of New York, as well as in every other large city in the United States where a substantial Jewish population of eastern European background is found.[7] Further-

[5]C. Daryll Forde, "Double Descent among the Yako," in *Kinship and Social Organization,* ed. Paul Bohannan and John Middleton (Garden City, N.Y.: Natural History Press, 1968), pp. 179-191.

[6]George P. Murdock, "Cognatic Forms of Social Organization," in *Social Structure in Southeast Asia.* ed. G.P. Murdock (Chicago: Quadrangle Books, 1960), p. 11.

[7]William E. Mitchell, *Mishnokhe: A Study of New York City Jewish Family Clubs* (The Hague: Mouton, 1978).

more, these descent groups are not survivals of an old eastern European, descent-based organization. Rather, they represent a social innovation designed to restructure and preserve the traditionally close affective family ties of the old eastern European Jewish culture in the face of continuing immigration to the United States, subsequent dispersal from New York City, and the development of significant social and even temperamental differences among their descendants. The earliest of these descent groups did not develop until the end of the first decade of the 1900s, some 40 years after the immigration of eastern European Jews began in earnest. Although some groups have disbanded, they generally have remained alive and vital right down to the present day.

The original Jewish descent groups in New York City are known as *family circles*. The potential members of a family circle consist of all living descendants, with their spouses, of an ancestral pair. In actuality, not all who are eligible actually join, so there is an element of voluntarism. But eligibility is explicitly determined by descent, using both male and female links, without set order, to establish the connection with the ancestral pair. Thus, individuals are normally eligible for membership in more than one group. To activate one's membership, one simply pays the required dues, attends meetings, and participates in the affairs of the group. Individuals can, and frequently do, belong at the same time to two or three groups for which they are eligible. Each family circle bears a name, usually including the surname of the male ancestor, each has elected officers, and each meets regularly throughout the year rather than just once or twice. At the least, the family circle as a corporation holds funds in common, and some hold title to burial plots for the use of members. Originally, they functioned as mutual aid societies, as well as for the purpose of maintaining family solidarity. Now, as the mutual aid functions have been taken over by outside agencies, the promotion of solidarity has become their primary goal. It will be interesting to see if reduced government funding for these agencies leads to a resurgence of the mutual-aid function of family circles.

In the years just prior to World War II, an interesting variant of the ambilineal descent group developed among younger generation descendants of east European Jewish immigrants. Being more assimilated into North American culture, some of them sought to separate themselves somewhat from members of older generations, who were perceived as being a bit old-fashioned. Yet, they still wished to maintain the traditional Jewish ethic of family solidarity. The result was the *cousins club*, which consists of a group of first cousins, who themselves share a common ancestry, their spouses, and their descendants. Excluded are parents and grandparents of the cousins, with their older views and life-styles. Ambilineal descent remains the primary organizing principle, but it has been modified by a generational principle. Otherwise, cousins clubs are organized and function in many of the same ways as family circles.

FORMS AND FUNCTIONS OF DESCENT GROUPS

Descent groups with restricted membership, regardless of how descent is reckoned, are usually more than mere groups of relatives providing warmth and a sense of belonging; in nonindustrial societies they are tightly organized working units providing security and services in the course of what can be a difficult, uncertain life. The tasks performed by descent groups are manifold. Besides acting as economic units providing mutual aid to their members, they may act to support the aged and infirm or help in the case of marriage or death. Often, they play a role in determining whom an individual may or may not marry. The descent group may also act as a repository of religious traditions. Ancestor worship, for example, is a powerful force acting to reinforce group solidarity.

LINEAGE

A **lineage** is a corporate descent group composed of consanguineal kin who trace descent genealogically through known links back to a common

Lineage: A corporate descent group whose members trace their genealogical links to a common ancestor.

ancestor. The term is usually employed where some form of unilineal descent is the rule, but there are similar ambilineal groups, such as the Jewish family circles just discussed.

The lineage is ancestor-oriented; membership in the group is recognized only if relationship to a common ancestor can be traced and proved. In many societies an individual has no legal or political status except as a member of a lineage. Since "citizenship" is derived from lineage membership and legal status depends on it, political and religious power are thus derived from it as well. Important religious and magical powers, such as those associated with the cults of gods and ancestors, may also be bound to the lineage.

The lineage, like General Motors or IBM, is a corporate group. Because it continues after the death of members as new members are continually being born into it, it has a perpetual existence that enables it to take corporate actions, such as owning property, organizing productive activities, distributing goods and labor power, assigning status, and regulating relations with other groups. The lineage is a strong, effective base of social organization.

A common feature of lineages is that they are exogamous. This means that members of a lineage must find their marriage partners in other lineages. One advantage of lineage exogamy is that potential sexual competition within the group is curbed,

promoting the group's solidarity. Lineage exogamy also means that each marriage is more than an arrangement between two individuals; it amounts as well to a new alliance between lineages. This helps to maintain them as components of larger social systems. Finally, lineage exogamy maintains open communication within a society, promoting the diffusion of knowledge from one lineage to another.

CLAN

In the course of time, as generation succeeds generation and new members are born into the lineage, its membership may become too large to be manageable, or too much for the lineage's resources to support. When this happens, **fission** will take place; that is, the lineage will split up into new, smaller lineages. When fission occurs, it is usual for the members of the new lineages to continue to recognize their ultimate relationship to one anoth-

Fission: The splitting of a descent group into two or more new descent groups.

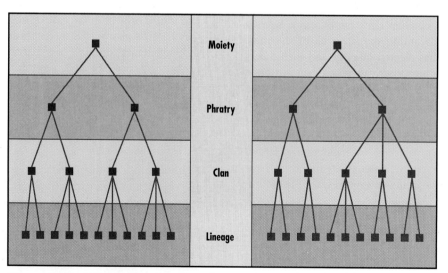

Figure 10.3   This diagram shows how lineages, clans, phratries, and moieties form an organizational hierarchy. Each moiety is subdivided into phratries, each phratry into clans, and each clan into lineages.

Clan: A noncorporate descent group with each member claiming descent from a common ancestor without actually knowing the genealogical links to that ancestor.

Totemism: The belief that people are related to particular animals, plants, or natural objects by virtue of descent from common ancestral spirits.

Phratry: A unilineal descent group composed of two or more clans that claim to be of common ancestry. If there are only two such groups, each is a moiety.

er. The result of this process is the appearance of a second kind of descent group, the **clan.** The term *clan,* and its close relative, the term *sib,* have been used differently by different anthropologists, and a certain amount of confusion exists about their meaning. The clan (or sib) will here be defined as a noncorporate descent group in which each member assumes descent from a common ancestor (who may be real or fictive), but is unable to trace the actual genealogical links back to that ancestor. This stems from the great genealogical depth of the clan, whose founding ancestor lived so far in the past that the links must be assumed rather than known in detail. A clan differs from a lineage in another respect: it lacks the residential unity that is generally—though not invariably—characteristic of the core members of a lineage. As with the lineage, descent may be patrilineal, matrilineal, or ambilineal.

Because clan membership is dispersed rather than localized, it usually does not hold tangible property corporately. Instead, it tends to be more a unit for ceremonial matters. Only on special occasions will the membership gather together for specific purposes. Clans, however, may handle important integrative functions. Like lineages, they may regulate marriage through exogamy. Because of their dispersed membership, they give individuals the right of entry into local groups other than their own. One is usually expected to give protection and hospitality to one's fellow clan members. Hence, these can be expected in any local group that includes members of one's own clan.

Clans, lacking the residential unity of lineages, depend on symbols—of animals, plants, natural forces, and objects—to provide members with solidarity and a ready means of identification. These symbols, called totems, are often associated with the clan's mythical origin and provide clan members with a means of reinforcing the awareness of their common descent. The word *totem* comes from the Ojibwa American Indian word *ototeman,*

meaning "he is a relative of mine." **Totemism** has been defined by A.R. Radcliffe-Brown as a set of "customs and beliefs by which there is set up a special system of relations between the society and the plants, animals, and other natural objects that are important in the social life."[8] Hopi Indian matriclans, for example, bear such totemic names as Bear, Bluebird, Butterfly, Lizard, Spider, and Snake.

Totemism is a changing concept that varies from clan to clan. A kind of watered-down totemism may be found even in modern North American society, where baseball and football teams are given the names of such powerful wild animals as bears, tigers, and wildcats. This extends to the Democratic Party's donkey and the Republican Party's elephant, to the Elks, the Lions, and other fraternal and social organizations. Our animal emblems, however, do not involve the same notions of descent and strong sense of kinship, nor are they associated with the various ritual observances associated with clan totems.

PHRATRIES AND MOIETIES

Other kinds of descent groups are phratries and moieties (Fig. 10.3). A **phratry** is a unilineal descent group composed of at least two clans that are supposedly related, whether or not they really are. Like individuals of the clan, members of the phratry are unable to trace accurately their descent links to a common ancestor, though they believe such an ancestor existed.

If the entire society is divided into two and only two major descent groups, be they equivalent to

[8]A.R. Radcliffe-Brown, "Social Organization of Australian Tribes," *Oceania Monographs,* No. 1 (Melbourne: Macmillan, 1931), p. 29.

Moiety: Each group that results from a division of a society into two halves on the basis of descent.

Kindred: A group of people closely related to one living individual through both parents.

clans or phratries, or at an even more all-inclusive level, each group is called a **moiety** (after the French word for "half"). Members of the moiety believe themselves to share a common ancestor, but are unable to prove it through definite genealogical links. As a rule, the feeling of kinship among members of lineages and clans is stronger than that felt among members of phratries and moieties. This may be due to the larger size and more diffuse nature of the latter groups.

BILATERAL DESCENT AND THE KINDRED

Important though descent groups are in many societies, they are not found in all societies, nor are they the only kinds of nonfamilial kinship groups to be found. Bilateral descent, a characteristic of Western society, as well as a number of food-foraging societies, affiliates a person with other close relatives through both sexes; in other words, the individual traces descent through both parents simultaneously and recognizes multiple ancestors. Theoretically, one is associated equally with all relatives on both the mother's and father's sides of

the family. Thus, this principle relates an individual lineally to all eight great-grandparents and laterally to all third and fourth cousins. Since such a huge group is too big to be socially practical, the group is usually reduced to a small circle of paternal and maternal relatives, called the **kindred**. The kindred may be defined as a group of people closely related to one living individual through both parents. Unlike descent groups, the kindred is laterally rather than lineally organized; that is, ego, or the focal person from whom the degree of each relationship is reckoned, is the center of the group (Fig. 10.4). North Americans are all familiar with the kindred; those who belong are simply called relatives. It includes the relatives on both sides of the family who are seen on important occasions, such as family reunions and funerals. Most people in the United States can identify the members of their kindred up to second cousins and grandparents.

The limits of the kindred, however, are variable and indefinite; no one can ever be absolutely certain which relatives to invite to every important function and which to exclude. Inevitably, situations arise that require some debate about whether or not to invite particular, usually distant, relatives. The kindred is thus not clearly bounded, and lacks the discreteness of the unilineal or ambilineal descent

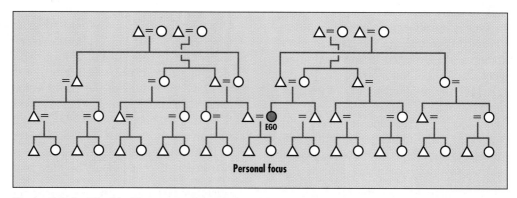

Figure 10.4   The kinship pattern of the kindred. These people are related not to a common ancestor but rather to a living relative—here, the sister and brother shown at the center of the bottom row.

Members of this baby's personal kindred shown here are her mother, father, father's mother, mother's father, mother's sister, and mother's sister's husband. Each of us has a unique kindred consisting of relatives on both our mother's and father's sides.

group. (It is also temporary, lasting only as long as the function it has been assembled to attend.)

The kindred possesses one feature that sets it apart from all descent groups: Because of its bilateral structure, a kindred is never the same for any two persons except siblings (brothers and sisters). Thus, no two people (except siblings) belong to the same kindred. Ego's father's kindred, for example, ranges lineally to the father's grandparents and laterally to cousins too distant for ego to know; the same is true of ego's mother, maternal and paternal aunts, and uncles. Thus, the kindred is not composed of people with an ancestor in common, but of people with a living relative in common—ego.

THE EGO: CENTER OF THE KINDRED

Kindreds are referred to as ego-centered or ego-focused groups because ego, or the person viewing the group, is at its center. Even in relation to ego, the membership of the group is constantly changing as ego moves through life. When one is young, it consists of one's parents, siblings, and other close consanguineal relatives, most of whom are older than ego is. As ego grows older and has children, the composition of the kindred changes; it consists of one's descendants and the remaining relatives of one's own generation. Thus, because of its vagueness, temporary nature, and changing personnel, the kindred cannot function as a group except in relation to ego. Unlike descent groups, it is not self-perpetuating—it ceases with ego's death. It has no constant leader, nor can it easily hold, administer, or pass on property. In most cases, it cannot organize work, nor can it easily administer justice or assign status. It can, however, be turned to for aid. In non-Western societies, for example, raiding or trading parties may be composed of kindred groups. The group is assembled, does what it was organized to do, shares the spoils, then disbands. It can also act as a ceremonial group for rites of passage: initiation ceremonies and the like. Thus, kindreds assemble only for specific purposes. Finally, they can also regulate marriage through exogamy.

Kindreds are frequently found in industrial societies such as that of the United States, where mobility weakens contact with relatives. Individuality is emphasized in such societies, and strong kinship organization is usually not as important as it is among non-Western peoples. On the other hand, the bilateral kindred may also be found in societies where kinship ties are important, and in some instances, they even occur alongside descent groups.

EVOLUTION OF THE DESCENT GROUP

Just as different types of families occur in different societies, so do different kinds of descent systems. Descent groups, for example, are not a common feature of food-foraging societies, where marriage acts as the social mechanism for integrating individuals within communities. In horticultural, pastoral, or many intensive agricultural societies, however, the descent group usually provides the structural framework upon which the fabric of the society rests.

It is generally agreed that lineages arise from extended family organization, so long as there are problems of organization that such groups help solve. All that is required, really, is that as members of existing extended families find it necessary to split off and establish new households elsewhere, they do not move too far away, that the core members of such related families (men in patrilocal, women in matrilocal, members of both sexes in ambilocal extended families) explicitly acknowledge their descent from a common ancestor, and that they continue to participate in common activities in an organized way. As this proceeds, lineages will develop, and these may with time give rise to clans and ultimately phratries.

Another way that clans may arise is as legal fictions to bring about the integration of otherwise autonomous units. The five Iroquoian Indian tribes of what now is New York State, for example, developed clans by simply behaving as if lineages of the same name in different villages were related. Thus, their members became fictitious brothers and sisters. By this device, members of, say, a "Turtle" lineage in one village could travel to another and be welcomed in and hosted by members of another "Turtle" lineage. In this way, the "Five Nations" achieved a wider unity than had previously existed.

As larger, dispersed descent groups develop, the conditions that gave rise to extended families and lineages may change. For example, economic diversity and the availability of alternative occupations among which individuals may choose may conflict with the residential unity of extended families and (usually) lineages. Or, lineages may lose their economic bases, if control of resources is taken over by developing political institutions. In such circumstances, lineages would be expected to disappear as

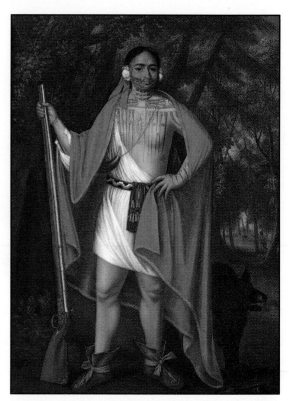

Iroquoian clans were a legal fiction that allowed people to travel back and forth between villages of the "Five Nations" in what is now New York state. This portrait, done in 1710, shows a member of the Mohawk Nation. Behind him stands a bear, which represents his clan.

important organizational units. Clans, however, might survive, if they continued to provide an important integrative function. In this sense, the Jewish family circles and cousins clubs that we discussed earlier have become essentially clanlike in their function. This helps explain their continued strength and vitality in the United States today: They perform an integrative function among kin who are geographically dispersed as well as socially diverse, but in a way that does not conflict with the mobility that is characteristic of North American society.

In societies where the small domestic units—nuclear families or single parent households—are of primary importance, bilateral descent and kindred organization are apt to be the result. This can be seen in modern industrial societies, newly emerging third-world societies, and many food-foraging societies throughout the world.

KINSHIP TERMINOLOGY AND KINSHIP GROUPS

Any system of organizing people who are relatives into different kinds of groups, be they descent-based or ego-oriented, is bound to have an important effect upon the ways in which relatives are labeled in any given society. The fact is, the kinship terminologies of other peoples are far from being the arbitrary and even capricious ways of labeling relatives that Westerners all too often take them to be. Rather, they reflect the positions individuals occupy within their society. In particular, kinship terminology is affected by, and adjusts to, the kinds of kinship groups that exist in a society. There are, however, other factors at work as well in each system of kinship terminology, which help differentiate one kin from another. These factors may be sex, generational differences, or genealogical differences. In the various systems of kinship terminology, any one of these factors may be emphasized at the expense of others, but regardless of the factors emphasized, all kinship terminologies accomplish two important tasks. First, they classify particular kinds of persons into single specific categories; second, they separate different kinds of persons into distinct categories. Generally, two or more kin are merged under the same term when similarity of status exists between the individuals. These similarities are then emphasized by the application of one term to both individuals.

Six different systems of kinship terminology result from the application of the above principles:

the Eskimo, Hawaiian, Iroquois, Crow, Omaha, and Descriptive systems, each identified according to the way cousins are classified.

ESKIMO SYSTEM

Eskimo kinship terminology, comparatively rare among all the systems of the world, is the one used by Anglo-Americans, as well as by a number of food-foraging peoples. The Eskimo or lineal system emphasizes the nuclear family by specifically identifying mother, father, brother, and sister, while lumping together all other relatives into a few gross categories (Fig. 10.5). For example, one's father is distinguished from one's father's brother (uncle); but one's father's brother is not distinguished from the mother's brother (both are called "uncle"). Mother's sister and father's sister are treated similarly, both being called "aunt." In addition, one calls all the sons and daughters of aunts and uncles cousin, without distinguishing the side of the family to which they belong, or even their sex.

Eskimo system: System of kinship terminology, also called lineal system, which emphasizes the nuclear family by specifically identifying mother, father, brother, and sister, while merging together all other relatives.

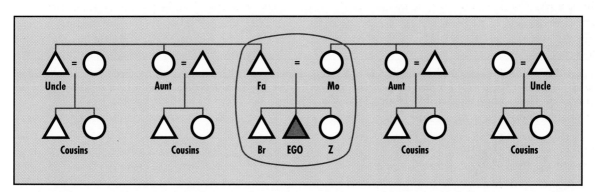

Figure 10.5 The Eskimo system of kinship terminology emphasizes the nuclear family (indicated by the red line). Ego's father and mother are distinguished from his aunts and uncles, and his siblings from his cousins.

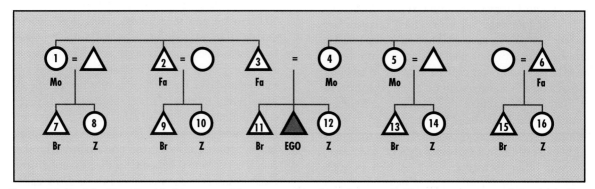

Figure 10.6   The Hawaiian kinship system. The men numbered 2 and 6 are called by the same term as father (3) by Ego; the women numbered 1 and 5 are called by the same term as mother (4). All cousins of Ego's own generation (7–16) are considered brothers and sisters.

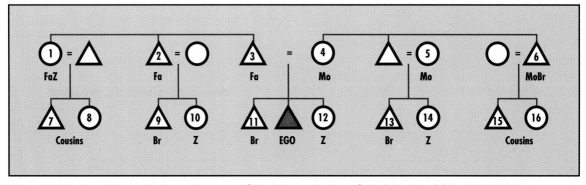

Figure 10.7   According to the Iroquois system of kinship terminology, father's brother (2) is called by the same term as father (3); mother's sister (5) is called by the same term as mother (4); but the people 1 and 6 have separate terms for themselves. Those people numbered 9–14 are all considered siblings, but 7, 8, 15 and 16 are cousins.

Unlike other terminologies, the Eskimo system provides separate and distinct terms for each member of the nuclear family. This is probably because the Eskimo system is generally found in societies where the dominant kin group is the bilateral kindred, in which only the members of the immediate family are important in day-to-day affairs. This is especially true of modern North American society, in which the family is independent, living apart from, and not directly involved with, other kin except on ceremonial occasions. Thus, people in the United States distinguish between their closest kin (parents and siblings), but lump together (as aunts, uncles, cousins) other kin on both sides of the family.

HAWAIIAN SYSTEM

The **Hawaiian system** of kinship terminology, common in Hawaii and other Malayo-Polynesian-speaking areas, but found elsewhere as well, is the least complex system, in that it uses the fewest terms. The Hawaiian system is also called the generational system, since all relatives of the same generation and sex are referred to by the same term (Fig. 10.6). For example, in one's parents' generation, the term used to refer to one's father is used as well for father's brother, and mother's brother. Similarly, one's mother, her sister, and one's father's sister are all lumped together under a single term. In ego's generation, male and female cousins are distinguished by sex and are equated with brothers and sisters.

The Hawaiian system reflects the absence of strong unilineal descent and is usually associated with ambilineal descent. Because ambilineal rules allow one to trace descent through either side of the family, and members on both the father's and the mother's side are looked upon as being more or less equal, a certain degree of similarity is created among the father's and the mother's siblings. Thus, they are all simultaneously recognized as being similar relations and are merged together under a single term. In like manner, the children of the mother's and father's siblings are related to oneself in the same way as one's brother and sister are. Thus, they are ruled out as potential marriage partners.

IROQUOIS SYSTEM

In the **Iroquois system** of kinship terminology, one's father and father's brother are referred to by a single term, as are one's mother and mother's sister; however, one's father's sister and mother's brother are given separate terms (Fig. 10.7). In one's own generation, brothers, sisters, and parallel cousins (offspring of parental siblings of the same sex, that is, the children of mother's sister or father's brother) of the same sex are referred to by the same terms, which is logical enough considering that they are the offspring of people who are classified in the same category as ego's actual mother and father. Cross-cousins (offspring of parental siblings of opposite sex, that is, the children of mother's brother or father's sister) are distinguished by separate terms. In fact, cross-cousins are often preferred as spouses, for marriage to them reaffirms alliances between related lineages.

Iroquois terminology is very widespread and is usually found with unilineal descent groups. It was, for example, the terminology in use until recently in rural Chinese society.

Hawaiian system: A mode of kinship reckoning in which all relatives of the same sex and generation are referred to by the same term.

Iroquois system: System of kinship terminology wherein one's father and father's brother are referred to by a single term, as are one's mother and mother's sister, but one's father's sister and one's mother's brother are given separate terms; parallel cousins are classified with brothers and sisters, but not with cross-cousins.

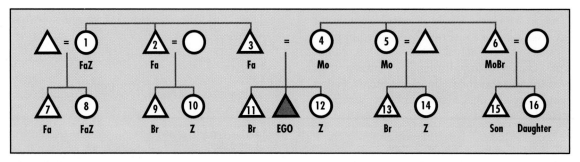

Figure 10.8   The Crow system is the obverse of the Omaha system, shown in Figure 10.9. Those numbered 4 and 5 are merged under a single term, as are 2, 3, and 7. Ego's parallel cousins (9, 10, 13, 14) are considered siblings, while mother's brother's children (15, 16) are equated with Ego's own children.

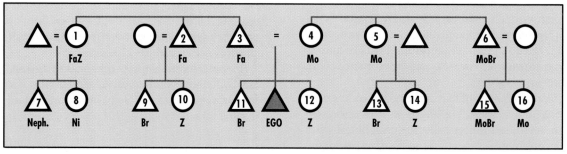

Figure 10.9   In the Omaha system, 2 is called by the same term as father (3); 5 is called by the same term as mother (4), but 1 and 6 have separate terms. In Ego's generation 9–14 are all considered siblings, but 7 and 8 are equated with the generation of Ego's children, while 15 and 16 are equated with the generation of Ego's parents.

CROW SYSTEM

In the preceding systems of terminology some relatives were grouped under common terms, while others of the same generation were separated and given different labels or terms. In the Crow system, another variable enters the picture: The system ignores the distinction that occurs between generations among certain kin.

The **Crow system,** found in many parts of the world, is the one used by the Hopi Indians. Associated with strong matrilineal descent organization, it groups differently the relations on the father's side and mother's side (Fig. 10.8). Cross-cousins on the father's side are equated with relatives on the parental generation while those on the mother's side are equated with the generation of ego's children. Otherwise, the system is much like Iroquois terminology.

To those unfamiliar with it, the Crow system seems terribly complex and illogical. Why does it exist? In societies like that of the Hopi, where individual identity is dependent on descent group affiliation, and descent is matrilineal, it makes sense to merge father's sister, her daughter, and even her mother together under a single term, regardless of generation. These are women through whom descent is traced in the lineage that sired ego, just as

a male ego's own children, along with those of his mother's brother, were sired by men of ego's own lineage. Thus, it makes sense for ego to equate his maternal cross-cousins with the generation of his own children.

OMAHA SYSTEM

The **Omaha system** is the patrilineal equivalent of the matrilineal Crow system. Thus, one's mother and one's mother's sister are designated by a single term, one's father and father's brother are merged together under another, while one's parallel cousins are merged with brothers and sisters (Fig. 10.9). Cross-cousins on the maternal side are raised a generation, while those on the paternal side are equated with the generation of ego's children. Thus, children born of women from one patrilineage, for the men of another, are lowered by one generation.

DESCRIPTIVE SYSTEM

Although the **descriptive system** is found among few of the world's societies, it has come to replace Iroquois terminology among rural Chinese. In this system, one's mother's brother is distinguished from one's father's brother, who is distinguished from one's father; one's mother's sister is distinguished from one's mother, as well as from one's father's sister. Each cousin is distinguished from all others, as well as from siblings. It is therefore more precise than any of the other systems (including that used by most Americans) which may be one reason it is so rare. In few societies are all one's aunts, uncles, cousins, and siblings treated differently from one another.

Chapter Summary

In nonindustrial societies, kinship groups commonly deal with problems that cannot be handled by families and households alone; problems such as those involving defense, the allocation of property or the pooling of other resources. As societies become larger and more complex, formal political systems take over many of these matters.

A common form of kinship group is the descent group, which has as its criterion of membership descent from a common ancestor through a series of parent-child links. Unilineal descent establishes kin group membership exclusively through the male or female line. Matrilineal descent is traced through the female line; patrilineal, through the male.

The descent system is closely tied to the economic base of a society. Generally, patrilineal descent predominates where the male is the breadwinner, matrilineal where the female is the breadwinner. Anthropologists now recognize that in all societies the kin of both mother and father are important elements in the social structure, regardless of how descent group membership is defined.

The male members of a patrilineage trace their descent from a common male ancestor. A female belongs to the same descent group as her father and his brother; but her children cannot trace their descent through him. Typically, authority over the children lies with the father or his elder brother. The requirement for younger men to defer to older men, and for women to defer to men as well as to the women of a household into which they marry are common sources of tension in a patrilineal society.

In one respect, matrilineal is the opposite of patrilineal descent, with descent being traced through the female line. Unlike the patrilineal pattern, which confers authority on men, matrilineal descent does not necessarily confer authority on women, although they usually have more of a say in the making of decisions than they do in patrilineal societies. The matrilineal system is common in societies in which women perform much of the productive work. This system may be a source of

family tension, since the husband's authority is not in his own household but in that of his sister. This, and the ease with which unsatisfactory marriages may be ended, often results in higher divorce rates in matrilineal than in patrilineal societies.

Double descent is matrilineal for some purposes and patrilineal for others. Ambilineal descent provides a measure of flexibility in that an individual has the option of affiliating with either the mother's or father's descent group.

Descent groups are often highly structured economic units that provide aid and security to their members. They may also be repositories of religious tradition, with group solidarity enhanced by worship of a common ancestor. A lineage is a corporate descent group made up of consanguineal kin who are able to trace their genealogical links to a common ancestor. Since lineages are commonly exogamous, sexual competition within the group is largely avoided. In addition, marriage of a member of the group represents an alliance of two lineages. Lineage exogamy also serves to maintain open communication within a society and fosters the exchange of information among lineages.

Fission is the splitting up of a large lineage group into new, smaller ones, with the original lineage becoming a clan. Clan members claim descent from a common ancestor but without actually knowing the genealogical links to that ancestor. Unlike lineages, clan residence is usually dispersed rather than localized. In the absence of residential unity, clan identification is reinforced by totems, usually symbols from nature, that remind members of their common ancestry. A phratry or moiety is a unilineal descent group of two or more clans that are supposedly related.

Bilateral descent, characteristic of Western, modernizing and many food-foraging societies, is traced through both parents simultaneously and recognizes several ancestors. An individual is affiliated equally with all relatives on both the mother's and father's sides. Such a large group is socially impractical and is usually reduced to a small circle of paternal and maternal relatives called the kindred. A kindred is never the same for any two persons except siblings.

Different types of descent systems appear in different societies. In societies in which the nuclear family is paramount, bilateral kinship and kindred organization are likely to prevail.

In any society, cultural rules dictate the way kinship relationships are defined. Factors such as sex, generational, or genealogical differences help distinguish one kin from another. The Hawaiian system is the simplest kinship system. All relatives of the same generation and sex are referred to by the same term. The Eskimo system, used by Anglo-Americans, emphasizes the nuclear family and merges all other relatives into a few large, generally undifferentiated categories. In the Iroquois system, a single term is used for an individual's father and father's brother, another for one's mother and mother's sister. In the Omaha and Crow systems, no distinction is made between generations among certain kinsmen. The relatively rare descriptive system treats all one's aunts, uncles, cousins, and siblings as different from one another.

Suggested Readings

Fox, Robin. *Kinship and Marriage in an Anthropological Perspective*. Baltimore, Md.: Penguin, 1968.
An excellent introduction to the concepts of kinship and marriage, outlining some of the methods of analysis used in the anthropological treatment of kinship and marriage. Updates Radcliffe-Brown's *African Systems of Kinship and Marriage* and features a perspective focused on kinship groups and social organization.

Goodenough, Ward H. *Description and Comparison in Cultural Anthropology*. Chicago: Aldine, 1970.
This is an important contribution to the study of social organization, which confronts the problem of describing kinship organization—kindred and clan, sibling and cousin—in such a way that meaningful cross-cultural comparisons can be made.

Keesing, Roger M. *Kin Groups and Social Structure*. New York: Holt, Rinehart and Winston, 1975.
This is a high-level introduction to kinship theory suitable for advanced undergraduate students. A strong point of the work is the attention given to nonunilineal, as well as unilineal, systems.

Schusky, Ernest L. *Variation in Kinship*. New York: Holt, Rinehart and Winston, 1975.
This book is an introduction to kinship, descent, and residence for the beginner. A reliance on a case-study approach leads the reader from basic data to generalizations, a strategy that helps remove some of the abstraction students of kinship organization sometimes find confusing.

Schusky, Ernest L. *Manual for Kinship Analysis*, 2nd ed. Lanham, Md.: University Press of America, 1983.
A useful book that discusses the elements of kinship, diagramming, systems classification, and descent, with specific examples.

11

GROUPING BY SEX, AGE,

COMMON INTEREST, AND

CLASS

CHAPTER PREVIEW

These young women of India exemplify the phenomenon of age grading, one of a number of means by which people may be organized into groups without recourse to kinship or descent.

WHAT PRINCIPLES, BESIDES KINSHIP AND MARRIAGE, ARE USED TO ORGANIZE PEOPLE WITHIN SOCIETIES? Grouping by sex, age, common interest, and position within a ranked hierarchy (class stratification) all may be used to deal with problems not conveniently handled by marriage, the family and/or household, descent group, or kindred. In addition, stratification is a means by which certain groups within society secure preferential treatment for themselves, at the expense of other groups.

WHAT IS AGE GRADING? Age grading—the formation of groups on the basis of age—is a means of organizing people that is widely used in human societies, including those of Europe and North America. In industrial societies, or nonindustrial societies in which populations are relatively large, age grades may be broken down into age sets—groups of people of approximately the same age who move as groups through the series of age grades.

WHAT ARE COMMON-INTEREST ASSOCIATIONS? Common-interest associations are formed to deal with specific problems. They acquire their members through an act of joining on the part of individuals. This act may range all the way from fully voluntary to compulsory. Common-interest associations have been a feature of human societies since the advent of the first farming villages several thousand years ago, but have become especially prominent in modern industrial or industrializing societies.

WHAT IS SOCIAL STRATIFICATION? Stratification is the division of society into two or more classes of people that do not share equally in basic resources, influence, or prestige. Such class structure is characteristic of all of the world's societies in which one finds large and heterogeneous populations with centralized political control. Among others, these include the ancient civilizations of the Middle East, Asia, Mexico, and Peru, as well as modern industrial societies, including the United States.

Social organization based on kinship and marriage has received an extraordinary amount of attention from anthropologists, and the subject usually is quite prominent in anthropological writing. There are several reasons for this: In one way or another, kinship and marriage operate as organizing principles in all societies, and, in the tribal and band societies so often studied by anthropologists, they are usually the most important organizational principles. There is, too, a certain fascination in the almost mathematical way in which kinship systems at least appear to work. To the unwary, all this attention to kinship and marriage may convey the impression that these are the only principles of social organization that really count. Yet it is obvious from the case of modern industrial societies that other principles of social organization not only exist but may be quite important. Those that we will examine in this chapter are grouping by sex, age, common interest, and class (stratification).

GROUPING BY SEX

As we have seen in preceding chapters of this book, some division of labor by sex is characteristic of all human societies. Although in some—the !Kung for example (Chapter 6)—many tasks undertaken by men and women may be shared, and people may perform work normally assigned to the opposite sex without loss of face, in some other societies, men and women are rigidly segregated in what they do. For instance, among the Mohawk, Oneida, Onondaga, Cayuga, and Seneca Indians of New York—the famous Five Nations Iroquois—society was divided into two parts consisting of sedentary women on the one hand, and nomadic men on the other. Living in villages were the women, who were "blood" relatives of one another, and whose job it was to grow the corn, beans, and squash on which the Iroquois relied for subsistence. Although

Among the Iroquois Indians of what is now New York, society was divided into sedentary women (whose work was carried out in or near the village) and nomadic men (whose work was carried out away from the village). This pattern still holds today, as men leave their villages for extended periods to do much of the high-steel work in the cities of North America.

houses and the palisades that protected villages were built by men, who also helped women to clear their fields, the most important work of men was pursued at some distance from their villages. This consisted of hunting, fishing, trading, warring, and engaging in diplomacy. As a consequence, men were transients in the villages, present for only brief periods of time.

Although masculine activities were considered to be more prestigious than those of women, the latter were regarded by all as the sustainers of life. Moreover, women headed the longhouses (dwellings occupied by matrilocal extended families), descent and inheritance passed through women, and ceremonial life centered on the activities of women. Although men held all positions of leadership outside of households, on the councils of the villages, tribes, and the league of Five Nations, it was the women of their lineages who nominated them for these positions and who held the power of the veto over them. Thus, male leadership was balanced by female authority. Overall, the phrase "separate but equal" accurately describes relations between the sexes in Five Nations Iroquoian society, with members of neither sex being dominant nor submissive to the other. Related to this seems to have been a low incidence of rape, at least among the Five Nations. Widely commented upon by outside observers in the nineteenth century was an apparent absence of rape within Iroquoian communities. On the other hand, earlier Jesuit missionaries do record its occurrence in association with the violence directed at peoples outside of the League of Five Nations, over whom the league wished to impose its dominance.

Although Iroquoian men were often absent from the village, when present they ate and slept with women. Among the Mundurucu, discussed briefly in Chapter 9, men not only work apart from women, but eat and sleep separately as well. All men from the age of 13 on live in a large house of their own, while women with their young children occupy two or three houses grouped around that of the men. For all intents and purposes, men associate with men, and women with women. The relation between the sexes, rather than being harmonious, is one of opposition. According to Mundurucu belief, sex roles were once reversed, women ruled over men, and controlled the sacred trumpets that are the symbols of power and represent the generative capacities of women. But because women couldn't hunt, they couldn't supply the meat demanded by the ancient spirits contained within the trumpets, enabling the men to take the trumpets from the women, establishing their dominance in the process. Ever since, the trumpets have been kept carefully guarded and hidden in the men's house, and no woman can see them under penalty of gang rape. Thus, Mundurucu men express fear and envy towards women, whom they seek to control by force. For their part, the women neither like nor accept a submissive status, and even though men occupy all formal positions of political and religious leadership, women are autonomous in the economic realm.

Although there are important differences, there are nonetheless interesting similarities between Mundurucu beliefs and those of traditional European (including American) culture. The idea of rule by men replacing an earlier state of matriarchy (rule by women), for example, was held by many nineteenth-century intellectuals. A major difference between Mundurucu and traditional European society is that, in the latter, women have not had control of their own economic activities. Although this is now changing, there is still a considerable distance to go before women in Western countries achieve economic parity with men.

AGE GROUPING

Age grouping is so familiar and so important that it and sex have sometimes been called the only universal factors in the determination of one's position in society. In North American society, one's first friends generally are children one's own age. Together they are sent off to school, where together they remain until their late teens. At specified ages they are finally allowed to do things reserved for adults, such as driving a car, voting, and drinking alcoholic beverages, and (if they are males) are required to go off to war if called upon to do so. Ultimately, North Americans retire from their jobs at some specified age and, more and more, live out the final years of their lives in "retirement communities," segregated from the rest of society. North

Age grading in modern North American society is seen in the educational system, which specifies that at six years of age all children must enter the first grade.

Americans are "teenagers," "middle-aged," "senior citizens," whether they like it or not, and for no other reason than their age.

The pervasiveness of age grouping in North American society is further illustrated by its effects on the Jewish descent groups that we discussed in Chapter 10. Until well into the 1930s, these always took on a more or less conventional ambilineal structure, which united relatives of all generations from the very old to the very young, with no age restrictions. By the late 1930s, however, younger generations of Jews of eastern European background were becoming assimilated into North American culture to such a degree that some of them began to form new descent groups that deliberately excluded any kin of the parental and grandparental generations. In these new cousins clubs, as they are called, descendants of the cousins are eligible for membership, but not until they reach legal majority or are married, whichever comes first. Here again, these newer descent groups contrast with the older family circles, in which membership can be activated at any age, no matter how young.

Age classification also plays a significant role in non-Western societies, where at least a distinction is made between the immature, mature, and older people whose physical powers are waning. Old age often has profound significance, bringing with it the period of greatest respect (for women it may mean the first social equality with men); rarely are the elderly shunted aside or abandoned. Even the Inuit, who are frequently portrayed as a people who quite literally abandon their aged relatives, do so only in truly desperate circumstances, where the physical survival of the group is at stake. In all nonliterate societies, the elders are the repositories of accumulated wisdom; they are the "living libraries" for their people. To cast them aside would be analogous to closing down all the archives and libraries in a modern industrial state.

In the United States we rely on the written word, rather than on our elders, for long-term memory. Moreover, we have become so accustomed to rapid change that some of us tend to assume that the experiences of our grandparents and those of their generation are of little relevance to us in "today's world." Indeed, retirement from earning a living implies to some that one has nothing further to offer society, and that one should stay out of the way of those who are younger. "The symbolism of the traditional gold

watch is all too plain: you should have made your money by now, and your time has run out. The watch will merely tick off the hours that remain between the end of adulthood and death."[1] The ultimate irony is that the ingenuity of modern science is often used to keep alive the bodies of individuals who have been shunted aside by society in virtually every other way.

In the institutionalization of age, cultural rather than biological factors are of prime importance in determining social status. All human societies recognize a number of life stages; precisely how they are defined will vary from one culture to another. Out of this recognition they establish patterns of activity, attitudes, prohibitions, and obligations. In some instances, these are designed to help the transition from one age to another, to teach needed skills, or to lend economic assistance. Often they are taken as the basis for the formation of organized groups.

INSTITUTIONS OF AGE GROUPING

An organized class of people with membership on the basis of age is known as an **age grade.** Theoretically speaking, membership in an age grade ought

[1]Colin M. Turnbull, *The Human Cycle* (New York: Simon & Schuster, 1983), p. 229.

Age grade: A category of people based on age; every individual passes through a series of such categories in the course of a lifetime.

---

to be automatic: One reaches the appropriate age, and so one is included, without question, in the particular age grade. Just such situations do exist, among the East African Tiriki, for example, whose system we will examine shortly. Sometimes, though, one has to buy one's way into the age grade for which one is eligible. By way of illustration, among some of the Indians of the North American plains, boys had to purchase the appropriate costumes, dances, and songs for age-grade membership. In societies where entrance fees are expensive, not all people eligible for membership in a particular age grade may actually be able to join.

Entry into and transfer out of age grades may be accomplished individually, either by a biological distinction, such as puberty, or by a socially recognized status, such as marriage or childbirth. Whereas age-grade members may have much in common, engage in similar activities, cooperate with one another, and share the same orientation and aspirations, their membership may not be entirely parallel with physiological age. A specific

In many societies it is common for children of the same age to play, eat, and learn together, like these Masai boys, who are coming together for the first time to receive instruction for their initiation into an age grade.

Age sets: Groups of persons initiated into age grades at the same time and who move through the series of categories together.

time is often ritually established for moving from a younger to an older grade. Although members of senior groups commonly expect deference from and acknowledge certain responsibilities to their juniors, this does not necessarily mean that one grade is better or worse or even more important than another. There can be standardized competition (opposition) between age grades, as between first-year students and sophomores on U.S. college campuses. One can, comparably, accept the realities of being a teenager without feeling the need to "prove anything."

In some societies, age grades are subdivided into **age sets.** An age set is a group of persons initiated into an age grade, who will move through the system together. For example, among the Tiriki of East Africa, the age group consisting of those initiated into an age grade over a 15-year period amounts to an age set. Age sets, unlike age grades, do not cease to exist after a specified number of years; the members of an age set usually remain closely associated throughout their lives, or at least through much of their lives.

A certain amount of controversy has arisen over the relative strength, cohesiveness and stability that go into an age grouping. The age-set notion implies strong feelings of loyalty and mutual support. Because such groups may possess property, songs, shield designs, and rituals, and are internally organized for collective decision making and leadership, a distinction is called for between them and simple age grades. We may also distinguish between transitory age grades—which initially concern younger men (sometimes women too), but become less important and disintegrate as the members grow older—and the comprehensive systems that affect people through the whole of their lives.

AGE GROUPING IN AFRICAN SOCIETIES

While age is used as a criterion for group membership in many parts of the world, its most varied and elaborate use is found in Africa, south of the Sahara. An example may be seen among the Tiriki, one of several pastoral nomadic groups who live in Kenya.[2] In this society, each boy born over a 15-year period becomes a member of a particular age set then open for membership. There are seven such named age sets, only one of which is open for membership at a time; when membership in one is closed, the next

[2]Walter H. Sangree, "The Bantu Tiriki of Western Kenya," in *Peoples of Africa*, ed. James Gibbs, Jr. (New York: Holt, Rinehart and Winston, 1965), pp. 69–72.

The diversity of common-interest associations is astounding. Shown here are a spokeswoman for an adoptive parents' group and a bikers' organization.

one is open for a 15-year period, and so on until the passage of 105 years (7 × 15), when the first once again takes in new "recruits."

Members of Tiriki age sets remain together for life, as they move through four age grades: advancement occurs at 15-year intervals, at the same time that one age set closes and another opens for membership. Each age grade has its own particular duties and responsibilities. The first, or "Warrior" age grade, traditionally served as guardians of the country, and members gained renown through fighting. Since colonial times, however, this traditional function has been lost with cessation of warfare, and members of this age grade now find excitement and adventure by leaving their community for extended employment or study elsewhere.

The next age grade, the "Elder Warriors," traditionally had few specialized tasks, but learned skills they would need later on by assuming an increasing share of administrative activities. For example, they would chair the post-funeral gatherings held to settle property claims after someone's death. Elder Warriors were also the ones who served as envoys between elders of different communities. Nowadays, Elder Warriors hold nearly all of the administrative and executive roles opened up by the creation and growth of a centralized Tiriki administrative bureaucracy.

"Judicial Elders," the third age grade, traditionally handled most tasks connected with the administration and settlement of local disputes. Today, they still serve as the local judiciary body. Members of the "Ritual Elders," the senior age grade, presided over the priestly functions of ancestral shrine observances on the household level, at subclan meetings, at semiannual community appeals, and at rites of initiation into the various age grades. They were also credited with access to special magical powers. With the decline of ancestor worship over the past several decades, many of these traditional functions have been lost and no new ones have

Common-interest associations: Associations not based on age, kinship, marriage, or territory that result from an act of joining.

arisen to take their places. Nonetheless, Ritual Elders continue to hold the most important positions in the initiation ceremonies, and their power as sorcerers and expungers of witchcraft are still recognized.

COMMON-INTEREST ASSOCIATIONS

The rise of **common-interest associations,** whether out of individual predilection or community need, is a theme intimately associated with world urbanization and its attendant social upheavals; the fondness of people in modern societies for joining all sorts of organizations is incontestably related to these societies' complexity. This phenomenon poses a major threat to the inviolability of age and kinship grouping. Individuals are often separated from their brothers, sisters, or age mates; they obviously cannot obtain their help in learning to cope with life in a new and bewildering environment, in learning a new language or mannerisms necessary for the change from village to city, if they are not present. But such functions must somehow be met. Because common-interest associations are by nature quite flexible, they are increasingly, both in the cities and in tribal villages, filling this gap in the social structure. Common-interest associations are not, however, restricted to modernizing societies alone; they are to be found in many traditional societies as well. There is reason to believe that they may have arisen with the emergence of the first horticultural villages.

Common-interest associations have traditionally been referred to in the anthropological literature as voluntary associations, but this term is misleading. The act of joining may range from being fully voluntary to being required by law. For example, in the United States, under the draft laws one sometimes became a member of the armed forces without choosing to join. It is not really compulsory to

join a labor union, but unless one does, one can't work in a union shop. What is really meant by the term *voluntary association* are those associations not based on sex, age, kinship, marriage, or territory, that result from an act of joining. The act may often be voluntary, but it doesn't have to be.

KINDS OF COMMON-INTEREST ASSOCIATIONS

The diversity of common-interest associations is astonishing. Their goals may include the pursuit of friendship, recreation, and the expression and distinction of rank, as well as governing function and the pursuit or defense of economic interests. Traditionally, associations have served for the preservation of tribal songs, history, language, and moral beliefs; the Tribal Unions of West Africa, for example, continue to serve this purpose. Similar organizations, often operating clandestinely, have kept traditions alive among North American Indians, who are undergoing a resurgence of ethnic pride despite generations of schooling designed to extinguish tribal identity. Another significant force in the formation of associations may be the supernatural experience common to all members; the Crow Indian Tobacco Society, the secret associations of the Kwakiutl Indians of British Columbia with their cycles of rituals known only to initiates, and the Kachina cults of the Hopi Indians are well-known examples. Among other traditional forms of association are military, occupational, political, and entertainment groups that parallel such familiar groups as the American Legion, labor unions, block associations, college fraternities and sororities, not to mention "co-ops" of every kind.

Such organizations are frequently exclusive, but a prevailing characteristic is their concern for the general well-being of an entire village or group of villages. The rain that falls as a result of the work of Hopi rainmakers nourishes the crops of members and nonmembers alike.

MEN'S AND WOMEN'S ASSOCIATIONS

For many years, women's contributions to common-interest associations were regarded by social scientists as less significant than men's. The reason is that men's associations generally have attracted more notice around the world than women's. Heinrich Schurtz's theory, published in 1902, that underlying the differentiation between kinship and associational groups is a profound difference in the psychology of the sexes, was widely accepted for years. Schurtz regarded women as eminently unsocial beings who preferred to remain in kinship groups based on sexual relations and the reproductive function rather than form units on the basis of commonly held interests. Men, on the other hand, were said to view sexual relations as isolated episodes, an attitude that fostered the purely social factor that makes "birds of a feather flock together."

In recent years, scholars of both sexes have shown this kind of thinking to be culture-bound. In some societies women have not formed associations to the extent that men have because the demands of raising a family and their daily activities have not permitted it, and because men have not always encouraged them to do so. Given the plethora of women's clubs of all kinds in the United States for several generations, however, one wonders how this belief in women as unsocial beings survived as long as it did. Earlier in this country's history, of course, when women were stuck at home in rural situations, with no near neighbors, they had little chance to participate in common-interest associations. Moreover, some functions of men's associations—like military duties—are often culturally defined as purely for men or repugnant to women. In a number of the world's traditional societies, however, the opportunities for female sociability are so great that there may be little need for women's associations. Among the Indians of northeastern North America (including the Five Nations Iroquois discussed earlier), the men spent extended periods off in the woods hunting, either by themselves or with a single companion. The women, by contrast, spent most of their time in their village, in close, everyday contact with all the other women of the group. Not only were there lots of people to talk to but there was always someone available to help with whatever tasks required assistance.

Still, as cross-cultural research makes clear, women do play important roles in associations of their own and even in those in which men predominate. Among the Crow Indians, women participated even in the secret Tobacco Society, as well as in

Common-interest associations are not limited to modern industrial societies. This 1832 picture shows a Mandan Indian Bull Dance. The Bulls were one of several common-interest groups that were concerned with both social and military affairs.

their own exclusive groups. Throughout Africa women's social clubs complement the men's and are concerned with educating women, with crafts, and with charitable activities. In Sierra Leone, where once-simple dancing societies have developed under urban conditions into complex organizations with a set of new objectives, the dancing *compin* is made up of young women as well as men, who together perform plays based on traditional music and dancing and raise money for various mutual-benefit causes. The Kpelle of Liberia maintain initiation, or "bush," schools for both young men and women; women also alternate with men in the ritual supremacy of a chiefdom. The cycle of instruction and rule (four years for males, three for females) that marks these periods derives from the Kpelle's association of the number four with maleness and three with femaleness, rather than from a notion of male superiority.

Women's rights organizations, so-called "consciousness-raising" groups, and professional organizations for women are examples of some of the associations arising directly or indirectly out of today's social climate. These groups cover the entire range of association forming, from simple friendship and support groups to political, guild-like, and economic (the publication of magazines, groups designed to influence advertising) associations on a national scale. If an unresolved point does exist in the matter of women's participation, it is in determining why women are excluded from associations in some societies, while in others their participation is essentially equal with that of men.

The importance of common-interest associations in areas of rapid social change is considerable. Increasingly, such organizations assume the roles and functions formerly held by kinship or age groups; in many areas they hold the key both to individual adaptation to new circumstances and to group survival. Where once groups were organized to preserve traditional ways and structure against the intrusion of the modern world, urban associa-

tions accept the reality of such intrusions and help their members to cope both socially and economically. Members may turn to associations for support and sympathy while unemployed or sick; the groups may also provide education or socialization. An important need met by many of these associations is economic survival; to achieve such ends they may help raise capital, regulate prices, discourage competition, and organize cooperative activities.

Always the keynote of these groups is adaptation. As Kenneth Little observes, adaptation implies not only the modification of institutions but also the development of new ones to meet the demands of an industrial economy and urban way of life.[3] Modern urbanism involves the rapid diffusion of entirely new ideas, habits, and technical procedures, as well as a considerable reconstruction of social relationships as a consequence of new technical roles and groups created. Age-old conventions yield to necessity, as women and young people in general gain new status in the urban economy. Women's participation, especially in associations with mixed membership, involves them in new kinds of social relationships with men, including companionship and the chance to choose a spouse by oneself. Young persons on the whole become leaders for their less Westernized counterparts. Even in rural areas, such associations thrive, reflecting the increasing consciousness of the outer world. The European contact that so frequently shattered permanent age and kinship groups has also, partly through the influence of education, helped to remove restrictions in association membership both in age and sex.

In contemporary North American culture, common-interest associations abound, such as women's clubs, street gangs, Kiwanis, Rotary, and the PTA. Elements of secret initiatory cults survive, to some extent, in the Masonic lodges and fraternity and sorority initiations. Women's associations recently seem to have proliferated. Although some people in North America may think of their own groups as more complex and highly organized than those of traditional non-Western societies, many of the new urban voluntary associations in Africa, for example,

[3]Kenneth Little, "The Role of Voluntary Associations in West African Urbanization," in *Africa: Social Problems of Change and Conflict*, ed. Pierre Van den Berghe (San Francisco: Chandler, 1964).

Stratified society: The division of society into two or more groups of people that do not share equally in the basic resources that support life, influence, and prestige.

---

are elaborately structured and rival many secular and religious organizations in the U.S. and Canada. Such traditional groups, with their antecedents reaching far back in history, may have served as models for associations familiar to North Americans; now, in becoming Westernized, they promise to outstrip those of the U.S. and Canada in complexity, an interesting phenomenon to watch as the non-Western countries become "modernized."

SOCIAL STRATIFICATION

The study of social stratification involves the examination of distinctions that strike us as unfair and even outrageous, but social stratification is a common and powerful phenomenon in some of the world's societies. Civilizations, in particular, with their large and heterogeneous populations, are invariably stratified.

Basically, a **stratified society** is one that is divided into two or more groups of people, and these groups are ranked high and low relative to one another. When the people in one such group or stratum are compared with those in another, marked differences in privileges, rewards, restrictions, and obligations become apparent. Members of low-ranked groups will tend to have fewer privileges than those in higher-ranked groups. In addition, they tend not to be rewarded to the same degree and are denied equal access to basic resources. Their restrictions and obligations, too, are usually more onerous, although members of high-ranked groups will usually have their own distinctive restrictions and obligations to attend to. In short, social stratification amounts to institutionalized inequality. Without ranking—high versus low—there is no stratification; social differences without this do not constitute stratification.

Stratified societies stand in sharp contrast to **egalitarian societies.** As we saw in Chapter 6,

One indicator of class standing in stratified societies is how people behave toward one another. Here a village chief in Nigeria has lower standing than the turbaned king, to whom he must pay homage.

Egalitarian societies: Social systems in which as many valued positions exist as there are persons capable of filling them.

societies of food-foraging peoples are characteristically egalitarian, although there are some exceptions. In such societies there are as many valued positions as there are people capable of filling them. Hence, individuals' positions in society depend pretty much on their own abilities alone. A poor hunter may become a good hunter if he has the ability; he is not excluded from such a prestigious position because he comes from a group of poor hunters. Poor hunters do not constitute a social stratum. Furthermore, they have as much right to the resources of their society as any other of its members. No one can deny a poor hunter a fair

Social class: A set of families that enjoy equal or nearly equal prestige according to the system of evaluation.

share of food, the right to be heard when important decisions are to be made, or anything else to which a man is entitled.

GENDER STRATIFICATION

Societies may be stratified in various ways, not just in terms of class and caste (discussed below). For instance, in our earlier discussion of sex as an organizing principle, we saw that in some (but not all) societies, men and women may be regarded as unequal, with the former outranking the latter. This we may speak of as gender stratification. Generally speaking, sexual inequality is characteristic of societies which are stratified in other ways as well; thus women have historically occupied a position of inferiority to men in the class-structured societies of the Western world. In addition, sexual inequality may sometimes be seen in societies that are not otherwise stratified; in such instances, men and women are always physically as well as conceptually separated from one another. On the other hand, as the Iroquoian case cited earlier in this chapter demonstrates, not all societies in which men and women are separated exhibit gender stratification.

CLASS AND CASTE

A **social class** may be defined as a set of families that show equal or nearly equal prestige according to the system of evaluation.[4] The qualification "nearly equal" is important, for there may be a certain amount of inequality even within a given class. If this is so, to an outside observer low-ranking individuals in an upper class may not seem much different from the highest-ranking members of a lower class. Yet there will be marked differenc-

[4]Bernard Barber, *Social Stratification* (New York: Harcourt, 1957), p. 73.

ANTHROPOLOGY APPLIED

ANTHROPOLOGISTS AND SOCIAL IMPACT ASSESSMENT

A kind of policy research frequently done by anthropologists are social impact assessments, which entail collection of data about a community or neighborhood for use by planners of development projects. Specifically, such assessments seek to determine the effect of a project by determining how and upon whom its impact will fall, and whether the impact is likely to be positive or negative. In the United States, any project requiring a federal permit or licence, or using federal funds, by law must be preceded by a social impact assessment, as part of the environmental review process. Examples of such projects include highway construction, urban renewal, water diversion schemes, and land reclamation. Often, such projects are sited so that their impact falls most heavily on neighborhoods or communities inhabited by people in low socioeconomic strata, sometimes because the projects are seen as ways of improving the lives of poor people, and sometimes because the poor people are seen as having less political power to block proposals that others conceive to be (sometimes rightly, sometimes wrongly) in "the public interest."

As an illustration of this kind of work, anthropologist Sue Ellen Jacobs was hired to carry out a social impact assessment of a water diversion project in New Mexico planned by the Bureau of Land Reclamation in cooperation with the Bureau of Indian Affairs. This would have involved construction of a diversion dam and extensive canal system for irrigation on the Rio Grande River. Affected by this would be 22 communities inhabited primarily by Hispanic Americans, as well as two Indian Pueblos. In the region, unemployment was high (19.1% in June, 1970), and the project was seen as a way of promoting a perceived trend to urbanism (which theoretically would be associated with industrial development), while bringing new land into production for intensive agriculture. What the planners failed to take into account was the fact that both the Hispanic and Indian populations were heavily committed to farming for household consumption, with some surpluses raised for the market,

using a system of established irrigation canals established as many as 300 years ago. This system is maintained by elected supervisors who know the communities as well as the requirements of the land and crops, water laws, and ditch management skills. Such individuals can allocate water equitably in times of scarcity, and can prevent and resolve conflict in the realm of water and land use, as well as community life beyond the ditches. Under the proposed project, this system would be given up in favor of one in which fewer people would control larger tracts of land, and water allocation would be in the hands of a government technocrat. One of the strongest measures of local government would be lost.

Not surprisingly, Jacobs discovered widespread community opposition to this project, and it was her report that helped convince Congress that any positive impact was far outweighed by negative effects.

> One of the major objections to the construction of the project is that it would result in the obliteration of the three-hundred-year-old irrigation system structures. Project planners did not seem to recognize the antiquity and cultural significance of the traditional irrigation system. These were referred to as 'temporary diversion structures.' The fact that the old dams associated with the ditches were attached to local descent groups was simply not recognized by the official documents.*

Other negative effects, besides loss of local control, were problems associated with population growth and relocation, loss of fishing and other river-related resources, and new health hazards, including increased threat of drowning, breeding of insects, and airborne dust. Finally, physical transformation of the communities' life space was seen likely to result in changes in the context of the informal processes of enculturation that go on within the communities.

*John Van Willigen, *Applied Anthropology* (South Hadley, Mass.: Bergain and Garvey, 1986), p. 169.

es when the classes are compared as wholes with one another. The point here is that class distinctions will not be clear-cut in societies like those of North America, where there is a continuous range of differential privileges, for example, from virtual

ly none to several. Such a continuum can be divided up into classes in a variety of ways. If fine distinctions are made, then many classes may be recognized. If, however, only a few gross distinctions are made, then only a few classes will be recognized.

Thus, some speak of North American society as divided into three classes: lower, middle, and upper. Others speak of several classes: lower-lower, middle-lower, upper-lower, lower-middle, and so forth.

A **caste** is a particular kind of social class, one in which membership is fairly fixed or impermeable. Castes are strongly endogamous, and offspring are automatically members of their parents' caste. The classic case is the caste system of India. Coupled with strict endogamy and membership by descent in Indian castes is an association of particular castes with specific occupations and customs, such as food habits and styles of dress, along with rituals involving notions of purity and impurity. The literally thousands of castes are organized into a hierarchy of four named groups, at the top of which are the priests or *Brahmins*, the bearers of universal order and values, and of highest ritual purity. Below them are the powerful—though less pure—warriors. Dominant at the local level, besides fulfilling warrior functions, they control all village lands. Furnishing services to the landowners, and owning the tools of their trade, are two lower-ranking landless caste groups of artisans and laborers. At the bottom of the system, owning neither land nor the tools of their trade, are the outcasts, or "untouchables." These most impure of all people constitute a large pool of labor at the beck and call of those controlling economic and political affairs, the land-holding warrior caste.

Although some argue that the term *caste* should be restricted to the Indian situation, others find this much too narrow a usage, since castelike situations are known elsewhere in the world. In South Africa, for example, blacks have traditionally been relegated to a low-ranking stratum in society, were until recent years barred by law from marrying non-blacks, and could not hold property except to a limited degree in specified "black homelands." While blacks perform menial jobs for whites, they were until recent years prohibited from living where whites do, swimming in the same water, or even holding the hand of someone who is white. All of this brings to mind the concepts of ritual purity

Outcast groups like India's "untouchables" are a common feature of stratified societies.

and pollution so basic to the Indian caste system. In South Africa, many whites have feared pollution of their purity through improper contact with blacks.

In India and South Africa, untouchables and blacks are categories of landless or near-landless people who constitute a body of mobile laborers always available to those in political control. A similar mobile labor force of landless men at the disposal of the state emerged in China as many as 2,200 years ago (caste, in India, is at least as old). Today, some social scientists have noted the emergence of a similar castelike "underclass" in U.S. society as automation reduces the need for unskilled workers. Its members consist of unemployed, unemployable, or drastically underemployed people who own little if any property, and who live "out on the streets" or in urban or rural slums. Lacking both economic and political power, it is argued, they have no access to the kinds of educational facilities that would enable them or their children to improve their lot. Meanwhile, their presence contributes to a high unemployment

Caste: A special form of social class in which membership is determined by birth and remains fixed for life.

Verbal evaluation: The way people in a stratified society evaluate other members of their own society.

rate, which makes those who do have jobs grateful, docile, dependent, and timid about pushing for higher wages or complaining about poor working conditions.

India, South Africa, China, and the United States—all very different countries, in different parts of the world, with different ideologies—and yet, a similar phenomenon has emerged, or may possibly be emerging, in each. Is there something about the structure of socially stratified states that sooner or later produces some sort of impoverished outcast group? The answer to this is clearly unknown, but the question is deserving of the attention of anthropologists and other social scientists.

The basis of social class structure is role differentiation. Some role differentiation, of course, exists in any society, at least along the lines of sex and age. Furthermore, any necessary role will always be valued to some degree. In a food-foraging society, the role of "good hunter" will be valued. The fact that one man may already play that role does not, however, prevent another man from playing it, too, in an egalitarian society. Therefore, role differentiation by itself is not sufficient for stratification. Two more ingredients are necessary: formalized evaluation of roles involving attitudes such as like–dislike, or attraction–revulsion, and restricted access to the more highly valued ones. Obviously, the greater the diversity of roles in a society, the more complex evaluation and restriction can become. Since great role diversity is most characteristic of civilizations, it is not surprising that stratification is one of its salient features.

Social classes are manifest in several ways. One is through **verbal evaluation**—what people say about others in their own society. For this, anything can be singled out for attention and spoken of favorably or unfavorably: political, military, religious, economic, or professional roles; wealth and property; kinship; personal qualities; community activity; and a host of other things. Different cultures do this differently, and what may be spoken of favorably in one may be spoken of unfavorably in another and ignored in a third.

Furthermore, cultural values may change, so that something regarded favorably at one time may not be at another. This is one reason why a researcher may be misled by verbal evaluation, for what people say may not correspond completely with reality.

Social classes are also manifest through patterns of association: not just who interacts with whom, but in what context, and how those who are interacting treat each another. In Western society, informal, friendly relations take place mostly within one's own class. Relations with members of other classes tend to be less informal and occur in the context of specific situations. For example, a corporation executive and a janitor normally are members of different social classes. They may have frequent contact with each other, but it occurs in the setting of the corporation offices and usually requires certain stereotyped behavior patterns.

A third way social classes are manifest is through **symbolic indicators.** Included here are activities and possessions indicative of class. For example, in North American society, occupation (a garbage collector has different class status than a physician); wealth (rich people generally are in a higher social class than poor people); dress (we have all heard the expressions "white-collar" and "blue-collar"); form of recreation (upper-class people are expected to play golf rather than shoot pool down at the pool hall—but they can shoot pool at home); residential location (upper-class people usually do not live in slums); make of car; and so on. The fact is that there are all sorts of status symbols indicative of class position, including such things as how many bathrooms one's house has. At the same time, symbolic indicators may be cruder indicators of class position than verbal indicators or patterns of association. One reason is that access to wealth may not be wholly restricted to upper classes, so that individuals can buy symbols suggestive of upper-class status, whether or not this really is their status. Conversely, a member of an upper class may deliberately choose a simpler life-style than is customary. Instead of driving a Mercedes, he or she may drive a beat-up Volkswagen.

Symbolic indicators: In a stratified society, activities and possessions that are indicative of social class.

Symbolic indicators of class or caste standing include factors of life-style, as illustrated here by ways of enjoying oneself on a hot day.

Symbolic indicators involve not only factors of life-style but also differences in life chances. Life is apt to be less hard for members of an upper class as opposed to a lower class. This will show up in a tendency for lower infant mortality and longer life expectancy for the upper class. One may also see a tendency to greater physical stature and robustness on the part of upper-class people, the result of better diet and less hardship.

The interplay of symbolic indicators, verbal evaluation, and especially patterns of association in a class-structured situation can be seen in the following Original Study. Its subject is the structure of society in Namibia, in southern Africa. Like all systems of stratification, this provided a means of dividing large numbers of people into a relatively few social categories, by means of which interaction between people could be organized.

ORIGINAL STUDY

THE STRUCTURE OF NAMIBIAN SOCIETY[5]

When I first did fieldwork in Namibia in the late sixties, apartheid was the reigning dogma, as in South Africa. Surely an extended discussion of the often horrendous implications of attempting to do fieldwork in such a milieu is superfluous in this context. It was, in the jargon of the trade, a structurally plural situation because the different "racial" and "ethnic" groups as defined by the state were differentially incorporated into the society, with the white group politically and economically dominant. In distinguishing the various "populations" which made up the aggregate that is Namibian society, I will use the folk model of types of people found in the territory. This folk model differentiates two main types of peoples, namely blacks (Africans) and whites, which will, following local usage, heuristically be called racial groups. Within this broad categorization there were a number of sub-categories, locally called tribes, peoples, nations, or other ethnic groups whom whites thought of as constituting racial groups. White conceptualizations of blacks or coloureds was based on a paucity of information concerning them which reflected quite accurately everyday life where blacks or coloureds were not treated by whites as part of the community or really differentiated as individuals. In Namibia this

was further accentuated by the fact that people claim to be able to recognize racial and ethnic groups quite easily on the basis of distinct physical features, dress, language usage, etc. But beyond the ability to easily recognize categories, real knowledge of the people in these categories was limited. These categories are important because they provide "a means of classifying a heterogeneous population into a limited number of meaningful social categories" and are meaningful because they "have the characteristics of organizing interaction between people."

How does social categorization organize interaction? In this situation it is primarily because of the strength of categorical social relationships. Categorical relationships take place between people whose interaction is patterned according to some social category which is mutually recognized. Categorical relationships have three levels of relevance. One occurs between strangers who do not interact directly and specifically; it is a tacit acknowledgment of relevant social categories allowing people to divide a crowd of strangers into familiar categories. Such a process of classification allows the individual to impose some sort of order on situations made up of heterogeneous strangers, and is a common phenomenon of social life in general and urban situations in particular where people from all sections of society are continually brought into contact. For example, an African woman walking down Kaiser Street in Windhoek, the capital of Namibia, passes many people: some belong to her own ethnic group, others belong to various African ethnic groups, some may be coloured, and others members of white ethnic groups. She will recognize to which categories the different people belong and in doing so she will impose some order on an otherwise unstructured situation.

The interaction of strangers or near-strangers in public places such as on the street, or in a shop, is a second aspect of the categorical relationship. In these situations the categories to which people belong may determine if they will talk to each other, ask directions, sit together, discuss the news or gossip. In a shop the social category of the customer versus that of the clerk may determine how the customer will be treated and what language will be spoken.

The categorical relationship also applies to people who are not strangers. They have perhaps seen each other many times in the same shop, they may belong to the same club or work together. However, due to the strength of categorical stereotypes, although they "know" each other, they may maintain social distance. The strength of categorical relationships constrains or on occasion strongly restricts the development of personal relationships between people of different social categories and acts as a boundary maintenance mechanism.

Most interaction between black and white was highly formalized. The South African government's policy of apartheid in Namibia was based on the premise that people of different origins cannot live together peacefully, therefore each "racial" or "ethnic" group must develop separately. Consequently, the territory was divided up into a number of differently named areas reserved for the occupation of specific ethnic groups; in the urban areas this was manifested in the forms of different townships. All the areas were administered by

whites appointed by the white-controlled government. Movement from one ethnic area to another, whether rural or urban, was controlled by an elaborate system of permits.

In accordance with government policy, education was by law racial and ethnic-group bounded. There were separate schools for each of the white language groups, African language groups, and "coloured" people (who speak Afrikaans). In the work sector, the job reservation policy had resulted in a pattern whereby the whites had all the skilled and managerial jobs and the blacks all the jobs under them. Whites could employ blacks to work for them but no black could have a white working under him.

The social and cultural life of whites and blacks was segregated. There were very few social occasions where black and white met. On those few occasions where they did come together, such as at sports' contests, they were spatially separated and given differential treatment. Informal social mixing between blacks and whites, while strictly speaking legal, was not practised due in part to the vagaries of certain laws, e.g. the Liquor Law, and in part to fear of being ostracized. Sexual intercourse and marriage between the two main "races" were forbidden by law. Blacks could not attend cinemas or eat at restaurants in white areas, nor could they use any of the recreational facilities in the white areas.

In sum, the possibilities of interaction between black and white were formally limited to the economic or money sphere. It was not the machine gun but the search for money which provided the glue of southern African society, as Max Gluckman once expressed it.

The social rules which governed interaction between white and black were deeply felt, at least by the whites. Minimal contact was the basic rule. Contact had to be avoided at all costs where possible and had only to be indulged in when it was "part of the job" or out of economic necessity. To quote two examples of how deeply felt these rules were: when blacks and whites were travelling together in the same car, the black was expected to occupy the backseat or, if it was a truck, to sit on the back. One white friend offered another R15 [15 Rands] to sit on the back of his truck, while he sat alone in the cab and drove through the town. The friend refused. In another case some urban blacks organized a beauty contest and asked the local white mayor if he would do them the honour of crowning the beauty queen. The mayor agreed, but later when some friends jokingly told him that it was customary to kiss the queen when he crowned her, he turned down the invitation.

It is impossible to describe all the intricacies of the rules of conduct, but a few examples can be given of the rules regulating language conduct in inter-racial interaction. The use of linguistic role markers indicated the superordinate position of the whites and the subordinate position of the blacks. Blacks primarily addressed whites as Baas (boss) or Master. Sometimes the Afrikaans term Meneer (Mister) was used, especially if both black and white were educated. But often this could result in a negative reaction from the white as the following case observed at a petrol station indicates: The coloured attendant had filled up a white's car and addressed him as Meneer; the white retorted

angrily. "Who do you think I am? A kaffir-missionary that you can call me Meneer?"

Similar cases were frequently observed in shops. Most blacks can relate stories of how when they addressed a white clerk in Afrikaans as "Meneer" the response would be an angry retort "Don't say Meneer to me; I am your Baas!" Rules such as not shaking hands, special ways to hand a cigarette, and not eating together are a few other examples of social distance mechanisms practised between whites and blacks at the time.

[5]Robert Gordon, "The Field Researcher as a Deviant: A Namibian Case Study," in *Truth Be in the Field: Social Science Research in Southern Africa,* ed. Pierre Hugo. (Pretoria: University of South Africa, 1990), pp. 72–74, 75–76.

MOBILITY

In all stratified societies there is at least some **mobility,** and this helps to ease the strains that exist in any system of inequality. Even in the Indian caste system, with its guiding ideology that pretends that all arrangements within it are static, there is a surprising amount of flexibility and mobility, not all of it associated with the recent changes that "modernization" has brought to India. As a rather dramatic case in point, in the state of Rajasthan, those who own and control most land, and who are wealthy and politically powerful, are not of the warrior caste, as one might expect, but are of the lowest caste. Their tenants and laborers, by contrast, are Brahmins. Thus, the group that is ritually superior to all others finds itself in the same social position as untouchables, whereas the landowners who are the Brahmins' ritual inferiors are superior in all other ways. Meanwhile, a group of leather-workers in the untouchable category, who have gained political power in India's new democracy, are trying to better their position by claiming that they are Brahmins who were tricked in the past into doing defiling work. Although individuals cannot move up or down the caste hierarchy, whole groups can move up or down depending on claims they are able to make for higher status, and how well they can manipulate others into acknowledging their

claims. Interestingly, the people at the bottom of India's caste system have not traditionally questioned the validity of the system itself, so much as their particular position within it.

Societies that permit a great deal in the way of mobility are referred to as **open-class societies.** Even in the United States, however, despite its "rags to riches" ideal, most such mobility involves a move up or down only a notch. If this continues over several generations, however, it may add up to major change. Generally, the culture makes much of those relatively rare examples of great upward mobility that are consistent with its cultural values, and tries to ignore those cases of little or no upward (not to mention downward) mobility.

The degree of mobility in a stratified society is related to the prevailing kind of family organization. In societies where the extended family is the usual form, mobility is apt to be difficult, the reason being that each individual is strongly tied to the large family group. Hence, for a person to move up to a higher social class, his or her family must move up as well. Mobility is easier for independent nuclear families in which the individual is closely tied to fewer persons. Moreover, under neolocal residence, individuals normally leave the family into which they were born. So it is, then, that through careful marriage, occupational success, and by disassociating one's self from a lower-class

Mobility: The ability to change one's class position.

Open-class societies: Stratified societies that permit a great deal of social mobility.

family in which one was raised, all of which are made possible by residential mobility, one can more easily "move up" in society.

DEVELOPMENT OF STRATIFICATION

Because social stratification of any kind tends to make life oppressive for large segments of a population, the misery of the oppressed may be eased by means of religion, which promises the faithful a tolerable existence in the hereafter. If they have this to look forward to, they are more likely to endure the "here and now." In India, belief in reincarnation and the existence of an incorruptible supernatural power that assigns people to a particular caste position as a reward or punishment for the deed, and misdeeds of past lives justifies one's position in this life. If, however, one performs the duties appropriate to one's caste in this lifetime, then one can expect to be reborn into a higher caste in a future existence. Truly exemplary performance of one's duties may even release one from the cycle of rebirth, to be reunited with the divinity from which all existence springs. In the minds of orthodox Hindus, then, one's caste position is something one earns, rather than the accident of birth that it appears to outside observers. Thus, while the caste system explicitly recognizes inequality between people, it is underlain with an implicit assumption of ultimate equality. This contrasts with the situation in the United States, where the equality of all people is explicitly avowed at the same time that various groups are treated as unequal.

In considering the origin of social stratification, we must reckon with such common tendencies as the desire for prestige, either for oneself or one's group. Although the impulse need not result inevitably in the ranking of individuals or groups relative to one another, it sometimes may. Among the Iroquois and Hopi Indians, the Sherente and Ugandan peoples, the superiority of some kinship lineages over others is recognized in electing chiefs, performing sacred rituals, and other special tasks, whether or not membership entails any economic advantages.

This sort of situation could easily develop into full-fledged stratification. Just such a development may have taken place among the Maya of Central America.[6] Indications are that these people began as horticulturists with a relatively egalitarian, kinship-based organization. In the last centuries B.C., elaborate rituals developed as a way of dealing with the very serious problems of agriculture, such as uncertain rains, vulnerability of crops to a variety of pests, and periodic devastation from hurricanes. As this took place, a full-time priesthood arose, along with some craft specialization in the service of religion. Out of the priesthood developed, in the last century B.C., hereditary ruling dynasties. In this developmental process, certain lineages seem to

---

[6]William A. Haviland, "The Ancient Maya and the Evolution of Urban Society," *University of Colorado Museum of Anthropology Miscellaneous Series*, 37, 1975; and William A. Haviland and Hattula Moholy-Nagy, "Distinguishing the High and Mighty from the Hoi Polloi at Tikal, Guatemala," in *Mesoamerican Elites: An Archaeological Assessment*, ed. Arlen F. and Diane Z. Chase (Norman, Okla.: University of Oklahoma Press, 1992).

Left: A portrayal of a Mayan king and his nobles. Among these people, stratification arose as certain lineages monopolized important offices. In South Africa, it emerged as conquerors excluded the conquered from positions of importance and restricted their access to basic resources. On the right is a South African squatter camp.

have monopolized the important civic and ceremonial positions, and so came to be ranked above other lineages, forming the basis of an upper class.

Just as lineages may come to be ranked differentially relative to one another, so may ethnic groups. In South Africa, for example, the whites came as conquerors, establishing a social order by which they could maintain their favored position. Even without conquest, though, ethnic differences often lead to diverse classes, as members of North American society have experienced through the racial stereotyping that leads to social and economic disadvantages.

Although the cost is great—social classes do, after all, make life oppressive for large numbers of people—classes nevertheless perform an integrative function in society. They may cut across some or all lines of kinship, residence, occupation, and age group, depending on the particular society, thus counteracting potential tendencies for society to fragment into discrete entities. In India, diverse tribal groups were incorporated into the larger society by certification of their leaders as warriors, and marriage of their women to Brahmins. The problem is that stratification, by its very nature, provides a means by which one, usually small group of people may dominate and make life miserable for large numbers of others, as in South Africa where 4.5 million whites have dominated 25 million nonwhites. In India, a succession of conquerors was able to move into the caste hierarchy near its top, as warriors. In any system of stratification, those who dominate proclaim their supposedly superior status, which they try to convert into respect on the part of the lower classes. In this they may be aided by an ideology that asserts that the social order is divinely fixed and therefore not to be questioned. Thus, they hope that members of the lower classes will thereby "know their place" and so not contest their domination by the "chosen elite." If, however, this domination is contested, the elite always have the power of the state to back them up in their privileged position.

Chapter Summary

Grouping by sex separates men and women to varying degrees in different societies; in some, they may be together much of the time, while in others, they may spend much of their time apart, even to the extreme of eating and sleeping separately. Although women are perceived by men to be their inferiors in some sexually segregated societies, in others they are perceived as equals.

Age grouping is another form of association that may augment or replace kinship grouping. An age grade is a category of persons, usually of the same sex, organized on the basis of age. Age grades in some societies are broken up into age sets, which include individuals who are initiated into an age grade at the same time and move together through a series of life stages. A specific time is often ritually established for moving from a younger to an older age grade.

The most varied use of grouping by age is found in African societies south of the Sahara. Among the Tiriki of East Africa, for example, seven named age sets pass through four successive age grades. Each age set embraces a 15-year age span, and so opens to accept new initiates every 105 years. In principle, the system resembles our college classes, where (say) the "Class of 1990" (an age set) will move through the four age grades: first year, sophomore, junior, senior.

Common-interest associations are linked with rapid social change and urbanization. They are increasingly assuming the roles formerly played by kinship or age groups. In urban areas they help new arrivals cope with the changes demanded by the move from the village to the city. Common-interest associations are also seen in traditional societies, and their roots are probably to be found in the first horticultural villages. Membership may range from voluntary to legally compulsory.

For a long time social scientists mistakenly viewed women's contributions to common-interest associations as less important than men's, largely because of culture-bound assumptions. A question

that remains to be resolved is why women are barred from associations in some societies, while in others they participate on an equal basis with men.

A stratified society is one that is divided into two or more categories of people who do not share equally in basic resources, influence, or prestige. This form contrasts with the egalitarian society, in which as many valued positions exist as there are persons capable of filling them. Societies may be stratified in various ways, as by gender, age, social class, or caste. Members of a class enjoy equal or nearly equal access to basic resources and prestige (according to the way the latter is defined). Class differences are not always clear-cut and obvious. Where fine distinctions are made in privileges, the result is a multiplicity of classes. In societies where only gross distinctions are made, only a few social classes may be recognized.

Caste is a special form of social class in which membership is determined by birth and fixed for life. Endogamy is particularly marked within castes, and children automatically belong to their parents' caste. Social class structure is based on role differentiation, although this by itself is not sufficient for stratification. Also necessary are formalized positive and negative attitudes toward roles, and restricted access to the more valued ones.

Social classes are given expression in several ways. One is through verbal evaluation, or what people say about other people in their society. Another is through patterns of association—who interacts with whom, how, and in what context. Social classes are also manifest through symbolic indicators: activities and possessions indicative of class position.

Mobility is present to a greater or lesser extent in all stratified societies. Open-class societies are those in which mobility is easiest. In most cases, however, the move is limited to one rung up or down the social ladder. The degree of mobility is related to the type of family organization that prevails in a society. Where the extended family is the norm, mobility tends to be severely limited. The independent nuclear family provides a situation in which mobility is easier.

Social stratification can be based on many criteria, such as wealth, legal status, birth, personal qualities, and ideology. A rigidly stratified society normally makes life particularly oppressive for large segments of a population.

Suggested Readings

Bernardi, Bernardo. *Age Class Systems; Social Institutions and Policies Based on Age*. New York: Cambridge University Press, 1985.
A cross-cultural analysis of age as a device for organizing society and seeing to the distribution and rotation of power.

Bradfield, Richard M. *A Natural History of Associations*. New York: International Universities Press, 1973.
This two-volume work is the first major anthropological study of common-interest associations since 1902. It attempts to provide a comprehensive theory of the origin of associations and their role in kin-based societies.

Hammond, Dorothy. *Associations*. Reading, Mass.: Addison-Wesley Modular Publications, 14, 1972.
This is a brief, first-rate review of anthropological thinking and the literature on common-interest associations and age groups.

Lenski, Gerhard E. *Power and Privilege: A Theory of Social Stratification*. New York: McGraw-Hill, 1966.
Who gets what and why is explained by the distributive process and systems of social stratification in industrial nations: the United States, Russia, Sweden, and Britain. Using a broadly comparative approach, the author makes heavy use of anthropological and historical material, as well as the usual sociological materials on modern industrial societies. The basic approach is theoretical and analytical; the book builds on certain postulates about the nature of humans and society, seeking to develop in a systematic manner an explanation of a variety of patterns of stratification. The theory presented is a synthesis of Marxian and functionalist theory.

Sanday, Peggy Reeves. *Female Power and Male Dominance: On the Origins of Sexual Inequality*. Cambridge: Cambridge University Press, 1981.
In this cross-cultural study, Professor Sanday reveals the various ways that male-female relations are organized in human societies, and demonstrates that male dominance is not inherent in those relations. Rather, it appears to emerge in situations of stress, as a result of such things as chronic food shortages, migration, and colonial domination.

SHAMAN'S

MASK, NORTH

AMERICA

PART IV

INTRODUCTION

IT IS AN IRONY OF HUMAN

LIFE THAT SOMETHING AS

FUNDAMENTAL TO OUR

EXISTENCE AS COOPERATION

SHOULD CONTAIN WITHIN IT

THE SEEDS OF ITS OWN

DESTRUCTION. IT IS

NONETHELESS TRUE THAT THE

GROUPS THAT PEOPLE FORM

TO TAKE CARE OF

▶ important organizational needs do not just facilitate cooperation among the members of those groups, they also create conditions that may lead to the disruption of society. A case in point is the escalating gang violence seen in many North American cities. The attitude that "my group is better than your group" is not confined to any one of the world's cultures, and it not infrequently takes the form of a sense of rivalry between groups: descent group against descent group, men against women, age grade against age grade, social class against social class, and so forth. This is not to say that such rivalry has to be disruptive; indeed, it may function to ensure that the members of groups perform their jobs well so as not to "lose face" or be subject to ridicule. Rivalry can, however, become a serious problem if it develops into conflict.

Social living inevitably entails a certain amount of friction—not just between groups, but between individual members of groups as well. Thus, any society can count on some degree of disruptive behavior on the part of some of its members, at some time or other. On the other hand, no one can know precisely when such outbursts will occur, or what form they will take. Not only does this uncertainty go against the

predictability that social life demands; it also goes against the deep-seated psychological need on the part of each individual for structure and certainty, which we discussed in Chapter 5. Therefore, every society must have means by which conflicts can be resolved and breakdown of the social order prevented Social control and political systems, which have as their primary function the maintenance of the social order, are the subjects of Chapter 12.

Effective though a culture may be in equipping, organizing, and controlling a society to provide for the needs of its members, there are always certain problems that defy solution through existing technological or organizational means. The response of every culture is to devise a set of rituals, with a set of beliefs to explain them, aimed at solving these problems through the manipulation of supernatural beings and powers. In short, religion and magic transform the uncertainties of life into certainties. At the same time, they may serve as powerful integrative forces through commonly held values, beliefs, and practices. Also important is religion's justification of the social order, which thereby becomes a moral order as well. Thus, there is a link

between religion and magic on the one hand, and political organization and social control on the other. Religion and magic are, then, appropriate subjects for discussion in Chapter 13 of this section on the search for order.

Like religion and magic, the arts also contribute to human well-being and help give shape and significance to life. Indeed, the relationship between art and religion goes deeper than this, for much of what we call art has come into being in the service of religion: myths to explain ritual practices, objects to portray important deities, music and dances for ceremonial use, and the like. In a very real sense, music, dance, or any other form of art, like magic, exploit psychological predispositions so as to enchant other people and cause them to perceive social reality in a way favorable to the interests of the enchanter. And like religion, art of any kind expresses the human search for order, in that some essentially formless raw material is given form by the artist. Accordingly, a chapter on the arts follows our chapter on religion, concluding this section.

CHAPTER

12

POLITICAL ORGANIZATION

AND SOCIAL CONTROL

Political organization in human societies takes many forms, of which the state is but one. Although states are often confused with nations, most states are not nations, nor are most nations states. While many states have not lasted very long, nations have shown extraordinary persistence over time—often despite ruthless suppression by modern states. Such was the case with Lithuanian nationalism, which re-emerged during the collapse of the Soviet Union. Here, a statue of Soviet Communist ruler Vladimir Lenin is hauled down in Vilnius, the capital of Lithuania.

WHAT IS POLITICAL ORGANIZATION? Political organization refers to the means by which a society maintains order internally and manages its affairs with other societies externally. Such organization may be relatively decentralized and informal, as in bands and tribes, or centralized and formal, as in chiefdoms and states.

HOW IS ORDER MAINTAINED WITHIN A SOCIETY? Social controls may be internalized—"built into" individuals—or externalized, in the form of sanctions. Built-in controls rely on such deterrents as personal shame and fear of supernatural punishment. Sanctions, by contrast, rely on actions taken by other members of society toward behavior that is specifically approved or disapproved. Positive sanctions encourage approved behavior, while negative sanctions discourage behavior that is disapproved. Sanctions that are formalized and enforced by an authorized political body are called laws. Consequently, we may say that laws are sanctions, but not all sanctions are laws. Similarly, societies do not maintain order through law alone.

HOW IS ORDER MAINTAINED BETWEEN SOCIETIES? Just as the threatened or actual use of force may be employed to maintain order within a society, so may it be used to manage affairs among bands, lineages, clans, or whatever the largest autonomous political units may be. Not all societies, however, rely on force, because there are some that do not practice warfare as we know it. Such societies generally have a view of themselves and their place in the world that is quite different from those characteristic of centrally organized states.

HOW DO POLITICAL SYSTEMS OBTAIN PEOPLE'S ALLEGIANCE? No form of political organization can function without the loyalty and support of those it governs. To a greater or lesser extent, political organizations the world over use religion to legitimize their power. In decentralized systems, loyalty and cooperation are freely given because everyone participates in making decisions. Centralized systems, by contrast, rely more heavily on force and coercion, although in the long run these may lessen the effectiveness of the system.

311

Louis XIV, it is reported, once proclaimed, "I am the state." With this sweeping statement, the king declared absolute rule over France; he held himself to be the law, the lawmaker, the courts, the judge, jailer, and executioner—in short, the seat of all political organization in France.

Louis took a great deal of responsibility on his royal shoulders; had he actually performed each of these functions, he would have done the work of thousands of people, the number required to keep the machinery of a large political organization such as a state running at full steam. As a form of political organization, the seventeenth-century French state was not much different from those that exist in modern times. All large states require elaborate, centralized structures, involving hierarchies of executives, legislators, and judges who initiate, pass, and enforce laws for large numbers of people.

Such complex structures, however, have not always been in existence, and even today there are societies that depend on far less formal means of organization. In some societies, flexible and informal kinship systems with leaders who lack real power prevail. Problems such as homicide and theft are perceived as serious "family quarrels," rather than affairs that affect the entire community. Between these two polarities of political organization lies a world of variety, including societies with chiefs, Big Men, or charismatic leaders, and segmented tribal societies with multicentric authority systems. Such disparity prompts the question: What is political organization?

The term *political organization* refers to those aspects of social organization specifically concerned with the management of a society's public policy, whether it be organizing a giraffe hunt or raising an army. In other words, political organization is the system of social relationships that provides for the coordination and regulation of behavior, insofar as that behavior is related to the maintenance of public order. Government, on the other hand, consists of an administrative system having specialized personnel that may or may not form a part of the political organization, depending on the complexity of the society. Some form of political organization exists in all societies, but it is not always a government.

KINDS OF POLITICAL SYSTEMS

Political organization is the means through which a society maintains social order and reduces social disorder. It assumes a variety of forms among the peoples of the world, but scholars have simplified this complex subject by identifying four basic kinds of political systems: bands, tribes, chiefdoms, and states. The first two are uncentralized systems; the latter two are centralized.

DECENTRALIZED POLITICAL SYSTEMS

Until recently, many non-Western peoples have had neither chiefs with established rights and duties nor any fixed form of government, as the citizens of modern states understand the term. Instead, marriage and kinship form the principal means of social organization among such peoples. The economies of these societies are of a subsistence type, and populations are typically very small. Leaders do not have real authority to enforce the society's customs or laws, but if individual members do not conform, they may be made the target of scorn and gossip, or even ostracized. Important decisions are usually made in a democratic manner by a consensus of

≠ Toma, a !Kung headman known to many North Americans through the documentary film *The Hunters*.

Band: A small group of related households occupying a particular region, that come together periodically on an ad hoc basis, but which do not yield their sovereignty to the larger collective.

---

adults, often including women as well as men; dissenting members may decide to act with the majority, or they may choose to adopt some other course of action, if they are willing to risk the social consequences. This form of political organization provides great flexibility, which in many situations confers an adaptive advantage.

BAND ORGANIZATION

The **band** is a small group of politically independent, though related, households, and is the least complicated form of political organization. Bands are usually found among food foragers and other nomadic societies in which people are organized into politically autonomous extended family groups, that usually camp together, although the members of such families may frequently go off in smaller groups for periods of time to forage for food or visit other relatives. Bands are thus kin groups, composed of men and/or women who are related (or assumed to be), with their spouses and unmarried children; the closeness of the group is indicated by the fact that most marriages are between members of the same band. Bands may be characterized as associations of related families who occupy a common (often vaguely defined) territory and who live there together, so long as environmental and subsistence circumstances are favorable. The band is probably the oldest form of political organization, since all humans were once food foragers, and remained so until the development of farming and pastoralism over the last 10,000 years.

Since bands are small in size, numbering at most a few hundred people, there is no real need for formal, centralized political systems. In egalitarian groups, where everyone is related to—and knows on a personal basis—everyone else with whom dealings are required, and where most everyone

values "getting along" with the natural order of life, there is reduced potential for conflicts to develop in the first place. Many of those that do arise are settled informally through gossip, ridicule, direct negotiation, or mediation. In the latter instances, the emphasis is on achieving a solution considered "just" by most parties concerned, rather than conforming to some abstract law or rule. Where all else fails, disgruntled individuals have the option of leaving the band to go live in another in which they have relatives. Decisions affecting a band are made with the participation of all its adult members, with an emphasis on achieving consensus, rather than a simple majority. Leaders become such by virtue of their abilities and serve in that capacity only as long as they retain the confidence of the community. Thus, they have neither a guaranteed hold on their position for a specified length of time, nor the power to force people to abide by their decisions. People will follow them only as long as they consider it to be in their best interests, and a leader who exceeds what people are willing to accept quickly loses followers.

An example of the informal nature of leadership in the band is found among the !Kung of the Kalahari Desert, whom we met in Chapter 6. Each !Kung band is composed of a group of families who live together, linked to one another and to the headman or, less often, headwoman, through kinship. Although each band has rights to the territory it occupies and the resources within it, two or more bands may range over the same territory. The head, called the *kxau* or "owner," is the focal point for the band's theoretical ownership of the territory. The headman or woman does not really own the land or resources, but symbolically personifies the rights of band members to them. If the head leaves a territory to live elsewhere, he or she ceases to be head, as people turn to someone else to lead them.

The head coordinates the band's movements when resources are no longer adequate for subsistence in a particular territory. This leader's chief duty is to plan when and where the group will move; when the move does take place, his or her position is at the head of the line. The leader chooses the site for the new settlement, and has the first choice of a spot for his or her own fire. There are no other rewards or duties. For example, a headman does not organize hunting parties, trading

---

Tribe: A group of nominally independent communities occupying a specific region, sharing a common language and culture, which are integrated by some unifying factor.

---

expeditions, the making of artifacts, or gift giving; nor does he make marriage arrangements. Instead, individuals instigate their own activities. The head man or woman is not a judge, and does not punish other band members. Wrongdoers are judged and regulated by public opinion, usually expressed by gossip among band members. A prime technique for resolving disputes, or even avoiding them in the first place, is mobility. Those unable to get along with others of their group simply move to another to which kinship ties give them rights of entry.

TRIBAL ORGANIZATION

The second type of decentralized or multicentric authority system is the **tribe,** in which separate bands or villages are integrated by pantribal factors, such as clans that unite people in separate communities, or age grades or associations that cross-cut kinship or territorial boundaries. In such cases people sacrifice a degree of household autonomy to some larger order group in return for greater security against attacks by enemies or starvation. Typically, though not invariably, a tribe has an economy based on some form of farming or herding. Since these methods of production usually yield more food than those of the food-foraging band, tribal membership is usually larger than band membership. Compared to bands, where population densities are usually less than one person per square mile, tribal population densities always exceed one person per square mile, and may be as high as 250 per square mile. Greater population density in tribes than in bands brings a new set of problems to be solved, as opportunities for bickering, begging, adultery, and theft increase markedly, especially among people living in sedentary villages.

Each tribe consists of one or more small autonomous local communities, which may then form alliances with one another for various purposes. As in the band, political organization in the tribe is informal and of a temporary nature. Whenever a situation requiring political integration of all or several groups within the tribe arises—perhaps for defense, to carry out a raid, to pool resources in times of scarcity, or to capitalize on a windfall which must be distributed quickly lest it spoil—they join to deal with the situation in a cooperative manner. When the problem is satisfactorily solved, each group then returns to its autonomous state.

Leadership among tribes is also informal. Among the Navajo Indians, for example, the individual did not think of government as something fixed and all-powerful, and leadership was not vested in a central authority. A local leader was a man respected for his age, integrity, and wisdom. His advice was therefore sought frequently, but he had no formal means of control and could not force any decision on those who asked for his help. Group decisions were made on the basis of public consensus, although the most influential man usually played a key role in reaching a decision. Among the social mechanisms that induced members to abide by group decisions were withdrawal of cooperation, gossip, criticism, and the belief that disease was caused by antisocial actions.

KINSHIP ORGANIZATION

In many tribal societies the organizing unit and seat of political authority is the clan, an association of people who believe themselves to share a common ancestry. Within the clan, elders or headmen are responsible for regulating the affairs of members and represent their clan in relations with other clans. As a group, the elders of all the clans may form a council that acts within the community or for the community in dealings with outsiders. Because clan members usually do not all live together in one community, clan organization facilitates joint action with members of other communities when necessary.

Another form of tribal kinship bond that provides political organization is the **segmentary lineage system.** This system is similar in operation to the clan, but it is less extensive and is a relatively rare form of political organization. The economy of the segmentary tribe is generally just above subsistence level. Production is small-scale, and the tribe has a labor pool just large enough to provide

Segmentary lineage system: A form of political organization in which a larger group is broken up into clans, which are divided into lineages.

necessities. Since each lineage in the tribe produces the same goods, none depends on another for goods or services. Political organization among segmentary lineage societies is usually informal: There are neither political offices nor chiefs, although older tribal members may exercise some personal authority. In his classic study of segmentary lineage organization, Marshall Sahlins describes how this works among the Nuer.[1] According to Sahlins, segmentation is the normal process of tribal growth. It is also the social means of temporary unification of a fragmented tribal society to join in particular action. The segmentary lineage may be viewed as a substitute for the fixed political structure, which a tribe cannot maintain.

Among the Nuer, who number some 200,000 people living in the swampland and savanna of East Africa (the southern Sudan), there are at least 20 clans. Each is patrilineal and is segmented into maximal lineages; each of these is in turn segmented into major lineages, which are segmented into minor lineages, which in turn are segmented into minimal lineages. The minimal lineage is a group descended from one great-grandfather or a great-great-grandfather.

The lineage segments among the Nuer are all equal, and no real leadership or political organization at all exists above the level of the autonomous minimal or primary segments. The entire superstructure of the lineage is nothing more than an alliance, active only during conflicts between any of the minimal segments. In any serious dispute between members of different minimal lineage segments, members of all other segments take the side of the contestant to whom they are most closely related, and the issue is then joined between the higher-order lineages involved. Such a system of political organization is known as complementary or balanced opposition.

Disputes among the Nuer are frequent, and under the segmentary lineage system, they can lead to widespread feuds. This possible source of social disruption is minimized by the actions of the "leopard-skin chief," or holder of a ritual office of conciliation. The leopard-skin chief has no political power and is looked on as standing outside the lineage network. All he can do is try to persuade feuding lineages to accept payment in "blood cattle" rather than taking another life. His mediation gives each side the chance to back down gracefully

Among the Nuer, the leopard-skin chief, standing outside the network of lineages, is able to persuade feuding lineages to accept payment of cattle to settle disputes. Having no power to enforce a settlement, he must rely solely on his prestige and powers of persuasion.

[1]Marshall Sahlins, "The Segmentary Lineage: An Organization of Predatory Expansion," *American Anthropologist, 63* (1961):322–343.

before too many people are killed; but if the participants are for some reason unwilling to compromise, the leopard-skin chief has no authority to enforce a settlement.

AGE-GRADE ORGANIZATION

Age-grade systems provide a tribal society with the means of political integration beyond the kin group. Under this system, youths are initiated into an age grade, following which they pass as sets from one age grade to another at appropriate ages. Age grades and sets cut across territorial and kin groupings and so may be important means of political organization. This was the case with the Tiriki of East Africa, whose age grades and sets we examined in Chapter 11. Among them, the warrior age grade guarded the country, while judicial elders resolved disputes. Between these two age grades were elder warriors, who were in a sense understudies to the judicial elders. The oldest age grade, the ritual elders, advised on matters involving the well-being of all the Tiriki people. Thus, political affairs of the tribe were in the hands of the age grades and their officers.

ASSOCIATION ORGANIZATION

Common-interest associations that function as politically integrative systems within tribes are found in many areas of the world, including Africa, Melanesia, and India. A good example of association organization functioned during the nineteenth century among the Plains Indians of the United States, such as the Cheyenne, whom we'll talk about again later in this chapter. The basic territorial and political unit of the Cheyenne was the band, but seven military societies, or warriors' clubs, were common to the entire tribe; the clubs functioned in several areas. A boy might be invited to join one of these societies when he achieved warrior status, whereupon he became familiar with the society's particular insignia, songs, and rituals. In addition to their military functions, the warriors' societies also had ceremonial and social functions.

The Cheyenne warriors' routine daily tasks consisted of overseeing movements in the camp, protecting a moving column, and enforcing rules

Melanesian Big Men, such as the one here wearing his ceremonial regalia, rely on their economic success and verbal skills to succeed as leaders.

against individual hunting when the whole tribe was on a buffalo hunt. In addition, each warrior society had its own repertoire of dances that the members performed on special ceremonial occasions. Since identical military societies bearing identical names existed in each Cheyenne band, the societies thus served to integrate the entire tribe for military and political purposes.[2]

The Melanesian Big Man

Throughout much of Melanesia there appears a type of leader called the Big Man. The Big Man combines a small amount of interest in his tribe's welfare with a great deal of self-interested cunning

[2]E.A. Hoebel, *The Cheyennes: Indians of the Great Plains* (New York: Holt, Rinehart and Winston, 1960).

and calculation for his own personal gain. His authority is personal; he does not come to office nor is he elected. His status is the result of acts that raise him above most other tribe members and attract to him a band of loyal followers.

Typical of this form of political organization are the Kapauku of West New Guinea. Among them, the Big Man is called the *tonowi,* or "rich one." To achieve this status, one must be male, wealthy, generous, and eloquent; physical bravery and skills in dealing with the supernatural are also frequent characteristics of a *tonowi,* but they are not essential. The *tonowi* functions as the headman of the village unit.

Kapauku culture places a high value on wealth, so it is not surprising that a wealthy individual is considered to be a successful and admirable man. Yet the possession of wealth must be coupled with the trait of generosity, which in this society means not gift giving but willingness to make loans. Wealthy men who refuse to lend money to other villagers may be ostracized, ridiculed, and, in extreme cases, actually executed by a group of warriors. This social pressure ensures that economic wealth is rarely hoarded, but is distributed throughout the group.

It is through the loans he makes that the *tonowi* acquires his political power. Other villagers comply with his requests because they are in his debt (often without paying interest), and they do not want to have to repay their loans. Those who have not yet borrowed from the *tonowi* may wish to do so in the future, and so they, too, want to keep his goodwill.

Other sources of support for the *tonowi* are apprentices whom he has taken into his household for training. They are fed, housed, given a chance to learn the *tonowi*'s business wisdom, and given a loan to get a wife when they leave; in return, they act as messengers and bodyguards. Even after they leave his household, these men are tied to the *tonowi* by bonds of affection and gratitude. Political support also comes from the *tonowi*'s kinsmen, whose relationship brings with it varying obligations.

The *tonowi* functions as a leader in a wide variety of situations. He represents his group in dealing with outsiders and other villages; he acts as negotiator and/or judge when disputes break out among his followers. Leopold Pospisil, who studied the Kapauku notes:

The multiple functions of a *tonowi* are not limited to the political and legal fields only. His word also carries weight in economic and social matters. He is especially influential in determining proper dates for pig feasts and pig markets, in inducing specific individuals to become co-sponsors at feasts, in sponsoring communal dance expeditions to other villages, and in initiating large projects, such as extensive drainage ditches and main fences or bridges, the completion of which requires a joint effort of the whole community.[3]

The *tonowi*'s wealth comes from his success at pig breeding (as we discussed in Chapter 2), for pigs are the focus of the entire Kapauku economy. Like all kinds of cultivation and domestication, raising pigs requires a combination of strength, skill, and luck. It is not uncommon for a *tonowi* to lose his fortune rapidly, because of bad management or bad luck with his pigs. Thus the political structure of the Kapauku shifts frequently; as one man loses wealth and consequently power, another gains it and becomes a *tonowi.* These changes confer a degree of flexibility on the political organization, and prevent any one *tonowi* from holding political power for too long a time.

CENTRALIZED POLITICAL SYSTEMS

In bands and tribes, authority is uncentralized, and each group is economically and politically autonomous. Political organization is vested in kinship, age, and common-interest groups. Populations are small and relatively homogeneous, with people engaged for the most part in the same sorts of activities throughout their lives. As a society's social life becomes more complex, however, as population rises and technology becomes more complex, as specialization of labor and trade networks produce surpluses of goods, the opportunity for some individuals or groups to exercise control increases. In such societies, political authority and power are concentrated in a single individual—the chief—or in a body of individuals—the state. The state is a form of organization found in societies in which each individual must interact on a regular

[3]Leopold Pospisil, *The Kapauku Papuans of West New Guinea* (New York: Holt, Rinehart and Winston, 1963), pp. 51–52.

Chiefdom: A regional polity in which two or more local groups are organized under a single chief, who is at the head of a ranked hierarchy of people.

basis with large numbers of people with diversified interests, who are neither kin nor close acquaintances.

CHIEFDOMS

A **chiefdom** is a regional polity in which two or more local groups are organized under a single ruling individual—the chief—who is at the head of a ranked hierarchy of people. An individual's status in such a polity is determined by closeness of one's relationship to the chief. Those closest are officially superior and receive deferential treatment from those in lower ranks.

The office of the chief is usually hereditary, passing from a man to his own or his sister's son, depending on how descent is reckoned. Unlike the headmen in bands and lineages, the chief is generally a true authority figure, and his authority serves to unite his people in all affairs and at all times. For example, a chief can distribute land among his community and recruit members into his military service. In chiefdoms, there is a recognized hierarchy consisting of major and minor authorities who control major and minor subdivisions of the chiefdom. Such an arrangement is, in effect, a chain of command, linking leaders at every level. It serves to bind tribal groups in the heartland to the chief's headquarters, be it a mud and dung hut or a marble palace.

On the economic level, a chief controls the economic activities of his people. Chiefdoms are typically redistributive systems; the chief has control over surplus goods and perhaps even the labor force of his community. Thus, he may demand a quota of rice from farmers, which he will redistribute to the entire community. Similarly, he may recruit laborers to build irrigation works, a palace, or a temple.

The chief may also amass a great amount of personal wealth and pass it on to his heirs. Land, cattle,

and luxury goods produced by specialists can be collected by the chief and become part of his power base. Moreover, high-ranking families of the chiefdom may engage in the same practice and use their possessions as evidence of status.

An example of this form of political organization may be seen among the Kpelle of Liberia, in West Africa.[4] Among them is a class of paramount chiefs, each of whom presides over one of the Kpelle chiefdoms (each of which is now a district of the Liberian nation). The paramount chiefs' traditional tasks are hearing disputes, preserving order, seeing to the upkeep of trails, and maintaining "medicines." In addition, they are now salaried officials of the Liberian government, mediating between it and their own people. Other rewards received by a paramount chief include a commission on taxes collected within his chiefdom, a commission for laborers furnished for the rubber plantations, a portion of court fees collected, a stipulated amount of rice from each household, and gifts brought by people who come to request favors and intercessions. In keeping with his exalted station in life, a paramount chief has at his disposal uniformed messengers, a literate clerk, and the symbols of wealth: many wives, embroidered gowns, and freedom from manual labor.

In a ranked hierarchy beneath each paramount chief are several lesser chiefs; one for each district within the chiefdom, one for each town within a district, and one for each quarter of all but the smallest towns. Each acts as a kind of lieutenant for his chief of the next higher rank, and serves as well as a liaison between him and those of lower rank. Unlike paramount or district chiefs, who are comparatively remote, town and quarter chiefs are readily accessible to people at the local level.

Stable though the Kpelle political system may be today, traditionally chiefdoms in all parts of the

[4]James L. Gibbs, Jr., "The Kpelle of Liberia," in *Peoples of Africa* (New York: Holt, Rinehart and Winston, 1965), pp. 216–218.

A Kpelle town chief settles a dispute.

world have been highly unstable. This happens as lesser chiefs try to take power from higher-ranking chiefs, or as paramount chiefs vie with one another for supreme power. In precolonial Hawaii, for example, war was the way to gain territory and maintain power; great chiefs set out to conquer one another in an effort to become paramount chief of all the islands. When one chief conquered another, the loser and all his nobles were dispossessed of all property and were lucky if they escaped alive. The new chief then appointed his own supporters to positions of political power. As a consequence, there was very little continuity of governmental or religious administration.

STATE SYSTEMS

The **state,** the most formal of political organizations, is one of the hallmarks of civilization. In the state, political power is centralized in a govern-

State: In anthropology, a centralized political system with the power to coerce.

ment, which may legitimately use force to regulate the affairs of its citizens, as well as its relations with other states. As anthropologist Bruce Knauft observes:

> It is likely . . . that coercion and violence as systematic means of organizational constraint developed especially with the increasing socioeconomic complexity and potential for political hierarchy afforded by substantial food surplus and food production.[5]

Associated with increased food production is increased population. Together, these lead to a filling in of the landscape, improvements such as irrigation and terracing, carefully managed rotation cycles, intensive competition for clearly demarcated lands, and rural populations large enough to support market systems and a specialized urban sector. Under such conditions, corporate groups that stress exclusive membership proliferate, ethnic differentiation and ethnocentrism become more pronounced, and the potential for social conflict increases dramatically. Given these circumstances, the institutions of the state, which minimally involve a bureaucracy, a military, and (usually) an official

[5]Bruce M. Knauft, "Violence and Sociality in Human Evolution," *Current Anthropology,* 32 (1991):391.

Symbolic of the state's authority over its citizens is the power to order executions—whether by electrocution, lethal injection, or gas as punishment for severe crimes, as in many modern-day states; by evisceration, decapitation, or burning of a sacrificial victim, as in the Aztecs' ritual offering to the sun god Huitzilopochtli; or by some other means.

Nation: Communities of people who see themselves as "one people" on the basis of common ancestry, history, society, institutions, ideology, language, territory, and (often) religion.

---

religion provide a means by which numerous and diverse groups can be made to function together as an integrated whole.

Although their guiding ideology pretends that they are permanent and stable, the fact is that, since their appearance some 5,000 years ago, states have been anything but permanent. Whatever stability they have achieved has been short-term at best; over the long term, they show a clear tendency to instability and transience. Nowhere have states even begun to show the staying power exhibited by more decentralized political systems, the longest-lasting social forms invented by humans.

An important distinction to make at this point is between **nation** and state. Today, there are roughly 200 states in the world, most of which did not exist before the end of World War II. By contrast, there are probably about 5,000 nations in the world today. "What makes each a nation is that its people share a language, culture, territorial base, and politi-

cal organization and history."[6] Today, states commonly have living within their boundaries people of more than one nation; for example, the Yanomami are but one nation within the state of Brazil (other Yanomami live within the state of Venezuela). Rarely do state and nation coincide, as they do, for example, in the case of Iceland.

An important aspect of the state is its delegation of authority to maintain order within and outside its borders. Police, foreign ministries, war ministries, and other bureaucracies function to control and punish disruptive acts of crime, terror, and rebellion. By such agencies, authority in the state is asserted impersonally and in a consistent, predictable manner.

Western forms of government, such as that of the United States, of course, are state governments, and their organization and workings are undoubtedly familiar to most everyone. An example of a state not so familar is afforded by the Swazi of Swaziland, a Bantu-speaking people who live in southeast Africa.[7] They are primarily farmers, but

[6]Jason W. Clay, "What's a Nation?" *Mother Jones,* 15, No. 7 (1990):28.

[7]Hilda Kuper, "The Swazi of Swaziland," in *Peoples of Africa,* ed. James L. Gibbs, Jr. (New York: Holt, Rinehart and Winston, 1965), pp. 479–512.

cattle raising is more highly valued than farming: the ritual, wealth, and power of their authority system are all intricately linked with cattle. In addition to farming and cattle raising, there is some specialization of labor; certain people become specialists in ritual, smithing, woodcarving, and pottery. Their goods and services are traded, although the Swazi do not have elaborate markets.

The Swazi authority system is characterized by a highly developed dual monarchy, a hereditary aristocracy, and elaborate rituals of kinship, as well as by statewide age sets. The king and his mother are the central figures of all national activity, linking all the people of the Swazi state: they preside over higher courts, summon national gatherings, control age classes, allocate land, disburse national wealth, take precedence in ritual, and help organize important social events.

Advising the king are the senior princes, who are usually his uncles and half-brothers. Between the king and the princes are two specially created *tinsila*, or "blood brothers," who are chosen from certain common clans. These men are his shields, protecting him from evildoers and serving him in intimate personal situations. In addition, the king is guided by two *tindvuna*, or counselors, one civil and one military. The people of the state make their opinions known through two councils: the *liqoqo*, or privy council, composed of senior princes, and the *libanda*, or council of state, composed of chiefs and headmen and open to all adult males of the state. The *liqoqo* may advise the king, make decisions, and execute them. For example, they may rule on such questions as land, education, traditional ritual, court procedure, and transport.

Government extends from the smallest local unit—the homestead—upward to the central administration. The head of a homestead has legal and administrative powers; he is responsible for the crimes of those under him, controls their property, and speaks for them before his superiors. On the district level, political organization is similar to that of the central government. The relationship between a district chief, however, and his subjects is personal and familiar; he knows all the families in his district. The main check on any autocratic tendencies he may exhibit rests in his subjects' ability to transfer their allegiance to a more responsive chief. Swazi officials hold their positions for life and are dismissed only for treason or witchcraft. Incompetence, drunkenness, and stupidity are frowned upon, but they are not considered to be sufficient grounds for dismissal.

POLITICAL LEADERSHIP AND GENDER

Irrespective of cultural configuration, or type of political organization, women have rarely held important positions of political leadership. Furthermore, when they do occupy publicly recognized offices, their power and authority rarely exceed those of men. Nevertheless, there have been exceptions, recent ones being Corazon Aquino, Sirimavo Badaranaike, Benazir Bhutto, Indira Gandhi, Golda Meir, and Margaret Thatcher, who have headed governments of the Philippines, Sri Lanka, Pakistan, India, Israel, and Great Britain, respectively. Historically, one might cite the occasional "squaw sachems" (woman chiefs) mentioned in early accounts of New England American Indians, or powerful queens such as Elizabeth I of England or Catherine the Great of Russia. When women do hold high office, it is often on account of their relationship to men. Thus, a queen is either the wife of a reigning monarch, or else the daughter of a king who died without a male heir to succeed him. Moreover, women in focal positions frequently must adopt many of the characteristics of temperament normally deemed appropriate for men in their societies. In her role as prime minister, Margaret Thatcher, for instance, displayed the toughness and assertiveness that, in Western societies, have long been considered desirable masculine qualities, rather than the nurturance and compliance often expected of women.

In spite of all this, it is a fact that in a number of societies, women regularly enjoy as much political power as men. In band societies, it is common for them to have as much of a say in public affairs as men, even though the latter more often than not are

This Seneca Chief, Cornplanter, participated in three treaties with the United States government in the late eighteenth century. Although Iroquoian chiefs were always men, they served strictly at the behest of women, whose position in society was equal to that of men.

the nominal leaders of their groups. Among the Iroquoian nations of New York state (discussed in Chapter 11), all positions of leadership above the household level were, without exception, filled by men. Thus they held all positions on the village and tribal councils, as well as on the great council of the League of Five Nations. However, they were completely beholden to women, for only the latter could appoint men to high office. Moreover, women actively lobbied the men on the councils and could remove someone from office whenever it suited them to do so.

As the above cases make clear, low visibility of women in politics does not necessarily exclude them from the realm of social control, or mean that men have more power in political affairs. Sometimes, though, women may play more visible roles, as in the dual sex systems of west Africa. Among the Igbo of Nigeria, in each political unit, separate political institutions for men and women give each sex their own autonomous spheres of authority, as

well as an area of shared responsibility.[8] At the head of each was a male *obi*, considered the head of government though in fact he presided over the male community, and a female *omu*, the acknowledged mother of the whole community, but who in practice was concerned with the female section of the community. Unlike a queen (though both she and the *obi* were crowned), the *omu* was neither wife of the *obi* nor the daughter of the previous one.

Just as the *obi* had a council of dignitaries to advise him, and act as a check against any arbitrary exercise of power, so was the *omu* served by a council of women, in equal number to the *obi's* male councilors. The duties of the *omu* and her councilors involved such things as establishing rules and regulations for the community market (marketing was a woman's activity), and hearing cases involving women brought to her from throughout the town or village. If such cases also involved men, then she and her council would cooperate with the *obi* and his. Widows also went to the *omu* for the final rites required to end their period of mourning for dead husbands. Since the *omu* represented all women, she had to be responsive to her constituency, and would seek their approval and cooperation in all major decisions.

In addition to the *omu* and her council, the women's government included a representative body of women chosen from each quarter or section of the village or town, on the basis of their ability to think logically and speak well. In addition, acting at the village or lineage level, were political pressure groups of women that acted to stop quarrels and prevent wars. These were of two types, one being of women born into a community, most of whom lived elsewhere since villages were exogamous and residence was patrilocal. The other consisted of women who had married into their

[8]Kamene Okonjo, "The Dual-Sex Political System in Operation: Igbo Women and Community Politics in Midwestern Nigeria," in *Women in Africa*, ed. Nancy Hafkin and Edna Bay (Stanford, Calif.: Stanford University Press, 1976).

community. Its duties included helping companion wives in times of illness and stress, as well as meting out discipline to lazy or recalcitrant husbands.

In the Igbo system, then, women managed their own affairs, and their interests were represented at all levels of government. Moreover, they had the right to enforce their decisions and rules by recourse to sanctions similar to those employed by men. Included were strikes, boycotts, and "sitting on a man" or woman. Anthropologist Judith Van Allen describes the latter:

> To "sit on" or "make war on" a man involved gathering at his compound, sometimes late at night, dancing, singing scurrilous songs which detailed the women's grievances against him and often called his manhood into question, banging on his hut with the pestles women used for pounding yams, and perhaps demolishing his hut or plastering it with mud and roughing him up a bit. A man might be sanctioned in this way for mistreating his wife, for violating the women's market rules, or for letting his cows eat the women's crops. The women would stay at his hut throughout the day, and late into the night if necessary, until he repented and promised to mend his ways . . . Although this could hardly have been a pleasant experience for the offending man, it was considered legitimate and no man would consider intervening. [9]

Given the high visibility of women in the Igbo political system, it is surprising to learn that when the British imposed colonial rule upon these people, they failed to recognize the autonomy and power possessed by those women. The reason for this is that the British were circumscribed by their Victorian values, which then were at their height. To them, a woman's mind was not strong enough for such supposedly masculine subjects as science, business, and politics; her place was clearly in the home. As a consequence, the British introduced changes that destroyed Igbo women's traditional forms of autonomy and power, without providing alternative forms in exchange. Far from enhancing the status of women in this case, Igbo women lost their equality and became subordinate to men. Nor is the Igbo situation unusual in this regard. Historically, in state-organized societies, women have usually been subordinate to men. Hence, when states impose their control on societies in which the sexes are equal to each other, the situation almost invariably changes to one in which women become subordinate to men.

POLITICAL ORGANIZATION AND SOCIAL CONTROL

Whatever form the political organization of a society may take, and whatever else it may do, it is always involved in one way or another with social control. Always it seeks to ensure that people behave in acceptable ways, and defines the proper action to take when they don't. In the case of chiefdoms and states, some sort of centralized authority has the power to regulate the affairs of society. In bands and tribes, however, people behave generally as they are expected to, without the direct intervention of any centralized political authority. To a large degree, gossip, criticism, fear of supernatural forces, and the like serve as effective deterrents to antisocial behavior.

As an example of how such seemingly informal considerations serve to keep people in line, we may look at the Wape people of Papua New Guinea, who believe that the ghosts of dead ancestors roam lineage lands, protecting them from trespassers and helping their hunting descendants by driving game their way.[10] These ghosts also punish those who have wronged them or their descendants by preventing hunters from finding game, or causing them to miss their shots, thereby depriving people of much-needed meat. Nowadays, the Wape hunt with shotguns, which are purchased by the community for the use of one man, whose job it is to hunt for all the others. The cartridges used in the hunt, however, are invariably supplied by individual members of the community. Not always is the gunman successful; if he shoots and misses, it is because the owner of the fired shell, or some close relative, has quarreled or wronged another person whose ghost relative is securing revenge by causing the hunter to miss. Or, if the gunman cannot even find game, it is because vengeful ghosts have chased the animals away. As a proxy hunter for the villagers, the gunman is potentially subject to

---

[9] Judith Van Allen, "Sitting on a Man: Colonialism and the Lost Political Institutions of Igbo Women," in *Women in Society*, ed. Sharon Tiffany (St. Albans, Vt.: Eden Press, 1979), p. 169.

[10] William E. Mitchell, "A New Weapon Stirs Up Old Ghosts," *Natural History Magazine*, December 1973, pp. 77–84.

ANTHROPOLOGY APPLIED

LAW AND ORDER IN PAPUA NEW GUINEA

When Papua New Guinea gained its independence in 1975, a major question was: What should be the national legal system of a country whose roughly 3.5 million people speak at least 750 mutually unintelligible languages, and maintain something like 1,000 customary legal systems? As an interim measure, the new government adopted the legal system under which people had lived while under Australian colonial rule, even though this often clashed with the customary law of indigenous groups. In order to develop a system more in accord with indigenous customs and traditions, the government established a Law Reform Commission.

The questions faced by the commission were twofold. First, could principles common to all indigenous legal systems be discovered? If so, then could the essence of systems that function smoothly in tribal societies, with their small and relatively homogenous populations, work in a large, pluralistic state? To help find the answers to these questions, the commission established the Customary Law Project,* which was to research the nature of customary law and the extent to which it could form the basis for a unique legal system for the country as a whole.

In 1979, the commission hired to head up this project a young anthropologist, Richard Scaglion, whose Ph.D. research a few years earlier had been a study of customary law and legal change among the Abelam. Scaglion's first job was to conduct an extensive bibliographical search and review of the literature. This revealed the need for more complete research on specific societies, for which students from the University of Papua New Guinea were

employed. Using standard anthropological techniques, usually in their home areas, these students gathered detailed data on all aspects of observed, remembered, and hypothetical cases. By the mid-1980s, roughly 600 case studies had been gathered from all parts of the country and were made available to legal researchers through a computer retrieval system. From these case studies, Scaglion and others have been able to abstract underlying principles, while legal practitioners have made use of them in actual court cases.

The reform of Papua New Guinea's legal system is an ongoing process. To date, Scaglion and his associates have not only supplied a body of precedent for legal scholars to draw on but have also helped draft legislation. For example, a Family Law Bill recognizes as legal customary marriage arrangements which, under Australian law, are not legal. Similarly, legislation was drafted to recognize the principle of customary compensation, by which a variety of conflicts were resolved, while regulating both claims and payments to control inflationary demands. Perhaps the most important accomplishment of the project has been to focus attention on underlying principles and procedures, which can be adapted to changing situations, as opposed to the kinds of inflexible statutory rules with which lawyers are so often preoccupied.

*Richard Scaglion, "Contemporary Law Development in Papua New Guinea," in *Anthropological Praxis: Translating Knowledge into Action,* ed. Robert M. Wulff and Shirley J. Fiske. Boulder, Colo.: Westview Press, 1987, pp. 98–108.

---

ghostly sanctions in response to collective wrongs on the part of those for whom he hunts.

For the Wape, then, successful hunting depends upon avoiding quarrels and maintaining tranquility within the community, so as not to antagonize anybody's ghost ancestor. Unfortunately, complete peace and tranquility are impossible to achieve in any human community, and the Wape are no exception. Thus, when hunting is poor, the gunman must discover what quarrels and wrongs have taken place within his village, in order to identify

the proper ancestral ghosts to appeal to for renewed success. Usually, this is done in a special meeting, in which confessions of wrongdoing may be forthcoming. If not, questioning accusations are bandied about until resolution occurs, but even if there is no resolution, the meeting must end amicably, in order to create no new antagonisms. Thus, everyone's behavior comes under public scrutiny, reminding everyone of what is expected of them and encouraging everyone to avoid acts that will cast them in an unfavorable light.

Sanctions: Externalized social controls designed to encourage conformity to social norms.

INTERNALIZED CONTROLS

The Wape concern about ancestral ghosts is a good example of internalized controls—beliefs that are so thoroughly ingrained that each person becomes personally responsible for his or her own good conduct. Examples of this can also be found in North American society; for instance, people refrain from committing incest not so much from fear of legal punishment as from a sense of deep disgust at the thought of the act and the shame they would feel in performing it. Obviously, not all members of North American society feel this disgust, or there wouldn't be a persistent incidence of incest, especially between fathers and daughters—but then, no deterrent to misbehavior is ever 100 percent effective. Built-in or internalized controls rely on such deterrents as the fear of supernatural punishment—ancestral ghosts sabotaging the hunting, for example—and magical retaliation. The individual expects to be punished, even though no one in the community may be aware of the wrongdoing.

EXTERNALIZED CONTROLS

Because internalized controls are not wholly sufficient even in bands and tribes, every society develops customs designed to encourage conformity to social norms. These institutions are referred to as **sanctions;** they are externalized social controls. According to Radcliffe-Brown, "a sanction is a reaction on the part of a society or of a considerable number of its members to a mode of behavior which is thereby approved (positive sanctions) or disapproved (negative sanctions)."[11] Sanctions may also be either formal or informal and may vary significantly within a given society.

Sanctions operate within social groups of all sizes. Moreover, they need not be enacted into law

Awards such as Olympic medals are examples of positive sanctions, by which societies promote behavior that is deemed exemplary.

in order to play a significant role in social control: "they include not only the organized sanctions of the law but also the gossip of neighbors or the customs regulating norms of production that are spontaneously generated among workers on the factory floor. In small-scale communities . . . informal sanctions may become more drastic than the penalties provided for in the legal code."[12] If, however, a sanction is to be effective, it cannot be arbitrary. Quite the opposite: sanctions must be consistently applied, and their existence must be generally known by the members of the society.

Social sanctions may be categorized as either positive or negative. Positive sanctions consist of such incentives to conformity as awards, titles, and recognition by one's neighbors. Negative sanctions consist of such threats as imprisonment, corporal punishment, or ostracism from the community for violation of social norms. One example of a nega-

[11]A.R. Radcliffe-Brown, *Structure and Function in Primitive Society* (New York: Free Press, 1952), p. 205.

[12]A.L. Epstein, "Sanctions," *International Encyclopedia of Social Sciences*, Vol. 14, 1968, p. 3.

Negative sanctions may involve some form of regulated combat, seen here as armed dancers near Mt. Hagen in Papua New Guinea demand redress in a case of murder.

tive sanction discussed earlier is the Igbo practice of "sitting on a man." If some individuals are not convinced of the advantages of social conformity, they are still likely to be more willing to go along with society's rules than to accept the consequences of not doing so.

Sanctions may also be categorized as either formal or informal, depending on whether or not a legal statute is involved. In the United States the businessman who wears tennis shorts to the office may be subject to a variety of informal sanctions, ranging from the glances of his supervisor to the chuckling of other employees. If, however, he were to show up without any trousers at all, he would be subject to the formal sanction of arrest for indecent exposure. Only in the second instance would he have been guilty of breaking the **law.**

Formal sanctions, like laws, are always organized, because they attempt to precisely and explicit-

---

Law: A social norm, the neglect or infraction of which is regularly met, in threat or in fact, by the application of physical force on the part of an individual or group possessing the socially recognized privilege of so acting.

---

ly regulate people's behavior. Other examples of organized sanctions include, on the positive side, such things as military decorations and monetary rewards. On the negative side are loss of face, exclusion from social life and its privileges, seizure of property, imprisonment, and even bodily mutilation or death.

Informal sanctions are diffuse in nature, involving spontaneous expressions of approval or disapproval by members of the group or community. They are, nonetheless, very effective in enforcing a large number of seemingly unimportant customs. Because most people want to be accepted, they are willing to acquiesce to the rules that govern dress, eating, conversation, even in the absence of actual laws.

As an example of how informal sanctions work, we may examine them in the context of power relationships among the Bedouins of Egypt's western desert (*see the opposite page*). The example is of especial interest, for it shows how sanctions not only act to control peoples' behavior, but serve to keep them in their place in a hierarchial society. Another agent of social control in societies, whether or not they possess centralized political systems, may be witchcraft. An individual would naturally hesitate to offend one's neighbor, when that neigh-

matter. His mother disapproved of splitting up the households. Eventually everyone calmed down. But it is likely that a few more incidents such as that will eventually lead the younger brother to demand a separate household.

Even a woman can resist a tyrannical husband by leaving for her natal home "angry" (*mughtáża*). This is the approved response to abuse, and it forces the husband or his representatives to face the scolding of the woman's kin and, sometimes, to appease her with gifts. Women have less recourse against tyrannical fathers or guardians, but various informal means to resist the imposition of unwanted decisions do exist. As a last resort there is always suicide, and I heard of a number of both young men and women who committed suicide in desperate resistance to their fathers' decisions, especially regarding marriage. One old woman's tale illustrates the extent to which force can be resisted, even by women. Náfla reminisced:

> My first marriage was to my paternal cousin [*ibn àmm*]. He was from the same camp. One day the men came over to our tent. I saw the tent full of men and wondered why. I heard they were coming to ask for my hand [*yukhultú fiyya*]. I went and stood at the edge of the tent and called out, "If you're planning to do anything, stop. I don't want it." Well, they went ahead anyway, and every day I would cry and say that I did not want to marry him. I was young, perhaps fourteen. When they began drumming and singing, everyone assured me that it was in celebration of another cousin's wedding, so I sang and danced along with them. This went on for days. Then on the day of the wedding my aunt and another relative caught me in the tent and suddenly closed it and took out the washbasin. They wanted to bathe me. I screamed. I screamed and screamed; every time they held a pitcher of water to wash me with, I knocked it out of their hands.
>
> His relatives came with camels and dragged me into the litter and took me to his tent. I screamed and screamed when he came into the tent in the afternoon [for the defloration]. Then at night, I hid among the blankets. Look as they might, they couldn't find me. My father was furious. After a few days he insisted I had to stay in my tent with my husband. As soon as he left, I ran off and hid behind the tent in which the groom's sister stayed. I made her promise not to tell anyone I was there and slept there.
>
> But they made me go back. That night, my father stood guard nearby with his gun. Every time I started to leave the tent, he would take a puff on his cigarette so I could see that he was still there. Finally I rolled myself up in the straw mat. When the groom came, he looked and looked but could not find me.
>
> Finally I went back to my family's household. I pretended to be possessed. I tensed my body, rolled my eyes, and everyone rushed about, brought me incense and prayed for me. They brought the healer [or holyman, *fgih*], who blamed the unwanted marriage. Then they decided that perhaps I was too young and that I should not be forced to return to my husband. I came out of the seizure, and

they were so grateful that they forced my husband's family to grant a divorce. My family returned the bride-price, and I stayed at home.

Náfla could not oppose her father's decision directly, but she was nevertheless able to resist his will through indirect means. Like other options for resistance by dependents unfairly treated, abused, or humiliated publicly, her rebellion served as a check on her father's and, perhaps, more important, her paternal uncle's power.

Supernatural sanctions, which seem to be associated with the weak and with dependents, provide the final check on abuse of authority. Supernatural retribution is believed to follow when the saintly lineages of Mrábtín are mistreated, their curses causing death or the downfall of the offender's lineage. In one Bedouin tale, when a woman denied food to two young girls, she fell ill, and blood appeared on food she cooked—a punishment for mistreating the helpless. Possession, as Náfla's tale illustrates, may also be a form of resistance.

All these sanctions serve to check the abuse of power by eminent persons who have the resources to be autonomous and to control those who are dependent upon them. At the same time, moreover, figures of authority are vulnerable to their dependents because their positions rest on the respect these people are willing to give them.

[13]Lila Abu-Lughod, *Veiled Sentiments: Honor and Poetry in a Bedouin Society* (Berkeley, Calif.: University of California Press, 1986), pp. 99–103.

---

bor might retaliate by resorting to black magic. Similarly, individuals may not wish to be accused of practicing witchcraft themselves, and so they will behave with greater circumspection. Among the Azande of the Sudan, people who think they have been bewitched may consult an oracle who, after performing the appropriate mystical rites, may then establish or confirm the identity of the offending witch.[14] Confronted with this evidence, the "witch" will usually agree to cooperate in order to avoid any additional trouble. Should the victim die, the relatives of the deceased may choose to make magic against the witch, ultimately accepting the death of some villager both as evidence of guilt and the efficacy of their magic. For the Azande, witchcraft provides not only a sanction against antisocial behavior but also a means of dealing with natural hostilities and death. No one wishes to be thought

of as a witch, and surely no one wishes to be victimized by one. By institutionalizing their emotional responses, the Azande successfully maintain social order. (For more on witchcraft, see Chapter 13.)

Another important social control, and one that is likely to be internalized, is the religious sanction. Just as a devout Christian may avoid sinning to avoid separation from God, so may other worshippers tend to behave in a manner intended not to offend their powerful supernatural beings. The threat of punishment—whether in this life or the next—by gods, ancestral spirits, or ghosts is a strong incentive for proper behavior. In some societies, it is believed that ancestral spirits are very much concerned with the maintenance of good relations among the living members of their lineage. Death or illness in the lineage may be explained by reference to some violation of tradition or custom. Religious sanctions may thus serve not only to regulate behavior but to explain unexplainable phenomena as well.

[14]E.E. Evans-Pritchard, *Witchcraft, Oracles and Magic among the Azande* (London: Oxford University Press, 1937).

In Western society, someone who commits an offense against someone else may be subject to a series of complex proceedings that attempt to determine and punish guilt. In non-Western societies, by contrast, the emphasis is often on reaching a settlement that both parties can live with.

SOCIAL CONTROL THROUGH LAW

Among the Inuit of northern Canada, all offenses are considered to involve disputes between individuals; thus, they must be settled between the disputants themselves. One way they may do so is through a song duel, in which they heap insults upon one another in songs specially composed for the occasion. Although "society" as such does not intervene, its interests are represented by spectators, whose applause determines the outcome. If, however, social harmony cannot be restored—and that, rather than assigning and punishing guilt is the goal—one or the other disputant may move to another band. Among the Inuit, the alternative to peaceful settlement is for one person to leave the group—depending on who is most uncomfortable staying. Ultimately, there is no binding legal authority.

In Western society, on the other hand, someone who commits an offense against another person is subject to a series of complex legal proceedings. In

criminal cases the primary concern is to determine guilt and punish the offender, rather than to help out the victim. The offender will be arrested by the police; tried before a judge and, perhaps, a jury; and, if the crime is serious enough, may be fined, imprisoned, or even executed. Rarely is there restitution or compensation for the victim. Throughout this chain of events, the accused party is dealt with by presumably disinterested police, judges, jurors, and jailers, who may have no personal acquaintance whatsoever with the plaintiff or the defendant. How strange this all seems from the standpoint of traditional Inuit culture! Clearly, the two systems operate under distinctly different assumptions.

DEFINITION OF LAW

Once two Inuit settle a dispute by engaging in a song contest, the affair is considered closed; no further action need be expected. Would we choose to describe the outcome of such a contest as a legal decision? If every law is a sanction, but not every sanction is a law, how are we to distinguish between social sanctions in general and those to which we will apply the label "law"?

The definition of law has been a lively point of contention among anthropologists in the twentieth century. In 1926, Malinowski argued that the rules of law are distinguished from the rules of custom in that "they are regarded as the obligation of one person and the rightful claim of another, sanctioned not by mere psychological motive, but by a definite social machinery of binding force based . . . upon mutual dependence."[15] An example of one rule of custom in our own society might be seen in the dictate that guests at a dinner party should repay the person who gave the party with entertainment in the future. A host or hostess who does not receive a return invitation may feel cheated of something thought to be owed, but there is no legal claim against the ungrateful guest for the $22.67 spent on food. If, however, an individual was cheated of the same sum by the grocer when shopping, the law could be invoked. Although Malinowski's definition introduced several important elements of law, his failure to distinguish adequately between legal and nonlegal sanctions left the problem of formulating a workable definition of law in the hands of later anthropologists.

An important pioneer in the anthropological study of law was E. Adamson Hoebel, according to whom "a social norm is legal if its neglect or infraction is regularly met, in threat or in fact, by the application of physical force by an individual or group possessing the socially recognized privilege of so acting."[16] In stressing the legitimate use of physical coercion, Hoebel de-emphasized the traditional association of law with a centralized court system. Although judge and jury are fundamental features of Western jurisprudence, they are not the universal backbone of human law. Some anthropologists have proposed that a precise definition of law is an impossible—and perhaps even undesirable—undertaking. When we speak of the law, are we not inclined to fall back on our familiar conception of

rules enacted by an authorized legislative body and enforced by the judicial mechanisms of the state? Can any concept of law be applied to such societies as the Nuer or the Inuit, for whom the notion of a centralized judiciary is virtually meaningless? How shall we categorize duels, song contests, and other socially condoned forms of self-help, which seem to meet some but not all of the criteria of law?

Ultimately, it seems of greatest value to consider each case within its cultural context. That each society exercises a degree of control over its members by means of rules and sanctions, and that some of these sanctions are more formalized than others, is indisputable; yet, in distinguishing between legal and nonlegal sanctions, we should not allow questions of terminology to overshadow our efforts to understand individual situations as they arise.

FUNCTIONS OF LAW

In *The Law of Primitive Man* (1954), Hoebel writes of a time when the notion that private property should be generously shared was a fundamental precept of Cheyenne Indian life. Subsequently, however, some men assumed the privilege of borrowing other men's horses without bothering to obtain permission. When Wolf Lies Down complained of such unauthorized borrowing to the members of the Elk Soldier Society, the Elk Soldiers not only had his horse returned to him but also secured an award for damages from the offender. The Elk Soldiers then announced that, to avoid such difficulties in the future, horses were no longer to be borrowed without permission. Furthermore, they declared their intention of retrieving any such property and administering a whipping to anyone who resisted their efforts to return improperly borrowed goods.

The case of Wolf Lies Down and the Elk Soldier Society clearly illustrates three basic functions of law. First, it defines relationships among the members of society, determining proper behavior under specified circumstances. Knowledge of the law permits each person to know his or her rights and duties in respect to every other member of society. Second, law allocates the authority to employ coercion in the enforcement of sanctions. In societies with centralized political systems, such authority is

---

[15]Bronislaw Malinowski, *Crime and Custom in Savage Society* (London: Routledge, 1951), p. 55.

[16]E. Adamson Hoebel, *The Law of Primitive Man: A Study in Comparative Legal Dynamics* (Cambridge, Mass.: Harvard University Press, 1954), p. 28.

generally vested in the government and its court system. In societies that lack centralized political control, the authority to employ force may be allocated directly to the injured party. Third, law functions to redefine social relations and to ensure social flexibility. As new situations arise, law must determine whether old rules and assumptions retain their validity and to what extent they must be altered. Law, if it is to operate efficiently, must allow room for change.

In actual practice, law is rarely the smooth and well-integrated system described above. In any given society, various legal sanctions may apply at various levels. Because the people in a society are usually members of numerous subgroups, they are subject to the various dictates of these diverse groups. Each individual Kapauku is, simultaneously, a member of a family, a household, a sublineage, and a confederacy, and is subject to all the laws of each. In some cases it may be impossible for an individual to submit to contradictory legal indications:

> In one of the confederacy's lineages, incestuous relations between members of the same clan were punished by execution of the culprits, and in another by severe beating, in the third constituent lineage such a relationship was not punishable and . . . was not regarded as incest at all. In one of the sublineages, it became even a preferred type of marriage.[17]

Furthermore, the power to employ sanctions may vary from level to level within a given society. The head of a Kapauku household may punish a member of his household by means of slapping or beating, but the authority to confiscate property is vested exclusively in the headman of the lineage. An example of a similar dilemma in our own society occurred a few years ago in Oklahoma, a state in which the sale of liquor by the drink is illegal. State officials arrested several passengers and workers on an Amtrak train passing through the state; these people knew their actions were legal under federal law but were unaware that they could be prosecuted under state law. The complexity of legal jurisdiction within each society casts a shadow of doubt over any easy generalization about law.

CRIME

As we have observed, an important function of sanctions, legal or otherwise, is to discourage the breach of social norms. A person contemplating theft is aware of the possibility of being captured and punished. Yet, even in the face of severe sanctions, individuals in every society sometimes violate the norms and subject themselves to the consequences of their behavior. What is the nature of crime in non-Western societies?

In Western society, a clear distinction can be made between offenses against the state and offenses against an individual. *Black's Law Dictionary* tells us that:

> The distinction between a crime and a tort or civil injury is that the former is a breach and violation of the public right and of duties due to the whole community considered as such, and in its social and aggregate capacity; whereas the latter is an infringement or privation of the civil rights of individuals merely.[18]

Thus, a reckless driver who crashes into another car may be guilty of a crime in endangering public safety. The same driver may also be guilty of a tort in causing damages to the other car, and can be sued for their cost by the other driver.

In many non-Western societies, however, there is no conception of a central state. Consequently, all offenses are viewed as offenses against individuals, rendering the distinction between crime and tort of no value. Indeed, a dispute between individuals may seriously disrupt the social order, especially in small groups where the number of disputants, though small in absolute numbers, may be a large percentage of the total population. Although the Inuit have no effective domestic or economic unit beyond the family, a dispute between two people will interfere with the ability of members of separate families to come to one another's aid when necessary, and is consequently a matter of wider social concern. The goal of judicial proceedings in most cases is to restore social harmony, instead of punishing an offender. In distinguishing between offenses of concern to the community as a whole

---

[17]Leopold Pospisil, *Anthropology of Law: A Comparative Theory* (New York: Harper & Row, 1971), p. 36.

[18]Henry Campbell Black, *Black's Law Dictionary* (St. Paul, Minn.: West, 1968).

Two means of psychological evaluation: a Kpelle trial by ordeal, and a Western polygraph, or lie detector.

Negotiation: The use of direct argument and compromise by the parties to a dispute to arrive voluntarily at a mutually satisfactory agreement.

and those of concern only to a few individuals, we may refer to offenses as public or private, rather than distinguishing between criminal and civil law. In this way we may avoid values and assumptions that are irrelevant to a discussion of non-Western systems of law.

Basically, disputes are settled in either of two ways. On the one hand, disputing parties may, by means of argument and compromise, voluntarily arrive at a mutually satisfactory agreement. This form of settlement is referred to as **negotiation** or, if it involves the assistance of an unbiased third party, **mediation.** In bands and tribes a third-party mediator has no coercive power and so cannot force disputants to abide by his decision, but as a person who commands great personal respect, he may frequently effect a settlement through his judgments.

In chiefdoms and states, an authorized third party may issue a binding decision, which the disputing parties will be compelled to respect. This process is referred to as **adjudication.** The difference between mediation and adjudication is basically a difference in authorization. In a dispute settled by adjudication, the disputing parties present their positions as convincingly as they can, but they do not participate in the ultimate decision making.

Although the adjudication process is not universally characteristic, every society employs some form of negotiation in the settlement of disputes. Often negotiation acts as a prerequisite or an alternative to adjudication. For example, in the resolution of U.S. labor disputes, striking workers may first negotiate with management, often with the mediation of a third party. If the state decides that the strike constitutes a threat to the public welfare, the disputing parties may be forced to submit to adjudication. In this case, the responsibility for resolving the dispute is transferred to a presumably impartial judge.

The work of the judge is difficult and complex. Not only must the evidence that is presented be sifted through but the judge must consider a wide

Mediation: Settlement of a dispute through negotiation assisted by an unbiased third party.

Adjudication: Mediation, with the ultimate decision made by an unbiased third party.

range of norms, values, and earlier rulings in order to arrive at a decision that is intended to be considered just not only by the disputing parties but by the public and other judges as well. In most tribal societies a greater value is placed on reconciling disputing parties and resuming tribal harmony than on administering awards and punishments. Thus, "tribal courts may . . . work in ways more akin to Western marriage conciliators, lawyers, arbitrators, and industrial conciliators than to Western judges in court."[19]

In many societies judgement is thought to be made by incorruptible supernatural, or at least nonhuman, powers, through a trial by ordeal. Among the Kpelle of Liberia, for example, where guilt is in doubt, an ordeal operator licensed by the government may apply a hot knife to the leg of a suspect. If the leg is burned, the suspect is guilty; if not, he is innocent. But the operator does not merely heat the knife and apply it. With his hand, he massages the suspect's legs and, once he has determined that the knife is hot enough, he strokes his own leg with it, without being burned, thus demonstrating that the innocent will escape injury. He then applies the knife to the suspect. What he has done up to this point—consciously or unconsciously—is to read the suspect's nonverbal cues: his gestures, the degree of tension in his legs, how much he perspires, and so forth. From this he is able to judge whether or not the accused is showing so much anxiety as to indicate his probable guilt; in effect, he has carried out a psychological stress evaluation. As he applies the knife, he manipulates it so as to either burn or not burn the suspect, once he has made his judgement. This manipulation is easily done by controlling how long the knife is in the fire, as well as by the pressure and angle at which it is pressed against the leg.[20]

Similar to this is the use of the lie detector (or polygraph) in the United States, although the guiding ideology is scientific rather than supernaturalistic. Still, an incorruptible nonhuman agency is thought to establish who is lying and who is not, whereas in reality the polygraph operator cannot just "read" the needles of the machine. What he or she must do is judge whether or not they are registering a high level of anxiety brought on by the testing situation, as opposed to the stress of guilt. Thus, the polygraph operator has much in common with the Kpelle ordeal operator.

POLITICAL ORGANIZATION AND EXTERNAL AFFAIRS

Although the regulation of internal affairs is an important function of any political system, it is by no means the sole function. Another is the management of external or international affairs—relations not just between states, but between different bands, lineages, clans, or whatever the largest autonomous political unit may be. And just as the threatened or actual use of force may be used to maintain order within a society, so may it be used in the conduct of external affairs.

WAR

One of the responsibilities of the state is the organization and execution of the activities of war. Throughout the last few thousand years of history, people have engaged in a seemingly endless chain of wars and intergroup hostilities. Why do wars occur? Is the need to wage war an instinctive feature of the human personality? What are the alternatives to violence as a means of settling disputes between societies?

War is not a universal phenomenon, for in various parts of the world there are societies in which warfare as we know it is not practiced. Examples include people as diverse as the !Kung of Africa, the Arapesh of New Guinea, and the Hopi of North America. Among those societies where warfare is practiced, levels of violence may differ dramatically. Of warfare in New Guinea, for example, the anthropologist Robert Gordon notes that:

> It's slightly more civilized than the violence of warfare which we practice insofar as it's strictly between two groups. And as an outsider, you can go up and interview people and talk to them while they're fighting and the arrows will miss you. It's quite safe and you can take photographs. Now, of course, the problem with modern warfare is precisely that it kills

[19]Max Gluckman, *The Judicial Process among the Barotse of Northern Rhodesia* (New York: Free Press, 1975).

[20]James L. Gibbs, Jr., Interview, *Faces of Culture* (Huntington Beach, Calif.: Coast Telecourses, 1983), Program 18.

In Iraq, as in many countries of the world, war has become commonplace as a government controlled by one ethnic group seeks to control other previously autonomous ethnic groups to gain access to their resources and labor. Shown here are Kurdish guerillas, who have been resisting the Iraqi government's attempts to destroy the Kurds as a people.

indiscriminately and you can't do much research on it, but at the same time, you can learn a lot talking to these people about the dynamics of how violence escalates into full-blown warfare.[21]

There is ample reason to suppose that war has become a problem only in the last 10,000 years, since the invention of food-production techniques, and especially since the invention of centralized states. It has reached crisis proportions in the last 200 years, with the invention of modern weaponry and increased direction of violence against civilian populations. Thus, war seems not to be so much an age-old problem as a relatively recent one. Among food foragers, with their decentralized political systems, although violence emerges sporadically, warfare is all but unknown. Because territorial boundaries and membership among food-foraging bands are usually fluid and loosely defined, a man who hunts with one band today may hunt with a neighboring band tomorrow. Warfare is further rendered impractical by the systematic interchange of women among food-foraging groups—it is likely that someone in each band will have a sister, a brother, or a cousin in a neighboring band. Where populations are small, property ownership is minimal and no state organization exists, the likelihood of organized violence by one group against another is virtually nonexistent.[22]

[21]Robert J. Gordon, Interview for Coast Telecourses, held in Los Angeles, December 4, 1981.

[22]Bruce Knauft, "Violence and Sociality in Human Evolution," *Current Anthropology*, 32 (1991):391–409.

World view: The conceptions, explicit and implicit, of a society or an individual of the limits and workings of its world.

Although there are peaceful farmers, despite the traditional view of the farmer as a gentle tiller of the soil, it is among such people, along with pastoralists, that warfare becomes prominent. One reason for this may be that food-producing peoples are far more prone to population growth than are food foragers, whose numbers are generally maintained well below carrying capacity. This population growth, if unchecked, can lead to resource depletion, one solution to which may be to seize the resources of some other people. In addition, the commitment to a fixed piece of land inherent in farming makes such societies somewhat less fluid in their membership than among people who are food foragers. In those societies that are rigidly matrilocal or patrilocal, each new generation is bound to the same territory, no matter how small it may be or how large the group trying to live within it.

The availability of virgin land may not serve as a sufficient detriment to the outbreak of war. Among slash-and-burn horticulturists, for example, competition for land cleared of virgin forest frequently leads to hostility and armed conflict. The centralization of political control and the possession of valuable property among farming people provide many more stimuli for warfare. It is among such peoples, especially those organized into states, that the violence of warfare is most apt to result in indiscriminate killing. This development has reached its peak in modern states.

Another difference between food-gathering and food-producing populations lies in their different **world views.** As a general rule, food foragers tend to conceive of themselves as a part of the natural world and in some sort of balance with it. This is reflected in their attitudes toward the animals they kill. Western Abenaki hunters, for example, thought that animals, like humans, were composed of a body and vital self. Although Abenakis hunted and killed animals to sustain their own lives, they

clearly recognized that animals were entitled to proper respect. Thus, when beaver, muskrat, or waterfowl were killed, one couldn't just toss their bones into the nearest garbage pit. Proper respect required that their bones be returned to the water, with a request that the species be continued. Such attitudes may be referred to as a naturalistic world view.

The Abenaki's respect for nature contrasts sharply with the kind of world view prevalent among farmers and pastoralists, who do not find their food in nature but impose their dominance upon it so as to produce food for themselves. The attitude that nature exists only to be used by humans may be referred to as an exploitative world view. With such an outlook, it is a small step from dominating the rest of nature to dominating other societies for the benefit of one's own. The exploitative world view, prevalent among food-producing peoples, is an important contributor to intersocietal warfare.

A comparison between the Western Abenakis and their Iroquoian neighbors to the west is instructive. Among the Abenakis warfare was essentially a defensive activity. These food foragers, with their naturalistic world view, believed that one could not operate in someone else's territory, since one didn't control the necessary supernatural powers. Furthermore, operating far below carrying capacity, they had no need to prey upon the resources of others. The Iroquois, by contrast, were slash-and-burn horticulturists who engaged in predatory warfare. Archaeological evidence indicates that significant environmental degradation took place around their settlements, suggesting over-utilization of resources. Although the Iroquois went to war in order to replace men lost in previous battles, the main motive was to achieve dominance by making their victims acknowledge Iroquoian superiority. The relation between victim and victor, however, was one of subjection, rather than outright subordination. The payment of tribute purchased "protection" from the Iroquois, no doubt helping to offset the depletion of resources near the village of the would-be protectors. The price of protection went further than this, though; it included constant and public ceremonial deference to the Iroquois, free passage for their war parties through the subjugated group's country, and the contribution of young men to Iroquoian war parties.

A comparison between the Iroquois and Europeans is also instructive. Sometime in the sixteenth century, five Iroquoian nations—the Mohawks, Oneidas, Onondagas, Cayugas and Sen-

ecas—determined to bring to an end warfare among themselves by the simple device of directing their predatory activities against outsiders, rather than each other. In this way the famous League of the Iroquois came into being. Similarly, in the year 1095, Pope Urban II launched the Crusades with a

Shown here are U.S. soldiers and tanks of Operation Desert Storm, the successful multinational drive to repulse Iraq's invasion of Kuwait. Since the end of World War II, no state has gone to war as often as has the United States.

speech in which he urged European barons to bring to an end their ceaseless wars against each other by directing their hostilities outwards, against the Turks and Arabs. In that same speech he also alluded to the economic benefits to be realized by seizing the resources of the infidels. Although viewed as a holy war, the Crusades clearly were motivated by more than religious beliefs alone.

Although the Europeans never did liberate the Holy Land, at least some of them did benefit from the booty obtained in battle, lending credence to the idea that people could live better than they had before by locating and seizing the resources of others. Thus, the state formation that took place in Europe in the centuries after A.D. 1000 was followed by expansion into other parts of the world. Proceeding apace with this growth and outward expansion was the development of the technology and organization of warfare.

The idea that warfare is an acceptable way to bring about economic benefits is still a part of the European cultural tradition, as the following excerpt from a letter-to-the-editor that appeared in New Hampshire's largest daily newspaper in the 1970s, illustrates: "If a war is necessary to stabilize the economy, then we shall have a war. It affects the everyday lives of most of us so little that we need hardly acknowledge the fact that it is going on. Surely the sacrifice of a son, husband or father by a hundred or so of our citizens every week is not that overwhelming. They will forget their losses in time."[23] Certainly, we would like to think that this kind of attitude is not widespread in the U.S., and perhaps it is not, but we do not know this for a fact. Nor do we really know the extent to which it is, or is not, held by members of those segments of U.S. society that tend to be influential in the setting of public policy. These are obviously important questions, and we need to find out more about them.

As the above examples show, the causes of warfare are complex; economic, political, and ideological factors are all involved. With the emergence of states (in not just Europe but other parts of the world as well) has come an increase in the scale of warfare. Perhaps this is not surprising, given the state's acceptance of force as a legitimate tool to use

in the regulation of human affairs, and its ability to organize large numbers of people. In the modern world, we are as far (if not farther) from the elimination of war as humanity ever has been, a fact reflected in the 120-odd shooting wars going on around the globe as of 1990. Moreover, value systems would seem to be as crucial as any element in the continued existence of warfare.

POLITICAL SYSTEMS AND THE QUESTION OF LEGITIMACY

Whatever form the political system of a society may take, and however it may go about its business, it must always find some way to obtain the people's allegiance. In decentralized systems, in which every adult participates in the making of all decisions, loyalty and cooperation are freely given, since each person is considered to be a part of the political system. As the group grows larger, however, and the organization becomes more formal, the problems of obtaining and keeping public support become greater.

In centralized political systems increased reliance is placed upon coercion as a means of social control. This, however, tends to lessen the effectiveness of a political system. For example, the staff needed to apply force must often be large and may itself grow to be a political force. The emphasis on force may also create resentment on the part of those to whom it is applied and so lessens cooperation. Thus, police states are generally short-lived; most societies choose less extreme forms of social coercion.

Also basic to the political process is the concept of legitimacy, or the right of political leaders to rule. Like force, legitimacy is a form of support for a political system; unlike force, legitimacy is based on the values a particular society believes most important. For example, among the Kapauku the legitimacy of the *tonowi*'s power comes from his wealth; the kings of Hawaii, and England and France before their revolutions, were thought to have a divine right to rule; the head of the Dahomey state of West Africa acquires legitimacy through his age, as he is always the oldest living male.

Legitimacy grants the right to hold, use, and allocate power. Power based on legitimacy may be

In the United States, despite an official separation of church and state, the president has always been sworn in over a Bible.

distinguished from power based on force alone: Obedience to the former results from the belief that obedience is "right"; compliance to power based on force is the result of fear of the deprivation of liberty, physical well-being, life, material property. Thus, power based on legitimacy is symbolic and depends not upon any intrinsic value, but upon the positive expectations of those who recognize and accede to it. If the expectations are not met regularly (if the head of state fails to deliver "economic prosperity" or the leader is continuously unsuccessful in preventing horse or camel theft), the legitimacy of the recognized power figure is minimized and may collapse altogether.

RELIGION AND POLITICS

Religion is intricately connected with politics. Religious beliefs may influence laws: acts that people believe to be sinful, such as sodomy and incest, are often illegal as well. Frequently it is religion that legitimizes the political order.

In both industrial and nonindustrial societies, belief in the supernatural is important and is reflect-ed in people's governments. The effect of religion on politics is perhaps best exemplified in medieval Europe. Holy wars were fought over the smallest matter; labor was mobilized to build majestic cathedrals in honor of the Virgin and other saints; kings and queens ruled by "divine right," pledged allegiance to the pope and asked his blessing in all important ventures, were they marital or martial. In the pre-Columbian Americas, the Aztec state was a religious state, or theocracy, which thrived in spite of more or less constant warfare carried out to procure captives for human sacrifices to assuage or please the gods. In Peru, the Inca emperor proclaimed absolute authority based on the proposition that he was descended from the sun god. Modern Iran has been proclaimed an Islamic republic, and its first head of state was the most holy of all Shiite Moslem holy men. In the United States the Declaration of Independence, a seminal expression of the social and political beliefs of this country, stresses a belief in a supreme being. The document states that "all men are created [by God] equal," a tenet that gave rise to American democracy, because it implied that all people should participate in governing themselves. That the President of the United States takes the oath of office by swearing on the Bible is another instance of the use of religion to legitimize political power, as is the phrase "one nation, under God" in the Pledge of Allegiance. On U.S. coins is the motto "In God We Trust"; many meetings of government bodies begin with a prayer or invoca-tion; and the phrase "So help me God" is routinely used in legal proceedings. Despite an official sepa-ration of church and state, religious legitimization of government remains.

Chapter Summary

Through political organization, societies maintain social order, manage public affairs, and reduce social disorder. No group can live together without persuading or coercing its members to conform to agreed-upon rules of conduct. To properly under-stand the political organization of a society, one needs to view it in the light of its ecological, social, and ideological context.

Four basic types of political systems may be identified. In order of complexity, these range from decentralized bands and tribes to centralized chief-doms and states. The band, characteristic of food-foraging and some other nomadic societies, is an association of politically independent but related families or households occupying a common terri-tory. Political organization in bands is democratic, and informal social control is exerted by public opinion in the form of gossip and ridicule. Band leaders are older men, or sometimes women, whose personal authority lasts only as long as members believe they are leading well and making the right decisions.

The tribe is composed of separate bands or other social units that are tied together by such unifying factors as descent, age grading, or common interest. With an economy usually based on farming or herding, the population of the tribe is larger than that of the band, although family units within the tribe are still relatively autonomous and egalitarian. As in the band, political organization is transitory, and leaders have no formal means of maintaining authority.

Many tribal societies vest political authority in the clan, an association of people who consider themselves to be descended from a common ances-tor. A group of elders or headmen regulate the affairs of members and represent their group in relations with other clans. The segmentary lineage system, similar in operation to the clan, is a rare form of tribal organization based on kinship bonds. Tribal age-grade systems cut across territorial and kin groupings. Leadership is vested in men in the group who were initiated into the age grade at the same time and passed as a set from one age grade to another until reaching the proper age to become elders.

Common-interest associations wield political authority in some tribes. A boy joins one club or another when he reaches warrior status. These organizations administer the affairs of the tribe. Another variant of authority in tribes in Melanesia is the Big Man, who builds up his wealth and political power until he must be reckoned with as a leader.

As societies include larger numbers of people and become more heterogeneous socially, political-ly, and economically, leadership becomes more centralized. Chiefdoms are ranked societies in which every member has a position in the hierar-chy. Status is determined by the individual's posi-tion in a descent group and distance of relationship to the chief. Power is concentrated in a single chief whose true authority serves to unite his community in all matters. The chief may accumulate great personal wealth, which enhances his power base, and which he may pass on to his heirs.

The most centralized of political organizations is the state. It has a central power that can legitimately use force to administer a rigid code of laws and to maintain order, even beyond its borders. A large bureaucracy functions to uphold the authority of the central power. The state is found only in societies with numerous diverse groups. Typically, it is a stratified society, and economic functions and wealth are distributed unequally. Although thought of as being stable and permanent, it is, in fact, inherently unstable and transitory. States differ from nations, which are communities of people who see themselves as one people with a common culture, but who may or may not have a centralized form of political organization.

Historically, women have rarely held important positions of political leadership, and when they have, it has sometimes been for lack of a qualified man to hold the position. Nonetheless, in a number of societies, women have enjoyed political equality with men, as among the Iroquoian tribes of New York state. Among them, all men held office at the pleasure of women, who not only appointed them but could remove them as well. Among the Igbo of midwestern Nigeria, women held positions in an administrative hierarchy that paralleled and balanced that of the men. Under centralized political systems, women are most apt to be subordinate to men, and when states impose their control on societies marked by sexual egalitarianism, the relationship changes to one in which men dominate women.

There are two kinds of social controls, internalized and externalized. Internalized controls are self-imposed by guilty individuals. These built-in controls, which include morality, rely on such deterrents as personal shame, fear of divine punishment, or magical retaliation. Although bands and tribes rely heavily upon them, internalized controls are generally insufficient by themselves. Every society develops externalized controls, called sanctions. Positive sanctions, in the form of rewards or recognition by one's neighbors, is the position a society, or a number of its members, takes toward behavior that is approved; negative sanctions, such as threat of imprisonment, corporal punishment, or "loss of face," reflect societal reactions to behavior that is disapproved.

Sanctions may also be classified as either formal, involving actual laws, or informal, involving norms but not legal statutes. Formal sanctions are organ-

ized and reward or punish behavior through a rigidly regulated social procedure. Informal sanctions are diffuse, involving immediate reactions of approval or disapproval by individual community members to one of their compatriot's behavior. Other important agents of social control are witchcraft beliefs and religious sanctions.

Sanctions serve to formalize conformity to group norms, including actual law, and to maintain each social faction in a community in its "proper" place. Some anthropologists have proposed that to define law is an impossible and perhaps undesirable undertaking. In considering law, it appears best to examine each society within its unique cultural context.

Law serves several basic functions. First, it defines relationships among the members of a society and thereby dictates proper behavior under different circumstances. Second, law allocates authority to employ coercion in the enforcement of sanctions. In centralized political systems this authority rests with the government and court system. Decentralized societies may give this authority directly to the injured party. Third, law redefines social relations and aids its own efficient operation by ensuring that there is room for change.

Western societies clearly distinguish offenses against the state, called crimes, from offenses against an individual, called torts. Decentralized societies may view all offenses as against individuals. One way to understand the nature of law is to analyze individual dispute cases against their own cultural background. A dispute may be settled in two ways, negotiation and adjudication. All societies use negotiation to settle individual disputes. In negotiation the parties to the dispute themselves reach an agreement, with or without the help of a third party. In adjudication, not found in some societies, an authorized third party issues a binding decision. The disputing parties present their petitions, but play no part in the decision making.

In addition to regulating internal affairs, political systems also attempt to regulate external affairs, or relations among politically autonomous units. In doing so they may resort to the threat or use of force.

War is not a universal phenomenon, since there are societies that do not practice warfare as we know it. Usually these societies are those that have some kind of naturalistic world view, an attitude that until recently had become nearly extinguished in modern industrial societies.

A major problem faced by any form of political organization is obtaining and maintaining people's loyalty and support. Reliance on force and coercion in the long run usually tends to lessen the effectiveness of a political system. A basic instrument of political implementation is legitimacy, or the right of political leaders to exercise authority. Power based on legitimacy stems from the belief of a

society's members that obedience is "right," and therefore from the positive expectations of those who obey. It may be distinguished from compliance based on force, which stems from fear, and thus from negative expectations.

Religion is so intricately woven into the life of people in both industrial and nonindustrial countries that its presence is inevitably felt in the political sphere. To a greater or lesser extent, most governments the world over employ religion to legitimize political power.

Suggested Readings

Bohannan, Paul, ed. *Law and Warfare, Studies in the Anthropology of Conflict*. Garden City, N.Y.: Natural History Press, 1967.
Examples of various ways in which conflict is evaluated and handled in different cultures are brought together in this book. It examines institutions and means of conflict resolution, including courts, middlemen, self-help, wager of battle, contest, and ordeal. It also has a selection discussing war—raids, organization for aggression, tactics, and feuds.

Cohen, Ronald, and John Middleton, eds. *Comparative Political Systems*. Garden City, N.Y.: Natural History Press, 1967.
The editors have selected some 20 studies in the politics of nonindustrial societies by such well-known scholars as Lévi-Strauss, S.F. Nadel, Marshall Sahlins, and S.N. Eisenstadt.

Fried, Morton. *The Evolution of Political Society: An Essay in Political Anthropology*. New York: Random House, 1967.
The author attempts to trace the evolution of political society through a study of simple, egalitarian societies. The character of the state and the means whereby this form of organization takes shape is considered in terms of pristine and secondary states, formed because preexisting states supplied the stimuli or models for organization.

Gordon, Robert J., and Mervyn J. Meggitt. *Law and Order in the New Guinea Highlands*. Hanover, N.H.: University Press of New England, 1985.
This ethnographic study of the resurgence of tribal fighting among the Mae-Enga addresses two issues of major importance in today's world: the changing nature of law and order in the third world and the nature of violence in human societies.

Johnson, Allen W., and Timothy Earle. *The Evolution of Human Societies, from Foraging Group to Agrarian State*. Palo Alto, Calif.: Stanford University Press, 1987.
Although written as a synthesis of economic and ecological anthropology, this is also a book on the evolution of political organization in human societies. Proceeding from family-level organization up through states, the authors discuss nine levels of organization, illustrating each with specific case studies, and specify the conditions that give rise to each level.

Nader, Laura, ed. *No Access to Law: Alternatives to the American Judicial System*. New York: Academic Press, 1980.
This is an eye-opening study of how consumer complaints are resolved in our society. After ten years of study, Nader found repeated and documented offenses by business that cannot be handled by present complaint mechanisms, either in or out of court. The high cost exacted includes a terrible sense of apathy and loss of faith in the system itself.

13

RELIGION AND THE

SUPERNATURAL

Ritual is one aspect of religion in action, and purificiation and prayer are common forms of ritual. Here, several men pray in the Ganges River at Benares, India.

WHAT IS RELIGION?

Religion may be regarded as the beliefs and patterns of behavior by which humans try to deal with what they view as important problems that cannot be solved through the application of known technology or techniques of organization. To overcome these limitations, people turn to supernatural beings and powers.

WHAT ARE RELIGION'S IDENTIFYING FEATURES?

Religion consists of various rituals—prayers, songs, dances, offerings, and sacrifices—through which people try to manipulate supernatural beings and powers to their advantage. These beings and powers may consist of gods and goddesses, ancestral and other spirits, or impersonal powers, either by themselves or in various combinations. In all societies there are certain individuals especially skilled at dealing with these beings and powers, who assist other members of society in their ritual activities. A body of myths rationalizes or "explains" the system in a manner consistent with people's experience in the world in which they live.

WHAT FUNCTIONS DOES RELIGION SERVE?

Whether or not a particular religion accomplishes what people believe it does, all religions serve a number of important psychological and social functions. They reduce anxiety by explaining the unknown and making it understandable, as well as provide comfort in the belief that supernatural aid is available in times of crisis. They sanction a wide range of human conduct by providing notions of right and wrong, setting precedents for acceptable behavior, and transferring the burden of decision making from individuals to supernatural powers. Through ritual, religion may be used to enhance the learning of oral traditions. Finally, religion plays an important role in maintaining social solidarity.

According to their origin myth, the Tewa Indians of New Mexico emerged from a lake far to the north of where they now live. Once on dry land, they divided into two groups, the Summer People and the Winter People, and migrated south along the Rio Grande. During their travels they made twelve stops before finally being reunited into a single community.

For the Tewa all existence is divided into six categories, three human and three supernatural. Each of the human categories, which are arranged in a hierarchy, is matched by a spiritual category, so that when people die, they immediately pass into their proper spiritual role. Not only are the supernatural categories identified with human categories; they also correspond to divisions in the natural world.

To those of some other religious persuasion, such beliefs may seem, at best, irrational and arbitrary, but in fact they are neither. Alfonso Ortiz, an anthropologist who is also a Tewa, points out that his native religion is not only logical and socially functional, it is the very model of Tewa society.[1] These people have a society that is divided into two independent moieties, each having its own economy, rituals, and authority. The individual is introduced into one of these moieties (which in this case are *not* based on kinship), and his or her membership is regularly reinforced through a series of life-cycle rituals that correspond to the stops on the mythical tribal journey down the Rio Grande. The rites of birth and death are shared by the whole community; other rites differ in the two moieties. The highest status of the human hierarchy belongs to the priests, who also help integrate this divided society; they mediate not only between the human and spiritual world but between the two moieties as well.

Tewa religion enters into virtually every aspect of Tewa life and society. It is the basis of the simultaneously dualistic/unified world view of the individual Tewa. It provides numerous points of mediation through which the two moieties can continue to exist together as a single community. It sanctifies the community by linking its origin with

the realm of the supernatural, and it offers divine sanction to those "rites of passage" that soften life's major transitions. In providing an afterworld that is the mirror image of human society, it answers the question of death in a manner that reinforces social structure. In short, Tewa religion, by weaving all elements of Tewa experience into a single pattern, gives a solid foundation to the stability and continuity of their society.

All religions fulfill numerous social and psychological needs. Some of these—the need to confront and explain death, for example—appear to be universal; indeed, we know of no group of people anywhere on the face of the earth who, at any time over the past 100,000 years, have been without religion. Unbound by time, religion gives meaning to individual and group life, drawing power from "the time of the gods in the Beginning," and offering continuity of existence beyond death. It can provide the path by which people transcend their arduous earthly existence and attain, if only momentarily, spiritual selfhood. The social functions of religion are no less important than the psychological functions. A traditional religion reinforces group norms, provides moral sanctions for individual conduct, and furnishes the substratum of common purpose and values upon which the equilibrium of the community depends.

In the nineteenth century the European intellectual tradition gave rise to the idea that science would ultimately destroy religion by showing people the irrationality of their myths and rituals. Indeed, many still believe that as scientific explanations replace those of religion, the latter should wither on the vine. An opposite tendency has occurred, however; not only do traditional, mainline religions continue to attract new adherents, but there has been a strong resurgence of fundamentalist religions. Examples include the Islamic fundamentalism of the Ayatollah Khomeini in Iran, with its marked anti-science bias. Moreover, an interest in astrology and occultism continues to be strong in North America (even among members of main-line religious denominations), and there are new religious options, such as sects derived from Eastern religions.

Science, far from destroying religion, may have contributed to the creation of a veritable religious boom. It has done this by removing many tradition-

[1]Alfonso Ortiz, *The Tewa World* (Chicago: University of Chicago Press, 1969), p. 43.

Far from causing the death of religion, the growth of scientific knowledge, by producing new anxieties and raising new questions about human existence, may contribute to its continuing practice in modern life. North Americans continue to participate in traditional religions, such as Judaism (top left) and evangelical Christianity (bottom left), as well as imported sects, such as Hare Krishna (right).

al psychological props, while at the same time creating, in its technological applications, a host of new problems—threat of nuclear catastrophe, health threats from pollution, fear of loneliness in a society that isolates us from our kin and that places impediments in the way of establishing deep and lasting friendships—to list but a few that people must now deal with. In the face of these new anxieties, religion offers social and psychological support.

The continuing strength of religion in the face of Western rationalism clearly reveals that it is a powerful and dynamic force in society. Although anthropologists are not qualified to pass judgement on the metaphysical truth of any particular religion, they can attempt to show how each religion embodies a number of truths about humans and society.

THE ANTHROPOLOGICAL APPROACH TO RELIGION

Anthropologist Anthony F.C. Wallace has defined **religion** as "a set of rituals, rationalized by myth, which mobilizes supernatural powers for the purpose of achieving or preventing transformations of

Religion: A set of rituals, rationalized by myth, which mobilizes supernatural powers for the purpose of achieving or preventing transformations of state in people and nature.

state in man and nature."[2] What lies behind this definition is a recognition that people, when they cannot deal with serious problems that cause them anxiety through technological or organizational means, try to do so through the manipulation of supernatural beings and powers. This requires ritual, which Wallace sees as the primary phenomenon of religion, or "religion in action." Its major function is to reduce anxiety and keep confidence high, all of which serves to keep people in some sort of shape to cope with reality. It is this that gives religion survival value.

Religion, then, may be regarded as the beliefs and patterns of behavior by which people try to control the area of the universe that is otherwise beyond their control. Since no known culture, including those of modern industrial societies, has achieved complete certainty in controlling the universe, religion is a part of all known cultures. There is, however, considerable variability here. At one end of the human spectrum are food-foraging peoples, whose technological ability to manipulate their environment is limited, and who tend to see themselves more as part, rather than masters, of nature. This is what we referred to in Chapter 12 as a naturalistic world view. Among food foragers, religion is apt to be inseparable from the rest of daily life. At the other end of the human spectrum is Western civilization, with its ideological commitment to overcoming problems through technological and organizational skills. Here religion is less a part of daily activities and is restricted to more specific occasions. Even so, there is variation. Religious activity may be less prominent in the lives of social elites, who see themselves as more in control of their own destinies, than it is to peasants or members of lower classes. Among the latter, religion may afford some compensation for a dependent status in society. On the other hand, religion is still important to elite members of society, in that it rationalizes the system in such a way that less advantaged people are not as likely to question the existing social order as they might otherwise be. After all, if there is hope for a better existence after death, then one may be more willing to put up with the difficulties of this life. Thus,

[2]Anthony F.C. Wallace, *Religion: An Anthropological View* (New York: Random House, 1966), p. 107.

religious beliefs serve to influence and perpetuate conceptions, if not actual relations, among different classes of people.

THE PRACTICE OF RELIGION

Much of the value of religion comes from the activities called for by its practice. Participation in religious ceremonies may bring a sense of personal transcendence, a wave of reassurance, security, and even ecstasy, or a feeling of closeness to fellow participants. Although the rituals and practices of religions vary considerably, even those rites that seem to us most bizarrely exotic can be shown to serve the same basic social and psychological functions.

SUPERNATURAL BEINGS AND POWERS

One of the hallmarks of religion is a belief in supernatural beings and forces. In attempting to control by religious means what cannot be controlled in other ways, humans turn to prayer, sacrifice, and ritual activity in general. This presupposes a world of supernatural beings that have an interest in human affairs and to whom appeals for aid may be directed. For convenience we may divide these beings into three categories: major deities (gods and goddesses), ancestral spirits, and nonhuman spirit beings. Although the variety of deities and spirits recognized by the world's cultures is tremendous, certain generalizations about them are possible.

GODS AND GODDESSES

Gods and goddesses are the great and more remote beings. They are usually seen as controlling the universe, or, if several are recognized, each has charge of a particular part of the universe. Such was the case of the gods and goddesses of ancient Greece: Zeus was lord of the sky, Poseidon was ruler of the sea, and Hades was lord of the underworld and ruler of the dead. Besides these three brothers, there were a host of other deities, female

The people of Bali believe in three worlds: an upper one inhabited by the gods, a middle one inhabited by people, and a lower one inhabited by demons. Elaborate rituals are the means by which the people keep the inhabitants of all three worlds in balance.

as well as male, each similarly concerned with specific aspects of life and the universe. **Pantheons,** or collections of gods and goddesses such as those of the Greeks, are common in non-Western states as well. Since states have frequently grown through conquest, their pantheons often have developed as local deities of conquered peoples were incorporated into the official state pantheon. Although creators of the present world may be included, this is not always the case; the Greeks, to cite but one example, did not include them. Another frequent though not invariable feature of pantheons is the presence of a supreme deity, who may be all but totally ignored by humans. The Aztecs of Mexico, for instance, recognized a supreme pair, to

Pantheon: The several gods and goddesses of a people.

whom they paid little attention. After all, being so remote, they were unlikely to be interested in human affairs. The sensible thing, then, was to focus attention on those deities who were more directly concerned in human matters.

Whether or not a people recognize gods, goddesses, or both has to do with how men and women relate to one another in everyday life. Generally speaking, in societies in which women are subordinate to men, the godhead is defined in masculine terms. Such societies are mainly those with economies based upon the herding of animals or intensive agriculture carried out by men who, as fathers, are distant and controlling figures to their children. Goddesses, by contrast, are apt to be most prominent in societies in which women make a major contribution to the economy, enjoy relative equality with men, and in which men are more involved in their children's lives. Such societies are most often those that depend upon farming, much or all of which is done by women. As an illustration, the early Hebrews, like other pastoral nomadic tribes of the Middle East, described their God in masculine terms. By contrast, goddesses played central roles in religious ritual and the popular consciousness of the agricultural peoples of the region. Associated with these goddesses were concepts of light, love, fertility, and procreation. Around 1300 B.C., the Hebrew tribes entered the land of Canaan and began to practice agriculture, requiring them to establish a new kind of relationship with the soil. As they became dependent upon rainfall and on the rotation of the seasons for crops and concerned about fertility (as the Canaanites already were), some of them adopted many of the Canaanite goddess cults. Although diametrically opposed to the original Hebrew conception, belief in the Canaanite goddesses catered to the human desire for security by seeking to control the forces of fertility in the interest of peoples' well-being.

Later on, when the Israelite tribes sought national unity in the face of a military threat by the Philistines, and they strengthened their identity as a chosen people, the goddess cults lost out to followers of the old, masculine conception of God. This ancient masculine concept of God has continued down to the present. As a consequence, this masculine model has played an important role in perpetuating a relationship between men and women in which the latter traditionally have been expected to submit to the rule of men at every level of Jewish, Christian, and Islamic society.

ANCESTRAL SPIRITS

A belief in ancestral spirits is consistent with the widespread notion that human beings are made up of two parts, a body and some kind of vital spirit. For example, the Penobscot Indians, whom we met in Chapter 5, maintained that each person had a vital spirit that could even detach itself and travel about apart from the body, while the latter remained inert. Given some such concept, the idea of the spirit being freed by death from the body and having a continued existence seems quite logical.

Where a belief in ancestral spirits exists, these beings are frequently seen as retaining an active interest and even membership in society. In the last chapter, for instance, we saw how ghost ancestors

of the Wape acted to provide or withhold meat from their living descendants. Like living persons, ancestral spirits may be benevolent or malevolent, but one is never quite sure what their behavior will be. The same feeling of uncertainty—How will they react to what I have done?—may be displayed toward ancestral spirits that tends to be displayed toward members of a senior generation who hold authority over the individual. Beyond this, ancestral spirits closely resemble living humans in appetites, feelings, emotions, and behavior. Thus, they reflect and reinforce social reality.

A belief in ancestral spirits of one sort or another is found in many parts of the world. In several African societies, however, the concept is particularly well developed. Here one frequently finds ancestral spirits behaving just like humans. They are able to feel hot, cold, and pain, and they may be capable of dying a second death by drowning or burning. They may even participate in family and lineage affairs, and seats will be provided for them, even though the spirits are invisible. If they are annoyed, they may send sickness or even death. Eventually, they are reborn as new members of their lineage, and in societies that hold such beliefs, there is a need to observe infants closely in order to determine just who it is that has been reborn.

Deceased ancestors were also important in the patrilineal society of traditional China. For the gift of life, a boy was forever indebted to his parents, owing them obedience, deference and a comfortable old age. Even after their death, he had to provide for them in the spirit world, offering food, money, and incense to them on the anniversaries of their births and deaths. In addition, collective worship of all lineage ancestors was carried out periodically throughout the year. Even the birth of sons was regarded as an obligation to the ancestors, as this ensured that their needs would continue to be attended to even after the present generation's death. To satisfy the needs of ancestors for descendants (and a man's own need to be respectable in a culture that demanded that he satisfy their needs), a man would go so far as to marry a girl who had been adopted into his family as an infant, in order to be raised as a dutiful wife for him, even when this arrangement went against the wishes of both parties. Furthermore, a man would readily force his daughter to marry a man against her will. In fact, a

The patriarchal nature of Western society is expressed in the Judeo-Christian creation story, in which a masculine God gave life to the first man, as depicted here on the ceiling of the Sistine Chapel. After this, God created the first woman out of the first man.

woman was raised to be cast out by her natal family, and yet, might not find acceptance in her husband's family for years. Not until after death, when her soul was carried in a tablet and placed in the shrine of her husband's family was she an official member of it. As a consequence, once a son was born to her, a woman worked long and hard to establish the strongest possible tie between herself and her son to ensure that she would be looked after in life.

Strong beliefs in ancestral spirits are particularly appropriate in a society of descent-based groups with their associated ancestor orientation. More than this, though, they provide a strong sense of continuity in which past, present, and future are all linked.

ANIMISM

One of the most widespread beliefs about supernatural beings is **animism,** which views nature as animated by all sorts of spirits. In reality, the term covers a wide range of variation. Animals and plants, like humans, may all have their individual spirits, as may springs, mountains, or other natural

Animism: A belief in spirit beings, which are thought to animate nature.

SIR EDWARD B. TYLOR

(1832–1917)

The concept of animism was first brought to the attention of anthropologists by the British scholar Sir Edward B. Tylor. Though not university-educated himself, Tylor was the first person to hold a chair in anthropology at a British university, with his appointment first as lecturer, then reader, and finally (in 1895) professor at Oxford. His interest in anthropology developed as a consequence of travels that took him as a young man to the United States (where he visited an Indian Pueblo), Cuba, and Mexico, where he was especially impressed by the achievements of the ancient Aztec and the contemporary blend of Indian and Spanish culture.

Tylor's numerous publications ranged over such diverse topics as the possible historical connection between the games of pachisi and patolli (played in India and ancient Mexico), the origin of games of Cat's Cradle, and the structural connections between post-marital residence, descent, and certain other customs such as in-law avoidance and the couvade (the confinement of a child's father following birth). It was also Tylor who formulated the first widely accepted definition of culture (see Chapter 12). The considerable attention paid to religious concepts and practices in his writings stemmed from a lifelong commitment to combat the idea, still widely held in his time, that so-called savage people had degenerated more than civilized people from an original state of grace. To Tylor, "savages" were intellectuals just like anyone else, grappling with their problems, but handicapped (as was Tylor in his intellectual life) by limited information.

features. So too may stones, weapons, ornaments, and so on. In addition, the woods may be full of a variety of unattached or free-ranging spirits. The various spirits involved are a highly diverse lot. Generally speaking, though, they are less remote from people than gods and goddesses and are more involved in daily affairs. They may be benevolent, malevolent, or just plain neutral. They may also be awesome, terrifying, lovable, or even mischievous. Since they may be pleased or irritated by human actions, people are obliged to be concerned with them.

Animism is typical of those who see themselves as being a part of nature rather than superior to it. This takes in most food foragers, as well as those food-producing peoples who recognize little difference between a human life and that of any growing thing. Among them, gods and goddesses are relatively unimportant, but the woods are full of all sorts of spirits. (For a good example, see the discussion of the Penobscot behavioral environment in Chapter 5.) Gods and goddesses, if they exist at all, may be seen as having created the world, and perhaps making it fit to live in; but it is spirits to whom one turns for curing, who help or hinder the shaman, and whom the ordinary hunter may meet in the woods.

ANIMATISM

While supernatural power is often thought of as being vested in supernatural beings, it doesn't have to be. The Melanesians, for example, think of *mana* as a force inherent in all objects. It is not in itself physical, but it can reveal itself physically. A warrior's success in fighting is not attributed to his own strength but to the *mana* contained in an amulet

Animatism: A belief that the world is animated by impersonal supernatural powers.

that hangs around his neck. Similarly, a farmer may know a great deal about horticulture, soil conditioning, and the correct time for sowing and harvesting, but nevertheless depend upon *mana* for a successful crop, often building a simple altar to this power at the end of the field. If the crop is good, it is a sign that the farmer has in some way appropriated the necessary *mana*. Far from being a personalized force, *mana* is abstract in the extreme, a power lying always just beyond reach of the senses. As R.H. Codrington described it, "Virtue, prestige, authority, good fortune, influence, sanctity, luck are all words which, under certain conditions, give something near the meaning. . . . *Mana* sometimes means a more than natural virtue or power attaching to some person or thing."[3] This concept of impersonal power was also widespread among North American Indians. The Iroquois called it *orenda*; to the Sioux it was *wakonda*; to the Algonquians, *manitu*. Though found on every continent, the concept is not necessarily universal, however.

R.R. Marett called this concept of impersonal power **animatism.** The two concepts, animatism (which is inanimate) and animism (a belief in spirit beings), are not mutually exclusive. They are often found in the same culture, as in Melanesia, and also in the Indian societies mentioned above.

People trying to comprehend beliefs in supernatural beings and powers frequently ask how such beliefs are maintained. In part, the answer is through manifestations of power. By this is meant that, given a belief in animatism and/or the powers of supernatural beings, then one is predisposed to see what appear to be results of the application of such powers. For example, if a Melanesian warrior is convinced of his power because he possesses the necessary *mana*, and he is successful, he may very well interpret this success as proof of the power of *mana*. "After all, I would have lost had I not

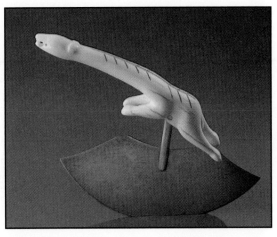

This Inuit carving is no mere inanimate object, but is thought to represent the spirit of the animal portrayed. To the Inuit, all living (and many non-living) things are animated by their own spirits.

possessed it, wouldn't I?" Beyond this, because of his confidence in his *mana*, he may be less timid in his fighting, and this could indeed mean the difference between success or failure.

Failures, of course, do occur, but they can be explained. Perhaps one's prayer was not answered because a deity or spirit was still angry about some past insult. Or perhaps our Melanesian warrior lost his battle—the obvious explanation is that he was not as successful in bringing *mana* to bear as he thought, or else his opponent had more of it. In any case, humans generally emphasize successes over failures, and long after many of the latter have been forgotten, tales will probably still be told of striking cases of the workings of supernatural powers.

Another feature that tends to perpetuate beliefs in supernatural beings is that they have attributes with which people are familiar. Allowing for the fact that supernatural beings are in a sense larger than life, they are generally conceived of as living the way people do, and are interested in the same sorts of things. For example, the Penobscot Indians believed in a quasi-human being called Gluskabe. Like ordinary mortals, Gluskabe traveled about in a canoe, used snowshoes, lived in a wigwam, and made stone arrowheads. The gods and goddesses of the ancient Greeks had all the familiar human lusts and jealousies. Such features serve to make supernatural beings believable.

[3]Quoted by Godfrey Leinhardt in "Religion," in *Man, Culture, and Society*, ed. Harry Shapiro (New York: Oxford University Press, 1960), p. 368.

The role of mythology in maintaining beliefs should not be overlooked. Myths, which are discussed in some detail in Chapter 14, are explanatory narratives that rationalize religious beliefs and practices. To North Americans, the word *myth* immediately conjures up the idea of a story about imaginary events, but the people responsible for a particular myth usually don't see it that way. To them myths are true stories, analogous to historical documents in modern North American culture. Myths invariably are full of accounts of the doings of various supernatural beings. Hence, they serve to reinforce beliefs in them.

RELIGIOUS SPECIALISTS

PRIESTS AND PRIESTESSES

In all human societies there exist individuals whose job it is to guide and supplement the religious practices of others. Such individuals are highly skilled at contacting and influencing supernatural beings and manipulating supernatural forces. Their qualification for this is that they have undergone special training. In addition, they may display certain distinctive personality traits that particularly suit them for their job. In societies with the resources to support full-time occupational specialists, the role of guiding religious practices and influencing the supernaturals belongs to the **priest** or **priestess**. He or she is the socially initiated, ceremonially inducted member of a recognized religious organization, with a rank and function that belongs to him or her as the tenant of an office held before by others. The sources of power are the society and the institution in which the priest or priestess functions. The priest, if not the priestess, is a familiar figure in Western societies; he is the priest, minister, pastor, rector, rabbi, or whatever the official title may be in some organized religion. With their God defined in masculine terms, it is not surprising that the most important religious positions in the Judaic, Christian, and Islamic religions have traditionally been filled by men. Only in societies in which women make a major contribution to the economy, and which recognizes goddesses as well as gods, are female religious specialists likely to be found.

SHAMANS

Societies that lack full time occupational specialization have existed far longer than those in which one finds such specialization, and in them there have always been individuals who have acquired religious power individually, usually in solitude and isolation, when the Great Spirit, the Power, the Great Mystery, or whatever is revealed to them. These persons become the recipients of certain special gifts, such as healing or divination; when they return to society they are frequently given another kind of religious role, that of the **shaman.**

In the United States perhaps millions of people may have learned something about shamans through reading either the popular autobiography of Black Elk, a traditional Sioux Indian "medicine man," or Carlos Castaneda's apparently fictional accounts of his experiences with Don Juan, the Yaqui Indian shaman. Few of them may realize, however, that the faith healers and many other evangelists in their own society correspond in every respect to our definition of the shaman. Thus, one should not get the idea that shamans are not to be found in modern, industrial societies, for they are. Furthermore, they may become more common, given the current revival of interest in the supernatural that is taking place in the United States.

Typically, one becomes a shaman by passing through stages commonly related by many myths. These stages are often thought to involve torture and violent dismemberment of the body; scraping away of the flesh until the body is reduced to a

Priest or Priestess: A full-time religious specialist.

Shaman: A part time religious specialist who has unique power acquired through his or her own initiative; such individuals are thought to possess exceptional abilities to deal with supernatural beings and powers.

Shown here is an evangelist in the United States healing a follower. Such faith-healers correspond in every respect to our definition of the shaman; hence, shamanism is by no means absent in modern industrial societies.

skeleton; substitution of the viscera and renewal of the blood; a period spent in a nether region, or land of the dead, during which the shaman is taught by the souls of dead shamans and other spirit beings; and an ascent to a sky realm. Among the Crow Indians, for example, any man could become a shaman, since there was no ecclesiastical organization that handed down laws for the guidance of the religious consciousness. The search for shamanistic visions was pursued by most adult Crow males, who would engage in bodily deprivation, even self-torture, to induce such visions. The majority of seekers would not be granted a vision, but failure carried no social stigma. While those who claimed supernatural vision would be expected to manifest some special power in battle or wealth, it was the sincerity of the seeker that carried the essential truth of the experience. Many of the elements of shamanism, such as transvestitism, trance states, and speaking in undecipherable languages, can just as easily be regarded as abnormalities, and it has been frequently pointed out that those regarded as specially gifted in some societies would be outcasts or worse in others. The position of shaman can provide a socially approved role for what in other circumstances might be unstable personalities.

The shaman is essentially a religious entrepreneur, who acts for some human client. On behalf of the client, the shaman intervenes to influence or impose his or her will on supernatural powers. The shaman can be contrasted with the priest or priestess, whose "clients" are the deities. Priests and priestesses frequently tell people what to do; the shaman tells supernaturals what to do. In return for services rendered, the shaman may collect a fee—fresh meat, yams, a favorite possession. In some cases, the added prestige, authority, and social power attached to the status of shaman are reward enough.

When a shaman acts for a client, he or she may put on something of a show—one in which the basic drama is heightened by a sense of danger. Frequently, the shaman must enter a trance-like state, in which he or she will be able to see and interact with spirit beings. Having achieved this state, the shaman seeks to impose his or her will upon these spirits, an inherently dangerous contest, considering the superhuman powers that spirits are usually thought to possess. In many human societies trancing is accompanied by sleight-of-hand tricks and ventriloquism. Among Arctic peoples, for example, a shaman may summon spirits in the dark

ANTHROPOLOGY APPLIED

RECONCILING MODERN MEDICINE WITH TRADITIONAL BELIEFS IN SWAZILAND

Although the biomedical germ theory is generally accepted in Western societies today, this is not the case in many other societies around the world. In southern Africa's Swaziland, for example, all types of illnesses are generally thought to be caused by sorcery, or by loss of ancestral protection. Even where the effectiveness of Western medicine is recognized, the ultimate question remains: why was the disease sent in the first place? Thus, for the treatment of disease, the Swazi have traditionally relied upon herbalists, diviner mediums through whom ancestor spirits are thought to work, and Christian faith healers. Unfortunately, such individuals have usually been regarded as quacks and charlatans by the medical establishment, even though the herbal medicines used by traditional healers are effective in several ways, and the reassurance provided patient and family alike through rituals that reduce stress and anxiety plays an important role in the patient's recovery. In a country where there is one traditional healer for every 110 people, but only one physician for every 10,000, the potential benefit of cooperation between physicians and healers seems self-evident. Nevertheless, it was unrecognized until proposed by anthropologist Edward C. Green.*

Green, who is now senior research associate with a private firm, went to Swaziland in 1981 as a researcher for a Rural Water-Borne Disease Control Project, funded by the United States Agency for International Development. Assigned the task of finding out about knowledge, attitudes, and practices related to water and sanitation, and aware of the serious deficiencies of conventional surveys that rely on precoded questionnaires (see Chapter 1), Green used instead the traditional anthropological techniques of open-ended interviews with key informants, along with participant observation. The key informants were traditional healers, patients, and rural health motivators (individuals chosen by their communities to receive eight weeks of training in preventive health care in regional clinics). Without such work, it would have

been impossible to design and interpret a reliable survey instrument, but the added payoff was that Green learned a great deal about Swazi theories of disease and its treatment. Disposed at the outset to recognize the positive value of many traditional practices, he was able to see as well how cooperation with physicians might be achieved. For example, traditional healers already recognized the utility of Western medicines for the treatment of diseases not indigenous to Africa, and traditional medicines were routinely given to children through inhalation and a kind of vaccination. Thus, non-traditional medicines and vaccinations might be accepted, if presented in traditional terms.

Realizing the suspicion which existed on both sides, Green and his Swazi associate Lydia Makhubu (a chemist who had studied the properties of native medicines) recommended to the Minister of Health a cooperative project focused on a problem of concern to health professionals and native healers alike: infant diarrheal diseases. These had recently become a health problem of high concern to the general public; healers wanted a means of preventing such diseases, and a means of treatment existed—oral rehydration therapy—that was compatible with traditional treatments for diarrhea (herbal preparations taken orally over a period of time). Packets of oral rehydration salts, along with instructions as to their use, were provided healers in a pilot project, with positive results. This helped convince health professionals of the benefits of cooperation, while at the same time, the distribution of packets to the healers was seen by them as a gesture of trust and cooperation on the part of the Ministry of Health. Since then, further steps at cooperation have been taken. What all this demonstrates is the importance of finding how to work in ways that are compatible with existing belief systems. To directly challenge traditional beliefs, as all too often happens, does little more than create stress, confusion, and resentment.

*Edward C. Green, "The Planning of Health Education Strategies in Swaziland," and "The Integration of Modern and Traditional Health Sectors in Swaziland," in *Anthropological Praxis: Translating Knowledge into Action*, ed. Robert M. Wulff and Shirley J. Fiske, Boulder, Colo.: Westview, 1987, pp. 15–25 and 87–97.

and produce all sorts of flapping noises and strange voices to impress the audiences. To some Western observers, this kind of trickery is regarded as evidence of the fraudulent nature of shamanism; but is this so? The truth is that shamans know perfectly well that they are pulling the wool over people's eyes with their tricks. On the other hand, virtually everyone who has studied them agrees that shamans really believe in their power to deal with supernatural powers and spirits. It is this power that gives them the right as well as the ability to fool people in minor technical matters. In short, the shaman regards his or her ability to perform tricks as proof of superior powers.

The importance of shamanism in a society should not be underestimated. For the individual members of society, it promotes, through the drama of the performance, a feeling of ecstasy and release of tension. It provides psychological assurance, through the manipulation of supernatural powers otherwise beyond human control, of such things as invulnerability from attack, success at love, or the return of health. In fact, a frequent reason for a shamanistic performance is to cure illness. Although the treatment may not be medically effective, the state of mind induced in the patient may be critical to his or her recovery.

What shamanism does for society is to provide a focal point of attention. This is not without danger to the shaman. Someone with so much skill and power has the ability to work evil as well as good, and so is potentially dangerous. Too much nonsuccess on the part of a shaman may be interpreted as evidence of malpractice, and result in his or her being driven out of the group or killed. The shaman may also help maintain social control through the ability to detect and punish evil-doers.

The benefits of shamanism for the shaman are that it provides prestige and perhaps even wealth. It may also be therapeutic, in that it provides an approved outlet for the outbreaks of an unstable personality. An individual who is psychologically unstable (and not all shamans are) may actually get better by becoming intensely involved with the problems of others. In this respect, shamanism is a bit like self-analysis. Finally, shamanism is a good outlet for the self-expression of those who might be described as being endowed with an "artistic temperament."

A Yanomami shaman speaking with spirits.

RITUALS AND CEREMONIES

Religious ritual is the means through which persons relate to the sacred; it is religion in action. Not only is ritual the means by which the social bonds of a group are reinforced and tensions relieved, it is also one way that many important events are celebrated and crises, such as death, made less socially disruptive and less difficult for the individuals to bear. Anthropologists have classified several different types of ritual, among them **rites of passage**, which pertain to stages in the life cycle of the

Rites of passage: Religious rituals marking important stages in the lives of individuals, such as birth, marriage, and death.

Rites of intensification: Religious rituals that take place during a real or potential crisis for a group.

---

individual, and **rites of intensification,** which take place during a crisis in the life of the group, serving to bind individuals together.

RITES OF PASSAGE

In one of anthropology's classic works, Arnold Van Gennep analyzed the rites of passage that help individuals through the crucial crises of their lives, such as birth, puberty, marriage, parenthood, advancement to a higher class, occupational specialization, and death.[4] He found it useful to divide ceremonies for all of these life crises into three stages: **separation, transition,** and **incorporation.** The individual would first be ritually removed from the society as a whole, then isolated for a period, and finally incorporated back into society in his or her new status.

Van Gennep described the male initiation rites of Australian aborigines. When the time for the initiation is decided by the elders, the boys are taken from the village, while the women cry and make a ritual show of resistance. At a place distant from the camp, groups of men from many villages gather. The elders sing and dance, while the initiates act as though they are dead. The climax of this

---

Separation: In rites of passage, the ritual removal of the individual from society.

Transition: In rites of passage, the isolation of the individual following separation and prior to incorporation.

Incorporation: In rites of passage, reincorporation of the individual into society in his or her new status.

---

part of the ritual is a bodily operation, such as circumcision or the knocking out of a tooth. Anthropologist A.P. Elkin says,

> This is partly a continuation of the drama of death. The tooth-knocking, circumcision or other symbolical act "killed" the novice; after this he does not return to the general camp and normally may not be seen by any woman. He is dead to the ordinary life of the tribe.[5]

The novice may be shown secret ceremonies and receive some instruction during this period, but the most significant element is his complete removal from society. In the course of these Australian puberty rites, the initiate must learn the tribal lore; he is given, in effect, a "cram course." The trauma of the occasion is a pedagogical technique that ensures that he will learn and remember everything; in a nonliterate society the perpetuation of cultural traditions requires no less, and so effective teaching methods are necessary.

On his return to society the novice is welcomed with ceremonies, as though he had returned from the dead. This alerts the society at large to the individual's new status—that he can be expected to act in certain ways and in return people must act in the appropriate ways toward him. The individual's new rights and duties are thus clearly defined. He is spared, for example, the problems of "American teenage," a time when an individual is neither adult nor child, but a person whose status is ill-defined.

In the Australian case just cited, boys are prepared not just for adulthood, but for *manhood.* In their society, for example, fortitude is considered an important masculine virtue, and the pain of tooth-knocking and circumcision help instill this in initiates. Similarly, female initiation rites help prepare Mende girls in West Africa for womanhood. After they have begun to menstruate, they are removed from society to spend weeks, or even months, in seclusion. There, they discard the clothes of childhood, smear their bodies with white clay and dress in brief skirts and many strands of beads. Shortly after their seclusion, they undergo surgery in which their clitoris and part of the labia minora are excised, something that is thought to enhance their procreative potential. Until their

---

[4]Arnold Van Gennep, *The Rites of Passage* (Chicago: University of Chicago Press, 1960).

[5]A.P. Elkin, *The Australian Aborigines* (Garden City, N.Y.: Doubleday, Anchor Books, 1964).

Circumcision is an important part of the rites of passage that initiate aboriginal Australian boys into adulthood. The trauma of the occasion is one of the things that helps make memorable the lore that they learn as part of their initiation.

return to society, they are trained in the moral and practical responsibilities of potential child bearers by experienced women in the Sande association, an organization to which the initiates will belong once their training has ended. This training is not all harsh, however, for it is accompanied by a good deal of singing, dancing, and storytelling, and the initiates are very well fed. Thus, they acquire both a positive image of womanhood and a strong sense of sisterhood. Once their training is complete, a medicine made by brewing leaves in water is used for a ritual washing, removing the magical protection that has shielded them during the period of their confinement.

Mende women emerge from their initiation, then, as women in knowledgeable control of their sexuality, eligible for marriage and childbearing. The pain and danger of the surgery, which was endured in the context of intense social support from other women, serves as a metaphor for childbirth, which, when it happens, may well take place in the same place of seclusion, again with the support of Sande women. It has also been suggested that, symbolically, excision of the clitoris (a rudiment of the male penis), removed sexual ambiguity.[6] Once done, a woman *knows* she is all woman. Thus, we have symbolic expression of gender as something important in peoples' cultural lives.

RITES OF INTENSIFICATION

Rites of intensification are those rituals that mark occasions of crisis in the life of the group, rather than an individual. Whatever the precise nature of the crisis—a severe lack of rain that threatens crops in the fields, the sudden appearance of an enemy war party, or some other force from outside that disturbs everyone—mass ceremonies are performed to allay the danger to the group. What this does is to unite people in a common effort in such a way that fear and confusion yield to collective action and a degree of optimism. The balance in the relations of all concerned, which has been upset, is restored to normal.

[6] Carol P. MacCormack, "Biological Events and Cultural Control", *Signs* 3(1977):98.

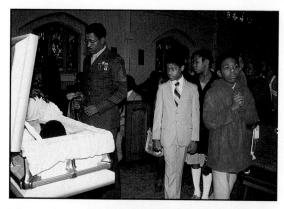

Viewing the body of the deceased is a common part of North American funeral rites. It is one expression of the desire to maintain a tie with the individual even after death. Other expressions of the same desire are common in the funeral rites of other cultures.

While the death of an individual might be regarded as the ultimate crisis in the life of an individual, it is, as well, a crisis for the entire group, particularly if the group is small. A member of the group has been removed, and so its equilibrium has been upset. The survivors, therefore, must readjust and restore balance. At the same time, they need to reconcile themselves to the loss of someone to whom they were emotionally tied. Funerary ceremonies, then, can be regarded as rites of intensification that permit the living to express in nondisruptive ways their upset over the death, while providing for social readjustment. A frequent feature of such ceremonies is an ambivalence towards the dead person. For example, one of the parts of the funerary rites of Melanesians was the eating of the flesh of the dead person. This ritual cannibalism, witnessed by anthropologist Bronislaw Malinowski, was performed with "extreme repugnance and dread and usually followed by a violent vomiting fit. At the same time, it is felt to be a supreme act of reverence, love, and devotion."[7] This custom, and the emotions accompanying it, clearly reveal the ambiguous attitude toward death: On the one hand, there is the desire to maintain the tie to the dead person, and on the other hand, one feels disgust and fear at the transformation wrought by death. According to Malinowski, funeral ceremo-

[7]Bronislaw Malinowski, *Magic, Science and Religion* (Garden City, N.Y.: Doubleday, Anchor Books, 1954), p. 50.

nies provide an approved collective means by which individuals may express these feelings, while at the same time maintaining social cohesiveness and preventing disruption of society.

The performance of rites of intensification does not have to be limited to times of overt crisis. In regions where the seasons differ enough so that human activities must change accordingly, they will take the form of annual ceremonies. These are particularly common among horticultural and agricultural people, with their planting, first-fruit, and harvest ceremonies. These are critical times in the lives of people in such societies, and the ceremonies express a reverent attitude toward the forces of generation and fertility in nature, on which peoples' very existence depends. If all goes well, as it often does at such times, participation in a happy situation reinforces group involvement. It also serves as a kind of dress rehearsal for serious crisis situations; it promotes a habit of reliance on supernatural forces through ritual activity, which can be easily activated under stressful circumstances when it is important not to give way to fear and despair.

RELIGION, MAGIC, AND WITCHCRAFT

Among the most fascinating of ritual practices is application of the belief that supernatural powers can be compelled to act in certain ways for good or evil purposes by recourse to certain specified formulas. This is a classical anthropological notion of magic. Many societies have magical rituals to ensure good crops, the replenishment of game, the fertility of domestic animals, and the avoidance or cure of illness in humans. Although Western peoples today, in seeking to objectify and demythologize their world, have often tried to suppress the existence of these fantastic notions in their own consciousness, they continue to be fascinated by them. Not only are books and films about demonic possession and witchcraft avidly devoured and discussed, but by 1967 (after some 40 years of poor sales) sales of ouija boards in the United States passed the two-million mark. Thirty years ago about 100 newspapers carried horoscope columns, but by 1970, 1,200 of a total of 1,750 daily newspapers regularly carried such columns. Anthropologist Lauren Kendall notes that "Many

In North America, an interest in and the practice of the occult have grown significantly over the past twenty years—often among highly schooled segments of society.

witches, wizards, druids, Cabalists, and shamans . . . practice modern magic in contemporary England and the United States, where their ranks are comfortably reckoned in the tens of thousands." Furthermore, "The usual magician is ordinary, generally middle class, and often highly intelligent—a noticeable number of them have something to do with computers."[8] Although it is certainly true that non-Western and peasant peoples tend to endow their world quite freely with magical properties, so do many highly educated Western peoples.

In the nineteenth century Sir James George Frazer, author of one of the most widely read anthropological books of all time, *The Golden Bough*, made a strong distinction between religion and magic. Religion he saw as "a propitiation or conciliation of powers superior to man which are believed to direct and control the course of nature and human life."[9] Magic, on the other hand, he saw as an attempt to manipulate certain perceived "laws" of nature. The magician never doubts that

[8]Laurel Kendall, "In the Company of Witches," *Natural History* 10/90 (1990):92.

[9]James G. Frazer, "Magic and Religion," *The Making of Man: An Outline of Anthropology*, ed. V.F. Calverton (New York: Modern Library, 1931), p. 693.

Sympathetic magic: Magic based on the principle that like produces like.

Contagious magic: Magic based on the principle that things once in contact can influence one another after separation.

the same causes will always produce the same effects. Thus, Frazer saw magic as a sort of pseudo-science, differing from modern science only in its misconception of the nature of the particular laws that govern the succession of events.

Frazer differentiated between two fundamental principles of magic. The first principle, that "like produces like," he called **sympathetic magic.** In Burma, for example, a rejected lover might engage a sorcerer to make an image of his scornful love. If this image were tossed into water, to the accompaniment of certain charms, the hapless girl would go mad. Thus, the girl would suffer a fate similar to that of her image.

Frazer's second principle was that of **contagious magic**—the concept that things or persons that have once been in contact can afterward influence one another. The most common example of contagious magic is the permanent relationship between an individual and any part of his or her body, such as hair, fingernails, or teeth. Frazer cites the Basutos of South Africa, who were careful to conceal their extracted teeth, because these might fall into the hands of certain mythical beings who could harm the owner of the tooth by working magic on it. Related to this is the custom, in Western societies, of treasuring things that have been touched by special people.

In the following Original Study, anthropologists Anthony Parades and Elizabeth Purdum argue that capital punishment in the United States, which they liken to Aztec rituals of human sacrifice, constitutes an institutional magical response to perceived disorder in the lives of North Americans.

ORIGINAL STUDY

BYE BYE, TED . . . [10]

In 1985, we presented a paper comparing capital punishment in modern-day Florida to Aztec rituals of human sacrifice in 16th century Mexico. Finding the usual explanations for capital punishment and its widespread support in the contemporary United States incomplete at best, we hypothesized that capital punishment in contemporary America functions as the ultimate validator of law, serving "to reassure many that society is not out of control after all, that the majesty of the Law reigns, and that God is indeed in his heaven," in much the same way the Aztec rituals reassured the population that the state was healthy and the Sun would remain in the heavens.

The idea of human sacrifice as a means of reaffirming the power and control of society as a whole is of course not new. Sir James Frazer in *The Golden Bough* chronicles a variety of customs whereby a person or an animal is killed, often after being both treated well and tortured, in order to rid society of its accumulated ills.

Bronislaw Malinowski observed that "there are no peoples however primitive without religion and magic," neither are there peoples so civilized that they are devoid of magic. All peoples turn to magic when knowledge, technology, and experience fail. In the face of evidence that capital punishment does no more to deter crime than the rituals of Tenochtitlan did to keep the sun in the sky, we concluded "that modern capital punishment is an institutionalized magical response to perceived disorder in American life and in the world at large, an attempted magical solution that has an especial appeal to the beleaguered, white . . . God-fearing men and women of the working class. And, in certain aspiring politicians they find their sacrificial priests."

In a 1987 revision, we cited as "emic" verification of our validation-of-law hypothesis a popular bumper sticker expressing resentment of a new Florida statute requiring automobile passengers to wear safety belts: "I'll buckle up when Bundy does; it's the law." The momentum was building for notorious, serial sex-murderer Theodore Bundy to become the central character in a contemporary mass-media morality play. When Bundy was executed in the electric chair on 24 January 1989, for the murder of a 12-year-old girl, public reactions to his execution seemed to confirm our ideas about capital punishment. Given the enormity of Bundy's crimes and the celebrity status he had received, his execution became a dramatic extravaganza casting into high relief the underlying psychological and social currents that swirl around capital punishment as a cultural trait.

It seemed a natural follow-up to our earlier paper to analyse newspaper data on the Bundy spectacle for evidence that might test our general hypothesis that "capital punishment . . . serves the psychosocial function of reassuring members of society that law reigns." Once we began work on this present paper we realized we had seriously underestimated the attention Bundy's execution had received in the Florida press.

There are 49 daily newspapers in Florida. For purposes of the present essay we rely upon a sample consisting of only the Miami, St. Petersburg, Orlando and Tallahassee newspapers. Together, these account for approximately one-third of the total circulation of all Florida daily newspapers. The papers were selected to represent political points of view as well as location. Our survey of four Florida newspapers has produced a rich corpus of data for anthropological analysis. We have only skimmed the surface of the complex and many-faceted themes found in 280+ items on Bundy from 40 days' worth of newspapers. What we present here is, perforce, rather broad, but, as we had hoped (we won't pretend otherwise), there is in the material much confirmation of our views on the psycho-social functions of capital punishment. Many other themes are represented as well.

Not all Floridians support the death penalty. This is amply evident in the newspaper data; even so, some early reports and commentaries claimed that capital punishment opponents were less active in connection with Bundy's execution than with others. Some of those opposing capital punishment did admit to having difficulty in remaining true to their position, faced with the heinousness of Bundy's crimes and noted, for example, "if ever a defendant met the criteria for Florida's death penalty, he [Bundy] did." Even so, the number of death penalty opponents attending the customary post-execution protest in the state capital the day after an execution was, in the Bundy case, three times the usual number.

In the last few days before Bundy was executed the story was dominated by two themes: legal manoeuvres to save Bundy from execution, and Bundy's confessions to murders in the far west. The latter were widely seen as a ploy to save his life. Bundy was portrayed by the state governor as trying to bargain over the bodies of his victims. Briefly, the governor and Bundy seemed locked together as mythic combatants, the governor standing firm to execute his duty—"it's the law"—and, incidentally, realizing a significant political credit. One state legislator declared that if Bundy were executed on schedule the governor would be "viewed as an archangel of justice." One columnist drew a parallel between the Governor and Jimmy Stewart in the role of "The Man who Shot Liberty Valance."

The final days before Bundy's death provided an opportunity for one last cliff-hanger of whether good would triumph over evil, whether the collective force of society would prevail over that deepest structural threat to social order: the categorical anomaly. Here was the bright, articulate, college-educated, handsome, former law student crisis counsellor, who looked "like a professional tennis player," but who was also a murderer, rapist, and sodomizer who beat his human prey with a club, tore at their flesh with his teeth, and tossed the remains of his last victim, a girl of twelve, into a "pigsty." In these terms, Bundy was that ultimate Judaeo-Christian anomaly of anomalies who, like the serpent in the Garden of Eden, is the creepiest of creeping things—truly Lucifer among us, according to one close observer.

With less and less chance that Bundy would win another reprieve, newspaper coverage shifted to accounts of the throng of news reporters converging on the "cow pasture" across from the Death Row prison. As if to heighten the drama, newspapers recounted details of Bundy's grisly crimes, of the anticipated execution procedures, of Bundy's mental condition, of his final interviews, of his turn to religion—"Bundy prays and reads Bible." In these final hours the stage was also set for the epilogue that was to follow.

A born-again Christian lawyer who had got to know Bundy through a prison ministry visited the condemned at length, urging that he confess his other crimes, and that he be given time to do so. But the lawyer had just been elected a district prosecutor, so his actions stirred great controversy among his constituents. Only when the prosecutor pressed for the death penalty in another case, weeks after Bundy's execution, did he seem to cleanse his reputation.

***

Once the sentence was carried out and Bundy's body was borne away—in one dramatic photo, a man reaches out to touch the hearse as if it were a passing icon in a religious procession—there followed a flood of sentiment giving native expression to the function of capital punishment as a validator of law. These sentiments were succinctly summarized by the frequently used phrase "The system works," often accompanied by reference to Bundy's "manipulation" of the system. "Bundy loomed as an evil genius. . . . who . . . play[ed] games with a judicial system that promises to protect us from the dark," declared one newspaperman. "Now people know that our system works," said one witness to the execution. Responding to a Boston criminal justice professor, one letter writer said that those "opposed to capital punishment need to be reminded that this is a nation of laws, not of men whose feelings distort justice; that laws form a basis of order, freedom, and the citizens' protection from criminals."

One of the most frequently recurring words to describe feelings after Bundy's execution was "relief, relief as simple as respite from constant speculation about Bundy's execution, to relief that the system really works," to a Hegelian sense of closure for the families of victims, to catharsis of a classic sort—"purging ourselves," as one columnist put it.

Not unrelated to the oft-cited sense of relief was a surprisingly unabashed release of vengefulness. "Hundreds celebrate execution," announced one news story. In the "cow pasture" on the morning of Bundy's death were many revellers—singing, drinking, carrying frying pans, selling "Burn Bundy Burn" T-shirts and producing a genuine carnival atmosphere—like Mardi Gras, said one reporter. Another writer, as if wanting to play into the hands of an anthropological analysis, described the celebrants as "acting in a savage manner." Even more pointed was an effigy execution carried out by some in the crowd, as if by magical emulation they, too, could participate in the killing of Bundy. Similarly, in some cities disc jockeys played requests for songs celebrating Bundy's execution, especially "Bye-Bye Ted Bundy" sung to the tune of Don McLean's early 1970s popular work "American Pie," a selection for parody in itself thick with symbolism. Among the most peculiar identifications with the execution was the Tallahassee bar-owner who presided over an execution party wearing a halo-like contraption representing Bundy's brains being burned.

One of the more surprising aspects of the Bundy spectacle was the extent to which some used the event to display their creativity—trying to "out comic" one another, as one writer put it. Often these expressions played on elements of popular culture of the most innocent genres—"Bundy Bar-BQ" on short-order menus, a bawdy parody of "On Top of Old Smokey," and, in reference to the sorority house murders, a chilling play on Walt Disney's seven dwarfs: "Chi O, Chi O, It's off to hell I go." Adding to the surreal quality of it all was the announcement of Salvador Dali's death juxtaposed to Bundy execution stories on the front page of several newspapers, including photographs of Dali's impish, mustachioed countenance.

Afterwards, execution celebration was a frequent subject for condemnation by both supporters of the death penalty and by those opposed. Much of the celebration did appear to be, as critics claimed, a tasteless expression of vengeful glee. Nonetheless, even among the more sober there was an implication that by his slaughter of innocents Ted Bundy had placed upon society a collective moral obligation to exact vengeance and retribution. As one headline announced, "Bundy Pays the Price." Vengefulness is not surprising given that, according to one account, the governor issued the final telephone order to kill Bundy "on behalf of the countless victims of Theodore Bundy both dead and living, across Florida and the nation."

Even in their condemnation, though, some tried to find an explanation for the macabre celebration surrounding Bundy's execution. One veteran reporter wrote, "perhaps it was an eruption of hatred for a criminal justice system that is too slow to right wrongs." One correspondent defended the cheering at Bundy's death saying, "The people of Florida and the rest of the United States did not cheer when Ted Bundy was electrocuted because they were bloodthirsty. They did so because justice finally prevailed over a flawed judicial system . . ." One of the more off-beat defences of post-execution revelry was the letter to the editor comparing those events to the jubilation of the Munchkins in the Land of Oz after Dorothy's house squashed the wicked witch of the East!

Many subthemes were woven around the central drama of the events of 24 January. Columnists, letter writers, and public figures used Bundy's execution as an opportunity to declaim on topics as varied as the venality of the legal profession, the arrogance of the "liberal elite,"

God's ordination of earthly governments, state pride for Florida having executed Bundy, alarm that the state's image would be damaged by having executed Bundy, the dedication and bravery of the police officers, the certainty that whatever else may be said an executed murderer never kills again, loss of civic innocence (echoing lines of Thorton Wilder's *Our Town*), apprehension that even in death Bundy was mocking society by his wish to have his ashes scattered over the Cascade Mountains where bones of many of his alleged victims were found, the abortion debate (those cheering the execution were probably pro-abortion, a writer suspected; another linked supporters of the death penalty to the "pro-lifers"), the pros and cons of the death penalty itself, the need for reform in the appeals process, the need to understand and protect ourselves from truly malevolent forces in our midst, and much more. At least two items even challenged Florida motorists to "buckle up," now that Bundy's sentence had in fact been carried out.

While we are far from a conclusive analysis of the drama surrounding Ted Bundy's final days, these preliminary observations suggest that many do take special comfort in the affirmation of authority and order which capital punishment seems to provide—especially when the executed is such a vile smart-aleck as the likes of Ted Bundy. Ironically, such an execution provides the stage for some to act out their own private rituals of rebellion and disorderliness.

Ding, dong, the witch is dead.

[10]J. Anthony Parades and Elizabeth D. Purdum, "Bye Bye, Ted. . .", *Anthropology Today* 6, No. 2 (1990):9–11.

WITCHCRAFT

Two hundred suspected witches were arrested in Salem, Massachusetts, in 1692; of these, 19 were hanged and one other was hounded to death. Nineteen years later the descendants of some of the victims were awarded damages, but not until 1957 were the last of the Salem witches exonerated by the Massachusetts legislature. Although many North Americans suppose that **witchcraft** is something that belongs to a less-enlightened past, in fact, it is alive and well in the United States today.

Witchcraft: An explanation of misfortune based on the belief that certain individuals possess an innate, psychic power capable of causing harm, including sickness and death.

Indeed, in the 1960s, witchcraft began to undergo something of a boom in this country. North Americans are by no means alone in this; for example, as the Ibibio of Nigeria have become increasingly exposed to modern education and scientific training, their reliance on witchcraft as an explanation for misfortune has increased. [11] Furthermore, it is often the younger, more-educated members of Ibibio

[11]Daniel Offiong, "Witchcraft among the Ibibio of Nigeria," in *Magic, Witchcraft and Religion*, ed. Arthur C. Lehmann and James E. Myers (Palo Alto, Calif.: Mayfield, 1985), pp. 152–165.

society who accuse others of "bewitching" them. Frequently, the accused are older, more traditional members of society; thus, we have an expression of the intergenerational hostility that often exists in fast-changing traditional societies.

IBIBIO WITCHCRAFT

Among the Ibibio, as among most peoples of sub-Saharan Africa, witchcraft beliefs are highly developed and are of long standing. A rat that eats up a person's crops is not really a rat, but a witch that changed into one; if a young and enterprising man cannot get a job or fails an exam, he has been bewitched; if someone's money is wasted away, if they become sick, if they are bitten by a snake, or struck by lightning, the reason is always the same: It is witchcraft. Indeed, virtually all misfortune, illness, or death is attributed to the malevolent activity of some witch. Their modern knowledge of such things as the role played by microorganisms in disease has little impact; after all, it says nothing about why these were sent to the afflicted individual. Although Ibibio religious beliefs provide alternative explanations for misfortune, they carry negative connotations and do not elicit nearly as much sympathy from others. Thus, if evil befalls a person, witchcraft is a far more satisfying explanation than something like "filial disobedience" or violation of some taboo.

Who are these Ibibio witches? They are thought to be those, male or female, who have within them a special substance acquired from some other established witch. This substance is made up of red, white, and black threads, needles, and other ingredients, and one gets it by swallowing it. From it comes a special power that causes harm, up to and including death, irrespective of whether its possessor intends to cause harm or not. The power is purely psychic, and witches do not perform rites, nor make use of "bad medicine." It gives them the ability to change into animals, to travel any distance at incredible speed to get at their victims, whom they may torture, or kill by transferring the victim's soul into an animal, which is then eaten.

To identify a witch, one looks for any person whose behavior is out of the ordinary. Specifically, some combination of the following may cause one to be labeled a witch: not being fond of greeting people; living alone in a place apart from others;

charging too high a price for something; enjoying adultery or committing incest; walking about at night; not showing sufficient grief upon the death of a relative or other member of the community; taking improper care of ones' parents, children, or wives; hard-heartedness. Witches are apt to look and act mean, and to be socially disruptive people in the sense that their behavior too far exceeds the range of variance considered acceptable.

Neither the Ibibio in particular nor Africans in general are alone in attributing most malevolent happenings to witchcraft. Similar beliefs can be found in any human society, including—as already noted—that of the United States. As among the Ibibio, the powers (however they may be gained) are generally considered to be innate and uncontrollable; they result in activities that are the antithesis of proper behavior, and persons displaying undesirable characteristics of personality (however these may be defined) are generally the ones accused of being witches. The Ibibio make a distinction between "black witches"—those whose acts are especially diabolical and destructive—and "white witches," whose witchcraft is relatively benign, even though their powers are thought to be greater than those of their black counterparts. This exemplifies a common distinction between what Lucy Mair, a British anthropologist, has dubbed "nightmare witches" and "everyday witches."[12] The nightmare witch is the very embodiment of a society's conception of evil, a being that flouts the rules of sexual behavior and disregards every other standard of decency. Nightmare witches, being almost literally the product of dreams and repressed fantasies, have much in common wherever they appear: The modern Navajo and the ancient Roman, for example, like the Ibibio, conceived of witches that could turn themselves into animals and gather to feast on their victims. Everyday witches are often the nonconformists of a community, who are morose, who eat alone, who are arrogant and unfriendly, but who otherwise cause little trouble. Such witches may be dangerous when offended and retaliate by causing sickness, death, crop failure, cattle disease, or any number of lesser ills; people thought to be witches are usually treated very courteously.

---

[12]Lucy Mair, *Witchcraft* (New York: McGraw-Hill, 1969), p. 37.

THE FUNCTIONS OF WITCHCRAFT

Why witchcraft? We might better ask, why not? As Mair aptly observed, in a world where there are few proven techniques for dealing with everyday crises, especially sickness, a belief in witches is not foolish; it is indispensable. No one wants to resign oneself to illness, and if the malady is caused by a witch's hex, then magical countermeasures should cure it. Not only does the idea of personalized evil answer the problem of unmerited suffering, it also provides an explanation for many of those happenings for which no cause can be discovered. Witchcraft, then, cannot be refuted. Even if we could convince a person that his or her illness was due to natural causes, the victim would still ask, as the Ibibio do, Why me? Why now? There is no room for pure chance in such a view; everything must be assigned a cause or meaning. Witchcraft provides the explanation, and in so doing, also provides both the basis and the means for taking counteraction.

Nor is witchcraft always malevolent; even during the Spanish Inquisition, church officials recognized a benevolent or "white" variety. The positive functions of even malevolent witchcraft may be seen in many African societies in which sickness and death are regarded as caused by witches. The ensuing search for the perpetrator of the misfortune becomes, in effect, a communal probe into social behavior.

A witch hunt is, in fact, a systematic investigation, through a public hearing, into all social relationships involving the victim of the sickness or death. Was her husband unfaithful, her son lacking in the performance of his duties; were her friends uncooperative or was she herself any of these things? Accusations are reciprocal, and before long just about every unsocial or hostile act that has occurred in that society since the last outbreak of witchcraft (sickness or death) is brought into the open.[13]

Through such periodic public scrutiny of everyone's behavior, people are reminded of what their society regards as both strengths and weaknesses of character. This encourages individuals to suppress as best they can those traits of personality that are looked upon with disapproval, for if they do not, they may at some time be accused of being a witch. A belief in witchcraft thus serves a function of social control.

PSYCHOLOGICAL FUNCTIONS OF WITCHCRAFT AMONG THE NAVAJO

Widely known among American Indians are the Navajo, who possess a detailed concept of witchcraft. Several types of witchcraft are distinguished. Witchery encompasses the practices of witches, who are said to meet at night to practice cannibalism and kill people at a distance. Sorcery is distinguished from witchery only by the methods used by the sorcerer, who casts spells on individuals, using the victim's fingernails, hair, or discarded clothing. Wizardry is not distinguished so much by its effects as by its manner of working; wizards kill by

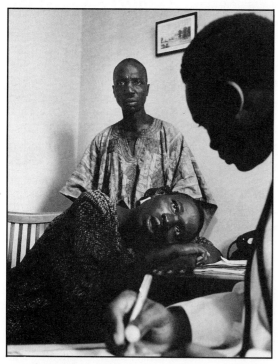

In many societies, witchcraft may be an important source of psychological assurance. Here we see a positive application of this possibility. The Nigerian man at the right is a trained psychiatrist; helping him treat his patient is the local "witch doctor," who has considerable skill in dealing with severe emotional upsets. He has been incorporated into the staff of the clinic under the title "native therapist."

[13]Colin M. Turnbull, *The Human Cycle* (New York: Simon & Schuster, 1983), p. 181.

Divination: A magical procedure by which the cause of a particular event, such as illness, may be determined or the future foretold.

---

injecting a cursed substance, such as a tooth from a corpse, into the victim's body.

Whether or not a particular illness results from witchcraft is determined by **divination,** a magical procedure by which the identity of the witch is also learned. Once a person is charged with witchcraft, he or she is publicly interrogated, possibly even tortured, until there is a confession. It is believed that the witch's own curse will turn against the witch once this happens, so it is expected that the witch will die within a year. Some confessed witches have been allowed to live in exile.

According to Clyde Kluckhohn, Navajo witchcraft served to channel anxieties, tensions, and frustrations that were caused by the pressures from Anglo Americans.[14] The rigid rules of decorum among the Navajo allow little means of expression of hostility, except through accusations of witchcraft. Such accusations funnel pent-up negative emotions against individuals, without upsetting the wider society. Another function of accusations of witchcraft is that they permit the direct expression of hostile feelings against people to whom one would ordinarily be unable to express anger or enmity.

THE FUNCTIONS OF RELIGION

Just as a belief in witchcraft may serve a variety of psychological and social functions, so too do religious beliefs and practices in general. Here we may summarize these functions in a somewhat more systematic way. One psychological function is to provide an orderly model of the universe, the importance of which for orderly human behavior is discussed in Chapter 5. Beyond this, by explaining

[14]Clyde Kluckhohn, "Navajo Witchcraft," *Papers of the Peabody Museum of American Archaeology and Ethnology*, 22, No. 2 (1944).

the unknown and making it understandable, the fears and anxieties of individuals are reduced. As we have seen, the explanations usually assume the existence of various sorts of supernatural beings and powers, which may potentially be appealed to or manipulated by people. This being so, a means is provided for dealing with crises: Divine aid is, theoretically, available when all else fails.

A social function of religion is to sanction a wide range of conduct. In this context, religion plays a role in social control, which, as we saw in Chapter 12, does not rely on law alone. This is done through notions of right and wrong. If one does the right thing, one earns the approval of whatever supernatural powers are recognized by a particular culture. If, on the other hand, one does the wrong thing, one may suffer retribution through supernatural agencies. In short, by deliberately *raising* peoples' feelings of guilt and anxiety, religion helps keep them in line. Religion does more than this, though; it sets precedents for acceptable behavior. We have already noted the connection between myths and religion. Usually, myths are full of tales of various supernatural beings, which in various ways illustrate the society's ethical code in action. So it is that Gluskabe, the Penobscot culture hero, is portrayed in the Penobscot myths as tricking and punishing those who mock others, lie, are greedy, or go in for extremes of behavior. Moreover, the specific situations serve as precedents for human behavior in similar circumstances. The Old and New Testaments of the Bible are rich in the same sort of material. Related to this, by the models it presents and the morals it espouses, religion serves to justify and perpetuate a particular social order. Thus, in the Jewish, Christian, and Islamic traditions, a masculine godhead along with a creation story in which a woman is responsible for a fall from grace justifies a social order in which men have exercised control over women.

There is a psychological function tied up in all this. The moral code of a society, since it is held to be divinely fixed, lifts the burden of responsibility for one's conduct from the shoulders of the individual members of society, at least in important situations. It can be a tremendous relief to individuals to know that the responsibility for the way things are rests with the gods, rather than with themselves.

Another social function of religion is its role in the maintenance of social solidarity. In our discussion of the shaman we saw how such individuals provide focal points of interest, thus supplying one ingredient of assistance in maintaining the unity of the group. In addition, common participation in rituals, coupled with a basic uniformity of beliefs, helps to bind people together and reinforce their identification with their group. Particularly effective may be their participation together in rituals, when the atmosphere is charged with emotion. The exalted feelings people may experience in such circumstances serve as a positive reinforcement in that they "feel good" as a result. Here, once again, we find religion providing psychological assurance, while providing for the needs of society.

One other area in which religion serves a social function is education. In our discussion of rites of passage, we noted that Australian puberty rites served as a kind of cram course in tribal lore. By providing a memorable occasion, initiation rites can serve to enhance learning and so help ensure the perpetuation of a nonliterate culture. And as we saw in the case of female initiation rites among the Mende, they can serve to ensure that individuals have the knowledge that they will need to fulfill their adult roles in society. Education may also be served by rites of intensification. Frequently such rites involve dramas that portray matters of cultural importance. For example, among a food-foraging people, dances may imitate the movement of game and techniques of hunting. Among farmers a fixed round of ceremonies may emphasize the steps necessary for good crops. What this does is to help preserve knowledge that is of importance to a people's material well-being.

RELIGION AND CULTURE CHANGE

Although the subject of culture change is taken up in a later chapter, no anthropological consideration of religion is complete without some mention of revitalization movements. In 1931, at Buka in the Solomon Islands, a native religious cult suddenly emerged, its prophets predicting that a deluge would soon engulf all whites. This would be followed by the arrival of a ship laden with European goods. The believers were to construct a storehouse for the goods and to prepare themselves to repulse the colonial police. Because the ship would

Young Melanesian men parade with mock rifles made of bamboo in a cargo cult ritual. Many of the believers are also Christians; the people see nothing contradictory in the two faiths.

arrive only after the natives had used up all their own supplies, they ceased working in the fields. Although the leaders of the cult were arrested, the movement continued for some years.

This was not an isolated instance. Such "cargo cults"—and many other movements that have promised the resurrection of the dead, the destruction or enslavement of Europeans, and the coming of utopian riches—have sporadically appeared throughout Melanesia ever since the beginning of this century. Since these cults are widely separated in space and time, their similarities are apparently the result of similarities in social conditions. In these areas the traditional cultures of the indigenous peoples have been uprooted. Europeans, or European-influenced natives, hold all political and economic power. Natives are employed in unloading and distributing Western-made goods, but have

Revitalization movements are not restricted to non-Western cultures. This picture was taken in San Diego, California.

no practical knowledge of how to attain these goods. When cold reality offers no hope from the daily frustrations of cultural deterioration and economic deprivation, religion offers the solution.

REVITALIZATION MOVEMENTS

From the 1890 Ghost Dance of many North American Indians to the Mau Mau of Kenya to the "cargo cults" of Melanesia, extreme and sometimes violent religious reactions to European domination are so common that anthropologists have sought to formulate their underlying causes and general characteristics. Yet **revitalization movements,** as they are now called, are by no means restricted to the colonial world, and in the United States alone hundreds of such movements have sprung up. Among the more widely known are Mormonism,

---

Revitalization movements: Social movements, often of a religious nature, with the purpose of totally reforming a society.

---

which began in the nineteenth century, the more recent Unification Church of the Reverend Sun Myung Moon, and the extreme of the Guayana "People's Temple" of the Reverend Jim Jones. As these three examples suggest, revitalization movements show a great deal of diversity, and some have been much more successful than others.

A revitalization movement is a deliberate effort by members of a society to construct a more satisfying culture. The emphasis in this definition is on the reformation not just of the religious sphere of activity, but of the entire cultural system. Such a drastic solution is attempted when a group's anxiety and frustration have become so intense that the only way to reduce the stress is to overturn the entire social system and replace it with a new one.

Anthropologist Anthony Wallace has outlined a sequence common to all expressions of the revitalization process.[15] First is the normal state of society, in which stress is not too great and there exist sufficient cultural means of satisfying needs. Under certain conditions, such as domination by a more powerful group or severe economic depression, stress and frustration will be steadily amplified; this ushers in the second phase, or the period of

[15]Anthony F.C. Wallace, *Culture and Personality,* 2d ed. (New York: Random House, 1970), pp. 191–196.

increased individual stress. If there are no significant adaptive changes, a period of cultural distortion follows, in which stress becomes so chronic
that socially approved methods of releasing tension
begin to break down. This steady deterioration of
the culture may be checked by a period of revitalization, during which a dynamic cult or religious
movement grips a sizable proportion of the population. Often the movement will be so out of touch
with reality that it is doomed to failure from the
beginning. This was the case with the Ghost
Dance, as practiced by the Sioux Indians, which

was supposed to make the participants impervious
to the bullets of the white men's guns. This was the
case also with the cult of the Reverend Jim Jones,
where the murder of a U.S. congressman was
followed by the suicide of Jones and many of his
followers. More rarely, a movement may tap long-
dormant adaptive forces underlying a culture, and a
long-lasting religion may result. Such was the case
with Mormonism. Indeed, revitalization movements lie at the root of all known religions, Judaism, Christianity, and Islam included. We shall
return to revitalization movements in Chapter 15.

CHAPTER SUMMARY

Religion is a part of all cultures. It consists of
beliefs and behavior patterns by which people try to
control the area of the universe that is otherwise
beyond their control. Among food-foraging peoples religion is a basic ingredient of everyday life.
As societies become more complex, religion is less a
part of daily activities and tends to be restricted to
particular occasions.

Religion is characterized by a belief in supernatural beings and forces. Through prayer, sacrifice,
and general ritual activity, people appeal to the
supernatural world for aid. Supernatural beings
may be grouped into three categories: major deities
(gods and goddesses), nonhuman spirit beings, and
ancestral spirits. Gods and goddesses are the great
but remote beings. They are usually thought of as
controlling the universe or a specific part of it.
Whether or not people recognize gods, goddesses,
or both has to do with how men and women relate
to one another in everyday life. Animism is a belief
in spirit beings other than ancestors who are
believed to animate all of nature. These spirit
beings are closer to humans than gods and goddesses and are intimately concerned with human activities. Animism is typical of peoples who see themselves as a part of nature rather than as superior to
it. A belief in ancestral spirits is based on the idea
that human beings are made up of a body and soul.
At death the spirit is freed from the body and

continues to participate in human affairs. Belief in
ancestral spirits is particularly characteristic of
descent-based groups with their associated ancestor
orientation. Animatism, as described by R.H. Codrington, may be found with animism in the same
culture. Animatism is a force or power directed to a
successful outcome, which may make itself manifest in any object.

Beliefs in supernatural beings and powers are
maintained, first, through what are interpreted as
manifestations of power. Second, they are perpetuated because supernatural beings possess attributes
with which people are familiar. Finally, myths serve
to rationalize religious beliefs and practices.

All human societies have specialists—priests and
priestesses and/or shamans—to guide religious
practices and to intervene with the supernatural
world. Shamanism, with its often dramatic ritual,
promotes a release of tension among individuals in
a society. The shaman provides a focal point of
attention for society and can help to maintain social
control. The benefits of shamanism for the shaman
are prestige, sometimes wealth, and an outlet for
artistic self-expression.

Ritual is religion in action. Through ritual acts,
social bonds are reinforced. Times of life crises are
occasions for ritual. Arnold Van Gennep divided
such rites of passage into rites of separation, transition, and incorporation. Rites of intensification are

rituals to mark occasions of crisis in the life of the group rather than the individual. They serve to unite people, allay fear of the crisis, and prompt collective action. Funerary ceremonies are rites of intensification that provide for social readjustment after the loss of the deceased. Rites of intensification may also involve annual ceremonies to seek favorable conditions surrounding such critical activities as planting and harvesting.

Ritual practices of peasant and non-Western peoples are often an expression of the belief that supernatural powers can be made to act in certain ways through the use of certain prescribed formulas. This is the classic anthropological notion of magic. Sir James Frazer saw magic as a pseudoscience and found two principles of magic—"like produces like," or sympathetic magic, and the law of contagion.

Witchcraft functions as an effective way for people to explain away personal misfortune without having to shoulder any of the blame themselves. Even the most malevolent witchcraft may function positively in the realm of social control. It may also provide an outlet for feelings of hostility and frustration without disturbing the norms of the larger group.

Religion (including magic and witchcraft) serves several important social functions. First, it sanctions a wide range of conduct by providing notions of right and wrong. Second, it sets precedents for acceptable behavior and helps perpetuate an existing social order. Third, religion serves to lift the burden of decision making from individuals and places responsibility with the gods. Fourth, religion plays a large role in maintaining social solidarity. Finally, religion serves education. Ritual ceremonies enhance learning of tribal lore and so help to ensure the perpetuation of a nonliterate culture.

Domination by Western society has been the cause of certain religious manifestations in non-Western societies. In the islands of Melanesia, cargo cults have appeared spontaneously at different times since the beginning of the century. Anthony Wallace has interpreted religious reformations as revitalization movements in which an attempt is made, sometimes successfully, to change the society. He argues that all religions stem from revitalization movements.

Suggested Readings

Kalweit, Holger. *Dreamtime and Inner Space: The World of the Shaman*. New York: Random House, 1988.
Written by an ethnopsychologist, this book surveys the practices and paranormal experiences of healers and shamans from Africa, the Americas, Asia, and Australia.

Lehmann, Arthur C., and James E. Myers, eds., *Magic, Witchcraft and Religion: An Anthropological Study of the Supernatural*, 2nd ed. Palo Alto, Calif.: Mayfield, 1988.
An anthology of readings, cross-cultural in scope and covering traditional as well as non-traditional themes. Well represented are both "tribal" and "modern" religions. A good way to discover the relevance and vitality of anthropological approaches to the supernatural.

Malinowski, Bronislaw. *Magic, Science and Religion, and Other Essays*. Garden City, N.Y.: Doubleday, 1954.
The articles collected here provide a discussion of the Trobriand Islanders as illustrative of conceptual and theoretical knowledge of humankind. The author covers such diversified topics as religion, life, death, character of "primitive" cults, magic, faith, and myth.

Norbeck, Edward. *Religion in Human Life: Anthropological Views*. New York: Holt, Rinehart and Winston, 1974.
The author presents a comprehensive view of religion based on twin themes: the description of religious events, rituals, and states of mind, and the nature of anthropological aims, views, procedures, and interpretations.

Wallace, Anthony F.C. *Religion: An Anthropological View*. New York: Random House, 1966.
This is a standard textbook treatment of religion by an anthropologist who has specialized in the study of revitalization movements.

14

THE ARTS

No human culture is known to be without some form of art, even though that art may be applied to a purely utilitarian object. Although not intended to be an object of art, this Philippine jeep certainly is artistic.

WHAT IS ART? Art is the creative use of the human imagination to interpret, understand, and enjoy life. Although the idea of art serving nonuseful, nonpractical purposes seems firmly entrenched in the thinking of modern Western peoples, in other cultures art often serves what are regarded as important, practical purposes.

WHY DO ANTHROPOLOGISTS STUDY ART? Anthropologists have found that art reflects the cultural values and concerns of a people. This is especially true of the verbal arts—myths, legends, and tales. From these the anthropologist may learn how a people order their universe, and may discover much about a people's history as well. Also, music and the visual arts, such as sculpture, may provide insights into a people's world view and, through distributional studies, may suggest things about a people's history.

WHAT ARE THE FUNCTIONS OF THE ARTS? Aside from adding enjoyment to everyday life, the various arts serve a number of functions. Myths, for example, set standards for orderly behavior, and the verbal arts generally transmit and preserve a culture's customs and values. Songs, too, may do this, within the restrictions imposed by musical form. And any form of art, to the degree that it is characteristic of a particular society, may contribute to the cohesiveness or solidarity of that society.

Art is the product of a specialized kind of human behavior: the creative use of our imagination to help us interpret, understand, and enjoy life. Whether one is talking about a Chinese love song, a Hopi pot, a Balinese dance, or an African woodcarving, it is clear that everyone involved in the activity we call art—the creator, the performer, the participant, the spectator—is making use of a uniquely human ability to use and comprehend symbols and to shape and interpret the physical world for something beyond a purely utilitarian purpose. After all, if a Hopi Indian wanted a useful container, a simple, undecorated pot would do just as well as a carefully shaped, smoothed, and elaborately painted one, and could be more quickly and easily made. Yet Hopi potters typically devote much time and technical skill to the production of pottery vessels that are aesthetically pleasing not just to other Hopi but to many non-Hopi peoples as well.

The idea of art serving nonuseful, nonpractical purposes seems firmly entrenched in the thinking of modern Western peoples. Today, for example, the objects from the tomb of the young Egyptian king Tut-ankh-amen are on display in a museum, where they may be seen and admired as the exquisite works of art that they are. They were made, however, to be hidden away from human eyes, where they were to guarantee the eternal life of the king, and protect him from evil forces that might enter his body and gain control over it. Or, we may listen to the singing of a sea chantey purely for aesthetic pleasure, as a form of entertainment. In fact, in the days of sailing, sea chanteys served very useful and practical purposes. They set the appropriate rhythm for the performance of specific shipboard tasks, and the same qualities that make them pleasurable to listen to today served to relieve the boredom of those tasks. Such links between art and other aspects of culture are common in human societies around the world.

To people today, the making of exquisite objects of gold and precious stones to place in a tomb might seem like throwing them away. Yet, something of the same sort happens when a Navajo Indian creates an intricate sand painting as part of a ritual act, only to destroy it once the ritual is over. Johann Sebastian Bach was doing the very same thing when, almost 300 years ago, he composed cantatas to be used in church services. These were "throw away" music, to be discarded after the religious services

for which they were written. Bach composed them not for posterity but for the glory of God. In many societies the "doing" of art is often of greater importance than the final product itself.

Whether a particular work of art is intended to be appreciated purely as such or to serve some practical purpose, as in the examples shown here, it will in every case require the same special combination of the symbolic representation of form and the expression of feeling that constitutes the creative imagination. Insofar as the creative use of the human ability to symbolize is universal and either expresses or is shaped by cultural values and concerns, it is properly and eminently an area of investigation for anthropology.

There appears to be no culture in the world without at least some kind of storytelling, singing, dancing, or other activity that gives aesthetic pleasure. Reasoning backward from effect to cause, some writers in recent times have proposed that humans may have an actual need or drive—either innate or acquired—to use their faculties of imagination. Just as we need food and shelter to survive, we may also need to nourish and exercise our active minds, which are not satisfied, except in times of crisis, with the mere business of solving the immediate problems of daily existence. Without the free play of the imagination there is boredom, and boredom may lead to a lack of productivity, perhaps even in extreme cases to death. It is art that provides the means and the materials for our imaginative play and thus helps to sustain life. Art is, therefore, not a luxury to be afforded or appreciated by a minority of aesthetes or escapists, but a necessary kind of social behavior in which every normal and active human being participates.

As an activity or kind of behavior that contributes to well-being and helps give shape and significance to life, art must be at the same time related to, yet differentiated from, religion. The dividing line between the two is not distinct: It is not easy to say, for example, precisely where art stops and religion begins in an elaborate ceremony involving ornamentation, masks, costumes, songs, dances, and effigies. And like magic, art, music, and dance may be used as a form of "enchantment" to exploit the innate or psychological biases of some other person or group causing them to perceive social reality in a way favorable to the interests of the "enchanter." Indeed, the arts may be used to manipulate a

Much of the world's art is created for functional rather than aesthetic purposes. Shown here are examples of art used to cure sickness (a Navajo sand painting), to express cultural identity (the Mardi Gras costume of one of New Orleans' "Black Indians"), and as political propaganda (a mural in Northern Ireland).

seemingly inexhaustible list of human passions, including desire, terror, wonder, cupidity, fantasy, and vanity.[1]

Although the distinction is not always easy to make, one is often made between secular and religious art. In what is called purely secular art, whether it is light or serious, it is clear that our imaginations are free to roam without any ulterior motives—creating and re-creating patterns, plots, rhythms, and feelings at leisure and without any thought of consequence or aftermath. In religious art, on the other hand, the imagination is working still, but the whole activity is somehow aimed at assuring our well-being through manipulation and acknowledgment of forces beyond ourselves. At any rate, whether categorized as secular or reli-

[1]Alfred Gell, "Technology and Magic," *Anthropology Today* 4, No. 2(1988):7.

gious, art of all varieties can be expected to reflect the values and concerns of the people who create and enjoy it; the nature of the things reflected and expressed in art is the concern of the anthropologist.

THE ANTHROPOLOGICAL STUDY OF ART

In approaching art as a cultural phenomenon, the anthropologist has the pleasant task of cataloguing, photographing, recording, and describing all possible forms of imaginative activity in any particular culture. There is an enormous variety of forms and modes of artistic expression in the world. Because people everywhere continue to create and develop in new directions, there is no foreseeable point of diminishing returns in the interesting process of

The world's earliest known pictorial art is from Australia, and is not unlike this example from Ayer's Rock.

collecting and describing the world's ornaments, body decorations, variations in clothing, blanket and rug designs, pottery and basket styles, architectural embellishments, monuments, ceremonial masks, legends, work songs, dances, and other art forms. The process of collecting, however, must eventually lead to some kind of analysis, and generalizations about relationships between art and culture.

Probably the best way to begin a study of this problem of the relationships between art and culture is to examine critically some of the generalizations that have already been made about specific arts. Since it is impossible to cover all forms of art in the space of a single chapter, we shall concentrate on just a few: verbal arts, music, and sculpture. We shall start with the verbal arts, for we have already touched upon them in our earlier discussions of religion (Chapter 13) and world view (Chapters 5 and 12).

VERBAL ARTS

The term **folklore** was coined in the nineteenth century to denote the unwritten stories, beliefs, and customs of the European peasant, as opposed to the traditions of the literate elite. The subsequent study of folklore, **folkloristics**, has become a discipline allied to but somewhat independent of anthropolo-

Folklore: A nineteenth-century term first used to refer to the traditional oral stories and sayings of the European peasant, and later extended to those traditions preserved orally in all societies.

Folkloristics: The study of folklore (as linguistics is the study of language).

gy, working on cross-cultural comparisons of themes, motifs, and structures, from a literary as well as ethnological point of view. Many linguists and anthropologists prefer to speak of the oral traditions and verbal arts of a culture rather than its folklore and folktales, recognizing that creative verbal expression takes many forms and that the implied distinction between folk and "sophisticated" art is a projection of the attitude of European (and European-derived) cultures onto others.

The verbal arts include narrative, drama, poetry, incantations, proverbs, riddles, word games, and even naming procedures, compliments, and insults, when these take structured and special forms. The narrative seems to be one of the easiest kinds of verbal arts to record or collect. Perhaps because it is also the most publishable, with popular appeal in North American culture, it has received the most study and attention. Generally, narratives have been divided into three basic and recurring categories: myth, legend, and tale.

MYTH

The word *myth*, in popular usage, refers to something that is widely believed to be true, but probably isn't. Actually, a true **myth** is basically religious, in that it provides a rationale for religious beliefs and practices. Its subject matter is the ultimates of human existence: where we and the things in our

---

Myth: A sacred narrative explaining how the world came to be in its present form.

---

world came from, why we are here, and where we are going. As was noted in Chapter 13, the myth has an explanatory function; it depicts and describes an orderly universe, which sets the stage for orderly behavior. Below is a typical origin myth traditional with the western Abenaki of northwestern New England and southern Quebec.

In the beginning, *Tabaldak,* "The Owner," created all living things but one—the spirit being who was to accomplish the final transformation of the earth. Man and woman *Tabaldak* made out of a piece of stone, but he didn't like the result, and so he broke them up. He tried again, this time using living wood, and from them came all later Abenakis. The one living thing not created by *Tabaldak* was *Odziózo:* "He Makes Himself from Something." This being seems to have created himself out of dust, but since he was more transformer than creator, he wasn't able to accomplish it all at once. At first, he managed only his head, body, and arms; the legs came later, growing slowly as legs do on a tadpole. Not waiting until his legs were grown, he set out to change the shape of the earth. He dragged his body about with his hands, gouging channels

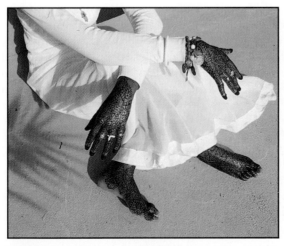

Perhaps the oldest means of artistic expression is body decorating. Shown here are a Moroccan woman, whose hands and feet are dyed with henna (to celebrate a royal wedding), and a tattooed Asian man.

that became the rivers. To make the mountains, he piled dirt up with his hands. Once his legs grew, *Odziózo's* task was made easier; by merely extending his legs, he made the tributaries of the main streams.

Anthropologist Gordon Day has described *Odziózo's* last act of landscape transformation as follows:

> It was Odziózo who laid out the river channels and lake basins and shaped the hills and mountains. Just how long he took is a subject which Abenakis, only recently deceased, used to discuss over their campfires. At last he was finished, and like Jehovah in Genesis, he surveyed his handiwork and found it was good. The last work he made was Lake Champlain and this he found especially good. It was his masterpiece. He liked it so much that he climbed onto a rock in Burlington Bay and changed himself into stone so that he could better sit there and enjoy the spectacle through the ages. He still likes it, because he is still there and used to be given offerings of tobacco as long as Abenakis went this way by canoe, a practice which continued until about 1940. The rock is also called Odziózo, since it is the Transformer himself.[2]

Such a myth, insofar as it is believed, accepted, and perpetuated in a culture, may be said to express a part of the world view of a people: the unexpressed but implicit conceptions of their place in nature and of the limits and workings of their world. (This concept we discussed in Chapters 5 and 12.) Extrapolating from the details of the Abenaki myth, we might arrive at the conclusion that these people recognize a kinship among all living things; after all, they were all part of the same creation, and humans were even made from living wood. Moreover, an attempt to make them of nonliving stone was not satisfactory. This idea of a closeness between all living things led the Abenaki to show special respect to the animals that they hunted in order to sustain their own lives. For example, when one killed a beaver, muskrat, or waterfowl, one couldn't unceremoniously toss their bones into the nearest garbage pit. Proper respect demanded that their bones be returned to the water, with a request that their kind be continued. Similarly, before eating meat, an offering of grease was placed on the fire to thank *Tabaldak*. More generally, waste was to

be avoided, so as not to offend the animals. Failure to respect their rights would result in their no longer being willing to sacrifice their lives, that people might live.

In transforming himself into stone, in order to enjoy his work for all eternity, *Odziózo* may be seen as setting an example for people; they should see the beauty in things as they are, and not seek to alter what is already so good. To question the goodness of existing reality would be to call into question the judgement of an important deity. It is characteristic of an explanatory myth, such as this one, that the unknown will be simplified and explained in terms of the known. This myth accounts in terms of human experience for the existence of rivers, mountains, lakes, and other features of the landscape, as well as for humans and all other living things. It also serves to sanction particular attitudes and behaviors. It is a product of creative imagination, and it is a work of art, as well as a potentially religious statement.

One aspect of mythology that has attracted a good deal of interest over the years is the similarity of certain themes in the stories of peoples living in separate parts of the world. One of these themes is the myth of matriarchy, or one-time rule by women. In a number of societies, stories tell about a time when women ruled over men. Eventually, so these stories go, men were forced to rise up and assert their dominance over women, in order to combat their tyranny or incompetence (or both). In the nineteenth century, a number of eminent scholars interpreted such myths as evidence for an early stage of matriarchy in the evolution of human culture, an idea that has recently been revived by some feminists. Although a number of societies are known in which the two sexes relate to each other as equals (Western Abenaki society was one), never have anthropologists found one in which women rule over, or dominate, men. The interesting thing about myths of matriarchy is that they are generally found in societies in which men dominate women, while at the same time the latter have considerable autonomy.[3] Under such conditions, male dominance is insecure, and a rationale is needed to justify it. Thus, myths of men overthrowing women and taking control mirror an existing paradoxical relationship between the two sexes.

[2]Gordon M. Day, quoted in William A. Haviland and Marjory W. Power, *The Original Vermonters: Native Inhabitants, Past and Present* (Hanover, N.H.: University Press of New England, 1981), p. 189.

[3]Peggy Reeves Sanday, *Female Power and Male Dominance: On the Origins of Sexual Inequality* (Cambridge: Cambridge University Press, 1981), p. 181.

Legends: Stories told as true, set in the post-creation world.

The analysis and interpretation of myths have been carried to great lengths, becoming a field of study almost unto itself. It is certain that myth making is an extremely important kind of human creativity, and the study of the myth-making process and its results can give some valuable clues to the way people perceive and think about their world. The dangers and problems of interpretation, however, are great. Several questions arise. Are myths literally believed or perhaps accepted symbolically or emotionally as a different kind of truth? To what extent do myths actually determine or reflect human behavior? Can an outsider read into a myth the same meaning that it has in its own culture? How do we account for contradictory myths in the same culture? New myths arise and old ones die. Is it then the content or the structure of the myth that is important? All of these questions deserve, and are currently receiving, serious consideration.

LEGEND

Less problematical, but perhaps more complex than myth, is the legend. **Legends** are stories told as true, set in the post-creation world. An example of a modern urban legend in the United States is one about a woman on welfare in Chicago. Supposedly, her ability to collect something like 103 welfare checks under different names enabled her to live lavishly. Although proven false, the story has continued to be told as if true, as all legends are. This particular legend illustrates a number of features all such narratives share: They cannot be attributed to any known author, they always exist in multiple versions, but in spite of variation, they are told with sufficient detail to be plausible, and they tell us something about the societies in which they are found. In this case, we learn something about racism in U.S. society (the story is generally told by whites, who identify the woman as a black), social policy (the existence of government policies to help the poor), and attitudes towards the poor (distrust, if not dislike).

American Indian peoples revere the earth as the source of all life, a concept reflected in this picture by Hopi artist Waldo Nootzka. In it, corn—the fruit of the earth—represents fertility.

As this example shows, legends (no more than myths) are not confined to nonliterate, nonindustrialized societies. Commonly, legends consist of pseudo-historical narratives that account for the deeds of heroes, the movements of peoples, and the establishment of local customs, typically with a mixture of realism and the supernatural or extraordinary. As stories, they are not necessarily believed or disbelieved, but they usually serve to entertain as well as to instruct and to inspire or bolster pride in family, tribe, or nation.

To a degree, in literate states such as the United States, the function of legends has been taken over by history. Yet much of what passes for history, as one historian has put it, consists of "the myths we develop to make ourselves feel better about who we are."[4] (The word *myth* is used here in its popular

[4]Mark Stoler, "To Tell the Truth," *Vermont Visions*, 82, No. 3 (1982):3.

Epics: Long oral narratives, sometimes in poetry or rhythmic prose, recounting the glorious events in the life of a real or legendary person.

---

sense.) The trouble is that history does not always tell people what they want to hear about themselves or, conversely, it tells them things that they would prefer not to hear. By projecting their culture's hopes and expectations onto the record of the past, they seize upon and even exaggerate some past events, while ignoring or giving scant attention to others. Although this often takes place unconsciously, so strong is the motivation to transform history into legend that states have often gone so far as to deliberately rewrite it, as when the Aztecs in the reign of their fifteenth-century king Itzcoatl rewrote their history in a way befitting their position of dominance in ancient Mexico. An example from the colonial past of the United States may be seen in the deliberate "slanting" (and in some cases destruction) of written documents by the Puritan authorities of colonial New England, so that their policies toward Indians might be seen in the most favorable light.[5] In modern times, the Soviet Union was particularly well-known for similar practices. Historians, in their attempts to separate fact from fiction, frequently incur the wrath of people who will not willingly abandon what they wish to believe is true, whether or not it really is.

Long legends, sometimes in poetry or in rhythmic prose, are known as **epics.** In parts of West and Central Africa there are remarkably elaborate and formalized recitations of extremely long legends, lasting several hours, and even days. These long narratives have been described as veritable encyclopedias of the most diverse aspects of a culture, with direct and indirect statements about history, institutions, relationships, values, and ideas. Epics are typically found in nonliterate societies with a form of state political organization; they serve to transmit and preserve a culture's legal and political precedents and practices. The Mwindo epic of the Nyanga people, the Lianja epic of the Mongo, and the Kambili epic of the Mande, for example, have

been the subject of extensive and rewarding study by French, British, and American anthropologists in the last several years.

Legends may incorporate mythological details, especially when they make appeal to the supernatural, and are therefore not always clearly distinct from myth. The legend about Mwindo follows him through the earth, the atmosphere, the underworld, and the remote sky, and gives a complete picture of the Nyanga people's view of the organization and limits of the world. Legends may also incorporate proverbs and incidental tales, and thus be related to other forms of verbal art as well. A recitation of the legend of Kambili, for example, has been said to include as many as 150 proverbs.

Below is an example of a short legend that instructs, traditional with the Western Abenakis of northwestern New England and southern Quebec.

> This is a story of a lonesome little boy who used to wander down to the riverbank at Odanak or downhill toward the two swamps. He used to hear someone call his name but when he got to the swamp pond, there was no one to be seen or heard. But when he went back, he heard his name called again. As he was sitting by the marshy bank waiting, an old man came and asked him why he was waiting. When the boy told him, the old man said that the same thing happened long ago. What he heard was the Swamp Creature, and [he] pointed out the big tussocks of grass where it hid; having called out, it would sink down behind them. The old man said: "It just wants to drown you. If you go out there you will sink in the mud. You better go home!"[6]

The moral of this story is quite simple: swamps are dangerous places; stay away from them. When told well, the story is a lot more effective in keeping children away from swamps than just telling them, "Don't go near swamps."

For the anthropologist, a major significance of the secular and apparently realistic portions of legends, whether long or short, is in the clues they provide to what constitutes approved or model ethical behavior in a culture. The subject matter of legends is essentially problem-solving, and the content is likely to include combat, warfare, confrontations, and physical and psychological tri-

---

[5]Francis Jennings, *The Invasion of America* (New York: Norton, 1976), p. 182.

[6]Gordon M. Day, quoted in the film *Prehistoric Life in the Champlain Valley,* by Thomas C. Vogelman and others (Burlington, Vt.: Department of Anthropology, University of Vermont, 1972).

als of many kinds. Certain questions may be answered explicitly or implicitly. Does the culture justify homicide? What kinds of behavior are considered to be brave or cowardly? What is the etiquette of combat or warfare? Is there a concept of altruism or self-sacrifice? Here again, however, there are pitfalls in the process of interpreting art in relation to life. It is always possible that certain kinds of behavior are acceptable or even admirable, with the distance or objectivity afforded by art, but are not at all so approved in daily life. In North American culture, murderers, charlatans, and rakes have sometimes become popular "heroes" and the subjects of legends; we would object, however, to the inference of an outsider that we necessarily approved or wanted to emulate the morality of Billy the Kid or Jesse James.

TALE

The term **tale** is a nonspecific label for a third category of creative narratives, those that are purely secular, nonhistorical, and recognized as fiction for entertainment, though they may draw a moral or teach a practical lesson, as well. Consider this brief summary of a tale from Ghana, known as "Father, Son, and Donkey":

> A father and his son farmed their corn, sold it, and spent part of the profit on a donkey. When the hot season came, they harvested their yams and prepared to take them to storage, using their donkey. The father mounted the donkey and they all three proceeded on their way until they met some people. "What? You lazy man!" the people said to the father. "You let your young son walk barefoot on this hot ground while you ride on a donkey? For shame!" The father yielded his place to the son, and they proceeded until they came to an old woman. "What? You useless boy!" said the old woman. "You ride on the donkey and let your poor father walk barefoot on this hot ground? For shame!" The son dismounted, and both father and son walked on the road, leading the donkey behind them until they came to an old man. "What? You

The telling of legends and tales is no less important in the education of children in the United States than it is on the Ivory Coast.

> foolish people!" said the old man. "You have a donkey and you walk barefoot on the hot ground instead of riding?" And so it goes. Listen: When you are doing something and other people come along, just keep on doing what you like.

This is precisely the kind of tale that is of special interest in traditional folklore studies. It is an internationally popular "numbskull" tale; versions of it have been recorded in India, the Middle East, the Balkans, Italy, Spain, England, and the United States, as well as in West Africa. It is classified or catalogued as exhibiting a basic **motif** or story

situation—father and son trying to please everyone —one of the many thousands that have been found to recur in world folktales. In spite of variations in detail, every version will be found to have about the same basic structure in the sequence of events, sometimes called the syntax of the tale; a peasant father and son work together, a beast of burden is purchased, the three set out on a short excursion, the father rides and is criticized, the son rides and is criticized, both walk and are criticized, and a conclusion is drawn.

Tales of this sort with an international distribution sometimes raise more problems than they solve: Which one is the original? What is the path of its diffusion? Could it be sheer coincidence that different cultures have come up with the same motif and syntax, or could it be a case of independent invention with similar tales developing in similar situations in response to like causes? A surprisingly large number of motifs in European and African tales are traceable to ancient sources in India. Is this good evidence of a spread of culture from a "cradle" of civilization, or is it an example of diffusion of tales in contiguous areas? There are, of course, purely local tales, as well as tales with such a wide distribution. Within any particular culture it will probably be found possible to catego-rize local types of tales: animal, human experience, trickster, dilemma, ghost, moral, scatological, non-sense, and so on. In West Africa there is a remark-able prevalence of animal stories, for example, with such creatures as the spider, the rabbit, and the hyena as the protagonists. Many were carried to the slave-holding areas of the Americas; the Uncle Remus stories about Br'er Rabbit, Br'er Fox, and other animals may be a survival of this tradition.

The significance of tales for the anthropologist rests partly in this matter of their distribution. They provide evidence for either cultural contacts or cultural isolation, and for limits of influence and cultural cohesion. It has been debated for decades now, for example, to what extent the culture of West Africa was transmitted to the southeast United-ed States. So far as folktales are concerned, one school of folklorists has always found and insisted on European origins; another school, somewhat more recently, points to African prototypes. The anthropologist is interested, however, in more than these questions of distribution. Like legends, tales very often illustrate local solutions to universal human ethical problems, and in some sense they state a moral philosophy. The anthropologist sees that whether the tale of the father, the son, and the donkey originated in West Africa or arrived there

The "little songs" of the Awlad Áli Bedouins punctuate conversations carried out while performing every day chores, like making bread, as these girls are doing.

from Europe or the Middle East, the very fact that it is told in West Africa suggests that it states something valid for that culture. The tale's lesson of a necessary degree of self-confidence in the face of arbitrary social criticism is therefore something that can be read into the culture's values and beliefs.

OTHER VERBAL ARTS

Myths, legends, and tales, prominent as they are in anthropological studies, turn out to be no more important than the other verbal arts in many cultures. In the culture of the Awlad 'Ali Bedouins of Egypt's western desert, for example, poetry is a lively and active verbal art, especially as a vehicle for personal expression and private communication. Among these people, there are two forms of poetry, one being the elaborately structured and heroic poems chanted or recited by men only on ceremonial occasions and in specific public contexts. The other is the *ghinnáwa*, or "little songs" that punctuate everyday conversations. Simple in structure, these deal with personal matters and feelings more appropriate to informal social situations, and are regarded by older men as the unimportant productions of women and youths. In spite of this official devaluation in the male-dominated society of the Bedouins, however, they play a vital part in peoples' daily lives. As is often true of folklore in general, they provide a sanctioned outlet for thoughts or opinions that are otherwise taboo.

ORIGINAL STUDY

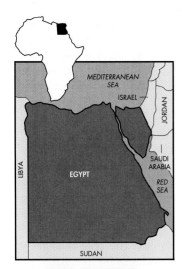

THE "LITTLE SONGS" OF THE AWLAD 'ALI[7]

It is clear that individuals are shielded from the consequences of making statements and expressing sentiments that contravene the moral system if they do so in poetry. By sharing these "immoral" sentiments only with intimates and veiling them in impersonal traditional formulas, they even demonstrate that they have a certain control, which actually enhances their moral standing. But if we turn from how individuals use poems to the poetry itself as a cultural discourse, as a set of rule-bound statements that represent a vision of reality, an even more intriguing set of questions presents itself. If the disjunction between the messages carried by the two discourses occurs not just on the individual level but on the cultural level as well, and if ordinary discourse is that generated in accordance with the values that support the dominant social and political system, then is poetry the discourse of antistructure? If poetry is associated with opposition to the system, why is it not condemned or repressed? Why is it glorified? The *ghinnáwa's* antistructural character is evident not just in the type of sentiments regularly carried by it, but in its association as well. Its closest association is with the traditional Bedouin romance. Poems are always included in love tales that celebrate the often tragic course of romance, a force usually condemned as threatening to the social system. Thwarted love, especially between a man and a woman from different tribes, is the theme of the most poignant Bedouin love stories, which are recounted as true tales of the distant past. In a few, cousins fall in love but are prevented from marrying by the girl's wealthy father who does not wish to let her marry his poor brother's son; from what I could gather, those stories usually ended happily with the young nephew triumphing. More commonly, the sweethearts are unrelated, and their love is thwarted by the girl's cousin, as in the following archetypal love story:

Once upon a time there was a boy and a girl who were in love with each other. The girl's father's brother's son heard about this and was furious. He swore she would never marry the boy and claimed her . . . for himself.

Now, the girl and the boy used to meet secretly to talk at the tent of an old lady, a neighbor of theirs. One day, the boy announced that he was leaving on a journey. He was going to the oasis of Siwa to get dates. He promised that after he returned, he would marry the girl. He said to her:

> Happiness in my absence is a failing
> and grief between us the sign of love . . .

With that he set off with a caravan of camels. He was away for a long time. On his way back, only two days from home, he fell ill and died. He had instructed his companion earlier, "If I die on the way, please carry my body home so my family can bury me." So his companion loaded his corpse on a camel and journeyed the rest of the way home.

When his family heard what had happened, they wailed and cried. Meanwhile, the girl had seen the camels returning to his camp but wondered, "Why don't I hear trilling and the firing of rifles [signs of celebration]?" She ran to find out, and when she did, she wailed and cried with his kinswomen.

Her cousin discovered that she had gone to her lover's camp and followed her. He ran in and grabbed her from among the mourners and started beating her. She tried to run away, but he chased her, beating her until she fell dead, right on the fresh grave of her sweetheart.

Her cousin was enraged. He swore at her," Even in death you're a slut!" He demanded that they not bury her near the boy, so they carried her about a kilometer away and buried her.

After a while, a palm tree sprang from the head of the boy's grave and a tree sprang from the head of the girl's. The trees grew and grew until their fronds crossed high in the sky. The cousin grew angry when he saw this, thinking, "She still can't keep away from him, even in death?" So he went to find a woodcutter to cut down the trees.

As the woodcutter was trying to chop down the tree that grew over her grave, the axe flew out of his hand and into his eye, blinding him. He went home and fell ill. In his sleep a vision of the boy came to him and said:

> May God cut you down, oh woodcutter,
> you cut the rope as they were filling [at the well] . . .

Then he parted with the words:

> Love must bring forth fruits
> which join each other in their sky . . .

This story has several remarkable features. It celebrates the desires of individuals against the demands of the system, as codified in the first cousin's right to his father's brother's daughter—the cousin seeks to enforce the system as the girl and her lover refuse to accept it. The

heroine is both defiant and a "slut," hence lacking in modesty; her tragic end may hold a lesson for Awlad 'Ali about the ultimate power of the system. At the same time, however, she and her sweetheart are heroic, and their defiance ends in a victory of sorts. People who listen to such tales admire the behavior of lovers and do not condemn it as immoral, and they appreciate the poetry that expresses the lover's feelings.

Poetry is associated with antistructure in ways other than this explicit link to romance and sexuality. People perceive poetry as un-Islamic and poetic recitation as impious, just as "crying" at funerals is wrong from a religious point of view (and so is not done by women who have been on the pilgrimage to Mecca). The fact that the very word "to sing" . . . cannot be said in mixed-sex company suggests its antistructural quality. Another indication is that people say they *tahashsham* or are embarrassed/ashamed/modest about singing in front of nonintimates, especially elders. Elders, too, avoid settings such as weddings and sheep shearings where, at least in the past, *ghinnáwas* were publicly sung. Even the rhetoric of poetry gives it an antistructural flavor, as if poetry were the language of the unsocialized child as opposed to the ordinary discourse of adult conformity. The final and most persuasive link is in who sings or recites *ghinnáwas*. Although older men occasionally recite them, *ghinnáwas* are most closely associated with youths and women, the disadvantaged dependents who least embody the ideals of Bedouin society and have least to gain in the system as structured. Poetry is, in so many ways, the discourse of opposition to the system and of defiance of those who represent it: it is antistructure just as it is antimorality.

The existence of dissident or subversive discourses is probably not unusual. What may be peculiar to Awlad 'Ali is that their discourse of rebellion is both culturally elaborated and sanctioned. Although poetry refers to personal life, it is not individual, spontaneous, idiosyncratic, or unofficial but public, conventional, and formulaic—a highly developed art. More important, this poetic discourse of defiance is not condemned, or even just tolerated, as well it might be given all the constraints of time and place and form that bind it. Poetry is a privileged discourse in Awlad 'Ali society. Like other Arabs, and perhaps like many oral cultures, the Bedouins cherish poetry and other verbal arts. Everyone listens attentively whenever poems are recited or sung. People memorize poems, repeat them, and are moved by them. For Awlad 'Ali, poetry represents what is best in their culture, what they consider distinctively Bedouin. Poetry is associated with the glorious past, when Awlad 'Ali lived without Egyptian government interference, migrating freely, herding sheep, riding horses, and being brave and tough.

People are thrilled by poetry. They are drawn to *ghinnáwas*, and at the same time they consider them risqué, against religion, and slightly improper—as befits something antistructural. This ambivalence about poetry is significant, and it makes sense only in terms of the cultural meaning of opposition. Because ordinary discourse is informed by the values of honor and modesty, the moral correlates of the ideology that

upholds the Awlad 'Ali social and political system, we would expect the antistructural poetic discourse with its contradictory messages, to be informed by an opposing set of values. This is not the case. Poetry as a discourse of defiance of the system symbolizes freedom —the ultimate value of the system and the essential entailment of the honor code.

In all cultures the words of songs constitute a kind of poetry. Poetry and stories recited with gesture, movement, and props become drama. Drama combined with dance, music, and spectacle becomes a public celebration. The more we look at the individual arts, the clearer it becomes that they are often interrelated and interdependent. The verbal arts are, in fact, simply differing manifestations of the same creative imagination that produces music and the plastic arts.

[7]Lila Abu-Lughod, *Veiled Sentiments* (Berkeley, Calif.: University of California Press, 1986), pp. 248–252

THE ART OF MUSIC

The study of music in specific cultural settings, beginning in the nineteenth century with the collection of folksongs, has developed into a specialized field, called **ethnomusicology.** Like the study of folktales for their own sake, ethnomusicology is at the same time related to and somewhat independent of anthropology. Nevertheless, it is possible to sort out from the various concerns of the field several concepts that are of interest in general anthropology.

In order to talk intelligently about the verbal arts of a culture, it is, of course, desirable to know as much as possible about the language itself. In order to talk about the music of a culture, it is equally desirable to know the language of music—that is, its conventions. The way to approach a totally unfamiliar kind of musical expression is to learn first how it functions in respect to melody, rhythm, and form.

In general, human music is said to differ from natural music—the songs of birds, wolves, and

Ethnomusicology: The study of a society's music in terms of its cultural setting.

whales, for example—in being almost everywhere perceived in terms of a repertory of tones at fixed or regular intervals from each other: in other words, a scale. We have made closed systems out of a formless range of possible sounds by dividing the distance between a tone and its first overtone or sympathetic vibration (which always has exactly twice as many vibrations as the basic tone) into a series of measured steps. In the Western or European system, the distance between the basic tone and the first overtone is called the octave; the interval leading to it consists of seven steps—five whole tones and two semitones —which are named with the letters A through G. The eighth step (*octo* = eight) is the overtone. The whole tones are further divided into semitones, for a total working scale of twelve tones. Westerners learn at an early age to recognize and imitate this system and its conventions, and it comes to sound natural. Yet the overtone series, on which it is based, is the only part of it that can be considered a wholly natural phenomenon.

One of the most common alternatives to the semitonal system is the pentatonic system, which divides the octave into five nearly equidistant tones. In Japan there is a series of different pentatonic scales, in which some semitones are employed. In Java there are scales of both five and seven equal steps, which have no relation to the intervals Europeans and European Americans hear as natural in their system. In Arabic and Persian music there

Tonality: In music, scale systems and their modifications.

are smaller units of a third of a tone (some of which Westerners may accidentally produce on an out-of-tune piano), with scales of 17 and 24 steps in the octave. There are even quarter-tone scales in India and subtleties of interval shading that are nearly indistinguishable to many a Western ear. Small wonder, then, that even when Westerners can hear what sounds like melody and rhythm in these systems, the total result may sound peculiar to them, or out of tune. The anthropologist needs a very practiced ear to learn to appreciate—perhaps even to tolerate—some of the music heard, and only some of the most skilled folksong collectors have attempted to notate and analyze the music of nonsemitonal systems.

Scale systems and their modifications comprise what is known as **tonality** in music. Tonality determines the possibilities and limits of both melody and harmony. Not much less complex than tonality is the matter of rhythm. Rhythm, whether regular or irregular, is an organizing factor in music, sometimes more important than the melodic line. Traditional European music is rather neatly measured into recurrent patterns of two, three, and four beats, with combinations of weak and strong beats to mark the division and form patterns. Non-European music is likely to move also in patterns of five, seven, or eleven, with complex arrangements of internal beats and sometimes polyrhythms: one instrument or singer going in a pattern of three beats, for example while another is in a pattern of five or seven. Polyrhythms are frequent in the drum music of West Africa, which shows remarkable precision in the overlapping of rhythmic lines. In addition to polyrhythms, non-European music may also contain shifting rhythms: a pattern of three, for example, followed by a pattern of two, or five, with little or no regular recurrence or repetition of any one pattern, though the patterns themselves are fixed and identifiable as units.

Although it is not necessarily the concern of anthropologists to untangle all these complicated

This man carries a West African talking drum under his elbow. Such drums "talk" by copying the distinctive speech patterns of West African languages, which are tonal.

technical matters, they will want to know enough to be aware of the degree of skill or artistry involved in a performance and to have some measure of the extent to which people in a culture have learned to practice and respond to this often important creative activity. Moreover, as with myths, legends, and tales, the distribution of musical forms and instruments can reveal much about cultural contact or isolation.

FUNCTIONS OF MUSIC

Even without concern for technical matters, the anthropologist can profitably investigate the function of music in a society. First, rarely has a culture been reported to be without any kind of music. Bone flutes and whistles up to 30,000 years old have been found by archaeologists. Nor have historically known food-foraging peoples been without their music. In the Kalahari desert, for example, a !Kung hunter off by himself would play a tune for himself on his bow simply to help while away the time.

While songs and dances are often performed in Western society for enjoyment, in non-Western societies they are often more important as adjuncts to ritual. At the top, people who live on the Sepik River in Papua New Guinea dance to mourn for a dead child.

(Long before anyone thought of beating swords into plowshares, some genius discovered—when and where we do not know—that bows could be used not just to kill, but to make music.) In northern New England, Abenaki shamans played cedar flutes to call game, lure enemies, and attract women. In addition, a drum over which two raw-hide strings were stretched to produce a buzzing sound, thought to represent singing, gave the sha-man the power to communicate with the spirit world. But however played, and for whatever rea-son, music (like all art) is an individual creative skill that one can cultivate and be proud of, whether from a sense of accomplishment or the sheer pleasure of performing; and it is a form of social behavior through which there is a communication or sharing of feelings and life experience with other humans. At the same time, because the individual's

creativity is constrained by the traditions of his or her particular culture, each society's art is distinc-tive and helps to define its members' sense of identity.

The social function of music is perhaps most obvious in song. Songs very often express as much as tales the values and concerns of the group, but they do so with the increased formalism that results from the restrictions of closed systems of tonality, rhythm, and musical form. Early investigators of non-European song were struck by the apparent simplicity of pentatonic scales and a seemingly endless repetition of phrases. They often did not give sufficient credit to the formal function of repetition in such music, equating repetition with repetitiveness or lack of invention. A great deal of non-European music was dismissed as primitive and formless, and typically treated as trivial.

Repetition is, nevertheless, a fact of music, including European music, and a basic formal principle. Consider this little song from Nigeria:

Ijangbon l'o ra,
Ijangbon l'o ra,
Eni r'asho Oshomalo,
Ijangbon l'o ra.
(He buys trouble,
He buys trouble,
He who buys Oshomalo cloth,
He buys trouble.)

Several decades ago, the Oshomalo were cloth sellers in Egba villages who sold on credit, then harassed, intimidated, and even beat their custom-ers to make them pay before the appointed day. The message of the song is simple, and both words and music are the same for three lines out of four; the whole song may be repeated many times at will. What is it that produces this kind of artistic expression and makes it more than primitive trivia? A single Egba undoubtedly improvised the song first, reacting to a personal experience or observa-tion, lingering on one of its elements by repeating it. The repetition gives the observation not empha-sis but symbolic form, and therefore a kind of concreteness or permanence. In this concrete form, made memorable and attractive with melody and rhythm, the song was taken up by other Egba, perhaps with some musical refinements or embel-lishments from more creative members of the group, including clapping or drumming to mark the rhythm. Thus a bit of social commentary was

Incessant repetition is found not only in non-Western music but in some Western music as well.

crystallized and preserved even after the situation had passed into history.

Whether the content of songs is didactic, satirical, inspirational, religious, political, or purely emotional, the important thing is that the formless has been given form, and feelings are communicated in a symbolic and memorable way that can be repeated and shared. The group is consequently united and has the sense that their experience, whatever it may be, has shape and meaning.

THE ART OF SCULPTURE

In the broadest sense, sculpture is art in the round. Any three-dimensional product of the creative imagination may be called a piece of sculpture: A ceremonial knife, a decorative pot, a handcrafted lute, an ornamental gate, a funerary monument, or a public building displays the same essential artistic process as a statue, a mask, or a figurine. All of these human creations represent an imaginative organization of materials in space. The artist has given tangible shape to his or her feelings and perceptions, creating or re-creating symbolically meaningful form out of formlessness. In a narrower

sense, sculpture means only those artifacts that serve no immediate utilitarian purpose and are fashioned from hard or semipermanent materials. It is, however, difficult to state unequivocally what may or may not qualify as a piece of sculpture, even with this limitation. Are the beautiful and highly imaginative tiny brass figurines of Ashanti, for example, formerly used as weights for measuring out quantities of gold, not to be considered sculpture, even though the somewhat larger brass figurines of comparable design in Dahomey, which have never had a practical use, are obviously to be so considered? Or should we perhaps now call the Ashanti figurines sculpture, as we now do, because they are no longer put to use?

ART AND CRAFT

Use of the word *sculpture* in English seems to impose a distinction between types of creative activity where none may in fact exist. One solution is to substitute the modern term "plastic art," but the phenomenon remains the same. Objects that are obviously skillfully made but still do not quite qualify as sculpture by virtue of being somewhat trivial, low in symbolic content, or impermanent—

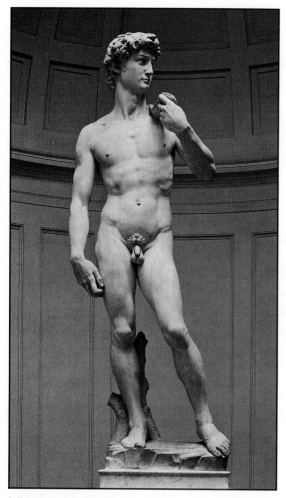

Michelangelo's *David.*

As a type of symbolic expression, sculpture may be representational, imitating closely the forms of nature—or abstract, drawing from natural forms but representing only their basic patterns or arrangements. Representational sculpture is partly abstract to the extent that it generalizes from nature and abstracts patterns of ideal beauty, ugliness, or typical expressions of emotion. Michelangelo's *David* is representational sculpture, clearly depicting a human being; it is also abstract insofar as it generalizes an ideal of masculine beauty, quiet strength, and emotional calm, therefore functioning symbolically. Henry Moore's gigantic women with holes through their midsections are abstractions, using nature but exaggerating and deliberately transforming some of its shapes for the purpose of expressing a particular feeling toward them.

WEST AFRICAN SCULPTURE

West African sculpture, only comparatively recently studied and described in adequate detail, is an especially rich non-Western tradition that may help illustrate some of the anthropological aspects of representational and abstract sculpture, its subjects, materials, and meanings.

Ancestor worship and reverence of royalty have found expression in a realistic or portrait-style sculpture throughout the region of the Niger and Zaire River basins. Probably the most dramatically realistic are the so-called Benin bronzes: hundreds of finely detailed heads of royal ancestors, produced first at the sacred Yoruba city of Ife (in present-day Nigeria) in the fifteenth century, and later in the Benin capital itself. Upon the death of a ruler of Benin, a memorial head was cast in bronze to be placed on the shrine of the departed ruler. Most of these heads were carried off to England at the end of the nineteenth century, and they have served as a forcible reminder to Westerners that the Mediterranean region is not the only source of fine realistic sculpture.

In addition to the Benin bronzes, the royal statues of the Bakuba kings in the Zaire River region, the ancestor figures of the Guro on the Ivory Coast, the secular and satirical representations of Europeans by the Yoruba in Nigeria, and the small brasses depicting the royalty and animals of the Fon in Dahomey are also naturalistic in detail, and are obviously often intended to repre-

by the standards of the culture—are generally known and considered as the products of craft (or, in modern times, industry). An automobile, for example, however beautifully it may be designed, however proudly it may be displayed in front of the house as an object for admiration, and however cleverly one may interpret its parts and its functions as symbolic in U.S. culture, is for North Americans above all a mass-produced consumable, and to treat it as sculpture would be misrepresenting its *usual* value in U.S. society. Furthermore, we must also consider the intention of the creator. What North Americans call sculpture or plastic art is not ordinarily artistic by accident or through after-the-fact interpretation, but by design on the part of some recognized "artist." General Motors does *not* intentionally produce sculpture.

Left: Head of one of the kings of Benin; cast in bronze at the time of his death. *Right:* A wooden figure made by the Yoruba of Nigeria, probably in the 1920s as a cult item. It served as a container for kola nuts used in divination ceremonies.

sent real persons or animals in characteristic moods or poses. Features and proportions may be somewhat stylized according to regional conventions of what is appropriate or possible in sculpture: Heads may be disproportionately large, necks elongated, and sexual parts either exaggerated or minimized. It is of note that most of these sculptures come from cultures in which subsistence techniques were efficient enough to produce a surplus, which was used to support a variety of occupational specialists. The artist was one such specialist, much of whose work was commissioned by other specialists, such as priests and government officials.

The majority of West African sculpture is abstract or expressionistic—giving form to human feelings and attitudes toward gods, spirits, other humans, and animals. Generalizations about the nonrepresentational styles and purposes for the region are, however, almost impossible. Every West African culture that produces or has produced sculpture has its own identifiable styles, and this artistic cohesion undoubtedly reinforces the sense of ethnic identity and social unity of the group. A Fon recognizes a Yoruba mask, and is disassociated from whatever symbolic significance it has for the Yoruba. Materials as well as styles differ in neighboring cultures. The most common material is wood, but there is also regional use of brass, iron, terra-cotta, mud, and raffia. Sculpture may be rubbed with ash, smoked in banana leaves, oiled, waxed, painted, and adorned with cowrie shells, teeth, iron or brass nails, strips of metal, or cloth.

ANTHROPOLOGY APPLIED

PROTECTING CULTURAL HERITAGES

In these last years of the twentieth century, the time is long past when the anthropologist could go out and describe small tribal groups in remote places that had not been "contaminated" by contact with Westerners. Not only are there few such groups in the world today, but those that do remain face strong pressures to abandon their traditional ways in the name of progress. All too often, tribal peoples are made to forfeit their indigenous identity and are pressed into a mold that allows them neither the opportunity nor the motivation to rise above the lowest rung of the social ladder. From an autonomous people able to provide for their own needs, with pride and a strong sense of their own identity as a people, they are transformed into a deprived underclass with neither pride nor a sense of their own identity, often despised by more fortunate members of some multinational state in which they live.

The basic right of groups of people to be themselves and not be deprived of their own distinctive cultural identities is and should be our paramount consideration, and will be dealt with in the final two chapters of this book. There are, however, additional reasons to be concerned about the disappearance of the societies with which anthropologists have been so often concerned. For one thing, the need for information about them has become steadily more apparent. If we are ever to have a realistic understanding of that elusive thing called human nature, we need reliable data on all humans. There is more to it than this, though; once a tribal society is gone, it is lost to humanity, unless an adequate record of it exists. When this happens, humanity is the poorer for the loss. Hence, anthropologists have in a sense rescued many such societies from oblivion. This not only helps to preserve human heritage, it may also be important to an ethnic group that, having become Westernized, wishes to rediscover and reassert its past cultural identity. Better yet, of course, is to find ways to prevent the loss of cultural traditions in the first place.

To the Pomo Indians of California, the art of basketmaking has been important for their sense of who they are since before the coming of European settlers. Recognized for their skilled techniques and aesthetic artistry, Pomo baskets—some of the finest in the world—are prized by both museums and private collectors alike. Nevertheless, the art of Pomo basketmaking was threatened in the 1970s by the impending construction of the Warm Springs Dam-Lake Sonoma Project to the north of San Francisco. The effect of this project would be to wipe out virtually all existing habitat for a particular species of sedge essential for the weaving of Pomo baskets. Accordingly, a coalition of archaeologists, Native Americans, and others with objections to the project brought suit in federal district court. As it happened, the U.S. Army Corps of Engineers had recently hired anthropologist Richard N. Lerner for its San Francisco District Office to advise on sociocultural factors associated with water resources programs in northwestern California. One of Lerner's first tasks, therefore, was to undertake studies of the problem, and to find ways to overcome it.*

After comprehensive archaeological, ethnographic, and other studies were completed in 1976, Lerner succeeded in having the Pomo basketry materials recognized by the National Register of Historic Places as "historic property," requiring the corps of engineers to find ways of mitigating the adverse impact dam construction would have. The result was a complex ethnobotanical project, developed and implemented by Lerner. Working in concert with Pomo Indians as well as botanists, 48,000 sedge plants were relocated onto nearly three acres of suitable lands downstream from the dam. By the fall of 1983, the sedge was doing well enough to be harvested, and proved to be of excellent quality. Since this initial harvest, groups of weavers have returned each year, and the art of Pomo Indian basketmaking appears to be safe for the time being.

*Richard N. Lerner, "Preserving Plants for Pomos," in *Anthropological Praxis: Translating Knowledge into Action*, ed. Robert M. Wulff and Shirley J. Fiske (Boulder, Colo.: Westview 1987):212–222.

Symbolic Content

In all these varieties of sculpture, whatever their style and material, anthropologists are interested in exactly what is abstracted from nature and why. They are also interested in the extent to which traditions are perpetuated, and what meanings may be developing or changing. It appears that any single piece of sculpture in West Africa may be interpreted in terms of its symbolic significance for

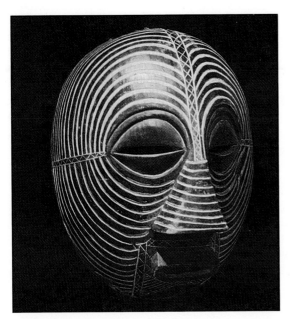

Mask made by the Baluba of Zaire.

the group, which is well known by the people who make and look at the sculpture. Consequently the anthropologist has only to ask.

A small wooden figure of a person, with a head, rudimentary limbs, and a large trunk purposely riddled with holes, may be found among the Balega of the northeast Zaire region. The figure is known as a *katanda*, meaning the scattering of red ants when attacked; it is interpreted as symbolizing the bad effect of internal fighting on the unity of local descent groups. The *kanaga* mask of the Dogon in Upper Volta is an elongated head with triangular eyes, long pointed ears and nose, and a cap surmounted with an enormous crest, four or five times the size of the head, in the form of a double-armed cross. For young initiates the cross symbolizes a bird with outstretched wings, the beginning of active flight into life, and for older initiates of high rank its structure symbolizes a synthesis of contradictory or competing life forces. The *akua'ba* dolls of the Ashanti in Ghana, flat disc-headed figures on a long, narrow, legless body with a simple crosspiece for arms, are said to symbolize an Ashanti ideal of beauty in the high, wide forehead; the dolls are tucked into the waistcloths of young girls, who carry them like real babies, perhaps as talismans to assure their own physical development or that of their children.

Ritual Masks

The widest variety of expression in African sculpture is certainly to be found in the ritual mask. Styles range from the relatively realistic and serene faces made by the Baule on the Ivory Coast to the frightening, violent, and extroverted faces with

The ritual nature of much art is exemplified by this African rock art. The subject matter of this art consists of the visions experienced by shamans in trance states.

protruding eyes produced by the neighboring Ngere of Liberia. Theories about the symbolism of the masks have arisen beside the explanations of local informants, particularly in cases where certain masks are no longer produced or known. One of the more interesting is the notion that the unnatural features of some of the masks representing spirits of the dead are made systematically unnatural in order to suggest that the other world, or the spirit world, is somehow an opposite of this one: Noses are long instead of short, ears are large rather than small, eye cavities are hollow rather than filled, and so on. The mask, as well as other sculpture, therefore becomes, as much as the myth, an expression of world view. The sculptor again gives shape and meaning to that which is unknown.

As in musical expression, sculpture also crystallizes feeling in a form that can be shared and perpetuated. Much, though not all, African sculpture is impermanent because of the impermanent nature of its materials (50 years has been suggested as an average lifetime for a wooden figure exposed to weather), but it is generally considered a great shame when a mask or piece of sculpture disintegrates. An important piece of sculpture may be replaced by imitation—copied and perpetuated so that the traditions and beliefs may be preserved. There is often a ritual in mask making, with great care taken to preserve and copy exactly the traditional specifications. Similarly, there is still in some places a special reverence in the process of sculpting in general, and the soul of the wood must be respected with attendant rituals and beliefs. Traditional West African sculpture is currently in decline, but it is not by any means everywhere dead. An excursion beyond the major urban centers reveals continuing activity in this important kind of symbolic creativity.

Chapter Summary

Art is the creative use of the human imagination to interpret, understand, and enjoy life. It stems from the uniquely human ability to use symbols to give shape and significance to the physical world for more than just a utilitarian purpose. Anthropologists are concerned with art as a reflection of the cultural values and concerns of people.

Oral traditions denote the unwritten stories, beliefs, and customs of a culture. Verbal arts include narrative, drama, poetry, incantations, proverbs, riddles, and word games. Narratives, which have received the most study, have been divided into three categories: myths, legends, and tales.

Myths are basically sacred narratives that explain how the world came to be how it is. In describing an orderly universe, myths function to set standards for orderly behavior. Legends are stories told as if true that often recount the exploits of heroes, the movements of people, and the establishment of local customs. Epics, which are long legends in poetry or prose, are typically found in nonliterate societies with a form of state political organization. They serve to transmit and preserve a culture's legal and political practices. In literate states, these functions have been taken over to one degree or another by history. Anthropologists are interested in legends because they provide clues as to what constitutes model ethical behavior in a culture. Tales are fictional, secular, nonhistorical narratives that instruct as they entertain. Anthropological interest in tales centers in part on the fact that their distribution provides evidence of cultural contacts or cultural isolation.

The study of music in specific cultural settings has developed into the specialized field of ethnomusicology. Almost everywhere human music is perceived in terms of a scale. Scale systems and their modifications comprise tonality in music. Tonality determines the possibilities and limits of melody and harmony. Rhythm is an organizing factor in music. Traditional European music is measured into recurrent patterns of two, three, and four beats.

The social function of music is most obvious in song. Like tales, songs may express the concerns of the group, but with greater formalism because of the restrictions imposed by closed systems of tonality, rhythm, and musical form.

Sculpture is any three-dimensional product of the creative imagination fashioned from hard or semipermanent materials. Sculpted objects, such as a statue, a ceremonial knife, or a public building, represent an imaginative organization of materials in space. A more modern term for sculpture is *plastic art*. Certain objects, although skillfully made, do not qualify as sculpture. This may be because by the standards of the culture they are seen as trivial, low in symbolic content, or impermanent. Such objects are generally considered as the products of crafts—or in modern times, industry. Sculpture may be representational, imitating the forms of nature—or abstract, representing only basic patterns of natural forms. West African sculpture illustrates some of the anthropological aspects of representational and abstract sculpture in its subject matter, materials, and meanings.

Suggested Readings

Boas, Franz. *Primitive Art*. Gloucester, Mass.: Peter Smith, 1962.
Reprint of an old classic, which gives an analytical description of the basic traits of "primitive" art. Its treatment is based on two principles: the fundamental sameness of mental processes in all races and cultural forms of the present day, and the consideration of every cultural phenomenon in a historical context. It covers formal elements in art, symbolism, and style and has sections on "primitive" literature, music, and dance.

Dundes, Alan. *Interpreting Folk Lore*. Bloomington: Indiana University Press, 1980.
A collection of articles that assess the materials folklorists have amassed and classified; seeks to broaden and refine traditional assumptions about the proper subject matter and methods of folklore.

Hannah, Judith Lynne. *Dance, Sex and Gender*. Chicago: University of Chicago Press, 1988.
Like other forms of art, dances are social acts that contribute to the continuation and emergence of culture. One of the oldest—if not the oldest—art forms, dance shares the same instrument, the human body, with sexuality. This book, written for a broad, nonspecialist audience, explicitly examines sexuality and the construction of gender identities as they are played out in the production and visual imagery of dance.

Hatcher, Evelyn Payne. *Art as Culture: An Introduction to the Anthropology of Art*. New York: University Press of America, 1985.
This handy, clearly written book does a nice job of relating the visual arts to other aspects of culture. Topics include "The Technological Means," "The Psychological Perspective," "Social Contexts and Social Functions," "Art as Communication," and "The Time Dimension." Numerous line drawings help the reader to understand the varied forms of art in non-Western societies.

Merriam, Alan P. *The Anthropology of Music*. Chicago: Northwestern University Press, 1964.
This book focuses upon music as a complex of behavior, which resonates throughout all of culture: social organization, aesthetic activity, economics, and religion.

Otten, Charlotte M. *Anthropology and Art: Readings in Cross-Cultural Aesthetics*. Garden City, N.Y.: Natural History Press, 1971.
This is a collection of articles by anthropologists and art historians, with an emphasis on the functional relationships between art and culture.

SPIRIT MASK,

PAPUA NEW

GUINEA

PART V

INTRODUCTION

WITHOUT THE ABILITY TO

CONCEIVE NEW IDEAS AND

CHANGE EXISTING BEHAVIOR

PATTERNS, NO HUMAN

SOCIETY COULD SURVIVE.

HUMAN CULTURE, THOUGH

NEVER STATIC, IS

REMARKABLY STABLE, BUT IT

IS ALSO RESILIENT AND

THEREFORE ABLE TO ▶

▶ adapt to altered circumstances.

Understanding the processes of change, the subject of Chapter 15, is one of the most important and fundamental of anthropological goals. Unfortunately, the task is made difficult by the cultural biases of most modern North Americans, which predispose them to see change as a progressive process leading in a predictable and determined way to where they are now, and even on beyond into a future to which they are leading the way. So pervasive is this notion of progress that it motivates the thinking of North Americans in a great many ways of which they are hardly aware. Among other things, it leads them to view cultures not like their own as backward and underdeveloped; as two well-known economists put it, "we . . . have the feeling that we are encountering in the present the anachronistic counterparts of the static societies of antiquity."[1] Of course, they are no such thing; as we saw in Chapter 6, no culture is static, and cultures may be very highly developed in quite different ways. A simple analogy with the world of nature may be helpful here. In the course of evolution, single-celled organisms appeared long before vertebrate animals, and land vertebrates like mammals are relative latecomers indeed. Yet, single-celled organisms abound in the world today, not as relics of the past, but as creatures highly adapted to situations for which mammals are totally unsuited. Just because mammals got here late doesn't mean that a dog is "better" or "more progressive" than an amoeba.

Belief in progress and its inevitability has important implications for North Americans as well as others. For people in the United States, it means that change has become necessary for its own sake, for whatever they have today is, by definition, not as good as what they will have tomorrow. Put another way, whatever is old is, by virtue of that fact alone, inadequate, and should be gotten rid of, no matter how well it seems to be working. This virtually guarantees the continuing existence of significant dissatisfaction within the U.S. For others, the logic runs like this: If the old must inevitably give way to the new, then societies that North Americans perceive as being "old" or "out of the past" must also give way to the new. Since the

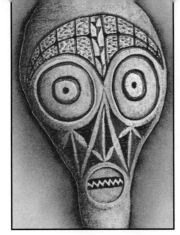

way of life in the United States is a recent development in human history, the U.S. must represent the new. "Old" societies must therefore become like that of the United States, or else it is their fate to disappear altogether. What this amounts to is a charter for massive intervention into the lives of others, whether they want this or not; the outcome, more often than not, is the destabilization and even destruction of other societies in the world at large.

A conscious attempt to identify and eliminate the biases of culture allows us to see change in a very different way. It allows us to recognize that, although people can respond deliberately to problems in such a way as to change their culture, much change occurs accidentally. This should not surprise us, though, when we consider that in biological evolution accidents (called mutations) are the ultimate source of all change. The historical record, too, is quirky, and full of random events. And while it is true that without change, cultures could never adapt to changed conditions, we must recognize that too much in the way of large-scale, continuing change may also place a culture in jeopardy. This is because it conflicts with the social need for predictability, discussed in Chapter 2; the need of individuals for regularity and structure, discussed in Chapter 5; and the need of populations for an adaptive "fit" with their environment, discussed in Chapter 6. In short, just as a runaway rate of mutation is a threat to the survival of a biological species, so is a runaway rate of change to a human society.

The more anthropologists study change and learn about the various ways people go about solving their problems of existence, the more aware they become of a great paradox of culture. While the basic business of culture is to solve problems, in doing so, inevitably, new problems are created, which themselves demand solution.

Throughout this book we have seen examples of this—the problem of forming groups in order to cooperate in solving the problems of staying alive, the problem of finding ways to overcome the stresses and strains on individuals as a consequence of their membership in groups, as well as the structural problems that are inherent in the division of society into a number of smaller groups, to mention but a few. It is apparent that every solution to a problem has its price, but so long as culture is able to keep at least a step ahead of the problems, all is reasonably well. This seems to have been the case generally over the past two million years.

When we see all of the problems that face the human species today (Chapter 16), most of them the result of cultural practices, we may wonder if we haven't passed some critical threshold where culture has begun to fall a step behind the problems. This is not to say that the future necessarily has to be bleak for the generations that come after us, but it would certainly be irresponsible to project some sort of rosy, science-fiction type of future as inevitable, at least on the basis of present evidence. To prevent the future from being bleak, humans will have to rise to the challenge of changing their behavior and ideas in order to conquer the large problems that threaten to annihilate them: overpopulation and unequal access to basic resources with their concomitant starvation, poverty, and squalor; environmental pollution and poisoning; and the culture of discontent and bitterness that rises out of the widening economic gap separating industrialized and nonindustrialized countries as well as the "haves" from the "have nots" within countries.

[1]Robert L. Heilbroner and Lester C. Thurow, *The Economic Problem*, 6th ed. (Englewood Cliffs, N.J.: Prentice-Hall, 1981), p. 607.

15

CULTURAL

CHANGE

CHAPTER PREVIEW

The capacity to change has always been important to human cultures. Perhaps at no time has the pace of culture change equaled that of today, as symbolized by this Kayapo Indian's use of a video camera. Faced by massive pressures from the industrialized world to change their ways, traditional people like the Kayapo are increasingly contesting these pressures and finding ways to control the way change affects their destinies.

WHY DO CULTURES CHANGE?

All cultures change at one time or another, for a variety of reasons. Although people may deliberately change their ways in response to some perceived problem, much change is accidental, including the unforeseen outcome of existing events. Or, contact with other peoples may lead to the introduction of "foreign" ideas, bringing about changes in existing values and behavior. This may even involve the massive imposition of foreign ways through conquest of one group by another. Through change, cultures are able to adapt to altered conditions; on the other hand, not all change is adaptive.

HOW DO CULTURES CHANGE?

The mechanisms of change are innovation, diffusion, cultural loss, and acculturation. Innovation occurs when someone within a society discovers something new that is then accepted by other members of the society. Diffusion is the borrowing of something from another group, and cultural loss is the abandonment of an existing practice or trait, with or without replacement. Acculturation is the massive change that occurs with the sort of intensive, firsthand contact that has occurred under colonialism.

WHAT IS MODERNIZATION?

Modernization is an ethnocentric term used to refer to a global process of change by which traditional, nonindustrial societies seek to acquire characteristics of industrially "advanced" societies. Although modernization has generally been assumed to be a good thing, and there have been some successes, it has frequently led to the development of a new "culture of discontent," a level of aspirations far exceeding the bounds of an individual's local opportunities. Sometimes it leads to the destruction of cherished customs and values people had no desire to abandon.

Culture is the medium through which the human species solves the problems of existence, as these are perceived by members of the species. Various cultural institutions, such as kinship and marriage, political and economic organization, and religion, mesh together to form an integrated cultural system. Because systems generally work to maintain stability, cultures are often fairly stable and remain so unless either the conditions to which they are adapted, or human perceptions of those conditions, change. Archaeological studies have revealed how elements of a culture may persist for long periods of time. In Chapter 6, for example, we saw how the culture of the native inhabitants of northwestern New England and southern Quebec remained relatively stable over thousands of years.

Although stability may be a striking feature of many cultures, none is ever changeless, as the cultures of food foragers, subsistence farmers, or pastoralists are all too often assumed to be. In a stable society, change may occur gently and gradually, without altering in any fundamental way the underlying logic of the culture. Sometimes, though, the pace of change may increase dramatically, causing a radical cultural alteration in a relatively short period of time. The modern world is full of examples as diverse as the disintegration of the Soviet Union, or what is happening to the native peoples of the Amazon forest, as Brazil presses ahead to "develop" this vast region. The causes of change are many and include the unexpected outcome of existing activities.

To cite an example from U.S. history, the settlement of what we now call New England by English-speaking people had nothing to do with their culture being better or more progressive than those of the region's native inhabitants. Rather, it was the outcome of a series of unrelated events that happened to coincide at a critical moment in time. In England, economic and political developments that drove large numbers of farmers off the land, occurring at a time of population growth, together favored an outward migration of people; that this happened shortly after the European discovery of the Americas was purely a matter of chance. Even at that, attempts to establish British colonies in New England ended in failure, until an epidemic of unprecedented scope resulted in the sudden death of about 90 percent of the native inhabitants of coastal New England. This epidemic did not hap-

Two Mayan women fire pottery vessels. The discovery that firing clay vessels makes them nearly indestructible (unless they are dropped or otherwise smashed) probably came about when clay-lined basins next to cooking fires in the Middle East were accidentally fired.

pen because without it, the British would be unable to settle, but rather because the American Indians had been in regular contact with European fishermen and fur traders—whose activities were independent of British attempts at colonization—from whom they contracted the disease. For centuries, up to this time, Europeans had been living under conditions that were ideal for the incubation and spread of all sorts of infectious diseases, but the Indians had not. Consequently, the Europeans had developed over time a degree of resistance to them, which American Indians lacked altogether.

To be sure, the consequences were inevitable, once direct contact between these people occurred; nonetheless, differential immunity did not occur in order to clear the coast of New England for English settlement. And even once those settlements were established, it is unlikely that the colonists would have been able to alienate the remaining natives from their land, had they not come equipped with the techniques for dominating other peoples previously used to impose their control upon the Scots, Irish, and Welsh. In sum, had not a number of otherwise unrelated phenomena come together by chance at just the right moment in time, English might very well not be the language spoken by most North Americans today.

Not just the unexpected outcome of existing activities, but other sorts of accidents, too, may bring about changes, if people perceive them to be useful. Of course, people may also respond deliberately to altered conditions, thereby correcting the perceived problem that made the cultural modification seem necessary. Change may also be forced upon one group by another, as happened in colonial New England and as is happening in many parts of the world today, in the course of especially intense contact between two societies. Progress and adaptation, on the other hand, are *not* causes of change; the latter is a consequence of change that happens to work well for a population, and the former is a judgement of those consequences in terms of the group's cultural values. Progress is whatever it is defined as.

MECHANISMS OF CHANGE

INNOVATION

The ultimate source of all change is through innovation: any new practice, tool, or principle that gains widespread acceptance within a group. Those that involve the chance discovery of some new principle we refer to as **primary innovations;** those that result from the deliberate applications of known principles are **secondary innovations.** It is the latter that correspond most closely with Western culture's model of change as predictable and determined, while the former involves accidents of one sort or another.

An example of a primary innovation is the discovery that the firing of clay makes it permanently hard. Presumably, accidental firing of clay took place frequently in ancient cooking fires. An accidental occurrence is of no account, however, unless some application of it is perceived. This actually happened about 25,000 years ago, for figurines were made then of fired clay. Pottery vessels were not made, however, nor did the prac-

Primary innovation: The chance discovery of some new principle.

Secondary innovation: Something new that results from the deliberate application of known principles.

tice of making things of fired clay reach southwest Asia; at least if it did, it failed to take root. Not until some time between 7000 and 6500 B.C. did people living in southwest Asia recognize a significant application of fired clay, at which time they began using it to make cheap, durable, easy-to-produce containers and cooking vessels.

As nearly as we can reconstruct it, the development of the earliest known pottery vessels came about in the following way.[1] By 7000 B.C., cooking areas in southwest Asia included clay-lined basins built into the floor, clay ovens, and hearths, making the accidental firing of clay inevitable. Moreover, people were already familiar with the working of clay, which they used to build houses, line storage pits, and model figurines. For containers, however, they still relied upon baskets and leather bags.

Once the significance of fired clay—the primary innovation—was perceived, then the application of known techniques to it—secondary innovation—became possible. Clay could be modeled in the familiar way into the known shapes of baskets, leather bags, and stone bowls and then fired, either in an open fire or in the same ovens used for cooking food. In fact, the earliest known southwest Asian pottery is imitative of leather and stone containers, and the decoration consists of motifs transferred from basketry, even though they were ill suited to the new medium. Eventually, shapes and decorative techniques more suited to the new technology were developed.

Since men are never the potters in traditional societies unless the craft has become something of a commercial operation, the first pottery was probably made by women. The vessels that they produced were initially handmade, and the earliest kilns were the same ovens that were used for cooking. As people became more adept at making pottery, there were further technological refinements. As an aid in production, the clay could be modeled on a mat or other surface, which the woman could move as work progressed. Hence, she could sit in one place while she worked, without having to get up to move around the clay. A further refinement was to mount the movable surface on a vertical rotating shaft—an application of a known

[1]Ruth Amiran, "The Beginnings of Pottery-Making in the Near East," in *Ceramics and Man*, ed. Frederick R. Matson, Viking Fund Publications in Anthropology, 1965, No. 41, pp. 240–247.

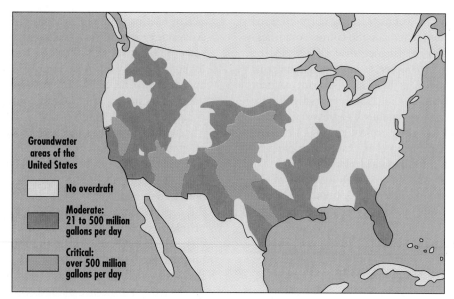

Figure 15.1   Human practices may or may not be adaptive. For example, it is not adaptive over the long run to deplete groundwater, yet this is being done in regions of the U.S. with fast-growing populations.

principle used for drills—which produced the potter's wheel and permitted mass production. Kilns, too, were improved for better circulation of heat by separating the firing chamber from the fire itself. By chance, it happened that these improved kilns produced enough heat to smelt some ores such as copper, tin, gold, silver, and lead. Presumably, this discovery was made by accident—another primary innovation—and the stage was set for the eventual development of the forced-draft furnace out of the earlier pottery kiln.

The accidents responsible for primary innovations are not generated by environmental change or some other "need," nor are they preferentially oriented in an adaptive direction (Fig. 15.1). They are, however, given structure by the cultural context in which they occur. Thus, the outcome of the discovery of fired clay by mobile hunters and gatherers 25,000 years ago was very different from what it was when discovered later on by more sedentary farmers in southwest Asia, where it set off a veritable chain reaction as one invention led to another. Indeed, given certain sets of cultural goals, values, and knowledge, particular innovations are almost bound to be made, as illustrated by the case of penicillin. This antibiotic was discovered in 1928 when a mold blew in through the window of

Sir Alexander Fleming's lab and landed on a microbial colony of staphylococcus, which it then dissolved. Fleming recognized the importance of this accident, because he had become aware of the need for more than antiseptics and immunization, the mainstays of medicine at the time, to fight infection. Of course, he was not alone in his awareness, nor was the accident involved at all unusual. Any physician who studied medicine in the early part of this century has stories about having to scrub down laboratories when their studies in bacteriology were brought to a halt by molds that persisted in contaminating cultures and killing off the bacteria. To them, it was an annoyance; to Fleming, it was a "magic bullet" to fight infection. Under the circumstances, however, had he not made the discovery, someone else would have before long.

Although a culture's internal dynamics may encourage certain innovative tendencies, they may discourage others, or even remain neutral with respect to yet others. Copernicus's discovery of the rotation of the planets around the sun and Mendel's discovery of the basic laws of heredity are instances of genuine creative insights out of step with the established needs, values, and goals of their times and places. In fact, Mendel's work remained obscure until 16 years after his death, when three scientists working independently rediscovered, all in the same year (1900), the same laws of heredity. Thus, in the context of turn-of-the-century Western culture, Mendel's laws were bound to be discovered, even had Mendel himself not hit upon them earlier.

While an innovation must be reasonably consistent with a society's needs, values, and goals, if it is to be accepted, this alone is not sufficient to assure its acceptance. Force of habit tends to be an obstacle to acceptance; people will generally tend to stick with what they are used to, rather than adopt something new that will require some adjustment on their part. An example of this can be seen in the continued British practice of driving on the left-hand side of the road, rather than on the right. Driving on the left is no more natural than driving on the right, but to someone from Britain it seems so, because of the body reflexes that have developed in the course of driving on the left. In this case the individual's very body has become adjusted to certain patterns of behavior that bypass any presumed "openness" to change. An innovation's chance of acceptance tends to be greater if it is obviously better than the thing or idea it replaces. Beyond this, much may depend on the prestige of the innovator and imitating groups. If the innovator's prestige is high, this will help gain acceptance for the innovation. If it is low, acceptance is less likely, unless the innovator can attract a sponsor who has high prestige.

DIFFUSION

When the Pilgrims established their colony of New Plymouth in North America, they very likely would have starved to death, had the Indian Squanto not showed them how to grow the native American crops—corn, beans, and squash. The borrowing of cultural elements from one society by members of another is known as **diffusion,** and the donor society is, for all intents and purposes, the "inven-

---

Diffusion: The spread of customs or practices from one culture to another.

One barrier to change is simple tradition and force of habit. Though Westerners may learn to use chopsticks, doing so requires both a reason and more effort than continuing to eat with fork, knife, and spoon.

tor" of that element. So common is borrowing that the late Ralph Linton, a North American anthropologist, suggested that borrowing accounts for as much as 90 percent of any culture's content. People are creative about their borrowing, however, picking and choosing from multiple possibilities and sources. Usually their selections are limited to those compatible with the existing culture.

In modern-day Guatemala, for example, Maya Indians, who make up over half of that country's population, will adopt Western ways if the value of what they adopt is self-evident and does not conflict with traditional ways and values. The use of metal hoes, shovels, and machetes has long since become standard, for they are superior to stone tools, and yet they are compatible with the cultivation of corn in the traditional way by men using hand tools. Yet certain other "modern" practices, which might appear advantageous to the Maya, tend to be resisted if they are perceived as running counter to Indian tradition. Thus, a young man in one community who tried his hand at truck gardening, using

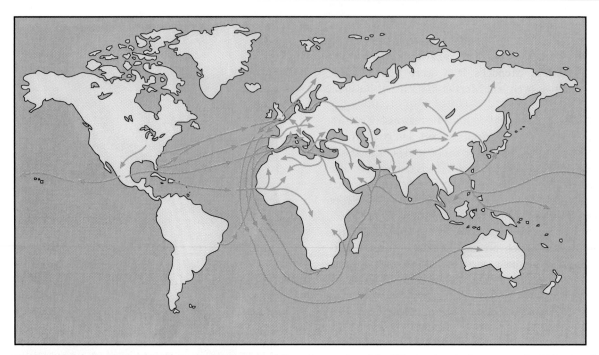

Figure 15.2   The diffusion of tobacco. Having spread from the tropics of the Western hemisphere to much of North and South America, after 1492 it rapidly spread to the rest of the world.

chemical fertilizers and pesticides to grow cash crops with market value only in the city—vegetables never eaten by the Maya—could not secure a "good" woman for a wife (a "good" woman is one who has never had sex with another man, who is skilled at domestic chores, not lazy, and willing to attend to her husband's needs). Upon abandonment of his unorthodox ways, however, he became accepted by his community as a "real man," no longer different from the rest of them and conspicuous (a real "man" is one who will work steadily to provide his household with what they need to live by farming and making charcoal in the traditional ways). Before long, he was well married.[2]

While the tendency toward borrowing is so great as to lead Robert Lowie to comment, "Culture is a thing of shreds and patches," the borrowed traits usually undergo sufficient modifications to make this wry comment more colorful than critical. Moreover, existing cultural traits may be modified to accommodate the borrowed one. An awareness of the extent of borrowing can be eye-opening.

Take, for example, the numerous things European Americans have borrowed from American Indians. Domestic plants that were developed ("invented") by the Indians—"Irish" potatoes, corn, beans, squash, tomatoes, manioc, and sweet potatoes—furnish something like half the world's food supply. Among drugs and stimulants, tobacco (Fig. 15.2) is the best known, but others include coca in cocaine, ephedra in ephedrine, datura in pain relievers, and cascara in laxatives. All but a handful of drugs known today made from plants native to the Americas were used by Indians, and over 200 plants and herbs that they used for medicinal purposes have at one time or another been included in the *Pharmacopeia of the United States* or in the *National Formulary*. Varieties of cotton developed by Indians supply much of the world's clothing needs, while the woolen poncho, the parka, and moccasins are universally familiar items. Not only has American literature been permanently shaped by such works as Longfellow's *Hiawatha* and James Fenimore Cooper's *Leatherstocking Tales*, but American Indian music has contributed to world music such "ultra-modern" devices as unusual intervals, arbitrary scales, conflicting rhythms, and hypnotic monoto-

[2]Ruben E. Reina, *The Law of the Saints* (Indianapolis: Bobbs-Merrill, 1966), pp. 65–68.

ny. These devices are so well integrated into modern North American culture that few people are aware that American Indian music is one source of them.

In spite of the obvious importance of diffusion, there are probably more obstacles to accepting an innovation from another culture than there are to accepting one that is "homegrown." In addition to the same obstacles that stand in the way of "homegrown" inventions is the fact that a borrowed one is, somehow, "foreign." In the United States, for example, this is one of the reasons why people have been so reluctant to abandon completely the old, established English system of weights and measures for the far more logical metric system, which has been adopted by just about every other government in the world. (The only holdouts besides the United States are Borneo and Liberia.) Hence, the ethnocentrism of the potential borrowing culture may act as a barrier to acceptance.

CULTURAL LOSS

Most often people tend to think of change as an accumulation of innovations; new things being added to those already there. They do so because this seems so much a part of the way they live. A little reflection, however, leads to the realization that frequently the acceptance of a new innovation leads to the loss of an older one. This sort of replacement is not just a feature of Western civilization. For example, back in biblical times, chariots and carts were in widespread use in the Middle East, but by the sixth century A.D., wheeled vehicles had virtually disappeared from Morocco to Afghanistan. They were replaced by camels, not because of some reversion to the past on the part of the region's inhabitants, but because camels, used as pack animals, worked better. By the sixth century, Roman roads had deteriorated, but camels, so long as they were not used as draft animals, were not bound to them. Not only that, their longevity, endurance, and ability to ford rivers and traverse rough ground without having to build roads in the first place made pack camels admirably suited for the region. Finally, there was a saving in labor: a wagon required a man for every two draft animals, whereas a single person can manage from three to six pack camels. Stephen Jay Gould comments:

In Western cultures, the wheel has become the symbol of technological progress, but wheeled transport is not always superior to other forms.

We are initially surprised . . . because wheels have come to symbolize in our culture the sine qua non of intelligent exploitation and technological progress. Once invented, their superiority cannot be gainsaid or superseded. Indeed, "reinventing the wheel" has become our standard metaphor for deriding the repetition of such obvious truths. In an earlier era of triumphant social Darwinism, wheels stood as an ineluctable stage of human progress. The "inferior" cultures of Africa slid to defeat; their conquerors rolled to victory. The "advanced" cultures of Mexico and Peru might have repulsed Cortés and Pizarro if only a clever artisan had thought of turning a calendar stone into a cartwheel. The notion that carts could ever be replaced by pack animals strikes us not only as backward but almost sacrilegious.

The success of camels reemphasizes a fundamental theme . . . Adaptation, be it biological or cultural, represents a better fit to specific, local environments, not an inevitable stage in a ladder of progress. Wheels were a formidable invention, and their uses are manifold (potters and millers did not abandon them, even when cartwrights were eclipsed). But camels may work better in some circumstances. Wheels, like wings, fins, and brains, are exquisite devices for certain purposes, not signs of intrinsic superiority.[3]

Often overlooked is another facet of the loss of apparently useful traits: loss without replacement. An example of this is the absence of boats among the inhabitants of the Canary Islands, an archipelago isolated in the stormy seas off the coast of West Africa. The ancestors of these people must have had

[3]Stephen Jay Gould, *Hen's Teeth and Horses' Toes* (New York: Norton, 1983), p. 159.

boats, for without them they could never have transported themselves and their domestic livestock to the islands in the first place. Later, without boats, they had no way to communicate between islands. The cause of this loss of something useful was that the islands contain no stone suitable for making polished stone axes, which in turn limited the islanders' carpentry.[4]

FORCIBLE CHANGE

Innovation, diffusion, and cultural loss all may take place among peoples who are free to decide for themselves what they will or will not accept in the way of change. Not always, however, are people left free to make their own choices; frequently changes that they would not willingly make themselves have been forced upon them by some other group, usually in the course of colonialism and conquest. A direct outcome in many cases is a phenomenon that anthropologists call acculturation.

ACCULTURATION

Acculturation occurs when groups having different cultures come into intensive firsthand contact, with subsequent massive changes in the original culture patterns of one or both groups. It always involves an element of force, either directly, as in the case of conquest, or indirectly, as in the implicit or explicit threat that force will be used if people refuse to make the changes that those in the other group expect them to make. Other variables include degree of cultural difference; circumstances, inten-

---

Acculturation: Major culture changes that people are forced to make as a consequence of intensive, firsthand contact between societies.

---

[4]Carleton S. Coon, *The Story of Man* (New York: Knopf, 1954), p. 174.

sity, frequency, and hostility of contact; relative status of the agents of contact; who is dominant and who is submissive; and whether the nature of the flow is reciprocal or nonreciprocal. It should be emphasized that acculturation and diffusion are not equivalent terms; one culture can borrow from another without being in the least acculturated.

In the course of acculturation, any one of a number of things may happen. Merger or fusion occurs when two cultures lose their separate identities and form a single culture, as expressed by the melting-pot ideal of American culture in the United States. Sometimes, though, one of the cultures loses its autonomy but retains its identity as a subculture, in the form of a caste, class, or ethnic group; this is typical of conquest or slavery situations, and there are examples in the United States in spite of its melting-pot ideology. One need look no farther afield than the nearest Indian reservation. Today, in virtually all parts of the world, people are faced with the indignity of forced removal from their traditional homelands, as entire communities are uprooted to make way for hydroelectric projects, grazing lands for cattle, mining operations, or the construction of highways. In Brazil's rush to develop the Amazon basin, for instance, whole villages are frequently relocated to "national parks," where resources are inadequate for so many people, and where former enemies are often forced to live in close proximity.

Extinction is the phenomenon in which so many carriers of a culture die that those who survive become refugees, living among peoples of other cultures. Examples of this may be seen in many parts of the world today; the closest examples are to be found in many parts of South America, again as in Brazil's Amazon basin. One particularly well-documented case occurred in the 1960s, when hired killers tried to wipe out the Cinta-Larga Indians. Using arsenic, dynamite, and machine guns from light planes, these killers chose a time when an important native ceremony was taking place to attack a Cinta-Larga village, seen as an obstacle to development. Violence continues to be used in Brazil as a means of dealing with native people; in 1987–88, for instance, at least 25 Yanomami were killed as cattle ranchers and miners continued to pour into northern Brazil. By 1990, 70 percent of the Yanomami's land in Brazil had been unconstitu-

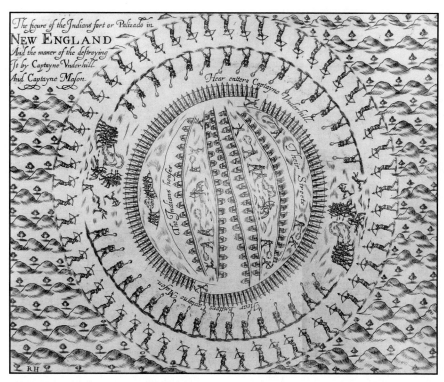

Genocide is not new in the world. This 1638 illustration shows English colonists joining with Narrangansett Indians (the outer ring of bowmen) to shoot down unarmed Pequot Indian men, women, and children attempting to flee their homes, which have been set afire.

tionally expropriated, their supplies of fish were poisoned by mercury contamination of rivers, and malaria, venereal disease, and tuberculosis were running rampant. The Yanomami were dying at the rate of 10 percent a year, and their fertility had dropped off to near zero. Many villages were left with no children or old people, and the survivors awaited their fate with a profound terror of extinction.[5] The attitude of the Brazilians to this and similar situations is illustrated by the reaction of their government when two Kayapó Indians and an anthropologist traveled to the United States, where they spoke with members of several congressional committees, as well as officials of the Department of State, the Treasury, and the World Bank about the destruction of their land and way of life caused by internationally financed development projects. All three were charged with violating Brazil's Foreign Sedition Act.

[5]Terry Turner, "Major Shift in Brazilian Yanomami Policy," *Anthropology Newsletter* 32, No. 5 (1991):1 and 46.

GENOCIDE

The case of the Brazilian Indians just cited raises the issue of **genocide**—the extermination of one group of people by another, deliberately and often in the name of "progress." Genocide is not new in the world, as we need look no farther than North American history to see. In 1637, for example, the Pequot Indians were effectively destroyed by the Naragansett Indians and English colonists, who joined to set afire their village at Mystic, Connecticut, and then shoot down all those—primarily women and children—who sought to escape being burned alive. To try to ensure that even their very memory would be stamped out, laws were passed to

Genocide: The extermination of one people by another, often in the name of "progress."

Two examples (out of many) of attempted genocide in the twentieth century: Hitler's Germany against Jews and Gypsies, during the 1930s and 1940s; and Saddam Hussein's Iraq against the Kurds, beginning in the 1980s.

make it illegal even to mention the Pequot's name. Several other massacres of Indian peoples occurred thereafter, up until the last one at Wounded Knee, South Dakota, in 1890. Of course, such acts were by no means restricted to North America; one of the most famous nineteenth-century acts of genocide was the extermination of the aboriginal inhabitants of Tasmania, a large island just south of Australia. In this case, the use of military force failed to achieve the complete elimination of the Tasmanians, but what the military could not achieve, a missionary could. George Augustus Robinson was able to round up the surviving natives, and at his mission station the deadly combination of psychological depression and diseases brought over by European settlers effected the demise of the last full-blooded Tasmanians in time for Robinson to retire to England a moderately wealthy man.

The most widely known act of genocide in recent history was the attempt of the Nazi Germans to wipe out European Jews and gypsies in the name of racial superiority. Unfortunately, the common practice of referring to this as "*the* Holocaust"—as if it were unique—tends to blind us to the fact that this thoroughly monstrous act is simply one more example of an all too common phenomenon. Moreover, genocide continues to occur in the world today in places like Iraq, where, in 1988, Iraqis used poison gas against Kurdish villagers, and (as we will see in Chapter 16) in Guatemala, to mention but two cases. If such ugly practices are ever to be ended, we must gain a better understanding of them than currently exists. Anthropologists are actively engaged in this, carrying out cross-cultural as well as individual case studies. One finding to emerge is the regularity with which religious, economic, and political interests are allied in cases of genocide.

In Tasmania, for example, wool growers wanted aborigines off the land so they could have it for their sheep. The government advanced their interests through its military campaigns against the natives, but it was Robinson's missionary work that finally secured Tasmania for the wool interests. In the 1970s and 1980s, the !Kung living in Namibia found themselves in a situation remarkably similar to that experienced earlier by the Tasmanians; a combination of religious (Dutch Reformed church), political (Namibia's Department of Nature Conservation), and economic (agricultural/pastoral and touristic) interests brought about the people's confinement to a place where disease and apathy caused death rates to outstrip birth rates. Other such cases might be cited; for example, a cooperative relationship among Oblate missions, the Royal Canadian Mounted Police, and the Hudson Bay Company was instrumental in bringing about the demise, in the 1950s, of the Ihalmiut who lived in Canada's "Barren Grounds" west of Hudson Bay.[6] The latter case is important, for it clearly illustrates that this is not always a deliberate act. It also occurs as the unforseen outcome of activities carried out with little regard for their impact on other peoples. For the people whose lives are snuffed out, however, it makes no difference; for them, the outcome is the same.

[6]Farley Mowat, *The Desperate People* (Boston: Little, Brown, 1959).

DIRECTED CHANGE

The most extreme cases of acculturation usually occur as a result of military conquest and displacement of traditional political authority by conquerors who know or care nothing about the culture they control. The indigenous people, unable to resist imposed changes and prevented from carrying out many of their traditional social, religious, and economic activities, may be forced into new activities that tend to isolate individuals and tear apart the integration of their societies. Such a people are the !Kung of Namibia, who have been rounded up and confined to a region where they cannot possibly provide for their own needs. In this situation, they are provided by the government with rations that are insufficient to meet their nutritional needs. In poor health and prevented from developing meaningful alternatives to traditional activities, the people have become argumentative and depressed and, as already noted, their death rate now exceeds their birth rate.

One byproduct of colonial dealings with indigenous peoples has been the growth of **applied**

Applied anthropology: The use of anthropological knowledge and techniques for the purpose of solving "practical" problems, often for a specific "client."

anthropology and the use of anthropological techniques and knowledge for certain "practical" ends. For example, British anthropology has often been considered the "handmaiden" of that country's colonial policy, for it typically provided the kind of information of particular use in maintaining effective colonial rule. In the United States, the Bureau of American Ethnology was founded toward the end of the nineteenth century, to gather reliable data on which the government might base its Indian policies. At the time, North American anthropologists were convinced of the usefulness of their discipline, and many who carried out ethnographic work among Indians devoted a great deal of time, energy, and even money to assisting their infor-

A common agent of change in many nonindustrial societies is the religious missionary. Although their intent is to improve the lives of indigenous peoples, such missionaries also seek to radically alter the beliefs that lie at the heart of such cultures and make life within them meaningful.

FRANZ BOAS

(1858–1942)

Born in Germany, where he studied physics and geography, Franz Boas came to the United States to live in 1888. His interest in anthropology began a few years earlier with a trip to Baffinland, where he met his first so-called primitive people. Thereafter, he and his students came to dominate anthropology in North America through the first three decades of the 1900s. Through meticulous and detailed fieldwork, which set new standards for excellence, Boas and his students were able to expose the shortcomings of the grandiose schemes of cultural evolution which had been proposed by earlier social theorists. His thesis that a culture must be judged according to its own standards and values, rather than those of the investigator, represented a tremendously liberating philosophy in his time. (The photo shows Boas posing as a Kwakiutl hanatsa dancer for a National Museum diorama, 1895).

mants, whose interests were frequently threatened from outside. In the present century the scope of applied anthropology has broadened. Early on, the applied work of Franz Boas, who almost single-handedly trained a generation of anthropologists in the United States, was instrumental in reforming the country's immigration policies. In the 1930s, anthropologists carried out a number of studies in industrial and other institutional settings, with avowedly applied goals. With World War II came the first efforts at colonial administration beyond U.S. borders, especially in the Pacific, made by officers trained in anthropology. The rapid recovery of Japan was due in no small measure to the influence of anthropologists in structuring the U.S. occupation. Anthropologists continue to play an active role today in administering the U.S. trust territories in the Pacific.

Today, applied anthropologists are in some demand in the field of international development, on account of their specialized knowledge of social structure, value systems, and the functional interrelatedness of third-world cultures targeted for development. The role of the applied anthropologists, however, is far from easy; as anthropologists, they respect the dignity of other peoples and the integrity of their cultures, yet they are being asked for advice on how to change certain aspects of those cultures. If the request comes from the people themselves, that is one thing, but more often than not, the request comes from some outside "expert." Supposedly, the proposed change is for the good of the targeted population, yet they don't always see it that way. Just how far applied anthropologistsshould go in advising how people—especially ones without the power to resist—can be made to embrace changes that have been proposed for them is a serious ethical question.

In spite of such difficulties, applied anthropology is flourishing today as never before. As the several "Anthropology Applied" features throughout this book illustrate, anthropologists now practice their profession in many different non-academic settings, in a wide variety of ways.

In the past few decades, Western countries have sent "technological missionaries" to teach people in other countries new ways of doing old tasks. Unless they have had anthropological training, however, such persons are apt to be unaware of the side effects their new ways will cause.

REACTIONS TO FORCIBLE CHANGE

The reactions of indigenous peoples to the changes that have been thrust upon them by outsiders have varied considerably. Some have responded by removing themselves to the nearest available forest, desert, or other inhospitable place, in hopes of being left alone. In Brazil, a number of communities once located near the coast took this option a few hundred years ago, and were successful until the great push to develop the Amazon forest began in the 1960s. Others, like the Ik of Uganda (discussed in Chapter 2) have lapsed into apathy. These former hunters and gatherers were rounded up, loaded into trucks, and transported out of their homeland virtually overnight; they are now, quite literally, dying out. Sometimes, though, people have managed to keep faith with their own traditions by inventing creative and ingenious ways of expressing them in the face of powerful foreign domination. This blending of indigenous and foreign elements

Syncretism: In acculturation, the blending of indigenous and foreign traits to form a new system.

into a new system is known as **syncretism,** and a fine illustration of it is the game of cricket as played by the Trobriand Islanders, some of whose practices we looked at in Chapters 7, 8, and 9.

Under British rule, the Trobrianders were introduced by missionaries to the rather staid British game of cricket, to replace the erotic dancing and open sexuality that normally followed the harvest of yams. Traditionally, this was the time when chiefs sought to spread their fame by hosting nights of dancing, in the course of which they provided food for the hundreds of young married people who participated. For two months or so, there would be night after night of provocative dancing, accompanied by chanting and shouting full of sexual innuendo, each night ending as couples disappeared off

ANTHROPOLOGY APPLIED

GROWING TREES IN HAITI

When foreigners go to Haiti, one of the things that impresses them is the massive deforestation that has taken place. Since colonial times, this country's population has swelled from fewer than half a million to more than six million—too many people for too little arable land. In their quest for fields, peasants have cut down all but a few stands of trees in remote areas. The resultant erosion, coupled with over-utilization of crop land has led to catastrophic declines in yields, sending many peasants into the capitol, Port au Prince, in search of other work. This in turn has created a growing demand for construction wood and charcoal in that city, which the rural poor are all too happy to satisfy by going after the country's few remaining trees. Responding to this crisis, international development organizations poured millions of dollars into studies of the problem, as well as into reforestation schemes, all to no avail. Not only were very few seedlings planted, but those that were quickly became forage for the goats of peasants, who were reluctant to devote any of their scarce land holdings to the growing of state-owned trees.

Faced with failure, the United States Agency for International Development (AID) in Haiti invited anthropologist Gerald F. Murray to develop an alternative approach to reforestation, and subsequently hired him as project director. Already familiar with peasant land usage in Haiti, Murray knew that typical reforestation projects, such as the planting of fruit trees by agents of the government for purposes of soil conservation, would not work. To peasants, fruit trees were of little commercial or nutritional value, especially if they were perceived as being state owned. What they needed was a cash crop which was theirs to do with as they wished. Accordingly, what Murray did was to make available, through nongov-ernmental organizations rather than state agencies, seedlings of leucaena, ocassia, and eucalyptus, fast-growing wood trees good for charcoal and basic construction material, for which there was a ready market. Moreover, the trees could be cut in some instances as early as four years after planting, and could be grown along borders of fields, or even intercropped among other plants, rather than in large unbroken uncropped stands. Thus, their growth was compatible with continued subsistence farming. Moreover, any potential loss from decreased food production was far offset by income the trees would generate.

The idea that trees were meant to be cut, while heretical to the international development "establishment," was extremely popular with the peasants. As Murray observes, "though it had taken AID two years to decide about the project; it took about twenty minutes with any group of skeptical but economically rational peasants to generate a list of enthusiastic potential tree planters . . . Cash-flow dialogues and ownership . . . were a far cry from the finger-wagging ecological sermons to which many peasant groups had been subjected on the topic of trees."* When first conceived, the planting of three million trees, on the land of six thousand peasants, was set as the project's four-year goal. In fact, by the end of the fourth year, 20 million trees had been planted by 75,000 peasants. Unlike bureaucratically conceived projects, this anthropologically conceived and carried out agroforestry project has turned out to be reasonably successful.

*Gerald F. Murray, "The Domestication of Wood in Haiti: A Case Study in Applied Evolution," in *Applying Anthropology, An Introductory Reader,* ed. Aaron Podolefsky and Peter J. Brown (Mountain View, Calif.: Mayfield 1989):151–152.

into the bush together. Since no chief wished to be outdone by any other (to be outdone reflected on the strength of one's magic), there was a strong competitive element to all of this dancing, and fighting sometimes erupted. To the missionaries, cricket seemed a good way to end all of this, in a way that would encourage conformity to "civilized" comportment in dress, religion, and "sportsmanship." The Trobrianders, however, were determined to "rubbish" (throw out) the British game, and turned it into the same kind of distinctly Trobriand event that their dance competitions had once been.[7]

The Trobrianders made cricket their own by adding battle dress and battle magic, and by incorporating erotic dancing into the festivities. Instead of inviting dancers each night, chiefs now arrange

[7]Annette B. Weiner, review of "Trobriand Cricket: An Ingenious Response to Colonialism," *American Anthropologist,* 79 (1977):506.

In 1979 Iran, the Ayatollah Ruhollah Khomeini led to power a revitalization movement that was in part revivalistic and in part revolutionary.

games of cricket. Pitching has been modified from the British style to one closer to their old way of throwing a spear. Following the game, they hold massive feasts, where wealth is displayed to enhance their prestige. Cricket, in its altered form, has been made to serve traditional systems of prestige and exchange. Neither "primitive" nor benignly accepted in its original form, Trobriand cricket was thoughtfully and creatively adapted into a sophisticated activity reflecting the importance of basic indigenous cultural premises. Exuberance and pride are displayed by everyone associated with the game, and the players are as much concerned with conveying the full meaning of who they are as with scoring well. From the sensual dressing in preparation for the game to the team chanting of songs full of sexual metaphors and to erotic chorus-line dancing between the innings, there is little doubt that each player is playing for his own importance, for the fame of his team, and for the hundreds of attractive young women who usually watch the game.

REVITALIZATION MOVEMENTS

Another common reaction to forcible change is revitalization, a process already touched upon in Chapter 13. Revitalization may be defined as a

deliberate attempt by some members of a society to construct a more satisfactory culture by the rapid acceptance of a pattern of multiple innovations. Once primary ties of culture, social relationships, and activities are broken, and meaningless activity is imposed by force, individuals and groups characteristically react with fantasy, withdrawal, and escape.

Examples of revitalization movements have been common in the history of the United States whenever significant segments of the population have found their conditions in life to be at odds with the values of "the American Dream." For example, in the nineteenth century, periodic depression and the disillusionment of the decades after the Civil War produced a host of revitalization movements, of which the most successful was that of the Mormons. In the twentieth century, movements have repeatedly sprung up in the slums of major cities, as well as in depressed rural areas such as Appalachia. By the 1960s, a number of movements were becoming less inward-looking and more activist, a good example being the rise of the Black Muslim movement. The 1960s also saw the rise of revitalization movements among the young of middle-class and even upper-class families. In their case, the professed values of peace, equality, and individual freedom were seen to be at odds with the reality of war, poverty, and constraints on individual action

Revivalistic revitalization movements are not restricted to third-world countries; in the United States, the Reverend Jerry Falwell served as the leader of one such movement, the Moral Majority.

imposed by a variety of impersonal institutions. Their reaction to these things was expressed by their use of illegal drugs; their outlandish or "freaky" clothes, hair styles, music, and speech; and their behavior toward authority and authority figures.

By the 1980s revitalization movements were becoming prominent even among older, more affluent segments of society, as in the rise of the Moral Majority. In these cases, the reaction is not so much against a perceived failure of the American dream as it is against perceived threats to that dream by dissenters and activists within their society, by foreign governments, by ideas that challenge the ideas that they believe, and by the sheer complexity of modern life.

Clearly, when value systems get out of step with existing realities, for whatever reason, a condition of cultural crisis is likely to build up that may breed some form of reactive movement. Not all suppressed, conquered, or colonized people eventually rebel against established authority, although why they do not is still a debated issue. When they do, however, resistance may take one of several forms, all of which are varieties of revitalization move-

ments. A culture may seek to speed up the acculturation process in order to share more fully in the supposed benefits of the dominant cultures. Melanesian cargo cults of the post-World War II era have generally been of this sort, although earlier ones stressed a revival of traditional ways. Movements that try to reconstitute a destroyed but not forgotten way of life are known as **nativistic** or **revivalistic movements.** One that attempts to resurrect a suppressed pariah group, which has long suffered in an inferior social standing and which has its own special subcultural ideology, is referred to as **millenarism;** the most familiar examples of this

---

Nativistic or revivalistic movement: A revitalization movement that tries to reconstitute a destroyed but not forgotten way of life.

Millenarism: A revitalization movement that attempts to resurrect a suppressed pariah group that has long suffered in an inferior social position and that has its own special subcultural ideology.

—————————————

Revolutionary: A revitalization movement from within, directed primarily at the ideological system and the attendant social structure of a culture.

—————————————

to Western peoples are prophetic Judaism and early Christianity. If the aim of the movement is directed primarily to the ideological system and the attendant social structure of a cultural system from within, it is then called **revolutionary**.

REBELLION AND REVOLUTION

When the scale of discontent within a society reaches a certain level, the possibilities for rebellion and revolution—such as the 1979 fundamentalist Iranian revolution, the unsuccessful 1989 student-led rebellion in China, or the 1990 Romanian revolution in which dictator Nicaloae Ceausescu was executed—are high.

The question of why revolutions come into being, as well as why they frequently fail to live up to the expectations of the people initiating them, is a problem. It is clear, however, that in spite of the political independence most colonies have gained since World War II, many of them continue to be exploited by more powerful countries for their natural resources and cheap labor, causing a deep resentment of rulers beholden to foreign powers.

Further discontent has been caused by the attempts of newly independent states to assert their control over peoples living within their boundaries who, by virtue of a common ancestry, possession of distinct cultures, persistent occupation of their own territories, and traditions of self-determination identify themselves as distinct nations and refuse to recognize the sovereignty of what they regard as a foreign government. Thus, in many a former colony, large numbers of people have taken up arms to resist annexation and absorption by imposed state regimes that would strip them of their lands, resources, and sense of identity as a people. One of the most important facts of our time is that the vast majority of the distinct peoples of the world have never consented to rule by the governments of states within which they find themselves living.[8] In

many a newly emerged country, such peoples feel they have no other option than to fight.

On the basis of an examination of four revolutions of the past—English, American, French, and Russian—the following conditions have been offered as precipitators of rebellion and revolution:

1. Loss of prestige of established authority, often as a result of the failure of foreign policy, financial difficulties, dismissals of popular ministers, or alteration of popular policies.
2. Threat to recent economic improvement. In France and Russia, those sections of the population (professional classes and urban workers) whose economic fortunes had previously taken an upward swing were "radicalized" by unexpected setbacks, such as steeply rising food prices and unemployment.
3. Indecisiveness of government, as exemplified by lack of consistent policy; such governments appear to be controlled by, rather than in control of, events.
4. Loss of support of the intellectual class. Such a loss deprived the prerevolutionary governments of France and Russia of philosophical support, thus leading to their lack of popularity with the literate public.
5. A leader or group of leaders with charisma enough to mobilize a substantial part of the population against the establishment.

Apart from resistance to internal authority, such as in the English, French, and Russian revolutions, many revolutions in modern times have been struggles against an authority imposed on them by outsiders. Such resistance usually takes the form of independence movements that wage campaigns of armed defiance against colonial powers. The Algerian struggle for independence from France and the American war for independence from England are typical examples. Of the 120 or so armed conflicts in the world today, 98 percent are in the economically poor third-world countries of Africa, Asia, and Central and South America, almost all of which were at one time under European colonial domination. Of these wars, 75 percent are between the state and one or more peoples within the state's

[8] Bernard Nietschmann, "The Third World War," *Cultural Survival Quarterly* 11, No. 3 (1987):3.

borders who are seeking to maintain or regain control of their persons, communities, lands, and resources in the face of what they regard as subjugation by a foreign power.[9]

Not all revolts are truly revolutionary in their consequences. According to Max Gluckman, rebellions:

> ". . . throw the rascals out" and substitute another set, but there is no attempt to alter either the cultural ideology or the form of the social structure. In political revolution, attempts are made to seize the offices of power in order to change social structure, belief systems, and their symbolic representations. Political revolutions are usually turbulent, violent, and not long-lasting. A successful revolution soon moves to re-establish a stable, though changed, social structure; yet it has far-reaching political, social, and sometimes economic and cultural consequences.[10]

Not always are revolutions successful at accomplishing what they set out to do. One of the stated goals of the Communist Chinese revolution, for example, was to liberate women from the oppression of a strongly patriarchal society in which a woman owed lifelong obedience to some man or other—first her father, later her husband and, after his death, her sons. Although some progress was made, the effort overall has been frustrated by the cultural lens through which the revolutionaries have viewed their work. A tradition of extreme patriarchy extending back at least 22 centuries is not easily overcome, and has unconsciously influenced many of the decisions made by China's leaders since 1949. In rural China today, as in the past, a woman's life is still usually determined by her relationship to some man, be it her father, husband, or son, rather than her own efforts or failures. What's more, women are being told more and more that their primary role is as wives and mothers. When they do work outside the house, it is generally at jobs with low pay, low status, and no benefits. Thus in spite of whatever autonomy they may achieve for a while, they become totally dependent in their old age on their sons. What we see here is that subversion of revolutionary goals, if it occurs, is not necessarily brought about by political opponents. Rather, it may be a consequence of the revolutionaries' own cultural background. In rural China, so long as women marry out, and land is held by families, daughters will always be seen as something of a liability.

It should be pointed out that revolution is a relatively recent phenomenon, occurring only during the last 5,000 years. The reason for this is that political rebellion requires a centralized political authority (or state) to rebel against, and the state has been in existence for only 5,000 years. Obviously, then, in those societies typified by tribes and bands, and in other nonindustrial societies lacking central authority, there could not have been rebellion or political revolution.

MODERNIZATION

One of the most frequently used terms to describe social and cultural change as these are occurring today is **modernization**. This is most clearly defined as an all-encompassing and global process of cultural and socioeconomic change, whereby developing societies seek to acquire some of the characteristics common to industrially advanced societies. If one looks very closely at this definition, one sees that "becoming modern" really means "becoming like us" ("us" being the United States), with the very clear implication that not being like us is to be antiquated and obsolete. Not only is this ethnocentric, it also fosters the notion that these other societies must be changed to be more like us, irrespective of other considerations. It is unfortunate that the term *modernization* continues to be so widely used. Since we seem to be stuck with it, the best we can do at the moment is to recognize its inappropriateness, even though we continue to use it.

The process of modernization may be best understood as consisting of four subprocesses, of which one is technological development. In the course of modernization, traditional knowledge and techniques give way to the application of

[9]Ibid., p. 7.

[10]E. Adamson Hoebel, *Anthropology: The Study of Man*, 4th ed. (New York: McGraw-Hill, 1972), p. 667.

Modernization: The process of cultural and socioeconomic change, whereby developing societies acquire some of the characteristics of Western industrialized societies.

Structural differentiation. Whereas most items for daily use were once made at home, as in this quilting party (*top*), almost everything we use today is the product of specialized production, as are the quilts shown in the linens boutique (*bottom*).

scientific knowledge and techniques borrowed mainly from the West. Another subprocess is agricultural development, represented by a shift in emphasis from subsistence farming to commercial farming. Instead of raising crops and livestock for their own use, people turn more and more to the production of cash crops, with greater reliance on a cash economy and markets for the sale of farm products and purchase of goods. A third subprocess is industrialization, with a greater emphasis placed on inanimate forms of energy—especially fossil fuels—to power machines. Human and animal power become less important, as do handicrafts in general. The fourth subprocess is urbanization, marked particularly by population movements from rural settlements into cities. Although all four subprocesses are interrelated, there is no fixed order of appearance.

As modernization takes place, other changes are likely to follow. In the political realm, political parties and some sort of electoral machinery fre-

quently appear, along with the development of a bureaucracy. In education, there is an expansion of learning opportunities, literacy increases, and an indigenous educated elite develops. Religion becomes less important in many areas of thought and behavior, as traditional beliefs and practices are undermined. The traditional rights and duties connected with kinship are altered, if not eliminated, especially where distant kin are concerned. Finally, where stratification is a factor, mobility increases as ascribed status becomes less important and achievement counts for more.

Two other features of modernization go hand in hand with those already noted. One, **structural differentiation,** is the division of single traditional roles, which embrace two or more functions, into two or more separate roles, each with a single specialized function. This represents a kind of fragmentation of society, which must be counteracted by new **integrative mechanisms,** if the society is not to disintegrate into a number of discrete units. These new mechanisms take such forms as new nationalistic ideologies, formal governmental structures, political parties, legal codes, labor and trade unions, and common-interest associations. All of these cross-cut other societal divisions and so serve to oppose differentiating forces. These two forces, however, are not the only ones in opposition in a situation of modernization; to them must be added a third, the force of **tradition.** This opposes the new forces of both differentiation and integration. On the other hand, the conflict does not have to be total. Traditional ways may on occasion facilitate modernization. For example, ru-

Structural differentiation: The division of single traditional roles, which embrace two or more functions (for example, political, economic, and religious) into two or more roles, each with a single specialized function.

Integrative mechanisms: Cultural mechanisms, such as nationalistic ideologies, formal governmental structures, political parties, legal codes, labor and trade unions, and common-interest associations, that oppose forces for differentiation in a society.

Tradition: In a modernizing society, old cultural practices, which may oppose new forces of differentiation and integration.

ral people may be assisted by traditional kinship ties as they move into cities, if they have relatives already there to whom they may turn for aid. One's relatives, too, may provide the financing that is necessary for business success.

One aspect of modernization, the technological explosion, has made it possible to transport human beings and ideas from one place to another with astounding speed and in great numbers. Formerly independent cultural systems have been brought into contact with others. The cultural differences between New York and Pukapuka are declining, while the differences between fishing people and physicists are increasing. No one knows whether this implies a net gain or net loss in cultural diversity, but the worldwide spread of anything, whether it is DDT or a new idea, should be viewed with at least caution. That human beings and human cultural systems are different is the most exciting thing about them, yet the destruction of diversity is implicit in the worldwide spread of rock-and-roll, socialism, capitalism, or anything else. When a song is forgotten or a ceremony ceases to be performed, a part of the human heritage is destroyed forever.

An examination of three traditional cultures that have felt the impact of modernization or other cultural changes will help to pinpoint some of the problems these cultures have met. The cultures are the Skolt Lapps of Finland, the Shuar Indians of Ecuador, and the Wauja of Brazil.

SKOLT LAPPS AND THE SNOWMOBILE REVOLUTION

The Skolt Lapps, whose homeland straddles the Arctic Circle in Finland, traditionally supported themselves by fishing and by herding reindeer.[11] Although they depended on the outside world for certain material goods, the resources crucial for their system were to be had locally and were for all practical purposes available to all. No one was denied access to critical resources, and there was little social and economic differentiation among people. Theirs was basically an egalitarian society.

[11]Pertti J. Pelto, *The Snowmobile Revolution: Technology and Social Change in the Arctic* (Menlo Park, Calif.: Cummings, 1973).

Of particular importance to the Skolt Lapps was reindeer herding. Indeed, herd management is central to their definition of themselves as a people. These animals were a source of meat, for home consumption or for sale in order to procure outside goods. They were also a source of hides for shoes and clothing, sinews for sewing, and antler and bone for making certain things. Finally, reindeer were used to pull sleds in the winter and as pack animals when there was no snow on the ground. Understandably, the animals were the objects of much attention. The herds were not large, but without a great deal of attention, productivity suffered. Hence, most winter activities centered on reindeer. Men, operating on skis, were closely associated with their herds, intensively from November to January, periodically from January to April.

In the early 1960s these reindeer herders speedily adopted snowmobiles, on the premise that the new machines would make herding physically easier and economically more advantageous. The first machine arrived in Finland in 1962; by 1971 there were 70 operating machines owned by the Skolt Lapps and non-Lapps in the same area. Although men on skis still carry out some herding activity, their importance and prestige are now diminished. As early as 1967 only four people were still using reindeer sleds for winter travel; most had gotten rid of draft animals. Those who had not converted to snowmobiles felt themselves disadvantaged compared to the rest.

The consequences of this mechanization were extraordinary and far-reaching. The need for snowmobiles, parts and equipment to maintain them, and a steady supply of gasoline created a dependency on the outside world unlike anything that had previously existed. As traditional skills were replaced by snowmobile technology, the ability of the Lapps to determine their own survival without dependence on outsiders, should this be necessary, was lost. Snowmobiles are also expensive, costing several thousand dollars in the Arctic. Maintenance and gasoline expenses must be added to this initial cost. Accordingly, there has been a sharp rise in the need for cash. To get this, men must go outside the Lapp community for wage work more than just occasionally, as had once been the case, or else rely on such sources as government pensions or welfare.

The argument may be made that dependency and the need for cash are prices worth paying for an improved system of reindeer herding; but has it improved? In truth, snowmobiles have contributed in a significant way to a disastrous decline in reindeer herding. By 1971 the average size of the family herd was down from 50 to 12. Not only is this too small a number to be economically viable, it is too small to maintain at all. The reason is that the animals in such small herds will take the first opportunity to run off to join another larger one. What happened was that the old close, prolonged, and largely peaceful relationship between herdsman and beast changed to a noisy, traumatic relationship. Now, when men appear, it is to come speeding out of the woods on snarling, smelly machines that invariably chase animals, often for long distances. Instead of helping the animals in their winter food quest, helping females with their calves, and protecting them from predators, the appearance of men now means either slaughter or castration. Naturally enough, the reindeer have become suspicious. The result has been actual de-domestication, with reindeer scattering and running off to more inaccessible areas, given the slightest chance. Moreover, there are indications that snowmobile harassment has adversely effected the number of viable calves added to the herds. What we have here is a classic illustration of the fact that change is not always adaptive.

The cost of mechanized herding—and the decline of the herds—has led many Lapps to abandon it altogether. Now, the majority of males are no longer herders at all. This constitutes a serious economic problem, since few economic alternatives are available. The problem is compounded by the fact that participation in a cash-credit economy means that most people, employed or not, have payments to make. Furthermore, this is more than just an economic problem, for in the traditional culture of this people, being a herder of reindeer is the very essence of manhood. Hence, the new

nonherders are not only poor in a way that they could not be in previous times, but they are in a sense inadequate as "men" quite apart from this.

This economic differentiation with its evaluation of roles is leading to the development of a stratified society out of the older egalitarian one. Differences are developing in terms of wealth, and with this, in life-styles. It is difficult to break into reindeer herding now, for one needs a substantial cash outlay. And herding now requires skills and knowledge that were not a part of traditional culture. Not everyone has these, and those without them are dependent on others if they are to participate. Hence, there is now restricted access to critical resources, where once there had been none.

THE SHUAR SOLUTION

Although the Skolt Lapps have not escaped many negative aspects of modernization, the choice to modernize or not was essentially theirs. The Shuar Indians, by contrast, deliberately avoided modernization, until they felt that they had no other option, if they were to fend off the same outside forces that elsewhere in the Amazon Basin have resulted in the destruction of whole societies. Threatened with the loss of their land base as more and more Ecuadoran colonists intruded into their territory, the Shuar in 1964 founded a fully independent corporate body, the Shuar Federation, to take control over their own future. Recognized by the government of Ecuador, albeit grudgingly, the federation is officially dedicated to promotion of the social, economic, and moral advancement of its members, and to coordination of development with official government agencies. Since its founding, the federation has secured title to over 95,000 hectares of communal land, has established a cattle herd of more than 15,000 head as the people's primary source of income, has taken over control of their own education, using their own language and mostly Shuar teachers, has established their own bilingual broadcasting station and a bilingual newspaper. Obviously, all this has required enormous changes on the part of the Shuar, but they have been able to maintain a variety of distinctive cultural markers, including their own language, communal land tenure, cooperative production and distribution, a basically egalitarian economy, and kin-based communities which retain maximum autonomy. Thus, for all the changes, they feel they are still Shuar, and quite distinct from other Ecuadorans.[12]

What the Shuar case shows us is that Amazonian Indian nations are capable of taking control of their own destinies even in the face of intense outside pressures, if allowed to do so. Unfortunately, until recently, few have had that option. Prior to European invasions of the Amazon, more than 700 distinct groups inhabited the region. By 1900 in Brazil, the number was down to 270, and today something like 180 remain.[13] Many of these survivors find themselves in situations not unlike that of the Yanomami, described earlier in this chapter. Nevertheless, many of these peoples are showing a new resourcefulness in standing up to the forces of destruction arrayed against them, as the following Original Study illustrates.

[12]John H. Bodley, *Victims of Progress*, 2nd ed. (Palo Alto, Calif.: Mayfield, 1982), pp. 172–174. Copyright 1982 by Mayfield Publishing Company. Reprinted by permission.

[13] *Cultural Survival Quarterly* 15, No. 4 (1991):38.

ORIGINAL STUDY

WAUJA ORGANIZATION IN DEFENSE OF THEIR HOMELAND[14]

An idea is spreading in the rain forests of central Brazil, perhaps even more rapidly than the fires of deforestation: that Indians as a group are politically powerful. Indians living in isolated rainforest villages throughout Amazonia are coming to think of themselves as sharing an identity as Indian people.

In February 1989, the Kayapó and their allies staged a historic peaceful demonstration against a proposed hydroelectric project at Altamira, Brazil. The project, to be funded by the World Bank, would have flooded vast areas of Kayapó land and destroyed most of their rivers for fishing. Outraged that they had not even been consulted, the Kayapó organized themselves and mounted a spectacular media event in protest. Their campaign was so creative and well-executed that the ensuing international outcry caused the World Bank to withdraw its support for the dam project. The success of this initiative at Altamira profoundly changed political reality and expectations for Indian people in Brazil and beyond. The stereotype of Indian as victim was broken.

One example of this legacy is the current effort of the Wauja of the Upper Xingu to reclaim peacefully, under Brazilian law, traditional fishing grounds and a sacred ceremonial site, Kamukuaka. Both are currently being invaded or occupied by ranchers and poachers.

The Wauja are a community of about 200 relatively traditional Arawak-speaking Indians who live by fishing and swidden horticulture in the Xingu National Park in Northern Mato Grosso. Although during the past generation their economy has become dependent on steel tools, fishhooks, and other manufactured goods, their involvement in the cash economy is still minimal and sporadic, limited mainly to sale of handicrafts.

In February of 1989, the Kayapo skillfully manipulated Western technology and the media when they organized a massive demonstration against the Altamira Hydro Project in Brazil. Their efforts were successful at halting this project, which would have destroyed vast parts of their homeland.

Like virtually all Indian people, during the early period of contact they suffered horrific population losses due to recurrent epidemics of introduced disease. Unlike most other Indians, however, much of their traditional land was reserved for them under law soon after regular contact began in the 1940s. Despite this measure of protection, an essential part of their traditional territory was left out of the park. This unprotected area includes fishing grounds; agricultural land; and, most important, Kamukuaka, the most sacred Wauja ceremonial site.

When the Wauja first began to understand that only part of their traditional territory fell within park boundaries, they protested to the government Indian agency, FUNAI, saying that the excluded area was essential to their survival as an Indian people. In response to the Wauja's most recent protests on the matter, FUNAI stated that a five-year study is needed before action can be taken.

The Wauja say that if nothing is done, in five years their ancestral land will be overrun and lost to them forever. Ranchers already occupy Kamukuaka, which is situated on the upper Batovi-Tamitatoala River. Atamai, political chief of the Wauja, describes the site as an extraordinary place, a great stone cavern beside a waterfall. At the mouth of the cavern are rock carvings made by ancestors of the Wauja, images of the parts of women that create life. The Wauja say the carvings have power to make living things increase and become abundant.

In addition, the Wauja revere Kamukuaka as the dwelling place of spirits. These spirits are respectfully addressed as kin, and referred to in the Wauja language as *inyākānāu*, "those who teach." The spirits guide the elders, appearing to them in visions and helping them heal the sick and maintain harmony within the village. To honor these spirits, the Wauja and their neighbors the Bacari have performed ceremonies at Kamukuaka for many generations. Wauja elders emphasize their most sacred ceremony, *kawika*, was performed at that place, and can proudly list deceased relatives who played kawika flutes at Kamukuaka. Mayaya, brother of Atamai and ceremonial leader of the Wauja, once sought to express his attachment to Kamukuaka without reducing it to words. An accomplished musician, he softly sang the melody of the sacred flute ceremony, concluding, "therefore that land means everything to us." In Wauja oral tradition, Kamukuaka has existed since the beginning of the world, before human beings were created. Chief Atamai says his late father took his children there before he died and told them the sacred story linked to that place, of how the Sun dwelt in the great stone house when he still walked the earth in human form. Atamai himself has seen the gaping hole in the side of the cavern where, according to the ancestors, the Sun tried to tear the house apart in those ancient times.

Today, the ranchers keep the Wauja out. The ancient ceremonies cannot be performed, and young people know Kamukuaka only through the stories of their elders. Even worse, the Wauja say, is the desecration the ranchers have brought:

> They have turned Kamukuaka into a cattle pasture. There used to be giant trees all around the stone cavern, right up to the waterfall, but the ranchers have ripped them all out, leaving the earth bare and pitiful. They graze cattle there now. Our ceremonial ground is covered with stinking cattle droppings. The whiteman has covered the dust of our ancestors with shit.

The loss of Kamukuaka has had economic consequences for the Wauja as well, since the area along the Batovi near Kamukuaka is the only source for certain essential raw materials, including ceramic pigments, medicinal plants, and shells used in trade.

But Kamukuaka is not the only area where outsiders are invading the Wauja's ancestral land. In 1988 and again in 1989, Atamai complained to government officials that poachers were penetrating deep into Wauja territory and taking commercial quantities of fish to sell in Brazilian towns along the upper Batovi River. The poachers enter Wauja waters in boats filled with heavily armed men, and transport the fish to small trucks waiting at designated locations outside Wauja territory.

Wauja attempts to keep poachers out have led to violent confrontations in which poachers have shot at Wauja fishermen without provocation. Because of poachers, ordinary overnight fishing

trips have suddenly become dangerous. Parents now discourage their adolescent boys from going on fishing trips unless accompanied by an elder who can be trusted to handle a threatening situation.

In addition to the physical danger posed by armed invaders, the sheer loss of fish is a serious problem, since the Wauja depend on fish for most of the protein in their diet. The areas currently being invaded by poachers are some of the best traditional fishing grounds. Generations of Wauja have relied on these areas to provide the large numbers of fish needed for ceremonial feasts. As a result of the continuing depredation by poachers, the Wauja say these areas are becoming "fished out." Poaching therefore threatens traditional Wauja economy, which is based in large part on communal sharing and ceremonial redistribution, not private profit and accumulated wealth.

The incident in early 1989, when the chief and other elders were shot at by poachers, was a turning point for the Wauja. That summer they decided the government would not defend their land and resources, and that they would have to do it themselves. They built a new village, Aldeia Batovi, within the park but near the area where the poachers and ranchers were penetrating. Gardens were cleared and planted; three large, traditional houses were built; and several families took up permanent residence there, maintaining contact with the main village at Lake Piyulaga by radio.

In June 1990, this new village was burned to the ground by an employee of a local rancher. The three houses were lost, along with all they contained: tools, stores of food, and medical supplies. Responding to letters of protest from abroad, the Brazilian government tried to minimize this incident, alleging the ranchers merely torched a make-shift campsite the Wauja had used overnight and abandoned. This is not the case. No temporary Wauja campsite has first-year gardens; the village was inhabited. Confrontation was avoided only because the occupants were away attending a ceremony at the main village during the attack.

The Brazilian government insists these incidents were not violent, even though shots were fired and houses burned. The Wauja do not agree. They consider themselves under attack, and blame the escalating violence on faulty demarcation of their territory years ago, when the Xingu National Park was created. To correct the situation, the Wauja say park boundaries must be moved south a distance of 30–40 km, to include critical parts of their traditional territory. The area of land is not large, but it is crucial to the Wauja and to peace in the region. Though it forms the outer margin of their territory, it is at the center of their traditions and their identity as Indian people.

The Wauja have already rebuilt their burned village and renamed it Aldeia Ulupuene. To maintain an increased presence in the area, they are adding an airstrip at the site of the attack. Soon after their village was burned, the Wauja asked the government to survey the land officially outside the park in order to have it included in the park and thereby protected. Officials replied that they lacked funds for such a project. In response, the Wauja, together with members of other indigenous communities, decided to survey the land themselves.

In August, a volunteer force of about 50 men drawn from Kayapó, Kajabi, Soya, Trumai, Yawalapiti, and Wauja communities assembled at the burned village site to survey the land. This in itself is a major achievement by the Wauja, and a credit to the volunteers. In the first half of this century, some of these communities fought pitched battles against each other, and in several well-remembered instances inflicted heavy casualties and took women and children captive. The men in this volunteer group are working close beside traditional enemies of their fathers and grandfathers. That they all are united in a common purpose bespeaks their determination to protect their shared future as Indian people.

The volunteers have begun clearing surveying sightlines and building the airstrip. The project is expected to take three to six months, depending on support from outside sources. Since the new village is six days' journey from the main village by dugout canoe, the Wauja need motorboats to transport people and supplies, as well as food to feed the volunteers.

The Rainforest Foundation, founded in 1988 by Kapapó chief Raoni and rock musician Sting to support Indian-initiated efforts to protect the rainforest, has taken on the Wauja project as a top priority. Olympio Serra, formerly director of the Xingu National Park and now working on the Rainforest Foundation's Brazilian board, Fundação Mata Virgem, reports that 4,000 liters of gasoline and food for the volunteers were shipped to the Wauja the first week of October 1990. These supplies should enable the Wauja to finish the job before the heavy rains arrive in December.

José Carlos Libânio at the Nucleus for Indigenous Rights (NDI) in Brasilia explains that surveying the area is an important step in protecting it for Indian people under Brazilian law. He says the Wauja's legal case, currently under preparation, stands to set a legal precedent on behalf of all Brazilian Indians. To expand the Xingu National Park boundaries, the Wauja's lawyers must challenge an administrative decree that currently prohibits altering existing boundaries of indigenous reserves. This decree works against Indians, denying them redress against boundary decisions made without their knowledge or consent.

Libânio says the Wauja case is strong, and he expects them to win it. However, it will take at least a year for the case to proceed through the Brazilian courts. During that time, the Wauja will need support from the international community. A public information and letter-writing campaign is currently being organized to help create a climate of opinion in Brazil favorable to a just resolution of the Wauja's legal case.

Although all Amazonian Indians are facing serious threats to their survival, the Wauja's case is crucial in several respects. First, their legal case stands to set a major precedent on behalf of all Brazilian Indians. If the Wauja win the right to reclaim traditional territory under law, all Brazilian Indians benefit.

Second, the Wauja campaign for nonviolent, legal reclamation of territory is setting a historical precedent as well. The Wauja have never attacked or killed Brazilian settlers. If they are successful in reclaiming

their territory through entirely nonviolent means, it will be a landmark victory for both Indian rights and rainforest conservation.

Third, the Wauja's case presents a unique opportunity simply because they stand a good chance of winning. The Yanomami situation is currently receiving worldwide attention; Survival International rightly calls it one of the great humanitarian campaigns of the late twentieth century. Both in numbers of people affected, and in severity of human rights violations, the Yanomami case outweighs the Wauja case. But the Yanomami campaign faces great odds, and will be very difficult to win. The gold miners are organized and determined; the political situation is complex and entrenched. The suffering of the Yanomami is so intense and unrelenting that it is a public relations problem to maintain enough optimism to keep the international community actively involved.

The Wauja case, on the other hand, is relatively straightforward and easy to win. A win for the Wauja will help the Yanomami as well, because success attracts optimism and support. The Yanomami situation seems almost hopeless, and this is a great part of the problem. If the Wauja create a well-publicized victory for indigenous rights in Brazil, the cause of the Yanomami and other Brazilian Indians will be advanced, just as the Wauja's own cause was advanced by the Kapapó victory at Altamira.

It is difficult to convey to members of an international community that is increasingly mobile and secular how the Wauja, and other people in traditional small-scale societies, are connected to their ancestral lands not only by economic necessity, but by far deeper bonds. The Wauja's land provides far more than food, tools, and shelter. It is the dwelling place of the spirits who guide them, the birthplace of their children, and the resting place of their ancestors. It is the sacred landscape of all their poetry, stories, songs, and prayers; it is their one place upon the earth. Everything needed for human life, everything sacred and precious, flows from that land. If it is ripped away from the Wauja, if they lose it, they lose their future as Indian people, a danger of which they are keenly aware.

[14] Emilienne Ireland, "Neither Warriors nor Victims, The Wauja Peacefully Organize to Defend Their Land." *Cultural Survival Quarterly* 15, No. 1 (1991):54–59.

MODERNIZATION AND THE THIRD WORLD

In the examples that we have just examined, we have seen how modernization has affected indigenous peoples in otherwise modern states. Elsewhere in the so-called third world, whole countries are in the throes of modernization. Throughout Africa, Asia, and South and Central America we are witnessing the widespread removal of economic activities from the family-community setting; the altered structure of the family in the face of the changing labor market; the increased reliance of young children on parents alone for affection, instead of on the extended family; the decline of general parental authority; schools replacing the family as the primary educational unit; the discov-

ery of a generation gap; and many others. The difficulty is that it all happens so fast that traditional societies are unable to adapt themselves to it gradually. Changes that took generations to accomplish in Europe and North America are attempted within the span of a single generation in developing countries. In the process they are frequently faced with the erosion of a number of dearly held values they had no intention of giving up.

Commonly the burden of modernization falls most heavily on women. For example, the commercialization of agriculture often involves land re-

Although many third-world countries have improved the educational levels of their populations remarkably, they are frequently unable to then provide the kinds of employment opportunities for which people have been educated. A consequence is widespread discontent, as people are unable to realize their aspirations.

forms which overlook or ignore traditional land rights of women. At the same time that this reduces their control of, and access to resources, mechanization of food production and processing drastically reduces their opportunities for employment. As a consequence, they are confined more and more to traditional domestic tasks which, as commercial production becomes peoples' dominant concern, is increasingly downgraded in value. To top it all off, the domestic workload tends to increase, as men are less available to help out, while tasks such as fuel gathering and water collection are made more difficult as common land and resources come under private ownership, and woodlands are reserved for commercial exploitation. In short, with modernization, women frequently find themselves in an increasingly marginal position. At the same time that their workload increases, the value assigned the work they do declines, as does their relative and absolute health, nutritional, and educational status.

In Guatemala, where these bananas are grown, agricultural development has caused increased levels of malnutrition. As in many developing countries, modernization of agriculture has meant the conversion of land from subsistence farming to the raising of crops for export, making it increasingly difficult for people to satisfy their basic nutritional needs.

MODERNIZATION: MUST IT ALWAYS BE PAINFUL?

Although most anthropologists see the change that is affecting traditional, non-Western peoples caught up in the modern technological world as an ordeal, the more widespread opinion has been that it is a good thing; that however disagreeable the "medicine" may be, it is worth it for the people to become just like "us" (i.e. the people of Europe and North America). This view of modernization, unfortunately, is based more on the hopes and expectations of Western culture than on reality. There is no doubt that many Western peoples would like to see the non-Western world attain the high levels of development seen in Europe and North America, as the Japanese in fact have done. Overlooked is that the standard of living in the Western world is based on a rate of consumption of nonrenewable resources, where far less than 50 percent of the world's population uses a good deal more than 50 percent of these resources. By the early 1970s, for example, the people of the United States—less than 5 percent (approximately) of the world's population—were consuming over 50 percent of all of the world's resources. Figures like this suggest that it is

not realistic to expect most peoples of the world to achieve a standard of living comparable to that of the Western world in the near future, if at all. At the very least, the countries of the Western world would have to cut drastically their consumption of resources. So far, they have shown no willingness to do this, and if they did, their living standards would have to change. Yet more and more non-Western people, quite understandably, aspire to a standard of living such as Western countries now enjoy, even though the gap between the rich and poor people of the world is widening rather than narrowing. This has led to the development of what anthropologist Paul Magnarella has called a new "culture of discontent," a level of aspirations that far exceeds the bounds of an individual's local opportunities. No longer satisfied with traditional values, people all over the world are fleeing to the cities to find a "better life," all too often to live out their days in poor, congested, and diseased slums in an attempt to achieve what is usually beyond their reach. Unfortunately, despite all sorts of rosy predictions about a better future, this basic reality remains.

Chapter Summary

Although cultures may be remarkably stable, culture change is characteristic to a greater or lesser degree of all cultures. Change is often caused by accidents, including the unexpected outcome of existing events. Another cause is the deliberate attempt of people to solve some perceived problem. Finally, change may be forced upon one group in the course of especially intense contact between two societies. Adaptation and progress are consequences rather than causes of change, although not all changes are necessarily adaptive. Progress is whatever a culture defines it as.

The mechanisms involved in cultural change are innovation, diffusion, cultural loss, and acculturation. The ultimate source of change is through innovation; some new practice, tool, or principle. Other individuals adopt the innovation, and it becomes socially shared. Primary innovations are chance discoveries of new principles, for example, the discovery that the firing of clay makes the material permanently hard. Secondary innovations are improvements made by applying known principles, for example, modeling the clay that is to be fired by known techniques into familiar objects. Primary innovations may prompt rapid culture change and stimulate other inventions. An innovation's chance of being accepted depends on its perceived superiority to the method or object it replaces. Its acceptance is also connected with the prestige of the innovator and imitating groups. Diffusion is the borrowing by one society of a cultural element from another. Cultural loss involves the abandonment of some trait or practice with or without replacement. Anthropologists have given considerable attention to acculturation. It stems from intensive firsthand contact of groups with different cultures and produces major changes in the cultural patterns of one or both groups. The actual or threatened use of force is always a factor in acculturation.

Applied anthropology arose as anthropologists sought to provide colonial administrators with a better understanding of native cultures, so as to avoid serious disruption of them, or as anthropologists tried to help indigenous people cope with outside threats to their interests. A serious ethical issue for applied anthropologists is how far they should go in trying to change the ways of other peoples.

Reactions of indigenous peoples to changes that are forced upon them vary considerably. Some have retreated to inaccessible places in hopes of being left alone, while some others have lapsed into apathy. Some, like the Trobriand Islanders, have been able to reassert their traditional culture's values by blending foreign and indigenous traits, a phenomenon known as syncretism. If a culture's values get widely out of step with reality, revitalization movements may appear. Some revitalization movements try to speed up the acculturation process in order to get more of the benefits expected from the dominant culture. In millenarism an attempt is made to resurrect a pariah group with its subcultural ideology. Nativistic or revivalistic movements aim to reconstitute a destroyed but not forgotten way of life. Revolutionary movements try to reform the culture from within. Rebellion differs from revolution, in that the aim is merely to replace one set of office holders with another.

Modernization refers to a global process of cultural and socioeconomic change by which developing societies seek to acquire characteristics of industrially advanced societies. The process consists of four subprocesses: technological development, agricultural development, industrialization, and urbanization. Other changes follow in the areas of political organization, education, religion, and social organization. Two other accompaniments of modernization are structural differentiation and new forces of social integration. An example of modernization is found in the Skolt Lapps of Finland, whose traditional reindeer-herding economy was all but destroyed when snowmobiles were adopted to make herding easier. In Ecuador, the

Shuar Indians modernized in order to escape the destruction that has been visited upon many other Amazonian peoples. So far they have been successful, and others are mobilizing their resources in an attempt to achieve similar success. Nevertheless, formidable forces are still arrayed against them, and on a worldwide basis, it is probably fair to say that modernization has led to a deterioration, rather than improvement, of people's quality of life.

Suggested Readings

Arensberg, Conrad M., and Arthur H. Niehoff. *Introducing Social Change: A Manual for Americans Overseas.* Chicago: Aldine, 1964.
An "oldie but goodie," this does an excellent job of showing Westerners that what appear to be bad or inefficient ways of doing things have purpose and meaning in the matrix of the particular culture, and that failure to understand such customs can lead to disaster when programs of change, no matter how well-meaning, are introduced.

Barnett, Homer G. *Innovation: The Basis of Cultural Change.* New York: McGraw-Hill, 1953.
This is the standard work on the subject, widely quoted by virtually everyone who writes about change.

Bodley, John H. *Victims of Progress,* 2nd ed. Palo Alto, Calif.: Mayfield, 1982.
Few North Americans are aware of the devastation that has been unleashed upon indigenous peoples in the name of progress, nor are they aware that this continues on an unprecedented scale today, or of the extent to which the institutions of their own society contribute to it. For most, this book will be a real eye-opener.

Kroeber, A.L. *Anthropology: Cultural Processes and Patterns.* New York: Harcourt, 1963.
Several chapters of this work are given over to excellent discussions of innovation and diffusion. Particularly good are sections dealing with the histories of specific inventions.

Magnarella, Paul J. *Tradition and Change in a Turkish Town.* New York: Wiley, 1974.
This book, one of the best anthropological community studies of the Middle East, is also an excellent introduction to the phenomenon known as modernization. There are none of the facile generalizations about modernization that one so often finds, and the author's view of the phenomenon, which is well documented, is quite different from that which was promoted in the optimistic days of the 1950s.

16

THE FUTURE

OF HUMANITY

CHAPTER PREVIEW

A child in Luanda, Angola, observes a state-sponsored 1990 rally for Marxist ruler José Eduardo dos Santos. Throughout the world, ethnic groups continue to retain and assert their distinctive identities and traditions. A common response of the artificially created state governments under which such people live is to exert repressive measures to maintain control over people who have never consented to that control.

WHAT CAN ANTHROPOLOGISTS TELL US OF THE FUTURE?

Anthropologists cannot any more accurately predict future forms of culture than biologists can predict future forms of life or geologists future landforms. They can, though, identify certain trends of which we might otherwise be unaware, and anticipate some of the consequences these might have if they continue. They can also shed light on problems already identified by nonanthropologists, by showing how these relate to each other as well as to cultural practices and attitudes of which "experts" in other fields are often unaware. This ability to place problems in their wider context is an anthropological specialty, and it is essential, if these problems are ever to be solved.

WHAT PRESENT-DAY TRENDS ARE TAKING PLACE IN THE EVOLUTION OF CULTURE?

One major trend in present-day cultural evolution is toward the worldwide adoption of the products, technology, and practices of the industrialized world. This apparent gravitation toward a homogenized, one-world culture is, however, opposed by another very strong trend for ethnic groups all over the world to reassert their own distinctive identities. A third trend, of which we are just becoming aware, is that the problems created by cultural practices seem to be outstripping the capacity of culture to find solutions to problems.

WHAT PROBLEMS WILL HAVE TO BE SOLVED IF HUMANITY IS TO HAVE A FUTURE?

If humanity is to have a future, human cultures will have to find solutions to problems of population growth, food and other resource shortages, pollution, and a growing culture of discontent. One difficulty is that, up to now, there has been a tendency to see these as if they were discrete and unrelated. Thus, attempts to deal with one problem, such as short food supplies, are often at cross-purposes with others, such as an inequitable global system for the distribution of basic resources. Unless humanity has a more realistic understanding of the "global society" than presently exists, it will not be able to solve the problems that are crucial for its future.

435

Anthropology is often described by those who know little about it as a backward-looking discipline. The most popular stereotype is that anthropologists devote all of their attention to the interpretation of the past and the description of present-day tribal remnants. Yet as we saw in Chapter 1, as well as in the "Anthropology Applied" features for Chapters 3 and 6, not even archaeologists, the most backward-looking anthropologists, limit their interests to the past, nor are ethnologists uninterested in their own cultures. Thus, throughout this book we have constantly made comparisons between "us" and "others." Moreover, anthropologists have a special concern with the future and the changes it may bring. Like many members of Western industrialized societies, they wonder what the postindustrial society now being predicted will hold. They also wonder what changes the coming years will bring to non-Western cultures. As we saw in the preceding chapter, when non-Western peoples are thrown into contact with Western industrialized peoples, their culture rapidly changes, often for the worse, becoming both less supportive and less adaptive. Since Westerners show no inclination to leave non-Westerners alone, we may ask, How can these cultures adapt to the future?

THE CULTURAL FUTURE OF HUMANITY

Whatever the biological future of the human species, culture remains the mechanism by which people solve their problems of existence. Yet some anthropologists have noted with concern—and interpret as a trend—that the problems of human existence seem to be outstripping culture's ability to find solutions. The main problem seems to be that in solving existing problems, culture inevitably poses new ones. To paraphrase anthropologist Jules Henry, although culture is "for" people, it is also "against" them. [1] As we shall see, this is now posing serious new problems for human beings. What can anthropologists tell us about the culture of the future?

Anthropologists—like geologists and evolutionary biologists—are historical scientists; as such,

they can identify and understand the processes that have shaped the past and will shape the future. They cannot, however, tell us precisely what these processes will produce in the way of future cultures, any more than biologists can predict future forms of life, or geologists future landforms. The cultural future of humanity, though, will certainly be affected in important ways by decisions that we humans will be making in the future. This being so, if those decisions are to be made intelligently, it behooves us to have a clear understanding of the way things are in the world today. It is here that anthropologists have something vital to offer.

To comprehend anthropology's role in understanding and solving the problems of the future, we must look at certain flaws frequently seen in the enormous body of future-oriented literature that has appeared over the past few decades, not to mention the efforts to plan for the future that have become commonplace on regional, national, and international levels. For one, rarely do futurist writers or planners look more than about 50 years into the future, and the trends they project into it, more often than not, are those of recent history. This predisposes people to think that a trend that seems fine today will always be so, and that it may be projected indefinitely into the future. The danger inherent in this is neatly captured in anthropologist George Cowgill's comment: "It is worth recalling the story of the person who leaped from a very tall building and on being asked how things were going as he passed the 20th floor replied, 'Fine, so far.'" [2]

Another flaw is a tendency to treat subjects in isolation, without reference to pertinent trends outside an expert's field of competence. For example, agricultural planning is often predicated upon the assumption that a certain amount of water is available for irrigation, whether or not urban planners or others have designs upon that same water. Thus—as in the southwestern United States, where more of the Colorado River's water has been allocated than actually exists—people may be counting on resources in the future that will not, in fact, be available. One would suppose that this would be a cause for concern, but as two well-known futurists put it, "if you find inconsistencies

[1] Jules Henry, *Culture against Man* (New York: Vintage Books, 1965), p. 12.

[2] George L. Cowgill, Letter, *Science*, 210 (1980):1305.

the model is better off without them."[3] These same two authorities, in editing a volume aimed at refuting the somewhat pessimistic projections of *Global 2000* (the first attempt at a coordinated analysis of global resources on the part of the U.S. government), deliberately avoided going into population growth and its implications, because they knew that to do so would lead their contributing authors to disagree with one another.[4] This brings us to yet another common flaw: A tendency to project the hopes and expectations of one's own culture into the future interferes with the scientific objectivity that one ought to bring to the problem.

Against this background, anthropology's contribution to our view of the future is clear. With our holistic perspective, we are specialists at seeing how parts fit together into a larger whole; with our evolutionary perspective, we are able to see short-term trends in longer-term perspective; with over 100 years of cross-cultural research behind us, we are able to recognize culture-bound assertions when we encounter them; and we are familiar with alternative ways of dealing with a wide variety of problems.

ONE WORLD CULTURE

A popular belief in recent years has been that the future world will see the development of a single homogeneous world culture. The idea that such a "one-world culture" is emerging is based largely on the observation that developments in communication, transportation, and trade so link the peoples of the world that they are increasingly wearing the same kinds of clothes, eating the same kinds of food, reading the same kinds of newspapers, watching the same kinds of television programs, and so on. The continuation of such trends, so this thinking goes, should lead North Americans, traveling in the year 2100 to Tierra del Fuego, China, or New Guinea, to find the inhabitants of these areas living in a manner identical or similar to theirs.

Certainly it is striking, the extent to which such things as Western-style clothing, transistor radios, Coca-Cola, and McDonald's hamburgers have

The worldwide spread of such products as Pepsi Cola is viewed by some people as a sign that a single homogeneous world culture is developing.

spread to virtually all parts of the world, and many countries—Japan, for example—have gone a long way toward becoming Westernized. Moreover, if one looks back over the past 5,000 years of human history, one will see that there has been a clear-cut trend for political units to become larger and more all-encompassing, while becoming at the same time fewer in number. A logical outcome of the continuation of this trend into the future would be the reduction of autonomous political units to a single one, encompassing the entire world. In fact, by extrapolation from this past trend into the future, some anthropologists have gone so far as to predict that the world will become politically integrated, perhaps by the twenty-third century, but no later than the year 4850.[5]

One problem with such a prediction is that it ignores the one thing that all large states, past and present, irrespective of other differences between them, share in common: a tendency to come apart.

[3]Constance Holden, "Simon and Kahn versus *Global 2000*," *Science,* 221 (1983):342.

[4]Ibid., p. 343.

[5]Carol R. Ember and Melvin Ember, *Cultural Anthropology*, 4th ed. (Englewood Cliffs, N.J.: Prentice-Hall, 1985), p. 230.

One recent, heroic example of the determination of national groups to run their own affairs came with the collapse of the Soviet Union. Here, Russian president Boris Yeltsin (waving) leads citizens in defying the abortive 1991 coup by Communist hard-liners, who sought to prevent the breakup of the Soviet Union into its constituent national republics.

Not only have the great empires of the past, without exception, broken up into numbers of smaller independent states, but countries in virtually all parts of the world today are showing a tendency to fragment. The most dramatic illustrations of this in recent years have been the breakup of the Soviet Union into several smaller, independent states, and the struggle of several Yugoslavian republics to regain their independence. It can also be seen in separatist movements, such as that of French-speaking peoples in Canada; Basque and Catalonian nationalist movements in Europe; Scottish, Irish, and Welsh nationalist movements in Britain; Tibetan nationalism in China; Kurdish nationalism in Turkey, Iran, and Iraq; Sikh separatism in India; Tamil separatism in Sri Lanka; Igbo separatism in Nigeria; Eritrean and Tigrean secession movements in Ethiopia; Namibian nationalism; and so on—this list is far from exhaustive. Nor is the United States immune, as can be seen from Puerto Rican nationalist movements and American Indian attempts to secure greater political self-determination and autonomy. These examples all involve peoples who consider themselves to be members of distinct nations by virtue of birth and cultural and territorial heritage, over whom peoples of some other ethnic background have tried to assert control. There are an estimated 5000 such national groups in the world today, as opposed to a mere 181 recognized states (up from fewer than 50 in the 1940s).[6] Although some of these groups are quite small in population and area—100 or so people living on a few acres, some are quite large. The Karen people of Burma, for example, number some 4.5 to 5 million, making them larger than 48 percent of United Nations member states.

Reactions of these peoples to attempts at annexation and absorption by imposed state regimes controlled by other peoples range all the way from the successful fight for independence from Pakistan on the part of Bangladesh (or the Igbos' unsuccessful fight for independence from Nigeria) to the nonviolence of Scottish and Welsh nationalism. Many struggles for independence have been going on for years, as in the case of Karen resistance to the Burmese invasion of their territory in 1948, or the

[6] *Cultural Survival Quarterly* 15, No. 4 (1991):38.

takeover of Kurdistan by Iraq, Iran, and Turkey in 1925. Even in cases of relative nonviolence, the stresses and strains are obviously there. Similar stresses and strains may even develop in the absence of ethnic differences, as regional interests within a large country come into increasing competition. Again, hints of this may be seen in the United States—for example, in arguments over access to Colorado River water, in attempts by oil- and gas-producing states to get the most out of their resources at the expense of other states ("Let the Bastards Freeze in the Dark" proclaimed bumper stickers in oil- and gas-producing states during the Arab oil embargo of the 1970s) or in the refusal in some states to curb smokestack emissions that cause acid rain, which is destroying resources and endangering the health of people in other states (not to mention other countries; Canada in particular).

Expansionist attempts on the part of existing states to annex all or parts of other states also seem to be running into difficulty, as in the case of the Iraqi attempt to take over Kuwait. It is just possible that we are reaching a point at which the old tendency for political units to increase in size, while decreasing in number, is being canceled out by the tendency to fragment into a greater number of smaller units.

THE RISE OF THE MULTINATIONAL CORPORATIONS

The resistance of the world to political integration seems to be offset, at least partially, by the rise of multinational corporations. Because these cut across the boundaries between states, they are a force for global unity in spite of the political differences that divide people. Situations like this are well known to anthropologists, as illustrated by this description of Zuni Indian integrative mechanisms:

> Four or five different planes of systemization crosscut each other and thus preserve for the whole society an integrity that would speedily be lost if the planes merged and thereby inclined to encourage segregation and fission. The clans, the fraternities, the priesthoods, the kivas, in a measure the gaming parties, are all dividing agencies. If they coincided, the rifts in the social structure would be deep; by countering each

other they cause segmentations which produce an almost marvelous complexity, but can never break apart the national entity.[7]

Multinational corporations are not new in the world (The Dutch East India Company is a good example from the seventeenth century), but they were comparatively rare until the 1950s. Since then they have become a major force in the world. These modern-day giants are actually clusters of corporations of diverse nationality, joined together by ties of common ownership and responsive to a common management strategy. More and more tightly controlled by a head office in one particular country, these multinationals are able to organize and integrate production across international boundaries for interests formulated in corporate board rooms, irrespective of whether or not these are consistent with the interests of the countries within which they operate. In a sense they are products of the technological revolution, for without sophisticated data-processing equipment, the multinationals could not keep adequate track of their worldwide operations.

So great is the power of multinationals that they are increasingly able to thwart the wishes of governments. Because the information processed by these corporations is kept from flowing in a meaningful way to the population at large, or even to lower levels within the organization, it becomes difficult for governments to get the information they need for informed policy decisions. For example, the U.S. Congress repeatedly expressed its frustration in trying to get from corporations the information that it needed in order to consider what federal energy policies should be. Beyond this, though, the multinationals have shown themselves able to overrule foreign-policy decisions, as when they got around a U.S. embargo on pipeline equipment for the now-defunct Soviet Union. While some might see this as a hopeful augury for the transcendence of national vices and rivalries, it raises the unsettling issue as to whether or not the global order should be determined by corporations interested only in their own profits.

If the ability of multinational corporations to ignore the wishes of sovereign governments is

[7]Alfred L. Kroeber, quoted in Edward Dozier, *The Pueblo Indians of North America* (New York: Holt, Rinehart and Winston, 1970), p. 19.

Brazil's Grand Carajas iron ore mine is an example of the kind of project often favored by states in their drive to develop. Not only does this introduce ecologically unsound technologies, it commonly has devastating effects on the indigenous people whose land is seized.

cause for concern, so is their ability to act in concert with such governments. Here, in fact, is where their worst excesses have taken place. In Brazil, for example, where the situation is hardly unique but is especially well documented, a partnership emerged, after the military coup of 1964, between a government anxious to proceed as rapidly as possible with "development" of the Amazon basin, a number of multinational corporations such as ALCOA, Borden, Union Carbide, Swift-Armour, and Volkswagen, to mention only a very few, and several international lending institutions, such as the Export-Import Bank, the Inter-American Development Bank, and the World Bank.[8] In order to realize their goals, these allies have introduced "inappropriate" technology and ecologically unsound practices into the region, which have already converted vast areas into semidesert. Far more shocking, however, has been the practice of uprooting whole human societies because they are seen as obstacles to economic growth. Literally overnight, people are deprived of the means to provide for their own needs and forcibly removed to places where they do not choose to live. Little distinction is made here between Indians and Brazilian small-holders who were brought into the region in the first place by a government anxious to alleviate acute land shortages in the northeast. Bad as this is for these Brazilian small-holders, the amount of disease, death, and human suffering unleashed upon the Indians can only be described as massive; in the process, whole peoples have been (and are still being) destroyed with a thoroughness not achieved even by Stalin during his Great Terror of the 1930s, or the Nazis in World War II. Were it not so well-documented, it would be beyond belief. This is "culture against people" with a vengeance.

The power of multinational corporations creates problems on the domestic as well as on the international scene. Anthropologist Jules Henry, in his classic study of life in the United States, argued that working for any large corporation—multinational or not—tends to generate "hostility, instability, and fear of being obsolete and unprotected. For most people their job was what they had to do rather than what they wanted to do. . . . taking a job, therefore, meant giving up part of their selves."[9]

[8]Shelton H. Davis, *Victims of the Miracle* (Cambridge: Cambridge University Press, 1982).

[9]Henry, *Culture*, p. 127.

Consumers, too, have their problems with big business. After a ten-year intensive study of relations between producers and consumers of products and services, the anthropologist Laura Nader found repeated and documented offenses by business that cannot be handled by present complaint mechanisms, either in or out of court. Viable alternatives to a failed judicial system do not seem to be emerging. Face-to-faceless relations between producers and consumers, among whom there is a grossly unequal distribution of power, exact a high cost: a terrible sense of apathy, even a loss of faith in the system itself.

These problems are exacerbated, and new ones arise in the "sprawling, anonymous, networks" that are the multinational corporations.[10] Not only are corporate decisions made in board rooms far removed from where other corporate operations take place but, given their dependence on ever more sophisticated data-processing systems to keep their operations running smoothly, many decisions can be and are being made by computers programmed for given contingencies and strategies. As anthropologist Alvin Wolfe has observed, "a social actor has been created which is much less under the control of men than we expected it to be, much less so than many even think it to be."[11] In the face of such seemingly mindless systems for making decisions in the corporate interest, employees become ever more fearful that, if they ask too much of the corporation, it may simply shift its operations to some other part of the globe where it can find cheaper, more submissive personnel, as has happened with some frequency with respect to labor forces. Indeed, whole communities become fearful that, if they do not acquiesce to corporate interests, local operations may be closed down.

In their never-ending search for inexpensive labor, multinational corporations more and more have come to favor women for low-skill assembly jobs. In third-world countries, as subsistence farming gives way to mechanical agriculture for production of crops for export, women are less able to contribute to their families' survival. Together with devaluation of the worth of domestic work,

In third-world countries, women have become a source of cheap labor for large corporations as subsistence farming has given way to mechanized agriculture, which is less labor-intensive. Unable to contribute to their families' well-being in any other way, they take on menial jobs for low wages.

this places pressure on women to seek jobs outside the household, in order to contribute to its support. Since most women do not have the time or resources to get an education, or to develop special job skills, only low-paying jobs are open to them. Corporate officials, for their part, may assume that female workers are strictly temporary, and high turnover means that wages can be kept low. Unmarried women are especially favored for employment, for it is assumed that they are free from family responsibilities until they marry, whereupon they will leave the labor force. Thus, the increasing importance of the multinationals in developing countries is contributing to the emergence of a division of labor in which gender segregation is prominent. On top of their housework, women hold low-paying jobs that require little skill; altogether, they may work as many as 15 hours a day. Higher-paying jobs, or at least those that require special skills, are generally held by men, whose workday may be shorter since they do not have additional domestic tasks to perform. Those men who lack special skills—and there are many—are often doomed to lives of unemployment.

In sum, multinational corporations have become a major force in the world today, drawing people more firmly than ever before into a system of

[10]David Pitt, "Comment," *Current . Anthropology,* 18 (1977):628.

[11]Alvin W. Wolfe, "The Supranational Organization of Production: An Evolutionary Perspective," *Current Anthropology,* 18 (1977):619.

relationships that is truly global in scope. While this brings with it potential benefits, it is also clear that it poses whole new sets of problems, which now must be solved.

ONE WORLD CULTURE: A GOOD IDEA OR NOT?

In the abstract, the idea of a single culture for all the world's people is one that has had a degree of popular appeal, in that it might offer fewer chances for the kinds of misunderstandings to develop that, so often in the past few hundred years, have led to wars. Some anthropologists question this, though, in the face of evidence that traditional ways of thinking of oneself and the rest of the world may persist, even in the face of massive changes in other aspects of culture. Indeed, one might argue that the chances for misunderstandings actually increase; an example of this is the Penobscot Indian land-claims case mentioned in Chapter 5. Many non-Indian residents of the state of Maine simply cannot comprehend how a people who look and act so much like themselves cannot see things as they do.

Some have argued that perhaps a generalized world culture would be desirable in the future, because certain cultures of today may be too specialized to survive in a changed environment. Examples of this situation are sometimes said to abound in modern anthropology. When a traditional culture that is highly adapted to a specific environment—such as that of the Indians of Brazil, who are well adapted to life in a tropical rain forest—meets European-derived culture and the social environment changes suddenly and drastically, the traditional culture often collapses. The reason for this, it is argued, is that its traditions and its political and social organizations are not at all adapted to "modern" ways. Here we have, once again, the ethnocentric notion (discussed in Chapter 15) that "old" cultures are destined to give way to the new. Since this is regarded as inevitable, actions are taken that by their very nature virtually guarantee that the traditional cultures will not survive; it is a classic case of the self-fulfilling prophecy.

A problem with this argument is that, far from being unable to adapt, traditional societies in places like Brazil's Amazon forest usually have been given

These Australian aborigines are calling relatives to ceremonies via a short-wave radio. Indigenous peoples can manage to adapt to the modern world without losing their own distinctive identity, provided they are given the chance to do so.

ANTHROPOLOGY APPLIED

ADVOCACY FOR THE RIGHTS OF INDIGENOUS PEOPLES

Anthropologists are increasingly concerned about the rapid disappearance of the world's remaining tribal peoples for a number of reasons, foremost among them a basic issue of human rights. In the world today there is a rush to develop those parts of the planet Earth that have so far escaped industrialization, or the extraction of resources regarded as vital to the well-being of developed economies. These efforts at national and international development are planned, financed, and carried out by both governments and businesses (generally the huge multinational corporations) and international lending institutions. Unfortunately, the rights of native peoples generally have not been incorporated into the programs and concerns of these organizations, even where laws exist that are supposed to protect the rights of such peoples.

For example, the typical pattern for development of Brazil's Amazon basin has been for the government to build roads, along which poor people from other parts of the country are settled. This brings them into conflict with Indians already living there, who begin to die off in large numbers from diseases contracted from the settlers. Before long, the settlers learn that the soils are not suited for their kind of farming; at the same time, outside logging, mining, and agribusiness interests exert pressure to get them off the land. Ultimately, the poor people wind up living in disease-ridden slums, while the Indians end up decimated by the diseases and violence unleashed upon them by the outsiders. Those who survive are usually relocated to places where resources are inadequate to support them.

In an attempt to do what they can to help indigenous peoples gain title to their land and avoid exploitation by outsiders, anthropologists in various countries have formed advocacy groups. The major one in the United States is Cultural Survival, Inc., based in Cambridge, Massachusetts. The interest of this organization is not in preserving indigenous cultures in some sort of romantic, pristine condition, so that they will be there to study or to serve as "living museum exhibits," as it were. Rather, it is to provide the information and support to help endangered groups to comprehend their situation, maintain or even strengthen their sense of self, and adapt to the changing circumstances. It does not regard "mainstreaming" these groups into national societies as necessarily desirable; rather, they should be allowed the freedom to make their own decisions about how they wish to live. Instead of designing projects and then imposing them on endangered societies, Cultural Survival prefers to respond to the requests and desires of groups that see a problem and the need to address it. Cultural Survival can suggest ways to help and can activate extensive networks of anthropologists, other indigenous peoples who have already dealt with similar problems, and those government officials whose support can be critical to success.

Most projects funded or assisted by Cultural Survival have been focused on securing the land rights of indigenous peoples and organizing native federations. It has also identified and funded a number of locally designed experiments in sustainable development, such as the Turkmen Weaving Project, which allows Afghan refugees to make a profitable income from traditional rug weaving; the Ikwe Marketing Collective, through which Minnesota Indians market wild rice and crafts; or Cultural Survival Enterprises, which has developed and expanded markets for such products as the nuts used in the popular Rain Forest Crunch. Of major importance was the success of Cultural Survival in getting the World Bank, in 1982, to require as a matter of policy that the rights and autonomy of tribal peoples and minorities be *guaranteed* in any project in which the bank is involved. In spite of such successes, however, much remains to be done to secure the survival of indigenous peoples in all parts of the world.

no chance to work out their own adaptations. That Amazonian Indians can adapt themselves to the modern world if left alone to do so, without losing their own distinctive ethnic and cultural identity, is demonstrated by the Shuar case, noted in the preceding chapter. In Brazil, however, the pressures to "develop" the Amazon are so great that whole groups of people are swept aside, as multinational corporations and agribusiness pursue their own particular interests. People do not have much chance to work out their own adaptations to the modern world if they are transported en masse from their homelands and deprived literally overnight of their means of survival, so that more acreage can be devoted to the raising of beef cattle. Few Brazilians get to eat any of this meat, for the bulk of it is shipped to Europe; nor do many of the profits stay in Brazil, since the major ranches are owned and operated by corporations based elsewhere. The process continues apace, nonetheless.

There is an important issue at stake in such situations, for what has happened is that some of the world's people have defined others—indeed, whole societies—as obsolete. This is surely a dangerous precedent, which if allowed to stand, means that any of the world's people may at some time in the future be declared obsolete by someone else.

ETHNIC RESURGENCE

In spite of the worldwide adoption of such things as Coca-Cola and the Big Mac, and in spite of pressure for traditional cultures to disappear, it is clear that cultural differences are still very much with us in the world today. In fact, there is a strengthening tendency for peoples all around the world to resist modernization, and in many cases retreat from it. Manifestations of this to which we have already alluded are the separatist movements around the world, and the success so far of the Shuar in retaining their own ethnic and cultural identity.

During the 1970s indigenous peoples around the world began to organize self-determination movements, culminating in the formation of the World Council of Indigenous Peoples in 1975. This now has official status as a nongovernmental organization of the United Nations, which allows it to present the case of indigenous people before the world community. Leaders of this movement see their own societies as community-based, egalitarian, and close to nature, and are intent upon maintaining them that way. Further credibility to their cause comes from the dedication of 1993 as the Year of Indigenous Peoples.

Many North Americans have difficulty adjusting to the fact that not everyone wants to be just like they are. People in the United States have traditionally been taught to believe that "the American way of life" is one to which all other peoples aspire, but it isn't only people like the Shuar who resist becoming "just like us." There are in the world today whole countries that, having striven to emulate Western ways, have suddenly backed off. The most striking recent case of such a retreat from modernity is Iran. With the 1979 overthrow of Shah Reza Pahlavi, a policy of deliberate modernization was abandoned in favor of a radical attempt to return to an Islamic republic out of a mythical "golden age." A somewhat similar, though far less radical, retreat from modernity seemed to be under way in the United States, which, in 1984 re-elected a government dedicated to a return to traditional values out of the American past. To note just two other broad parallels between the two situations, in the United States, the analogue to the control of the Iranian government by a fundamentalist Islamic leader is the sympathy shown by members of the Reagan administration, as well as some members of Congress, to fundamentalist Christian views;[12] the analogue to Iran's outlawing of Western-style dress for women, who were ordered to return to traditional-style clothing, was the directive to women on the White House staff that pants were no longer acceptable dress, and that skirts must be worn.

CULTURAL PLURALISM

If a single homogeneous world culture is not necessarily the wave of the future, what is? Some see **cultural pluralism**, in which more than one culture exists in a given society, as the future condition of humanity. Cultural pluralism is the social and political interaction within the same society of people with different ways of living and thinking. Ideally, it implies the rejection of bigotry, bias, and racism in favor of respect for the cultural traditions of other peoples. In reality, however, it has rarely worked out that way.

Cultural pluralism: Social and political interaction within the same society of people with different ways of living and thinking.

---

[12]Joan Marsella, "Pulling It Together: Discussion and Comments," in *Confronting the Creationists*, ed. Stephen Pastner and William A. Haviland, Northeastern Anthropological Association, Occasional Proceedings, No. 1 (1982):79–80.

All large North American cities contain pockets of immigrant cultures. Shown here is a produce market in New York's Chinatown.

Elements of pluralism are to be found in the United States, despite its melting-pot ideal. For example, in New York City there are neighborhoods where Puerto Ricans, with their own distinctive cultural traditions and values, exist side by side with other New Yorkers. Besides living in their own *barrio*, the Puerto Ricans have their own language, music, religion, and food. This particular pluralism, however, may be of a temporary nature, a stage in the process of integration into standard American culture. Thus, the Puerto Ricans, in four or five generations, like many Italians, Irish, and east European Jews before them, may also become Americanized to the point where their life-style will be largely indistinguishable from others around them. On the other hand, some Puerto Ricans, Asian Americans, American Indians, Hispanics, and others have strongly resisted abandoning their distinctive cultural identities. Whether this marks the beginning of a trend away from the melting-pot philosophy and toward pluralism, however, remains to be seen.

Some familiar examples of cultural pluralism may be seen in Switzerland, where Italian, German, and French cultures exist side by side; in Belgium, where the French Walloons and the Flemish have somewhat different cultural heritages; and in Canada, where French- and English-speaking Canadians live uneasily in a pluralistic society. In none of these cases, though, are the cultural differences of the magnitude seen in many a non-Western pluralistic society. We may look at the Central American country of Guatemala as an example of one such society and its many attendant problems.

GUATEMALAN CULTURAL PLURALISM

Guatemala, like many another pluralistic country, came into being through conquest. In Guatemala's case the conquest was about as violent and brutal as it could be, given the technology of the time, as a rough gang of Spanish adventurers led by a man known even then for his cruelty and inhuman treatment of foes defeated a people whose civilization was far older than Spain's. The aim of the conquerors was quite simply to extract as much wealth as they could, primarily for themselves but also for Spain, by seizing the riches of those they conquered and by putting the native population to work extracting the gold and silver they hoped to find. Although the treasures to be had did not live up to the expectations of the conquerors (no rich deposits of ore were found), their main interest in their new possession continued to be in whatever they could extract from it that could be turned into wealth for themselves. Over the nearly 500 years since, their Ladino descendants have continued to be motivated by the same interests, even after independence from Spain.

Following its conquest, there was never substantial immigration from Spain, or anywhere else in Europe, into Guatemala. The conquerors and their descendants, for their part, wished to restrict the spoils of victory as much as possible to themselves, even though those spoils did not live up to advance expectations. There was, in fact, little to attract outsiders to the country. Thus, Indians have always outnumbered non-Indians in Guatemala, and continue to do so today. Nonetheless, Indians have never been allowed to hold any important political power at all; the apparatus of state, with its instruments of force (the police and army) remained firmly in the hands of the Ladino minority. This enabled them to continue exacting tribute and forced labor from Indian communities.

In the nineteenth century, Guatemala's Ladino population saw the export of coffee and cotton as a new source of wealth for themselves. For this, they took over huge amounts of Indian lands to create their plantations, at the same time placing Indians in a situation where they had no option but to work for the plantation owners at wages cheap beyond belief. Any reluctance on the part of these native laborers was dealt with by brute force.

In the 1940s democratic reforms took place in Guatemala. Although Indians played no role in bringing them about, they benefitted from them; for the first time in over 400 years native peoples could hold municipal offices in their own communities. In the 1950s the Roman Catholic church began to promote agricultural, consumer, and credit cooperatives in rural areas (which, in Guatemala, are predominantly Indian).

With the military coup of 1954 this brief interlude, in which the government recognized that Indians had social, economic, and cultural rights, came to an end. As before, the Indians stayed out of politics except within their own villages. And for

In Guatemala, "model villages" like this one are inhabited by refugees from communities that have been destroyed by the army. Thrown together with people from different regions, who often speak different languages, such refugees have been deprived of the ability to sustain themselves and have become utterly dependent upon a government that neither trusts nor respects them.

the most part, they remained aloof from the guerrilla activities that arose in reaction to a succession of military regimes. But because the guerrillas operated in the countryside, these regimes came to regard all rural people, most of whom are Indian, with deep suspicion. Inevitably, the latter were drawn into the conflict, for reasons elucidated in the following Original Study (*opposite*) by an anthropologist with long experience in rural Guatemala.

What Carmack's case study describes has become commonplace in rural Guatemala. Indeed, as recently as December of 1990 an army massacre took place in Santiago Atitlán, 11 people were killed in February 1991 in Quiché province in a single incident, and in just the first weekend of March, 19 bodies turned up throughout Guatemala.[13] Whole communities have been wiped out, and an estimated 2,000,000 people have been displaced. One would like to think that Guatemala represents the exception rather than the rule so far as pluralistic societies go, but unfortunately cases like it abound, in South and Central America and other parts of the world. A few random examples from

[13]James Louckey and Robert Carlsen, "Massacre in Santiago Atitlán," *Cultural Survival Quarterly*, 15, No.3 (1991):70.

ORIGINAL STUDY

**THE INDIANS
BECOME
GUERRILLAS: A
QUICHÉ CASE**[14]

Santa Cruz del Quiché produced no authentic guerrillas before 1980. This does not mean that there were no sympathizers, peasant organizations, or even some contacts with guerrillas.

In September of 1980 a terrorist act occurred in Santa Cruz that revolutionized the Indians of Santa Cruz. On the 23rd of September, 1980, Santa Cruz' first Indian *alcalde* [mayor] after centuries of Ladino rule was assassinated while riding home on his bicycle. His name was Abelino Zapeta y Zapeta. He was an acculturated Indian who lived in a hamlet a few kilometers from town, practiced carpentry, and was deeply committed to the Catholic Action movement of the community.

I interviewed Alcalde Zapeta the morning of his assassination. He related an incident of great interest to me, telling of some Indians in one of his hamlets, La Estancia, who had become guerrillas. According to him, men from that hamlet had been harassed by the Army. Some were even killed. They consequently took up arms to defend themselves. Though Catholics, he said, they became guerrillas and would fire on the Army as it passed alongside the hamlet on maneuvers. This was the first reliable testimony I had received that there were guerrillas in Santa Cruz.

By 1980 La Estancia was a large community, numbering about 4,000 persons, all Indians. It was heavily agricultural, approximately 63% of the families subsisting primarily from the cultivation of traditional highland crops. Weaving was an important secondary means of subsistence; some 25% of the families lived from the sale of weavings. Another 10% of the families made a living as travelling merchants, and another few (perhaps 2% of the families) owned trucks and pickups and made money through transportation.

Few of the La Estancia Indians worked on Pacific Coastal plantations. Such work was unnecessary because, through the use of fertilizers, cooperatives (La Estancia had five), and other progressive means the Indians of La Estancia were relatively wealthy. Most of the families earned from $1,000 to $3,000 per year. Thus, while the hamlet was overwhelmingly peasant, the vast majority owned lands and lived comfortably through income earned from agriculture and/or crafts.

The peasant Indians of La Estancia were overwhelmingly involved in the Catholic Action movement. At least 80% of the families were active—almost all agriculturalists and weavers. The merchants were comparatively secular in their beliefs. There were only a handful of traditionalists in the community and only a single family of Adventists.

As might be expected, the Christian Democratic party received a wide majority of votes from the Indians of La Estancia, especially in national elections; the two conservative parties polled only about 25% of the votes. The religious and political unity of most La Estancia Indians gave the community a strong collective spirit.

The collective spirit of the community is seen even more clearly in the strength of the Peasant Organization, CUC (Committee for Peasant Unity). CUC came to La Estancia in 1974. In 1980 almost everyone except the merchants had joined. CUC appears to have gradually replaced the Catholic Action organization as the collective secular structure of La Estancia; all its leaders came directly out of the Church leadership. Though originally set up under the direction of outside peasant leaders, it later became locally autonomous. While not directly militarized, it functioned to provide vigilance against outside interference, to gather intelligence information, to coordinate activities with peasants from other Santa Cruz hamlets and the region, and to promote political education—especially to awaken the Indians to their subordinate position as peasants in Guatemalan society. In La Estancia CUC was not seen as Marxist or revolutionary, but as a local organization necessary to protect the vast majority of inhabitants against an increasingly hostile government.

Incredible as it may seem, given the conditions outlined above, before the end of 1980 the entire community of La Estancia, some 4,000 individuals, except for a few families in an isolated mountainous zone, had disappeared. A band of about 40 young men and women had joined the EGP (Guerrilla Army of the Poor) guerrillas. The rest of the people had become refugees, scattered throughout Guatemala and neighboring countries; all had become guerrilla sympathizers. The situation was actually much more radical than Alcalde Zapeta had understood. How did this incredible transformation take place?

One big step, as noted before, was the assassination of Indian leaders like Alcalde Zapeta. Zapeta's family had seen the Ladino assassins, who were picked up by a speeding Army jeep shortly after the assassination. A few months before, one of the cooperative leaders from La Estancia had also been assassinated. The murder was highly symbolic, for the young man was killed in front of the Utatlan ruins, where the ancient Quiché capital had been. On that occasion too, the assassins were seen by Indian witnesses; they were once again Ladinos affiliated with the Army. The killing of Alcalde Zapeta and the cooperative leader, neither of whom were revolutionaries, greatly alarmed and angered the Indians of La Estancia. Little did they know that the terror directed against them by their own government was just beginning.

Three days after the assassination of Alcalde Zapeta some thirty to fifty armed men arrived in jeeps at La Estancia early in the morning. In a house to house search, using lists, they tracked down the Catholic Action, CUC, and cooperative leaders of the hamlet. By the time they completed their assignment, fifteen people including several adolescents, had been massacred. One CUC-Catholic Action leader was crucified between two trees, his side pierced with a knife. According to witnesses from La Estancia, these paramilitary assassins were Ladinos from the Oriente.

The terrified La Estancia Indians redoubled their vigilant guard. The men guarded by night, the children by day. At that time, many of the men began to sleep together, occupying a different house each night. They still had no modern weapons, and armed themselves with slings, machetes, and stones.

In November, Guatemalan soldiers arrived in force, this time by a different road (though they sent a jeep as a decoy along the same route the paramilitary assassins had come). Starting from the southern end of the hamlet, the soldiers systematically began searching homes for arms. According to witnesses, one of the Lieutenants was black, and many of the soldiers were Indians. Entire families, unarmed, were killed in cold blood, riddled with machine gun bullets as they cowered or slept in their beds. In all, fifty people were killed, including many women and children; they even killed a seventy-year-old man.

The dazed La Estancia Indians buried their dead in large holes dug in the ground—to have brought coffins from the town center for proper burial would have been seen as subversive. It was not even possible to officially report the killings.

The women of the hamlet collectively beat to death a suspected informer in the marketplace of a nearby town, and a band of 30–40 youth left for the north to join the guerrillas. Then, as the rain poured down, the remaining inhabitants of La Estanica broke into families and silently left their homes. A community that had existed for a thousand years disappeared!

[14]Robert M. Carmack, "Indians and the Guatemalan Revolution," *Cultural Survival Quarterly*, 7 (Summer 1983):52–54.

---

elsewhere will make the point. In Yugoslavia, ethnic Croats rose in revolt against a repressive regime controlled by another ethnic group, the Serbs. In South Africa, despite recent gains by blacks, a white minority government still makes use of force to maintain its grip over a black majority. In southeast Asia, Indonesians maintain their control over the people of East Timor and western New Guinea by force of arms. In the 1980s, on average, states borrowed more money to fight peoples within their boundaries than for all other programs combined. Nearly all debt in Africa, and nearly half of all other third-world debt, comes from the purchase of weapons by states to fight people claimed to be citizens by those very same states.[15]

Switzerland may be about the only country in the world where pluralism has worked out to the satisfaction of all parties to the arrangement—perhaps because, in spite of linguistic differences,

[15]*Cultural Survival Quarterly*, 15, No. 4 (1991):38.

they are all heirs to a common European cultural tradition. In Northern Ireland, on the other hand, being heirs to a common tradition has not prevented violence and bloodshed. The more divergent cultural traditions are, the more difficult it appears to be to make pluralism work.

ETHNOCENTRISM

The major problem with cultural pluralism has to do with ethnocentrism, a concept introduced in Chapter 2. To function effectively, a culture must instill the idea that its ways are best, or at least preferable to those of all other cultures. It provides individuals with a sense of pride in and loyalty to their traditions, from which they derive psychological support, and which binds them firmly to their group. In societies in which one's self-identification derives from the group, ethnocentrism is

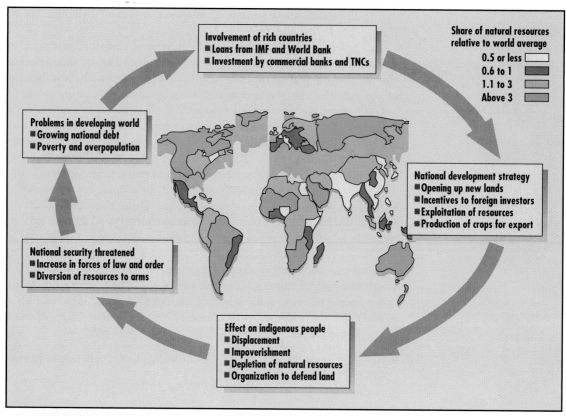

Figure 16.1   A high gross national product (*highlighted areas on map*) is sustained in the industrial countries in part by a flow of mineral and other raw wealth purchased from other lands.

essential to a sense of personal worth. The problem with ethnocentrism is that it can all too easily be taken as a charter for manipulating other cultures for the benefit of one's own, even though—as we saw in Chapter 12—it does not have to be taken as such. When it is, however, unrest, hostility, and violence commonly result.

A typical expression of ethnocentrism is provided by President James Monroe's view, expressed in 1817, of American Indian rights:

> The hunter state can exist only in the vast uncultivated deserts. It yields to the . . . greater force of civilized population; and of right, it ought to yield, for the earth was given to mankind to support the greater number of which it is capable; and no tribe or people have a right to withhold from the wants of others, more than is necessary for their support and comfort.[16]

[16]Quoted in Jack D. Forbes, *The Indian in America's Past* (Englewood Cliffs, N.J.: Prentice-Hall, 1964), p. 103.

This attitude is, of course, alive and well throughout the world today, and the idea that no group has the right to stand in the way of "the greater good for the greater number" is frequently used by governments to justify the development of resources in regions occupied by subsistence farmers, pastoral nomads, or food foragers—irrespective of the wishes of those peoples. But is it the greater good for the greater number? A look at the world as it exists today as a kind of global society, in which all the world's peoples are bound by interdependency, raises serious questions.

"GLOBAL APARTHEID"

Apartheid, once the official policy of the government of South Africa (but now undergoing change), consists of programs or measures that aim to

Under apartheid, South African blacks have had to live in separate reserves, like the one shown here. Because these "Bantustans" were not self-supporting, whites had available a pool of cheap labor to perform menial work.

maintain racial segregation.[17] Structurally, it serves to perpetuate the dominance of a white minority over a nonwhite majority through the social, economic, political, military, and cultural constitution of society. Nonwhites are denied effective participation in political affairs, are restricted as to where they can live and what they can do, and are denied the right to travel freely. Whites, by contrast, control the government including, of course, the military and police. Although there are 4.7 nonwhites for every white, being white and belonging to the upper stratum of society tend to go together. The richest 20 percent of South Africa take 58 percent of the country's income and enjoy a high standard of living, while the poorest 40 percent of the population receive but 6.2 percent of the national product.

What has South Africa to do with a global society? Structurally, the latter is similar—though there is obviously no stated policy of global apartheid. In the world society about two-thirds of the population is nonwhite and one-third white. In the world as a whole, being white and belonging to the upper stratum tend to go together. Although this upper stratum has not been a homogeneous group, being divided until recently into Communist and non-Communist peoples, neither is the upper stratum of South African society, where there is friction between the English, who control business and industry, and the Afrikaners, who control the government and military. In the world, the poorest 40 percent of the population receive about 5.2 percent of the world product, while the richest 20 percent take about 71.3 percent of world income (Fig. 16.2). Life expectancy, as in South Africa, is poorest among nonwhites. Most of the world's weapons of warfare, like most of its technology, are owned by whites: the United States, Russia, France, and Britain. As in South Africa, death and suffering from war and violence are distributed unequally; in the world, the poorest 70 percent of the population suffer over 90 percent of violent deaths in all categories.

One could go on, but enough has been said to make the point: the cursory parallels between the current world situation and that in South Africa are

[17]Material on global apartheid is drawn from Gernot Kohler, "Global Apartheid," *World Order Models Project Working Paper* 7 (New York: Institute for World Order, 1978).

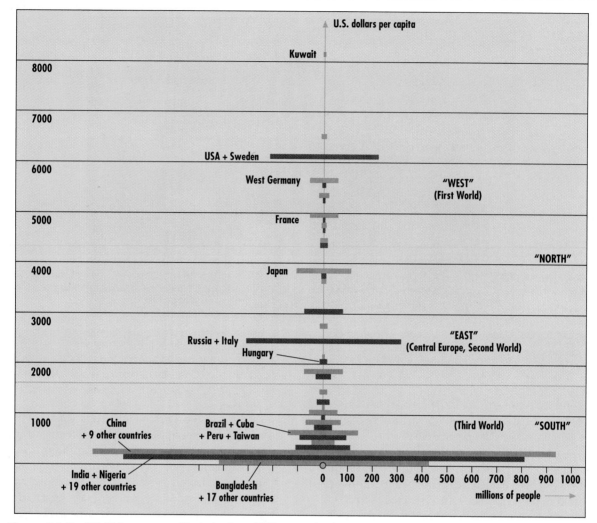

Figure 16.2   World income tree. Vertical axis = GNP per capita (U.S.$), intervals of 100. Horizontal axis = number of persons living at each income level.

striking. We may sum up "global apartheid" as a condition of world society which combines socio-economic and racial antagonisms and in which (1) a minority of whites occupies the pole of affluence, while a majority composed of other races occupies the pole of poverty; (2) social integration of the two groups is made extremely difficult by barriers of complexion, economic position, political boundaries, and other factors; (3) economic development of the two groups is interdependent; (4) the affluent white minority possesses a disproportionate share of the world society's political, economic, and

military power. "Global apartheid" is thus an unplanned condition of extreme inequality in cultural, racial, social, political, economic, military, and legal terms, as in South Africa's official apartheid.[18]

Around the world, condemnation of South African apartheid has been close to universal, and South Africa itself is now in the process of dismantling apartheid. Since "global apartheid" is, if anything, even more severe, it may be argued that we ought to be much more concerned about it than we have been up to now.

[18]Ibid., p. 4.

PROBLEMS OF "STRUCTURAL VIOLENCE"

One of the consequences of a system of apartheid, be it official or unofficial, national or global, is a great deal of **"structural violence"**: devastation that is brought about by situations, institutions, and social, political, and economic structures. A classic instance of "structural violence" is the accident that occurred in December of 1984, when gas released from Union Carbide's plant in Bhopal, India, killed 2,000 people and seriously injured at least 200,000 more. The effect of this disaster on its victims was lethal, even though the cause was not a hostile act committed by any individual. The source of the violence was anonymous, and this is what "structural violence" is all about. In what remains of this chapter, there is not sufficient space to go into all its aspects, but we can look at those aspects that have been of particular concern to some anthropologists. They are of concern to other specialists, too, and anthropologists draw on the work of these specialists as well as their own, thereby fulfilling their traditional role as synthesizers (discussed in Chapter 1). Moreover, anthropologists are less apt than other specialists to see these occurrences of "structural violence" as discrete and unrelated. Thus, they have a key contribution to make to our understanding of such modern-day problems as overpopulation, food shortages, pollution, and widespread discontent in the world.

WORLD HUNGER

As frequently dramatized by events in Ethiopia and other parts of Africa, a major source of "structural violence" in the world today is the failure to provide food for all of its people. Not only is Africa losing the capacity to feed itself; by 1980, 52 countries worldwide were producing less food per

---

"Structural violence": Violence exerted by situations, institutions, and social, political, and economic structures.

In April of 1986, an explosion and fire in the Soviet Union's Chernobyl nuclear power plant released massive amounts of radioactivity into the atmosphere over the USSR and Europe. Fallout from this devastated the reindeer-herding economy of Scandinavian Lapps: a classic example of structural violence.

capita than they were ten years previously, and in 42 countries, available supplies of food were not adequate to supply the caloric requirements of their populations.[19] One factor that has contributed to this food crisis is a dramatic growth in the world's population.

Population growth is more than a simple addition of people. If it were just that, the addition of 20 people a year to a population of 1,000 would result in that population's being doubled in 50 years; but because the added people produce more people, the doubling time is actually much less than 50 years. Hence, it took the whole of human history and prehistory for the world's population to reach one billion people, which it had done by 1850 (Fig. 16.3). By 1950, world population had reached almost 2.5 billion, representing an annual growth rate of about 0.8 percent. Between 1950 and 1960, the rate of growth had climbed to 1.8 percent (doubling time 39 years), and in the 1960s fluctuated between 1.8 percent and 2 percent (doubling time 35 years at 2 percent). There are now over five billion people in the world, with growth rates ranging from less than 1 percent (Europe and North America) to 2.4–2.6 percent (South Asia, Central and South America) to close to 3 percent (Africa).

[19]John H. Bodley, *Anthropology and Contemporary Human Problems*, 2nd ed. (Palo Alto, Calif.: Mayfield, 1985), p. 114.

Figure 16.3   The greatest population growth today is in those parts of the globe that seem to "skyrocket" here.

The obvious question arising from the burgeoning world population is: Can we produce enough food to feed all of those people? The majority opinion among those in the field of agriculture is that we can do so, although we probably won't be able to in the future, if populations continue to grow as they have. In the 1960s, a major effort was launched to expand food production in the poor countries of the world by introducing new high-yield strains of grains. Yet in spite of some dramatic gains from this "green revolution"—India, for example, was able to double its wheat crop in six years and was on the verge of grain self-sufficiency by 1970—and in spite of the impressive output of North American agriculture, millions of people on the face of the globe continue to face malnutrition and starvation. In the United States, meanwhile, about $85 million worth of *edible* food is thrown out every day (far more food than is sent out for famine relief), and farms are going out of business in record numbers.

The immediate cause of world hunger has less to do with food production than with food distribution. For example, millions of acres in Africa, Asia, and Latin America, which once were devoted to subsistence farming, have been given over to the raising of cash crops for export, to satisfy the desire in "developed" countries for such things as coffee, tea, chocolate, bananas, and beef. Those who used to farm the land for their own food needs are relocated, either to urban areas, where all too often there is no employment for them, or to other areas that are ecologically unsuited for farming. In Africa such lands are often occupied by pastoral nomads; as these are encroached upon by farmers, insufficient pasturage is left for livestock. The resultant overgrazing, coupled with the clearing of the land for farming, leads to increased loss of both soil and water, with disastrous consequences to nomad and farmer alike. In Brazil, which is highly dependent on outside sources of fossil fuels for its energy needs, millions of acres in the northeast part of the

Hunger stalks much of the world as a result of a world food system geared to satisfy an affluent minority in the developed nations of the world.

country were taken over for sugar production, which could be used to make alcohol to fuel the vehicles in Rio. The people who were displaced by this were given small holdings in the Amazon, where they are now being uprooted to make way for huge ranches on which beef is raised for export.

One strategy urged upon third-world countries, especially by government officials and development advisors from the United States, is to adopt the practices that have made North American agriculture so incredibly productive. On the face of it, this seems like a good idea; what it overlooks is the fact that it requires investment in expensive seeds and chemicals that neither small farmers nor poor countries can afford. Intensive agriculture on the U.S. model requires enormous inputs of chemical fertilizers, pesticides, and herbicides, not to men-

tion fossil fuels needed to run all the mechanized equipment. Even where high production lowers costs, the price is likely to be beyond the reach of poor farmers. And there are other problems: farming U.S.-style is energy inefficient. For every calorie that is produced, at least 8—some say as many as 20—calories go into its production and distribution.[20] By contrast, an Asian wet rice farmer using traditional methods produces 300 calories for each one expended. North American agriculture is wasteful of other resources as well: about 30 pounds of fertile topsoil are ruined for every pound of food produced.[21] Meanwhile, toxic substances from chemical nutrients and pesticides pile up in unexpected places, poisoning ground and surface waters, killing fish, birds, and other useful forms of life, upsetting natural ecological cycles, and causing public-health problems. In spite of its spectacular short-term success, there are questions about whether such a system of food production can be sustained over the long run, even in North America.

POLLUTION

It is ironic that a life-sustaining activity such as food production should constitute a health hazard, but that is precisely what it becomes, as agricultural chemicals poison soils and waters, and food additives (over 2,500 are or have been used) expose people to substances that all too often turn out to be harmful. This, though, is but a part of a larger problem of environmental pollution. Industrial activities are producing highly toxic waste at unprecedented rates, and emissions from factories are poisoning the air. For example, smokestack gases are clearly implicated in "acid rain," which is causing damage to lakes and forests all over northeastern North America. Air containing water vapor with a high acid content is, of course, harmful to the lungs, but the health hazard is greater than this. As surface and ground waters become more acidic, the solubility of lead, cadmium, mercury, and aluminum increases sharply. The increase of dissolved aluminum, in particular, is becoming truly

[20]Ibid., p. 128.
[21]Barbara H. Chasin and Richard W. Franke, "U.S. Farming: A World Model?," *Global Reporter*, 1, No. 2 (1983):10.

massive, and aluminum has been found to be associated with senile dementia and Alzheimer's and Parkinson's diseases. Today, these rank as major health problems in the United States.

As with world hunger, the "structural violence" that results from pollution tends to be greatest in the poorer countries of the world, where chemicals banned for use in countries like the United States are still widely used. Moreover, the industrial countries of the world have taken advantage of lax environmental regulations of third-world states to get rid of hazardous wastes. For instance, the president of Benin (in West Africa) recently signed a contract to dump toxic and low-grade radioactive waste from a European waste company on the lands of his tribal opposition.[22] And as manufacturing shifts from the developed to the less developed countries of the world, a trend also encouraged by fewer safety and environmental regulations to comply with, disasters such as the one already mentioned at Bhopal, India, may be expected to increase. Indeed, development itself seems to be a health hazard; it is well known that indigenous peoples in Africa, the Pacific Islands, South America, and elsewhere are relatively free from diabetes, obesity, hypertension, and a variety of circulatory

[22]*Cultural Survival Quarterly,* 15, No. 4 (1991):5.

diseases until they adopt the ways of the developed countries. With this, rates of these "diseases of development" escalate dramatically.

Modern humanity knows the causes of pollution and realizes it is a danger to future survival. Why, then, can humanity not control this evil by which it fouls its own nest? At least part of the answer lies in the misuse of philosophical and theological traditions. As we saw in Chapter 12, Western industrialized societies often abuse the Biblical assertion that they have dominion over the earth with all that grows and lives on it. It is these societies that contribute most to global pollution. One North American, for example, consumes hundreds of times the resources of a single African, with all that implies with respect to waste disposal and environmental degradation.

The exploitative world view, characteristic of all civilizations, extends to all natural resources. Only when problems have reached crisis proportions have people protected or replaced what greed and acquisitiveness have prompted them to take from the environment. In recent years, recognizing the seriousness of the environmental crisis people were creating for themselves, authorities have passed laws against such activities as hunting whales out of existence, dumping toxic wastes into streams and rivers, and poisoning the air with harmful fumes.

"Progress" comes to the Amazon: Illegal gold mining on Yanomami territory has caused widespread pollution.

That these laws have been at best only partially successful is illustrated by attempts to deal with the destruction of the earth's protective ozone layer that is being caused by the chlorofluorocarbons used in aerosol sprays, refrigerators, air conditioners, and the manufacture of styrofoam. First, a ban was imposed on the use of these chemicals in sprays, in spite of which deterioration of the ozone layer proceeded about twice as fast as scientists predicted it would, even in the absence of the ban. More recently, an international treaty restricting the use of chlorofluorocarbons has been ratified, but even this will merely slow down, rather than halt, further deterioration. Obviously, many more people will have to suffer from skin cancers than presently do before more meaningful steps will be taken, by which time it could be too late.

A large part of the problem in this and similar situations is a reluctance to perceive as disadvantageous practices that previously seemed to work well. What frequently happens is that practices carried out on one particular scale, or that were suited to one particular context, become unsuitable when carried out on another scale or in another context. Because they are trained to look at customs in their broader context, anthropologists would seem to have an important role to play in convincing people that solutions to many problems require changed behavior.

Indigenous peoples, in particular, are apt to stand in awe of natural forces, bestowing on them a special place in their religious system. For example, many people believe that rushing rapids, storms, the mountains, and the jungles possess awesome powers. This is also true of fire, which both warms and destroys. For farmers, the sun, rain, and thunder are important to their existence and are often considered divine. Such world views are not foolproof checks to the kind of environmental manipulation that causes severe pollution, but they certainly act as powerful restraining influences.

POPULATION CONTROL

Although the problems we have discussed so far may not be caused by population growth, they are certainly made worse by it. For one thing, it increases the scale of the problems; thus, the waste generated by a small population is far easier to deal with than that generated by a large one. For

Replacement reproduction: When birth and death rates are in equilibrium; people produce no more offspring than necessary to replace themselves when they die.

another, it often nullifies efforts made to solve the problems, as when increased food production is offset by increased numbers of people to be fed. While solving the problem of population growth will not by itself make the other problems go away, it is unlikely that those other problems can be solved unless population growth is arrested.

As our earlier look at population demonstrated, the world's population has grown enormously since the beginning of the industrial age. With the exception of European and North American populations, there was no sign of a significant decline in birth rates prior to 1976. The reason that poor people, in particular, have so many children is simple: Children are the main resource of the poor. They provide a needed pool of labor to work farms and they are the only source of security for the elderly; hence, to have lots of offspring makes sense. Historically, people are apt to limit the size of their families only when they became wealthy enough that money replaces children as their main resource; at that point, children actually *cost* them money. Given this, we can see why birth rates remain so high in the poorer countries of the world. To those who live in poverty, children are seen as the only hope. Nevertheless, since 1976 there have been some encouraging signs, as in China, where there has been a steep decline in birth rates. In Africa, southern Asia, and much of Central and South America, however (again, the poorer countries of the world), the impact on fertility of programs to reduce birth rates is yet to be felt. In these countries, growing populations make it difficult even to maintain their present per capita share of food and other resources. Even if, through some miracle, those countries having policies aimed at population control were able to bring about an immediate balance between birth and death rates **(replacement reproduction)**, their populations would continue to grow for the next 60 years or so. The case of India—a country that has been working for some time to curb population growth—

A state-sponsored billboard for China's "one child" family policy. Necessary though population control may be, existing cultural practices may make it difficult to carry out.

illustrates the problem. This country's population currently is about one-ninth of the world total, and is growing by 13,000,000 people per year. If by 25 years from now India achieved replacement reproduction, its population would continue to grow for another 60 years, making it 2.5 times its present size.

The severity of the problem becomes clear when it is realized that the present world population of over 5 billion people can be sustained only by using up what are really nonrenewable resources, which is like living off income-producing capital. It works for a time, but once the capital is gone, so is the possibility of even having an income to live on. In recognition of the importance of bringing population growth under control, some 59 developing countries have programs for the dissemination of birth-control information. By contrast, in 1984, the United States government, under budgetary constraints, cut off all funding for the U.N. Fund for Population Activity and International Planned Parenthood, the only multinational agencies that work directly with governments to provide support for family planning services in more than 140 countries.

Evident though the problem is, efforts to bring about reduced birth rates face enormous cultural and structural obstacles. Some of these, as well as the kinds of new problems that may arise, are well illustrated by China's much-publicized policy to forcibly foster one-child families. While this has slowed the rate of growth of China's population (which nevertheless continues to grow at a rate of 17,000,000 per year), it has given rise to some serious new problems. The difficulty stems from a basic contradiction with another policy, to raise agricultural productivity by granting more economic autonomy to rural households, and the continued existence of families, which (as in old China) are strongly patriarchal. Within such families, men are responsible for farm work. Perpetuation of the male line of descent is considered essential to everyone's well-being, and postmarital residence is strictly patrilocal. Under these circumstances, the birth of male children is considered essential; without them, the household will not have the workforce it needs and will suffer economically. Furthermore, the parents will have no one to support them, once they are too old for physical labor. Daughters are of little use to them, since they will marry out of the household and can offer little aid to their parents. Since married couples are supposed to have only one child, the birth of a daughter is greeted with dismay, for if the couple tries again for a boy, tremendous pressures will be brought to bear by local officials of the state for the woman to have an abortion, and for her or her husband to undergo sterilization.

Not surprisingly, in the face of all this, female infanticide is on the rise in China, and women who bear daughters are often physically and mentally abused by their husbands and mothers-in-law, sometimes to the point of committing suicide (although the state teaches that men determine the sex of a baby, most rural Chinese believe that the woman is still responsible for the outcome of birth, perhaps through her diet and behavior). Women pay in other ways with their bodies; when a second pregnancy occurs, it is the woman who must have the abortion, and it is usually she who is sterilized (surgical intervention in men in their prime is discouraged owing to the importance of their labor in agriculture). This leaves the man free to coerce his daughter-bearing wife into a divorce, so that he can try again for a son with a new wife, leaving the old one of no use to anyone and with no son to care for her in old age. In a married woman, one means by which unauthorized pregnancy is prevented is through placement of an intrauterine device (IUD) in her womb. This cannot be removed without official permission, which is hard to get even in the face of compelling medical reasons to do so, since removal is contrary to official policy. Nor is an attached cord for removal provided, all of which has led to proliferation of back-alley practitioners who remove IUDs with improvised hooks, often leading to infection and death.

THE CULTURE OF DISCONTENT

In spite of the difficulties, stabilization of the world's population appears to be a necessary step if the problems of the future are ever to be solved. Without this, whatever else is done, an inability to provide enough food seems inevitable. Up until about 1950, growth in the world's food supply came almost entirely from expanding the amount of land under cultivation. Since then, it has come

The demand for resources on the part of industrialized countries condemns many people to lives of misery. In Bolivia, tin is the primary export. It is mined by Quechua Indians, who work for the equivalent of one U.S. dollar a day. Rarely do they live more than seven years after entering the mines.

increasingly from high energy inputs in the form of chemical fertilizers upon which new high-yield varieties of crops depend, pesticides and herbicides, as well as fuel to run tractors and other mechanical equipment, including irrigation pumps. The source of almost all this energy is oil, yet while the demand for food is projected to rise until at least the middle of the twenty-first century, oil supplies are diminishing and will surely decline over this same period. Insufficient supplies of food are bound to result in increased structural violence in the form of higher death rates in the "underdeveloped" countries of the world. This will surely have an impact on the "developed" countries, with their relatively stable populations and high standards of living. It is hard to see how such countries could exist peacefully side by side with others experiencing high death rates and abysmally low living standards.

Necessary though it may be in solving problems of the future, there is no reason to suppose that birth control will be sufficient by itself. The result would be only to stabilize things as they are. The problem is twofold. Over the past several years, the poor countries of the world have embraced the belief that they should enjoy a standard of living comparable to that of the rich countries, while at the same time the resources necessary to maintain such a standard of living are running out. As we saw in Chapter 15, this situation has led to the creation of a culture of discontent, whereby people's aspirations far exceed their opportunities. The problem involves not just a case of population growth outstripping food supplies; it is also one of unequal access to decent jobs, housing, sanitation, health care, and adequate police and fire protection. And it is one of steady deterioration of the natural environment as a result of increasing industrialization.

What are required are some dramatic changes in values and motivations, as well as in social institutions. The emphasis on individual self-interest, materialism, and conspicuous production, acquisition, and consumption, needs to be abandoned in favor of a more humane self-image and social ethic, which can be created from values still to be found in many of the world's cultures and religions. These include a world view that sees humanity as a part of nature rather than superior to it. Included, too, is a sense of social responsibility that recognizes that no individual, people, or state has the right to expropriate resources at the expense of others. Finally, there is needed an awareness of the importance of the supportive ties among individuals, such as are seen in kinship or other associations in the traditional societies of the world.

Chapter Summary

Since future forms of culture will be shaped by decisions humans have yet to make, they cannot be predicted with any accuracy. Thus, instead of trying to foretell the future, a number of anthropologists are trying for a better understanding of the existing world situation, so that those decisions may be made intelligently. Anthropologists are especially well suited to do this, owing to their experience at seeing things in context, their long-term evolutionary perspective, their ability to recognize culture-bound biases, and their familiarity with cultural alternatives.

However humanity changes biologically, culture remains the chief means by which humans try to solve their problems of existence. Some anthropologists are concerned that there is a trend for the problems to outstrip culture's ability to find solutions. Rapid developments in communication, transportation, and world trade, some believe, will link people together to the point that a single world culture will result. Their thinking is that such a homogenized superculture would offer fewer chances for conflict between peoples than in the past. A number of anthropologists are skeptical of such an argument, in view of the recent tendency for ethnic groups to reassert their own distinctive identities, and in view of the persistence of traditional ways of thinking about oneself and others, even in the face of massive changes in other aspects of culture. Anthropologists are also concerned about the tendency for many of the world's traditional societies to be treated as obsolete when they appear to stand in the way of "development."

Another alternative is for humanity to move in the direction of cultural pluralism, in which more than one culture exists in a society. To work, cultural pluralism must reject all bigotry, bias, and racism. Some anthropologists maintain that pluralistic arrangements are the only feasible means for achieving global equilibrium and peace. A problem preventing cultural pluralism is group ethnocentrism. All too often, it has led one group to impose its control on others, often leading to prolonged, violent, and bloody political upheavals, including genocide.

Adopting a global perspective, a picture emerges that is broadly similar to South Africa's official system of apartheid. A white minority dominates over a nonwhite majority, through the social, economic, political, military, and cultural makeup of the global society. One consequence of any system of apartheid is a great deal of "structural violence" exerted by situations, institutions, and social, political, and economic structures. Such violence involves things like overpopulation and food shortages, which some anthropologists are working to understand and help alleviate. One challenge the world over is to provide food resources to keep pace with the burgeoning population. The immediate problem, though, is not so much one of overpopulation as it is a food-distribution system that is geared to the satisfaction of desires of "rich" countries at the expense of poorer nations.

Pollution has become a direct threat to humanity. People have protected their environments only when some crisis forced them to do so; they have felt no long-term responsibilities toward the earth or its resources. Societies can learn much from those peoples who see themselves as integral parts of the earth.

Meeting the problems of "structural violence" that beset the human species today probably can be done only if we are able to reduce the birth rate. Effective birth-control methods are now available. Whether or not these methods are used on a vast enough scale depends on their availability and acceptance. Many of the world's developing countries have policies aimed at controlling population growth, but these sometimes conflict with other policies, and give rise to new kinds of problems. Even if replacement reproduction were immediately achieved, their populations would continue to grow. Over the past two decades, United States government policy has been to curtail its funding for family planning efforts in other countries.

Solving the problems of the global society depends also on lessening the gap between the living standards of poor and developed countries. This will call for dramatic changes in the materialistic, consumer orientation found in many industrialized societies. All people need to see themselves as a part of nature, rather than as superior to it. Also needed are a social responsibility that recognizes that no people has a right to expropriate important resources at the expense of others, and an awareness of the importance of supportive ties between individuals.

Suggested Readings

Bodley, John H. *Anthropology and Contemporary Human Problems,* 2nd ed. Palo Alto, Calif.: Mayfield, 1985.
Anthropologist Bodley examines some of the most serious problems in the world today: overconsumption, resource depletion, hunger and starvation, overpopulation, violence, and war.

Bodley, John H. *Victims of Progress,* 2nd ed. Palo Alto, Calif.: Mayfield, 1982.
Explores the impact of industrial civilization on the indigenous peoples of the world, and how the latter are organizing to protect themselves.

Davis, Shelton H. *Victims of the Miracle.* Cambridge: Cambridge University Press, 1982.
An anthropologist looks at Brazil's efforts to develop the Amazon region, the motivations behind those efforts, and their impact on indigenous peoples. Davis pays special attention to the role played by multinational corporations, how they relate to the Brazilian government, and who benefits from it all.

Maybury-Lewis, David, ed. *The Prospects for Plural Societies* (1982 Proceedings of the American Ethnological Society.) American Ethnological Society, 1984.
In 1982, a group of anthropologists met to discuss one of the most crucial issues of our time, the prospects for multiethnic societies. What emerged as the villain of the conference was the state; not particular countries but states as a kind of political structure and the hold that they have over modern thought and political action. Maybury-Lewis confronts this issue in the concluding essay, which by itself makes this volume worth getting hold of.

Wolf, Eric R. *Europe and the People Without History.* Berkeley: University of California Press, 1982.
As far back as the Crusades, Eric Wolf argues, Europeans learned that seizure of external resources allowed them to live better than before, and they have been living beyond their means ever since. In this book, Wolf looks at the role of Europeans as part of a global community, and how this has made the world what it is today.

BIBLIOGRAPHY

Aberle, David F., Urie Bronfenbrenner, Eckhard H. Hess, Daniel R. Miller, David H. Schneider, and James N. Spuhler, 1963. "The Incest Taboo and the Mating Patterns of Animals," *American Anthropologist*, 65:253–265.

Aberle, David F., 1961. "Culture and Socialization," in F. Hsu, ed., *Psychological Anthropology: Approaches to Culture and Personality*. Homewood, Ill.: Dorsey Press, pp. 381–399.

Abu–Lughod, Lila, 1986. *Veiled Sentiments: Honor and Poetry in a Bedouin Society* Berkeley, Cal.: University of California Press, pp. 99–103.

Adams, Robert McC., 1966. *The Evolution of Urban Society*. Chicago: Aldine.

Al–Issa, Ihsan, and Wayne Dennis, eds., 1970. *Cross-cultural Studies of Behavior*. New York: Holt, Rinehart and Winston.

Alland, Alexander, Jr., 1970. *Adaptation in Cultural Evolution: An Approach to Medical Anthropology*. New York: Columbia University Press.

Alland, Alexander, Jr., 1971. *Human Diversity*. New York: Columbia University Press.

Allen, Susan, 1984. "Media Anthropology: Building a Public Perspective," *Anthropology Newsletter*, 25:6.

Amiran, Ruth, 1965. "The Beginnings of Pottery-Making in the Near East," in *Ceramics and Man*, ed. Frederick R. Matson, Viking Fund Publications in Anthropology, No. 41, pp. 240–247.

Arensberg, Conrad M., 1961. "The Community as Object and Sample," *American Anthropologist*, 63:241–264.

Arensberg, Conrad M., and Arthur H. Niehoff, 1964. *Introducing Social Change: A Manual for Americans Overseas*. Chicago: Aldine.

Balandier, Georges, 1971. *Political Anthropology*. New York: Pantheon.

Banton, Michael, 1968. "Voluntary Association: Anthropological Aspects,"

International Encyclopedia of the Social Sciences, 16:357–362.

Barber, Bernard, 1957. *Social Stratification*. New York: Harcourt.

Barfield, Thomas J., 1984. "Introduction," *Cultural Survival Quarterly*, 8:2.

Barnett, H., 1953. *Innovation: The Basis of Cultural Change*. New York: McGraw-Hill.

Barnouw, Victor, 1963. *Culture and Personality*. Homewood, Ill.: Dorsey Press.

Barth, Frederik, 1960. "Nomadism in the Mountain and Plateau Areas of South West Asia," *The Problems of the Arid Zone* (UNESCO), pp. 341–355.

Barth, Frederick, 1961. *Nomads of South Persia: The Basseri Tribe of the Khamseh Confederacy*. Boston: Little, Brown.

Bascom, William, 1965. "The Forms of Folklore-Prose Narratives," *Journal of American Folklore*, 78:3–20.

Bascom, William R., 1965. "Folklore and Anthropology," in Allan Dundes, ed., *The Study of Folklore*. Englewood Cliffs, N.J.:Prentice-Hall. pp. 25–33.

Bascom, William, 1969. *The Yoruba of Southwestern Nigeria*. New York: Holt, Rinehart and Winston.

Bates, Daniel G., and Fred Plog, 1991 *Human Adaptive Strategies*. New York: McGraw-Hill.

Bateson, Gregory, 1958. *Naven*. Stanford, Cal.: Stanford University Press.

Beals, Alan R., 1972. *Gopalpur: A South Indian Village*. New York: Holt, Rinehart and Winston.

Beattie, John, 1964. *Other Cultures: Aims, Methods and Achievements*. New York: Free Press.

Beidelman, T. O., ed., 1971. *The Transition of Culture: Essays to E. E. Evans–Pritchard*. London: Tavistock.

Belshaw, Cyril S., 1958. "The Significance of Modern Cults in Melanesian Development," in William Lessa and Evon Z. Vogt, eds., *Reader in Comparative Religion: An Anthropological Approach*. New York: Harper & Row, pp. 486–492.

Benedict, Ruth, 1959. *Patterns of Culture*. New York: New American Library.

Bennett, John W., 1964. "Myth, Theory and Value in Cultural Anthropology," in E. W. Caint and G. T. Bowles, eds., *Fact and Theory in Social Science*. Syracuse, N.Y.: Syracuse University Press.

Berdan, Frances F., 1982. *The Aztecs of Central Mexico*. New York: Holt, Rinehart and Winston.

Bernard, H. Russell, and Willis E. Sibley, 1975. *Anthropology and Jobs*. Washington, D.C.: American Anthropological Association.

Bernardi, Bernardo, 1985. *Age Class Systems: Social Institutions and Policies Based on Age*. New York: Cambridge University Press.

Bernstein, Basin, 1961. "Social Structure, Language and Learning," *Educational Research*, 3:163–176.

Berreman, Gerald D., 1962. *Behind Many Masks: Ethnography and Impression Management in a Himalayan Village*. Ithaca, N.Y.: Society for Applied Anthropology.

Berreman, Gerald D., 1968. "Caste: The Concept of Caste," *International Encyclopedia of the Social Sciences*, 2:333–338.

Bicchieri, M. G., ed., 1972. *Hunters and Gatherers Today: A Socioeconomic Study of Eleven Such Cultures in the Twentieth Century*. New York: Holt, Rinehart and Winston.

Bidney, David, 1953. *Theoretical Anthropology*. New York: Columbia University Press.

Birdwhistell, Ray, 1970. *Kinesics and Context*. Philadelphia: University of Pennsylvania Press.

Black, Henry Campbell, 1968. *Black's Law Dictionary*. St. Paul, Minn.: West.

Boas, Franz, 1962. *Primitive Art*. Gloucester, Mass.: Peter Smith.

Boas, Franz, 1966. *Race, Language and Culture*. New York: Free Press.

Bodley, John H., 1985. *Anthropology and Contemporary Human Problems*, 2d ed. Palo Alto, Cal.: Mayfield.

Bodley, John H., 1982. *Victims of Progress*, 2d ed. Palo Alto, Cal.: Mayfield.

Bohannan, Paul, 1966. *Social Anthropology*, New York: Holt, Rinehart and Winston.

Bohannan, Paul, and George Dalton, eds., 1962. *Markets in Africa*. Evanston, Ill.: Northwestern University Press.

Bohannan, Paul, and John Middleton, eds., 1968. *Kinship and Social Organization*. Garden City, N.Y.: Natural History Press.

Bohannan, Paul, and John Middleton, eds., 1968. *Marriage, Family, and Residence*. Garden City, N.Y.: Natural History Press.

Bohannan, Paul, ed., 1967. *Law and Warfare: Studies in the Anthropology of Conflict*. Garden City, N.Y.: Natural History Press.

Bolinger, Dwight, 1968. *Aspects of Language*. New York: Harcourt.

Bornstein, Marc H., 1975. "The Influence of Visual Perception on Culture," *American Anthropologist*, 77(4):774–798.

Bradfield, Richard, 1973. *A Natural History of Associations*. New York: International Universities Press.

Braidwood, Robert J., and Gordon R. Willey, 1962. *Courses Toward Urban Life: Archeological Consideration of Some Cultural Alternatives*. Chicago: Aldine.

Braidwood, Robert J., 1960. "The Agricultural Revolution," *Scientific American*, 203:130–141.

Brew, John O., 1968. *One Hundred Years of Anthropology*. Cambridge, Mass.: Harvard University Press.

Brinton, Crane, 1953. *The Shaping of the Modern Mind*. New York: Mentor.

Brown, Donald E., 1991. *Human Universals*. New York: McGraw-Hill.

Bruner, Edward M., 1970. "Medan: The Role of Kinship in an Indonesian City," in William Mangin, ed., *Peasants in Cities: Readings in the Anthropology of Urbanization*. Boston: Houghton Mifflin.

Burling, Robbins, 1970. *Man's Many Voices: Language in Its Cultural Context*. New York: Holt, Rinehart and Winston.

Burling, Robbins, 1969. "Linguistics and Ethnographic Description," *American Anthropologist*, 71:817–827.

Butzer, K., 1971. *Environment and Anthropology: An Ecological Approach to Prehistory*, 2d ed. Chicago: Aldine.

Campbell, Bernard G., 1988. *Humankind Emerging*, 5th ed. Boston: Little, Brown.

Carmack, Robert, 1983. "Indians and The Guatemalan Revolution," *Cultural Survival Quarterly*, 7(2):52–54.

Carneiro, Robert L., 1961. "Slash and Burn Cultivation among the Kuikuru and Its Implications for Cultural Development in the Amazon Basin," in J. Wilbert, ed., *The Evolution of Horticultural Systems in Native South America: Causes and Consequences*. Caracas: Sociedad de Ciencias Naturales La Salle, pp. 47–68.

Carneiro, Robert L., 1970. "A Theory of the Origin of the State," *Science*, 169:733–738.

Carroll, John B., ed., 1956. *Language, Thought and Reality: Selected Writings of Benjamin Lee Whorf*. New York: Wiley.

Cashdan, Elizabeth, 1989. "Hunters and Gatherers: Economic Behavior in Bands," in *Economic Anthropology*, edited by Stuart Plattner. Stanford, Cal.: Stanford University Press, pp. 21–48.

Chagnon, Napoleon A., and William Irons, eds., 1979. *Evolutionary Biology and Human Social Behavior*. North Scituate, Mass.: Duxbury Press.

Chagnon, Napoleon A., 1988. *Yanomamo: The Fierce People*. 3rd ed., New York: Holt, Rinehart and Winston.

Chambers, Robert, 1983. *Rural Development: Putting the Last First*. New York: Longman.

Chasin, Barbara H., and Richard W. Franke, 1983. "U.S. Farming: A World Model?," *Global Reporter*, 1, No. 2:10.

Chodorow, Nancy, 1971. "Being and Doing: A Cross-Cultural Examination of the Socialization of Males and Females," in *Woman in Sexist Society*, Vivian Gornick and Barbara K. Moran, eds. New York: Basic Books, pp. 173–197.

Clark, W. E. LeGros, 1960. *The Antecedents of Man*. Chicago: Quadrangle Books.

Clay, Jason W., 1988. "Genocide in the Age of Enlightenment," *Cultural Survival Quarterly* 12, No. 3.

Clay, Jason W., 1990. "What's a Nation," *Mother Jones*, 15, No. 7:28.

Clough, S. B., and C. W. Cole, 1952. *Economic History of Europe*, 3d ed. Lexington, Mass.: Heath.

Codere, Helen, 1950. *Fighting with Property*. Seattle: University of Washington Press.

Cohen, Ronald, and John Middleton, eds., 1967. *Comparative Political Systems*. Garden City, N.Y.: Natural History Press.

Cohen, Myron L., 1967. "Variations in Complexity among Chinese Family Groups: The Impact of Modernization," *Transactions of the New York Academy of Sciences*, 295:638–647.

Cohen, Myron L., 1968. "A Case Study of Chinese Family Economy and Development," *Journal of Asian and African Studies*, 3:161–180.

Cohen, Yehudi, 1968. *Man in Adaptation: The Cultural Present*. Chicago: Aldine.

Collier, Jane Fishburne, and Sylvia Junko Yanagisako, eds., 1987. *Gender and Kinship: Essays Toward a Unified Analysis*. Stanford, Cal.: Stanford University Press.

Collier, Jane, Michelle Z. Rosaldo, and Sylvia Yanagisako, "Is There a Family? New Anthropological Views," in *Rethinking the Family: Some Feminist Problems*, Barrie Thorne and Marilyn Yalom, eds. New York: Longman, 1982, pp. 25–39.

Connelly, John C., 1979. "Hopi Social Organization" in *Handbook of North American Indians Vol. 9*, Southwest, ed. Alfonso Ortiz. Washington, D.C.: Smithsonian Institution, pp. 539–553.

Coon, Carleton S., 1954. *The Story of Man*. New York: Knopf.

Coon, Carleton S., 1948. *A Reader in General Anthropology*. New York: Holt, Rinehart and Winston.

Coon, Carleton S., 1958. *Caravan: The Story of the Middle East*, 2d ed. New York: Holt, Rinehart and Winston.

Coon, Carleton S., 1971. *The Hunting Peoples*. Boston: Little, Brown.

Cornish, Andrew, 1987. "Participant Observation on a Motorcycle," *Anthropology Today* 3(6).

Cottrell, Fred, 1965. *Energy and Society: The Relation between Energy, Social Changes and Economic Development*. New York: McGraw-Hill.

Courlander, Harold, 1971. *The Fourth World of the Hopis*. New York: Crown.

Cowgill, George L., 1980. Letter, *Science*, 210:1305.

Cox, Oliver Cromwell, 1959. *Caste, Class and Race: A Study in Dynamics*. New York: Monthly Review Press.

Crane, L. Ben, Edward Yeager, and Randal L. Whitman, 1981. *An Introduction to Linguistics*. Boston: Little, Brown.

Cultural Survival Quarterly, 1983. "Death and Disorder in Guatemala." *Cultural Survival Quarterly*, 7(1).

Dalton, George, ed., 1967. *Tribal and Peasant Economics: Readings in Economic Anthropology*. Garden City, N.Y.: Natural History Press.

Dalton, George, 1971. *Traditional Tribal and Peasant Economics: An Introductory Survey of Economic Anthropology*. Reading, Mass.: Addison-Wesley.

Dalton, George, ed., 1967. *Economic Anthropology and Development: Essays on Tribal and Peasant Economics*. New York: Basic Books.

Darwin, Charles, [1859], 1967. *On the Origin of Species*. New York: Atheneum.

Davenport, 1959. "Linear Descent and Descent Groups." *American Anthropologist*, 61:557–573.

Davis, Susan S., 1983. *Patience and Power: Women's Lives in a Moroccan Village*. Cambridge, Mass.: Schenkman.

Davis, Shelton, 1982. *Victims of the Miracle*. Cambridge: Cambridge University Press.

Deevy, Edward S., Jr., 1960. "The Human Population," *Scientific American*, 203:194–204.

Despres, Leo A., 1968. "Cultural Pluralism and the Study of Complex Societies," *Current Anthropology*, 9:3–26.

Devereux, George, 1963. "Institutionalized Homosexuality of the Mohave Indians," in Hendrik M. Ruitenbeck, ed., *The Problem of Homosexuality in Modern Society*. New York: Dutton.

Dobyns, Henry F., Paul L. Doughty, and Harold D. Lasswell, eds., 1971. *Peasants, Power, and Applied Social Change*. London: Sage.

Douglas, Mary, 1958. "Raffia Cloth Distribution in the Lele Economy," *Africa*, 28:109–122.

Dozier, Edward, 1970. *The Pueblo Indians of North America*. New York: Holt, Rinehart and Winston.

Draper, Patricia, 1975. "!Kung women: Contrasts in Sexual Egalitarianism in Foraging and Sedentary Contexts," in Rayna Reiter, ed., *Toward an Anthropology of Women*. New York: Monthly Review Press, pp. 77–109.

Driver, Harold, 1964. *Indians of North America*. Chicago: University of Chicago Press.

Dubois, Cora, 1944. *The People of Alor*. Minneapolis: University of Minnesota Press.

Dundes, Alan, 1980. *Interpreting Folk Lore*. Bloomington: Indiana University Press.

Durkheim, Emile, 1965. *The Elementary Forms of the Religious Life*. New York: Free Press.

Durkheim, Emile, 1964. *The Division of Labor in Society*. New York: Free Press.

duToit, Brian M., 1991. *Human Sexuality: Cross Cultural Readings*. New York: McGraw Hill.

Eastman, Carol M., 1990. *Aspects of Language and Culture*, 2nd ed. Novato, Cal.: Chandler and Sharp.

Edmonson, Munro S., 1971. *Lore: An Introduction to the Science of Folklore*. New York: Holt, Rinehart and Winston.

Eggan, Fred, 1954. "Social Anthropology and the Method of Controlled Comparison," *American Anthropologist*, 56:743–763.

Ehrlich, Paul R., and Anne H. Ehrlich, 1970. *Population, Resources, Environment*. San Francisco: Freeman.

Eiseley, Loren, 1958. *Darwin's Century: Evolution and the Men Who Discovered It*. New York: Doubleday.

Eisenstadt, S. N., 1956. *From Generation to Generation: Age Groups and Social Structure*. New York: Free Press.

Elkin, A. P., 1964. *The Australian Aborigines*. Garden City, N.Y.: Doubleday/Anchor Books.

Ellison, Peter T., 1990. "Human Ovarian Function and Reproductive Ecology: New Hypotheses," *American Anthropologist* 92, pp. 933–952.

Ember, Melvin, and Carol R. Ember, 1971. "The Conditions Favoring Matrilocal vs. Patrilocal Residence," *American Anthropologist*, 73:571–594.

Epstein, A. 1968. "Sanctions," *International Encyclopedia of the Social Sciences*, Vol. 14.

Erasmus, C. J., and W. Smith, 1967. "Cultural Anthropology in the United States since 1900," *Southwestern Journal of Anthropology*, 23:11–40.

Erasmus, C. J., 1950. "Patolli, Pachisi, and the Limitation of Possibilities," *Southwestern Journal of Anthropology*, 6:369–381.

Ervin-Tripp, Susan, 1973. *Language Acquisition and Communicative Choice*. Stanford, Cal.: Stanford University Press.

Esber, George S., Jr., 1987. "Designing Apache Houses with Apaches," in *Anthropological Praxis: Translating Knowledge into Action*, edited by Robert M. Wulff and Shirley J. Fiske. Boulder, Co.: Westview Press, pp. 187–196.

Escholtz, Paul, Alfred Rosa and Virginia Clark, eds., 1986. *Language Awareness*, 4th ed. New York: St. Martin's Press.

Evans, William, 1968. *Communication in the Animal World*. New York: Crowell.

Evans-Pritchard, E. E., 1968. *The Nuer: A Description of the Modes of Livelihood and Political Institutions of a Nilotic People*. London: Oxford University Press.

Evans-Pritchard, E. E., 1937. *Witchcraft, Oracles, and Magic among the Azande*. London: Oxford University Press.

Falk, Dean, 1975. "Comparative Anatomy of the Larynx in Man and the Chimpanzee: Implications for Language in Neanderthal," *American Journal of Physical Anthropology*, 43(1):123–132.

Farsoun, Samih K., 1970. "Family Structures and Society in Modern Lebanon," in Louise E. Sweet, ed., *Peoples and Cultures of the Middle East*, Vol. 2. Garden City, N.Y.: Natural History Press, pp. 257–307.

Fei Hsiaotung, 1939. *Peasant Life in China*. London: Kegan, Paul, Trench and Truber.

Firth, Raymond, 1952. *Elements of Social Organization*. London: Watts.

Firth, Raymond, 1957. *Man and Culture: An Evaluation of Bronislaw Malinowski*. London: Routledge.

Forbes, Jack D., 1964. *The Indian in America's Past*. Englewood Cliffs, NJ: Prentice-Hall, p. 103.

Firth, Raymond, 1963. *We the Tikopia*. Boston: Beacon Press.

Firth, Raymond, ed., 1967. *Themes in Economic Anthropology*. London: Tavistock.

Forde, C. Daryll, 1968. "Double Descent among the Yako," in Paul Bohannan and J. Middleton, eds., *Marriage, Family and Residence*. Garden City, N.Y.: Natural History Press, pp. 179–192.

Forde, C. Daryll, 1963. *Habitat, Economy and Society*. New York: Dutton.

Forde, C. Daryll, 1955. "The Nupe," in Daryll Forde, ed., *Peoples of the Niger-Benue Confluence*. London: International African Institute (Ethnographic Survey of Africa. Western Africa, part 10), pp. 17–52.

Fortes, Meyer, and E. E. Evans-Prichard, eds., [1940], 1962. *African Political Systems*. London: Oxford University Press.

Fortes, Meyer, 1950. "Kinship and Marriage among the Ashanti," in A. R. Radcliffe-Brown and C. Daryll Forde, eds., *African Systems of Kinship and Marriage*. London: Oxford University Press, pp. 252–284.

Fortes, Meyer, 1969. *Kinship and the Social Order: The Legacy of Lewis Henry Morgan*. Chicago: Aldine.

Fossey, Dian, 1983. *Gorillas in The Mist*. Burlington, Mass.: Houghton Mifflin.

Foster, G. M., 1955. "Peasant Society and the Image of the Limited Good," *American Anthropologist*, 67:293–315.

Fox, Robin, 1967. *Kinship and Marriage in an Anthropological Perspective*. Baltimore, Md.: Penguin.

Fox, Robin, 1968. *Encounter with Anthropology*. New York: Dell.

Fraser, Douglas, 1962. *Primitive Art*. New York: Doubleday.

Fraser, Douglas, ed., 1966. *The Many Faces of Primitive Art: A Critical Anthology*. Englewood Cliffs, N.J.: Prentice-Hall.

Frazer, Sir James George, 1931. "Magic and Religion," in V. F. Claverton, ed., *The Making of Man: An Outline of Anthropology*. Westport, Conn.: Greenwood, pp. 693–713.

Frazer, Sir James George, 1961 reissue. *The New Golden Bough*. New York: Doubleday/Anchor Books.

Freeman, J. D., 1960. "The Iban of Western Borneo," in G. P. Murdock, ed., *Social Structure in Southeast Asia*. Chicago: Quadrangle Books, pp. 65–87.

Freidl, Ernestine, 1975. *Women and Men: An Anthropologist's View*. New York: The Crossing Press, pp. 17–40.

Fried, Morton, 1960. "On the Evolution of Social Stratification and the State," in S. Diamond, ed., *Culture in History: Essays in Honor of Paul Radin*. New York: Columbia University Press, pp. 713–731.

Fried, Morton, Marvin Harris, and Robert Murphy, 1968. *War: The Anthropology of Armed Conflict and Aggression*. Garden City, N.Y.: Natural History Press.

Fried, Morton, 1972. *The Study of Anthropology*. New York: Crowell.

Fried, Morton, 1967. *The Evolution of Political Society: An Essay in Political Anthropology*. New York: Random House.

Frye, Marilyn, 1983. "Sexism," in *The Politics of Reality* New York: The Crossing Press, pp. 17–40.

Gamst, Frederick C., and Edward Norbeck, 1976. *Ideas of Culture: Sources and Uses*. New York: Holt, Rinehart and Winston.

Geertz, Clifford, 1965. "The Impact of the Concept of Culture on the Concept of Man," in John R. Platt, ed., *New Views of Man*. Chicago: University of Chicago Press, pp. 93–118.

Geertz, Clifford, 1963. *Agricultural Involution: The Process of Ecological Change in Indonesia*. Berkeley: University of California Press.

Geertz, Clifford, 1984. "Distinguished Lecture: Anti Anti-Relativism," *American Anthropologist*, 86:263–278.

Geertz, Clifford, 1968. "Religion: Anthropological Study," *International Encyclopedia of the Social Sciences*, Vol. 13. New York: Macmillan, pp. 398–406.

Gellner, Ernest, 1969. *Saints of the Atlas*. Chicago: University of Chicago Press.

Gennep, Arnold Van, 1960. *The Rites of Passage*. Chicago: University of Chicago Press.

Gibbs, James L., Jr., 1965. "The Kpelle of Liberia," in James L. Gibbs, ed., *Peoples of Africa*. New York: Holt, Rinehart and Winston, pp. 197–240.

Gleason, H. A., Jr., 1966. *An Introduction to Descriptive Linguistics*, rev. ed. New York: Holt, Rinehart and Winston.

Gluckman, Max, 1955. *The Judicial Process among the Barotse of Northern Rhodesia*. New York: Free Press.

Godlier, Maurice, 1971. "Salt Currency and the Circulation of Commodities among the Baruya of New Guinea," in George Dalton, ed., *Studies in Economic Anthropology*. Washington, D.C.: American Anthropological Association.

Goodall, Jane, 1990. *Through a Window: My Thirty Years with the Chimpanzees of Gombe*. Boston: Houghton Mifflin.

Goodall, Jane, 1986. *The Chimpanzees of Gombe: Patterns of Behavior*. Cambridge, Mass.: Belknap Press.

Goode, William, 1963. *World Revolution and Family Patterns*. New York: Free Press.

Goodenough, Ward, 1961. "Comment on Cultural Evolution," *Daedalus*, 90:521–528.

Goodenough, Ward, 1990. "Evolution of the Human Capacity for Beliefs," *American Anthropologist*, 92:597–612.

Goodenough, Ward, 1970. *Description and Comparison in Cultural Anthropology*. Chicago: Aldine.

Goodenough, Ward, ed., 1964. *Explorations in Cultural Anthropology: Essays in Honor of George Murdock*. New York: McGraw-Hill.

Goodenough, Ward, 1965. "Rethinking Status," and "Role: Toward a General Model of the Cultural Organization of Social Relationships," in Michael Banton, ed., *The Relevance of Models for Social Anthropology, ASA Monographs I*. New York: Praeger, pp. 1–24.

Goodman, Mary Ellen, 1967. *The Individual and Culture*. Homewood, Ill.: Dorsey Press.

Goody, Jack, ed., 1972. *Developmental Cycle in Domestic Groups*. New York: Cambridge University Press.

Goody, Jack, 1969. *Comparative Studies in Kinship*. Stanford, Cal.: Stanford University Press.

Goody, Jack, 1976. *Production and Reproduction: A Comparative Study of the Domestic Domain*. Cambridge: Cambridge University Press.

Goody, Jack, 1983. *The Development of the Family and Marriage in Europe*. Cambridge: Cambridge University Press.

Gordon, Robert, 1990. "The Field Researcher as a Deviant: A Namibian Case Study," in *Truth Be in the Field: Social Science Research in Southern Africa*, edited by Pierre Hugo. Pretoria: University of South Africa, pp. 70–85.

Gordon, Robert J., and Mervyn J. Meggitt, 1985. *Law and Order in the New Guinea Highlands*. Hanover, N.H.: University Press of New England.

Gorer, Geoffrey, 1943. "Themes in Japanese Culture," *Transactions of the New York Academy of Sciences*, Series II, 5.

Gorman, E. Michael, 1989. "The AIDS Epidemic in San Francisco: Epidemiological and Anthropological Perspectives," in *Applying Anthropology, An Introductory Reader*, Aaron Podolefsky and Peter J. Brown, eds. Mountain View, Co., Mayfield: 197–198.

Gornick, Vivian, and Barbara K. Moran, eds. 1971. *Woman in Sexist Society*. New York: Basic Books.

Gould, Stephen Jay, 1983. *Hen's Teeth and Horses' Toes* New York: Norton.

Gould, Stephen Jay, 1989. *Wonderful Life*. New York: Norton.

Graburn, Nelson H., 1971. *Readings in Kinship and Social Structure*. New York: Harper & Row.

Graburn, Nelson H., 1969. *Eskimos Without Igloos: Social and Economic Development in Sugluk*. Boston: Little Brown.

Graham, Susan Brandt, 1979. "Biology and Human Social Behavior: A Response to van den Berghe and Barash," *American Anthropologist*, 81(2):357–360.

Green, Edward C., 1987. "The Planning of Health Education Strategies in Swaziland," in *Anthropological praxis: Translating Knowledge into Action*, Robert M. Wulff and Shirley J. Fiske, eds. Boulder, Co.: Westview, pp. 15–25.

Green, Edward C., 1987. "The Integration of Modern and Traditional Health Sectors in Swaziland," in *Anthropological Praxis: Translating Knowledge into Action*, Robert M. Wulff and Shirley J. Fiske, eds. Boulder, Co.: Westview, pp. 87–97.

Greenberg, Joseph H., 1968. *Anthropological Linguistics: An Introduction*. New York: Random House.

Gulliver, P., 1968. "Age Differentiation," *International Encyclopedia of the Social Sciences*, 1:157–162.

Hafkin, Nancy, and Edna Bay eds. 1976. *Women in Africa*. Stanford, Cal.: Stanford University Press.

Hall, Edward T., and Mildred Reed Hall, 1986. "The Sounds of Silence," in *Anthropology 86/87*, Elvio Angeloni, ed. Guilford, Ct.: Dushkin, pp. 65–70.

Hallowell, A. Irving, 1955. *Culture and Experience*. Philadelphia: University of Pennsylvania Press.

Hammond, Dorothy, 1972. *Associations*. Reading, Mass.: Addison-Wesley.

Harlow, Harry F., 1962. "Social Deprivation in Monkeys," *Scientific American*, 206:1–10.

Harris, Marvin, 1965. "The Cultural Ecology of India's Sacred Cattle," *Current Anthropology*, 7:51–66.

Harris, Marvin, 1968. *The Rise of Anthropological Theory: A History of Theories of Culture*. New York: Crowell.

Hart, Charles W., and Arnold R. Pilling, 1960. *Tiwi of North Australia*. New York: Holt, Rinehart and Winston.

Hatcher, Evelyn Payne, 1985. *Art As Culture: An Introduction to the Anthropology of Art*. New York: University Press of America.

Haviland, W. A., 1983. *Human Evolution and Prehistory*, 2d ed. New York: Holt, Rinehart and Winston.

Haviland, W. A., 1972. "A New Look at Classic Maya Social Organization at Tikal," *Ceramica de Cultura Maya*, 8:1–16.

Haviland, W. A., 1970. "Tikal, Guatemala and Mesoamerican Urbanism," *World Archaeology*, 2:186–198.

Haviland, W. A., 1975. "The Ancient Maya and the Evolution of Urban Society," *University of Northern Colorado Museum of Anthropology, Miscellaneous Series*, No. 37.

Haviland, W. A., 1974. "Farming, Seafaring and Bilocal Residence on the Coast of Maine," *Man in the Northeast*, 6:31–44.

Haviland, William A. and Hattula Moholy–Nagy, 1992. "Distinguishing the High and Mighty from the Hoi Polloi at Tikal, Guatemala," in *Mesoamerican Elites: an Archaeological Assessment*, ed. Arlen F. and Diane Z. Chase. Norman, Ok.: University of Oklahoma Press.

Haviland, William A., and Marjory Power, in press. *The Original Vermonters* 2nd ed. Hanover, N.H.: University Press of New England.

Hays, H. R., 1965. *From Ape to Angel: An Informal History of Social Anthropology*. New York: Knopf.

Heichel, G., 1976. "Agricultural Production and Energy Resources," *American Scientist*, Vol. 64, 64–72.

Heilbroner, Robert L., and Lester C. Thurow, 1981. *The Economic Problem*, 6th ed. Englewood Cliffs, NJ: Prentice-Hall.

Helm, June, 1962. "The Ecological Approach in Anthropology," *American Journal of Sociology*, 67:630–649.

Henry, Jules, 1965. *Culture against Man*. New York: Vintage Books.

Henry, Jules, 1974. "A Theory for an Anthropological Analysis of American Culture," in Joseph G. Jorgensen and Marcello Truzzi, eds., *Anthropology and American Life*. Englewood Cliffs, N.J.: Prentice-Hall, pp. 6–22.

Henry, Jules, 1966. "The Metaphysic of Youth, Beauty, and Romantic Love," in *The Challenge to Women*, ed. Seymour Farber and Roger Wilson. New York: Basic Books.

Herskovits, Melville J., 1964. *Cultural Dynamics*. New York: Knopf.

Herskovits, Melville J., 1952. *Economic Anthropology: A Study in Comparative Economics*, 2d ed. New York: Knopf.

Hewes, Gordon W., 1973. "Primate Communication and the Gestural Origin of Language," *Current Anthropology*, 14:5–24.

Hickerson, Nancy Parrot, 1980. *Linguistic Anthropology*. New York: Holt, Rinehart and Winston.

Hjelmslev, Louis, 1970. *Language: An Introduction*, Francis J. Whitfield, trans. Madison: University of Wisconsin Press.

Hodgen, Margaret, 1964. *Early Anthropology in the Sixteenth and Seventeenth Centuries*. Philadelphia: University of Pennsylvania Press.

Hoebel, E. A., 1954. *The Law of Primitive Man: A Study in Comparative Legal Dynamics*. Cambridge, Mass.: Harvard University Press.

Hoebel, E. A., 1960. *The Cheyennes: Indians of the Great Plains*. New York: Holt, Rinehart and Winston.

Hoebel, E. A., 1972. *Anthropology: The Study of Man*, 4th ed. New York: McGraw-Hill.

Hogbin, Ian, 1964. *A Guadalcanal Society*. New York: Holt, Rinehart and Winston.

Holden, Constance, 1983. "Simon and Kahn versus *Global 2000*," *Science*, 221:342.

Hostetler, John, and Gertrude Huntington, 1971. *Children in Amish Society*. New York: Holt, Rinehart and Winston.

Hsiaotung, Fei, 1939. *Peasant Life in China*. London: Kegan, Paul, Trench and Truber.

Hsu, Francis L., 1977. "Role, Affect, and Anthropology," *American Anthropologist*, 79:805–808.

Hsu, Francis L., 1961. *Psychological Anthropology: Approaches to Culture and Personality*. Homewood, Ill.: Dorsey Press.

Hsu, Francis L., 1979. "The Cultural Problems of the Cultural Anthropologist," *American Anthropologist*, 81:517–532.

Hubert, Henri, and Marcel Mauss, 1964. *Sacrifice*. Chicago: University of Chicago Press.

Hunt, Robert C., ed., 1967. *Personalities and Cultures: Readings in Psychological Anthropology*. Garden City, N.Y.: Natural History Press.

Hymes, Dell, ed., 1972. *Reinventing Anthropology*. New York: Pantheon.

Hymes, Dell, 1964. *Language in Culture and Society: A Reader in Linguistics and Anthropology*. New York: Harper & Row.

Inkeles, Alex, 1966. "The Modernization of Man," in Myron Weiner, ed., *Modernization: The Dynamics of Growth*. New York: Basic Books.

Inkeles, Alex, and D. J. Levinson, 1954. "National Character: The Study of Modal Personality and Socio-cultural Systems," in G. Lindzey, ed., *Handbook of Social Psychology*. Reading, Mass.: Addison-Wesley, pp. 977–1020.

Ireland, Emilienne, 1991. "Neither Warriors nor Victims, The Wauja Peacefully Organize to Defend Their Land." *Cultural Survival Quarterly* 15, No. 1, pp. 54–60.

Jennings, Francis, 1976. *The Invasion of America*. New York: Norton.

Johanson, Donald, and James Shreeve, 1989. *Lucy's Child: The Discovery of a Human Ancestor*. New York: Avon.

Johanson, Donald C., and Maitland Edey, 1981. *Lucy, The Beginnings of Humankind*. New York: Simon & Schuster.

Johnson, Allen. 1989. "Horticulturalists: Economic Behavior in Tribes," in Stuart Plattner, ed., Economic Anthropology. Stanford, Cal.: Stanford University Press, pp. 49–77.

Johnson, Allen W., and Timothy Earle, 1987. *The Evolution of Human Societies, from Foraging Group to Agrarian State*. Stanford, Cal.: Stanford University Press.

Johnson, Dirk, 1991. "Polygamists Emerge From Secrecy, Seeking Not Just Peace But Respect," *New York Times*, April 9, p. A22.

Jolly, Alison, 1985. "The Evolution of Primate Behavior," *American Scientist* 73(3):230–239.

Jolly, Allison, 1985. *The Evolution of Primate Behavior*, 2nd ed. New York: Macmillan.

Jolly, Allison, 1991. "Thinking Like a Vervet," *Science*, 251:574.

Jopling, Carol F., 1971. *Art and Aesthetics in Primitive Societies: A Critical Anthology*. New York: Dutton.

Jorgensen, Joseph, 1972. *The Sun Dance Religion*. Chicago: University of Chicago Press.

Joyce, Christopher, 1991. *Witnesses from the Grave: The Stories Bones Tell*. Boston: Little, Brown.

Kahn, Herman, and Anthony J. Wiener, 1967. *The Year 2000*. New York: Macmillan.

Kalwet, Holger, 1988. *Dreamtime and Inner Space: The World of the Shaman*. New York: Random House.

Kaplan, David, 1972. *Culture Theory*. Englewood Cliffs, N.J.: Prentice-Hall.

Kaplan, David, 1968. "The Superorganic: Science or Metaphysics," in Robert Manners and David Kaplan, eds., *Theory in Anthropology: A Sourcebook*. Chicago: Aldine.

Kardiner, Abram, and Edward Preble, 1961. *They Studied Men*. New York: Mentor.

Keesing, Roger M., 1976. *Cultural Anthropology: A Contemporary Perspective*. New York: Holt, Rinehart and Winston.

Keesing, Roger M., 1975. *Kin Groups and Social Structure*. New York: Holt, Rinehart and Winston.

Kendall, Laurel, 1990. "In the Company of Witches," *Natural History* 10/90, p. 92–95.

Kerri, James N., 1976. "Studying Voluntary Associations as Adaptive Mechanisms: A Review of Anthropological Perspectives," *Current Anthropology*, 17(1), pp. 23–47.

Kessler, Evelyn, 1975. *Women*. New York: Holt, Rinehart and Winston.

Kleinman, Arthur, 1982. "The Failure of Western Medicine," in David Hunter and Phillip Whitten, *Anthropology: Contemporary Perspectives*. Boston: Little, Brown, pp. 266–269.

Kluckhohn, Clyde, 1970. *Mirror for Man*. Greenwich, Conn.: Fawcett.

Kluckhohn, Clyde, 1944. *Navajo Witchcraft*. Cambridge, Mass.: Harvard University Press.

Knauft, Bruce, 1991. "Violence and Sociality in Human Evolution," *Current Anthropology*, 32: 391–409.

Kohler, Gernot, 1978. "Global Apartheid," in *World Order Models Project, Paper 7*. New York: Institute for World Order.

Krader, Lawrence, 1965. *Formation of the State*. Englewood Cliffs, N.J.: Prentice-Hall.

Kroeber, A. L., 1963. *Anthropology: Cultural Processes and Patterns*. New York: Harcourt.

Kroeber, A., 1958. "Totem and Taboo: An Ethnologic Psychoanalysis," in William Lessa and Evon Z. Vogt, eds., *Reader in Comparative Religion: An Anthropological Approach*. New York: Harper & Row, pp. 57–62.

Kroeber, A. L., and Clyde Kluckhohn, 1952. *Culture: A Critical Review of Concepts and Definitions*. Cambridge, Mass.: Harvard University Press.

Kroeber, Alfred L., quoted in Edward Dozier, 1970. *The Pueblo Indians of North America*. New York: Holt, Rinehart and Winston.

Kroeber, A. L., 1939. "Cultural and Natural Areas of Native North America," *American Archaeology and Ethnology*, Vol. 38. Berkeley, Cal.: University of California Press.

Kuhn, Thomas 1962. *The Structure of Scientific Revolutions*. Chicago: University of Chicago Press.

Kuper, Hilda, 1965. "The Swazi of Swaziland," in James L. Gibbs, ed., *Peoples of Africa*. New York: Holt, Rinehart and Winston, pp. 479–511.

Kurath, Gertrude Probosch, 1960. "Panorama of Dance Ethnology," *Current Anthropology*, 1:233–254.

Kushner, Gilbert, 1969. *Anthropology of Complex Societies*. Stanford, Cal.: Stanford University Press.

LaBarre, Weston, 1945. "Some Observations of Character Structure in the Orient: The Japanese," *Psychiatry*, 8:319–342.

Laguna, Grace A. de, 1966. *On Existence and the Human World*. New Haven, Conn.: Yale University Press.

Landes, Ruth, 1982. "Comment," *Current Anthropology*, 23:401.

Lanternari, Vittorio, 1963. *The Religions of the Oppressed*. New York: Mentor.

Lévi-Strauss, Claude, 1963. *Structural Anthropology*. New York: Basic Books.

Lévi-Strauss, Claude, 1966. *The Savage Mind*. Chicago: University of Chicago Press.

Lévi-Strauss, Claude, 1969. *The Elementary Structures of Kinship*. Boston: Beacon Press.

Lévi-Strauss, Claude, 1963. *Totemism*. Boston: Beacon Press.

Lévi-Strauss, Claude, 1971. "The Family," in Harry L. Shapiro, ed., *Man, Culture and Society*. London: Oxford University Press, pp. 333–357.

Leach, Edmund, 1963. "The Determinants of Differential Cross-cousin Marriage," *Man*, 63:87.

Leach, Edmund, 1961. *Rethinking Anthropology*. London: Athione Press.

Leach, Edmund, 1982. *Social Anthropology*. Glasgow: Fontana Paperbacks.

Leach, Edmund, 1962. "On Certain Unconsidered Aspects of Double Descent Systems," *Man*, 214:13.

Leach, Edmund, 1962. "The Determinants of Differential Cross-cousin Marriage," *Man*, 62:238.

Leach, Edmund, 1965. *Political Systems of Highland Burma*. Boston: Beacon Press.

Leacock, Eleanor, 1981. *Myths of Male Dominance: Collected Articles on Women Cross Culturally*. New York: Monthly Review Press.

Leacock, Eleanor, 1981. "Women's Status in Egalitarian Society: Implications for Social Evolution," in *Myths of Male Dominance: Collected Articles on Women Cross Culturally* New York: Monthly Review Press, pp. 133–182.

Leap, William L., 1987. "Tribally Controlled Culture Change: The Northern Ute Language Renewal Project" in *Anthropological Praxis: Translating Knowledge into Action*, edited by Robert M. Wulff and Shirley J. Fiske. Boulder Co.: Westview, pp. 197–211.

Leavitt, Gregory C., 1990. "Sociobiological Explanations of Incest Avoidance: A Critical Review of Evidential Claims," *American Anthropologist* 92:973, pp. 971–993.

LeClair, Edward, and Harold K. Schneider, eds., 1968. *Economic Anthropology: Readings in Theory and Analysis*. New York: Holt, Rinehart and Winston.

Lee, Richard B., 1984. *The Dobe !Kung: Foragers in a Changing World*. New York: Holt, Rinehart and Winston.

Lee, Richard B., and Irven DeVore, eds., 1968. *Man the Hunter*. Chicago: Aldine.

Leeds, Anthony, and Andrew P. Vayda, eds., 1965. *Man, Culture and Animals: The Role of Animals in Human Ecological Adjustments*. Washington, D.C.: American Association for the Advancement of Science.

Lees, Robert, 1953. "The Basis of Glottochronology," *Language*, 29:113–127.

Lehmann, Winifred, 1973. *Historical Linguistics, An Introduction*, 2d ed. New York: Holt, Rinehart and Winston.

Lehmann, Arthur C., and James E. Myers, eds., 1988. *Magic, Witchcraft and Religion: An Anthropological Study of the Supernatural.* 2d ed. Palo Alto, Cal.: Mayfield.

Leinhardt, Godfrey, 1964. *Social Anthropology.* London: Oxford University Press.

Leinhardt, Godfrey, 1971. "Religion," in Harry Shapiro, ed., *Man, Culture and Society.* London: Oxford University Press, pp. 382–401.

LeMay, Marjorie, 1975. "The Language Capability of Neanderthal Man," *American Journal of Physical Anthropology,* 43(1):9–14.

Lenski, Gerhard, 1966. *Power and Privilege: A Theory of Social Stratification.* New York: McGraw-Hill.

Leonard, William R., and Michelle Hegman, 1987. "Evolution of P3 Morphology in *Australopithecus afarensis,*" *American Journal of Physical Anthropology,* 73:41–63.

Lett, James., 1987. *The Human Enterprise: A Critical Introduction to Anthropological Theory.* Boulder, Co.: Westview.

LeVine, Robert, 1973. *Culture, Behavior and Personality.* Chicago: Aldine.

Lewin, Roger, 1986. "New Fossil Upsets Human Family," *Science,* 1986, 233:720–721.

Lewin, Roger, 1987. "Four Legs Bad, Two Legs Good," *Science,* 1987, 235:969.

Lewin, Roger, 1987. "The Earliest 'Humans' Were More Like Apes," *Science,* 236:1062–1063.

Lewin, Roger, 1988. "Molecular Clocks Turn a Quarter Century," *Science,* 239:562.

Lewis, I.M., 1965. "Problems in the Comparative Study of Unilineal Descent," in Michael Banton, ed., *The Relevance of Models for Social Organization.* London: Tavistock, pp. 87–112.

Lewis, I. M., 1976. *Social Anthropology in Perspective.* Harmondsworth, Eng.: Penguin.

Linton, Ralph, [1936], 1964. *The Study of Man: An Introduction.* New York: Appleton.

Little, Kenneth, 1964. "The Role of Voluntary Associations in West African Urbanization," in *Africa: Social Problems of Change and Conflict,* ed. Pierre Van den Berghe. San Francisco: Chandler, pp. 325–345.

Livingstone, Frank B., 1973. "The Distribution of Abnormal Hemoglobin Genes and Their Significance for Human Evolution," in C. Loring Brace and James Metress, eds., *Man in Evolutionary Perspective.* New York: Wiley.

Louckey, James, and Robert Carlsen, 1991. "Massacre in Santiago Atitlán," *Cultural Survival Quarterly,* 15, No. 3. pp. 65–70.

Lounsbury, Floyd 1964. "The Structural Analysis of Kinship Semantics," in Horace G. Lunt, ed., *Proceedings of the Ninth International Congress of Linguists.* The Hague: Mouton, pp. 1073–1093.

Lowie, Robert H., 1966. *Culture and Ethnology.* New York: Basic Books.

Lowie, Robert H., 1948. *Social Organization.* New York: Holt, Rinehart and Winston.

Lowie, Robert H., 1956. *Crow Indians.* New York: Holt, Rinehart and Winston.

Lustig–Arecco, Vero, 1975. *Technology: Strategies for Survival.* New York: Holt, Rinehart and Winston.

MacCormack, Carol P. 1977 "Biological Events and Cultural Control," *Signs* 3:93–100.

MacNeil, Robert, 1982. *The Right Place at the Right Time.* Boston: Little, Brown.

Magnarella, Paul J., 1974. *Tradition and Change in a Turkish Town.* New York: Wiley.

Mair, Lucy, 1969. *Witchcraft.* New York: McGraw-Hill.

Mair, Lucy, 1971. *Marriage.* Baltimore, Md.: Penguin.

Malefijt, Annemarie de Waal, 1969. *Religion and Culture: An Introduction to Anthropology of Religion.* London: Macmillan.

Malefijt, Annemarie de Waal, 1974. *Images of Man.* New York: Knopf.

Malinowski, Bronislaw, 1945. *The Dynamics of Culture Change.* New Haven, Conn.: Yale University Press.

Malinowski, Bronislaw, 1954. *Magic, Science and Religion.* Garden City, N.Y.: Doubleday/Anchor Books.

Malinowski, Bronislaw, 1951. *Crime and Custom in Savage Society.* London: Routledge.

Malinowski, Bronislaw, 1922. *Argonauts of the Western Pacific.* New York: Dutton.

Marano, Lou, 1982. "Windigo Psychosis: The Anatomy of an Emic-Etic Confusion," *Current Anthropology,* 23:385–412.

Marsella, Joan, 1982. "Pulling It Together: Discussion and Comments," in *Confronting the Creationists,* ed. Stephen Pastner and William A. Haviland, Northeastern Anthropological Association, Occasional Proceedings, No. 1, pp. 77–80.

Marshack, Alexander, 1976. "Implications of the Paleolithic Symbolic Evidence for the Origin of Language," *American Scientist,* 64:136–145.

Marshall, Lorna, 1961. "Sharing, Talking and Giving: Relief of Social Tensions among !Kung Bushmen," *Africa,* 31:231–249.

Mason, J. Alden, 1957. *The Ancient Civilizations of Peru.* Baltimore, Md.: Penguin.

Maybury–Lewis, David, 1960. "Parallel Descent and the Apinaye Anomaly," *Southwestern Journal of Anthropology,* 16:191–216.

Maybury–Lewis, David, 1984. *The Prospects for Plural Societies.* 1982 Proceedings of the American Ethnological Society.

Maybury–Lewis, David, 1985. "A Special Sort of Pleading: Anthropology at the Service of Ethnic Groups," in *Advocacy and Anthropology,* Robert I. Paine, ed., St. John's Newfoundland: Institute of Social and Economic Research, Memorial University of Newfoundland.

McHale, John, 1969. *The Future of the Future.* New York: Braziller.

Mead, Margaret, 1963. *Sex and Temperament in Three Primitive Societies,* 3d ed. New York: Morrow.

Mead, Margaret, 1928. *Coming of Age in Samoa.* New York: Morrow.

Mead, Margaret, 1970. *Culture and Commitment.* Garden City, N.Y.: Natural History Press.

Meadows, Donella H., Dennis L. Meadows, Jorgen Randers, and William W. Behrens III, 1974. *The Limits to Growth.* New York: Universe Books.

Mellars, Paul, 1989. "Major Issues in the Emergence of Modern Humans," *Current Anthropology,* 30:349–385.

Merriam, Alan, 1964. *The Anthropology of Music.* Chicago: Northwestern University Press.

Mesghinua, Haile Michael, 1966. "Salt Mining in Enderta," *Journal of Ethiopian Studies,* 4(2).

Middleton, John, ed., 1970. *From Child to Adult: Studies in the Anthropology of Education.* Garden City, N.Y.: Natural History Press.

Mitchell, William E., 1973. "A New Weapon Stirs Up Old Ghosts," *Natural History Magazine,* December, pp. 77–84.

Mitchell, William E., 1978. *Mishpokhe: A Study of New York City Jewish Family Clubs.* The Hague: Mouton.

Montagu, Ashley, 1964. *Man's Most Dangerous Myth: The Fallacy of Race,* 4th ed. New York: World Publishing.

Morgan, Lewis H., 1877. *Ancient Society.* New York: World Publishing.

Mowat, Farley, 1959. *The Desperate People.* Boston: Little Brown.

Mowat, Farley, 1981. *People of the Deer.* Toronto: Bantam Books.

Murdock, George P., 1956. "How Culture Changes," in Harry L. Shapiro, ed., *Man, Culture and Society.* Chicago: University of Chicago Press, 319–332.

Murdock, George P., 1965. *Social Structure.* New York: Free Press.

Murdock, George, 1960. "Cognatic Forms of Social Organization," in G. P. Murdock, ed., *Social Structure in Southeast Asia.* Chicago: Quadrangle Books, pp. 1–14.

Murphy, Robert, 1971. *The Dialectics of Social Life: Alarms and Excursions in Anthropological Theory.* New York: Basic Books.

Murphy, Robert, and Leonard Kasdan, 1959. "The Structure of Parallel Cousin Marriage," *American Anthropologist,* 61:17–29.

Murray, Gerald F., 1989. "The Domestication of Wood in Haiti: A Case Study in Applied Evolution," in *Applying Anthropology, An Introductory Reader,* Aaron Podolefsky and Peter J. Brown, eds. Mountain View, Cal.: Mayfield.

Myrdal, Gunnar, 1974. "Challenge to Affluence: The Emergence of an 'Under-class,'" in Joseph G. Jorgensen and Marcello Truzzi, eds., *Anthropology and American Life.* Englewood Cliffs, N.J.: Prentice-Hall, 52–61.

Nader, Laura, ed., 1980. *No Access To Law: Alternatives to the American Judicial System.* New York: Academic Press.

Nader, Laura, ed., 1965. "The Ethnography of Law," *American Anthropologist,* Part II, 67(6).

Nader, Laura, ed., 1969. *Law in Culture and Society.* Chicago: Aldine.

Naroll, Raoul, 1973. "Holocultural Theory Tests," in Raoul Naroll and Frada Naroll, eds., *Main Currents in Cultural Anthropology.* New York: Appleton, pp. 309–384.

Nash, Manning, 1966. *Primitive and Peasant Economic Systems.* San Francisco: Chandler.

Needham, Rodney, ed., 1971. *Rethinking Kinship and Marriage.* London: Tavistock.

Needham, Rodney, 1972. *Belief, Language and Experience.* Chicago: University of Chicago Press.

Nesbitt, L. M., 1935. *Hell-Hole of Creation.* New York: Knopf.

Netting, R.M., R.R. Wilk and E.J. Arnould, eds., 1984. *Households: Comparative and Historical Studies of the Domestic Group.* Berkeley, Cal.: University of California Press.

Nettl, Bruno, 1956. *Music in Primitive Culture.* Cambridge, Mass.: Harvard University Press.

Newman, Philip L., 1965. *Knowing the Gururumba.* New York: Holt, Rinehart and Winston.

Nietschmann, Bernard, 1987. "The Third World War," *Cultural Survival Quarterly* 11 (3):1–16.

Norbeck, Edward, Douglas Price–Williams, and William McCord, eds., 1968. *The Study of Personality: An Interdisciplinary Appraisal.* New York: Holt, Rinehart and Winston.

Norbeck, Edward, 1974. *Religion in Human Life: Anthropological Views.* New York: Holt, Rinehart and Winston.

Nye, E. Ivan, and Felix M. Berardo, 1975. *The Family: Its Structure and Interaction.* New York: Macmillan.

O'Mahoney, Kevin, 1970. "The Salt Trade," *Journal of Ethiopian Studies,* 8(2).

Obler, Regina Smith, 1980. "Is the Female Husband a Man? Woman/Woman Marriage Among the Nandi of Kenya," *Ethnology* 19: 69–88.

Offiong, Daniel, 1985. "Witchcraft among the Ibibio of Nigeria," in *Magic, Witchcraft and Religion,* ed. Arthur C. Lehmann and James E. Myers. Palo Alto, Cal.: Mayfield, pp. 152–165.

Okonjo, Kamene, 1976. "The Dual-Sex Political System in Operation: Igbo Women and Community Politics in Midwestern Nigeria," in *Women in Africa,* ed. Nancy Hafkin and Edna Bay. Stanford, Ca.: Stanford University Press, pp. 45–58.

Oliver, Douglas Z., 1964. *Invitation to Anthropology.* Garden City, N.Y.: Natural History Press.

Ortiz, Alfonso, 1969. *The Tewa World.* Chicago: University of Chicago Press.

Oswalt, Wendell H., 1970. *Understanding Our Culture.* New York: Holt, Rinehart and Winston.

Oswalt, Wendell H., 1972. *Habitat and Technology.* New York: Holt, Rinehart and Winston.

Oswalt, Wendell H., 1972. *Other Peoples Other Customs: World Ethnography and Its History.* New York: Holt, Rinehart and Winston.

Otten, Charlotte N., 1971. *Anthropology and Art: Readings in Cross-cultural Aesthetics.* Garden City, N.Y.: Natural History Press.

Ottenberg, Phoebe, 1965. "The Afikpo Ibo of Eastern Nigeria," in James L. Gibbs, ed., *Peoples of Africa.* New York: Holt, Rinehart and Winston, pp. 1–39.

Otterbein, Keith F., 1971. *The Evolution of War.* New Haven, Conn.: HRAF Press.

Parades, J. Anthony and Elizabeth D. Purdum, 1990. "Bye Bye, Ted . . .," *Anthropology Today* 6, No. 2, pp. 9–11.

Parker, Seymour, and Hilda Parker, 1979. "The Myth of Male Superiority: Rise and Demise," *American Anthropologist,* 81(2):289–309.

Partridge, William, ed., 1984. *Training Manual in Development Anthropology.* Washington, D.C.: American Anthropological Association.

Pastner, Stephen, and William A. Haviland, eds., 1982. "Confronting the Creationists," *Northeastern Anthropological Association Occasional Proceedings,* I.

Patterson, Francine, and Eugene Linden, 1981. *The Education of Koko.* New York: Holt, Rinehart and Winston.

Peacock, James L., 1986. *The Anthropological Lens: Harsh Light, Soft Focus.* New York: Cambridge University Press.

Pelto, Pertti J., 1966. *The Nature of Anthropology.* Columbus, Ohio: Merrill.

Pelto, Pertti J., 1973. *The Snowmobile Revolution: Technology and Social Change in the Arctic.* Menlo Park, Cal.: Cummings.

Penniman, T. K., 1965. *A Hundred Years of Anthropology.* London: Duckworth.

Peters, Charles R., 1979. "Toward an Ecological Model of African Plio-Pleistocene Hominid Adaptations," *American Anthropologist,* 81(2):261–278.

Peterson, Frederick L., 1962. *Ancient Mexico, An Introduction to the Pre-Hispanic Cultures.* New York: Capricorn Books.

Piddocke, Stuart, 1965. "The Potlatch System of the Southern Kwakiutl: A New Perspective," *Southwestern Journal of Anthropology,* 21:244–264.

Pilbeam, David, 1986. *Human Origins.* David Skamp Distinguished Lecture in Anthropology, Indiana University.

Pitt, David, 1977. "Comment," *Current Anthropology,* 18: 628.

Polanyi, Karl, 1968. "The Economy as Instituted Process," In E. E. LeClair, Jr., and H. K. Schneider, eds., *Economic Anthropology: Readings in Theory and Analysis.* New York: Holt, Rinehart and Winston, pp. 122–167.

Pope, Geoffrey, 1989. "Bamboo and Human Evolution," *Natural History*, Vol. 98., 10/89, p. 56.

Pospisil, Leopold, 1971. *Anthropology of Law: A Comparative Theory*. New York: Harper & Row.

Pospisil, Leopold, 1963. *The Kapauku Papuans of West New Guinea*. New York: Holt, Rinehart and Winston.

Powdermaker, Hortense, 1966. *Stranger and Friend: The Way of an Anthropologist*. New York: Norton.

Price–Williams, D. R., ed., 1970. *Cross-cultural Studies: Selected Readings*. Baltimore, Md.: Penguin.

Prins, A. H., 1953. *East African Class Systems*. Gronigen, The Netherlands: J. B. Walters.

Radcliffe–Brown, A. 1952. *Structure and Function in Primitive Society*. New York: Free Press.

Radcliffe–Brown, A. R., and C. D. Forde, eds., 1950. *African Systems of Kinship and Marriage*. London: Oxford University Press.

Radcliffe–Brown, A. R., 1931. "Social Organization of Australian Tribes," *Oceania Monographs*, No. 1. Melbourne: Macmillan.

Rappaport, Roy, 1984. *Pigs for the Ancestors*, new enlarged ed. New Haven, Conn.: Yale University Press.

Rappaport, Roy A., 1969. "Ritual Regulation of Environmental Relations among a New Guinea People," in *Environment and Cultural Behavior*, ed. Andrew P. Vayda. Garden City, NY: Natural History Press. pp. 181–201.

Rathje, William L., 1974, "The Garbage Project: A New Way of Looking at the Problems of Archaeology," *Archaeology*, 27:236–241.

Rathje, William, and Cullen Murphy, 1992. *Rubbish!: The Archaeology of Garbage*. New York: HarperCollins.

Redfield, Robert, Ralph Linton, and Melville J. Herskovits, 1936. "Memorandum of the Study of Acculturation," *American Anthropologist*, 38:149–152.

Reina, Ruben, 1966. *The Law of the Saints*. Indianapolis: Bobbs-Merrill.

Reiter, Rayna, ed., 1975. *Toward an Anthropology of Women* New York: Monthly Review Press.

Rice, Don S., and Prudence M. Rice, 1984, "Lessons from the Maya," *Latin American Research Review*, 19 (3):7–34.

Rindos, David, 1983. *The Origins of Agriculture: An Evolutionary Perspective*. New York: Academic Press.

Rodman, Hyman, 1968. "Class Culture," *International Encyclopedia of the Social Sciences*, Vol. 15. New York: Macmillan, pp. 332–337.

Rowe, Timothy, 1988. "New Issues for Phylogenetics," *Science*, 239:1184.

Sahlins, Marshall, 1972. *Stone Age Economics*. Chicago: Aldine.

Sahlins, Marshall, 1968. *Tribesmen*. Englewood Cliffs, N.J.: Prentice-Hall.

Sahlins, Marshall, 1961. "The Segmentary Lineage: An Organization of Predatory Expansion," *American Anthropologist*, 63:322–343.

Salzman, Philip C., 1967. "Political Organization among Nomadic Peoples," *Proceedings of the American Philosophical Society*, 3:115–131.

Sanday, Peggy Reeves, 1981. *Female Power and Male Dominance: On the Origins of Sexual Inequality*. Cambridge: Cambridge University Press.

Sangree, Walter H., 1965. "The Bantu Tiriki of Western Kenya," in James L. Gibbs, ed., *Peoples of Africa*. New York: Holt, Rinehart and Winston.

Sapir, E., 1917. "Do We Need a Superorganic?" *American Anthropologist*, 19:441–447.

Sapir, E., 1921. *Language*. New York: Harcourt.

Sapir, E., 1916. *Time Perspective in Aboriginal American Culture: A Study in Method*. Ottawa: Geological Society of Canada.

Sapir, E., 1924. "Culture, Genuine or Spurious?" *American Journal of Sociology*, 29:401–429.

Scaglion, Richard, 1987. "Contemporary Law Development in Papua New Guinea," in *Anthropological Praxis: Translating Knowledge into Action*, edited by Robert M. Wulff and Shirley J. Fiske. Boulder, Co.: Westview Press. pp. 98–108.

Scheflen, Albert E., 1972. *Body Language and the Social Order*. Englewood Cliffs, N.J.: Prentice-Hall.

Scheper–Hughes, Nancy, 1979. *Saints, Scholars and Schizophrenics*. Berkeley: University of California Press.

Schlegel, Alice, 1977. "Male and Female in Hopi Thought and Action," in *Sexual Stratification*, ed. Alice Schlegel New York: Columbia University Press, pp. 245–269.

Schrire, Carmel, ed., 1984. *Past and Present in Hunter-Gatherer Studies*. Orlando, Fla.: Academic Press.

Schurtz, Heinrich, 1902. *Alterklassen und Männerbünde*. Berlin: Reimer.

Schusky, Ernest L., 1983. *Manual for Kinship Analysis*, 2d ed. Lanham, Md.: University Press of America.

Schusky, Ernest L., 1975. *Variation in Kinship*. New York: Holt, Rinehart and Winston.

Schwartz, Jeffrey H., 1984. "Hominoid Evolution: A Review and a Reassessment," in *Current Anthropology* 25(5):655–672.

Sen, Gita, and Caren Grown, 1987. *Development, Crisis, and Alternative Visions: Third World Women's Perspectives*. New York: Monthly Review Press.

Service, Elman R., 1966. *The Hunters*. Englewood Cliffs, N.J.: Prentice-Hall.

Service, Elman R., 1971. *Primitive Social Organization: An Evolutionary Perspective*, 2d ed. New York: Random House.

Seymour, Dorothy Z., 1986. "Black Children, Black Speech," in *Language Awareness*, 4th ed., ed. Paul Escholz, Alfred Rosa and Virginia Clark. New York: St. Martin's Press, p. 74.

Shapiro, Harry, ed., 1960. *Man, Culture and Society*. New York: Oxford University Press.

Sharp, Lauriston, 1952. "Steel Axes for Stone Age Australians," in Edward H. Spicer, ed., *Human Problems in Technological Change*. New York: Russell Sage, pp. 69–90.

Shaw, Dennis G., 1984. "A Light at the End of the Tunnel: Anthropological Contributions Towards Global Competence," *Anthropology Newsletter*, 25:16.

Sheets, Payson, 1987. "Dawn of a New Stone Age in Eye Surgery," in *Archaeology: Discovering Our Past*, by Robert J. Sharer and Wendy Ashmore. Palo Alto, Cal.: Mayfield, pp. 230–231.

Shimkin, Dimitri B., Sol Tax, and John W. Morrison, eds., 1978. *Anthropology for the Future*. Urbana, Ill.: Department of Anthropology, University of Illinois, Research Report No. 4.

Shinnie, Margaret, 1970. *Ancient African Kingdoms*. New York: New American Library.

Shostak, Marjorie, 1981. *Nisa: The Life and Words of a !Kung Woman*. Cambridge, Mass.: Harvard University Press.

Sjoberg, Gideon, 1960. *The Preindustrial City*. New York: Free Press.

Slobin, Dan I., 1971. *Psycholinguistics*. Glenview, Ill.: Scott, Foresman.

Smith, Raymond, 1970. "Social Stratification in the Caribbean," in Leonard Plotnicov and Arthur Tudin, eds., *Essays in*

Comparative Social Stratification. Pittsburgh: University of Pittsburgh Press, pp. 43–76.

Snowden, Charles T., 1990. "Language Capabilities of Nonhuman Animals," *Yearbook of Physical Anthropology*, 33: 215–243.

Speck, Frank G., 1935. "Penobscot Tales and Religious Beliefs," *Journal of American Folk-Lore*, 48(187):1–107.

Speck, Frank G., 1940. *Penobscot Man*. Philadelphia: University of Pennsylvania Press.

Speck, Frank G., 1920. "Penobscot Shamanism," in *Memoirs of the American Anthropological Association*, 6:239–288.

Spiro, Melford E., 1966. "Religion: Problems of Definition and Explanation," in Michael Banton, ed., *Anthropological Approaches to the Study of Religion*. London: Tavistock, pp. 85–126.

Spradley, James P., 1979. *The Ethnographic Interview* New York: Holt, Rinehart and Winston.

Spuhler, James N., 1979. "Continuities and Discontinuities in Anthropoid-Hominid Behavioral Evolution: Bipedal Locomotion and Sexual Reception," in *Evolutionary Biology and Human Social Behavior*, ed. N. A. Chagnon and William Irons. North Scituate, Mass.: Duxbury Press. pp. 454–461.

Stacey, Judith, 1990. *Brave New Families*. New York: Basic Books.

Stahl, Ann Brower, 1984. "Hominid Dietary Selection Before Fire," *Current Anthropology*, 25:151–168.

Stanner, W. E., 1968. "Radcliffe–Brown, A. R.," *International Encyclopedia of the Social Sciences*, Vol. 13. New York: Macmillan, 285–290.

Stephens, William N., 1963. *The Family in Cross-cultural Perspective*. New York: Holt, Rinehart and Winston.

Steward, Julian H., 1972. *Theory of Culture Change: The Methodology of Multilinear Evolution*. Urbana: University of Illinois Press.

Stocking, George W., Jr., 1968. *Race, Culture and Evolution: Essays in the History of Anthropology*. New York: Free Press.

Swartz, Marc J., Victor W. Turner, and Arthur Tuden, 1966. *Political Anthropology*. Chicago: Aldine.

Tannen, Deborah, 1990. *You Just Don't Understand: Women and Men in Conversation*. New York: William Morrow, pp. 231–234 and 241–244.

Tax, Sol, ed., 1962. *Anthropology Today: Selections*. Chicago: University of Chicago Press.

Tax, Sol, 1953. *Penny Capitalism: A Guatemalan Indian Economy*, Smithsonian Institution, Institute of Social Anthropology, Pub. No. 16. Washington, D.C.: Government Printing Office.

Tax, Sol, Sam Stanley, and others, 1975. "In Honor of Sol Tax," *Current Anthropology*. 16:507–540.

Thomas, W. L., ed., 1956. *Man's Role in Changing the Face of the Earth*. Chicago: University of Chicago Press.

Thompson, Stith, 1960. *The Folktale*. New York: Holt, Rinehart and Winston.

Thorne, Barrie, and Marilyn Yalom, eds., 1982. *Rethinking the Family: Some Feminist Problems*. New York: Longman.

Tiffany, Sharon, ed., 1979. *Women in Africa*. St. Albans, Vt.: Eden Press.

Trager, George L., 1964. "Paralanguage: A First Approximation," in Dell Hymes, ed., *Language in Culture and Society*. New York: Harper & Row.

Tuden, Arthur, 1970. "Slavery and Stratification among the Ila of Central Africa," in Arthur Tuden and Leonard Plotnicov, eds., *Social Stratification in Africa*. New York: Free Press, pp. 47–58.

Tumin, Melvin M., 1967. *Social Stratification: The Forms and Functions of Inequality*. Englewood Cliffs, N.J.: Prentice-Hall.

Turnbull, Colin M., 1961. *The Forest People*. New York: Simon & Schuster.

Turnbull, Colin M., 1983. *The Human Cycle*. New York: Simon & Schuster.

Turnbull, Colin M., 1983. *Mbuti Pygmies: Change and Adaptation*. New York: Holt, Rinehart and Winston.

Turnbull, Colin M., 1972. *The Mountain People*. New York: Simon & Schuster.

Turner, V. W., 1957. *Schism and Continuity in an African Society*. Manchester, Eng.: The University Press.

Turner, V. W., 1969. *The Ritual Process*. Chicago: Aldine.

Turner, Terry, 1991. "Major Shift in Brazilian Yanomami Policy," *Anthropology Newsletter* 32, No. 5, pp. 1 and 46.

Tylor, Edward Burnett, 1871. *Primitive Culture: Researches into the Development of Mythology, Philosophy, Religion, Language, Art and Customs*. London: Murray.

Tylor, Sir Edward B., 1931. "Animism," in V. F. Calverton, ed., *The Making of Man: An Outline of Anthropology*. New York: Modern Library.

Valentine, Charles A., 1968. *Culture and Poverty*. Chicago: University of Chicago Press.

Van Allen, Judith, 1979. "Sitting on a Man: Colonialism and the Lost Political Institutions of Igbo Women," in *Women in Society*, ed. Sharon Tiffany. St. Albans, Vt.: Eden Press, pp. 163–187.

Van Gennep, Arnold, 1960. *The Rites of Passage*. Chicago: University of Chicago Press.

Van Willigan, John, 1986. *Applied Anthropology*, South Hadley, Mass.: Bergin and Garvey, pp. 128–129 and 133–139.

Vansina, Jan, 1965. *Oral Tradition: A Study in Historical Methodology*, H. M. Wright, trans. Chicago: Aldine.

Vayda, Andrew P., 1961. "Expansion and Warfare among Swidden Agriculturalists," *American Anthropologist*, 63:346–358.

Vayda, Andrew, ed., 1969. *Environment and Cultural Behavior: Ecological Studies in Cultural Anthropology*, Garden City, N.Y.: Natural History Press.

Vayda, Andrew P., 1961. "A Re-examination of Northwest Coast Economic Systems," *Transactions of the New York Academy of Sciences*, 2d. series, 23:618–624.

Vayda, Andrew, ed., 1969. *Environment and Cultural Behavior: Ecological Studies in Cultural Anthropology*. Garden City, New York: Natural History Press.

Vogelman, Thomas C., et al., 1972. Film: *Prehistoric Life in the Champlain Valley*. Burlington, Vt.: Department of Anthropology, University of Vermont.

Voget, F. W., 1975. *A History of Ethnology*. New York: Holt, Rinehart and Winston.

Voget, F. W., 1960. "Man and Culture: An Essay in Changing Anthropological Interpretation," *American Anthropologist*, 62:943–965.

Vogt, Evon Z., 1990. *The Zinacantecos of Mexico, A Modern Maya Way of Life*, 2nd ed. New York: Holt, Rinehart and Winston.

Wagner, Philip L., 1960. *A History of Ethnology*. New York: Holt, Rinehart and Winston.

Wagner, Philip L., 1960. *The Human Use of the Earth*. New York: Free Press.

Wallace, Anthony F., 1956. "Revitalization Movements," *American Anthropologist*, 58:264–281.

Wallace, Anthony F. C., 1970. *Culture and Personality*, 2d ed. New York: Random House.

Wallace, Anthony F. C., 1965. "The Problem of the Psychological Validity of Componential Analysis," *American Anthropologist, Special Publication*, Part 2, 67(5):229–248.

Wallace, Anthony F. C., 1966. *Religion: An Anthropological View*. New York: Random House.

Wallace, Ernest, and E. Adamson Hoebel, 1952. *The Comanches*. Norman, Ok.: University of Oklahoma Press.

Wardhaugh, Ronald, 1972. *Introduction to Linguistics*. New York: McGraw-Hill.

Weiner, Annette, 1988. *The Trobrianders of Papua New Guinea*. New York: Holt, Rinehart and Winston.

Weiner, Annette B., 1977. "Review of *Trobriand Cricket: An Ingenious Response to Colonialism*," *American Anthropologist*, 79:506.

Westermarck, Edward A., 1926. *A Short History of Marriage*. New York: Macmillan.

Whelehan, Patricia, 1985. "Review of *Incest, a Biosocial View*," *American Anthropologist* 87:677–678.

White, Douglas R., 1988. "Rethinking Polygyny: Co-Wives, Codes and Cultural Systems," *Current Anthropology* 29:529–572.

White, Leslie, 1940. "The Symbol: The Origin and Basis of Human Behavior," *Philosophy of Science*, 7:451–463.

White, Leslie, 1959. *The Evolution of Culture: The Development of Civilization to the Fall of Rome*. New York: McGraw-Hill.

White, Leslie, 1949. *The Science of Culture: A Study of Man and Civilization*. New York: Farrar, Strauss.

Whiting, John W. M., and Irvin L. Child, 1953. *Child Training and Personality: A Cross-cultural Study*. New Haven, Conn.: Yale University Press.

Whiting, Beatrice B., ed., 1963. *Six Cultures: Sudies of Child Rearing*. New York: Wiley.

Wilson, A. K., and V. M. Sarich, 1969. "A Molecular Time Scale for Human Evolution," *Proceedings of the National Academy of Science* 63:1089–1093.

Wingert, Paul, 1962. *Primitive Art: Its Tradition and Styles*. London: Oxford University Press; New York: World.

Wirsing, Rolf L., 1985. "The Health of Traditional Societies and the Effects of Acculturation," *Current Anthropology* 26(3):303–322.

Wolf, Margery, 1985. *Revolution Postponed-Women in Contemporary China*. Stanford, Cal.: Stanford University Press.

Wolf, Margery, 1972. *Women and the Family in Rural Taiwan*. Stanford, Cal.: Stanford University Press.

Wolf, Eric, 1982. *Europe and the People without History*. Berkeley: University of California Press.

Wolf, Eric, 1966. *Peasants* Englewood Cliffs, N.J.: Prentice-Hall.

Wolfe, Alvin W., 1977. "The Supranational Organization of Production: An Evolutionary Perspective," in *Current Anthropology*, 18:615–635.

Wolpoff, Milford H., 1982. *"Ramapithecus* and Hominid Origins," *Current Anthropology*, 23:501–522.

Woolfson, Peter, 1972. "Language, Thought, and Culture," in Virginia P. Clark, Paul A. Escholz, and Alfred F. Rosa, eds., *Language*. New York: St. Martin.

World Bank, 1982. *Tribal Peoples and Economic Development*. Washington, D.C.: World Bank.

Wright, Robin, 1984. "Towards a New Indian Policy in Brazil," *Cultural Survival Quarterly* 8,(1):76–78.

Wulff, Robert M., and Shirley J. Fiske, 1987. *Anthropological Praxis: Translating Knowledge into Action*. Boulder, Co.: Westview.

INDEX

Terms in **boldface** type are defined in the running glossary definitions on the text pages indicated with **boldface numbers.** Photograph and figure page numbers are in *italic* type.

PERMISSIONS
AND ACKNOWLEDGMENTS

Illustrations for the cover and the part openers were created by Rebecca Rüegger. The illustration for Part I was based on a photo by Robert Frerck, Odyssey Productions. The illustration for Part V was based on a photo by Wolfgang Kaehler.

The author is indebted to the following for photographs and permission to reproduce them. Copyright for each photograph belongs to the photographer or agency credited, unless specified otherwise.

Chapter 1

1-1 (page 5), The Thomas Gilcrease Institute of American History and Art, Tulsa, Oklahoma; 1-2a (7), The Granger Collection; 1-2b (7), The Granger Collection; 1-3 (8), Dr. W. Montague Cobb; 1-4a (10), Will and Deni McIntyre/Photo Researchers; 1-4b (10), James Newberry; 1-5 (12), Peter Arnold; 1-6 (13), Mel Konner/Anthro-Photo; 1-7 (17), Al Danegger/Courtesy of the University of Maryland; 1-8 (19), Galen Rowell © 1985/Peter Arnold, Inc.; 1-9 (20), AP/Wide World Photos; 1-10a (21), The Bettmann Archive; 1-10b (21), The Granger Collection; 1-10c (21), Culver Pictures; 1-11 (22), Richard B. Lee, Department of Anthropology, University of Toronto; 1-12 (25), Luke Holland

Chapter 2

2-1 (29), L. Dennis/The Image Bank; 2-2a (31), Julie Ades/Visions; 2-2b (31), Karen Holsinger Mullen/Unicorn Stock Photos; 2-3 (32), Susan Meiselas/Magnum; 2-4 (33), Blair Seitz; 2-5 (36), Gorilla Foundation; 2-6 (36), University of Michigan; 2-7 (37), UPI/Bettmann Newsphotos; 2-8 (38), John Lewis Stage/Image Bank; 2-9 (40), Lowie Museum, Berkeley, CA; 2-10 (42), Annette Weiner, Department of Anthropology, New York University; 2-11 (44), Alec Duncan/Taurus Photos; 2-12a (46), Archive Photos; 2-12b (46), Blair Seitz; 2-13 (48), Chris Brown/Sipa Press; 2-14 (49), Colin Turnbull

Chapter 3

3-1 (53), Eric & David Hosking/Photo Researchers; 3-2 (54), Mark Phillips/Photo Researchers; 3-3 (56), L & D Klein/Photo Researchers; 3-4 (59), Gerry Ellis/The Wildlife Collection; 3-5 (60), Gerry Ellis/The Wildlife Collection; 3-6 (64), Margo Crabtree/*Science*; 3-7 (65), Peter Drowne/E. R. Degginger; 3-8 (66), Townsend P. Dickinson/Comstock; 3-9 (69), David L. Brill © 1985 by permission of Owen Lovejoy; 3-10 (69), Tim White, Department of Anthropology, University of California at Berkeley; 3-11 (70), David L. Brill © 1985, by permission of the National Museum of Kenya, Nairobi; 3-12 (72), David L. Brill; 3-13 (74), Anthro-Photo; 3-14 (75), Geoffrey G. Pope, Department of Anthropology, University of Illinois, Champaign/Urbana; 3-15 (76), David L. Brill © 1985/Musee de l'Homme, Paris; 3-16a (78), David L. Brill; 3-16b (78), Chris Stringer; 3-17 (81), Rapho/Photo Researchers

Chapter 4

4-1 (89), Gale Wrausman; 4-2 (91), Gunter Ziesler/Peter Arnold, Inc.; 4-3 (92), Megan Biesele/Anthro-Photo; 4-4 (96), Bob Daemmrich/The Image Works; 4-5 (98), John Chellmann/Animals Animals; 4-6a (99), Terry Madison/The Image Bank; 4-6b (99), The Image Bank; 4-6c (99), Eric L. Wheater/The Image Bank; 4-7 (104), Sipa Press; 4-8 (105), Klaus Franke/Peter Arnold; 4-9 (111), Will and Deni McIntyre/Photo Researchers; 4-10 (111), Frances M. Roberts; 4-11a (113), Comstock; 4-11b (113), Comstock

Chapter 5

5-1 (117), Wolfgang Kaehler; 5-2 (118), Martin Bell/Mary Ellen Mark Library; 5-3a (120), Mark Jenike/Anthro-Photo; 5-3b (120), Irven DeVore/Anthro-Photo; 5-4 (123), UPI/Bettmann; 5-5 (125), Anthony Bannister/Earth Scenes; 5-6 (126), The Native American Painting Reference Library; 5-7 (127), E. R. Degginger; 5-8 (129), Tronick/Anthro-Photo; 5-9 (132), N. Chagnon/Anthro-Photo; 5-10 (133), The Granger Collection; 5-11a (135), J. L. Stage/The Image Bank; 5-11b (135), Dan Cabe/Photo Researchers; 5-12 (137), Museum of the American Indian, Heye Foundation; 5-13 (141), Joseph Schuyler/Stock Boston

Chapter 6

6-1 (145), Julian Engelsman/Tony Stone Worldwide; 6-2 (146), Roy A. Rappaport, Department of Anthropology, University of Michigan; 6-3 (148), William W. Bacon III/Photo Researchers; 6-4 (149), Mark Sasahara/The Burlington Free Press; 6-5 (152), University of Illinois; 6-6 (154), 20th Century Fox; 6-7 (155), Super Stock; 6-8 (155), Anita de L. Haviland; 6-9 (158), Stan Washburn/Anthro-Photo; 6-9b (158), Marvin E. Newman; 6-9c (158), Richard B. Lee, Department of Anthropology, University of Toronto; 6-10 (165), Andy Sacks/Tony Stone Worldwide/Chicago Ltd.; 6-11 (167), David Austen/Woodfin Camp & Associates; 6-12 (168), Super Stock; 6-13 (170), D. Donne Bryant; 6-14 (172), American Museum of Natural History; 6-15 (173), J. Blank/H. Armstrong Roberts

Chapter 7

7-1 (177), Gary Rogers/The Image Bank; 7-2 (178), Annette Weiner, Department of Anthropology, New York University; 7-3a (180), Allen Russell/Profiles West; 7-3b (180), Loren McIntyre/Woodfin Camp & Associates; 7-4 (182), Eric Kroll/Taurus; 7-5a (183), D. Donne Bryant; 7-5b (183), Byron Augustin/D. Donne Bryant; 7-6 (184), David R. Frazier/Photo Researchers, Inc.; 7-7 (187), Stan Washburn/Anthro-Photo; 7-8a (190), Annette Weiner, Department of Anthropology, New York University; 7-8b (190), Annette Weiner, Department of Anthropology, New York University; 7-9 (192), Super Stock; 7-10 (194), Larry Tackett/Tom Stack & Associates; 7-11 (197), Brad Crooks; 7-12 (198), Elsa Peterson; 7-13 (199), David H. Wells/The Image Works; 7-14 (201), Colin Turnbull

Chapter 8

8-1 (209), Michael Salus/The Image Bank; 8-2a (210), Annette Weiner, Department of Anthropology, New York University; 8-2b (210), Annette Weiner, Department of Anthropology, New York University; 8-3 (211), Warren & Genny Garst/Tom Stack; 8-4 (214), Giraudon/Art Resource; 8-5 (215), AP/Wide World Photos; 8-6 (217), Ermakoff/The Image Works; 8-7 (221), Anthro-Photo; 8-8a (222), E. J. Camp/Onyx; 8-8b (222), The Bettmann Archive; 8-9a (223), Stephanie Dinkins/Photo Researchers; 8-9b (223), Topham/The Image Works; 8-10 (228), Annette Weiner, Department of Anthropology, New York University; 8-11 (229), John Eascott & Eva Momatiuk/Woodfin Camp & Associates; 8-12 (231), Linda Bartlett/Photo Researchers

Chapter 9

9-1 (235), Joel Halpern/Anthro-Photo; 9-2 (236), B. W. Hoffmann/Envision; 9-3 (237), Scala/Art Resource; 9-4 (243), Irven de Vore/Anthro-Photo; 9-5 (244), F. B. Grunzweig/Photo Researchers; 9-6 (245), Aldona Salralis/Photo Researchers; 9-7 (246), John Eastcott/Yva Momatiuk/The Image Works; 9-8 (247), Blair Seitz/Photo Researchers; 9-9a (248), Robert Frerck/Odyssey; 9-9b (248), Joe Cavanaugh/D. Donne Bryant Stock; 9-10 (249), Courtesy Museum of New Mexico; 9-11 (250), Annette Weiner, Department of Anthropology, New York University; 9-12 (251), Lila AbuLughod/Anthro-Photo; 9-13 (252), Peter Simon/Stock Boston; 9-14 (255), Comstock

Chapter 10

10-1 (259), British Museum; 10-2 (261), The Bettmann Archive; 10-3a (263), Culver; 10-3b (263), The Bettmann Archive; 10-4 (268), Photo Archive of New Mexico; 10-5 (270), Hanna Schreiber/Photo Researchers; 10-6 (275), Innervisions; 10-7 (276), Public Archives of Canada

Chapter 11

11-1 (285), Pam Hasegawa; 11-2b (286), Richard Hill; 11-2c (286), Kanien'kehaka Raotitiohka Cultural Center; 11-3 (288), Kevin Horan/Stock Boston; 11-4 (289), Bruce Davidson/Earth Scenes; 11-5a (290), Jack Deutsch/Innervisions; 11-5b (290), Charles Gatewood/The Image Works; 11-6 (293), The Granger Collection; 11-7 (295), Marc & Evelyn Bernheim/Woodfin Camp & Associates; 11-8a (297), Nondial Tank/Taurus Photos; 11-8b (297), Jeffrey D. Smith/Woodfin Camp & Associates; 11-9a (299), Bill Bachman/Photo Researchers; 11-9b (299), Jan Halaska/Photo Researchers; 11-10a (303), Hillel Burger/Peabody Museum; 11-10b (303), M. Courtney-Clarke/Photo Researchers

Chapter 12

12-1 (311), East News-Sipa Press; 12-2 (312), Documentary Educational Resources; 12-3 (315), Bross/Anthro-Photo; 12-4 (316), George Holton/Photo Researchers; 12-5 (319), Jacques Jangoux/Peter Arnold; 12-6a (320), Susan McElhinney; 12-6b (320), American Museum of Natural History; 12-7 (322), New York Historical Society; 12-8 (325), J. P. Laffont/Sygma; 12-9 (326), Fred McConnaughey/Photo Researchers; 12-10 (327), Anthro-Photo; 12-11 (331), Michael Heron/Woodfin Camp & Associates; 12-12a (334), Dr. James Gibbs; 12-12b (334), Hans Halberstadt/Photo Researchers; 12-13 (336), Teit Hornback/Impact

Visuals; 12-14 (338), Dennis Brack/Time Magazine; 12-15 (340), Ira Wyman/Sygma

Chapter 13

13-1 (345), A. D'Argzien/The Image Bank; 13-2a (347), Blair Seitz/Photo Researchers; 13-2b (347), Jeff Jacobson/Deborah Brown & Associates; 13-2c (347), Michael Heron/Woodfin Camp & Associates; 13-3 (349), Super Stock; 13-4 (351), Scala/Art Resource; 13-5 (352), Culver Pictures; 13-6 (353), Chris Arend/Alaska Stock Images; 13-7 (355), Steve McCurry/Magnum; 13-8 (357), Victor Englebert; 13-9 (359), Fritz Goro/Time-Life Picture Agency, Time, Inc.; 13-10 (360), Alon Reininger/Woodfin Camp & Associates; 13-11 (361), Cheetham/Magnum; 13-12 (368), Mark & Evelyn Bernheim/Woodfin Camp & Associates; 13-13a (370), Kal Muller/Woodfin Camp & Associates; 13-13b (370), Kal Muller/Woodfin Camp & Associates; 13-14 (371), Jerry Schad/Photo Researchers

Chapter 14

14-1 (375), Harold Sund/The Image Bank; 14-2a (377), Museum of the American Indian; 14-2b (377), Anita de L. Haviland; 14-2c (377), Sydney Byrd; 14-3 (378), Robert Frerck/Odyssey Productions; 14-4a (379), Denis Stock/Magnum; 14-4b (379), Alan Carey/The Image Works; 14-5 (381), Private Collection, Photo Native American Painting Reference Library; 14-6a (383), Mark & Evelyn Bernheim/Woodfin Camp & Associates; 14-6b (383), Gabe Kirchheimer/Impact Visuals; 14-7 (384), Anthro-Photo; 14-8 (389), Annette Coolidge; 14-9a (390), George Holton/Photo Researchers; 14-9b (390), Luis Castaneda/The Image Bank; 14-10 (391), James Bland; 14-11 (392), Scala/Art Resource; 14-12a (393), The Bettmann Archive; 14-12b (393), R. B. Pickering; 14-13 (395), F. B. Grunzweig/Photo Researchers; 14-14 (395), Daniele Pellegrini/Photo Researchers

Chapter 15

15-1 (403), Nair Benedicto/f4/D. Donne Bryant Stock; 15-2 (404), D. Donne Bryant; 15-3 (407), Richard B. Levine; 15-4 (409), Lila AbuLughod/Anthro-Photo; 15-5 (411), Chapin Library; 15-6a (412), The Bettmann Archive; 15-6b (412), Smithsonian Institution; 15-7 (414), Smithsonian Institution; 15-8 (413), D. Donne Bryant; 15-9 (415), Richard Wood/Taurus; 15-10 (417), A. Keler/Sygma; 15-11 (418), Jeff Jacobson/Deborah Brown & Associates; 15-12a (421), The Bettmann Archive; 15-12b (421), Jack Deutsch/Innervisions; 15-13 (425), Sue Cunningham Photographic; 15-14 (430), Wolfgang Kaehler; 15-15 (431), Alon Reininger/Woodfin Camp & Associates

Chapter 16

16-1 (435), Robert Harbison © 1991/The Christian Science Publishing Society; 16-2 (437), Beryl Goldberg; 16-3 (438), UPI/Bettmann; 16-4 (440), Sue Cunningham Photographic; 16-5 (441), Tom Davenport/Photo Researchers; 16-6 (442), Irven DeVore/Anthro-Photo; 16-7 (445), E. R. Degginger; 16-8 (446), Joe Cavanaugh/D. Donne Bryant; 16-9 (451), A. Tannenbaum/Sygma; 16-10 (453), Sygma; 16-11 (455), Mary Ellen Mark; 16-12 (456), Sue Cunningham Photographic; 16-13 (458), Alon Reininger/Woodfin Camp & Associates; 16-14 (459), Benjamin Porter

Tables and Figures

Chapter 5

Table 5.1 (140), "Highlight 3.5" from *Abnormal Psychology and Modern Life,* 8/e by Robert C. Carson, et al, p.85. Copyright (c) 1988, 1984 by Scott, Foresman and Company. Reprinted by permission of HarperCollins Publishers.

Chapter 7

Figure 7.1 (179), Figure 1, "A Sociocultural Analysis of a Midwestern American Flea Market," by John F. Sherry. *The Journal of Consumer Research,* Vol. 17, (June 1990). Reprinted by permission of The University of Chicago Press.

Chapter 8

Figure 8.1 (218), "Estimated global distribution of adult HIV infections —early 1992" by courtesy of the World Health Organization.

Chapter 16

Figure 16.1 (450), Source: *The Gaia Atlas of First Peoples* by Julian Burger. Published in the United States of America by DOUBLEDAY. Reproduced with the permission of GAIA BOOKS, LONDON.
Figure 16.3 (454), Source: *The Gaia Atlas of First Peoples* by Julian Burger. Published in the United States of America by DOUBLEDAY. Reproduced with the permission of GAIA BOOKS, LONDON.